JOHN ASHBERY was born in Rochester, New York, in 1927. His books of poetry include *Breezeway*; *Quick Question*; *Planisphere*; *Notes from the Air: Selected Later Poems*, which was awarded the 2008 International Griffin Poetry Prize; *A Worldly Country*; *Where Shall I Wander*; and *Self-Portrait in a Convex Mirror*, which received the Pulitzer Prize for Poetry, the National Book Critics Circle Award, and the National Book Award. The winner of many prizes and awards both nationally and internationally, in 2011 he received the Medal for Distinguished Contribution to American Letters from the National Book Foundation, and in 2012 he received a National Humanities Medal, presented by President Obama at the White House. He lived in New York until his death, aged ninety, in 2017.

MARK FORD, editor, is the author of three acclaimed collections of poetry, *Landlocked*, *Soft Sift*, and *Six Children*; his *Selected Poems* was published in 2014. His book-length interview, *John Ashbery in Conversation with Mark Ford*, was published in 2003. His most recent book is *Thomas Hardy: Half a Londoner* (2016).

JOHN ASHBERY

John Ashbery

COLLECTED POEMS 1991–2000

Mark Ford, *editor*

chronology by Mark Ford and David Kermani

CARCANET

First published in Great Britain in 2018 by

Carcanet Press Ltd
Main Library, The University of Manchester,
Oxford Road, Manchester, M13 9PP
www.carcanet.co.uk
First published in the USA in 2017 by The Library of America.

Volume compilation, notes, and chronology by Mark Ford and
David Kermani copyright © 2017 by Literary Classics of the United
States, Inc., New York, N.Y. All rights reserved.

*Flow Chart, Hotel Lautréamont, And the Stars Were Shining,
Can You Hear, Bird, Wakefulness, Girls on the Run, Your Name Here,*
and uncollected poems copyright © 1991, 1992, 1994, 1995, 1998, 1999,
2000 by John Ashbery. The right of John Ashbery to be identified
as the author of these works has been asserted in accordance with the
Copyright, Designs and Patents Act of 1988. All rights reserved.

A CIP catalogue record for this book is available
from the British Library, ISBN 978 1 78410 525 9.

The publisher acknowledges financial assistance
from Arts Council England.

Printed and bound in England by SRP Ltd.

Contents

FLOW CHART, 1

HOTEL LAUTRÉAMONT
  Light Turnouts, 227
  And Forgetting, 227
  The Large Studio, 228
  The Garden of False Civility, 230
  Autumn Telegram, 231
  Notes from the Air, 232
  Still Life with Stranger, 234
  Hotel Lautréamont, 235
  On the Empress's Mind, 237
  The Phantom Agents, 238
  From Estuaries, from Casinos, 239
  Cop and Sweater, 241
  Musica Reservata, 242
  Susan, 244
  The King, 245
  The Whole Is Admirably Composed, 246
  By Forced Marches, 248
  Autumn on the Thruway, 249
  The Little Black Dress, 254
  Part of the Superstition, 255
  The Art of Speeding, 257
  American Bar, 258
  From Palookaville, 259
  Another Example, 261
  Avant de quitter ces lieux, 262
  The White Shirt, 264
  Baked Alaska, 265
  Private Syntax, 269
  Not Now but in Forty-Five Minutes, 270
  In Another Time, 272
  Withered Compliments, 272
  The Wind Talking, 273
  Joy, 276
  Irresolutions on a Theme of La Rochefoucauld, 276

A Call for Papers, 278
Love's Old Sweet Song, 279
Wild Boys of the Road, 281
Le mensonge de Nina Petrovna, 282
Of Linnets and Dull Time, 284
Korean Soap Opera, 284
A Driftwood Altar, 286
Poem at the New Year, 289
Central Air, 290
The Youth's Magic Horn, 292
Brute Image, 293
Of Dreams and Dreaming, 294
Seasonal, 296
Kamarinskaya, 297
Elephant Visitors, 299
The Great Bridge Game of Life, 300
The Departed Lustre, 301
Villanelle, 303
A Sedentary Existence, 304
Erebus, 305
The Old Complex, 307
Where We Went for Lunch, 308
As Oft It Chanceth, 311
Retablo, 312
A Mourning Forbidding Valediction, 314
I Found Their Advice, 315
French Opera, 316
A Stifled Notation, 317
Haunted Stanzas, 318
Livelong Days, 320
Quartet, 321
[untitled], 324
Oeuvres Complètes, 324
Just Wednesday, 325
In My Way / On My Way, 327
No Good at Names, 330
Film Noir, 331
In Vain, Therefore, 332
The Beer Drinkers, 333
That You Tell, 334
A Hole in Your Sock, 336

And Socializing, 337
Revisionist Horn Concerto, 338
The Woman the Lion Was Supposed to Defend, 339
Harbor Activities, 341
It Must Be Sophisticated, 341
Alborada, 345
How to Continue, 346

AND THE STARS WERE SHINING
Token Resistance, 351
Spring Cries, 351
The Mandrill on the Turnpike, 352
About to Move, 353
Ghost Riders of the Moon, 354
The Love Scenes, 355
Just What's There, 356
Title Search, 357
Free Nail Polish, 357
Till the Bus Starts, 358
The Ridiculous Translator's Hopes, 359
The Story of Next Week, 360
A Hundred Albums, 361
A Waltz Dream, 362
Falls to the Floor, Comes to the Door, 363
The Lounge, 364
The Improvement, 365
"The Favor of a Reply, 366
A Held Thing, 366
Strange Things Happen at Night, 368
World's End, 368
Ice Cream in America, 369
Works on Paper I, 369
Local Time, 370
Well, Yes, Actually, 371
My Gold Chain, 373
Footfalls, 374
Weather and Turtles, 375
Sometimes in Places, 375
William Byrd, 376
Assertiveness Training, 378
Like a Sentence, 378
Two Pieces, 380

CONTENTS

The Friendly City, 381
The Desperate Hours, 382
The Decline of the West, 383
The Archipelago, 384
Gummed Reinforcements, 385
Spotlight on America, 386
What Do You Call It When, 387
Pleasure Boats, 388
Pretty Questions, 389
Pathless Wanderings, 390
On First Listening to Schreker's *Der Schatzgräber*, 391
Dinosaur Country, 392
Leeward, 393
Paraph, 394
Not Planning a Trip Back, 395
Myrtle, 395
Man in Lurex, 396
In the Meantime, Darling, 397
Just for Starters, 398
Bromeliads, 398
Commercial Break, 399
Sicilian Bird, 400
Mutt and Jeff, 400
Coventry, 402
And the Stars Were Shining, 403

CAN YOU HEAR, BIRD

A Day at the Gate, 423
A New Octagon, 423
A Poem of Unrest, 424
A Waking Dream, 424
Abe's Collision, 426
Allotted Spree, 426
Angels (you, 427
Anxiety and Hardwood Floors, 428
At First I Thought I Wouldn't Say Anything About It, 428
At Liberty and Cranberry, 429
Atonal Music, 430
Awful Effects of Two Comets, 430
. . . by an Earthquake, 431
By Guess and by Gosh, 435
Can You Hear, Bird, 436

Cantilever, 436
Chapter II, Book 35, 437
Chronic Symbiosis, 438
Collected Places, 439
Coming Down from New York, 440
Dangerous Moonlight, 440
Debit Night, 442
Do Husbands Matter?, 445
Dull Mauve, 446
Eternity Sings the Blues, 447
Fascicle, 450
Five O'Clock Shadow, 451
From the Observatory, 452
Fuckin' Sarcophagi, 453
Getting Back In, 454
Gladys Palmer, 455
Hegel, 456
I Saw No Need, 456
I, Too, 458
In an Inchoate Place, 459
In Old Oklahoma, 459
Limited Liability, 460
Love in Boots, 462
Love's Stratagem, 463
Many Are Dissatisfied, 464
Military Pastoral, 464
My Name Is Dimitri, 465
My Philosophy of Life, 467
Nice Morning Blues, 469
No Earthly Reason, 469
No Longer Very Clear, 471
Obedience School, 471
Ode to John Keats, 472
Of a Particular Stranger, 473
Operators Are Standing By, 473
Others Shied Away, 474
Palindrome, 476
Penthesilea, 476
Plain as Day, 477
Point Lookout, 478
Poor Knights of Windsor, 479

Quick Question, 480
Reverie and Caprice, 481
Safe Conduct, 481
Salon de Thé, 482
See How You Like My Shoes, 483
Sleepers Awake, 484
Something Too Chinese, 485
Swaying, the Apt Traveler Exited My House, 486
Taxi in the Glen, 488
The Blot People, 489
The Captive Sense, 490
The Confronters, 491
The Desolate Beauty Parlor on Beach Avenue, 492
The Faint of Heart, 493
The Green Mummies, 494
The Latvian, 495
The Military Base, 496
The Peace Plan, 497
The Penitent, 497
The Problem of Anxiety, 498
The Sea, 499
The Shocker, 500
The Waiting Ceremony, 500
The Walkways, 501
The Water Carrier, 503
Theme, 504
Three Dusks, 505
Today's Academicians, 506
Touching, the Similarities, 507
Tower of Darkness, 508
Tremendous Outpouring, 508
Tuesday Evening, 509
Twilight Park, 525
Umpteen, 526
What the Plants Say, 526
When All Her Neighbors Came, 527
Where It Was Decided We Should Be Taken, 528
Woman Leaning, 529
Yes, Dr. Grenzmer. How May I Be of Assistance to You? What! You Say the Patient Has Escaped?, 530
Yesterday, for Instance, 532

You Dropped Something, 533
You, My Academy, 535
You Would Have Thought, 537
Young People, 538

WAKEFULNESS
Wakefulness, 541
Baltimore, 542
Palindrome of Evening, 542
Cousin Sarah's Knitting, 543
Last Night I Dreamed I Was in Bucharest, 545
Added Poignancy, 545
Quarry, 547
Laughing Gravy, 547
From Such Commotion, 548
Moderately, 549
Alive at Every Passage, 551
The Burden of the Park, 552
At the Station, 554
Another Kind of Afternoon, 555
Tangled Star, 556
Deeply Incised, 558
Tropical Sex, 558
The Friend at Midnight, 560
Stung by Something, 560
The Last Romantic, 562
Shadows in the Street, 563
The Earth-Tone Madonna, 564
Dear Sir or Madam, 566
The Laughter of Dead Men, 566
Discordant Data, 567
Bogus Inspections, 568
Floatingly, 570
Tenebrae, 570
Outside My Window the Japanese . . . , 571
Any Other Time, 573
Probably Based on a Dream, 574
The Village of Sleep, 574
In My Head, 576
The Spacious Firmament, 576
Proximity, 578
Going Away Any Time Soon, 578

Like America, 580
New Constructions, 580
Whiteout, 583
A French Stamp, 583
One Man's Poem, 584
The Pathetic Fallacy, 585
From Old Notebooks, 586
Many Colors, 587
Autumn in the Long Avenue, 588
Snow, 589
Within the Hour, 591
The Dong with the Luminous Nose, 591
Come On, Dear, 593
Gentle Reader, 594
Homecoming, 595

GIRLS ON THE RUN, 597

YOUR NAME HERE
This Room, 649
If You Said You Would Come with Me, 649
A Linnet, 650
The Bobinski Brothers, 650
Not You Again, 651
Terminal, 652
Merrily We Live, 653
Brand Loyalty, 654
Rain in the Soup, 655
Bloodfits, 656
Implicit Fog, 657
Dream Sequence (Untitled), 657
What Is Written, 658
Caravaggio and His Followers, 659
Industrial Collage, 660
Frogs and Gospels, 662
Weekend, 663
Get Me Rewrite, 664
Invasive Procedures, 665
Paperwork, 666
The History of My Life, 667
Toy Symphony, 668
Memories of Imperialism, 669

Strange Occupations, 670
Full Tilt, 671
The File on Thelma Jordan, 672
Two for the Road, 675
Heartache, 676
The Fortune Cookie Crumbles, 677
Onion Skin, 678
Redeemed Area, 678
Variations on "La Folia," 679
De Senectute, 681
The Gods of Fairness, 683
Who Knows What Constitutes a Life, 683
Sacred and Profane Dances, 684
Here We Go Looby, 685
Avenue Mozart, 687
Life Is a Dream, 687
Vowels, 688
Beverly of Graustark, 688
The Pearl Fishers, 690
They Don't Just Go Away, Either, 691
Conventional Wisdom, 692
And Again, March Is Almost Here, 693
A Descent into the Maelstrom, 695
Sonatine Mélancolique, 695
Stanzas Before Time, 696
A Postcard from Pontevedra, 697
A Suit, 697
Crossroads in the Past, 698
The Water Inspector, 699
Cinéma Vérité, 700
The Old House in the Country, 701
Autumn Basement, 702
Hang-Up Call, 702
Lost Profile, 703
How Dangerous, 704
Humble Pie, 705
More Hocketing, 706
Amnesia Goes to the Ball, 708
Railroaded, 708
Honored Guest, 710
Our Leader Is Dreaming, 710

Last Legs, 712
Lemurs and Pharisees, 712
The Underwriters, 714
Pale Siblings, 715
Nobody Is Going Anywhere, 716
Poem on Several Occasions, 716
Slumberer, 717
Pot Luck, 719
Short-Term Memory, 721
Vendanges, 721
Small City, 723
Vintage Masquerade, 724
To Good People Who Should Be Going Somewhere Else, 725
Another Aardvark, 725
Has to Be Somewhere, 726
The Don's Bequest, 728
Strange Cinema, 729
A Star Belched, 730
When Pressed, 730
The Impure, 731
Crowd Conditions, 732
Enjoys Watching Foreign Films, 733
Fade In, 734
Over at the Mutts', 734
Pastilles for the Voyage, 735
Of the Light, 736
Your Name Here, 737

UNCOLLECTED POEMS
Hoboken, 741
Call It "Untitled," 745
Le singe d'une nuit d'été, 746
Fruit and Tea, 747
Two Norwegian Moods, 748
Tahiti Trot, 748
Tin Steamboat, 749
My Favorite Dress, 750
Yes, I Have Been Reading, 750
Often in Sorting Out, 752
The Dissolving Bride, 752
Shadows on the Street, 753
Media Runner, 754

The Hailstorm in Belgrade, May 24th, 1937, 755
Victrola floribunda, 756
The Green Dress, 756
Hierarchy of the Unexpected, 757
Welcome to Entropy, 758
Invitation to a Wooing, 759
These Symptoms I Know So Well, 760
Vauban, 761
Greased Lightning, 762
A Leap in Time, 763
Befuddled, 764
A Lot of Catching Up to Do, 766
The Lyricist, 766

Chronology, 771
Note on the Texts, 787
Notes, 791
Index of Titles and First Lines, 809

FLOW CHART

For David

I

Still in the published city but not yet
overtaken by a new form of despair, I ask
the diagram: is it the foretaste of pain
it might easily be? Or an emptiness
so sudden it leaves the girders
whanging in the absence of wind,
the sky milk-blue and astringent? We know life is so busy,
but a larger activity shrouds it, and this is something
we can never feel, except occasionally, in small signs
put up to warn us and as soon expunged, in part
or wholly.
        Sad grows the river god as he oars past us
downstream without our knowing him: for if, he reasons,
he can be overlooked, then to know him would be to eat him,
ingest the name he carries through time to set down
finally, on a strand of rotted hulks. And those who sense something
squeamish in his arrival know enough not to look up
from the page they are reading, the plaited lines that extend
like a bronze chain into eternity.
                      It seems I was reading something;
I have forgotten the sense of it or what the small
role of the central poem made me want to feel. No matter.
The words, distant now, and mitred, glint. Yet not one
ever escapes the forest of agony and pleasure that keeps them
in a solution that has become permanent through inertia. The
   force
of meaning never extrudes. And the insects,
of course, don't mind. I think it was at that moment he
knowingly and in my own interests took back from me
the slow-flowing idea of flight, now
too firmly channeled, its omnipresent reminders etched
too deeply into my forehead, its crass grievances and greetings
a class apart from the wonders every man feels,
whether alone in bed, or with a lover, or beached
with the shells on some atoll (and if solitude
swallow us up betimes, it is only later that
the idea of its permanence sifts into view, yea

later and perhaps only occasionally, and only much later
stands from dawn to dusk, just as the plaintive sound
of the harp of the waves is always there as a backdrop
to conversation and conversion, even when
most forgotten) and cannot make sense of them, but he knows
the familiar, unmistakable thing, and that gives him courage
as day expires and evening marshals its hosts, in preparation
for the long night to come.
                      And the horoscopes flung back
all we had meant to keep there: *our* meaning, for us, yet
how different the sense when another speaks it!
How cold the afterthought that takes us out of time
for a few moments (just as we were beginning to go with the
    fragile
penchants mother-love taught us) and transports us to a
    stepping-stone
far out at sea.
              So no matter what the restrictions, admonitions,
premonitions that trellised us early, supporting this
artificial espaliered thing we have become, by the same token no
subsequent learning shall deprive us, it seems, no holy
sophistication loosen the bands
of blessed decorum, our present salvation, our hope for years
    to come.
Only let that river not beseech its banks too closely,
abrade and swamp its levees, for though the flood is always terrible,
much worse are the painted monsters born later
out of the swift-flowing alluvial mud.
                            And when the time for
    the breaking
of the law is here, be sure it is to take place in the matrix
of our everyday thoughts and fantasies, our wonderment
at how we got from there to here. In the unlashed eye of noon
these and other terrible things are written, yet it seems
at the time as mild as soughing of wavelets in a reservoir.
Only the belated certainty comes to matter much,
I suppose, and, when it does, comes to seem as immutable as roses.
Meanwhile a god has bungled it again.
                                Early on
was a time of seeming: golden eggs that hatched

into regrets, a snowflake whose kiss burned like an enchanter's
poison; yet it all seemed good in the growing dawn.
The breeze that always nurtures us (no matter how dry,
how filled with complaints about time and the weather the air)
pointed out a way that diverged from the true way without
    negating it,
to arrive at the same result by different spells,
so that no one was wiser for knowing the way we had grown,
almost unconsciously, into a cube of grace that was to be
a permanent shelter. Let the book end there, some few
said, but that was of course impossible; the growth must persist
into areas darkened and dangerous, undermined
by the curse of that death breeze, until one is handed a skull
as a birthday present, and each closing paragraph of the
    novella is
underlined: *To be continued*, that there should be no peace
in the present, no sleep save in glimpses of the future
on the crystal ball's thick, bubble-like surface. No you and me
unless we are together. Only then does he mumble confused words
of affection at us as the barberry bleeds close against the frost,
a scarlet innocence, confused miracle, to us, for what we have
    done
to others, and to ourselves. There is no parting. There is
only the fading, guaranteed by the label, which lasts forever.

This much the gods divulged before they became too restless,
too preoccupied with other cares to see into the sole fact the
present allows, along with much ribbon, much icing
and pretended music. But we can't live with them in their day:
the air, though pure, is too dense. And afterwards when others
come up and ask, what was it like, one is too amazed to behave
    strangely;
the future is extinguished; the world's colored paths all lead
to my mouth, and I drop, humbled, eating from the red-clay floor.
And only then does inspiration come: late, yet never too late.

It's possible, it's just possible, that the god's claims
fly out windows as soon as they are opened, are erased from
    the accounting. If one is alone,
it matters less than to others embarked on a casual voyage

into the promiscuity of dreams. Yet I am always the first to know
how he feels. The inventory of the silent auction
doesn't promise much: one chewed cactus, an air mattress,
a verbatim report. Sandals. The massive transcriptions with which
he took unforgivable liberties—hell, I'd sooner join the project
farther ahead, retaining all benefits, but one is doomed,
repeating oneself, never to repeat oneself, you know what I
    mean?
If in the interval false accounts have circulated, why,
one is at least unaware of it, and can live one's allotted arc
of time in feasible unconsciousness, watching the linen dresses
    of girls,
with a wreath of smoke to come home to. There is nothing
    beside the familiar
doormat to get excited about, yet when one goes out in loose
    weather
the change is akin to choirs singing in a distance nebulous with
    fear
and love. Sometimes one's own hopes are realized
and life becomes a description of every second of the time it
    took;
conversely, some are put off by the sound of legions milling
    about.
One cultivates certain smells, is afraid to leave the charmed
    circle
of the anxious room lest uncommitted atmosphere befall
                                                  and
    the oaks
are seen to be girdled with ivy.

Alack he said what stressful sounds

More of him another time but now you
in the ivory frame have stripped yourself one by one of your earliest
opinions, polluted in any case by bees, and stand
radiant in the circle of our lost, unhappy youth, oh my
friend that knew me before I knew you, and when you came
    to me
knew it was forever, *here* there would be no break, only I was
so ignorant I forgot what it was all about. You chided me

for forgetting and in an instant I remembered everything: the
schoolhouse, the tent meeting. And I came closer until the day
I wrote my name firmly on the ruled page: that was a
time to come, and all happy crying in memory placed the stone
in the magic box and covered it with wallpaper. It seemed our
 separate
lives could continue separately for themselves and shine like a
 single star.
I never knew such happiness. I never knew such happiness
 could exist.
Not that the dark world was removed or brightened, but
each thing in it was slightly enlarged, and in so seeming
 became its
true cameo self, a liquid thing, to be held in the hollow
of the hand like a bird. More formal times would come
of course but the abstract good sense would never drown in
 the elixir
of this private sorrow, that would always sing to itself
in good times and bad, an example to one's consciousness,
an emblem of correct behavior, in darkness or under water.
How unshifting those secret times, and how stealthily
they grew! It was going to take forever just to get through
the first act, yet the scenery, a square of medieval houses, gardens
with huge blue and red flowers and solemn birds that dwarfed
the trees they sat on, need never have given way to the fumes
 and crevasses
of the high glen: the point is one was going to do to it
what mattered to us, and all would be correct as in a painting
that would never ache for a frame but dream on as
 nonchalantly as we did.
Who could have expected a dream like this to go away for
 there are some
that are the web on which our waking life is painstakingly
 elaborated:
there are real, bustling things there and the burgomaster of success
stalks back and forth, directing everything
with a small motion of a finger. But when it did come,
the denouement, we were off drinking in some restaurant,
too absorbed, too eternally, expectantly happy to be there or
 care.

That inspiration came later, in sleep while it rained,
urgently, so that lines of darkness interfered with the careful
arrangement of the dream's disguise: no takers? Anyway,
sleep itself became this chasm of repeated words,
of shifting banks of words rising like steam
out of someplace into something. Forget the promises the stars
    made you: they were half-stoned, and besides
are twinned to no notion that can have an impact
on our way of thinking, as crabbed now
as at any time in the past. A forlorn park stood before us
but there was no way to want to enter it, since the guards
had abandoned their posts to slate-gray daylight
flowing into your heart as though it were a blotter, confounding
or negating the rare survival of wit into our century:
these, at any rate, are my children, she intoned,
of whom I divest myself so as to fit into the notch
of infinity as defined by a long arc of crows returning to the
    distant
coppice. All's aglow. But we see by it that some mortal
material was included in the glorious compound, that next to
nothing can prevent its mudslide from sweeping over us
while it renders the pitted earth smooth and pristine and
    something
like one's original idea of it, only so primitive
it can't understand us. Meanwhile the coat I wear,
woven of consumer products, asks you to pause and inspect
the still-fertile ground of our once-valid compact
with the ordinary and the true. It wants out and
we shall get it even with decreased services and an increased
number of spot-checks, since all of it, ourselves included,
is in our own interests to speak up for and deny when the
    proper
moment arrives. Now, nothing further remains to be done except
to sleep and pray, saving the pieces for a slightly
later time when they shall be recognized as holy remnants of the
    burnished
mirror in which the Almighty once saw Himself, and wept,
realizing how all His prophecies had come true for His people
at last and no one was any wiser for it as they walked the wide
shadowless streets with no eyelids or memory when it came to

intersecting the itineraries of other, similarly blessed creatures
(blessed for having no name, no preconceived strategies
unless they lay underground, too unprofitable to dig up
until the requisite technologies had been developed some
decades down the road and nodding as though in
    acknowledgment of
an acquaintance one doesn't remember yet is not sure of
having ever formally renounced either: was it on land or at sea
that that bird first came to one, many miles from the nearest
    anything?).

What we are to each other is both less urgent and more
perturbing, having no discernible root, no raison d'être, or else
    flowing
backward into an origin like the primordial soup it's so easy to pin
anything on, like a carnation to one's lapel. So it seems we must
stay in an uneasy relationship, not quite fitting
together, not precisely friends or lovers though certainly not
    enemies, if
the buoyancy of the spongy terrain on which we exist is to be
    experienced
as an ichor, not a commentary on all that is missing from the
    reflection
in the mirror. *Did I say that? Can this be me?* Otherwise the
    treaty will
seem premature, the peace unearned, and one might as well
    slink back
into the solitude of the kennel, for the blunder to be read as
    anything
but willful, self-indulgent. And meanwhile everything around
    us is already
prepared for this resolution; the temperature, the season are
    exactly right
for it all not to be awash with sentiments expelled from some
    impossibly
distant situation; some episode from your childhood nobody
    knows about and
even you can't remember accurately. It is time for the long beds
then, and the extra hours to be spent in them, but surely
    somebody can

find something spontaneous to say before it all fizzles, before
    the incandescent
tongs are slaked in mud and the tender yellow shoots of the
    willow
dry up instead of maturing having concluded that the moment
is inappropriate, the heroes gone to their rest, and all the plain
folk of history foundered in the subjective reading of their
    lives
as expendable, the stuff of ordinary heresy, shards of common
    crockery
interesting only because unearthed long after the time had
    come for a
decision on what to do at the very moment they disappeared
    into timelessness,
one of innumerable such tramping exits that no one hears,
so long as they may be promptly and justly forgotten,
subtracted like the soul we never knew we had and replaced
    with something
young, and easier, climate of any day and of all the days,
    postmillenarian.

Just so, some argue, some still are
nurtured by their innocence, a wanton
formula a nursemaid gives them. They grow up to be slim,
and tall, but often it seems something is lacking,
some point of concentration around which a person can collect
    itself,
and be neither conscious nor uncaring, be neutral.
And when the pitcher
is emptied of milk, it is not refilled, but washed and put away
    on a shelf.
Conversations are still initiated,
haltingly, under the leaves, around an outdoor table,
but they insist on nothing and are remembered
only as disquieting examples of how life might be
in that other halting yet prosperous time
when games of strength were put away.
And each guest rises
abruptly from the table, a star at his or her shoulder.
For then, in smeared night, no blotch or defect can erase it,

the wonderful greeting you heard in the morning
and heard yourself reply to.

                             But at times such as
these late ones, a moaning in copper beeches is heard, of regret,
not for what happened, or even for what could conceivably
    have happened, but
for what never happened and which therefore exists, as dark
and transparent as a dream. A dream from nowhere. A dream
with no place to go, all dressed up with no place to go, that an
    axe
menaces, off and on, throughout eternity. Or ships, lands
which no one sees, islands scattered like pebbles
across the immense surface of the ocean; this is what it is
to believe and not see, to implore dreaming, then to arrive home
by cunning, stricken and exhausted, a framed picture of
    oneself. The ads
didn't tell you this, they were too busy with their own
    professional sleight-of-hand
to notice those farther out in deep water ("*when such a destin'd wretch*
as I, wash'd headlong from on board"), decorating the
    maelstrom with
someone's (I wish I knew whose) notion of what is right, or cute.
Soon the dark chairs and tables stand out sharply in front of strange
green-striped walls, gulls circle in the sky, smoke
from piles of old tires set alight at strategic points throughout
    the city
sifts through the crack where the pane doesn't quite join the
    sill—
is this, I ask you, a mute entreaty on the part of some
    well-intentioned
but shy deity meant to take the temperature of the lives being
    squandered
by the few left here below? Ask, rather, why the clock slows down
a little more each day, necessitating double, triple and even
    quadruple tintinnabulations
in order for its fundamentally banal intentions to be elucidated
so that one may settle down to enjoying the usufruct of the
    sparse,

shattering seconds, the while looking forward to retiring at ninety
on a comfortable income without rueing the day one first took
    up the odd
gambit that has projected us into a lifetime of self-loathing and
    shallow interests.
One lives thus, plucking a mean sort of living from the rubbish
    heaps
of history, unaware that the parallel daintiness of the lives of
    the rich,
like fish in an ocean whose bottom is dotted with the rusted
    engines and debris
of long-forgotten wrecks, unfolds; yes, "*And I in greater depths
    than he*," I suppose,
yet it doesn't help deliver one back either to the after all sane
    and helpful blank square
one is always setting out from, having in the meantime
    forgotten those other
precepts, sane and insane, that intrude as soon as one begins to
    think
about anything at all. It is always on the rim of some fleshpot
    briefly
mentioned in the Bible one is seen to squirm, a pinned worm,
    so that
one is pitted against others as against oneself: lonesome, hungry,
and a little bit thirsty until the day of doom universally
    misconstrued as a
time of relief and pillars of dust rising straight up out of the
    desert valleys
where one's feet take one, and all that mythology of broken tracks,
jettisoned equipment, and the long-uninhabited wadi whose
    watering-trough
is merely mud now and a few puddles of camel-stale, materializes.

Latest reports show that the government
still controls everything but that the location of the blond
    captive
has been pinpointed thanks to urgent needling from the
    backwoods constituency
and the population in general is alive and well. But can we dwell

on any of it? Our privacy ends where the clouds' begins, just
    here, just at
this bit of anonymity on the seashore. And we have the right
to be confirmed, just as animals or even plants do, provided we
    go away and leave
every essential piece of the architecture of us behind. Surely then,
    what we work for must be met
with approval sometime even though *we* haven't the right to
    issue any
such thing. There are caves and caves, and almost none
of them has been explored yet. That doesn't give us much
to go on, yet we insistently cry that someone else's rondo is
    already
being played, and that over and over, so how come nobody
    does anything about it,
relaxes us in our shoes and tells us about bedtime? Surely, in
    my younger
days people acted differently about it. There was no
    barnstorming, just quiet
people going about their business and not worrying too much
    about
being rewarded at the end when it came down to that. No, we
    were wandering
away, too busy for such things, toward the altar,
or better yet into the nave whose fruit-and-flower
decoration led unostentatiously and facilely into the outdoors it
anticipated. No use just sitting around juicing the lemon
or the orange for that matter as long as one was intending to
    get up and play
again. And now that the time of reckoning nears, it wears a
    changed coat;
its color is brighter. No but there must be some structural
    difference as well
in the ordering of the colors and how they were laid on, only
no one can conceivably care enough about this to talk about it.
    Well I do
and can, but the un-nice fractions almost always assert
    themselves
above the din of this great city and I have trouble remembering

even my name until some passing girl kindles its fancy, what my
    name was
to me when I first began to think about other things. There is
    not postage for
        this boredom either really so that it keeps
returning, might be said never to have gone away at all,
except for the media with which it keeps getting compared. I
    say, the other
reaches really tickle you, when you have a chance. And all this
    time
I thought he was only farting around disinclined to have a
    serious opinion
on anything, and even more so to give it vent or utterance.
    And my sight clears
for the first time in a thousand years and it's true, I can see up
    ahead
where no one waits and the long flags flap and droop in the
    dust of sunsets
and so may it be forever and ever till we get it right. Mine's
    isn't the option to
show you how to escape or comfort you unduly but with a little
    time
and a little patience we shall make this thing work. Even
    though you thought
everything you touched was doomed to fall apart or not start,
    time has
a few surprises up its sleeve and deserves to be spat on for not
    having more,
or would, if it didn't. Yet it does. There are promises clad with
    the finest
silk you can imagine and silver ornaments hitherto undreamed
    of, if only you can
match them with something of equal loveliness and curiosity
    from your own
secret collection. And of course this does take time, but in the
    end one
senses it more richly bedizened than ever before, and in line for
    a promotion
out of the ranks of futility into the narrow furrows of bliss and
    total sublimity

crystallized in good humor that took over early on in the
    century. Of course,
no one is aware of this. Yet. But give
everybody time, even no-shows, and it will all flow backwards,
    that
caparisoned night, a trial for some, and otherwise it all gets out
into your childhood and the beach that was its launching pad
    before
hunger and fears took over even as delight fostered the notion that
there was going to be enough for everybody, for children to pause
and have a happy home no one talks about anymore. Best to
    rest, sleep and laugh
about it to someone who no longer matters and then you'll
    find that you are indeed
in it and have been all along, only that the show was on a kind
    of treadmill moving
at the same leaden pace as your jokes and ambitions, which is
    why you
never knew about it and therefore consented to come along anyway
on this dangerous outing to the very sources of time. Don't
excuse yourself, nothing could.

I've never really considered telling you. And now. He hated
doing it—he wasn't sure why. And so just as the mirthless
    sequel was being
disinterred, a feeling of rage came over him, but also of relief,
    because
you couldn't do it now. They're lost somewhere out there
    between the trees
and muck, besides all cars have them now. And the colorful
    glasses and telephone
are there; he came for a fitting. It was proper, and in its time.
    But no
matter what you do someone will be malevolent about it, and try
    to stop you,
though there is no stopping them. He came for the fitting and
    tried
it on and it fit, just like that. What a laugh. Oh yes she laughed
    out
of the closet I'll be there in a minute dear. You see

how fond of him she was, and he, well he just took it,
like most things, change, pretzels. And she thought he was
so good at it it kind of faked her when the last windshield
    whizzed
by and it was all over as though in a rush. And as meat is sung,
and lips only slowly parted for the alphabet of night chimes to come
clanging down like an immense ring of keys, so with the gale-
whipped morsel, notion of itself, that dogs us and all humans,
    and we never
quite get out from under it, there is always a thread of it attached
    to you
and when you remove that, another one as though magnetized
    takes its place.
Begorrah it was dumb to be in the pit with him, for then the
    sentence . . .
But who knows what all they may have tried before, what
avenues exhausted before it was time to mend and really be the
    interloper,
and for all its sparks it was never considered dangerous.
Everybody gets such ideas on occasion, but here was the little
    shot-glass
of night, all ready to drink, and you spread out in it
even before it radiates in you. It doesn't matter whether or not
you like the striations, because, in the time it takes to consider
    them,
they will have merged, the rich man's house become a kettle,
    the wreath
in the sink turned to something else, and still the potion holds,
prominent. And you want to see it and to have it be talked
    about this way,
not drool aimless compassion. So on that night we were almost
    boarded up,
packed off to a vacation—where? Moreover no men heard of it,
only teen-age girls and male adolescents with fruited
    complexions and scalps,
who were going to make it difficult for one should an occasion
    arise.
        But a funny
thing happened, none of us were around to count, all
    incommensurate with our

duties as we should forever be, and not wanting much training.
    The dark
was like nectar that evening, rising in the mouth; you thought
    you had never heard
so pretty a sound. Then, of course, quietism was again broached
and that soon, and quite soon the pink of the salmon ignited
    the whey
of the plover's egg and the black of old, scarred metal; then,
    how it
feels relaxes one like a warm, numbing bath, and her argument,
    and yours,
and all of theirs—why, why not just consider, or better yet, just
hold, hold on to them? For the speed of light is far away,
and you, sooner or later, must return
to a deteriorated situation, and, placing your hand in the fire, say
just what it means to you to be connected
and over, and kiss the burning edges of the unfolded, stiff
card, and be unable to avoid doing anything about it or
    acknowledging it
when we have passed, when all is past.
                                        And why did
he, by what was he it? Why, we push our little tales around
and back and forth and so on
by which time it literally *implodes,* I mean by then he was
    settling in
and no one called his attention to it. In your repertory of
    groans is one
glottal one—you'll feel the difference. And if it can't liberate
    itself from us,
just turns to dust in the air floating with the kind of negative
    majesty one thought
one would not see again in one's life. But I had the horn—we
    had a deal we agreed on, yet
no record of its existence is sketched, and I am all I am
in the meanwhile and 13,000 fucking miles away like a planter
on his porch. And so I am unaware of the flambeaux and,
    possibly, the stealth
that brought me here. And abandoned me—I—
I'm awfully sorry, big boy, but my plans concern George and
    his wife over by the other side

of the lake slipping into a nervous breakdown, and I, we, well
    as you know, we
sit here determined, not like the rind
of the melon but not liking to say anything about it into the
    miraculous dawn
that—gasp—gathers us into its stocking. A pervasive air about
    him of studious
lyricism avoided us, and he turned, ever so quickly, to the hen
    house, and off
in the open was seen running, and then, it's so easy, was
    probably not recorded
except between the trees of a clearing. And who, what patron
    saint, will pick up
the pieces of the glittering lighthouse and restore us to them in
    a kind
of Roman calm, that we were meant for? And suddenly SHIT
    it's the fire and
glass breaking everywhere—it's as though you were never born
    but you must somehow
drink a toast to the small nucleus of watch-springs or confusion
    that
lords it over you now but will be less than an unconsumed coal
    among ashes, soon,
until the dryer's fixed. And then all out and along the
cinder path that led so alluringly down to the bayou, all we can
    know is hope
and fevers for a coming tomorrow of saffron and moist rage
    under the corner
of someone's hat that wasn't meant to like you. Me, I
rest in the sun regardless. We saw a car drive on to the city that
is the password. Ice-cubes played tag up and down my spine. I'm
here to collect the reward. Obey my every command, no matter
how strange it may seem, otherwise we'll have been banished
    before the judgment,
not know how fortunate we were in our old simplicity. Other
    vanished
zinnias were interviewed and nobody had anything, good or
    bad, to say about us,
which doesn't cause any tears yet one wonders: what if one
    were back there again?

On whom might one rely? What distractions would be
  concocted for us
if we had strayed? And who is the baron that manipulates our
  daily lives
from afar? Why even depend on industry and innocence when
  rebellion is growing
in the ditch just outside? Who knows about us? Who ever did?
  Weren't we
lying to ourselves when we thought we caught someone being
  just slightly
interested in us one day, and if so, whose fault is it? That we came
too late to an overgrown baseball diamond? And in the meantime
  shacks had vanished
without a trace from the face of the globe
and now the evening star was combing her hair at the attic
  window
and no one is to blame, just be calm, don't
rush, it's all over or soon will be or just was, in any
other language sufficient to tell it in—just like it was.

It has long been my contention that jackals,
unlike other denizens of the epistemic forest, are able to predict
the future of metabolizing some kind of parasite that grows on
  other people's
children and devours them. The eyes are a profound cobalt
  blue, accepting
of moral dilemmas and sprouting proverbs
slowly, like crystals,
but no, not innocent,
and not lacking in character. Twenty years ago, you will recall,
  the eyes
thought they made a difference, were glazed, forgetting and
  impudent,
relieved of parenting. Arenas were quite happy to comply
though a little bewildered. At first at least. One very chewy
  advanced proposition
seemed to falter, then faded into the background noise, but—
  here's the thing—
continued, to this day. Bald and bleeding. I don't like it, no one
is obliged to, everyone may *bon gré mal gré* ignore it, yet it peaks

and in so doing has its say. The manageress was adamant, but I
    had the horrible idea
of prolonging beyond night and dawn one's predilection for
    quoting old
dispatches and getting into hot water, and then? The sullen
    bathroom
question lasted, I was too far out into it, out of pocket, plus
    the by no means negligible
question of my own comfort to be decoded, and all other
    arguments
suddenly collapsed, like a dream of homecoming. How stung
    my myth;
my dream wasn't over, we were only such a dream. By this time
    all the caissons
of power had been turned inside out anyway; it was considered
    correct to despise it
and rightly so, but how often can one shamble
back to the vegetable gunk and still retain at least a superficial
    appearance of contrition?
As often as the clock seems to say I love you and boulders
turn in their sleep and sigh and the cat is forever running away.
    It took
two weeks to lead up to this. The stores are quiet now.
I say lie down in it. I already asked Santa about it.
And then, you see, it became part of our cultural history. We
    can't ignore it
even though we'd like to, it's so mild and hurtless. And you
    thought
you had it bad, or good. With as many associations as that
to keep thumbing through, one winks at the legal filigrane that
    penetrates every
page of the mouldering sheaf down to the last one, like a spike
through a door. Somebody dust these ashes off, open
the curtains, get a little light on the subject: the subject
going off on its own again. Yes but if home were only light
sliding down darkened windows in rivulets, inhabiting their
concavities and generally adapting itself to the contours of
    what is already there,
one could understand that,
lie back on the stiff daybed shading one's eyes from

omnipresent bleary dawn that acts as an uncle's remonstrance:
  do this
not for me or for yourself but for your mother the way an
  empty circle
of daisies seeks to promote plausibility and is simultaneously
  too distraught
and ashamed to articulate the siren call crisply and sinks, it too,
into the foam of reliably not taking itself seriously. I wish you
  well darling always
especially days when the gray pain lifts for a moment like fog
  trapped under
a layer of warmer air, then sags definitively not knowing what
  to do
with itself or about anything. Days when the pointed freshness
  of forests
above the snowline
can consider itself numb, when the friendly gurgling of rills talks
back and one listens but never heeds
that desire for perfectability. Hey, it was here only a moment ago
I think or somebody misled me, as sometimes happens, yet
  with as many
associations as that some of it is bound to come down, to
  crumble, to be reduced
to a vexing powder but natural like dust, and that
within all our lifetimes. Local businessmen bristled. New painless
methods were introduced but somehow made it all thick and
  rubbery, an unwanted anthem.
No one said it. Care was off and running, the divorce courts
overflowing for once, and no one was going to take issue,
  dispute the power vacuum
that was walking around shaking hands, acting for all the world
  like a candidate.
But you feel it don't you? How come nobody
has anything nice
to say, I mean you striped ball, even for a testimonial dinner on
  a commercial, then they all
run back, must have been a mistake. Yes, we have it here.

Anyway, where are they? I am violently opposed to the little
  pieces

of the puzzle getting in on the act; slobbering, as it were,
any more than I can see Little Red Riding Hood climbing Mt.
    McKinley.
But as for the horror of it—we are, look, all of us, undisciplined so
when it's time to take the kids somewhere or subvert the boss's
    ego the light
goes out of us for an instant. Oh I know we can patch it up,
    always successfully,
later. But out of the fine deposit of the encounter there is
    surely something
that is required reading, though seldom in focus. Good gravy, it
gives me the creeps just telling you about it. And after we had
    sunbathed
the mist was on time, dull and fathomable. That's no reason to
    return home, to
our roots, of course, yet neither can it be construed as an
    invitation. You see
everything you see on television is a fraud, is planted there to
    confuse distraught
patriots like yourself, and though we enter into it no wiser and
    leave
resolved to mend our ways, something like an actual misprint
    occurs. We are no
longer in charge of our propriety; jackdaws have launched
    nearby and the elms have seen
better days. Why is it that just because I'm a child I can
warn no one of this, except by speaking in tongues? Oh I know
    formulating
bright, snazzy, fabulous demands isn't the same thing as being
    a teacher
and picking up on the slowness of your student. I can
    rhapsodize about that
too, but there comes a point when having aimed
accurately and reaped the reasonable rewards is more than
    something to
sing about, is the entity, no I mean the accretion—is indeed the
fantastic fact. It was like being run over when I
first thought of this. And now sad to say our limbs
aren't as important; we have witnessed an entire tennis match
    and candles

are coming on, there's a hint
of fall in the air, soggy and bored. *O I have to keep fighting
back to find you, and then when you're still there, what is it I know?*
Nothing about the future and no more about you, either, honey,
I was going to say. Have you noted how things
have a way of working out but have you also noted how rarely
    this constitutes a satisfying
set of circumstances, especially when we dream, not plan, them?
    In my house
no one is rude but that's no excuse;
I think footfalls
are approaching, circling round, then moving away
to some other sun, some direction? I care more
yet it's there.

Despite handicaps trading continues,
natural horns bleat. The fog may be messing up traffic today
but in offices chic outfits signal that for sure violence too has its
    calm
aspects, when things get done in dozens, or even scores. The
    museum
guards must have known something was up, yet here too, only
    silence stammers.
Don't ask your partner what to think. He may have noticed
that the weathervane has jammed even as crowds of daytrippers
move on out of the city in gaily painted carts, and by noon
    something just
too awful had come between us. I called John but he couldn't
    come to the phone
nor did his assistant have any clue as to what the barking, the clatter
of falling jewelry were all about. It occurs to me in my home
    on the beach
sometimes that others must have experiences identical to mine
and are also unable to speak of them, that if we cared
enough to go into each other's psyche and explore
around, some of the canned white entrepreneurial brain food
could be reproduced in time to save the legions
of the dispossessed, and elephants. But—
what is a waiting room for, after all? If not to
live out one's life scarily to the borders of altered lawns

with red leaves nestled on them. Home becomes more than a
    place, more even than
a concept for this elite minority, and then singles them out
by pointing so that some symbol of their shame never
goes away, until the paper it is written on has rotted
over thousands of years, by which time new insects will have
    been introduced,
new forms of dandruff, holes that are really shoes. A thin
    puddle of air
rules over us; all obeisances are made that way, all
curtsies and notions seem to point into that vortex
of fear just as the alarm goes off. But is it
fear, or only an unpleasant hum? And jaywalkers gravitate there,
are seen to believe. The old man had no enemies. Why, then?
    Because a handful
of ages knew of his connection to poetry via the wet, fissured
    rocks far below
in the cave and took revenge for their own knowingness to
    create an unpleasant
situation that would probably have gone away if nobody had
    said anything about it,
but now—well you just can't ask people to keep silent
about something they've seen, and the forces that prodded
us on to victory are staging an uncharacteristic fast.
Only the intrusion of tomorrow's light will have been
    recognized as a new note
in the negotiations, which will in any case by that time be in
    the public
domain, and no further recruiting be deemed necessary, or
    undertaken.
I can't shake the hunch that this is what the stuff is all about
and no one cares to
know, let alone be a witness to further legal horse-trading.
That's what caused all the trouble.

Words, however, are not the culprit. They are at worst a placebo,
leading nowhere (though nowhere, it must be added, can
    sometimes be a cozy
place, preferable in many cases to somewhere), to banal if
    agreeable note-spinning.

Covering reams of foolscap with them won't guarantee success,
yet neither will it automatically induce ruination; wheel on the
    guillotine;
leave, in the middle distance, something like an endless morgue,
    a lake of regret.
It's better though to listen to the strange chirps of the furniture.
Listening is a patented device whose manifold uses have
    scarcely begun to be explored,
that one should practice on as many occasions as are deemed
    profitable. Bore your friends,
wine them, show them a grand time: other, more auspicious
occasions are sure to be evoked; nights when, from the
    grandstand, tremendous plumes
of steam plummeted straight into the basalt sky. Days of
    conversation, and, at the end,
a feeling of progress in sorting out mutual feelings and actually
    partly
resolving certain discords came to seem as though it were
    happening
and the treehouse was split apart by rays plunging out of the
    incandescent
core of tangled concerns and resolves and the handcar of an
    important relationship
was steered onto the right track out of the city into a
    shadowed, mostly empty
peripheral zone of tears for anointed and angry memories,
    defused now,
ready for twilight. It's something Eagle Scouts used to discuss
by the campfire, a page that somehow got ripped out of the
    record, to be
as though it had never been. Just because cows and horses
    stand around much as they always have,
it is as though we were contemplating a set of sealed
    instructions:
now the bridge will never be built,
if that is all time had in the wallet at his back. Scaled-down surprises
here and there, a puttering about in dust, and once again it
    seems as though it
were all up to us. Well, why not? The gravel underfoot is a little
    finer

this time round. And nobody yells at you. The words have, as
   they
always do, come full circle, dragging the meaning that was on
   the reverse side
all along, and one even
expects this, something to chew on. I'm rubber
and you're glue, whatever you say bounces off me and sticks to
   you; in which gluey
embrace I surrender. We are both part of a living thing now.

A decade later he stumbled or became confused.
There was no one else along on this outing, so why was he
always flailing his arms majestically? Talking to the walls?
   Whenever someone'd
cross over to be kind to him it was as though he'd never seen a
   human face before;
the eyes were runny, the nose ditto, the words were like
   chopped cotton wool
after he'd forced them out. To drag meaning like this behind
   one is bad
enough, but to have it beside one is worse, worse than
   knowing what to do.
Finally, the memory became an object
to be passed around for displays of connoisseurship to ignite; thus,
one can live in the same house with one's ambitions and
drives and still have the luxury of feeling alone: oh come off it, no
one wants to be alone. And even, you know, accept the
   occasional invitation
but also slog on unshod, solitary, except for casual greetings from
even more casual acquaintances.

Harder to explain is the disparity between what is loved
and the energy with which one goes about doing it, and harder
   still
to understand or appreciate the astonishingly thin gruel
which serves its hunger *de tous les jours* and with which
it gives every appearance of being satisfied. I suppose if one
were born and grew up on a desert island, knowing
of nothing better or even different, one might coincide
with the four walls that contain one and see no anomaly, no

grotesquerie, in the result. This mound of cold ashes that we call
for want of a better word the past wouldn't inflect the horizon
as it does here, calling attention to shapes
that resemble it and so liberating them into the bloodstream
of our collective memory: here a chicken coop, there a
    smokestack,
farther on an underground laboratory. These things then wouldn't
depress (or, as sometimes happens, exalt) one, and living would
    be just that:
a heavenly apothegm leading to a trance on earth. Yet one scolds
the horizon for having nothing better to offer. *Did I order that?*
And when the bill comes, tries to complain to the management
but at that point the jig, or whatever, is up. Yes I've seen many
    fine
young girls in my time take that path and wonder afterwards
what went wrong. I've seen children, taken from their homes
at too early an age, left to wander about like Little Nell,
not knowing that they were never obliged to do this thing. O
paradise, to lie in the hammock with one's book and drink,
not hearing the murmur of consternation as it moves
    progressively
up the decibel scale. Yet I see you are uncertain where to locate
    me:
here I am. And I've done more thinking about you than you
    perhaps realize,
yes, a sight more than you've done about *me*. Which reminds me:
when are we going to get together? I mean really—not just for a
drink and a smoke, but *really*
invade each other's privacy in a significant way that will make sense
and later amends to both of us for having done so, for I am
short of the mark despite my bluster and my swaggering,
have no real home and no one to inhabit it except you
whom I am in danger of losing permanently as a bluefish slips off
the deck of a ship, as a tuna flounders, but say, you know all that.
What kind of a chump do you think I am, anyway? I would like
    your
attention, not just your eyes and face. I would like to tell you
how much I love you. I'm a sap for trying, but down deep
in the bowels of the ship we hear something, don't you agree, that
tells us where we went off course and what we must do to

get back on it only now it's too late, all the
spars have erupted like apple blossoms, hitting the reef: I would
like to go on for a while anyway, but wonder under the
   circumstances whether
it wouldn't be like setting out on a long journey in rain so heavy
it takes your breath away. Even one step is out of the question,
I think, now. I no longer have the energy to breathe
on the windowpane so that the frost will transform it into garlands
of chiseled steel that draw one out
like a rapt interlocutrix. No it's
heavy out here today; the wind serves only to remind one of
   other possible
beginnings and an end, if one were likely to pass this way again.

I see.
I'll try another ticket. Meanwhile thanks for the harmonium: its
inoffensive chords swept me right off my feet near the railroad
and—nice—are returning to bloom tomorrow and each day
   after that.
I thought nobody needed a confessor any more, but I was
   wrong I guess,
so, old stump, I'm off until tomorrow or some day early next
   week, I mean
how much more can I say, giving myself away, without negating
the positive meaning of what I wanted to say and which has
   now subtly changed
back to an elementary precept or something else one doesn't
   much want to hear:
how we flowered, and lost, and rose up thin again with our
   thoughts
to distract us but not too much and so approached the shambling
roadbed and placed one sole in front of another, slowly but not
   tentatively,
and then the lean-to, the buttercups and the ring of blue
   mountains hove
into view as though to say but that's what I asked you last time
and now you will be forced to give a different answer
even though the wind has dropped. I thought I saw someone
   over there.
No, it's just the wind egging the trees on

into battle with dusk, and I can
still see how it's still you there, only with such a difference I almost
didn't have time to trust my space. But we know now and have
    had it true
to be us, for the asking, for the begging, for the just one more
    time.

In winter it was generally a slow blizzard of piano rags, while in
    summer
or some such season gentian shadows on the tapioca fields
    looked themselves
good enough to eat, and always in a locker downstairs was this
    pocket
mirror with *the* thumbprint on it, a source of shame, but how
can I deny my true origin and nature even if it's going to get
    me into a lot of
trouble later? At any rate, no notice was taken of anything and
maids pushed their prams and policemen stopped cars and it
    was getting to be spring
or it wasn't, but the bare trees looked oddly barbed, and perhaps
    that
was something, and it seemed to be starting to rain. I sit here
wringing my hands but what good does it do
if *I* am the ghost this time despite
the reassuring activity that surrounds me? And if I am to be
    cast off, then
where? There has to be a space, even a negative one, a slot
for me, or does there? But if all space is contained within me, then
there is no place for me to go, I am not even here, and now,
    and can join
no choir or club, indeed I am the sawdust of what's around but
    nobody can
even authorize that either. My Collected Letters will I
    somehow
feel vindicate me but even there the onion skin cannot be split
    and I'll go on
being a postscript written in invisible ink until some day several
    centuries from now
when they open a time capsule and enthusiastic fresh air will
    rush out to inform

the world and one can rise from one's nap in time for bed. The
    great apartment
fronts will put their heads together and sunset will seem an
    enormous conflagration,
but vindicate one at what price? Where are the children now
    who wanted
to hear that story? Why, the youngest of them passed away
    years ago
on the west coast surprised that anyone should remember and
    the slow
torrent of the glacier got piped in efficiently to fill the slightest
    hairline
fissure. Its job is done. We all live in the past now. And so the
    children
must still hang on somewhere, though no one is quite sure where
    or how many
or what paths there are to be taken in darkness. Only the fools,
    the severed heads, know.

So my old mother became a niche in time, and she, too,
    preferred not to get out of it:
as long as it was going to be, it wasn't this bad, says the antique
    adage. And these
three or four others came of it. No one asked them in but they
    came in anyway,
prepared to play. And somehow a chapter was written about
    this. It all
boils down to keeping quiet and having a good time. As long
    as you don't abuse
the orange trees standing in their pots so civil, well all will be
    yours next time too
and let's hear it for those who never won anything, whose time
    came and went
like the tide leaving curious bones behind, and they were never
    cheated on and never
lied, without telling anyone the truth. And behind these,
    interlopers
and more interlopers, a vast frame of them, too facile to be
    derided.
And bananas stand around stiffly, at attention. Is this

the gray way I once knew? And if so, where are the standard
   bearers? Why
have our values been lost? Who is going to pay for any of this?
Pottsville is too small for a man of your caliber. Full many a flower
is born to blush unseen, and waste its fragrance on the arctic air
outside the Shady Octopus saloon, and then some.
If all is going to be reorganized, the charming irregularities of
   the days
ahead may as well go too, the song of plaintive songs choke off
   the ingress
while alleviating the drip, as the old man, hypotenuse-like, touches
an extremity that soon burns out of control, surrounds
the town on the down and all rush together, those who
hated each other suddenly finding good reason for the
   slobbering embrace.
Whether it's more fun to feel in one's own underpants
or strike out on the highroad to professional success, all
   pavilions a-flutter,
all portholes glinting, before the thing sinks in the mouth of
   the river, memory
has been transformed into corpses and while we stand discussing
   the news the unmanageable
outline of something much bigger and more profuse is
   struggling to understand
itself (it will be years before it gets around to us and by then
what faces will we be? Who's going to take care of the
   association headquarters
and, likelier still, revert with us to the narrow-gauge railroad
   track that steals
through yellow viburnum and buried cinders as though to
   point the finger of guilt
at the very beginning, the origin that is still a baby, learning to cry
as the lights are blown out and darkness like a swift film of oil
   closes down
to the brilliant crack at the horizon's outcome?). No two
   employees know it.

I thought, and this much remained hidden from me:
the beloved canker that was always there, willing to give you all
   of "Queen Mab"

for a quarter, or turn on the rusty heel of one boot and be off, whistling
into such nether parts of the sky as are deemed scarcely fit for consumption
here on our poor earth; the Christmas lights, each blinking in the triumph of its
individual color toward the benefit of the whole; the stars and so on brought forth
each night as a sop to the unweeded intellect, though much
more remains to be read into them; polar bears, relaxing each on his floe in the arctic section
of the zoo or rolling off it into the green, greasy water; people with pencils
in their hands; a selection of erotic attractions for this week including stiletto heels
and rubber miniskirts; carloads of whatever thundered past in the night; juleps
on porches; and the most extravagant collection of whodunit compliments one
was ever gifted with, out of the nightfall of a dream, freeflowing as the meanders
of a great stream, and every bit as meaningless and ominous; and finally a choice
of purgations, each not necessarily appropriate to the instance; i.e., electrocution for the theft
of a needle; simple tears for aggravated manslaughter; a necklace of boar's teeth
for blaspheming; added lines in the forehead for poaching, or preaching; a fountain
of mud on the front lawn of one who fondled his daughter's best friend's breasts;
and, for the discreetly ambitious, a monotonous horizon. As it all bore in
on me I started to awake, then thought better of it, then rushed to the phone to call
my broker, but it was too late: an osselet of meaning in the lizard's tail
of eternity had clicked into place, become pure and unattainable, while I, goof

that I am, simultaneously realized just how sensational it was
    and how a fortune could
be made by being first with the revelation as the bank closed its
    doors and the market suspended operations.

True, they managed to save Hitler's brain before it destroyed
    the world
with *zuppa inglese*. (Just look in the milk can and you'll find
    out why.) But sometimes
walking away from a cure may not be the best way to get rid of
    it. Sure, you feel
fine. Today, and tomorrow as well. By next week you're feeling better
than you have in a long time. And as the medication gradually
    dissipates, the feeling of
well-being takes over, an arbiter for generations to come. Only
    long after your death
will the life you so busily led be imputed to the cornerstone of
    rot that was
the secret, driving force in it: something everyone at the time
    found to be OK.
And as gravel sinks slowly with the aquifer's depletion, those
not in the know will begin to stir in their sleep; it will gradually
    dawn on them
(in dreams of "cheese, toasted mostly") how the ingenious theory
    was flawed; indeed
it was flaws that produced the dazzling quicksilver sheen that
    attracted
so many to it for so long. If that's the case, why tarry on rutted
    goat-paths
from whence even the nearest foothills are shrouded, by mists,
    from view? The animals
are incredible; there's even a dog named Bruce. One can retool
    the context, but slowly,
slowly, and of course there is no positive guarantee of a successful
    outcome; one
should think of it as a virtuoso spinning-song whose relentless
    roulades promise minor
disturbances among the cobwebbed rafters but perhaps nothing
    much to weave

one-armed nightshirts with for the wild swans, your brothers: only
try to forget the slow upward
path to perfectness and let its mirror-image
come to install its truly sensitive surface within you, during the
    night
of deft dreams and bad brushes with dolor. Fear of the dark
    causes it,
but by then to have been around and been of it will have
    carried over into lunch.
Do you think there's some connection between this and that
    which happened before?
Perhaps not. Perhaps there is none, but the Patagonians will like
    it, all 499,500 of 'em.

Without further ado bring on the subject of these
negotiations. They all would like to collect it always, but since
that's impossible, the Logos alone will have to suffice.
A pity, since no one has seen it recently. Others crowded the
    opening, hoping
to catch a glimpse, but the majority saw the occluded expatriate
    ragtag representation and
decided to not even try. To this day no one knows the shape or
    heft of the thing,
and that's the honest truth thrown out of court, exhibiting
    abrasions,
muffled. And the story of how we ran out of it.

So, "marrying little with less," *meliora probant, deteriora
sequuntur*, they footdrag in oblivion, lingering over steaks to
    analyze
the latest inquiry.

My biological father thought enough of it to see that I was
    posited, demanding
names omitted from the roster, either from carelessness or
    intent to harm: *we'll*
see that the thing gets done! And moreover, as I was asking her
    about her car
a quiet moment of fatigue slipped in leaving faces drained,
    moments of pleasure

unexamined. It was all because I told him he should change his
    shirt. He got mad
and went out and I didn't see him again for thirty years, by
    which time both of us had aged
considerably but were still reasonably attractive, some might
    even say more so. I
reminded him of the shirt thing and he just laughed, said
    supermarkets sell them now
and besides you shouldn't worry about a little dirt, it's the spice
    of life, he said.
And we had set aside Siberia
for us and for a few beloved friends
but the bureaucracy and the logistics of it all defeated us, why
    we were tied
up in red tape for 2½ years and after that I just wanted out, no
place is worth that much worry. Besides it's quite quiet and
    confusing at home, thank you
very much. Yet I was still hung up on his idea of me, I thought
    I was becoming that person
I didn't even know or want to know very much about, and all
    of my
déjà-vus were ones that could have occurred to him. Still, life is
    reasonably absorbing
and there's a lot of nice people around. Most days are well
    fed
and relaxing, and one can improve one's mind a little
by going out to a film or having a chat with that special friend;
    and before
you know it it's time to brush your teeth and go to bed. Why
    then, does that feeling
of emptiness keep turning up like a stranger you've seen dozens
    of times, out-of-focus
usually, standing toward the rear of the bus or fishing for coins
    at the newsstand? I'm
sure it's all coincidence, but it
does have a way of rattling things, like a constant draft through
    the house, rustling
papers, riveting one's eye on the clock. So what's
to feel nervous about? We all know that we have to live for a
    certain time and then

unfortunately we must die, and after that no one is sure what
   happens. Accounts vary. But we
most of us feel we'll be made comfortable for much of the time
   after that, and get credit
for the (admittedly) few nice things we did, and no one is
   going to make too much
of a fuss over those we'd rather draw the curtain over, and
   besides, we can't see
much that was wrong in them, there are two sides to every
   question. Yet the facts
fascinate one, we become one of those persons who are only
   satisfied with thoroughly
reliable information—the truth, if there ever could be such a
   thing. Our journey
flows past us like ice chunks, maybe it is we that are stationary.
O so much God to police everything and still be left over to
   flatter one's
harmless idiosyncrasies, the things that make us *us*, which is
   precisely
what is fading like paint on a sign, no matter how much one
   pretends it's the same
as yesterday. And children talk to us—*that*, surely, must be a plus?

It's the lunatic frequency this time. One man, taking his kids to
   the ball
game, reverted and was found playing cards at a friend's house.
   In spring the tips of
the apple branches graze the trailer and it's time for a new round
robin of progressive delicacies and returned thank-you letters.
   Out in the open
by the gym it was never a question of keep your pants on we're
   all getting someplace, getting
to be someone. Those were perspectives too limned to shoot
   along and the people thanked
the baseball player who invented them. Inactivity is as a syrup
   to these people, some of them,
they bank on mistrust and in the end are amazed to find their
   land has been overgrazed
by herds of yak, each of the quadrupeds spaced almost
   equidistant from its

nearest neighbor, as far as the eye can see, to Labrador and beyond
into the topaz twilight of the Urals. Oh some will say
you can't trust them let alone see them coming, let alone avoid
   a collision
with jarring implications for the future of humanity. Even its
   garish exterior
isn't as uncompromising as one might
at first conclude, and then they have ashtrays and can see, no
   one makes extraordinary
demands on them as long as they go on living, and in April
that doesn't seem an impossible feat. To those residing on the
   outskirts of some
city or suburb it gets to be even more of a tease—were *they*
   included in the survey, and,
if so, who are they? Shooting-gallery ducks waiting to be
   flattened, probably.
What if one crosses the sea
to descend at the pier where one's sweetheart bade farewell to
   one several years ago and finds
her there to greet one, not all that changed? And if the parents
   of both parties pronounce it
a suitable match, why there you are, another union has been
   consecrated, another
two people been driven from loneliness into the reciprocal
   dawn of each other's arms
as if it were long ago, and tidings spread throughout the land
   and ordinary people
came to appreciate and savor and go back into the narrow,
   closetlike conundrum of their own
slender existences and be thankful there was for once
   something to talk about and then
mutually agree on. A pact with the forces that be—nothing
   less, and that
is saying a good deal. So in all eras bargains have been struck,
horns blown, and in some strange, silly way each of us is the
   stronger for it. We made
our tea and then we drank it. This is an honorable instance of
   how shame can disappear
in the dust and the confusion, the aftermath. And if an executive
can teeter on his perch all day long from dawn to dusk, a wren

can say to him, why don't you go on an organized outing, stop
fooling yourself, this world-situation isn't nonsense though
   realpolitik may not be
the accurate term for it either, so why explode like a timebomb
   that was set long ago
and may no longer be operable? But you see so many
of us are like that bird, that man I mean, that for but a few can
   life resonate with
anything like serious implications. So many were hung out to
   dry, or, more accurately, to rot.
And these marginalia—what other word is there for them?—are
   the substance of the text,
by not being allowed to fit in. One can proceed like a ghost
along corridors and find that doors are closed to one, and then
what good is being invisible? It all goes to show how our
   parents taught us many things,
including the right one, that we should untie
gently, like a knotted shoelace, and then little expressions of
   relief occur in the whorls,
and many things, incipient ones, besides. Yet on the shoals of this
   time
everyone believes himself righteous and lost, that the view is
   only a way
in all directions, and one must have a timepiece to unravel
   ramifications that
in fact do not exist, but like a gold toothpick are merely on hand
   to see that they
get talked about and maybe some club will invite one of them
   to speak. It is an air
strangely purged of magnolias, and quicklime, and anyone
can be called to take a seat. Best to enjoy it,
not turn up in the unwritten part as a miser or scavenger few
   would have taken seriously
as a person, but just as many might have feared. We live in an
   age when terror
opens like breadfruit and one *must* pick and choose—the seeds
   and proverbs just
aren't that numerous. Everybody must vote. Everybody's vote
   must be accepted into the

tilting radio tower that is collapsing in one's own best interest
   in one
dark swoop of mingled horror and relaxed apprehension: to
   accomplish
anything more would be a joke, yet
the boy
still stands there, hasn't gone away; by any
other standards a misadventure yet one is going to be firm and
   tame and positive
in searching out the old prescription, scratching one's
first initial idly in the wood of the door and only then
going away, to be something else in some other town when
   newspapers bearing
that day's date finally arrive and the citizenry, perplexed, still
   goes about its business
carrying news of new situations into inaccessible corners of this
   bland
and stultified universe, only to be someone
isn't then their top priority: getting to be tall in late afternoon is.
The arrogance of these people! Anyone who's been around
   understands, and that
includes most of us: barristers . . . Out of one's loneliness it's
   hard not to forgive
the girl who longs to be seen, and the guy who wishes only to
   be left alone. Forest
dithers protect us a lot of the time, but for those moments
   when one is thrust willy-
nilly into the spotlight, then oh dear! I wish I had something
   more sizable to say—
couldn't my part be rewritten? But that's over too before long.
   And the forest comes to
seem more like a commodity, somewhere one can live and tie
   rope around oneself.
The annals, if there are any, transform this into glamour and
   chrysoprase, two
adjacent keys of a piano pressed down one after the other. And
   one's modesty—
well it's all here, in this manila folder. I was going to talk about
   that, tree

of the deep, tree of being beautiful of, of lost promise and hopes
that still flutter in the distance, and you know somehow . . .
　　But in the end it got mistreated,
the happy moments streaked with sadness, but perhaps they
　　always were.
Perhaps it says a great deal that there were any, and so
out of tune with the rest that was going on, like a canary in a
　　zoo, and I said
why give any guarantees if it can be rescinded without notice, if
　　entreaties are to
become comments, and you know what he said, he said, well,
　　it's reasonable for you to expect that
but it's not unreasonable for anyone else to pay it no mind, so
　　there! I was
crushed. The one person I thought understood. But it's all right,
　　he can go on paying,
meanwhile I am scarcely alone, though it *is* lonesome.
　　However, when I start
feeling blue I can just stand up like everyone else and lay my
　　cards on the table: look,
it says so, it's all here, written in this book. So I'm never
　　completely at a loss,
only a little disconcerted, thrashing about, sometimes. In the
　　rival cesspool
of other nations they may think they have it better, but I know
　　that here the
uncertainty is pure. And so I often take the afternoon off, read,
　　write or gaze
intently out of the window for long periods of time. And then
　　you take tea
in the afternoon, that is you make it and then drink it. Oh I'm
　　so sorry, golly, how
nothing ever really comes to fruition. But by the same token I
　　am relieved of manifold responsibilities,
am allowed to delegate authority, and before I know it, my
　　mood
has changed, like a torn circus poster that becomes pristine
　　again in reverse cinematography,
and these moments of course matter, and fall by the wayside in
　　a positive sense.

Perplexed by myopia one still enjoys it, and in the autumn of
    life cackles somewhat unrestrainedly
before writing off one's accurate perception
of all that has gone before in the heroic period when books are
    friends. Nature
wants you to do it. No seism infinitesimal enough not to
    register in the growing
tornado of disapproval when mountains crash in the rubble,
    electricity bisects the sky, and
shrill ululations burst forth from caverns deep in the earth's
    surface. But I'm
getting ahead of my story, we're talking about how you, a
    wanderer, like it,
and how to escape. Oh my dear, I've tried that. But if it
    interests you
you can browse through this catalog and, who knows, perhaps
    come up with a solution that will apply
to your complicated case, just conceivably, or perhaps you
    know someone better informed
in the higher echelons where the view is distant and severe,
the ground blue as steel.

II

But how trivial the music. All this. Yet it is where part of the
    gender first starts to
emerge and become a blur. The various members
of both sexes never seem to get hurt: theirs is a life that drifts
    peaceably along
as on a stream and they can wave
to each other like boats and join in the fun and never be
    forgotten. Possibly
a door opens far down in the wall to admit a lover
who as silently departs later. Possibly there is more to it all than
    this,
but if we can decipher even what the fair-minded man wants us
    to, what about the rest,
poverty and disclaimers? And who sees the mountain-mad man
    through goatshine
and never confesses to an early blunder concealed, to having
    left a child in the cold once?
And as they marginally edge each other, new and good truths
    and others, older
and not so good, begin to appear along the bicycle-trail of
    their itinerary
through space, here on earth. One was a Spanish
    longshoreman's daughter,
a laughing girl, who, when told the truth, deliberately spat on
    it. Another,
young too, and in the full flower of "the devil's beauty," had
    good cause to come up and grab
an arm, an elbow resting on a newspaper as it happened, and
    tickle the thing
half to death. And in the interval of slide, or portamento, a lot
    of laughing does
get to be heard, only it's like you're not doing it, it's the boys
on the other side of the ridge obeying their zeal again. The
    moon abruptly decides to set
and kids pester their parents for more firecrackers, in the
    crevices, where eyes
lately peeked out—O bored hero,
why not return to earth for a while? We have forgiven thee

what was construed as negligence rather than rancor, so in
 return we
should be taught by thy knee. Later when she comes to throw
 out the table scraps there it will be,
a little sliver of haven made and purposely rigged for you
to come and go many times without noticing, slinging your
 coat over your shoulder
as you go along looking in the dirt for a whistle. But that day
it was all roses. And it turned out that the inquiry was silenced,
deliberately erased from the file.
And if a man wanted this, and got it, how about the heathen
 rest of us
who wait in silence for food
as though a drug got planted in one's abdomen? Sooner or
 later, boys and girls declare, there
will be someone on whom a care like this could devolve,
a woman made to see through, analyze, and correct the errant
 circuitry
and in doing so bring us back to the harbor of recollection
from which we strayed so long ago, but it was a mistake in a dream.
The formula is now reconstituted.
From the awfulness of times long gone by it wrests
a polite excuse, small even by its standards, but alive to us, and
 harsh, dry, a wrong prism.

Or stand: all right, lowering the teabag into the mug until
 something
comes of it, is plumbed, but meanwhile what of zombies
 standing around in clinging seersucker
in frigid temperatures, awaiting your decision? When the curse
arrives, are you prepared to deal with it? Apologies don't
 matter any more; it's
a question of biting off the end, spitting it out, and sucking the
 poison through a small tube
if you want to go that way. Otherwise, listless years of atrophy
 could be your fate
though there are undoubtedly worse ones. Pick a channel,
 explore, document it—
please take *all* the evidence into account in your report, when
 you write it:

you'll find your story isn't so different from any honest man's, nor
   less
bizarre and compelling: was it always a savage rite? Weren't there
   times
in childhood when one felt neutral, a shy appraiser gazing
   unendangered into
the reflecting globe, and when you turned back, moments
   later, the horrible clashes
hadn't gone away, but you were somehow separated, a person
   with things to do? And if
the urgency thinned out in later decades, why be compromised?
   Because these others
were waging war on things and people with words and things
   does it follow that your employment
was slighted, that you weren't free to clean out your desk? Sullen
   newsprint blows back and forth, a double sheet of it is
   suddenly tossed six stories high
and drops back, heavy as a sinker: does this have something
to do to you; more to the point, are you alive severed from it?
   The old ghouls
will have to be derided before one faces up to the specter of
   the empty stadium
at dusk, bare branches aquiver. How about your friend
in the hospital: did you call him? How many bridges between
   here and the end of that journey?
Over wells, along walls, silently one creeps along. Employment
   is difficult: I mean
it's difficult for me to hold a job long, not that I'm not
   efficient, it's, well,
so easy not to understand, to take full possession of one's
   unawareness and
then refuse to leave, a squatter in one's own house. And so much
   will
have happened by the time even this minor wrangle is settled.
   It's impossible
to keep abreast of the times, and yet we still think of wings.

How soft were those mute,
eloquent colors; even the plaids were like subtle hints. One
   baked

under trees, too lazy to notice the fading hour, until
the alarm sounded, the park went berserk, and then?
    Meanwhile a decision about keeping and
refinancing the old records had been reached, sure enough,
    just as one arrived home out
of breath. They said no one will ever speak to you now.
    Because in the dark
you knew something and didn't tell it, though the darkened
    spaces under the trees were at that
point intolerable, their bulk like mere hulls in the shattered
    night light. Better
to go into exile early rather than late, you thought, not saying
    anything, but the notion
became a battle-cry and soon everybody was trying to
    disconnect his life and seal it
off, unsuccessfully. The idea had occurred to you during a
    performance of a high-school play.
You weren't ashamed to take credit for it—why should you be?
    And thus a field
got sorted out; all the husks, shadows and little bells counted
    and clear in the rising
tide of shadow that steeped and proclaimed it: here was
    another place
to take orders in, to be from if convenient; only don't die
yet, we'll need you for the next act; it suited everybody.

Not on the agenda was the piercing squeal of puffins
newly released from captivity—but we'd get to that, later. Now
    the news
was of inflation. How to combat it? Is there any world-power
    so stupid it thinks it
must have the answer, or that an answer actually exists? You
    can bet there isn't,
which isn't a reason for a lot of ink and newsprint not to get
    chewed up in the approach
to an argument on the subject. Those peaceful voices, rising
    tier on tier
in the storied gothic cathedral, go unheard. Nobody thinks it's
    time for them,
and so, when one has become a little more exhausted, one

sinks down with one's lunch under a lofty elm in the breathless,
    shrunken noon.
Did one perhaps oversell oneself,
and if so how many instances are left? Miss Winslow was just
    telling us about your island
and its cormorants and the—er—other problems. How do the
    natives feel
about what you're doing? Is there any way to escape butchery
before it's too late, except in the exploding haystacks? But I get
    ahead of myself—I'll
do anything—that is, anything I can—to avoid the appearance
    of inequity, only please,
please call those spear-carriers or whatever you call them off.
Once two were saddled with each other's lies which became as
    a sacramental trust
for them. They listened, they put forth feelers, pouted on cue,
    but in due
course banshees exploited the situation. And once the climate
    of trust is destroyed
only lust for vengeance can take its place—or so *one* would
    have us believe.
After school I told some of the parents about it. On this site
exactly ten years ago stood an oblong wooden toll booth. Now
    there's not
a trace to indicate anything ever existed here. Kind of makes
    you wonder how
this place will look when you're gone. Oh you needn't throw bones
at it, the attendants are churlish enough—still, I've got to see
    one of those
so-called ant men before I leave here, which better be quick.
    But don't drag us
back to the water hole, I can see my reflection just fine in this
    bent
piece of aluminum. My hair, today, is beautifully combed. I am
    on a roll, I guess, and two
medicine men are coming to tea, and their letters of
    recommendation have already been mailed,
and so for two years out of vanity I shifted my position on the
    stool, pretending indifference

to everything, though I knew, in my heart of hearts, this wasn't
    the way
to gain their trust, or mine. And now that it's time to give out
    prizes, why
there just isn't any gumption left, only wheezes, so we all must
    stay and then go
away unsatisfied. It was no good grumbling about the weather;
it always came just the same, and left us
feeling vaguely unsatisfied.
A proud pair they were: unscathed for a day.
Interestingly, he hadn't done all the things he said he had.
Which doesn't solve the problem of white-glove inspections
    and seeds that roll
after they have been planted. Should he have been feeling more
    anxiety? Nah. Generating
trust? Depends on whose. Any one of several roadblocks could
    have deterred whatever
was escaping, and she (in green dress) was doing a masterful
    job of distracting the parking-
lot attendant. On the morning of the following day we found
    ourselves confronted with the
familiar problem of too much desert and too little time.
    Friends—you know the feeling—
are going to insist on knowing whose story it is. Better tell
    them. But wait—
you can't relate something and then connect it to some specific
    person. No job
says you ought to. But, heavy with garlands, we were being
    followed by the police
into a set-up storefront. Here, it all ends. Not so fast—we may
    have other information
to absolve wage-earners of paying dues
to your rotten club with all its intimate signs and shivers
of remorseless joy. Thought you had me. You'll face the
    Luftwaffe—alone. Now there's
a young woman outside says she has some important
    information about Mrs. Butterfield.
Young lady, is this a trick? What about the spiders that drilled
    all day, maneuvers

that took up so much time the judge never got around to
 depositing the check and the
bingo night went kerflooey, what with the sounds of drenching
 rain, leaks in the shutters,
pivotal oilcloth sentiments peeling, junked party ornaments, a
 woman who says he's a size 11
and other gadabouts, listless ones, too revealing to report on?
 The chimney seemed about to collapse,
disguising the fact that a mountain of sludge was moving on
the hysterical town, all of whose gaily decorated ridgepoles
 were in danger, only now no one
stopped to think about it, the more massive southwestern face
 being turned toward one
and all, who, mesmerized by the silence of death, made sure their
 seams
were straight. It seemed but a few moments later though
 actually it was probably more like
years that the evangelist profited and whispered: all of his
town made sense, his relatives enjoyed positions of respect, and so
what trouble could there be? No, there is no knocking in the
 walls, nothing
like that. The operation is a success from the point of view of
 the furthest tangle
of violet cliff-face that sometimes flashes toward one, far across
 the valley, as though revealing
an ecstatic, deep-buried message. This is the price we have to
 pay,
it seems to say, and though all future debts will have been
 incurred gladly, one must
shoulder the burden of the interest payments NOW, otherwise
 there'll be such a scare
in the curriculum as only the oldest ones will want to get out,
 the others
impeded or impeached by the books they have a right to read
in this our own time. Only I say to you, don't look askance at
 the singers
just because they're not responsible for the awful libretto,
 bearing in mind the tropes
each had to traverse to get here, and now their music delights
 the eye

and the mind as well as the ear, they have surely calibrated their
    longings to us;
there will be more surprises to come and the well-nursed fantasy
    expands, blooms
with the hair of their yearning, turning desire to a trick and love
    to its own advantage.
Yet come speak with me behind the screen of the waterfall's
    Holophane, yet be not too
distant lest the muggers suspect us and the children bear away
    our burden, our only
secret. For nurseries have their news agencies as surely as garlic
    repels vampires
among others. Today a tree talked to us. What it said was don't
plunge too deeply into the microbe-infested waters, there may
    be an alternate plan
which will allow us to save more lives and so become our own
    resurrection of sorts
on the simple chart. Pin it here, it says, this place is the most
    valuable and least
congested with shit and other rungs of the ladder of hysterical flight
from the pages of a magazine to the dime-store trophy that is
    your secret, haunted
by memories both reluctant and relaxed, as long as it wants to
    take you away. But beware
the instant in which it doesn't: utopias can crumble
in that split-second, and you may wake up finding you have
    more than you ever wanted to own,
but by that time the dream is falling in on itself in slow motion
    or someone is dismantling it.

Here at Shadowlawn the question is always: O what awful thing
    are they doing now?
What make-believe? Idiotic proposals are advanced, then they
    blab it,
it won't work. It doesn't work. Not that anyone is what I
    would call conceited, or
outgoing either, I guess. There's a certain image . . . But that
    went out in 1971. No one has
been back there since. A small road leads to it, called "the
    esplanade." In small groups

they recur, since the fence was last painted, and are up to
    discussing it—who knows,
maybe an interesting idea will emerge, yet the handwriting on
    the wall seems to indicate otherwise:
return to your abstractions, it said, life
has no need of you just yet. I was sitting in my car
and suddenly I could see down the whole distance I had come,
    and the fog-shrouded destination
became clear again, as it has so many times over the past weeks.
    I thought I should
sharpen my appearance, for that way lies light, lies life, and yes
    I am
talking about new clothes as well. He wore a black suit—
that's what image those threads project? Arts & leisure—80
    bucks! As quiet as my
contentment is the voice at my shoulder: make it over. Perhaps
    not a total
from-the-ground-up rehab, perhaps only a few cosmetic
    touches
would have an earth-shaking impact, in this instance. It's what
    you *can* do that matters
more than the whole picture, but the older we grow, the more
    unused to the idea of dying—
and I'm sorry I brought the subject up—we become. We are
    set in our ways. The breath
of autumn is vast again, we see vague but kind-hearted auguries
in it, then forget. It's the way our silhouette gets projected on
    invisible nature
that seduces one to come down from the top of the leaf-pile.
    By then it's dark,
of course. One's sedan's not on schedule, and the rear-view
    mirror is brittle, too
polished to shine, just visible enough to see the hairs
on one's face by. Is it going to cripple
our image of our self-esteem? Where were we in the dark? Can
    you see it? Positive?

Not so nice now, as the deep cranberry-colored berries linger
on the trees though shriveled and cold—surely not till
    summer? But that's

ages away and I have to finish my story, and character
is what I forgot to add. O but it will change
the negative nature of it, put in something we don't need all right,
gigantic though it be. Still, and though the leaves are only
    threaded on the branches now,
someone has to look after it. I never had a servant. Always, I
    was accustomed
to doing my own cleaning, even as others were not. Heck, what
    creeps
are these? And I forgot the way back, forgot the back of the story,
perhaps for the better, since I was refreshed and could
    remember nothing,
nothing of what happened so long ago, on a certain evening
in July. We called across
shallow lagoons to each other; it seemed to help. Now to expunge
the revenge-motif, and get it all right for once. Life is an
    embroidery-frame, and what you put
into it gets left there, there are so many kinds of designs,
    literally millions of them
and the combinations of these—well. So perhaps what
    happened at Nuremberg in 1658 is
of some importance to me, but surely
the burden of proof doesn't rest on you. It's all I can do
for you baby now that I have to get going, but think
of the diminishing tiers of clouds clustered to the ever-more-
    distant horizon: do you want
our heritage? Or should you invest in something? And as one
    tendril
after another unclasps, what more is there to say? I can see you
in the ski-picture, as dazed and clean as in the old days behind
    the laundry,
and yet each word of what we said to each other matters, pulls,
    I don't know, away
like a sheet from the substance, and what are you going to get
    after that?
What me, huh?

I wish I could hear birdsong in those old days,
you know, the kind there used to be. It seemed every thorn
    was alight.

Here there is nowhere near the expansive atmosphere
we imagine we miss. Only a sullen waiter
in a soiled white jacket who slams down the coffee cups in
 front of you and then walks away.
I was told about it on a Sunday. By Monday the dogs were
 back, fighting over some used
excrement, half in the water. Wow. What a dumb thing. Only I
 hear he used to go behind
the other building, and no one knew him. But he can't say for
 sure. It's like a chicken.
I'm sure Babs remembers the time of the arguments we used to
 go through.
That's ancient history now, though. And, like history, it has a
 definite interest,
like Thebes. Curiously I was just talking
about it professor, to get it not quite wrong again, and you
 came up and asked me
how my theorem was and I blurted out the truth. It's all okay.
 It's not going to be divided,
not divided up among several participants anyway.

It was decided to proceed another way
while I was out of the room.
The startling freshness of it blinkered me
opposing me to many angles of lights
that fell before the door frame. A weathered quince
asked to be included. Round shrubs duly unwrapped
after winter and how do you get hold of these? Sipping a glass
 of brandy
my mother high above the city shooed
inset chimes to their places; how far
and how many balloons see the light of morning each time this
 year
and one must have a peg to hang it on, and something to walk
 upon,
yet it got no worse,
the time between the horse's lazily but abruptly twitched tail to
the flies from off the stable:
fellows who hurry by you,
they are taking you, out of the catalog, to

obnoxious rendezvous. Meetings. Was it ever a catbird that
   called thus,
got us late after school, how much we were loving it, instant
in each other's arms, and one thin one called down, that was a
   wave of air
to take the place away. And you and I, in our sun-kit,
we must have mastered many foreign dances,
been seen tall at the fair, for one or more of them to recognize
   us outside
the precinct, and to have got off scot-free for a wad
of cloth, roll of hair brushed from the comb, that's
all we were meant to see. But in the dark you see more,
especially if you're a child, and know instinctively what goes on
   there,
how matchbooks are bent open backwards, what warts they all
came to learn, in thin haze
out over San Francisco. I said you are my teacher Herr Schmidt,
I am the toad and pupil, you are after all all
you set out to be and it's true isn't it? It's come true, look? And
   his puppy-eyes
appraised mine, I was won over instantly, from that day
never thought forward, looked backward, rain
or shine, from that anointed moment
I first kissed a king in you. What reflections!
We are lucky to have this
yet one doesn't want to go, makes
excuses not to, toe twisting in door-jamb.
You flattered me I was higher up on the ladder
than any of the other pupils, and when I came to be eight, straight
as two twigs in the barn after love,
the waters receded and left.
Now's the time. But my fatal shyness overcame me
once again. I hurried out, threw
myself down the street. You see I wasn't going to be a good boy.
They just came. Took me. Now I angle pleasantly
toward the surface, thinking a good, fat dream: oh to be stuck
in there again. But the fire-engine
won't let me, the banging hurtling toward a concussion
on rocks, a broken pedestal and here,
here we stand, the breeze is pleasant so let's take

our time and sing one more song, eyes rolling,
and roam at will, timeless:

indeed I have no doubt it can be so.
Oh I don't know, do you?
What is it makes the window-maker go off on his own, if not
this sacred season of lips,
gray moisture that squeezes down on us so hard. And we are never
on our own. Because someone decreed we were not to be. And
    in glacial
pockets of this repercussion were still not meant to be ourselves,
    until
some cruel stranger forces us to be, and leaves. Ah, but then,
    what new
problems, taxis, taking years to get an accounting, while daffodils,
    long dead, continue
to droop sideways. Meanwhile the same film strip
is projected endlessly across one's forehead. One has seen it so
    many times!
Yet one dares to admit there are details, each time, that escaped
    one before,
like the title on the spine of the book laying on the table: The
    Taming of the Shrew. Once
mastered all this can still instruct far into the pale vacuum
one wants so much to come to know. It is strangely familiar,
    like a woodcutter
eating bread *dans un bois solitaire*: O my friends and sisters,
    haven't you
ever taken the position that what knows, grows? And familiar
    noodles are served.
One wants, not to like, but to live in, the structure of things,
    and this is
the first great mistake, from which all the others, down to the
    tiniest
speck, bead of snot on a child's nose, proceed in brisk military
    fashion, encouraging
to some on a chilly afternoon in March. What they have to say
    about you never recurs;
the fräulein, in the nadir of a pause, takes up some other
    subject. It's jewels.

Or a foray into the unexplained outside. We can never have
   tears enough,
in fact, so why regret the sun's pointing
these acerated surfaces? Once, a whale will be kind, and no
   other grief can exist after
that. You just have to choose, making sure all the choices are
   wrong, and the sky then
of your own privacy caves in on you, collapses, is comfortable
   as sleep. In that distant
forest nothing can live separate, and it's a dream. A difficulty.
   For one.
For one exchanging one neutral memory for another.

And one fans out over the abyss. This is spring, the warning:
herring may never happen again, and if one gray suit bulges
   before your eyes be sure
to take it in again: others may be found wanting, the gold rush
   having resumed, and operas
are once again in demand. By the time I got to the movies it
   was incredibly
quiet in the dark, only birds peeped, the silent man turned, and
   the chrome angle
of one's glasses inaccurately suggested the thirties to legions
   half-ignorant of their own
birthplaces, let alone metal screening. One has done so much
   for others; must it be?
No hint of lavender, of cirrus, of citrus? No but the lemmings
   trot back, you can see for yourself
how much potential was invested there, and what came of it.
It's time to swing out on one's own and, if perennial pathos
   isn't your dish,
make a stew of something else—nimbus, or limbo. Anything so
   long as it's not caused by neighbors
whose potential for wrecking your life is greater now than at
   any point in the future
provided you let them get away with it and are not angry to
   relinquish
the paws that go on escaping. Talk it over with your gardener, see
the bright shoots, forget that you will live long, that all thrives,
   apace and at the same rate.

Or bright facets could interrupt, reflectors
left out on lawns not live to see the dawning of new, earthen
    flowers
and yet be called to resume again, for dull
is not dull enough and we wish these stones to have duration
    even as fatigue palls
on the island in the sunset,
and flamingos fall over each other in the luxury of getting away.

I would assemble
landscapes from insect-tunneled wood and go live in a hole
    somewhere
lest pleasant anomalies impose bumptious charades promoting
    peace to others and to all comers,
seal it in a chest, rip it open, scatter the powder of life on the
    dead sawdust
to watch it blink, and then pound with my fists as hard as I can
    on the saga of
the sheepgirl and her friend the pelican merchant: how they
    became friends long after
ceasing to know each other, when both were blind and living
    in unfatally dingy
circumstances somewhere near Clapham Common: when
    autumn flickers, curves in
on the unfinished lunch, may it rest established early. To graduate
from sultry "other woman" parts to hell itself, which is
    infinitely more far-reaching
and beautiful than you might ever imagine, isn't the first step,
but something more like the emerging at the top of the
    monument, that lets you see
in the vastest if not the least clotted vistas and places
no value-judgment on your being there, on the fact of your
    being there, though
it might if you weren't alone, innocent
as a lintel. Back into the past, they sob, the others; it's necessary
    in order to
flush out the present as it were, yet one can't envy them the
    pained, coming-apart-in-high-velocity-winds feeling
or be surprised that one's reassurances are ignored. That would
    belong to an earlier

grand idea of the importance of one's actions, while now
almost any input is suspect, even the most cost-efficient, so that
    it seems other men's
gardens get all the moisture and sunlight. We on the other
    hand have
only sterile notions of staying included to ruffle through, and
    one never tires
of this retrograde motion, even as one fears the consequences
    of standing still
and becoming like an old chromo on a wall.
                                                And yet, dozens
of others experience it, no stigma is attached, only rolling over
    and over like a marble
that can never stop rolling and here we are, still doing it only
    advised of our interlocutor's
growing lack of patience, and permanently eager for the end of
    the run,
dog bite dog, it doesn't so much say it on the advertisement as
what do you think, where do you come from; more doses of
    advice
from shaggy-haired strangers.
                                    And all lock themselves in at night,
desperately vamping where a half-turn to see who's behind in
    that tree might
have been deemed more appropriate, if equally ineffective.
    What brio in your chat, how
do you keep going next time?
                                    And I told him for half a dime
    I'd quit and screw
you too, only that's not done, the very
pillars of our civilization would crumble and Osiris would again
    have to punish
the unwary who danced jigs in our shadow, we the keepers of
    the trust who have to
somehow find the missing key that at this moment is within
    the grasp of a leper
who plays with it, not knowing.

And flies still tax us with their lessons: when will we give up? In
    order to land on that shred

of inhospitable strand one is forced to jettison certain
much-beloved possessions, including, I'm afraid, that key. O if
    only one belonged to something,
life would be harder perhaps but we'd have the strength to go
    along with whatever they
wanted us to say and we'd have rivalry at the end, sure, but
    cunning as well in the abstract
clockface of accusations from the various points of the compass,
    and who knows, if one got
away, how much sicker the other would get? Perhaps not much.
    Perhaps if you had
a little compassion in your yard things would grow staler and
    the calm
of the original compact wouldn't capsize it, leading to distant
    benefits and premises.
I told you his name was Max you were the one who thought
    otherwise and well
it's just as well as the gunwale unkisses faster the tires nailed to
    the dock
of departure and all our plans and ammo were scuttled, at the
    threshold
of this adamantine resort where two
can lie but no more, reprisals splash into the night. It must surely
    have come
from over there, those dried grasses. More power to them, for
    what must never
seem to have taken place on an afternoon once. As we kindle
    interest in that old past, what
astonishing trills one hears, what blistering swamp flowers
    thrust open; furry
sea-creatures invade the royal compound and next week the
    clock will strike
exactly at twelve o'clock, you'll be free of a long-tendered
    obligation.
Since then I've been sleeping better too, but your shoes aren't
    getting fed properly, there are
spots on whatever one is called to drink, and curse it, no
water in the watering-trough. Yes but the horse said he didn't
    want any, besides
his harness is torn and angry,

a proverb for the industrious. Oh we've known a long time
   how much her
trail was costing her and others and now it's time for definitive
   common knowledge, only
nothing is so sure anymore it wants to be reminded. Maybe it
   never knew at all. Maybe
we deduced it out of guilt, and now it's we on the run, my
   goodness how the unrolling
scenery veers past. Was it even we
who were meant to start on this race? Might it have been for
   the others, all for them,
and so one is let off lightly, or so it seems, with a reprimand
and a startling dream? I told someone at the start of this
I wouldn't play faster than my nearest neighbor. Now look
what's become of him. I wouldn't want to end up at a finish
   line unwashed
and looking like that. I go. I come later. You all land at the
   bottom of a crowded funnel
and so whatever joke is cracked coincides with your defense.
   Not everyone was made to wear
what we choose to wear. The colors, rinsed, insistent, return;
   the pink is for you,
not just to wash and wish desperately into something else that
   in any case
was probably never meant to be understood, and it smiles, and
   salvages
what little it can from the eternal barren beginning of March.
   Just two;
the alibi would only cover two; it's over; we are lost
in the habit, smiling in a foxglove tent; but the doves requested
   permission to weave over us
like psalms and sometimes the sun is good, but it just seems
   like it won't go away
the way a song does, leaving a slightly hollowed path behind.
   We could follow,
but the brimming lake on the horizon is more likely to join us
   if we
don't absolve ourselves, recklessly dreaming. In time all excuses
   merge in an arch
whose keystone overlooks heaven, and

we must be patient if we are to live that far, at our own expense,
    this time, without that.

Bet there was some falling off there; still, amid the hoo-ha
    concerning new appointments and
such there was no time to discern; new people there, android
    sleep rains down
on pinched neighbors like ingots of silver, and there's no mess,
    only a poking among reeds.
The last recognizable mentor left; it was up to the remains of
    his flock to reconstitute,
but left to their own devices many fled the comparative safety
    of the coop for used-
car lots, car washes, drive-in banks, in order so to speak to get
    their heads together.
I was the only one of my squadron to count them as they left
    in single file,
but not being able to do much about it, or keep records, soon
    I too was lost—well, not exactly,
but tethered expectations always result when you go a little too
    far in one direction, not
enough in another, and betimes one spots the calendar on the
    office wall: think, it says.
Like a plangent river my life has unrolled this far, to a fraction
    of this place,
and I have commandeered motor launches, but it has all been
    in vain, this celebration: listen,
what do children think of you now? Suddenly everyone is
    younger, and many of them not all
that young, either, and who, do you suppose, loves you? It's a
    variant of the shell game
again; not all its premises are suicidal, but where is the one who
    takes out the ashes,
leaves the key behind? Up through the frantic town he rages
    ("It works, it's bent
but it works!") like the wing of a plane but we always knew it
    was here, sure we did, Ma I'll tell you later
in the meantime and lilac bushes are a kind of promise. Aren't
    they? And wine,

and noisemakers, and all the little things we thought good at a
  hinge in space: they're
not like that now, are they? And all the kids, and people who
  came over: now salted
in their time, and we try to break out of ours, I guess, and still
  the animals stampede toward
headquarters. I was depressed when I wrote that. Don't read it.
  Still, if you must, take
note of certain exemptions in the
fourth paragraph where I was high: they said it shouldn't enter,
  but I succeeded in decoding the big top
so that someday all children should live like this, have what was
  at last ours,
only I succeeded and a train roared by: *that man*, it seems to
  say. And then it is past,
after it is flagged down. A sore spot in my memory undoes
  what I have just written
as fast as I can write; weave, and it shall be unraveled; talk, and
  the listener response
will take your breath away, so it is decreed. And I shall be
  traveling on
a little farther to a favorite spot of mine, O you'd like it, but no
  one can go there. The mummy
said so. I have to keep in the shadows yet a little longer, until
  you will wisely see how I
fit under here and so must leave any day now.
                              The boskets were
   blue, I remember; only
a few ships in the distance now, and a tall flag beckons
  me in another direction. Dammit, I'll stick to this one, this is
    the one they meant
for me to take all along, and I don't see why I should take that
  other one. My child,
you must do as you wish; to do otherwise would insult God's
  rule, and you do
care for Him, don't you? Only give no thought to the
  morrow—
it will presently arrive and take care of itself, you'll see.
  Meanwhile, if a new hat

might seem appropriate, then why not? Oh father I was looking
    out the window
but this time doesn't seem such a long one, mightn't we return
to the old cabin, just for a glimpse of the driveway? But that,
as the parrot said, is another story. Sooner or later you go blind
    staring at platinum
and the reverberations that warned against it can themselves no
    longer be distinguished
in the thudding and fog, and if all comes to be eclipsed at some
date in the not-too-near future, then why does it say I'm a
    salesman with a tie trying to
interest you in this new product, that can go out of control? It's
    the Cotswolds
for me, but no, he has the name tag in his pants and this string
    flying behind him
into what you were told would be a void, which is his study.
    Heaven help jerks, they need
it worse than we, yet always something funny acts as a short
    prelude to disaster, and then afterwards
everybody is relieved; it's still a high school; there's nothing no
    longer wrong with it
and the shade acts as a puddle
from which froglike eyes protrude, if it is indeed this occasion,
    and this is 901½ McKinstry
Place, and you are Judson L. Whittaker, oh take this
    wheelbarrow far from my sight and bury it
on yonder height, so impatient have my clones become, and I,
    in the light,
of this new development am all but induced to come along with
    you. The stones
forbid it though. Fire that does not burn? Tell it to the no longer
    prematurely
gray slab of expanse, file it in "explanations which leave much
    unexplained," but leave me my
dance, the one underpraised porcelain object on the stand.

In the western districts greetings proliferate
and I'm already starting to look better. When was I not
a paramilitary brother in some sense? Who coined this
    nickname? For I see

far, in looking, out over a life, the strange, wrenching mess of
    it, yet which has
some undistressed surfaces and unscaled peaks, or bumps, along
    with much that was fey and
witless as it went by. Where *are* those files now? Is it possible
    they can have been deleted
in the very mouth of time? Grenades pop, rockets vomit their
    lucklessness into the sky,
and which of us wants to bear the responsibility of having looked
    something up? which is why
the unplanted cabbages stand tearful out of the mist, there is no
    reason to go on ploughing the garden once winter has begun, yet
what else is there to do, except sweep the floor
    with automatic hand, pondering certain dun sins of omission, if
    twilight really is a jewel
as you turned out to be (never fear, the rain
won't rob you of your distinctive personality though I saw it
    streaming
the other day, down your clothes, you paused and seemed not
    to know what to think, but I,
I in my compartment knew: damaged hair, tattered kneecaps, a
    pimple
or two, and as automatically as one uncloses a window
you filed your report, and the court was amazed, emptied in a
    moment before
the order of dismissal came. Out of respect I should say I didn't
    see you very closely;
you were too far down for that, not coinciding with anyone's
    notion of a "person" yet livelier
still for it; oh you showed 'em how to fit into the barrel of an
    ignored idiosyncrasy and
still have room left over for passages of devastating wit that nightly
bring the house down. And if sleep is narrower after that, it's
    also more pointed,
slanted like the harrow's tooth, to bring up what may be
    coming along
any second now) and it is, in feathers all over the floor, only
    now it's the maid's turn
and we may never see what stays groping in her eyes. The floor
    is lovely, though, passionate

and filled with bright ideas like a bride only what it says about
   us isn't forthcoming.
Outside the river is magenta and some sunbeams got caught
   upside down in it, just their
(our) luck I guess. Meanwhile I have received your postcard. I
   wanted to tell you
how much I thought it shouldn't change, but dairies (diaries?)
   got in the way and exchanged notes
at which time the judgment was all but unreadable, jointures
   charged with embalming fluid,
for it is written that whatever is not glue may be pressed into
   service as such, and
the trip gets merrier just before a sudden decision is reached
   concerning the child-pests
we thought we'd seen the last of.
                              And for one moment, when
   apple-dust hangs
in your hair you move that glider over an inch, to be
in shade. Dawn, an egg, comforts one only with the idea of its
   shape. Later we
are in the round and full of fears: did we confuse that shape
with something else, and if so was it congruent, or like a pair of
   trousers, wavering
in the breeze? And then when you come down to it nobody
   matters any more.
There is nothing like the old beach. The old tables.
Once, an avalanche of cuties threatened our meeting. Fred
   bypassed it.
Now the season, "a boundless and festive rejoicement," is on
   track. I, too, voted for it.
But a subtle form of harassment overtakes, by undermining, each
   new claim as fast
as it is put in the docket. Case dismissed. Is it then true that it
   does not matter,
or that women give birth to children as easily as a fruit
   disgorges its seeds?
Salt in the cure-all dilutes both qualms and unheeded label
cautions, and when called upon, comes outside in a suit,
   prepared to play the reasonable

inquisitor, listen to shouts. Toward evening a stitch is dropped
    and the blindly desiring
run together like syrup and milk: the only ethos, cranes
severing horizon from water with the great sawing motion that
    always instills awe
around wreaths for buddies, and in time your tome will tell
    them too
about the never leaving off.
                            Surely that last tragedy will be
    enough
and the wind must drop, and it does; a single leaf falls circling,
alights on the water's swiftly moving mirror as the chorus picks
    up on hope
in the black promise facing us. Blood oozing under every door,
    now tell us
if we can get this way again by remembering and so turn to
    glass citizens.
Let the cycle of greed begin again, the sheer poetry of it will
    win over all but a few
viewers and those servants who choose not to look into the
    path being proposed for all of us
to follow—we'll tell them how—and it has just started to sprinkle
a few seconds ago, just before I arrived here in some confusion
    but now am
dressing the bare stone, as was long ago ordered,
and can complain, really, of nothing—of my head, square as a box,
receptacle for fools' tools? But it was I who brought them here,
    taught them to scratch out a rough living from the soil. Of
    birdsong or caterwauling
in the night? No, I was just living it. Now that it's time for
    repairs I'm not sure I
had to be brought to the very edge of the indignant abyss, but
    no matter, if it doesn't fly
off on its own, sloth will overtake it, sleep bend the branch to
    earth.

Yet always in fear of some complaint we adjust dials
to those who lie on their side stricken with the power of the
    floor, uninhibited;

uninhibited cross farms for gain or planted shapes.
But, "no habitation unless one linger." You were afraid of
   setting out shoots.

But now that sugared April crosses blink, the shining squalls
   and yellow
plumes imaginably stuck in hair, and one returns to heaven,
   under what conditions

does one sort out the waterfall? For always, dark spirits and
   connivance
underlay the people-mover as it spiraled ever higher beyond

the counterpane of colored wooden cows, to the continental
   divide.
And here one would take some comfort in the waved gesture
   that told how far the sun had shriveled

since we began our climb, the hazards put away under our
   feet.
"The sun was still high in the heavens," yet a narrow ruffle of
   flux edged the huge

saucer-like plain, and one began to think of other sets of
   conditions:
the old people in the house, a long day away; the carbons of
   pets and other mooted toys,

so long away from us it barely became time to think and they
   had fallen away;
whispering in the organ loft, after you had begun to tell it and
   now, nothing

could ever interrupt you. You were an impossible storm from space
bearing down on us and each individual's name was clearly
   marked on the serpent's

whitish flank. Oh not we too, and how did we too come to be
   in here?
So pleasant and eager were the first steps

and even later in a rare descending moment
there was some strict mood that sustained you. Later, after all
    had been truly lost

for a long time, fragments of the monument's original intention
    surfaced,
were cleaned off, polished, and thought a wonder. Only on
    alternate days,

though, was the artifact then visible for the mind, a substance
    one partook of
until the next rot shut it down. Oh there were

brilliant chasms for the attention available even then. But as the
    slope flattened out
the higher we grew, in time a contentious stratum like
    chalk

came to soak up the forest of all we knew. We knew we were
    living there, but moving on
to a widest horizon where collective destinies sank like motes,
    and even the tonic

future was hollow, because suggestible; where dramas were
    played out as though a carpet
and were nothing the clear-eyed ever saw. Eventually, then,
    destiny comes to seem a frank,

level extension of oneself, while nothing in the blue-green noon
    gleam casts a shadow.
Later, the fits and starts are predictable, rude

awakenings redden every eye, but it's OK since colloquial:
    remember how grand was that
vernacular, how suited to living in. But now, look, the needle
    has plummeted

into something once again; there are barest chances for holding
    out

and another repulsive dream of a kitchen with handlebars
    offered to the grip

and an appendix that writes itself: all was put away here, once,
    but as often,
men came to disturb the mounds, gravely insulting the local
    deities,

who, empowered thus, wrought their vengeance on all the
    land, out of proportion to the gravity
of the offence as it seemed then, yet this too was part of the plan:

nobody ever said it was going to be equable. What we did
    know was that it would be gentle
in its unfolding, only ruthless after that, and that one's notion
    of "civilization," i.e.,

what we think we've got coming to us, would be rudely
    transformed, not shattered,
into a desolate plain whose unblinking design brings us low,
    parallel

to the lives of plants and insects we had never wondered about.
And lo, this makes you a caring member of your species. You
    can't see

any more, but that's all right; you are locked up in the original
    cipher
to be told as you are if an occasion ever arises, unless, trampled
    by demons, you return

to the condition of dust floating not disagreeably in middle airs
    where, at least,
you can never be separated from what drowned you some
    twenty days previously

or motion at a stranger in a hat who thinks he knows you from
    somewhere, but it scarcely
matters since you are separating amiably now again, forever, it
    seems, and the clues we

all leave behind are fated not to be found this time,
or if they are it will resemble something a squirrel laid there, a
 good while ago; but since charm can never

be quite rinsed from these bones it befits us to go along with
 it, congratulate it
at last for having had something to say and not said it, as
 torrents frazzle a canyon

without contributing to its demise unless one chooses to
 consider inexorably
slow processes that score even the cosmic mind at rarest
 intervals, and superficially;

secure in the adding up of all things
into a block of hay from which no strand is permitted to
 extrude.

And while the fire-mind tries out its images on us one last time
 an unsettling tableau
of doom constructs itself from greenish chalk on the green
 blackboard, but not yet

for these eyes, while the brandy decanter is bent and yards of
 cretonne
smother the schoolyard and take their place among the
 popping trees, yet unendorsably, O nargileh.

Long ago the earth rendered this pablum unholy or at least
 unappetizing.
Then the men began to speak in unison: why not sacrifice
 something
ordinary, such as a hairnet, and if that doesn't work one can
 consider what steps
are to be taken, but usually it suffices to
part with some insignificant possession. That leaves nothing to
 sniff at, later
when details are to be worked out, and as a matter of fact in
 most cases

the god will make you a gift of it or forget about it, going about
 his business, casehardened,
even as we humans do in strange lands. Of course the
 troublesome minority of
plaintiffs sometimes chases him back to his hole, and, oddly
 enough, often celebrates this
"triumph" with a drinking feast, little suspecting
how the god likes to wait and catch his enemies off balance,
 and then, woe to the litigious
and even their associates when he hits the comeback trail, nostrils
 aflare, only
it was funny this time, nobody seemed anxious to stir up
 hostilities on either side.
A few warning shots were fired, in the air, but even these might
 easily have been produced
by a car backfiring, or random firecrackers—that sort of thing.
Meanwhile the god licks his wounds, fiercely abiding: or so, at
 any rate, we have been taught
to believe, hunkered down in the fallout shelter, awaiting
 pestilence, a rain of arrows, or whatever
the chef may have whipped up for us today.
Yet in fact nothing of the kind has ever happened. We even *feel*
 pure and not devoid
of merit; our neighbors are nice as pie to us; even strangers
 salute us decorously in the street,
beautifully dressed, for this is indeed a secular feast day.
Shouts, the smoke from campfires almost drown it out. We
 have almost leveled off;
there is so much to say, but cisterns enclose the precious
 substance, not much will escape.
Oddly, under giant trees we seem smaller to each other, though
 the hopes the great race kindled
burn even more majestically than before the roll-call
that went on so many centuries to the accompaniment of
 battle-axes and cats-o'-nine-tails,
before such courtesies as we now command became acceptable
 to that god, the dew-weeper, and civilization began to
 grovel
in the dust for torn sausage-casings and bits of shrimp. But any
 pedigree

is by definition a long one, so that now it must seem to some
    called to be aristocrats as if
the whole shining night were stitched together to hide their
    port-wine stains
and even gnomes have some inner sense of nobility that will
    save the world
when it does begin to fall apart as, at last report, it hadn't yet
    done, the boiler-plate
contradictions ennobled in it being such as can last millenniums
    without exhibiting the slightest signs of wear,
though we have only ourselves to thank for that. When the
    convention finally assembles
there may be flak to take on that score. In which case we can
    always plead ignorance of the law,
that noblest, since most artless, of defenses, and dig our heels
    in and ask the cliff
to explain itself and the ferns erupting from its crevices: I too
    have stood here faceless and seemingly angry for a long time,
    yet for all that
don't feel it time to intimidate someone, make him or her feel
    lonesome just because there is
indeed a horizon, but prefer to sit back on my haunches,
    contemplating my navel to see what good
if any will come of it. Frightening noises are in poor taste;
    silence must be sorted out
however, its path followed back to where the tucks gather, and
    each random furrow
be gaily explored in a spirit of setting out to conquer the world
    someday. That's all.
I have no further bread and cheese for you; these days I count
    little
but the linens folded in my scented cedar closets, folded up
    against time, in case
I ever have a use for them; and you, you others, have only to
    break away
like chunks of ice from the much larger iceberg to accomplish
    your destiny, that day in court
the monkeys and jesters seemed to promise you—or was it a
    bad dream? But now, surely,
your mettle has been tested; let the perfume of burning archives

assault our olfactory sense once more as radically as the grape
    hyacinth in the fond gullies of spring.

Access to the poll-takers is limited, yet there are times, I feel,
    when this artificial barrier
along with so many others ought to be rescinded. Once in the
    booby hatch the setting sun
drilled its powerful horizontal rays, as strong as any you'd ever
    want to see at noon, through my
window just above the sill, striking this sheet of paper with the
    shadows of a flower pot
and an old faucet, that were lying there, with so much force
    that they seemed about to be embedded in it,
like a sentiment above a door. At such times, one gathers
that gravity isn't about to save us, that it wasn't installed as some
    sort of built-in smoke alarm
to discourage us from rash actions. We evolve naturally in its
    aura, there is so much
to say it gets weighted down like a pear tree with fruit, so that
    when the branch
breaks and the fruit must be harvested at once or discarded, we
    get stage fright and do imitations
of opera singers or anything to break the monotony of the pace
set for us by its metronome. And yes, it's like living in an
    atmosphere one can breathe, but
at the same time one can never take it for granted; like air, it
    slips by too easily
for anyone to care, once the dust has settled, what that minor
    commotion betokened. The giant
umbrella creations of our history of knowledge have that
    disconcerting side-effect. So one
concentrates on the line tangential to the thick, pebbled bulge
    of the fruit's skin: know it and
one can understand everything's the theory, though in practice
things don't go as smoothly as that. The top of a tower that is
    visible one minute
may be only a straw blowing across a courtyard the next; so, at
    any rate, has patience, deduction's
handmaid, taught us, and when we go out of doors, we never
    exhibit bad manners or any kind of feeling,

envy in particular. What enters your gate is my own inference, not some
colossal steed pawing the dust in a protracted spasm of preparedness, for what voyage
can any of us undertake until the lotus moon has risen to vanquish
squibs or rumors concerning its eligibility that blew up while one was seated, somewhat
taken aback, disinclined to candor that day, or anything that might compromise intelligent
speculation about the origin of dreams. So one sees couples
turn back from the altar, it not being quite right for them, and as quickly, cities,
ghouls, ghost ships bite the bullet and plunge from sight, to be resuscitated in some more
"normal" atmosphere where telling tall tales comes under the head of bystander entertainment,
a special budget item subsumed under crass though meticulous ganders at what the staff
has been up to in one's absence, how it looks, what it feels like. And the dark mahogany
of his mood, how one loved all that! Why is it too late to be simple,
out riding, pointing at something, when all you loved was there anyway? Too late
to be inventoried or caressed, as one lays in a stock of family anecdotes for the future,
poses to assume, frippery, harmless tomfoolery, until in a cocoon
made of commas it will all seem to come right, but the ashes have been left far behind
on a nameless road, in whose ruts glass still flashes magisterially,
not merrily short-circuited as when we were among people, but a thing on its own now,
to weep over rather than think of saving? If only we could get the message out further,
yet here all kinds of sacred cows hinder one, so there is no longer any point
in pursuing the implications today. Tomorrow will be good enough for that. The stationary
saraband of our considering it but deciding not to put it to a vote absorbs any

hint of the disorder that highmindedness sometimes trails in its
    wake like a wisp of
something in the sky, and in any case, our hands, our faces are
    clean, our plates empty
and brimming with moonlight, a pious reminder to the unwashed
    and unready that we will come
again someday and make sense of this arbitrary and tangled
    forest of misplaced
motives and other shades of imperfect sympathies that do not
    compromise us perhaps
as yet, yet I feel their aura, Mother, like a water table
    ascending,
and I haven't the answer, don't know if I'll ever have it, yet it
    looks so young,
pitiful and hopeless in morning light that one tries to suppress
    the intuition that to go
forward will be to do battle with some angry titan, sooner or
    later, and all one's
bad reactions will confront at every one of the house's apertures:
    slay me and then
leave me here, if that's going to help; just don't stand around
looking at me that way, that's all. Am I some kind of a freak?
    No. Am I disingenuous? Maybe,
but the case hasn't been proved; only an executioner could
    decide it, and besides I feel too well
to get into other feral arrangements when the night and its
    night-light are still
not far off. And besides other people are too interested right
    now, the ambiance can never
be gauged accurately enough in the feverish commotion that
    surrounds this, and our other
travel plans. There is no point in giving them the slip. It is
    never too late to mend
no matter how we clamor to redo everything from the ground
    up; the chatter never subsides
but like the tide of dust of the oceans, returns and retreats,
    forever opaque, forever itself:
a longing one does not subdue.

Yet time, for all that, hadn't abandoned
the grotty little amusement park though the wind now seethed
 through every rent
in its shell, and others now had plans which didn't take it into
 account:
in the foundry he sang it once and here was this sudden
 magnificent opportunity
to create a forum, an audience for oneself! Gosh, it's so long
 ago! Still, one must hold back,
feigning disinterest until the proper moment, and then, and then,
it shall fall into our hands and seem what the Lord probably
 meant for us, would have,
without a doubt, if we were known to Him. Which brings up
 . . . But anyway, it would all get
fixed up and then we'd hold a contest and people would learn
 about it through that, and we'd have
more people than we knew what to do with queuing up and
 asking questions, wanting to get involved,
to pledge something, anything, even a nickel a week, it's the
 thought that counts
and don't you ever forget that. Try sleeping on it. And then
 we'd have a nice car
and options about things to do; we'd entertain beggars and
 watch them come back for more,
and that's part of the fun, forgetting just what you have done,
 have given someone, in
the intoxication of your and everyone else's finally winning
 something in the free-for-all
of life just like Betty and your father said, only please don't
 release it all over me now,
I have to think some. Here, this chair ought to mean
 something, if I intuit
your philosophy correctly, or maybe it's me, maybe I'm a chair,
 that's what you
meant isn't it? Swift as a missile the cloud leaves the horizon, rising
 in our direction to blanket the city in a minute, and sure,
 somebody will think of something;
sunlight does continue to drizzle on us, but by God we
haven't any right to it, we haven't figured out one thing, and

darkness will too arrive soon and be more unexpectedly
 lasciviously than you thought. How do
you wriggle out of the knowledge that we shall all have to
 answer separately
for our truths if such they are when dying, and meanwhile
 music wants to take the load
off our chests and point the way to a possible recreation
 period? Oh, but there were nights . . .
Your father and I were away much of the time;
it was like not having a home, string, and wads of serge to stuff
 in the cracks,
yet there were so many of them! I don't wonder now that it all
 didn't get done,
that practically nothing did, and I don't blame anyone or
 myself either. At this time in one's
life it's permissible not to point the finger, and if we are
 cautionary, then to hell with it.
I'd like some more too yet don't feel I'll get any, and that's OK
 because I wasn't the only one
engaged in tearing down the gnarled structure, exposing the
 pores of the evidence
for all to see and I won't be the most unsurprised when it
 rattles and will have evidently all
taken place on the sly, at once, and no beekeepers mourn the
 autumnal splendor of our robes
or come to visit when snow stains them with its truth, a truth
 like another, yet it's
all strangeness, into solitude, and woebegone one sees so little
of what is passing that it's like a show of truth, merely an ad,
 that spoke volumes
however and would let no one off the hook, even if one were
 on special assignment: that probably
triggered it all anyway. So grouches reform, the day shakes
 cracked emeralds out of its lap
into grooves at the edge of the pavement. Probably this is a
 true story of how we were united.
If so we shouldn't resent ourselves, not until the new moon
has bent its playful bow at least, and this moment too passes
 with a special suddenness, for showing

us what it's like. And other cares will unravel while one is
    dressing so that the differences
more or less cancel each other at the moment of presentation:
    it's like candy, like a star
that doesn't matter, like one's feet bouncing to a joyful rhythm,
    a warning next time to any who might think of writing.

No one has to re-invent himself at each new encounter with
    something different or slightly new.
Nowhere does it say that results will issue from a recent
    overhauling.
We don't know what hamlets lie in our path, or how much
    grumbling will occur
when we knock over something metallic and it makes a loud
    clang, audible on the stairs below,
or whether there will be a comic ending to this. We can see into
    the future
as into a dimple, and nothing says not to proceed, to go on
    planning,
though we know this cannot be taken as an authorization, even
    less as approval of the morass
of projects like half-assembled watches, that surrounds us. No
    but there is a logic
to be used in such situations, and only then: a curl of smoke or
    fuzziness in distant trees
that tempts one down the slope, and sure enough, there is a
    village, festive preparations,
a votive smile on the face of each inhabitant that lets you pass
    through
unquestioned. And we thought we were lucky back there in
    the silence! Here, civilization takes over,
at its highest, a new trope that dazzles without intimidating,
    like a scroll, is ready for us
and however many more of us it takes to change moods, build
    the palace of reason our
inconsequence has promised for so long now, out of trued
    granite blocks fired with chips of mica,
and so get over feeling oppressed, so as to be able to construct
    the small song, our prayer

at the center of whatever void we may be living in: a romantic,
   nocturnal place
that must sooner or later go away. At that point we'll have
   lived, and the having done so would
be a passport to a permanent, adjacent future, the adult
   equivalent of innocence
in a child, or lost sweetness in a remembered fruit: something
   to tell time by.
By then we'll know, as surely as if parents catechized us, the
   empty drum that offers itself
to any yearning, the daily quotient, the resolution, but also
   bare facts scattered on a plain
of fires, data that cannot be checked, dictates to live by, unlikely
   as it now seems.
And scattered over these, the dust of heavens that incorporates
   some of the good things and others
you'll most likely want to avoid, if you can, otherwise torpor
   builds up in plumes
on the horizon, and when you go
to convert your notes into hard currency, something will be
   lacking though the columns
of figures add up correctly, and there seems to be no mystery
to it, beyond a pleasant, slightly numbed sense of wonderment
   which was in any case
on your original want list. Although we mattered as children,
   as adults we're somehow counterfeit
and not briefed as to what happened in the intervals to which
   this longing led us,
which turns out to be not so tragic after all, but merely baroque,
   almost functional.
Yet there can be no safety in numbers: each of us wants and
   wants to be
in the same way, so that in the end none of us matters, and in
   different ways
we cannot understand, as though each spoke a different language
   with enough cognates
to make us believe in deafness—*their* deafness—as well as in
   our own reluctance
to dramatize, leaving our speech just sitting there, unrinsed,
   untasted, not knowing us,

or caring to. Each day the ball is in our court, and worse,
this is probably unromantic and proper procedure, *fons et origo,
nemine dissentiente.*

Hours, years later, we were together.
The moon unbarred its hold, the thickness of brambles was
  compacted
just in time to prevent the closing of the door as if by magic—
  "It always
happens that way, and then no one can find it. Pretty please,
not in the terrarium, but outdoors, that vague nest,
and others will conspire to push the lawnmower, make coffee,
  as long as these
and ours are spared and stand along the walk in rows. We
  might never
get out alive otherwise. Besides, there's all that to see,
all that and more, you see, not including
the glint in someone's eye when you tell them that, and
  afterwards, well, it's back to
your tunnel or whatever you care to call where it is you stay
in the afternoons, then morning, if all goes well. And if we two
  inhabit
a daffy teacup, are adept at crowd-pleasing, then what about
  the rest,
star-gazers in their midst, who make up the electorate? Say it
  was long ago,
say nothing further need be said, that even a memory will
  traipse
across the crossed hairs and be shot down, only the comfort
  in it
will be, will not have been
for many years, and though these die
with a sheen on them there is not very much to mark
of that past, no stones to leave on the trail, which isn't the same
as having an alderman in your living room and cats wherever
  you look,
fond George."
                Then it said it was supposed to come back
to an eyrie or some sort of enclosed space, it wasn't too clear
about that, but definitely would walk to meet us

whether we were here, or far. It would meet us. And so on. If living
was going to be like that, give me back my clothes, my crown
of gold, and just let me out before I have had a chance to put them on,
regal when partially naked, and you can bet the next one that comes along
will have his say, and then we are gay, and be under a mushroom
the livelong day, because no one wants to play
any more. The mouse ran up the clock, the clock struck one, and it all lurched
into motion again like an ancient conveyor belt an unseen hand flicks on. And trials,
pumpkin-colored ships in the street, disturb the busman's accident long ago,
having no sense of humor, or just barely. The frightened sleep in parks,
though motionless palm fronds announce a quiet evening. You can get over
bouts of humor best by not going indoors
when the moon is full. The lion stood by the bridge
so long it might have been a sculpture, but in the end loped sheepishly away.
And we have to figure out what these coins mean, not knowing the language.

It might be—still, there's no point in being greedy
before one means to—has to—but if it was a game in the beginning
it must be still, despite inertia. It's getting to be the end of a dance marathon
and though people keep cutting in, they do so with an air of resignation.
No point in taking further lessons, just at the moment anyway.
An enormous sense of release hushes the impatience
in the grass, the wayward chirruping about something. One can still stand up,
and that's plenty, under the circumstances. Besides, we'll not leave you alone yet;

the bench you warmed for us looks inviting; soon stars will be out
and you can walk home peering into the distance, hoping
someone will pick us up. Easy now, the stair treads
have come along again, and soon, soon
the bed will drench us with sleep and the surprising leap into
    the middle of a dream,
striking pennants, pavilions, bringing all natural activity to a
    halt as it wonders
about this, tests the current, supposes everything
must be OK or we'd have heard. In the next town there's a
    grist mill and a blacksmith,
or was that part of a dream, or did it really exist in a past
one can focus on, extracting its kernel until, like a ship, the
    shell turns round,
advances on us and speculation is undone for today. And we
    sobbed into those sails
sometimes, yet the gryphon never wavered until the third blast
    of a trombone
soothed it and it fell asleep. Now the dangers were tiny ones,
    but everywhere;
it would have been a good time to stay home, but alas that was
    a concept
foreign to these steep, peripheral times, these crags like
    sandpaper
dividing a no-good, swamp-green sky, and all the while
you were just a bit younger, enough to complain and not
    understand
why all the women stifled sobs and I was appointed to meet you
and bring you to this place, locus of many diagonals
without beginning or end except for the sense of them a place
    of confluence
provides. So, as is the custom here, I pulled the hood down to
    cover most of my face.
In a twinkling the mood had changed. The hiatus in the
    manuscript
buttoned itself up.   And there were many sets of fraternal twins
    on earth
to share in a new sense of disparity and reward everyone for
    what they would have

done anyway, inasmuch as there always comes a time when
    congratulations fall
just short of the doormat, loved ones are sorely tried, and
    associates
go blindly about their business, some business at any rate, all to
    keep the shelving
from imminent collapse by destroying relationships
that were good in the past but have now come to naught
as we see each day in the papers. And if one swoons, another
    will follow suit
until the entire populace is restive. And surely no one can
    locate the good in that
except by poring over miles of yellowing folios, which seems
    unlikely, so it's back
into bed with us again, and that's the way it has to keep happening
for any of us to remain unaware very long of secret provisions
    and codicils
in the charter it is imperative not to mention—not, you
    understand, out of a spirit
of fair play but in the ultimate interests of a deeper yet darker
    strain of being
we have to live toward if anyone is to get any good out of the
    colossal, foundering
experiment, the braintrust of fiends and werewolves who lie
    perched just out of
the reach of sleep, ready to reclaim territories surrendered in a
    moment
of temporary insanity, and others as well that were never in
    question
until they became bones of contention just seconds ago in the
    new climate
of sharpened political awareness that hungers always for new
    victims
like a minotaur, and whose mad thirst for the blood of
    innocent bystanders can never
be slaked, least of all by tepid gestures toward understanding
seen in a mirror and wrongly interpreted, or lives entirely given
    over to sacrifice
and austerity, for it is there, cautions the tome, that the greatest
    losses, the worst

atrocities will be instigated and immediately tallied. For such is
    the life of a young man
these days; there is still time to leave the boat, which at last
    report
was committed to its moorings, but of course to quit now
would be to miss the whole spectacle, and that, after all, is what
we came for, and shall insist on staying for, once the dirt has
    settled
and the bats flown back into the trees. And the cicadas stopped
    stuttering.

As dead wood floats, the expanding afternoon exhales
its mousy fragrance, battening on the memory of countless
    similar
ones it thinks are in the heads of those going about in this one,
and so the structure stands, without any apparent support.
    Doors are left open
as in spring, and beyond them float tunnel-vision landscapes
brought from somewhere else, and none recognizes the clever
    substitution.
Here a man carries bags
out to his truck, and makes the same trip over and over. There,
    windows shine.
And on a far-off hilltop someplace a living sacrifice gleams, red
in the puddled haze, and all eyes are cast downward, defrocked,
speechless. And though one can hear the traffic's swish
as it cuts from one side of the island to the other, one is
    transfixed,
facing an army of necessary revisions. "How would it be if I
    said it this way,
or would so-and-so's way be better, easy on the adjectives?" And
    if I told you
this was your life, not some short story for a contest, how
    would you react?
Chances are you'd tell me to buzz off and continue writing, except
it's so difficult; we barely begin and paralysis takes over, forcing
    us out
for a breath of fresh air. Meanwhile the vengeful deity whose acts
are being recorded has all the time in the world. "OK, that's it
    for today," as if

one weren't busy on other fronts too, such as writing letters
to friends in Panama and Hawaii. Not to mention keeping
 track of expenses
in a ledger acquired for just this purpose. But though reams of
 work do get done,
not much listens. I have the feeling my voice is just for me,
that no one else has ever heard it, yet I keep mumbling the litany
of all that has ever happened to me, childish pranks included,
 and when the voluminous
sun sets, its bag full, one can question these and other
 endeavors silently:
how far wrong did I go? Indeed, one can almost see the
 answers spelled out
in quires of the sky: Why? it enthuses, and immediately some of
 the metal trim
falls off, the finish has gotten gooey, but we persevere, and just
 as the forms
begin to float away like mesmerized smoke, the resolution, or
 some resolution, occurs.

We are no longer on that island. Here, the inmates
treat us harshly, but like adults, and though as usual no rest is
 authorized,
one can without too much difficulty keep pace with the
 majority of them
and see one's old clothes reflected in that mirror. And shoots
 keep popping up;
birds are pecking excitedly in the dirt for something, and your
 shoes
have grown too small; it will be time to change them soon. Of
 course, one is too old
to be a waif, yet that issue never surfaces; one is judged fairly
though without this set of complex circumstances being taken
 into account,
and that's something, more than you think, for by evening
the pronounced moan will have been deadened, and we are
 free to take our ease,
reveling in the glow, the surface of things, like water nourished
 on fading light.
You see, we have escaped. But one always goes back voluntarily

before the next roll-call, and that bittersweet dream of complete and utter
laziness is postponed once again, confirmed and postponed. And I write my diary
by street-light, because it's better that way; I may not have to look too closely
at my handwriting, yet I can feel it, all around and on me
like a garment or a sheet, and this too seems like a good idea.
   Well, doesn't it?

It does. But remember, one isn't obliged to love everything
and everybody, though one ought to try. One way is to accept the face they
present to you, but on consignment. Then you may find yourself falling in love
with the lie, sinister but endearing, they fabricated to win acceptance
for themselves as beings that are crisp and airy, with an un-self-conscious note of rightness
or purpose that just fits, and only later take up the guilt behind the façade
in the close, humid rooms of whatever goes down in their struggle (or hundreds
of struggles) against fate, and perhaps buy that too someday
when their manners are out of the way. I have obtained gratifying results in both instances
but I know enough not to insist, to keep sifting a mountain of detritus
indefinitely in search of tiny yellow blades of grass. Enough
is surely enough, in spite of what religion teaches us. I'm happy to be back with others
at the fairgrounds, without disparaging them too much, and when someone asks me
what I think of him or her, reply without false naïveté that I really love them
very much, but it might be time to take other factors into account, my own
well-being, for example, and how far along the path to survival my unselfish
instincts have moved me. Usually it's both farther and not as far as we imagine,

i.e., taking a wrong turning and then after a fretful period
    emerging in some nice
place we didn't know existed, and would never have found
    without being misled
by the distracted look in someone's eyes. It's mostly green
    then; the waves are peaceful;
rabbits hop here and there. And the landscape you saw from
    afar, from the tower,
really is miniature, it wasn't the laws of perspective that made it
    seem so,
but for now one must forgo it in the interests of finding an
    open, habitable space,
which isn't going to be easy. In fact it's the big problem one
    was being led
up to all along under the guise of being obliged to look out for
    oneself
and others: the place isn't hospitable, though it can support
    itself and one or two
others, but really it would be best to start all over again from
    the beginning
and find some really decent area that reflects a commitment to
    oneself.
But where? In a bubble under the surface of the ocean? Isn't it
    all going to be a fiction
anyway, and if so, what does it matter where we decide to settle
    down?

III

That was the first time you washed your hands,
and how monumental it seems now. Those days the wind blew
    only from one quarter;
one was forced to make snap judgments, though the norms
    unfolded naturally enough,
constructing themselves, and it wasn't until you found yourself
    inside a huge pen
or panopticon that you realized the story had disappeared like
    water into desert sand,
although it still continued. I guess that was the time I
    understood enough
to seize one of the roles and make it mine, and knew what I
    heard myself saying,
but not whose yellow hair it was. Mélisande? Oh, I'd
come before to let you in, and saw only a chipmunk, and so
    . . . But now it's nice
to sing along, and read the newspapers together, and try on
    funny hats: only
be aware that at daybreak there must be no trace of you, or the
    cock might not crow
and there'd be hell to pay. Besides, you wouldn't wish it
even if we were together, as someday we may be. I say
    "someday"
for the sound of it, like a drop of water landing, but I also
    meant it, but now I'm
standing just outside unafraid, listening. So much is wrapped in
    soot,
that now I'm no longer blind
and can denounce any aggressor, but I won't, because I'm
    afraid to, and besides,
what if the attic door slammed shut? Much remains unknown
in these calm countries. A bridge erects itself into the sky, all
    trumpets and twisted steel,
but like the torso of a god, too proud to see itself, or lap up
the saving grace of small talk. And when these immense structures
    go down, no one hears:
a puff of smoke is emitted, a flash, and then it's gone,
leaving behind a feeling that something happened there once,

like wind tearing at the current, but no memory and no crying
    either: it's just
another unit of space reduced to its components. An empty salute.

It's like the wind has taken over,
except that one can be aware of, keep an eye on oneself in that
    medium:
this one is more like a pock-marked wall, in which spalling
    occurs due to stress
and anxiety at regular, key points in one's career
(if it can be called that—"progress" is a better word, implying a
    development
but not necessarily a resolution at the end), and which enfolds
    you even as you
marvel at its irregular surface before you feel yourself beginning
    to sink into it,
toes first. Then, usually, one wakes up and everything seems
    ordinary.
Which is no miracle either, only one's daily ration
of satisfaction after a plenitude of endurance, even as it puts
    springiness in the gait
and a deceptive, fleeting zest for life until one encounters it
    again, muddied
and forgotten on the side of a hill above a large city. Which way
    did they go, it wonders,
and horsemen ride up as though on cue, and the rustlers
    disappear over the ridge,
and the spring trash is freighted with penance yet there is a
    satisfaction in knowing it
all comes true again and I wave into the flag. How many knives
    in the corridor
of them one traverses at the rate of one inch per minute, and
    do those in charge know
what to do with them? Do they even know where they are?
    Not at the last point where speech coincided
with the much-embraced hem of someone's robe as it swept by
    too fast for compliments
to occur in near-zero-degree temperature with a wind-chill
    factor of minus 51 degrees Fahrenheit

but too slow for cognitions relative to our positive but neutral,
    spreadeagled stance
re the conniption chambers of this world and our frequent
    encounters with them,
give or take a year or two, and then it's gone, again. There was
    no one to tell us what it meant
when it meant what it did; we had to rely on quasi-secret
    details of costume encoded
into the larger blank that would do us harm but remains stalled
    off the coast, O
sister of my worst enemy, to know how it talked back to us
    when we were no longer there
to receive the ice cream and the short shrift, but when we did
    get back there was nothing
but a well-dressed old gentleman waiting in the lobby who told
    us we ought to apply
for an emigration visa but did nothing to help us solve the
    vexed question of directions,
oil the bureaucratic wheels; thus in one kind of mess one
    dreams of others, perhaps
more serious, but which have the attraction of occupying the
    middle distance; meanwhile
all the porters have shuffled away, under the erroneous
    impression we haven't the coin
to pay them no doubt, yet it's not true, we would pay them if
    we could, but just look
how they have left the funhouse mirror clearly visible for
    perhaps the first time
and we can at last admire our billowing hips and hourglass
    waists through which
the background music of the street pours at an exponential
    rate, quite enough
to deafen less serious characters than we, who benefit from
    being put in our place
without imagining the successes with which we were daubed in
    earliest childhood
and which continue to stick to us long after they have worn off
in the eyes of some, preachers and paupers alike, but did it ever
    occur to them we aren't

as they imagine us, or even as we imagine ourselves, but more
    like bales
of hay, already harvested but still sitting around, waiting for
    someone to put them
in the barn before rain and rodents have their way with them?
    Surely, no one
creeps, no one speaks, yet one can't call this silence,
there are too many ships on the horizon, and besides, a pea
blinded me the last time I tried to look for significance in it,
    and then lots
of people are ready to tell you you've gone astray, but what
    about the rest of them:
they may not think so, although they say nothing. Our words
    are interpreted left
and right as they become speech, and so it is possible at the
    end that a judgment may be
formed, and yet the intrepid
listener does no such thing, hypnotized by his reflection, and it
    is up
to us to file the final report on the decision in many cases. As
    flax is blue,
I desire your toes, and in the final
harbor our destinies though parallel are too closely linked to be
    seen as such, my
boulder that rushes to me yet hangs suspended
like mistletoe and we all go often to a place we are familiar
    with,
though it seems strange and uncompromising. So much was I
    taken aback by
the rules of the prostitute, it seemed for a while we should
    never reach the oval lake's
opposite shore, but then we did, suddenly; it was like looking
    for a lost object
and finding it in the palm of your hand. Out of the sad spring,
    no heart-clenching chime
then or ever; the development was muted, then fudged; but
    one had been warned to play
within the enclosure on the off chance that something slightly
    singular would occur; this

took the form of accidental meetings with old acquaintances.
    Never mind, it said, about how to
give dignitaries the slip; your job is to play with responses, until,
    elsewhere, they are changed
to raw greetings and obtuse expressions about how this or that
    influenced one's gradual ascent
to greatness with not so much as a look back in any direction,
    and when these "come true,"
when the future has arrived, not be the last to put in your
    consent to what, in actual fact,
transpired long ago when noses were buried in manuscripts
    and lampshades
ornamented our own landscape quite sufficiently, or so it is
    claimed in reference
works by forgotten but reliable authorities. The sheen, like that
    of silk, on the night air,
and the days, plain old miserable days scanned by a gas engine's
    rattle, or, worse,
afternoons in a canoe, with the quality of rebounding off
    yourself as you write
in water the name of the beloved, and later get a chance to see
    it on vellum, in blood-red.
No task actually kept us here; besides it was much too airy, but
    I want
to single out certain elements in the role indifference played in
    all our lives, winding down
toward a town that continues to hold our attention
after seven centuries of interaction of the divine with the sparse
    sentinels, posted
here and there, of our attention to portents high and low
    issued from a cave
on the edge of Main Street and therefore able to transport us
    instantaneously to the region
of whatever happens to be interesting to six or more people
    just then: a steeply shelving
lawn purplish with black gargoyle-like shadows and lesser
    animadversions, weak though sincere
ones, and we have to get off here, it's our stop. But we *will*
    come back, no question

of it, some other time when all the right numbers have come
    up, conflated with calls for
truth and decency at whatever street corners they may abound:
    so is it likened by clerics
to what had never gone before, except to say, I still love you.
    The barn has begun
to tarnish and it would not do to stay any longer, even though
    you were posted here:
it is essential that you leave this very evening, that you not look
    back
or ever give a thought to the circumstances that transported
    you to this place
of easy definitions and only so-so resolutions, because all
that was going to name you has been shunted aside, and it
    beseems us to act modest in turn, lest
our very lack of success be turned into an accusation of failure,
    and the loved things
spiral off to the rungs of distance, as the sandpiper pecks at the
    shore when the sea rushes out.
The panel impelled consideration of the question. So sure there
    are some that stay home
and mope, taking the path of least resistance, as
their dreams go to the opera and out to supper afterward,
    having a marvelous time, one
imagines, coming home at dawn. But for all the good this does
    anyone, ask the fairies,
and the record is eloquent on this point: no fire sales, none at
    all, before the end
of friendship. It was the day-to-day banter, you see. Besides,
    whose business is it if none
of us turns up, we signed no agreement, life gets along quite
    well without us, don't
you suppose, and if the sky is rarely green at evening, the water
    often is, when there is
an overlay of gold leaf and nothing too disgusting shreds one's
    patience as it did
the last time these books were taken out. Really, my dear, I
don't see any point in disturbing people about a few pencil-
    shavings on the desk-top

any more than your dead tea-leaves annoy *me*. Why then,
    should people swing toward people
in groups, and when some collide and others keep on going,
    misstate the occasion?
Either it's a social event or it isn't. You can't get away
with having two kinds of activity back to back: it just won't
    work. Otherwise
we'd all be happy, or blissfully out of our minds is more like it,
    but work
has to get done in the cracks, joists be visible, for it to matter,
    and happen: you know
the shed was bare in the morning, and when you crept back to
    it at noon, it still was
and was obviously going to be again when twilight arrived,
    broom in hand. Now the shocked clocks
jangle otherwise, but back there, when it was doing its being,
    who thought about time?
Who cared about being caught red-handed when there was so
    much to hear and complain about,
so many bodies sitting in drafts, backs bared for our added
    enjoyment when a man with a pipe
tiptoes in, and abruptly one felt uneasy, one's mood blunted by
    this seemingly unrelated
conundrum. It was then we got up to go. One simply stormed
    out of the baroque palace
in arctic weather, clad in a filmy negligee, with no thought for
    the morrow,
not the least concern for where cash or food were going to
    come from. Call it a happy ending,
there is much to praise in a decidedly mixed climate of coming-
    of-age films and old
bear masks, one would say, especially insofar as the current
    underlying it was cool,
not having made up its mind yet. The few who did escape were
    considered dangerous
and were put down, so that for a long time there was no really
    reliable account of what went on
in there: besides, who knew? Even belated guests having fun in
    a fit of champagne

and ruled legal paper were undercut by their own memories of
what this would have been
in a past that can make no sense to them, now. Besides, if *you*
said it one of them might obey
and there would be an end of it. Can you imagine? Nothing
but ecstatic rooms,
one after the other, and strong possibilities of *becoming* one's
desire and thereby
mastering it and one's own plans for the future before they
begin to drift,
causing the consternation that we know. Come to think of it,
why couldn't we all play at
savoring how the sun seems to grow aware of us gradually,
until late in the evening
when one is excused, and can go and write down one's
impressions? At least,
I thought that's what it was all about. You may contradict me,
but I *see* life
in the dead leaves beginning to blow across the carpet, paraffin
skies, the beetle's forlorn
wail, and all at once it recognizes me, I am valid again, the
chapter can close
and later be mounted, as though on a stage or in an album.
Really not too much does get
left out, if you count it to the end, not including the hopes and
desires that intervened
and made you think of it, but only the smooth moments that
were ours, O
don fatale, as someone said, and I agree, and now I must post
this, feeling you
in my hands and along my arms, as though it were all going to
stop and begin
a few minutes after the alarm sounded. Much of it is there,
intact and around.
Someone could start it up again. I know. We were all cute kids
once.
Lately I have this feeling you were avoiding me. We could sum
it all up as a bunch
of nerves, little people peeing around, but there goes my
Doberman's tether, he's off and running,

not to put too fine a point on it. And the cooling-off period
    ended, dirty,
this time. As these strangers of our waking existence are
    consumed, their outlines darken
and are suddenly stronger. We'll never get rid of them. They
    erupt as you start to move,
become your belt or maxim, ride roughshod over the ancient
    imperatives,
and there is nothing to see. You are inside the box. It couldn't
    have happened
in a more convenient interval. Yet life
is after all very much what they are all about:
why drag it out, sniff and whine, merely to remain
    perpendicular
to the afterlife, buying that notion. Visions at sea: the old
    promontories are there,
an argument I had with my father, the store that sells antique
    tools, and only a little
about cleaning up my act, really sitting down and just doing
    the job. Then the abandoned
projects need pampering too. So I walk out into the street,
    wearing a shirt,
and buy something. And the cake is eaten. No crumb is left
    over. There were never going to
be any, since what was predicted has already happened. You can
    turn off that appetite now.

Girls, I don't know, there were a lot of them but no special one.
Boys handed cigarettes around.
The newspaper had just hit the stands. The airplane was
    mentioned in it.

No one had come to shake hands. Besides they were just
    walking. A basin or two. That
shattering discharge of light just when sunset is supposed to
    occur, striking
terror into your heart, but gone the next moment. To be born
    eclectic is, I suppose, to die
into my idea of what you are, a basso-profundo fibrillation, an
    idea like a pit.

Here, I can't hold it up by myself, you've got to help. One can,
 one does exist like this
but what a thin home it makes. No place to put my despair.
 Never mind, we'll unpack it later.
Meanwhile I haven't told you what the kids said
about the airplane, and how their place on it was nice. Lots of
 people told stories.
It was grand, a truly grand homecoming: lifers off the sauce,
 raccoons that dodge, cheese
and pastry for everybody, canons praised, until the knife came
and sat on the chopping block, which was a bit problematical,
 but we figured out a way
to include it in our rounds, so it never got bored or lonesome.
 The bigger children had fits.
Soon all was gray, and gay. Honeybunch had never seen
so many distasteful lives intertwined, and Mary Ellen hadn't
 either. When the fray comes
undone, and the world is a frump, why it's time to make hay in
 the rain, leaving
the door closed, that tells its own story: a world of pimps, a
 season on a pink beach,
mauve twilights that plop down on you in the tropics and then
 ask *you* the way out, insist
on the recipe—still, one could have a fine time or two,
then. We were younger, but not as rich. By the time we were
 old, everyone cared,
and it was time to try something new, but the wine had taken
 over, what was supposed to be a lark
ended in the dark, and then how do you count them? The
 waivers, I mean
the insects, in the bloody awful place you brought me to. I
 suppose I could forgive you,
given the era, but then they all shouted. It was supposed to be
 embarrassing for me,
coming back, I mean. So I just put on the halter and waited,
 for what seemed
like tall summer afternoons, and a breeze came and kissed me
 on the head, and I was out of it,
finally, free to collect my things—you know how that feels. So
 I swaggered

over to the bar, was refused admission. Then I lay on my back
    in the street
for a while, gazing up at the stars, but soon tired of that too.
    So I got up, traded places
with a beggar standing next to me, and set out in rags to see
    the world itself,
a pretty tired place by that time. And so arrived home without
    further incident, "the trip
was uneventful," as they say, except in between I need more
    time with you, and primroses,
which I collect. There was a bad day too at school, but you see
    this
no longer concerns me, I am kind of semi-retired now, and
    don't wish to go pushing people
or putting on airs. Some of the young people came to stay. It
    was lovely, then.

But I'll tell you one thing: it wasn't easy. Mornings, I'd be at
    the library
while it was still dark outside, straining my eyes over useless
    newsprint, all
in the interests of some dumb theory I was trying to prove,
even after I'd forgotten what it was. There'd be times I thought
    I'd hit on something—
eureka! And then I'd realize I'd ignored an important bit of
    chronology, for instance
that A and B weren't even alive during the same century, and
    I'd be forced to backtrack,
treading water, then as always. Sometimes an important fact
    would come to light
only to reveal itself as someone else's discovery, while I felt my
    brain getting chafed
as everything in the reading room took on an unreal, somber
    aspect. But outside, the streetscape
always looked refreshingly right, as though scene-painters had
    been at work, and then,
at such moments, it was truly a pleasure to walk along,
    surprised yet not too surprised
by every new, dimpled vista. People would smile at me, as
    though we shared some pleasant

secret, or a tree would swoon into its fragrance, like a freshly
    unwrapped bouquet
from the florist's. I knew then that nature was my friend. "We
    do it," the contractor said,
"routinely." And sure enough, it was as though everything were
    posing for a photographer,
helping you to get the right angle. A snowy panorama would
    automatically appear framed
by a lych-gate; parked cars would reveal carved wooden heads,
    of unknown origin, affixed
to the house behind them. Beautiful girls wearing peasant aprons
    would sink, laughing,
in a circle on the grass, one of them tilting her head thoughtfully
    upward
as she chewed on a spear of hay. You can bet this helped me
    along with my work. Or if
the water in a vase appeared clouded, someone would have
    replaced it
the next time you noticed, and gone on to other happy,
    thankless tasks. I kept my counsel
as I continued to write, and then, because that is the way I do
    it, would greet
or compliment someone when they weren't expecting it, and
    you know something—I do it
because they expect me to, and that's the way I want everything
    to be. Because when
darkness does come we'll need advice, and the only way we'll
    get it is by looking at what
we wrote down a long time ago, thinking it of no importance
    and laying it
in a shallow box or drawer. But when you do really need to know
    the essential
nature of a thing, recognize it by its texture only, the cup by
    the handle, the gas
from its sudden volatility, you'll be glad you
wasted so much time in youth jotting down seemingly
    unrelated random characteristics of things,
rested on your elbows at the windowsill looking out over
    everything that was going to be night,

as dismay took two steps backward into curiosity and brought
    momentary relief in the form
of an incorrect solution that might be read later on as a stain
on your record, before everything became justified by age,
    antiquity
having usurped a moral force hitherto in suspension, now
    focused
on all the manifold exploits of men and animals. And not a
    moment too soon—the page
that was waiting to be turned had grown heavy as a barren
    mountain range, and armies
of civil engineers equipped with the latest in pulleys, winches,
    sprockets and windlasses
were just at that moment attempting to negotiate its sheer
    sides, with little success,
until in your sleep you muttered the word that released them,
    it sank, and all returned
to normal for a while. Music had gotten caught in the chinks of
    their argument,
that is, their history: it too disengaged itself and flew off,
    lapwing-wise, into the air
and the sun came out as though to congratulate earth on the
    felicitous result which
might so easily have proved far other, setting the race to
    humanity back a couple of hundred
years. At such times we are allies, rejoicing to feel the firm
    pavement under our feet.
And when things stagnate we can easily stir them up to
    produce an evocation
of freshness, until the next major change is called for. You'd
    better believe we can
bestir ourselves when necessary, though leisure is always
    productive, too,
leading, at the end, to truths it was never possible to envisage,
    or, even now, to formulate.
Let the weather of it all wash over me like a wall, I am not
    foolish, only a little
fanatical, but I do not intend to let that hinder me or
    discourage all of us

from taking ourselves down a peg, if needful; I have only the
    world to ask for, and,
when granted, to return to its pedestal, sealed, resolved, restful,
    a thing
of magic enmity no longer, an object merely, but one that watches us
secretly, and if necessary guides us
through the passes, the deserts, the windswept tumult that is to
    be our home
once we have penetrated it successfully, and all else has been
    laid to rest.

And the river threaded its way as best it could through sharp
    obstacles and was sometimes not there
and was triumphal for a few moments at the end. I put my
    youth and middle age into it,
and what else? Whatever happened to be around, at a given
    moment, for that is the best
we have; no one can refuse it, and, by the same token,
    everyone must accept it,
for it is like a kind of music that comes in sideways and
    afterwards you aren't sure
if you heard it or not, but its effects will be noticed later on,
    perhaps in
people you never heard of, who migrated to other parts of the
    country
and established families and businesses there. Yet sometimes
    too it'd seem like a moraine,
filled with rocks and bloom, a mammoth postscript
to whatever you thought your life had been before.
At no time did the music seem remotely interesting. You must
    always keep listening, though,
otherwise you might miss out on something. And there is
    something lovely
about haunting voices filling the high vaults of a basilica:
just the idea that they want to sing leads to a fork in the path,
and that can never be used against you because there are
    already far too many old men
to count as a reproach, with downcast eyes,
following the path wherever it leads now. Besides, it's
    impossible to be young enough

anyway, and the leaping intervals of the music don't so much
   consecrate youthful hopefulness
as excuse the follies of old age, as, running around like chickens
   with our heads cut off,
we try to excommunicate everyone including ourselves from
   society: even the word "society"
is something each of us eventually gets a stranglehold on,
   forcing it to say "uncle"—there,
I'm glad I did, and you can go away now. Such are dried fruits,
   a pleasant treat
perhaps in some afternoon that can be, but as I sit here it doesn't
   seem anything
can establish itself as the slab of meaning I feel central to my
   situation and all unwary,
unprepared to do anything. Looking out at the bay
one imagined one had seen it before.

Did I say that thing to you? I hope not—
but if I did, please forgive me—it wasn't the real me, but in any
   case
we have to get on with our lives somewhat, make swift
   compromises
for all the world to see, and sparrows fly off, and it shall be as
   perhaps it was before
when night tickled the very notion of seeing without artificial
   light, and finally
it began to rain past thirst, past any notion of seedlings, of
   decay, of posterity
and protocol, wherever they have fled now. Beyond horses and
   the island.
It would all be just as you were going to have it in a moment.
   No boys unloaded then.
The poor sailor seeking the familiar is still lost, and no one
   appears to know
anything about our circumstances. At least until we have been
   coaxed past the limit
of civilized performance. All else fades. Here is my pen. I am
   resolved to write
no more, until this business be settled, one day or the other.
   Cancel all my appointments.

Remember to water the dieffenbachia. And please, curl your
   hair. It's getting stretched-
looking. There are biscuits in a container under the counter.
   Otherwise, why
it's plenty being out in the air and watching others run.
   Someone came down
from upstate to see me, and that was fine. We rummaged in
   drawers for a spell. My, how
that bush has grown. Aren't you tempted too in the sweet part
   of the night
to give up your secret by whispering it and then roll over,
convinced nothing can ever repair the climate? And when, in
   the morning, everything
suddenly looks so frighteningly reassuring, and you
   automatically reach for the note
on the night table and find it gone, is this despair because it
   meshed better,
or is it all just animals in tall grasses, not so much as a sapling
   on the horizon,
that is one we have never seen before, though it all looks
like something I saw once in a waking dream, in Minnesota,
   perhaps? And you find you can't
add any more; somebody starts to sympathize and that
   frightens you, you run away
for a while, then stop and rest,
because where could you get to, anyway? Only if *he* authorized
   it, which is unlikely,
will we ever see those towering organ-pipe cactuses like deco
   skyscrapers in a city
one always wanted to live in, but if he comes back maybe he'll
   do something
about all the others who pestered an infant once, and, when it
   was time to go,
didn't say they'd had a nice time or anything. If, indeed, I am
   findable under the lens
of this disinterested red-haired scientist, and if he is willing to
   exchange me for
a hostage, why then I will go, no question of it. If, however, it
   is only to force me
to "take my medicine," then I'll stay. It's that simple. It's decided. We

have no way of forcing others to cooperate except by vaguely
    acquiescing
to their most intimate desires and pretending we don't know
    what it's all about, what
we are doing, and who are they? I thought one was the
    milkman. But it doesn't
matter because while still enrolled in a course at a local
    community college I happened
once to overhear a conversation between two boys in the next
    row of lockers, and it
sounded, well, suspicious. I thought I should tell somebody
    something, and ran out,
but the office was closed, although it was only a little after four,
    and a tremendous
black bruise stood up in the sky. This was definitely not
    something to kid about,
I thought as I ran the few blocks to a stationery store, which
    was closed too—damn!
No wonder kids can't get their schoolwork done. And then I
    noticed every window in every
single-story house was like an eye with a trembling eyelid, and
    knew that the hour
had come to deliver my speech, and did, the gist of it being:
    where, assuming
it can be located at all, when you came from the well, gingerly
making your way along the low masonry wall in the side of the
    bluff, did you expect the others
to be, if not in the roofless enclosure they called a house and
    were planning to enlarge
someday? Why didn't Dad reach for his shotgun then, instead
of putting some of them out of the house and grabbing the
    others and forcing them back
inside? Another roll of the glass paperweight and snow
    shoots up
out of the sagebrush, engulfing the bunkhouse: now see
here, is this what you ordered the man to be? Not if you have a
    warrant,
it isn't, and can't be exchanged or refunded, its name is a great
    hiss of waters
rolling toward, then past us. And just see how

the fire ants got washed away, in a red cloud on the surface of
   the billows,
their mandibles pawing the air pathetically, since after all it was
   the life force
that impelled them, as it does us, and now they are gone, and
   we have lasted
but are no better for it. Shit, let's go home. I mean, I forgot my key.
And the road has no survivors. They are probably with him in
   the jeep up ahead.
One dives at one, then at another, asking, beseeching an
   explanation
that is not forthcoming. If they were my kids, I'd discipline
   them different
but nobody can predict, when the day's work is done,
how much vomit would cover the stone surface and where
   you'd get 'em even if you had 'em.
Nice boys at school. It don't do much to mess with the
   vegetation leastwise
when it clambers like this and could be leaves or part of a tree
or a house in a miniseries. Therefore all ends in disappointment.
   And if you did
good that's fine, but if you did bad it don't make no difference,
   you're equal
same as the others, and the devil don't give a shit who you are
or whether your name has an umlaut to it. But we can rest,
   smooth from the attack,
until wit returns, and you shine
the little copper ring and something good will come of it. Few,
   however,
were interested in doing so, because of having already done it,
   and nothing
behind them. One little scholar however did observe
how odd it was to see two people here—you see, no one told
us about other names being on the list. It was, in effect, highly
   unusual,
though no more so than circumstantial evidence or grass being
   covered up. Here
a moral dilemma socks one: is it better to remain single,
   conscious of the many
overlapping half-lives that with luck add up to one, or should

we be planted at many listening posts ready to radio vital
   information back to whoever
stands at the long bar? And will my genuine if respectful
   indifference militate
against the neutrality of my performance? Is a conflict of
   interest shaping up, or what?
Or will these woolly, ball-like constituents of my flock teeter
permanently on the edge of forgiveness, of having something
   to say
even when I'm down the fire stairs preparing to exit into the
   alley, before losing
myself in the turbid flood of passersby that wearily
accosts one in the major thoroughfare it empties into? People
   that look like the Gov and Min
in a more strained version: the colors are soiled even when the
   long coats are clean,
and move swiftly past to tea or some such tropical rendezvous.
They've had it with us, seems to be the universal psalm
   emanating from some debris' psaltery:
and anyway, who dat man wid de fish? Is he the one who must
   drive death's wagon for a year
until somebody else dies and has to take over the job? (And
   how spidery the *attelage*,
the incomplete wheels.) Oh we must be ever saying and sighing
until what's-its-name gets you up there again, to turn the ever-
   accomplished phrases
once more and file out having been paid; then there's an
   argument, a stout middle-aged woman accuses a
weasely person of trying to grab her handbag and all hell
   breaks loose:
fat Irish policemen in outdated uniforms frantically blow on tin
   whistles until
a phantom paddy wagon drawn by six slavering horses careens
   down the narrow, muddied street.
It's all over for today; you can go home. Wait, the woman
still wants to know about her change purse; it wasn't in the
   retrieved handbag.
Things go from bad to worse; it sickens one when one
thinks about it for a second; yet having to explain to one's
   kindly interlocutor

that it's the crisis of humanity, not this isolated incident, is a
    fate worse than death,
almost. Here, we can duck into this café. You'll feel better
in a moment, but it's best not to take these things too seriously,
not be so thin-skinned. Honest. A rose is blowing over there.
    The baker comes out of his shop
and smiles, rubbing his hands on his floury apron, and the wind
picked up the veil off that woman's face and revealed her beauty
before she hastily jammed the hat down over her forehead and
    trotted swiftly off.
O my fellow members in the secret society, do you see what
    secrecy has brought us to,
do you know that shad are running in the river, that dams are
    collapsing in Italy,
and about other fields of interest? For me, it's not so much
    enough that someone brought me
here to my senses, as that the recent past is almost dead, that
    some other
people, though no officials, have struggled to greet me despite
    the dust storm's
increased severity, that no tax can ever be legitimately imposed
    on this period
of my uncertainty, that a score of bloopers hasn't imperiled my
    career—yet.
And that these elements combine thrillingly, almost
    diabolically, to
disarm the cryptogram, making us all well again in each other's
    arms, for as long
as one fancies time or happiness endures—check one. Well I see I've
not outstayed my welcome, that on the contrary quite a few
    people are waiting
in the anteroom to shake my hand. And with this reassurance,
    nothing ever quite seems
complete again. Yet it isn't exasperating. No furniture-bashing
    please.
And as we congregate this way, the actual lists of heaven seem
    roseate
anew. Flames lick the pulpit. This is the way to go—here. This
    the place
to be.

IV

I had
many ties to the region. And yes, life has a way of sidling on in
   rain-slick afternoons
like this as though nothing were amiss, as though we had just
seen each other five minutes ago and that tantrum was all for
   naught. As for the rusted
tackle on the rickety wooden dock, that's hardly our affair, is it?
   Is it
even worth the bother of trying to locate the owner? Think
   about the mountains,
their motto, "We grow the best for all the rest," and then ask
   yourself why it is you fall
out with those you love most, saving the look on your face for
   casual acquaintances, or,
better yet, complete strangers who are still pure and
   unrewarded: such society
as the place afforded, and as I took my seat among them, knew
   it wasn't my lot to be privy
to barbs and conversations about tilefish such as this, but
   would hold on for a time,
as tomorrow beckoned, and today would soon be then. And
   minutes still trail
by, loitering. As my cock hardens I can make out a group of
   primitive wattled structures
just below the horizon, and am allowed to wonder why, in
   such circumstances, anybody
would want to live from one day to the next, without
   assurances, no sketch
or dream of the morrow, and then it's gone. It disappears from
   view.
Patiently you again show me my name in the register where I
   wrote it.
But I'll be off now, there's no point in thanking me for what I
   haven't done, nor in
my thanking you for all the things you did for me, the good
   things and the less good.
In riper times of trial we stayed together. But in this kind of
   bleached-out crisis-

feeling, the best one can do is remain polite while dreaming of
    revenge in another key, even
with a different cast of characters who know nothing of the life
    you came from,
that neat trajectory that gradually became confused and later
    submerged in th'encroaching
gloom of everybody's opinion of what you should do to prevent it.

I suppose it does congeal slowly, like those footprints a primate
made one morning zillions of years ago, and that says
    something about spontaneity
as well as one's right to privacy. It's not like it was fused in a
    furnace;
it slowly ebbed into its permanent state just by appearing every
    so often
unchallenged; its absences too were seldom commented on,
    even as they grew less infrequent,
so that it became one's privileged daily routine without anyone's
    being the wiser.
The man told us that first-off. No one can plead ignorance,
    therefore,
and any other plea-bargain seems out of the question, though my
backers will tell you otherwise. And I can see no outcome but
    further fractioning
as precious time elapses, and a totally unexpected split decision
    that benefits no one
except perhaps those it lulls to sleep with promises of "good
    times"
long after its half-truths have been assimilated by the rabble it
    now seeks to contain
with only partial success. Our love, that we didn't know about,
    mitigated
our reception at the outset; the misunderstanding could only
    grow, so that it seems
desolation and solitude were the point we had set out for, the
    times of mirth
forgotten now, recorded in disappearing ink that doesn't outlast
    winter
and its holidays, its occasions. If I said to you now, let's go out
    somewhere, you know

what you would think; it's hardly worth disturbing even the
    sour calm of whatever fell
from day to day, like a croquet ball tentatively negotiating a
    stair, all cakes and notions
of pleasure screened by the past, the evergreens that shot up
in the twenty years you were away. Does it look like
I care now, that it matters still? Or is it the calm
of a moment of eternity, not something one lives in, fusses
    over, but only builds?
I must ask you to leave now. It seems we are fresh out of
    turnips.
The big spider of the day is broken. Who could repair it?
"Whatever things men are doing shall germ
the motley subject of my page." And that shall leave a great
    deal after it
in the way of trails. Besides, as trails go, we are pretty
    incompetent
except to watch the sun slide away, and the trellis of clouds
with it, while the city's modest spires stay put, again, as usual.
The madhouse statuary seemed to dispel the pre-life we gave it
in sleep, to become the one bauble rescued from that hoard,
    whose shapes
no one now will know. It cannot be said they existed. Yet
surely there was life once in those seams, life the daughters of
    the iron teeth
of time gave it, and swallows flew over it. One might say,
    casually,
that there was variation in it, that there was texture. More,
    though,
one still couldn't say. Yet one day the sanitation department
    decreed
it was coming through, a nice day in May with the usual
    blossoms, though these
were only accessories, having no bearing on the tale or
its context, petal-like, in fact, like a cat's nose, but the judge
happened by just then and told them to stop it. They went
    away and someone,
a bushy-haired man, came back and said it was OK, they could
    keep on doing it
if they wanted to, but not to say he said so, but that it was OK.

I long meanwhile for the confines of any other principality, but
    can't abandon
working even if I wanted to, it's like play to me though I get
    no pleasure from it
except pausing at odd moments to watch the rill for a few
    seconds,
and then it's back to work again, more work, lots of it, and the
    pollution
attendant on it, like Hebe to the rainbow's gauzy showers, or
    web, and I
can't stand on tradition nor beside it. Here it suits me, boys, to
    turn
over a new leaf like a chunk of recalcitrant granite. I know no
    other gadfly
who berates me so much; I love it; the woman came back to
    say she was in the way
and would we go away please it was four o'clock. Not on your
    life thundered the
hangman, and so it became a kind of ritual, then a game, and
    every day
someone came to ask after the stone, and someone would
    stand up to say
it has gone away, go lose yourself in studies or the wilderness;
    more none can say. He just came up that day,
had a look round, and left. We aren't even sure
we saw him. It could have been wildflowers in the wallpaper
or stray ashes in the grate, no more. Then the bird came back
    and shat
on the stone, and that proved it was there for a while, but
    somehow
that got forgotten and we were thrust out of doors to play in
    the rain
and sleet, and somebody got hold of the key, we entered, and
    presto, no one
was there, it was a different room, another empty one too, and had
obviously been vacated pretty recently. A smell of kippers
hung in the front hall. OK, I said, we must press on to the last
    house
they were seen in in the next block. The green cement one.
    But my

companions whispered why, let's ditch him at the first
    opportunity, no
let's not even wait that long, which is why I came across the
    lawn bruised
and moist, and trembling with pity to be let in, and you came
and let me in. Nowhere did I have anything to say again, but
    that
was not noticed until yesterday, too late to have us do anything
    about it.
One source said it was the tulips, against the nice gesture to be
    led and fed
and have others shut up about it. But one said, you can't have
    that
and not condone the listless others who don't know yet they're
    walking
in your tracks and will be sorry when they find out, but
    another man joined
the woman and said you could too talk about it, it was just a
    subject
and therefore forgotten, i.e. dead. And Joan she said
too it was like being dead only she didn't care, she might as
    well be anyway, for all
she cared, and then someone came back with beef. And said
    here
put a rose on this, you're not afraid, you do it, and someone
    said, O if the law
decree it he must do it. So the one went in and the others
    stayed out and waited.
And if you're not going to do it, and if it's none of your
    business, why are
you going to do it, the first one said, to which that one said:
    begone. You are my
business in any case and it behooves me not to be in the
    shadow of you
while I wait. And then one who came from a great distance
    said, why does it suit you
to be ornery, if others cannot join the general purgative
    exodus, to which that one inside
said, and so it becomes you, if it become you. And then in the
    shade they put their heads

together, and one comes back, the others being a little way off,
    and says, who
do you think taught you to disobey in the first place? And he
    says, my father.
And at that they were all struck dumb
and left that place falling all over each other
in their haste to get away, and it was all over for that day.
But another day came and the rice was still laying
on the ground, next to the dust ball. And one took it up, saying,
this is all that shall be till I get back from my trip.
And the others were amused because he had never mentioned
    a trip before,
but he spat at them, saying, you are too powerful now for my
    injunction to take hold,
but just wait till the others see you in my chamois costume,
    because if you think it's too late
now what will you think when it has gotten really out of hand
like a vine that grows and grows and cannot stop growing, or
    a fire
deep in a coal mine that burns for centuries before anyone can
    do anything
about it. So he stepped down at last. And the others, charred
and unrecognizable, concurred that something extraordinary
    had taken place and that there
was nothing to be done about it. And so he went away.

Love that lasts a minute like a filter
on a faucet, love that is always like headlights in the glistening
    dark, heed
the pen's screech. Do not read what is written. In time
it too shall become incoherent but for the time being it is good
just to tamper with it and be off, lest someone see you. And
    when this veil
of twisted creeper is parted, and the listing tundra is revealed
behind it, say why you had come to say it: the divorce. The no
    reason, as
the plane dives up into the sky and is lost. All that one had so
    carefully polished
and preserved, arranged in rows, boasted modestly to the
    neighbors about,

is gone and there is nothing, repeat nothing, to take its place.
    Only should we
wander a bit and then return without expectations, does some
    faint impulse twitch at its
base before expiring, and a lesbian truth rise up for a split
    second, and the faint
material truth dies again, and then flickers like a post-mortem
    arrangement
until the rabble of the skies cries and all is assumed to be
    productive.
Get your ass out of here. But it is time
to work again, but a sad, a tragic time, a time of trifles
and vast snowbanks, and so
you put on your hat backwards and decipher it again dutifully;
    it's the home stretch
but dare I say more before you think it's time to go and they
    think so
but they say only, is no more time to stay *here*, in any case we
    would have gone
if we knew where to go, but we have a place to go, so we will
    go there. And behind
the barn it behooves us again to take up the principle, so like
    the art
of tragedy and so unlike, and so we let it rest carefully, and
    someone says
he would like to be off, and the others agree, it ignites a
    general stampede
before the clock closes down. In the old corners of why the
    situation
was ever allowed to come into existence in the first place, the
    nasal whining
is first heard, then perturbed groans and idle retreats into
    shuttered
middle distances and auxiliary alcoves. Aw, shucks, someone
seems to be repeating, we could stay here all night if we
    wanted to
but that couldn't bring the child back into being, and I say, I
    suppose so.
One's gone for some grants. Be back
when the coal trestle is finished, and idle

against the apricot lamé of the distance here. And boys I know
the distance between your empty bellies and the jobs that will
    not fill them,
but I still maintain you are better here, but better off far from
    here
where the choo-choo whistles and a deadly white wind stoops
    to take a few prisoners,
where we shall be pleasant once the future has had its way with
    us. And you know,
he said, sure, that's the way to hell and its conundrums if that's
    the way
you want to go, and they all said we know, we are going that way
cautiously approved of in the introduction, only it seems so full
    of asperities now.
And he said that's the way it was, it was a tangle and will never
    be anything
more than a diagram pointing you in a senseless direction
    toward yourself.
Sure, they come with snacks you have foreseen,
but that doesn't excuse you for having been caught in this
    place. And they all said
giddyap, let's go on to the next
place on the side, for having won, and being here to count up
    our winnings, which are
surely all right with us. Watch it, he said.

So the initial exuberance departed. But that was fine, because
    surely
the beginning of a festival is a nice place to be, if it's Asia, and
    more hogs
were brought down. But when he saw the hogs, the owner of
    the grain elevator was angry
and went out. Now, there were two others who were there.
    And they were
each determined to get what was coming to them. The master
    returning, said OK boys,
never let it be said you didn't ask for it. And in that moment a
    fuzz of bloom
was on them. Each spring the desert comes alive with birds and
    flowers,

a breathtaking view at the foot of the famed Superstition
   Mountains,
reported home of the Lost Dutchman Mine with its still
   undiscovered caches of gold.
And all around it is nice too. The mineral springs I wanted so
   much to exploit—what
does any of it matter now, now that I have found my home in a
   narrow cleft
stained with Indian paintbrush and boar's blood, from which
   an avenue eventually leads
to the flatter, more civilized places I have no quarrel with
   either. After all,
we *have* to go in once or twice a month to pick up supplies, the few
articles we don't grow such as coffee, to which I'm still
   addicted by the way, and
records too from a local music shop, which are important to
   have—no man
needs to live by his own law in the wilderness after all, but even
   if he is going
to try it is best not to let the old world slip too casually. Rather
   it should come about
naturally, without too much fuss or horn tooting. And then, by
   and by, if he sees
he likes it, why then there is always time to make such decisions
   later on as regards
one's insurance, and such, and peter out from there—trickle
   accurately
into the sand so that each drop is utilized to the max, and then
   we'll see
how the desert is improving—only "improve" is a word I don't
   want to use too much
either. For after all everything is good of its kind to start with.
   It's all a
question only of finding out what the kind is and letting the
   thing ferment
in its own bile for a few decades. By then
it should become apparent to whoever has been watching how
   much the land owes us,
and how we re-distribute it wisely, if only we ever stop to think
   about it. Don't

you agree? I mean, don't you see the silhouetted foothills too?
    How bland and discordant,
yet after all how deeply satisfying in one's rage—and then too
    the pods fall off
all at once eventually, and must rot
if the seeds are to get into the ground, providing they are still
    alive and haven't rotted too.
So in all ways I think it's a question of a man coming—he had
a chicken or something on his arm. And when he arrived, the
    expected salutation
rang out like a shot; people took cover. I don't mean
I did, though. I stood up to him, just like a man, the man I
    was, or is, and he, he just
looked back at me, kind of funny and defiant-like, but he wuz
    saying nothing.
Too smart for that.

Since the last heist I sense a quintessential weariness; I can
neither lay my barrel down nor look directly into it; I think I'll
    have a go at the food—
h'mm, squirrel ragout again. No, I'll opt, I'll ope my eyelids for
    this next one
coming, without food. It was the cutest darn haunted house
    you ever saw. It had blue
shutters with squirrel cutouts in them. Inside everything was
    clean and neat.
But haunted houses are like whores—there's no such thing as a
    nice one, no matter
how prim they act, or how the spotted sun greets them as the
    warm morning is painted.
And then such a one, some other one, would want to know
    why in the name of thunder
these repairs were necessary. After all, the place looked all right.
    Even the bailiff
who lived next door said so. In the event of a storm or flood,
    the door
could be shut, and there was an end to it. But it never occurs
    to anyone that when the
light of the sun does reach the deep pools which are almost always
    bathed in shadow,

why then a short plop is heard and two people are unable to
    occupy the same space.
It sounds simple enough in my book. Someone on lead feet
    looked out
the upstairs window, astonished at the loud knocking below,
    and then withdrew.
Whether or not this person was actually coming downstairs to
    answer the door was unclear,
at least at first, as minutes and then hours seemed literally to go
    by. At
midnight the door slowly opened a crack: "Who's there?" Who
    wants to know?
It would be better if you returned to whatever kingdom you
    came from. But if you sincerely
want to know, bring me boiling water in a paper hat at three
    minutes before two, and that
without spilling a drop. Then I may let you in on my age-old
    secret, which, of course,
isn't mine. I'm only one of a group of seven or eight people who
    are in on it,
until then.
                I could hear the hissing of soda water in the seltzer
    bottle and the roar
of the wind in the trees, the cat scratching at the back door, the
    mice rotating
in place like dust mice, the jangle
of keys the size of fenceposts and the thunk of cylinders as the
    lock—what was
all the fuss about?—goes through the motions and the
    clipclopping door falls silent
again. Inside the place reeked of mildew and decay though it
    looked pretty tidy
considering no one had set foot there for twenty years. A
    newspaper, still dangling
precariously from the rim of the mail slot, hadn't aged. There
    was a coffeepot, still warm,
on the stove.
            Presently they began the rudimentary preparations
    for the raindance
everyone knew was to follow in order for the séance to take place. I'll

double you. That's what you think. You can have the two-spot, but please,
leave me the domino with my head scratched into it. Thus the bidding opened,
and it was to be years before it died down again, years that were not unpleasant
on the whole, as many owls stared in amazement at what was happening underneath.
What kind of place is this, anyway, to let such things occur in silence?
Surely there must come a time toward the end when an old man gets up
and says what needs to be said? But a rose, or, more precisely, a cactus, could do that
just as well and still leave time for whatever else wanted to get recognized.

There is no truth, saith the judge, and one is obliged to concur,
if by truth one means that an occasion has been fitted to an event, and it all came
about just so. If, however, one accepts a broader definition along the lines of
something being more or less appropriate to its time and place, then, by gosh, one is
pretty darn sure of having to own up to the fact that, yes, it does exist
here and there, if only in the gaudy hues of the diaphanous wings
of some passing insect. That is enough, however, to send the scribes back to their tablets.
I don't know where this one came in—but wait,
it is of myself I speak, and I do know! But the looks I got convinced me I was someone
else as I walked in, not at all sure of myself or (rightly, as it turned out) of
the reception I would be getting. There were framed silhouettes hanging on the walls
of the hall, depicting different forms of mild corporal punishment. A large vase
of pussy willows dominated the sitting room—it was here that the occupants

came to cry, out of vexation or frustration, and whence, having
    experienced some relief,
they departed to seek out others and compare notes
on the battle of time being waged in spiral notebooks and the
    dour feeling of
banging them shut. There was never any apparent politeness,
but the children sometimes talked with each other for a long
    time, and, though
conclusions were not ordinarily reached, it shook down some
    of the stuffing in the mattress
of each one's ego, for a time at least. A kettle boiled happily
on the hob. But it was too dark and, above all, too damp to
    read by. Tall
figures like the shadows of men had been blended into the
    viscosity of the plastered
walls; in short it was a jungle in there, and though for some
    reason one sometimes felt
tempted to stay, it was obvious that no discussion of the
    circumstances would ever
be possible. That's when I happened in, wearing a hat, with
    some sweet breath
of the streets perhaps still clinging to me, and had my say,
    without being too brusque
about it either, and afterward was shown the tremendous
    walk-in closets
they build in those climates, those conditions, conditions
which, I want you to understand, aren't all that real. But what's
    a poor penguin to do?
Meanwhile, fate was simmering down below in its cauldron like
    some delicious stew
that would never be ready in time; signs of haste in the form of
    bitten fingernails
and scribbled messages were everywhere apparent, and I have
    this thing
I must do without knowing what it is or whether anyone
will be helped or offended by it. Should I do it? And there, it
    was gone.
It will never be printed on a banner in a political demonstration
or fed to rabbits first to see whether they die, and as I live in a
    house,

am so bound to its principles, in the corners, that coming and
    going
are very much the same thing to me, in which I no doubt
    resemble the baby-boomers
who have not let me in peace a single moment since I was
    thirty years old. Oh,
the good old days! If only we could have received permission
    to stay a little longer!
But it wasn't to be. So, sadly, I changed into my plain woollen suit
and moved off toward the crest, attitude upgraded. It was a
    kind of lumber
room, full of boxes filled with papers ("John's report cards")
    and branches
of artificial holly from Christmases past. It seemed the ghosts
had taken a particular dislike to this room; it felt colder than
    the others,
though the cold was the result of natural causes. Sunlight,
    however, warmed the sill.
And I thought of all my lost days and how much more I could
    have done with them,
if I had known what I was doing. But does one ever? Perhaps
    it's best
this way, and a riper, more rounded you could only be the
    product
of so much inefficiency, hence these pear-shaped tones;
    conversely,
too much planning could have produced a meticulous but dry
    outline
of what my speech sketches in the rooms, ghost-like, like
    clouds of steam
on a day of bitter cold, and the minimal progress beyond life's
    friendly mess
would have meant a severe reckoning and probably an audit
later when it doesn't matter, when only sleep seems of any
    importance.
At least, that's my reading of it. But what if there were other,
adjacent worlds, at one's very elbow, and one had had the sense
    to ignore one's
simulacrum and actually wade into the enveloping mirror, the
    shroud

of a caress, and so end up imbued with common sense but on a
 slightly higher level,
one step above this one, and then everything you were going
 to say and
everything they were going to say to you in reply would erupt
in lightning, a steely glitter chasing shadows like a pack
of hounds, once they tasted the flavor of blood, and then this
 light would gradually
form prickly engraved letters on a page—*but who would read
 that!*
Who, indeed, would want to know what could have been if
 one had made the slightest
exertion in another direction? So it is always a relief to come
 back
to the beloved home with its misted windows, its teakettle, its
 worn places on the ceiling,
for better or worse, to the end where battle will be joined
cum frumentum, and heaven commingle in the wide smile of
 its disheveled
tolerance, and the inspectors, at last, be called in,
though the point was to be done with it without diluting it.
 How far does that take you? For the whole
is so pasted over with rags of old posters that only a Bedouin
 could intuit any rationale,
if then, in its insalubrious confusion. Yet, viewed on another
 day, there does seem to
be the beginning of a point in how it's boxed in, the hidden
 partitions commenting help-
lessly on what game of linings and the scarcely appreciable
 removes that make them the undersides
this was starting to become. Just as one longs for a solitary
 hole to call one's own,
so one is horrified at the prospect of being immured in it: that,
 at any rate,
was my take on the setup this winter. Once past March, the
 addition
seems not to be complete, to be rambling on to the horizon.
 So one can lose a good idea
by not writing it down, yet by losing it one can have it: it
 nourishes other asides

it knows nothing of, would not recognize itself in, yet when
   the negotiations
are terminated, speaks in the acts of that progenitor, and does
recognize itself, is grateful for not having done so earlier.
When all is
demented, no one individual stands out as enormously
   opinionated. So it goes, and my
goodness, I don't see how we are expected to live with it, but
   the fact of the matter
is we do and might even consider ourselves improved in respect
   to the way we were
quite recently, if only we could remember how we looked even
   this morning, forget
last year or even two or more years ago, so quickly do they pass
   even in the formal
chronologies and chronicles, I'm
not even talking about the sloppy kind of record-keeping that
   goes on all the time
without anyone there to be aware of or compliment it.

So seven years passed in whose hollows small, twinkling lights
   could sometimes be perceived
on dark and stormy nights, and the farther one proceeded from
   one's destination
the closer it seemed and in fact was, though most people took
   no notice of it
and read newspapers and glanced at swallows exactly as if in
   Sezession Vienna and there
was nothing to think about except one's bowels and the
   miserable climate.
Breakfasts were consumed; houses were put up for sale; and the
   whole sad, bad shimmer of it
charmed viewers the way a cobra is mesmerized and waves
   deliciously to and fro
in the temperate breeze, the while sinkholes open up, and
   K Marts fall into them,
as icebergs are delivered up to the whims of oceans. It wasn't
   bad while one stood,
but as soon as you sat down you appeared vulnerable; issues
   were raised; and from feeling

it all a mild annoyance but a mere formality, as when a stranger
   stops you to ask directions
and begins asking pointed questions about your religion, it
   quickly escalated
into a nightmare that waking would not heal. Retreat, retreat!
   was all they ever
said, and seemed sometimes not to know what they meant.
   Thus night
appears to have existed always, and to one's surprise one finds
   oneself
adapting to it as though one had never known anything else,
   and growing fangs and howling
at the moon and avoiding questions from loved ones and
   overreacting.
Now it was time to be tall too, a further complication. But we
   were taught that everything
is unexpected. Yes, but this is not the moment for recollecting
   that and even less
to be pondering the reasons for it. Besides we are merely in the
   middle of it
and can turn our heads to left and right like weathercocks, in
   deaf amazement
at all that anyone was ever going to do for us and then stopped
   mentioning.
The orchard that was right for you has stiffened, another
   autumn is coming
to place its hand across the sun; geese ruffle their feathers and
   there are whitecaps on the pond
and daybreak still eludes us. What could be the point of
   counting, or counting on anything?
The rich *facture* of the trusses and supports is admirable, of course,
knew what it was doing, and burgeoned suddenly, before one
   had any inkling of it,
drawing alarmed gasps of admiration from the besotted
   throng. Anyway, it was life,
one had to agree, but all the same could have been better
   written, with more attention
to niceties of style and fewer obscure references, though the
   concept,
always, was beyond reproach.

Wrapped in shawls, was it? And beyond the wharf where
    sometimes a rope of water
twisted though not for long, the password leading into danger
was "crotchet"—none of us was too sure of what it meant. We
    knew the reception
we'd get with it, though—a pattern of smiles opening down
    along the body,
gentle acquiescence to our most childish demands. We came
    there to be pampered
once in a while, and weren't disappointed. But the lips of the
    fish, speaking
out of fog, told us another story, which we were bound to
    recall afterwards
when fires blazed and groups, both sitting and standing,
    collected around them.
There was this well you looked down into and saw shadows
of bodies caught in trees or washed up on the beach, but the
    townspeople
never acknowledged anything was amiss: they'd look fixedly at
    you
if you hinted otherwise, and walk swiftly away muttering
    something about pearls
or children down there, and how long it takes to really mature
    anyhow
and who is to be the judge of that? Years later you'd run into
    one of them at a party,
recall what it was, and there'd be only that odd, dank furor of
    attention,
a glimmer, and then the time frame would change.

In some way the woman knew she was the pivot here, yet it
    was enough just
being adorable in the sun. A memory of a wish would pass
    over, but it was a bird-shadow,
giving way to frank sunlight the next moment, wholesome in
    its steady decline
as all things that seek a way out must be—fresh as radishes or
    Lucerne.
It is time I explained certain tenets of the land

to you, but you see we can never revel in passing back and
    forth across it:
the understanding has got to be dumb so that others
will think there is a settlement here, and condone development
    and repairs,
until one day it will be just another paved-over place without
    sensors:
there is no cause for alarm in this, nor for complacency either,
    yet it must give way.
Negatively, the posthorn striates the morning gloom since all
    things have a beginning
in something, and it falls back on itself, to material shores,
    clusters
of formal and market gardens, and there there ought to be an
    end to it
while the firm old peasant stands, head bowed, cap in hand,
    but the shrill voices
of children run past him into the near wilderness, and all is
    scattered again.
My fear is like a small house: you can come visit me
but it will not go away, or will itself into an education; the
    bonds are loosed,
the pattern lost, and who is to say if I made it up
or someone who was here before and departed, leaving no
    trace
of his passing, no flicker of ashes in the grate? Or by that time
the note has changed; hereditary enemies greet each other
like long-lost friends; snows melt; the incomprehensible
    messages
of tree-frogs explicate each other; perspectives, by shifting,
    have subtly changed
the profiles that stand inside them, and we may not be put to
    the test
until further legal angles have been explored and resolved, a
    long way
from here, at some distant point in eternity. Then it will be time
to live off one's resources, but for now one must do battle
with the elements, and stereotypes, and not expect to be called
    on the carpet

of others' anxious dreams of what is best for us. Go back
    inside;
it's still chilly out here; the fruit is unripe, and no one knows
    what time it is.
Pity the seer who gets it right, for he only abideth long,
but at the end is shut out or becomes the toy of others of like
    condition,
persistent animator. Do, and as I say, so shall the city even
take up the cry and track that one to his lair which is nowhere,
not even eight miles away. The drive, the lunch,
cost more than we knew then, bleary mountain ranges
    mobilized
against the flight of capital, yet it was hard to see how they
    could cost more even at home
and remain the same, nurse of the arcades to warn the soldiers
    of potential defeat,
for they came on, blinded by water. The day arrives for him to
    begin
to grow, but others
in the habitat are puzzled. Wasn't it just such a gentleman,
    once,
who made the transition from scarecrow to sergeant at arms
    without anyone's
being the wiser? Has he returned now to sup, yes you too get
    on with it as you must;
a place is made for him at the table, ere conversation is stilled
    and a heavy black hand
float above on the wall—no! for if it was my error it was a
    smallish one, he too then beside
us at the deck water pours into. For the one and only is a flower
of the mountaintop and cannot imagine the wrong we have
    done. They handed us over to it
and we were alone.

Soon all the animals acclaimed the victor, still in bed with
    pilgrims, drunk
with the wine of defeat, and easygoing, like the hero he never
    had the wisdom
to set out to be. And the line of supplicants led down to some
    graceless bushes

on fire, for virtue wears many masks. And when it came time to ask him
for the antidote, the dolmens appeared robed in white, and backlit,
and they thought it was an optical illusion. But it was a joke as old as the centipede
at the base of the morass. And seven questioners came, but they too fell to gazing
at the hearty snack he had left untouched, and were troubled. Then before you knew it
urchins ran screaming away, it had all been a prank! But some, I believe, were convinced,
and to this day swear that a beast had come out of that lair and looked around
and wandered apathetically away, seeing no reason to stay
on and become a weightlifter or *ouvreuse*, but the rest saw it for what it
was, a charade in which they had no part, and began backtracking. And great viaducts crashed
of their own accord; supertankers were upended; the cotillion was cancelled
in favor of life-saving exercises, but nobody knew how many, or where the implicit tone
or structure was leading. And they turned away stiff-necked. So we were able
to buy a few provisions from the locals, and that is how we got here, and why
we can't stay but a minute, but will see you
on the other side, after the rain, God willing.
And so revived, forgotten, into the long day
angling its shadows at a wider denouement
each time. What would it think of us, if it could think:
mere signers of petitions, names in a long list? Are we tractable
or blotted into the day's fabric like new boys' shouts, the careless exhaust?
Will our pain matter too, and if so, when?

For one pesky minute the wilderness stuck out its tongue
and that was all. Too schooled in its ways to feel adrift for long,
    I sat

naked and disconsolate at a corner of a crevice, hat in hand,
    fishing,
for who can tell what God intends for us next? And if a little
    girl can call
and run, her dog twirl, why not be able to slide a leg over the
    board
barrier that disconnects us from all that is really happening,
    that hive
of activity as you think of it? From funky, overexposed
    moments to plain truths, it is
all there, actually, which isn't to say you desire it yet.
Once the teeth have smiled and the lights been doused yet
    again, though, it's like
stones caring, and you think, what if that big one up there fell
    on my head?
Life, read my life, would be over, the jig up, so what's the point
even of moving off somewhere else? Something else could
    always trigger it.
But I don't want to back off, partly because it isn't
my nature. I think I'll wait behind this old counter, maybe a
    noise
will remind me a thing isn't right and I'll get
in the groove again. Besides, the wind is a punisher. Tonight
all the old ghosts are back on the radio. How sad that some
    people have to be unhappy
to keep the rest of us barely alive, breathing, I think. I was
in my dressing room and didn't hear it. It must have gone
    through the house like a bird's swoop
yet I am innocent, my clothes, the ones I've hardly worn,
    barely on.
Now the official announcement, probably. These dustcatchers
    . . . Look, if you're going to swear
you may as well leave, you can come with me, I'm leaving this
    place.
I've had it. Twenty centuries is too much. Just drifting, like a
    leaf, is more
than I bargained for, at the beginning when the tin was new,
    the smoke clean, and
a bramble's red could scorch your heart, leaving you alone, and
    now it's too late

for pie and others. All's stranded. The pergola in the plaza beckons still but it's the smile
of a latecomer, all candy and cigarettes, no more insulation for the cheers and puffery
we assumed would be forthcoming until he sets down his tray and it was empty
except for a dirty napkin and an orange stick; whose business are you playing
with now, in front of the old microphone? Painted
a bit more lugubriously now, true, but the busboys, the brunch crowd want danger; zero in
on sloth; what's a poor old fright to do? Suicide? No, I don't think you . . .

It was then I discovered the pavements were made of the same flagstones found underseas
except there they were arranged more brightly in schools; here, clusters
are the thing. School is for kids. I think I'll go, Miss MacGregor, honest
I will, this time or bust? You have cleared out my lounge . . .
There is no place to talk, no amphitheater
under which we can put our heads, deducing all-too-violent theorems, yet
I quite like it, one is active. Besides, didn't I hear you say our daddy was once picked up
here by the secret police, and shaved heads are no longer the thing inside the gates,
and the stand of birch is there, but it is all, there is nothing left over
to eat a sandwich next to? If he had tried too soon, if the sun
 . . . But plus or minus
is unimportant; beware of negative thoughts. The ewe and the prunes are mine
anyway; insistence on finer points is the stuff highwaymen's dreams are made on, until
the lost chord; it sounded so brittle back there. Come to my desk, we'll talk it out
and by George the next time it will come round, in a dress, and we'll all thank our

premonitions and the power of staying up alone
in a rain-lashed stadium with the TV on. So much power, at
    such a distance. But it glows.

All along I had known what buttons to press, but don't
you see, I had to experiment, not that my life depended on it,
but as a corrective to taking the train to find out where it
    wanted to go.
Then when I did that anyway, I was not so much charmed as
    horrified
by the construction put upon it by even some quite close
    friends,
some of whom accused me of being the "leopard man" who
    had been terrorizing
the community by making howl-like sounds at night, out of
    earshot
of the dance floor. Others, recognizing my disinterest,
    nonetheless accused
me of playing mind-games that only the skilled
should ever attempt. My reply, then as always, was that
    ignorance
of the law, far from being no excuse, is the law, and we'll see
    who rakes in
the chips come Judgment Day. I can see why someone who
    didn't know me
might be kind of appalled at this flip attitude, but was
    unprepared for the chorus
of condemnatory shrieks from the entourage, as though *they*
    hadn't been through
much of it themselves, and could cast the first stone. Once
    upon a time,
however, I was new to it and felt the land catching up to me
as on the outskirts of a town where one is seeking a night's
    lodging
unprepared for whatever consequences may befall. I spent a
    week once
in someone's house in a small town in Pennsylvania, without ever
learning whose it was, or addressing anyone by name. Another
    time, in Maine,
I found myself face to face with a wolf at sunset. So you see, my

rationale is that I've taken my lumps as well as enjoyed the
    good times
now and then, and don't see what difference it makes to old
    soldiers,
of which I'm proud to count myself one. On at least one
    occasion
when I felt I hadn't slaked the lime sufficiently, so to speak, it
    all seemed
to be going from bad to worse. I had my companions, and my
    kit,
and was ready to pack it in as soon as morning arrived, glad
to escape with my skin intact. But then a curious thing
    happens:
an old guy comes up to you and tells you, reading your mind,
    what a magnificent
job you've done, chipping away at the noble experiment, and
    then, abruptly,
you change your plans, backtrack, cancel the rest of the trip
that was going to promise so much good health and diversion
    for you; you suddenly
see yourself as others see you, and it's not such a pretty sight
    either, but at
least you know now, and can do something to repair the
    damage, perhaps by
looking deeper into the mirror, more thoroughly
to evaluate the pros and cons of your success and smilingly
    refuse all
offers of assistance, which would be the wrong kind anyway, no
    doubt, and set out
on your own at the eleventh hour, into the vast yawn or cusp
    that sits
always next door. And when we have succeeded, not know
    what to do with it
except break it into shards that get more ravishing as you keep
    pounding them. See,
I am now responsible though I didn't make it. And you
can come back, I'm harmless now. Anyway, that's how it
    pleases me to
detect myself. When the blossoms reappear, as they can, and
    the consumers,

someone must pay to keep it poignant. Otherwise one of you
    will remain an outrider.
Go finance the rigged deal then, and it can't hurt.

It worked. Now both of us were attracted.

Let me by way of introduction hopefully
try to extricate myself from this peculiar bunch of
    circumstances,
the slough. Incidentally I am a gentleman
for some of my dealings. Nor do I believe in one set of laws for
    the rich,
another for the poor, nor in one thing over another, one
    mother-in-law,
one pasture for ducks, another for swans. Permit me to posit,
though, another way of looking at the situation, awful now,
as it has been in the past when they had less hygiene but more
    spirit of things
than is alas now the case. What if you let everything bounce off
    you except those
things whose nature it is to imbed themselves in you? Like a
    sharpened pencil forever
flailing the dark with one's own tangles, one nears an edge.
    There are two possibilities:
ignore it or cross it anyway. In either case we'll be
rid of our relatives' nosiness and can get down to business
    quite quickly. I say "I"
because I'm the experimental model of which mankind is still
    dreaming, though to myself
I'm full of unworked-out bugs and stagefright, yet manfully I
    put aside those twenty years
to imagine some croft or bourne in which a few of us can
    weep, as flute-notes play,
and others can come round nodding approval and must then
    be on their way.
But—by heaven!—I think we almost knew just then what it
    meant to be together
without too many people around, how it could challenge the
    universe's bluster,
the hee-hawing ages in the time it takes to put an idea together

from its unlikely components, package it, and go on being the
   genius one was anyway
but not for too long, or without general consent. It's enough
   if—
my friend's mother is the one who believes in me and
   understands me better
than anybody, but I'm not going to let it delude me. There's a
   world out there.
So, drunk, we come back to the dollhouse open to the
   elements,
its scuffed paper furniture, to try to feed on newsprint once
   more,
unsuccessfully. But the old lady wants to explain what
   happened, indeed
there's no way to ignore her account of what happened, so let's
   just
sit still and listen. This, according to her, is what did:

slippery harmonies abound. In fact, I can't be sure I'm not
   addressing myself
to one or within one right now, but that's no matter. I've got
   to tell this
in whatever time remains to me. You and I were young, at
   lunch, we jumped up
in that mad way one has of wanting to see how things will
   react, wanting to see them
turn out, as it were—an ancient, though harmless, temptation.
   Wait, there was more:
after the gentleman had gone, leaving me his card, I stood in
   the hall
for a long time, unable to go back to the kitchen or up the
   stairs
I knew so well. I reflected on all the ways we have of quietly
getting each other's goat, of stewing over inconsequential
   things. The morning
had passed without event, and now, on the threshold of
   afternoon, I could lean out
into the bowl of eternity, like a poster
plastered to the wall of a house, advertising a brand of cigars,
   as the future

came dripping back with intent, impregnating me like a wick
    with its contradictory
or spurious commands, futile innuendo, explosions of choices
    before one is ready
to choose, like team-colors. And as I stood, contemplating the
    card, sinking
into the primness of outline for which I seemed to have turned
    into a walking or
at any rate standing testimonial, and the years mounted the
    wick, I see I am as ever
a terminus of sorts, that is, lots of people arrive in me and
    switch directions but no one
moves on any farther; this being, in effect, the end of the line, a
    branch-line
at that, and no one is interested in guessing, in passing through
    you
or fancying they spy more copious rewards you are presumably
    keeping them from accepting,
once they have come of age. True, a few dawdlers will move on
    briskly, then turn
back officiously to salute you, as though polite gestures could
    dilute the heavy
water of eternity, or what's left of it, which, it is naturally
    assumed, is inferior
to what has gone before—and then manage to insult your
    prudence by ignoring it
on this windblown platform you share with pigeons, not even
another bona fide passenger. And one's dream of escaping
    weighs on your
shoulders, like a yoke of steel. Could one even contemplate it
now? Now that so many other things and soldiers are coming
    to be
what must be, and in fact has always been? A towering tree?
    But, speechless,
we make it over into miniatures of itself, like miniature
    automobiles. Then
a perfectly sweet, sickly stench bears this notion over to the
    main table,
numbers it, sets it down with the others, while the concept of
    an alphabet can

still be sustained (but the curtain is falling on that particular
    misunderstanding, and on
much else as well, including some factors I would like to
    conserve in the new,
stripped-down, presumably more functional civilization the
    alphabet-wand
seemed to want to announce), walks hurriedly out of the great
    gare, without
so much as a backward glance, into a post-Wagnerian,
    impressionist world of rivers
and dreaming washerwomen, and stones at the edge. Well,
    whose maelstrom
was it, and what are you talking about? I think to see a bulb
    blooming; a little mote
in the sunlight, if that's it, would be fine for this morning. (Oh,
    you do,
do you?) And afterwards shut up about it. It's in the mail
    anyway.
A fine thing that nobody talks to me or his parents. How am I
    supposed to know which
ticket goes with which entrance portal? *And the woman with
    orange-pink hair stood silently by.*
And, not knowing, to whose parents am I to address the
    grievance form?
Believe that a change infuses the young, though they aren't
    enthusiastic.
For it is not a shifting of gears nor a vrooming of motors that
    is the note
one hungers after, but just as the distracted dripping of a
    stalactite produces,
in the fullness of time, a perfectly viable stalagmite, so one's
    fretting and anxious
reverberations are but the negative space that gives birth to this
    invisible but densely
compacted mass of fibers that filter truth: the Last Judgment
    (text enclosed).
Paganini on his cloud fiddles; lambs gambol; appealing
    nonsense would seem to have
had the last word again. Yet when you see from a great distance
    how it forms a

pattern, then other conditions have to be taken into account,
   their probability admitted
into the record, a court order produced putting it all on hold
   and speedily overruled as the
dynamics gets into your blood and you find you can live
   without it. Yes, but
meaningfully? No, the hold order is still in effect, though it was
   supposed
to have been lifted; the tape is blank. But I thought those were
unimportant details somebody else was supposed to see about?
   Sure they were
but time is up now, and the pugilists have returned to their
   corners. Write about it,
if you were going to be interested in it, right now, if not
otherwise involved with its destiny. It's the old "elaborate
   charade" accusation
again, and I'm not going to have any truck with it, or with you
   either. I don't
know how many times I've spelled the B-word accurately
   without being credited,
so in the time of doppelgangers I be a lost bairn—without
   spelling, I mean,
though I used to do well in the spelling bees.
                                        Which reminds
      me,
how are Alf and Al? Did I leave anything out? Does the lagoon
still stink? Or did somebody drain it after all those years of
   miasma
and not-too-amusing going about one's business, sometimes
with a handshake or a smile?

But if one's destiny is enclosed in one's brain, or brain pan,
   how about free will
and predestination, to say nothing of self-determination? Just
   how do they
fit together? I know I explained this once but
that was a cold while ago and now this upstart rephrasing of it
   seems to be
causing a lot of attention, I don't know why. It's only a
   re-working, a scissors-and-paste

job; the wording is almost identical, and still there are some
   benighted souls
who follow it, day by day in its lumbering, tumbrel-like
   progress across edifices,
burial sites, unnamed and unnamable sumps, for all the world
to see in its glory, for all the world as though something were
   emerging
and they were going to a circus or a party. Too bad the old
   people couldn't have
known about it before it was actually announced. Some of the
   young too were
tempted to skip until I stepped down from my soap-box to
   have a go at lecturing them
in real earnest, though with a joke or two added as leavening,
   or gilding the
pill as you might say. For if they had known first
they wouldn't have minded not knowing after it had all
   happened, in vain,
one supposes, again. It's too bad there aren't more students
or even a few customers. The weather and the rushes scare
   tourists away
and waste sets in. The season is spectacular. Here, take my viola
da gamba, that dump again, it had a . . . Sipping ouzo is
   something.
But in all the thirty-nine territorial states drains are backing up;
for the first time something like resentment is making itself felt
in the trees, on the lawns. It's still possible to chat with one's
   neighbor over
the back fence, but the quality of life has been imperceptibly
   diminished
by too much arguing over the status of life today—that is, how
   is it felt subtly
in one's veins, how does it differ from before, how is it that one
   day we think we see it
and the next day it seems gone, gone forever? Yet we do go on
   living—how does
that work? In the next field, a farmer is driving a rig of some
   kind—who is
expected to pay for the difference between what he sees up
   close and what is in the skies

now, with better labeling? More importantly, are they gone,
   the old familiar faces?
In time living on into a new share of English promise, some of
the junior ones went over the wall, and that was the last we saw
of *them*.

Still, it's a chance. One can easily side with some who offer no
moral incentive to cling together, who are, in their own words,
   "racked up,"
meaning blighted, for as long as cosmopolitan history chooses
   to entertain them, and no
offense either. That is, some are neanderthal diehards, you
   always get a few, but in
a notable number of instances there is no or not much
   prejudice; the eyes, wiped clean,
are ready for the prepared statement as it sings in the street like
   a serpent.
There isn't much you can do, and it's
a little darker. Tell it the time. And on no account lose your
   bearings
unless you want to wash up like a piece of polyester at the
   gulf's
festering edge. That tanker took on more water. The consensus
   was there *would* be a
symposium, if anyone could be found to host it. Meanwhile
   things are getting a little better
on that front too, which includes romance. It too
is highly nutritious. Homey. Just in time for some fun, pranks,
   feelings; it may
be time to get off now, to swap it for a bigger parcel, trade up
to new ruthless schoolroom dreams while keeping the coded
   receipt just in case
we may make another big slip and water cannot satisfy
   competing demands.
We'll still have an area with water, but like I say, juvenile
   bombast and highjinks bid fair
to drown out the other uproar, domesticate it and pass it on to
   their offspring
in Rome, where the dahlias blow, and sweet crocuses and cats
   by the score as the spring

billboard begins again. But *durch ein ander*. Smell it yourself
   he said my gosh.

And admit of sexual practices? Proclivities? The right to kill and
   maim? I suppose . . .
Night was floral at that post. It was fashionable to throw out
   last year's buggery
along with the rented skis, and hope no one saw you. Besides,
   what could be said
about those mosaics? That they looked on, wore down, smooth
   as old storks' nests,
witnesses to so much casual butchery, that a stringy music rose
   out of it
to command our measured pace back into history and then see
   it alive, tobacco- and
offal-stained, till we knew not who we were but only what we
   had to do.

The thunder could be heard all over the city.
Sometimes it is taken to extremes; the "extreme mind" thinks it can
understand what it means to it. The peculiar magic
of our idiom so enchanted her, with the vacuum of each
   thought,
that it even seemed permissible to escape around the edges and
   start running away,
though that is another story. What matters to us is that an
   unstable air
of permissiveness was in the streets, close, like a thick mist
or mitt, on the tongue, leading in some instances to crushes.
Little was ever made of the anomaly that we grew up here; indeed
it was never factored into the partial account that we succeeded
   only after
many demands in having read aloud, in a halting tone, next to
   a fountain, so that the tumbling
of pebbles obscured our larger words, in some cases replicating
   them in miniature,
obsequious to a fault. The ham-handed rendition made a botch
   of the layers
of meaning and the layers of bread, satisfying neither reporters
   nor hierophants.

We all returned home anxious
to get the night over with.

And end it did, yet scarcely
in the ways one had imagined, but with a finality as
inexplicable as its itinerant birth some years back down the
    creek. First,
there was a lot of hammering. Then a blonde woman got out
    of the car to take pictures.
H'mm, this must be *the* night, a lot of people mistakenly
    assumed. Then the thunder
again—I can't possibly tell you what was in it for me, so rounded
were its periods, like an architecture erupting from the earth;
like a repertory of trees, from which emerged cries,
or so it seemed. That these were the damned of the earth
in whose look colorful arcs beat the meaning down
to size, proud of being duly noted, was acknowledged by no
    one of rank.
Feathers first, then dust, then flourishes
in a signature, with the bad taste to insist on the letter of
    personality lessons
taken at some charm school in hell, were the note struck, and
    that you
were a few years older than me, and that sufficed to bring the
    argument
to a graceful dead-end near where the coats were. Yet
    sometimes in the quietism
I miss your cracked precision, knowing it could have taken us
    this far
in the storm's well-oiled chariot without making a production
    number
of it and we should have been well equally, only now
what does it matter? I mean, whose shortcomings are we
    talking about,
except it's better to go over at the last
moment and make your peace, whatever that can be.

There was something I liked in the way of beginning
and something also in the way of returning, though it made us
    sad.

Next spree though, try to find us a different decade: this one's
    already full.
The twaddle dispensary's reopened. The French still say
    "hailstones big as pigeon's
eggs," and poets are retreating into—or is it out of?—
    academia, beset by the
usual pit-bulls and well-meaning little old ladies in tennis shoes.
    And discovering
and assimilating new bastions of indifference and
    comprehension. What else?
That was some storm we had last week. The webs intersect at
    certain points where baubles
are glued to them; readers think this is nice. What else? Oh,
    stop badgering—
where were *you* in the fifties?

Indeed. Alvin and the chipmunks made nice ambient music for
    what
I was fussing over, or masticating, and I had to find a way out
    of the woods.
Now, in some cases, this is easy—you just walk straight along a
    road and pretty soon
you're out of the woods and there are suburban backlots. In my case,
though, it wasn't that simple, though it wasn't extraordinarily
    demanding either—I
just lay down in a boat and slept, Lady-of-Shalott style. Soon I
    was gliding among you,
taking notes on your conversations and otherwise making a
    pest of myself.
I pretended to be angry when onlookers jeered and cows
    mooed and even the heralds told me to shut up,
yet at bottom I was indifferent. I knew my oracles
for what they were—right about 50% of the time—and I also
    knew their accuracy wasn't
an issue. It was the repeating of them that interested me.
    Repetition makes reputation.
Besides, it's something you can build with. You need no longer
    inspect the materials
when you buy them in bulk; they are as a territory. What gets
    built happens

to be in that territory, though beside it. Your reputation as a builder
is the one interesting thing.
                            In the sixties new dresses were newer.
The humbler children were clad in dimity, and bird-cheerful.
    Airlines seldom
overbooked. My imagination was trying to get its act together,
    I mean really see
itself. But like the site of Carthage, which was circumscribed by
    strips of some
animal's hide, it could not really accept itself for all it was
    because of the
possibility that a trick was involved. And yet, shaking its hair
and staring at its crystal reflection in some drop of dew, it also
    knew it wasn't
nothing, and something had to account for this. I think the
    constant costume changes
caused it to mistrust itself, yet there was a game to be played,
    and rules to abide by—
so what? It's true in other walks of life . . . But it all led
    rapidly to the crunch
of where the fuck do you think you're going? *This* is the frontier.
Beyond lies civility, a paradise of choices—maybe. But it wasn't
    made to be tested
by such primitive assaying tools as you, and only you, come
    equipped with.

*I saw your face on some bookjacket. It looked beautiful. May I
    write to you?*
*I wouldn't really swallow poison if I was you. Meanwhile I have
    the rain*
*to experience with the others, each of us finding it uncomfortable
    though seldom*
*talking about it, as there are more important subjects. Fishing, for
    example.*
I have to get home before the music disappears. I love you.
I thought I said never to come in this café?

Finally all will survive because of fierce determination. I mean,
they're tough, people are. Hey guys,
what accounts for losses along the way? The house is built,

the beds made, and see how it comes undone, but then an
    enormous ray of sunlight,
like a minor flood, imbues the room, and once again we are
    saved from ourselves
as something rings down the curtain on us gloriously. One
    lived principally by one's wits
and therefore was not surprised by this sudden reversal: it
    always has something
of us in it, so I signed it. It wasn't long in coming, but was just
    my hope,
ironed and carefully hung on a hanger in a closet, and it was
    endearing, but that wasn't
why I loved it. All loves are quite pleasant, and this one, being
    for myself,
was especially so. Now that so much has simply dropped out of
    life, more
than one can take the pulse of, one isn't sure, in this rout, this
    retreat
from a great city, how much of it is left in there. It seems only
    yesterday
that one could find cheap walkup apartments in the East 50s,
    and modest restaurants
such as the Cloisters, with $1.95 complete lunches, or
    luncheons. When was the last
time you had luncheon? The atmosphere was thinner, but
    more abundant, and well worth
the few extra cents. Besides, I had begun working on
    something like
my autobiography, I was going to distill whatever happened to
    me, not taking into account
the terrific things that didn't, which were the vast majority, and
    maybe if I reduced it
all sufficiently, somebody would find it worth his while, i.e.,
    exemplary. And then in the rush
to evacuate I left the precious notebook behind; there simply
    wasn't time to look for it;
but I could have reconstructed it, drop by drop, from what I
    remembered, having
kept close watch over what went in, yet this would in some way
    have falsified

everything, one of the points being that one makes a show of
    what one rejects,
the better to flaunt what one enshrines, but that
can only happen once in the way of things happening. Yet that
    was more than a generation ago,
or more, depending on how you define a generation now.
    What are you saving it for?
And a horn screeched. Particles turn nasty. The other
is there, besides. We cannot move. The fullness in the house at
    night
is only a diagram (but cling to it, anyway) of where things
    were, and though
we can remember what things, they are gone now; only their
    relation
to one another subsists, and I am as a dog. It seems I can't
    think. I remember once under trees
receiving the warm but peculiar and complicated presence, like
    Leda her swan;
I smiled convulsively and in an instant was left
somehow darkened, though the pressure
was relieved and since then has never been a problem. But I, as
    the other (as I now
see myself to have been), was no wiser and certainly no better
for the terrible irruption into my life. It has made everything
    I've said since
sound silly, yet I won't debate the point, which after all is
nothing more than that a light, and some warmth, stood in my
    life for five minutes once
and ever afterward has remained unto me, though I often
    forget it for decades at a time, yet am forgiven
when it turns up again, like a smile. These seem like facts
to me; no politics attaches to it; yet in the stalemate of
    centuries it could
turn once to me and utter my name. That's all I ask. I'd be
    forgiven
then, and focus my energies on something more important like
    rebuilding our wall,
expecting nothing in return but the verdict, and then I'd go down
into the vicarious city expecting nothing but vibrations, the
    verdict: the one

you always said you couldn't stay to see me get, it would be too
    confusing
and painful to our house, too unexpected: inexcusable. (That
    word.)

Last night you weren't so sure. And it goes on:
There was once a shopping mall
at my place. Kids went to it. Mottled houseplants were sold to
    alert
home-makers, in that light. You could buy quantities of them
and leave them in your yard. Or mix them with others; try to
    get the most out of
the variety, as it sifts down to you: the great speckled hen
on the lookout, or the hyena I dreamed of last night, or
    salmon leaping in their beds:
all are abrupt elements in the sum listening leads to, cannot
    renege on
unless *you* backtrack, become the slightly less valuable person
    of a few minutes ago
with the feathered headdress and baubles. That one. But the
    sum will get lost anyway
in the crowd, unless drastic measures are taken. And who is to
    take them?
Because you, walking around comparison-shopping, are its
    infrastructure
and the only one who will bring it to the edge of a cross-
    section of the people's imaginings.
See, there might be already a little canopy over the pier
but more likely not; it's still early in the season; the river's rank
    winter smell
still pierces the air's musky crevices; the grass isn't right and
there's too much pre-freshness. The real thing won't be around
for days, even weeks. And we're supposed to get on with the
    project, somehow,
settle down in the logic these lines always left space for,
    between them, but which
was rarely visited by any save sandwich men and vagrants,
    more's the pity when you see how
idle folk get well off and we stand hands clasped to breasts still
    worrying about the

back taxes that were never paid one year, because this isn't
    forgotten by anybody
but becomes one of those rust-colored lots thieves and
    innocent children hang out in,
like the one where Mercury slew Argus for vulgar reasons,
reasons of his own imagining. Now that the moon's up
they say there won't be any rutabagas
till next year. But go on, I have to go out and fight
about it with everybody, even my superiors
in my place of employment
which is dry and casually tidy as the next person's. Only I do so
    out of a great fear
the man I entered may not be enough, may thoughtlessly
send me back to the end of the line that meanders
from here to the desolate, reedy horizon. What did I ever do to
    resent you, open your calm
caresses like oysters? And then is it right to save them? Might I be
reading a magazine when it all happens to me, this time, and
    now I stand up
baffled by the sandstorm, because how did I know it was
    zeroing to this
ungainly end, not see any danger signs, not shut off the hose,
    though I am gifted
with a suit of eyes and can foretell the near future and recall the
    recent past? Is it
that I'm a sort of jerk?
                            No, oceans were hiding, waiting
on your bald spot; pencils with chewed points told us all we'd
    need to know
until the twenty-first century, whereupon we'd all come out of
    our lairs, mew
and make up. And now that doesn't seem such a good idea,
    that stronghold
has got to last. Otherwise midnight and the fires
jabbering, like we were taught, will ruin all chances of an
    application
before it's forwarded. And stones come down from trees. No
    kidding it's a splendid
series; no way would you want to miss out on it. I have to
    grow though.

I must go back in time. It's not the way you heard it
in the alley or over the transom. For though hard work is
 indeed
a key ingredient, no one can know the outcome until all are
 banished by ill will
or saved and the mongrel idiot takes the credit for it
and then sleeps, it too, for the path is what you call freckled
 with blemishes.
No ape nor man stands alone who knows it,
who can recite it backwards. In the orchard, and that's the least
of my worries. I have to put you on hold again.

But what do we know? We're not authentic crime-busters,
only pals of the accused from school. When he wrote those
seemingly contradictory rules, he never dreamed we'd end up
following them, and him, into the oblivion he decreed for us.
Now it all seems an antique space in which they talked
much as we do, feared God, forgave
each other the endless trouble someone was always causing—
 not that
it wasn't justified in some instances by the confusion of late
 spring and early summer.
We heard each case. Then, if punishment was in order it was
 meted out
impartially and the whole business quickly forgotten, in the
 interests
of the children. Wait, there were arguments on both sides—
but it seems as though a stormy prelude had gotten out of
 hand; suddenly
everyone was running. But you know what I mean. They were
 like super-gullible
and had to be made to understand, even through tears,
 thrashings, moans.
Then I like the idea of coming out at the top
for a brief time to survey what's happened down below
and retreat, the better to tidy up loose ends, weave reports
around this affair that brought us so much ridicule, so much
 deserved
attention. Besides, the plaster arches had taken on an air of
 permanence

long ago and were in danger of being confused with the real
    thing; one had to
shuffle the cards, put a brave face on it; otherwise we ourselves
    might have ended up
imagining we stood at the apogee of empire and power and
    forgotten to go in at night
or take temporary precautions. Then when the collapse finally
    maneuvered itself
into being we'd have no one to blame but ourselves, and be
    forced back
into a primary mood of spells and rituals. You didn't want that.
    That's how we
ended up winning, which is another story. Had we
however mistaken the early chirpings for pre-emptive strikes
    there's a good chance we
might have ended up contemplating the sky from the other
    side, its stickers and warnings
looking interchangeable thanks to the tame minority decisions
    we'd endorsed,
never having run up against any precedents for dealing with
    superannuated, frayed
systems until they'd been polished to look like the present and
    were therefore
of no use to us or to anyone else either. How far we'd
strayed from the bend in the stream, but the current
seemed to push us forward, whispering words of
    encouragement, and the poplars laughed
and danced and smiled seemingly at us, but that was a pathetic
    fallacy,
of course. They never saw us. Not even once. Not us.

Quick—the medication. But the house had no sense at all, and
    having
become a limited partner in my own disestablishment, I
    watched in terror
as it moved on us, dull plumage of another kind,
condensed around doors and windows, with a sense of
    authority
still, like a wishbone in the throat, the docket
whose very plainness might be

adjudged a virtue. What is this? A frigid sense
of isolation, tarnished beyond knowledge? Yes, and the others tell
it differently, and their version too is the truth, or it is truthful.
And many of these were going up
into the house where he watched the city, and then
these others were below, but they did not matter so much. I
    was basking
on my sunlit shelf, like a tomato plant. *That* mattered. And the
    fact that there were so many
more speaking rationally mattered. And they began to scream,
    shrieking things like
where were you born, who got you started anyway? And in truth
I fumbled the question now, and the answer came from all
    over, randomly inclusive.
A ruthless teen dissolves equations you can't bear to look at
before it's all over but the shouting, and others prod
the old trunk, wanting some credit, like graffiti artists, shouting
    too.
I thought I was immune to it, having been stung once,
but I'm not. And I ask you, in the name of all that's
    reasonable . . .

Others were shot. As I see it the main difficulty is getting used
to the gradual increase in light increments, walking home in
    the early evening
after a day at the office, and being back
in the apartment again, if only for the night.

And the mounting green. Each year, spring is more powerful,
gaps in its front are fewer, sizable runs on the arsenal at the
    observatory more remarked.
And the truth sits rigid. What does it have to contribute after
    all?
No charm, certainly. And precious little of the bread one weeps
    eating
having taken the cross, and all else is "nice" or "interesting" in
    that lurch
before one sees. Truly sees, that is when it is too late
even for memories and rumors, the starched ballgown, the
    paymaster's slips,

and when it's too late, it's too good too. Otherwise they'd
    follow us
into this dawn, ask us misleading questions, like liars. Well,
some of us have to be. We'd see about that. "Anon." I asked
    about the witches' society
but you'll have to grovel, to find out where they put it, where
    they're
off to next, unless a lucky blight disclose as a side-effect the thrust
of its situation we're leading down to. Yes, the harvest home
    had no walls at all.
And I got off at the corner. I hear America snowing. I want it to
confront me, not my fate, with the possibilities of the next
    change, but we pretend there are
reasons not to blur the wall between them and us, not to step
    down,
and become one in a group of opportunists like ourselves, and
    so matter peculiarly
before tomorrow's decision, the battle of compromise. Yes, and
    you took over.

Not that I think for a moment that . . . And grasping that
    quiddity like an ox's neck, without
warning he came at me. Relentlessly the minutes, some of them
    golden, touched.
His task force inserted itself. It was almost lazy how the spars
    of flame floated
down, and continued to burn on the grass, but this was a kind
of joke, a celebration. The hundred-year-old ivy marked the
    ridges on the tegument
where nodules of revolutionary thought were beginning to
    form, and splinter, leaving
the dark, obdurate mass of negative energy, confined in a ball,
    to point to
having its day in the near future—quite soon, mind you—and
    bill collectors
in an outer room. Reading, apparently. Then a wolf-moan, in
    guise of roll-call,
blew up the ammunition dump. There were artificial legs
    everywhere
and kindly geezers standing under umbrellas, softly asking things

like where is the next scrunched-up ball of paper and can my
    daughter-in-law, who lives
alone, touch any benefits from the sick behemoth's collapse,
    who was
never particularly outgoing in his day but now wants to be part
    of the birthday celebration
just as kings and princes do. And with that on my mind, I
    searched the grass
for signs of the coming progress. And they all went back into
    their houses
and that was all for that day.

But I am prepared now for the drone that submerges grace-
    notes in the conviction
of its being. To listen only for a moment is to bathe
in it as in a possibility—the first one—and you can shut your
    ears anyway
from the tirade in its later stages, assuming one wants to
not get off until the sudden unnatural brightness that indicates
    the last stage of the
voyage has been inaugurated, that we're in for some fun and
    enlightenment
now which takes the form of bad dreams—you know that one
    you're terrified of having
again, and it always turns out to be rather nice
at the end? Besides, a delegation of schoolchildren has come to
    thank you for it,
for having it, and thus allowing yet another generation to grow
    up unmenaced
by the plans of bureaucrats for civilization a few years down the
    pike, every year
or so. You see it is part of your plan, gestates with you,
because of you, and in you—never mind that it's too shrill for
    some ears to pick up
on, that's what protects us during the periods of ritual slump
    and restores
some of one's original dignity like a lost lace christening-robe—
    besides,
they weren't very fat in those days, or somebody had to wear
    those things.

There were governesses and servants then, which seems almost
    magical now, almost
beyond belief. Simple lives were also led. In short the world
    was a great
circus ring in which one could witness proud doings and
    glimpse one's fellow
spectators on the opposite side, and everything turned to song
    like fire, hustled
into the furnace of energetic living, and the sad birds
walked away, were seen no more. Thus evening
when it arrived took on an orgiastic purity that was understood
    as of a piece
with the fabric, dim and buried in spray as it might have appeared
sometimes, until the truth will out, and vociferousness have its
    day, as is
only right, and we should think about it, and come back to it
    sometimes, at other times.

I now find it deeper, though quieter, to prepare this
and have come belatedly to realize that sex has very little to do
    with any of it,
that is directly, except insofar as it makes you do something
    you hadn't thought about
because it brought you to a place you hadn't thought of
    visiting,
some quiet corner of a garden, unnoticed before, whose
    perfection of design
no longer now seems a threat, but rather a greeting instead.
I was hurrying on my way as usual, too bored to notice the
    look of calm self-esteem
of those who circulated near me, nor give back what I had
    accepted as readily
as a drop of rain, token of the neutral benevolence that waits
    and pours
at certain corners where the road is taken up again
like a shuttle. There will always be someone to share the
    burden; even
oxen are true, as under burnished leaves they sidle
forth at morning, or return at evening without much
    commotion, without

making too much of it. And our dreams are scanned and
   dissolved in these seemingly
pointless rituals (unless the point is to release us as they smash
   the perfect design,
for mere symmetry is death, and their rounds would be that if
   shattered wreaths
didn't loom in the wake of their indifferent passage). But there
   I go,
attributing impartial goodness to the coils of superstitious
   industriousness that shored
me for a moment and let me down easy: bunches of grapes
the fox didn't even bother to shrug at, passing into the golden
   dust-clouds,
the clank of arms and clumsy restitutions, of that middle
   distance
where old man and girl alike play, and the shadow can never
   creep near enough
to explode the myth of the day we have, the scale to be played.

No matter that it didn't make me look ridiculous—the point is
   I could easily have managed
that without assists from bunnies and wood-sprites if
   something not of my own construing,
something I rejected, hadn't interposed a feline quickness and
   fur just before the fatal
gradient, and I stepped back and stared, and in that moment
   saw myself on a visit to myself,
with quite a few me's on a road receding sharply into a distance
   spiked with blue
fantastic crags that had castles perched on them and were
   honeycombed with grottoes. I could as easily
have missed it and arrived blind at my destination, this room
where I entertain a stranger as dusk deepens and silence settles in,
and never known my own two shoes, what to make of them,
as they scoured hills as well as dales in search of the person they
belonged to instead of staying parked under this plain wooden
   table.
Something else will break fruitfully
the allotted chain of associations, and it will serve as well—only
   don't try to pass it off as

an impulse, sincerity. Too much of the city remains standing
    for that
and the canker must burn in the memory, red as loganberries,
    for the lever
to cancel the fulcrum, for a new age of nothing to come into being,
attracting as little attention as possible,
that all may live
to do justice to the gods that set us in motion! Hesperides!

Any day now you must start to dwell in it,
the poetry, and for this, grave preparations must be made, the
    walks of sand
raked, the rubble wall picked clean of dead vine stems, but what
if poetry were something else entirely, not this purple weather
with the eye of a god attached, that sees
inward and outward? What if it were only a small, other way of
    living,
like being in the wind? or letting the various settling sounds we
    hear now
rest and record the effort any creature has to put forth to
    summon its spirits for a moment and then
fall silent, hoping that enough has happened? Sometimes we
    do perceive it
this way, like animals that will get up and move somewhere and
    then drop down
in place again, we hear it and especially we see it—some
    whitecap curdles
in a leaden expanse of water and we are aware this moment
has done its share, that we shall not be needing this batch of
    insight again.
Yet other times it all comes stampeding into the foreground,
    crushing one's toes, a question
like the question of what to wear, and then we fall back,
    confused, we know we are not
smart enough, that we can never anticipate all the trials that
    will have been administered
just now, forget those to come when we and our kind have
    been forgotten
in some memorial dump of time, with stone lotuses and iron
    epaulets, and they called you

a wheeler and dealer, and yes that is what fate reserves for the
    most capable,
even; they called you a leader and here you are, with us in the
    kingdom of ghosts; only don't
tarry too long with your inaugural address: others are waiting
    to mount the lectern.

Yet there are other times as in a quarry where no breeze stirs;
    nothing
indicates it; poetry scarcely drips from vines, the weather is
    hugely oppressive, yet
you do know something is at work in you, something else: take
    death away and still
a vast alteration remains to be made. We know this decade
    doesn't fit,
that we can do nothing about it except swear, yet it *will* do, it
    will have to. A fly
dies, and then? Who are we to speculate on the delicious
    paradoxes that will outlive us,
embroiled in street things, squeezing a pimple until some richly
    satisfying
pus comes out? Were we needed then?
                                    Almost casually, gigantic
    cardboard cutouts
of mammoths and hydras appear in the wings, and one knows,
    not having done one's homework,
that the spells will materialize as dots joined together, and the
    casual
whirlwind that vaporizes moods and intensity of expression was
    an astrologer's error;
here, it sits on a doorstep, waiting for the "back in five
    minutes" tenant to materialize
with all the lawsuits and indecent percentages in its wake, but
    that's no matter,
it's a river and one must keep up with it.

Another time I was just sitting, on a rung.
Some kids were playing ball. I asked what it meant that we
never did anything, were content to let others do things and play,
as though it were for us. He said, sure thing. I said I'd had a nap,

what I wanted now more than anything was that someone
    would come and play with me;
I'd then decide whether to or not. She said, but this is all some
    kind of love ambush.
The boys don't play with you, they have to play with
    themselves. You're supposed to find some
kind of message in it, when the weather takes you away for a
    day
and delivers you back home, as though from a fishing trip, and
    no one can say
you are any different, or notice a different twinkle in the eye.
    But it is all changed
even though you and they would prefer not to admit it.
You're a grown man now, but must sit in a tub. I agreed that it
    was so,
but said I'd always imagined that this was how things would be
and therefore wasn't it a surprise? Things aren't supposed to
    happen according
to plan and thus when they do it's a small dislocation in the
    universe; clocks
are delayed a millisecond and this causes phenomena to run
    counter to their usual course,
so I should be washed free of all blame. And even if it were
    otherwise,
arriving someplace and forgetting one's speech isn't such a
    grand or unique occasion;
it's like chess. The same things happen over and over again
    under such different guises,
but you think you're keeping up with them. That serves to
    salve
the individual conscience and suppress the crowd's roar as
    effectively
as a bell-jar would. I washed the jug in some water, then
wiped it clean with a cloth. I was thinking again about all the
    suffering and dying
that goes on all around us, in hospitals especially. Somehow the
    face of the mentally
retarded woman came back to haunt me. "Oh, no, not you
    again!" But she was all the time
talking quietly to herself and couldn't have heard me anyway

with that thick partition of glass between us. But even
if she could have it wouldn't have mattered; it'd have sounded
    like consolation
or agreement (so there was no point in attempting these either,
    they'd have
been transformed into static. Best not to hear). But you can
    never ignore
for long the pain that comes over you from such a person, how
    all the wishing
in the world would only make things worse. Yes, and you are a
    voyeur, too,
unfortunately, and the purity of your desire could hardly be
    extricated
from all that. You are a voyeur with a conscience, the last thing
    anyone should be,
I swear. No use trying to cover your tracks using archaic words
    like "leman"; the sense
kills and you have the refrain to remind you. Sure but I was
    just drifting
anyway, faintly out of tune, nothing scared could have
    happened to me.
                        On a treadmill
it would have been different, I'd have had the reward of seeing
    shining eyes,
knowing them directed at me. How I'd have fulfilled my
    promise if I'd been let go
or not, but that's a small cataclysm in a landscape now
that's no matter. I just want to be left at home—maybe
    something perky or melodic
will come along, who knows, and in the meantime I can irritate
    myself without causing
discomfort to others.
                        As on a darkling strand when the weather
    improves a bit,
there was a little more to be seen than was apparent at first.
    The groan of pebbles
lugged back and forth by the undertow, which at first seemed
    temporary and quickly
turned out to be eternal wasn't made to displease me, no more
    than were

the hanks of pubic seaweed deposited at intervals that might
    well have been
predetermined, though of course they were not, no more than
    were the houses
irregularly staggered up the street that led away from all this,
    but not
too far away. I had just been having my first nightmare at the
    age of 59, and awoke refreshed
to the ordinariness of the way things didn't want to shake
    hands with me; it
was pleasant in my sight.
                          "Wait here a moment, I'll be right
    back," she called
over her shoulder. Things had been regularly falling into place
for some time, but this wasn't one of them: "Look how
little shore there's actually left." But it wasn't true, there was a
    broad shelf
spattered with puddles of water extending quite a ways, glittering
in the softly veiled sunlight. Does she think you too
are going to come around to her notion of things, when we
    touch, and glance
at each other? Or will there positively not be any sequel
to it this time? But songs, yes. They cascade
into one another. It's getting dark, I fear. We should go back
though not until you—her—have answered the riddle of the
    miracle, why it crests
just at this point every year, and then ceases to speak, and the
    silence extends it
even as far as the forever with telling tears and twilights. Tell
    me, did
I ever come to you, talking like this, and you received me into
    you, and I dwell
with you? O we were never a couple, but at last
the lantern-light pierces the horn of distress, of mayhem: you
    may want to
rearrange the facts now that they're getting scarce. All this
    points to only one
perpetrator, and that person is—and a shot rang out. The
    intruder sprawled

in his new pants, a helpless look on his visage, as when one
    from outdoors rushes in,
sees the truth, and confesses; but surely more is to come, the
    stain
sang in the wall, and the wall buckled. And it was all up to us
    co-conspirators: more
even an uncle and an aunt couldn't ask. And veiled day paled,
    even
as it drained into the catch basin of our collective unconscious:
    just who were
we to feel this way anyway, and why had anyone asked? A
    mystery. The clerk
sharpened his pen and put it away. But as for coming back
    tomorrow, that was wonderful,
and also in the succeeding days ahead when the losses should
    be more acutely visible
and the burns too. The stone house man had built upon the
    shore, with the station-master
in it.

Speaking of which the weary sap next comes to your door.
What right have you to consider yourself anything but an
    enormously eccentric though
not too egocentric character, whose sins of omission haven't
    omitted much,
whose personal-pronoun lapses may indeed have contributed
    to augmenting the hardship
silently resented among the working classes? If I thought that
    for a minute I'd . . . yet,
remembering how you didn't want to get up today, how warm
    the bed was and cozy, you
couldn't really begin with a proletarian, accustomed as they are
    to backbreaking
toil and so (you'd like to think) don't feel it that much. Besides
    they never read Henry James' novels.
Just for the sake of argument let's say I've never done an
    honest day's work
in my life. It's hardly heartbreaking news, not
a major concern. Calling shots

is something I've done a lot of, and I'm here to tell you as
 referee that too much
isn't enough, and that coldness must get boxed out by
 somebody
or the universe would get derailed. Besides, maybe they do feel
 it less, as infants
and the feeble-minded are said to. My first concern (in any
 case) was to build up
a graduated series of studies, leading to the alchemical
 perfection of one who says,
I can do that. The fabrication of it lasted nearly a lifetime,
leaving me, at the end, unable to perform the most banal act
 such as tying my shoelaces
in a double knot, and vulnerable to the japes of skeptics
who would have preferred to die a thousand deaths rather than
 undertake the course
of study I had so painstakingly elaborated. And as for me, sad
 to say,
I could never bring myself to offer my experiments the gift of
 objective, scientific
evaluation. Anything rather than that! So I feel I have
wandered too long in the halls of the nineteenth century: its
 exhibits,
talismans, prejudices, erroneous procedures and doomed
 expeditions are but too familiar
to me; I must shade my eyes from the light with my hands, the
 light of the explosion
of the upcoming twentieth century. Nobody asked me whether
 I wanted to be born here,
whether I liked it here, but that's hardly an excuse for cobbling
 a palace of mendacious *rêves*
into something like existence. The entry is inconspicuous,
 more like a sentry's box,
but the grand regularity of the insides, spoilt by a profusion of
 ornament, is
(however) my main contribution to the history of sitting and
 licking.
         Over the door
a weathered board scratched with impossible-to-make-out
 letters, and for this

he was a child and we grew up knowing him, at least some did, and he
was fair as any, and stood in open cornfields sometimes
to give the scale
to his dreaming, and the dreams of one vast civilization.
We can see the effects now in devices we use in everyday life without thinking of them,
in traces of the slightly altered climate and the
    disproportionately enormous effect it has had
on geography, roads and productivity. Someone in his class
should have made him a marshal. Still, he never had the
    courage to follow his bent
to the exclusion of petty distractions, nor they to follow him
    when the wind stood
in his sails, and he on the poop deck, calling, *Arise,*
ye unchained millions, and realize your consequences
only before it's too late! I'm afraid it's all busywork
for the historian of manners, now. Trash and understanding.
    When they collected
on the balcony, some curious, it was only to listen to the
    upward whoosh! of air, to learn
how the week of seminars had gotten canceled due to
    circumstances beyond our control,
but out of spite, actually. Whose? His or the provost's? When
    they said, *Does it buzz?*
he replied, yes it does. And there was an end to making
    arrangements. Many had
already mounted the homeward trail, headed for a warm bath
    and a good fuck. Others
noted a change in the atmosphere: surely it was lighter, but
    thinner?
So you tell yourself you're going to show yourself and say no
    to yourself
before witnesses are dragged in to recant. It works so well—
    how *do* you manage it,
dear? Being able to go in and out at any point, I mean. In this
    case
it's back to the hurricane. When we last looked in though
there were party streamers suspended from ceiling fixtures, and
    everything

seemed to be in full swing. Now, Marsha's baby occupies center
   stage.
Whodunit? Dunno. But let's listen in: "For the fourth time I
   want you
to go over there where the washing is and stand the nasty
   question on its head.
I mean, what are mussels?" And so it goes, down to the
   loading and unloading,
the pretty bleak exteriors. For some, it causes eye cramps. But
   the boldest line
on today is Cedric's "Hey how'd we get this way, eyeful? And
   the fault of whose buns
ran it aground in Norwalk, if only you'd had an antenna out
   for the main, the central
occasion and dash after it like a slaphappy Weimaraner and
   diddle it, 'cos
it's ours, dig? Of course, after I was 'slimed' for the first time,
   and by
you, no less, I became increasingly withdrawn for years and the
   case dragged
through the courts before finally being settled. And by what right
do I imagine you this spring day?"
                                         Mostly the others are more
   secretive, or were,
until this new bombshell hit the stands. Now, full of remorse,
   we ask ourselves
what we could have done to prevent the calamity. But there
   was nothing,
of course, beyond waiting it out, under a dripping awning, on
   the beach.
The "elegancy" which Malone imposed upon it was in the
   direction of that generalization
dear to the eighteenth-century heart, which the modern
   temperament finds
so uncongenial. Clearly we were to blame in some way we
   cannot know
other than by divination or recourse to charlatans, which, I'd
   better say
right off, is totally out of the question. But when fear pelts down
one forgets such resolves. I was ever

determined not to reveal myself a stoolie. I had sat in a metal
    chair before,
yet had always assumed that with age a mingled straggling
    peace and dignity
came along. Even in my late forties I patiently awaited
this. After dinner she played Kjerulf. We sipped tea, looking at
    each other.
I find appealing the quality of danger
inherent in thunder, though of course it's actually in the
    lightning,
which I don't much like at all. I'll take my jacket off now, and
    be off.
Another day we read the thunder its own prepared statement.
The effect was stupefying. I always do get that feeling
of being prepared for anything but this, usually followed by a
    postscript
about deciding to mend my ways, abjure evil delight, from this
    day forward.
This, however, was something else. I may never speak the truth
    again,
knowing it to be compounded of false mottoes and *aperçus*,
    and that trying
should be good enough. You get A for effort, but the road to
    hell is paved
with good intentions. But I'll take the blight,
thanks. I'm good at working under pressure,
as indeed we all must be.

Sure, he was still at it by the time the others left. Some
    protection.
We had just time to get out. I had mislaid the thermometer.
    And pill. I bet
your sweet life I had to do it, to come up with something, for
    weren't we all equals
under the law? And how much should I let that excuse him?
    Ethical questions
were never my strong suit, but I wished to pass the gravy
    anyway, and in that
I was successful. Never to come round here again. Listen to
    politics

or someone filing on the word, and then a gush as from a well
occurs and no one is fit to stretch anymore. The old bomb
    was
having its say, I didn't know they allowed that, I thought it was
    still
that they outmoded it, sometime in the fifties. But to me, the
    last war
is World War II. I thought youth began then, is still going on,
    but for printing that
I'd be "libel" to legal action, so I pretend it's not like my youth
    anymore,
that things have grown up and gray. One or two friends and I,
    well we
get together and talk about it no oftener than once a month.
    You see,
the colors are in here in the dark too, only you can't see them,
    just feel them.
Don't touch. But these are in some way more satisfying than
    the others,
though also more eclectic. Did I say hectic? Yes, they are that
    too . . .

The wheat was the color of old men, the robin . . . Well these
    are what I had got
to offer you; I suppose it doesn't make any difference now
    because you have something new
that was not in the catalog I have. Something sweet, turning
    over, something unbuttoned.
But now there is no dose you can tolerate, no
sitting in the sun like a chunk of wood or a large broken
    fungus; it scarcely
matters which. See, I'm like you, a believer. At the same time I
    want to believe in things
that are endless, even though we don't get to see them every
    day, that are
what color is to a colorless surface, which I believe I have
    inhabited
once, or once upon a time. My politics shouldn't matter. It's
    my finger
that should—it's here I'll take my stand. I want over and over

to tell you what we are is *digital*, that no other form exists, at
    least if it does it
is as a function to the other great, existing forms, and they are
    already published,
it seems, in places. I have no desire other than to survive the
    endless extremes
of heat and cold. For a dollar I could put it in the mail to you,
my little tract, but so many others wanted it and spurned it.
    But I'm
thinking of you anyway, shall not go away, lest another be
    duller
than I'm, and I'm not trusting myself to get away
except on a lawn roller moving one to two miles per hour, and
    that
means we shall have to change when we get there, if we're
    tired, or be hired
by some straw boss and be sent to the rockpile for our pains,
    our talents
in getting lively others to talk about ourselves, how
they came down from Canaan in a wood car, and all was a
    frozen dump.
Why don't any of you want to come back with me,
where I see, from nesting, where the tree is? Long I've
    labored . . .
But others come along and do the job so much quicker, I'm almost
out of breath, and arranged to go home with them for the night.
I'd like more children around,
but that's it, not everything can be right, there must be a small
    hole
near the base, and all must get along, and not try to cover it
with anything. A shawl or turban would of course help.
But what does it matter if no one sees,
if there is no one to take attendance, and meanwhile the dam is
    overflowed
by some water, even as it comes rolling even to your feet. And
    what do you say
about it then, what ask for? If there are ideals in this society, let
    them speak
or afterward hold their peace since no job is going to get done
    until whoever

is here has explained the technical language in ways that I
and a chambermaid can understand. We've had so little help,
of late, been so understaffed, that even quite important logs
have rolled into the fireplace unbidden, and I
was never going to screw again, though there may have been
    error there, until the time
inscribed in colored crayons, upon the wall. And a distant
sister comes to take over, nurse you back to health and heresy
of your time, put one interest ahead of all others: staying still!
    Not talking! Pretty soon
it's everyone's job, the obligation to have a work-force be here
at times when no one else's is. Peace, and a thread of breath:
    that's all
they want; there's no reason to be excited
by their shout. And the poor little ones get some attention; it's
    as well,
you might think, and are sent off to the hills
once they have recuperated a bit from the noise and accident;
    oh what
disaster is closer to us today, and how do some others cope
in the meantime, until the vice-president can be here? And
    what cops
are talking together outside? Under the grape-arbor? Ah well
    it's no more of a season
now than it ever was; this year has got to be flooded out, and
    then it's
up to who can play. The morris-dances
are superseded, and others, who wish to join in, cannot. That is
    all what our rime is about,
we who are running, falling, reacting. In case the coat of burrs
    got overstated
we can sing operetta, or resurrect pliant golfers,
trying one's hand too at vanity in order to catch everything
    else.

Meanwhile the meat has been prepared and divided.
It was time to climb up, to pull the ladder up, having
    construed pith in the latest verbal
assaults from onlookers who wished to be crowned too. And
    that was really all it was about:

why, then, did it get blown out of context? In another decade
    there'd be no duel,
no stony silence in the media, only a little sunlight and
    frowning
before standing up again, past true forgetting. But in the
    meantime
its warped head wanders; there can never be a peaceful
    settlement, only further
reprisals and squeamishness, each day a curdled dawn, and no
    one remembers
why we were angry, only that a strict vengeance must be
    enacted. Even those
on the deck of a steamer departing for new free ports whose
    stone breakwaters will not have learned
of the mystery before are like sleepwalkers amid the gaiety, the
    greetings: did we say
it was to end here? And the sky of late spring and promising
    summer, deeply
saturated as always during times of war and occupation,
    promises no quick unraveling
of the skein of secret misery lobbed from generation to
    generation, though it does promise
much in the way of atmospheres and easy repose, and so may
    lighten the
burden for future cliff-dwellers, when it shall be seen and
    printed that all our care
is quaint anachronisms or prompt-scripts for retro chic. Yet
    they too, followers,
become lost in ever-narrowing canyons as day wanes, unwilling
to relinquish the post of court-historian to a younger and
    grubbier clientele,
and so history constantly dwindles, although one can still feel
    remarkably fit and well-adjusted
to life in an era more decadent than anything that has preceded
    it. These stylized
floral motifs the world offers aren't meant to be consumed,
    mindlessly,
before the waltz ends and fashion begins again; neither
is it a comment on one to have lost them, to arrive without
    memory at twilight,

which in any case spares no one. Blips from the maritime
provinces made it all disturbingly real: that anyone should have
   to die
so that we may stay on here, sodden but alive, fortunate
to be able to contemplate our mortality from a distance amid
   kindness
and late imperial emblems, golden dregs of another civilization
than the one we gulped down just a short time ago.
Its vanity pardons no one though, and there are other cudgels
   for defending
one's secret inclination than wisps of hope, transplanted, never
   acclimated,
that betray you at the end. How fast the children have grown
   this year!
No lovers undefeated? No time to return to the technical
   college? Then
you should have made a promise not to seek redress. The
   charm can't contain you now.
Apologies to all and sundry, and for the green that impedes
whatever I do in my writing, like a bias. *Why* hold that tiger?
   Or perform six other
acts before lunch, when all writing is putting aside something
in one's lap, like a sandwich, juggling priorities? But at least in
   this case it went well
until the long, late-afternoon-solemn street led first
to a shiver beyond it and next to a ship absurdly bedded in the
   snow, like a guidepost.
And then, finally, the year's shifting gears got to me, though I
   know
enough to be prepared for whatever explodes in your face.
   Still,
nobody amuses me anymore. I think now that in another time
   less would have been made
of all this. Formerly I was of a different opinion. But we
   moderns have to "leave our mark"
on whatever we say and do; we can let nothing pass without a
   comment
of some kind. Even rural lapses like water provoke us
to exquisite nitpicking, and then we don't know where we are
   when we stop

for the night. It could be one of the United States, it could be
    a European country.
But we are so riled at what has come secretly to possess us that
    it can't make any difference
to the maggot in one's sight, the flea in one's ear: all is basically
    kindling for the late
greater conflagration in which we think we shall see our
    destiny: our fate and death
as one. And when a shining thing approaches, rush out to meet
    it half-cocked
and laughing hysterically with worry. "This is my psychopomp;
    I ordered it!" But all that
is writing at the margin where daddy-long-legs tend to
    congregate. When we need
wackier prescriptions, we'll let you know. Meanwhile, be one of
    those
on whom nothing is lost. Organize your thoughts in random
    lines and, later on
down the road, paginate them. You'll see bluebells and
    cowslips on every hill; even
dragonflies will have become a thing of wonder, as long
as you don't get too close, and let water run through it all.
    What the hell! We're
in here having a fine time, our satisfaction pierces heaven's
    summit, and there are only
a few more who need to be drugged or convinced. As long as
    we're on this planet
the thrill never ceases. Even a garage can be a propitious place;
    a mechanic's
whistle from under a car can add to the spectrum of
    consternation suspended, and
making faces in the weeds. As long as we are never who we are
    ever going to be
the bind obtains and life on the edge of a knife has its own
    kind of remuneration,
so tenuous is the balance that keeps one foot caught in a
    misunderstanding
of someone's making. On the other
hand to walk away from it is the grave good face to austerity
    and fundamental

decisions that were reached long ago in the childhood of
    ambassadors in the nursery
of stars, and we can't avoid our reflection in these. It's come to
    get us, to take us
to the ceremony.

To the "newness" then, all subscribe, albeit with a few
    reservations. We have been living
in Herkimer for some time. The quiet plenitude exuded by fat,
    lettuce-colored stalks
is one thing, a haven, yet always in the imagination a hasp is loose,
something catches. One might, it is true, have preferred isles
    edged for miles and miles
with seabirds' feathers, and a smart-looking interior. But to
    give up what
has been offered is not a man's way. Similarly, when a drunken
    interlocutor
gets you and your best friend mixed up, the question is not
    whether to proceed into
the misunderstanding, but how to extend the frame
more or less grouping us as we sat before.
                            There was no luster
    then. But the suggestiveness
of both, blowhard and gawker, made it seem that a real
    element of choice
were sequestered, down there, near the root, as the shadow of
    an elegy fanned out
over the slag, enormous to this day. And just as one can
    remember a foreign
word but not the synonym for it in one's own language, it
    became a misleading
index of one's intelligence, just a little too imposing to be taken
    home
and placed on exhibit there. I talked to the governor's men
but though I could make myself understood in any language, it
    was without the foundation
that hope supplies when something is going well. Further
    negotiations were useless.
Besides, it seemed that the cinnabar headlands were not now a
    convergence;

that trophies other than this one would be talked about when
  the time came for that,
that no more daunting voyage could have shaken the recruit's
  resolve; meanwhile the press-gang
cheered on the puny efforts at repeal that I and my wimpish
  cohorts advocated, then
resolved to push through the ratification process. And,
  unfortunately, we all looked alike; hence,
no one took us seriously or thrust chicken sandwiches on us. It
  was all a sad day,
though a merry one insofar as we were going home, albeit
  unwillingly. "Unwillingly,
O queen, I left your shore." Yet she saw that none of us left
  empty-handed; I still have
that souvenir, and therefore cannot decry the fate that brought
  me to this pass, alone,
untended, with still some forty miles to go before I can call my
  journey ended.
There were some who mocked us, and some that threw
  pebbles at our backs. But these
we scarcely noticed, buckled into our seats, laughing at the
  dream that took us back to the
foundations of real fear where the story must be lived if it is to
  matter at all to others.
That of course was no concern of ours; we thought *we* were
  the others, observing
our exemplary adventures through a wall
of water that splits from time to time, revealing the real nature
  of the operation, that it is not
a place of entertainment, rather a swamp, from which one emerges,
before lying on the grass for a long time, getting one's bearings
  and indeed doing anything
to buy time and fool our jailers until the moment that becomes
  a nocturne and precipitates
the glabrous drop that will satiate us and send us home,
  muttering
of the winds and suchlike. Inside this privileged attitude a
  revolutionary spark asserted
its rights; a trail of powder blazed there where but a moment
  before cool arches

led from one to the other and the view of hillsides wavered as
    in a bath
of sodium silicate, and seemed permanent. But that was the
    governor's trick to trip you up,
make you confess what he already knew, before returning
overwhelmed to your alcove. All these officials had a stake in
    the matter, and it was
moreover their tactic to give you rope enough to hang
    yourself; if you wanted to braid a ladder
with it, why that was all right too, provided somebody saw it
    and wrote about it. So for
sixteen years I dazzled the constituents with sayings of a
    country I had never seen; they knew I
raved but thought it must always be so when men dreamed,
    but my darker
purpose never surfaced. And on the day when I was set free on
    the sand
and told to run no one could remember my name; as soon as I
    realized I was beyond
the range of their small arms I could relax and saunter, or, as
    the mood progressed,
bury my face in my hands trying to remember what it was,
    what gable had afflicted me now, or
how I should be caring about the move across the ever-
    shrinking circles, as though
I was going to enter 'em, and not let the enemy hear of any
    further predicament
regarding me or those I formerly associated with as long as
    everyone kept silent as
their part of the bargain, and I too dreamed, loosely, because I
    didn't want the
landscape and hares to remember they'd once seen me if asked.
    And the landmark decision I
helped instigate came tolling through the last several years of
    thatch and plaster and was as
my trademark; everybody knew me and I had only to walk
    through a hole
for it to become named as a piece of the life I was hoping to
    publish. No there were some

who were unhappy with this, and not content with tormenting
    me, actually made me see
there was no difference, no other way I could have gone on
    being
what once I had been. But the echoes of my calm egocentricity
    rolled over them too;
it was as if I had never held on to the blank stubs of my raffle
    tickets; in my composure
anything odd I said turned over and was revealed as the reverse
    of a truth that was something else,
and in such wise I was able to live for close to a year, in my
caboose, and no one suspected my ruse or fatal intelligence;
    they had other things to do,
and besides it was obvious I wasn't such a bad sort, we should
    all have to cotton to each other
and in so doing satisfy the chain destiny had prepared for us,
    the note
about to fall due. And I laughed
at the leaves floating in the cistern, that they too were my
    reward, and someday
all of us would come together in joyful earnest, for what it
    could do, and then my plans
would be better laid, and the daughters of those that were
    around us
would thrive specially too, and in becoming lead me into the
    cloud of chaff that was
to be my recompense, besides anything I really cared to do,
which could always be arranged, and anyway the future would
    be better for it
if I could just take my feet off the pedals and keep them there
    awhile.
And behold it all became good, and everybody recognized it.
    And the historians have had their say,
only now is too much done about it, and there is defeat, and
    fears about not
remembering. And so it will not pass away.

V

Nothing is required of you, yet all must render an accounting.
I said I was out hunting in the forest. How can it be that a man
can sup his fill, and still all around him find emptiness and
    drowsiness,
if he must go to the grave this way, unattended? Yet certainly
there are some bright spots, and when you listen to the
    laughter
in the middle of these it makes for more than a cosmetic truth,
    an invitation
to chivalry ringed by the dump fires of our deliberate
    civilization that has
got some things going for it—that invented neighborliness, for
    instance?
Then the paltry painted guest goes away, leaving behind the
    screed
she omitted to read. What's in it for us? Out of this school was
    sucked a philosophy
that didn't impel to action. A back-burner sort of thing. But if
    people had but
kept track of it that would have been something, someone
    could have framed
a memorandum. But they quickly find out what the traffic will
    bear
and are soon asleep in the midst of it, and the next call to
    action is considered passé
and no one will believe you represent the right cause. A piece
    of webbing
is nailed to the ground; ring-grass
invades its orient extremity; even these criteria have to be put away
until later. The hangar gets unbearably hot and very smelly.
Meanwhile the new green cascades silently and as it were
    invisibly.
Something has been said. You're right about that. But no two
    people
can agree on what it means, as though we were sounding
    boards
for each childish attempt at wireless communication the gods
    can invent,

and so return to our refectory. But I didn't know but what if I
didn't hang around a little longer the thrust
would be vouchsafed to *me* this time and of course as its public
repository I would use it to further the interests of all men and
women,
not just some. And it left the same message. It was as though
it never got my previous message. Sure, I'm still not yet
compromised
but there was so much in those fierce screens that ought to
have lived
as an example to conceal more and then to have it break out of
control and be put
down again if ever I could will myself to wish it, instead of
lingering
like a daisy on muck. Take out my tricycle for a spin and
return it
before anyone missed me. Yet, as I said, I didn't know. The old
men at the urinal
spat, not wanting word to get out. All my links with a certain
past were severed.
I let fall the book I had been reading, *The Radiator Girls at
Strapontin Lodge,*
as so much gift to the giver of idiosyncrasies which when
adopted
sift down like bran on rutted earth to accumulate
in whorls, and I thought how I could give no account
of these latest days. It was as though I had gone through a
bout of amnesia.
Now I was ready to put the gloves on again, but wasn't it too
late?
Wasn't the amnesty or amnesia of my own decreeing and
applicable not even
to one, to me, and in that case weren't we all excused
from class? And yet the board of governors certified me; I
became a vicious citizen,
not even to blame for what ills dunces harbored
in God knows what unimaginable slums, for as long as I chose
to occupy my seat
cooperating with the forces of eternal law and order yet
unwilling

to compromise friends, neighbors, orderlies, the giraffe at the
   zoo,
who even now moves toward me on unbending legs,
though his designs are far from clear. From whatever is happy
   and not
unholy, lead: the plan of the porch is quite an obvious one, and
   you know
what sliding doors mean and wherefore gutters conduct rain
to the abject earth, and turn around and absorb the shock of
   hearing the truth
told, once more, on an unforgettable day in early June,
which shall be all we need ever know of hearing quarrels inside
   out and then
reversing them so the abstract argument is pure and just again,
   a joy to many.

How much luckier I am, though, than they, who can see where
   I'm stumbling to during the day
and can rein in at night, between hedges. It's like
dangling far above the city streets, a kind of peace if you don't
   spoil it
by losing patience. Sure enough, other fun began while I was
   gone, a kind of imaginative
recycling of the days I'd crumpled and tossed out, and then
   their
dated shenanigans came to
seem crisp and well-presented, focussed, cropped; none of the
   "careful draftsman" in me could
cavil at that. Besides it was nice just being outdoors with
   something to say. An excuse
like a birthmark arose and flowered, still swimming upward
   past
the layers of the different civilizations, to Sun Lake. I could
   trundle my shopping cart past
the wicket and still be there, off the hook. I don't mind being
   mesmerized even for
fairly long periods but this was like playing tic-tac-toe with an
   automated
stone saint; the mock-orange note in it was strong and I'd
   come, I

remembered, chiefly to see my own reflection. Now, where was
    I? Where'd I put that
ticket of readmission to the bathers, who by this time were
    streaming out
in twos and threes. "Show us how to open a book like that."
    We gave them coffee
when it didn't go fast enough. Things seemed to pick up after
    that, though I felt a twinge:

was it going to do it for me, this time, and them? Might we be
    forced to split up,
and if so, which half of the ladder is left standing? You don't
    want to hear it. And still
the cloister extends, deeper and deeper into the dream of
    everyday life that was our
beginning, and where we still live, out in the open, under
    clouds stacked up in a holding pattern
like pictures in a nineteenth-century museum: forgive us
    our stitch of frivolity in the fabric of eternity if only so that
    others
can see how shabby the truth isn't and make their depositions
    accordingly, regulating
the paths over which we have no control now, speaking out of
    concentrated
politeness into an ear which wishes to hear, but once we have
    finished
what we had to say (and we have nothing to say) the moment
    and any afterthoughts are scooped up
as though by a steam shovel and deposited *over there*, not out
    of sight.
And the contentious are sometimes with us as a smooth pavane
    on glassy but profoundly
turbulent waters. How to keep it going
when all is trembling violently anyway, the air and all things in
    it? Shouldn't we
abandon them? But no these are
pointlessly fussy caveats sunk, so as to test one, in the great
    gray
fabric of the unwinding highway: don't let its apparent dignity
    fool you, and besides

they're free, and can and do say whatever they want to you;
    that doesn't
mean you have to respond in kind, but it helps. Someone is
    working on it,
providing heat in summer and air conditioning in winter, and
    get-well
notes arrive in every post; the top
of the volcano has been successfully glued back on, and who is
    to say we aren't
invited? The invitation, after all, arrived too, that was your
    name
beautifully chiselled into it. And ideas like fire
struck too quickly from flint seem to matter: your house or my
    house,
this time?
           I really think it's my turn,
but the variations don't let you proceed along one footpath
    normally; there are
too many ways to go. I guess that's what I meant. Why I was
    worried,
all along, I mean, though I knew it was superfluous and that
    you'd love me for it
or for anything else as long as I could sort out the strands that
    brought us together
and dye them for identification purposes further on, but you
didn't have to remain that generalized. A few anomalies
are a help sometimes, confetti that gets lost in the cracks
of some conversation and then you have to take it back again
    to the beginning
and start all over again, but that's normal, it's no cause for
    alarm, there are
more people out there than before. If you can think
    constructively, cogently,
on a spring morning like this and really want to know the
    result in advance, and can
accept the inroads colorful difficulties can sometimes make as
    well as all the
fortunate happening, the unexpected pleasures and all that,
    then there's no reason not to
rejoice in the exterior outcome, sudden

mountain-face, the abrupt slide
into somewhere or other. It will all twist us
closer together, under heaven, and I guess that's what you
    came about. See these
polished stones? I want them and I want you to have them. It's
    time, now.

So that's it, really. How all that fluff got wedged in with the
    diamonds in the star chamber
makes for compelling reading, as does the heading "Eyesores,"
    though what comes under it,
e.g., "Nancy's pendant," is a decidedly mixed bag. The proper
    walk must be aborted
and tangled hope restored to its rightful place in the hierarchy
    of dutiful devotions
for it to matter at all to "the likes of" us, and get booted to the
    rear
of the compartment. We were talking about cats. I said you
    should have one
not so much for companionship as for the extreme urgency of
    not letting it out of the bag,
if you should be so lucky as to possess one of those too. You
    always thank me
for my suggestions even when I can see they haven't gone over
    too well, and this
was one of those times. We chatted some more about cats and
    other pets
and then parted on an amiable note, what I would call one.
    And all during the succeeding
weeks there was no word, nothing on the radio, what we call
    the wireless. You'd think a line
like "HUNT MISSING GIRL" might have turned up in the
    papers, but the actual situation
was otherwise. A standoff. A phantom so strange in its
    implications it defies
. . . classification. Otherwise, how his beans were cooked
made absolutely no difference to him. In fact he seemed to lose
    interest in his surroundings
daily. I remember including that in one of my reports. If he
    asked for a nail file

it would be to stab playfully at the pillow, or occasionally to
    clean his nails,
never to file them. Once I even saw him reading a detective
    novel upside down.
I was too upset to include *that* in my report, as you may
    imagine. And secretly he
wheedles favors out of us; the older nurses are more
    susceptible. If he wants to
wind up sidelined, in the dugout, that is OK with me, but I
    don't see why *I* should be expected
to sign the warrant for his release. I have other, more
    important, things to do, besides.
Getting that bit of lacquer repaired is just one of them, but you
    get my drift,
I fear, then too I've traditionally been the indulgent, mild-
    mannered one,
who thought nothing of taking an afternoon off to play golf if
    the weather was right
as it is so seldom in this inclement land. When I asked about
    the new monitors
someone brought in I wasn't expecting a sermon on the
    necessity of staking out one's
territory the very same day, but there it came, with a hurricane
    in its pocket for good measure.
And when no one was betting on horses, there were the nags
    to feed,
the grooms' quarters to be kept in proper order, liveries to be
    pressed—it all came
gushing down on me like a bushel of affectionate children. It is
    lucky I am
old enough to keep my head, faced with the demands on my
    time. Even a computer
would get riled sometimes. Now I am more interested in "easy
    living,"
though more than ever feeling a need to keep up appearances,
    impress the neighbors
with the latest electronic *trouvaille*. Yet I never let down my
    defenses
for a moment. I am what some people would call "hard,"
    though

I'm really a pussycat underneath the austere façade. Speaking of
   cats, when was the last
time you spoke to one, calling it by its name? Out here on the
   prairie things are much too quiet
though we all know each other and share memories and
   stratagems
for coping with loneliness and disloyalty from time to time. In
   some ways
it's a life, or something you'd have no difficulty recognizing as
   such, but I wonder,
how are they going to fit me in at the end? Will my birdcage be
   draped
with some expensive Liberty fabric to suggest eternal peace,
   just as I was getting used
to the lively round of tea-parties and exhibits
some are over-attached to, but when you think
about it, what's wrong with a little pudding? Sprinkled with
   coconut, perhaps?
And then in the evening you get down to business, but you
   can't think clearer then.
Here there is no mist to admonish one, no pretzel sticks either,
and one knows very well what one wants to be
and can imagine a fancier existence anywhere. This has to get
   broken off here
for the reason things do get broken off: it's amusing. Love,
The Human Pool Table.

Sometimes to stimulate interest in other titles we
try to encourage a different angle such as the Near East with its
   walled, secret gardens,
jacaranda petals that fall all day into the basin. And the hours,
peeled off one after the other like onion skin, yet there is
   always more:
some curve up ahead. In fact
we never see all there is to see
which is good for business too: keeps the public returning
these days of swiftly eroding brand loyalty, so you can say: I
   beat him up,
my competitor, and now I'm ready to do business with him
   again: such

is the interesting climate we live in, all
shocks one minute, all smiles and surprises the next. I think I'll
    have the chicken salad oriental. I'll
wager you haven't one client in seven who can identify this,
    though the whole world knows of it,
this quite tiny key to success I hold in my hand. When the codger
returns I'll brusquely bring the question up again and you'll
    see. It's cooler
over here; the light forms a film at the windows
I first took for a curtain, a rash that won't wear off. Wait, now
he's ready to talk business. I have, sir, a handle on the truth
that could be of keen interest to you, a matter of considerable
    importance.
You can feel it when the lake is up and swans go flapping off
on various absurd errands, or when the phone rings and you
    hear his voice
before picking up the receiver, saying, It's me, I'm glad I waited
till you were in a different frame of mind, for truly this makes
    all the difference; no one
calls the woman who walks silently away, but later in the night
there are twists of tears and it seems as if someone shares your
    nervousness
about the awkward pauses that might ensue and has arrived at
    a plan of drastic action:
whisking the tablecloth off the laden table without disturbing a
    spoon is only part of it.
Giving up habits like compulsive hand-washing is another.
    Because you have no idea how
imperious their demands are; nothing can get closer to you as
    long as they are in the car-port
even though they too have nothing to say
and cannot justify their existence.

Other pleasures are folding the pillow and gazing mournfully
    into the face of the electric clock
when everything springs apart quite naturally and scrawled
    forms of people
are seen pacing the square in different directions; sometimes
one will hold on to another's head and then let go: it's my
    Sonata

of Experience, and I wrote it for you. Here's how it goes: the
 first theme is announced,
then fooled around with for a while and goes and sits over
 there. Soon the second
arrives, less appealing than the first or so it seems but after you
 get to know it you find
it deeper and somehow more human, like the plain face of an
 old lady who has seen much
but who has never been known to utter an opinion on
 anything that happens to her: quite
extraordinary, in fact. Then comes a hiatus in the manuscript:
the last bits of it keep seeming to move farther and farther
 away, like houses
on a beach one is leaving in a speeding motorboat: wait, though!
 isn't that them we're approaching now? Of course—we had
 been going around in a circle
all the time, and now we have arrived at the place of resolution.
 The stakes are high
now, but you couldn't tell it from the glum air of things: bored
 crows, seedlings.
And then, what passion
brought you to your knees? Suddenly your whole face is bathed
 in tears, though no one
saw you cry. This kind of makes me review my whole plan of
 action up to now; fishing around
for a handkerchief to hand someone does that to a person, I
 think, don't you?
And it will mean staying up later which in turn will screw up
tomorrow's well-laid plans, and then suddenly everything ends
 in a climax, or a cataract.
I think this *is* the way it was supposed to be, though I can't be
 sure now, so much has happened;
it will look better on a cassette, which is where I wanted it anyway,
 so I guess
we can go home now, each to his own bed, for each of us has
 one: that's what "calling it a night" means.
But I never meant to disturb anything, or harm a hair on your
 head: that would have been false
to our beginnings, and nothing could stand up to that, nothing
 good I mean.

As it builds, the power changes too, but in the
same direction it was carelessly aimed in long ago, before any of us got involved
with what we now consider our living, when it was free. And the strain grows, steadily,
though there are many scenes played for comic relief and the classic agendas are still
re-enacted when people get together. Not quite late-twentieth-century panic, but sobering in its
simple difference which can scarcely be demonstrated. All the people we knew and the songs
we sang are on our side, sinking imperceptibly
along with us into Old Home Week. Except it's not. And we cannot see the bottom
of these issues; they have outgrown us; which made the eye in the church shine even brighter
when it finally opened. Meanwhile, over the scruffy skies of New York, a doubt hangs
like a jewel, a melancholy melon-color that could be the correct shade of mourning
in heaven, pitting all that we said against us. Why, it's right there in the *procès verbal*,
only I don't feel too good. I just want to be absorbed in countries you were never
allowed to develop a taste for, yet I have no reason to go anywhere,
to be at your side, every place seems as mortally insipid
as every other place, and I've got used to living, like a toothache; I can stand
what's coming, but that doesn't mean I don't have to like it. Some mornings are quite pleasant:
a Florentine wonderment drips from the sky as putti with picnic baskets descend
to the enameled sward, and I don't have to ask you how near you think that lighthouse is,
or the blond warehouse: you find me in them. Is it asking too much
to want to be loved, just a little, and then to be satisfied with that? Of course not,

but the police are everywhere. You can't even order a drink
    without feeling one of them breathing
down your neck. And you apologize profusely, like the
    ridiculous twit you are.
Where is it written that men must go out in the afternoon
    without a hat?

In the real world things were going along about as well as
    could be expected, that is,
not quite satisfactorily. We were deceived in our reckoning,
but could still salvage some things like a decent emolument
    and self-respect. But in many ways
things were different now. Even the coastline had changed,
and the protective vacuum-packing around long-established
    major confrontations was no longer
mandatory. One sat at a kind of grillwork that used to be the
    kitchen table,
while outside hives exploded and buzzing insects darkened the
    air and we thought we knew
the year we graduated from high school, yet everything was
    suspended in an agitated trance.
Only, I knew where I wanted to go: to some mountains in the
    south covered with pine forests
and creeper. There, the silence causes you to will what you
    wanted to know without
exactly knowing if it was OK.   Here, curvaceous rocks brandish
    us; the squeals of "Put me *down!*"
are mere grace-notes in this battle of stupid titans. Strangely, a
    few amenities do survive,
enough to seem to give the lie to so much stinking chaos
    which, since it hasn't overturned
everything, is therefore perhaps not what its pennant in the sky
    proclaims it to be:
walks by creeks, for instance. Yet by enabling all creatures to
    become something different,
not necessarily their opposite, the proposed bifurcating leads in
    time to impossible
extremities one could never apostrophize anticipating a benign
    outcome due to the dreamlike

imaginings at the center that produced them. Waves, like
    weather currents on the map,
drift and coagulate above us, like "the swan-winged horses of
    the skies,
with summer's music in their manes," absolving the map of all
    responsibility to present itself,
to be read as a guide, and offering in its stead only the inane
    fumes of incense
spiritual masturbation set alight, long ago, and this is the
    bread, the palaces of the present,
a time that cannot tend itself. Each year the summer dwindles
    noticeably, but the Reagan
administration insists we cannot go to heaven without drinking
    caustic soda on the floor
of Death Valley as long as others pay their rent and have
    somewhere to go without thinking,
behind the curtain of closing down all operations. It's all right, I
like doing the housework naked and can see nothing wrong with it,
nor do I feel ashamed of it. I'll be all right when the
    government goes away; its
police state may not recognize me, or, if it does, may just
    shrug. What can I want,
anyway? Besides cashing in my federal insurance policy, that is.
    But as usual life is a dream
of blackbirds slowly flying, of people who come to your door
    needing help or merely
wanting to attack you so they can go away and say contact was
    made and it's your day in the barrel.
                                          Those of us who did
    manage to keep control over our personal affairs
before it was all over are obviously not going to testify anyway.
    What would we have said?
That we confronted the monster eyeball to eyeball and blinked
    first but only
after a decent interval had elapsed and were then excused from
    completing the examination
before defenestration became an issue? I thought I knew all
    about you and everything
everybody could do to me but this hiatus is sui generis and I
    know not how to read it

like braille and must forever remain behind in my solicitations,
    derelict in my duties,
until a child explains it all to me. And then I'll weep
at mountainscapes, if it isn't too late. But say,
where are you going, and why do you walk that way? Oh, I'll
    be all right, provided
you shut up and don't read too much into the dog's picture. After all,
the mutt said he wanted it taken, and in the backyard, so how
    was I to know
there'd be hell to pay for even this seeming indulgence? And
    how did I get away
after fourteen years? I'm afraid that's one you'll have to save for
    the answer man, besides,
my time is up and nothing too terrible has happened, only
    clouds, wind, stone, sometimes
a distant engine, purring in the morning fog, before the others
    are up, but I can see it.
It unwinds shelteringly.
                        *But there were dreams to sell, ill didst thou
buy:*
not the man walking, the woman sitting on the toilet, the tuba-
    player unscrewing the mouthpiece
of his instrument and blowing into it, not the azaleas blooming
    in tubs; but the three policemen and the man
scratching his groin, turning to say something to someone you
    couldn't see; the women
who wandered up to you at a cookout, waiting for you to give
    them an affectionate
peck on the cheek; the marching band in Rio, and the one in
    New Orleans, who knew
the music very well, and played it as they walked; the African
    violets you called *violettes*
du Cap, white, pink and blue, doing nicely in a northern
    window: these, for your trouble,
you may have mastered and accomplished much else besides,
    not least turning yourself from a
slightly unruly child into a sophisticated and cultivated adult
    with a number of books
to his credit and many more projects in the works; as well as
    the unattractive dreamer,

stained with sleep, who grasps at these as they elude him, and
    grasps at still others
which elude him not, all the time swilling the taste of one in
    his mouth. Forgetful,
you hang up the receiver allowing others to get through: in
    your garden
there may have been much confusion but also attentive things
    growing, now cut adrift,
floundering for lack of direction from you. And we see it even
    in the tall houses
that fan out from here: each has its family
who are not much concerned with you, but to whom a truce
    was offered, and who missed out on it
because of misplaced consideration for you; and then in the
    dark forests that slant down
ravines quite close to the town, whose emptiness you could
    have peopled
merely by taking them up, in conversation; and the vast, greenish-
    gray seas punctuated
with scudding whitecaps that are a mystery and will always
    remain so, but you could have
addressed yourself to that, at least, included them in some
    memorial address
at the proper time, and so saved a speck of righteousness for
    your otherwise unproductive antics, summoned
dazed spirits "out of hell's murky haze, heaven's blue hall,"
    accommodated them even
as you sat beside me, reading or listening to music. Thus, it
    becomes time to relax
e'en so. Funny, isn't it? The last thing on your list, and now
it is being approached even as afternoon makes room for
    evening, when all our
aspirations shall be quietened. And if no post arrives, no hens
    cluck,
then it shall be just as if it had happened. Why? Because it's
    completed. Don't you
see the light, seeing the light? Now you see it, now you don't,
is about right, having given up all lust, all hope.
                                      There is a time
    for trying on new clothes.

Yet the spirits are still angry that you woke them, if that's what
   you did.
Dreaming a dream to prize—way to go, Thomas L. It matters
   not how puke-encrusted
the areaway, how charged with punishments the jazz-inflected
   scroll—this *is* your time, by golly,
so change your clothes and get it right. THIS IS AN
   ILLUSTRATION OF SOMETHING.
What people never really wanted to talk about—Stonehenge.
   Last year it was a phantom's
breath upset you. Incorporate it—no second chance will be given
but what an old man said, quietly sitting at a coffee table, eyes
   shielded from the light.
A blast of gramophone music veers into the shutters from time
   to time. In those days and
in that time you had to have a sister and brother and be
   known. Now anyone
may play, but the stakes, alas, are much higher. Few
can afford to lose. Yet you see brothers, and sons, caught in the
   lure of it,
swapping new clothes for food, in short doing all the things you
   were warned against,
like talking to strangers. I like that. I only wish more of 'em
   would listen to me, but they
too have their business to attend to, curious as it seems, even as
   your mouth waters
at the sight of one of them, who hurries on, unfeeling. It's at
   night they come back,
once they know they've got you, or can have you, and then the
   caterwauling begins
unchecked. How would you like a plastron front to wear with
   this? Of course you wouldn't,
but that don't keep none of them from trying to play the Ripper,
   more shitted against
than shitting, so then they *do* rise up, and it can be one hell of
   a sight,
especially for those unaccustomed to it. I prefer to sit here and
   "rest" my eyes.
Usually my hunches are good, but last week comes one of 'em,
   and they always

asks you for something, begs a little jam or some string, and
    once you give it
you're in their power. But you knew *that*. Then the fun begins
    in earnest, blows rain
down from all over, chopping-block sounds, you think
    mechanically of Mary Stuart and Lady
Jane Grey, holding on to your forelock, cap in hand, of course.
    I don't know how long
the mist and smog have overlain this city, the dreaded heat,
    rising out of the sewers,
that can seem like the odor of fresh-baked buttered rolls. Then
    you must go to it again
and fill out a new application, for they have mislaid the
    first.
   We nightingales
sing boldly from our hearts, so listen to us:

First, a saxophone quartet told me we have lived too much
in the minds of others, have too much unguaranteed capital on
    deposit there.

Why are you here? Why did you scream?

Only that one told me a new-laid owl's egg is sovereign
against the gripes, and now I find you here too. I have found
    you out. You seem
convinced the killer is one of us. Why? Did a drowned virgin
tell you that, or Tim the ostler, or the one-eyed hay-baler
with a hook for a hand? Or was it something else—some letter
you might have received from some distant land
where all is peace under the umbrella-pines and a serpent guards
the golden apples still? Seal it didst thou,
to send it back across the water as a sigh
to those unknowable?
I'll be perfectly frank with you. Though the sun's crisply
    charred
entrails have slumped behind yonder peak, no one has stepped
    forward to claim
the amazing sum promised by the clerk. You know not one
    minnesinger has ever

reneged on a pledge. Until today, that is. When by the loose
    curtain's distracted
fall I spy the contour of an ankle, and the ferrous glint
of a meat-cleaver. Go to the judge! Tell him what you have
    told me
and your daughter! Implore his mercy! Then if you dare
look round to see what impression your sudden fit of sincerity
    hath produced. I'll wager you
no one leaves the room, and that the tool chest be empty! Go
    on! Try it! Last one in's
a rotten apple, or a—a booby. That's my last offer. Chain me to
    the iron bedstead
and electrocute me, so help me, that's all you're going to get
    out of me, harden my arteries
to obsidian as they will, let the mostly empty bottles
be drained till not one drop remaineth in them. Now that the
    killer is caught
you can return the map to Mr. Isbark.

A little loathing,
a cautious wind that pads softly
like a cat about thine loin
and argues persuasively for a cease-fire, in which one might read
much if one were wide awake and made aware, in whose bright fire
hell's thistle gleams, a league or so away. Marry, save that alibi
for your autobiography. Serve me fresh drink, I'll drink on't.
They were getting closer to your name in the list; now,
nothing will remove that stain. So how's about a walk around
    the old neighborhood?
Eleanor's here too. You remember Eleanor. So, nice and easy,
until it becomes something like grub, or a slug, something
    shapeless and horrible
you can talk back to, even scream invective at—you've got the
    time. And meanwhile our balls and
asses got to shamble on. But the daddies were keen on it.
They all liked it. Yon dork in the petting zoo,
Who, what, is it?

Two nights ago when I was complaining about all the weather
    we've been having lately,

and about how no one can do anything about it—much as I'd
   like to—
I was still happy, but today it turns out the drought has been
   secretly installed for weeks:
we're only beginning to feel the brunt of it. Of course,
   measures will be taken

but that's scarcely the point. It won't like you any better for it.
And what about mud? If we lose it, we lose everything.
Distinctions would no longer get muddied. There'd be nothing
   in life to wriggle out of,
no ooze to drop back into. We need water, heaven knows, but
   mud—it's so all over the place,
like air, that the thought of its not being there is even scarier.
Like a home that must be abandoned quickly, whose carpets
   and wallpaper get that faintly
distressed look, earth would go on without us, leave us waiting
   in space
for a connection that never comes. Somehow we'd survive—we
   always do—but at what cost
of mud and cosmetics. Different forms of address
would have to be adopted. Manners would become pallid, and
   the plot of one's life
like a thin membrane in which one can still recognize the shapes
that brought us here, and lure us on, but stronger too, to
   survive business,
and that would wreck our average partygoing.
I live at the bottom of the sea now.
But I can still sense a stranger
even when far off
and count the threads of partings still to be formalized.

And later when we stayed talking quietly apart
in the roofless outdoor room, she had discovered
my beloved: "Well! *Improvvisatore!* It would seem God's wrath
has taken us both down a peg. I have my money. And you, I
   suppose, will wing it
as in the past of windy Marches and stifling Augusts we have
   known
together, nor regretted them once past, but say,

if not some thread, a token then, a coupon
for pats and fondlings? Was this thy gratitude for pats and
    fondlings,
to die like any other mortal ass?
And why, O dearest, could'st not keep thy legs,
that sacred pair, sacred to sacred me?" Why, then, risk it?
Why go after it? Anyhow, I left it in the crypt.

And all that time was much fussing, to-ing and fro-ing, and
    above all waiting
to see the result on the street next day. As it happened, it was a
    lady
in yellow, with nice legs, who turned to me and said: "Haven't
    you anything better to do?"
I wanted to cry back at her: "Yes! And these are those things! Let's
discuss your legs!" But I knew she couldn't imagine herself
filling more than the allotted space, one for her and one for
    herself,
so I said nothing, and she resumed her walking. *You*
understand it, though, don't you? I mean how objects,
    including people, can be one thing
and mean something else, and therefore these two are subtly
    disconnected? I don't see how
a bunch of attributes can go walking around with a coatrack
    labeled "person" loosely tied
to it with apron strings. That blows my mind. I see that you
    want to mean it, though.
Yes, I love it, but that doesn't mean . . .

A girl named Christine asked me why I have so much trouble
    at the office.
It's just that I don't enjoy taking orders from my inferiors, and
    besides,
there are so many other, nicer things to be doing! Sleeping
    while the navigator
is poised, adrift, and sucking each other's dicks is only one.
Travel is another. Dinard! Was ever such a place? And when
    you are tired
but not yet ready to return home, you can be that person
    again, the one who dragged you

here. And we made love on a car-seat
in the moonlight, except there wasn't much of it. And I was
 the only one!
These adventures had passed through my head while I was alone
and I thought I was having them. But you need an audience
for them to reach the third dimension. Spooks in the manor
won't do, no pre-school-age children. That night in the car,
 though . . .
Then we clambered down some rocks. There was a girl there
 who spoke of finance, of how
it's going to be the next most important thing. I said nothing,
 but wondered if I could
take my stories with me when that happens, maybe read them
 to others
who would appreciate them in the new financial age that offers
 better reception
to things of the future, like mine. False dewdrops starred her
 eyelashes,
and I realized we were no better off in this age than in any
 other, except
perhaps the Ice Age. How if we are always going to be doing
 things for each other
why then of course we'll miss the point, since what happens,
 happens off in a trailer
and we really know no more of each other than ever, and that
 is what
ought to be our tree, our piece of happening.
My *standing*, in the French sense of the word. How everybody
 accepts me
and knows they are going to see a nice sight. Forget it. None
 of it matters
except what I am as I am to others. Trees floating around.
 Hard-ons
and what to do about them. But it is arranged so that you
 cannot begin to play.
Knowing the rules doesn't help, in fact it's better if you don't.
 You have to
be *in* on it already. And if you aren't you can die very quickly,
 or spend the decades
shattered. Out of touch even with yourself.

How can I tell them that . . . or that *La Fille mal gardée* is
   my favorite piece of music?
I'm sorry. Look guys. In the interests of not disturbing my
   fragile ecological balance
I can tell you a story about something. The expression will be
   just right, for it will be adjusted
to the demands of the form, and the form itself shall be
   timeless though
hitherto unsuspected. It will take us down to about now,
though a few beautiful archaisms will be allowed to flutter in
   it—"complaint,"
for one. You will be amazed at how touched you will be
   because of it, yet
not tempted to find fault with the author for doing so
   superlative a job that it leaves
his willing but breathless readers on the sidelines, like people
   waiting for hours
beside a village street to see the cross-country bicycle riders
   come zipping through
in their yellow or silver liveries, and it's all over so fast you're not sure
you even saw it, and go home and eat a dish of plain vanilla ice
   cream. Noises that bit me,
would-be fanciers skulking around, after an autograph or a
   piece of your hair, no doubt.
And indeed there's no point in worrying about the author's
   tender feelings as he streaks along
and sees no shame in it, nor any point in your concern for his
   injured vanity, not that you don't
already love him enough, more than any writer deserves. He
   won't thank you for it.
But you won't mind that either, since his literature will have
   performed its duty
by setting you gently down in a new place and then speeding
   off before
you have a chance to thank it. We've got to find a new name
   for him. "Writer" seems
totally inadequate; yet it is writing, you read it before you knew
   it. And besides,
if it weren't, it wouldn't have done the unexpected and by
   doing so proved that it was quite

the thing to do, and if it happened all right for you, but wasn't
    the way you
thought it was going to be, why still
that is called fulfilling part of the bargain. And by doing so
he has erased your eternal debt to him. You are free. You can
    go now.
But the last word is always the author's so you might want to
    dwell a bit
more on the perfections of form adjusted to content, and vice
    versa too, by Jove! The gate
to the corral is open, and he's in there now, running around
    and around it
in a paroxysm of arrival that holds the attention of every last
    member of that little audience.

We're interested in the language, that you call breath,
if breath is what we are to become, and we think it is, the
    southpaw said. Throwing her
a bone sometimes, sometimes expressing, sometimes expressing
    something like mild concern, the way
has been so hollowed out by travelers it has become cavernous.
    It leads to death.
We know that, yet for a limited time only we wish to pluck the
    sunflower,
transport it from where it stood, proud, erect, under a bungalow-
    blue sky, grasping at the sun,
and bring it inside, as all others sink into the common mold.
    The day
had begun inauspiciously, yet improved as it went along, until
    at bed-
time it was seen that we had prospered, I and thee.
Our early frustrated attempts at communicating were in any
    event long since dead.
Yet I had prayed for some civility from the air before setting
    out, as indeed my ancestors had done
and it hadn't hurt them any. And I purposely refrained from
    consulting *me*,

the *culte du moi* being a dead thing, a shambles. That's what
    led to me.

Early in the morning, rushing to see what has changed during
    the night, one stops to catch one's breath.
The older the presence, we now see, the more it has turned
    into thee
with a candle at thy side. Were I to proceed as my ancestors
    had done
we all might be looking around now for a place to escape from
    death,
for he has grown older and wiser. But if it please God to let me
    live until my name-day
I shall place bangles at the forehead of her who becomes my
    poetry, showing her
teeth as she smiles, like sun-stabs through raindrops. Drawing
    with a finger in my bed,
she explains how it was all necessary, how it was good I didn't
    break down on my way
to the showers, and afterwards when many were dead
who were thought to be living, the sun
came out for just a little while, and patted the sunflower

on its grizzled head. It likes me the way I am, thought the
    sunflower.
Therefore we all ought to concentrate on being more "me,"
for just as nobody could get along without the sun, the sun
would tumble from the heavens if we were to look up, still self-
    absorbed, and not see death.
It doesn't matter which day of the week you decide to set out
    on your journey. The day
will be there. And once you are off and running, it will be there
    still. The breath
you decide to catch comes at the far end of that day's slope,
    when her
vision is not so clear anymore. You say goodbye to her anyway,
    for the way
gleams up ahead. You don't need the day to see it by. And
    though millions are already dead
what matters is that they didn't break up the fight before I was
    able to get to thee,
to warn thee what would be done

to thee if more than one were found occupying the same bed.

Which is how we came to spend the night in the famous bed
that James VI of Scotland had once slept in. On its head the
    imperial sunflower
was inscribed, amid a shower of shooting stars. I say "imperial,"
    though by day
he was a king like any other, only a little more decent perhaps.
    And next morning the sun
came slashing through the crimson drapes, and I was like to
    have died. Although my death
would have encouraged a few, it did not happen then, or now,
    and still that me
as I like to call him saunters on, caring little for the others, the
    past a dead
letter as far as he's concerned. So that I wrote to her
asking if *she* cared anything about the way
he was going about it, and did she know what others had done
to stop him in similar circumstances. Her reply, brought to me
    late at night, when no breath
of wind stirred in the treetops outside, caught me unawares.
    "If to thee

he offers neither apology nor protest, then for him it is a good
    thing. For thee,
on the contrary, it augurs ill. If I were thee I'd stay in bed
from dawn to evening, waiting, at least until the sun
disappears from our heavens and goes to hector those cringing
    in the house of the dead.
There can be no luck in harvest-time, no tipping of the scales,
    while yet he draws breath."
I thanked her emissary and tiptoed out without telling him
    what I thought of her.
How extraordinary that as soon as one settles on a plan of
    action, whether it be day
or darkest midnight, someone will always try to discourage
    you, citing death
as a possible side-effect. Yet I could not, would not, dismiss my
    beloved boy. No way

would I proceed along the sea with no one to bounce my ideas
   off of but me.
And so we two rode together. It was almost late afternoon by
   the time we reached "The Sunflower,"
as the gigantic, decaying apartment complex was named. A
   noted architect had done

it right once, with open spaces, communal nurseries, walkways.
   Yet when he had done,
no one liked it. People refused to move in. It was cold and
   impersonal. To thee,
however, it seemed a paradise. The long, alienating corridors
   which the sun
sliced through at regular intervals were as confusing as a
   casbah; the dead
tennis-courts and watchtowers seemed a present sent by death
to distract you while you waited, always for her
touch. That said, there was plenty to do at night, while during
   the day-
long siesta one dreamed, and brooded not, and felt fairly good.
   No hog's breath
stirred the rusting weeds in the little yard in front of the
   veranda. Like me
you too chose to put a better construction on these things than
   perhaps the case warranted; at any rate, bed
always solves everything, at least for the time being. I went out
   and plucked a sunflower
but it was empty, the birds had eaten all the seeds. Surely
   there's a way

to avoid feeling lonesome *and* sorry for oneself, but up until
   today, no way
has opened before me, I'm *both* those things, though one
   would suffice. What's done
is done, they say, yet I can't help wondering whether, on a
   different day,
you might have turned around and walked back to where I was
   lying face down in bed
and told me all the love, all the respect you had for me, that
   was like a shining in you at me,

and we could have gone off to analyze our situation and add
 up the particulars. *Your* breath
was your own private property, of course, and you cared little
 for mine, but in the case of her
father being in the news and so many other officials who had
 turned out to be dead,
perhaps in a few years' time we would have forgotten all that,
 to live, sunflower
and sun, in periods of rain and drought, as they do in Africa,
 and never fear the sun.
It is written, and played on the African thumb-piano, that
 those who to thee
go, and return, unremembering, are earmarked for a lonely,
 unpleasant death,

and those to whom thou goest never grumble, even at the
 prospect of death.
Therefore it is urgent that we all, pursuers and pursued, be
 moving in the common way,
for that is the only way to outwit death, none-too-clever
 though he may be. To thee,
I say, stand, as though on a ladder picking apricots; your back
 should be to the sun,
and all will pass. You'll be satisfied, you'll see. No need to shake
 the sunflower
husk for dried kernels. Indeed, all the grasses are long dead;
the reaching angles of the thorn-tree branches barely jerk
 erratically in the breath
of the savannah. If I thought for one instant that the day
of the week spelled out protection for me, or that my own
 misdeed would trickle off me
like water from a duck's back, sure and I'd have done what any
 decent-minded preacher would have done:
I'd place bunches of fresh rue and meadowsweet in glass jars
 filled with water near the bed.
I'd point with my stick not at her sins but to the shy, closed
 flower of her womanhood, her

puckered glen of swansdown, and there would have been an
 end to it, unless her

parents had some say in the matter. We two have lasted almost
    until death,
and still nothing shields us from the aspirations of the
    sunflower;
even at night you can hear its ever-unquiet breath
that makes of life a station on some suburban railway.
Too bad you did what you did; I, meanwhile, was lying in bed
and caught the rumble of the vans of approaching day.
"This is my day, even though it belong as well to many who are
    dead.
I say it not in a spirit of possessiveness, only as a fact. Indeed, I
    pass it to thee
as generations of aspiring lovers and writers before me have done.
Look, this is what was done to me, written on me. Take it from
    me."
She stood up and began to do a little dance, then as abruptly
    stopped, noting the sun

had passed the zenith, and was waiting to be relieved by a
    replacement-sun.
In all our lives I still continue to try to make headway, and
    though to her
what I do never makes much sense, I do it anyway, for thee.
Scratching around one is sure to uncover bits of the ancient way;
meanwhile I am reasonably well-fed, clothed and happy and
    spend nights in a bed
that seems beautiful to me. We used to laugh; with every
    breath
we'd take, some new funny thing would point a moral and
    adorn the day,
until at last the earth lay baking in the heat, and the sunflower
had the last laugh. "Be strong, you that are now past your
    prime! When you are dead
we'll talk again and see how you understand this thing men call
    death,
that is in reality but a shadow of what God has done
to others, to the sun and to me."

I awoke, yet I dreamed still. It seemed that all had been
    destined for me

all along, and as I had traveled in fear, and alone, always the sun
traveled with me. At night one sleeps in fear of wetting the bed
but he makes amends for that by pointing to our eventual death
as a teacher would point with a wand to the solution of a
    problem on a blackboard. His way
is as inscrutable as a fox's. He brings to full bloom the
    cornflower and the sunflower,
then lets them slip into oblivion. Why? If I knew the answer, I
    wouldst tell thee,
but since thou sufferest much, I'll vouchsafe that the way of
    the dead
is as a lightness to our dreaming, a sense of gaiety, of
    irresponsibility. She in her
longing realizes much, and would tell it to us, but the breath
is gone. Still, there'll come a time and not too far off when all
    we have done
returns to charm us; we can go back, taste, repeat it any day.

So for the moment, although tomorrow is our day,
the sun shines through the meshes. You can have me
for anything I am, or want to be, and I'll replace you with me,
    introduce you to the sun.
When summer calls, and people wish they only had a way,
and nights are too thick, and days have barely begun to be
    spoiled, I'll riddle thee
about what we heard before we came here, how much is
    already done.
The moral of the story however is that the ubiquitous
    sunflower
knows the secret and cares. As a door on its hinges, so he in his
    bed
turns and turns, and in his turning unlocks the rusted padlock
    of death,
that flies apart and at once I am shriven. Take me in, teach me
    her
ways, but above all don't leave me for dead:
I live, though I draw only a little breath.

The story that she told me simmers in me still, though she is
    dead

these several months, lying as on a bed. The things we used to
   do, I to thee,
thou to me, matter still, but the sun points the way inexorably
   to death,
though it be but his, not our way. Funny the way the sun
can bring you around to her. And as you pause for breath,
remember it, now that it is done, and seeds flare in the
   sunflower.

And left it that way, and then it kind of got shelved. It was a
   missing increment,
but as long as no one realized it was missing, calm prevailed.
   When they did, it was well
on the way to being a back number of itself. So while people
   cared, and some even wept,
it was realized that this was a classic, even a generic, case, and
   soon
they called attention to other aspects of the affair. No one ever
   explained how a trained
competitor of long standing would just bar itself from the case
   that way, there being no
evidence of self-interest, except insofar as loving a sun
   constitutes one. They shied away
from this one, and it was with no love
or self-pity in its heart that it betook itself then down the few
   stone steps leading
to the crypt. Here, at least, peace of a sort reigned, better than
   the indifferent bog
of schnorrers and nay-sayers it had kept company with for so
   long, a whole season, and the unlovely
atmosphere that had soured that season at its close was not
   recognized here: it was a currency
no one had any use for. If this left one like sailcloth, with the
   grained and toned
texture of one who has seen much, and still wishes to help,
   why all the better: one could go
farther and fare worse than entertain the possibility of such a
   journey, a *voyage d'affaires*
that will consistently be fun at any given moment. And so,
   though stalks heavy with the

mothy, mopheaded bloom may tremble next August, that is a
    thing of the past; the sun
purges its mind of all negative thoughts, granting
equanimity with the largesse of one who has too much, and
causes people to re-examine their attitudes. Maybe get some
    rain?
Are sherbets more glorious now than formerly? So this small,
    piecemeal uncurling exposes
vast sheets of preoccupations that the sun's firmness can in
    many cases
cause to evaporate before their expiration date. A hound-
    shaped fragment of cloud rises
abruptly to the impressive center of the heavens only to fold
    itself
behind itself and fade into the distance even as it advances
bearing news of the channel coast. That is the archetypal kind
    of development
we're interested in here at the window girls move past
    continually. Something
must be happening beyond the point where they turn
and become mere fragments. But to find out what that is,
we should be forced to relinquish this vantage point, so
deeply fought for, hardly won.

VI

Yes, others chorused, and
we'll see to it that good use is made of it once they find you. Sea
so dark, O harvester, is it possible they could have brought you
    and me together
after so long, only to be separated in an instant? There must
    have been some purpose to this,
some idea hiding in the vacuity, the regular oblongs that
    comprise
your adverse assessment of my capabilities, like building blocks?
    But no,
it says, please sit down, you're upsetting the others. With my
    cant,
my stammer, I suppose? Oh all right, I'll go peaceably, but
    when you next see me,
rigged out in nickel armor to do battle with the
    henchpersons—it doesn't matter
whose—you'll descry in me a note of alarming mildness that I
    was saving
for just such an occasion. After all, *I*
can go on living here, and I don't mind emptiness, but you
must fill your days with satisfying chatter. Then, just as the
    moon's cloak
grazes the tits of some remote foothills, we'll engage
each other constructively, your energy will flow into me and
    vice versa, and behold,
all will have been in vain, the warring, the contusions, the
    peacemongering:
we'll have only ourselves, and only ourselves to blame.

Excellent is the peach, and stirring the tales
of battle, the calls to emulation. But excellent also is the spat-
    out pit, the ideal
of zero growth, when it comes to that. I think all men should
    argue, and then give in, for it
takes time to really make up one's mind about certain matters.
    Days of mourning
in particular.

Then when somebody comes to ask you if you have freshened
    up, or would like to,
the whole freight train of associations is set in motion, lumbers
    gracelessly
along the clacking tracks, and it isn't so much as if you *had*
    made up your mind, indeed
had done so quite some time ago, thank you, but as if it's all
    off
and running: the race to the pageant, stiff competition among
    the ushers,
the stagehands. And now I want it to be the way
it was. I'm very particular about the trivia I associate with,
but for which I'd long ago have passed out from boredom.
    Which brings me to you: how do *you*
like it, and could you care if you saw a sample of it escaping
    from the mass
to go inform other, unenlightened souls of whom we spoke
    and thought were past
redemption and caring but who shine like the night breezes
in this direction, the dew on them is genuine, and are those
tears? Who said it that way? I'll go another way. And she'll
    have me
then, there'll be no recourse, and we shall be happy after all,
    that's all there is to it, you'll
see.

It will never make any difference now, but
it remains to note how the change will affect your work. Empty
    slots in the zodiac
presage no good, nor the giant pebble at its center, but who
    knows, with patience
and a little hunger one makes one's way. From here you can see
    the town,
bustling with various kinds of sleepy activity. Old trucks in the
    squares.
Above it a few celestial blips, comparing different depths in
    space, how it feels
against a sky of tinfoil, and seemingly just emptied, but it has
    always been thus.

Gradually, heads appear around the rim of the crater, blotted in
 the sunlight.
Just gentle, happy suds, and the time to be missing:
all the time in the world, he liked to say,
and I'd recriminate too if I had escaped but it's not clear that I
 have. I stumbled
into an abandoned pigpen just now, and they are watching,
 which is all
anybody ever does. If I had books here I'd read.

Characterizing this rebuttal as "hogwash," the senator strode
 swiftly through the marble rotunda,
commenting the day's happenings without missing a beat. We
 have seen that the police
charge you more for delivering a baby when it's clement
 outdoors. We have seen
signs of life in the land of waiting, but it's too soon to rejoice;
 we'll
let you know. Others may have been after him to unzip the
 course, which wouldn't explain
dance orchestras in the rainy plaza or the unquestioning look
 of one child whose doll
came in second. In the hayloft the air was pure and fresh
and I could remember how once all of existence was as
 painfully expectant, careless of duration
as the mayflies trying to just get by, and how this curdled at
 evening with the smell of socks
and underarm deodorant so that that desperate patch seemed a
 nice place to be. Anyway it
had tested our mettle, whatever that is. Warnings boiled up
 seemingly out of the ground
but it was difficult to know what to make of them, or even to
 know who they were meant for.
Was it the last train? No pass to the way home from school? It
 was hard too to decode the missing,
who had apparently been seen as recently as this morning,
 turning away after being turned away.
Their locks are always a little more opalescent, their gussets
 straighter. Hygiene

is always a problem in the jungle, but you can stay here for
    decades and never appear
flushed, or flustered. Something about the thinness of the
    topsoil. They stand you
up and march you away and nobody looks afraid, just bored,
    and the majesty of the larkspur
performs annually. Refreshments are on a first-come, first-
    served basis. We have seen the cage
and the humdrum animals it contains. We have seen the house
    of the leader,
a little farther off. And the numbered apples on his trees.
It can never be anything but symbolic.
By that I mean it can never cause utterance in outsiders,
only second thoughts and self-doubt. For the discourse (and by
    discourse I mean *lively* discourse)
to take place on a meaningful level, that is, outside someone's
    brain, a state of artificial
sleep would have to be induced, first of all. Then the skills for
    measuring reflexive
response would have to be sharply honed. Finally, the patient's
    automatic, and therefore healthy,
impulse toward duplicity would have to be sorted out, strand
    by strand, in order that the
viable negative attempts to ward off phenomena like the
    empurpled dais of the approaching
twilit gloom might be measured, both as to sincerity and
    effectiveness. This technically
not unrealizable state of affairs would then bring us closer, but
    only a little, to a vantage
point from which the abiding, negative (but in the sense of
    "passive") sheathing of the soul might
offer an overview of what might be mounted inside that, but
    the view our telescope afforded
would be that of an episode which happened several trillion
    light-years ago, a fleeting
one at that, a grace-note in some cosmic oratorio from which
    one would then try to extrapolate
a sense of all that comes after, and how it jibes with the average
    mind of today,

its feeding habits, outbursts, and so on. The attempt is
    certainly worth making, even
if it only corroborates the central dark thesis about the purely
    symbolic, anti-functional
nature of the universe as a setting for the countless doomed
    initiatives that flourish
in it to supply compost for the core-concept, a somewhat
    antiquated but still functioning
regulatory system that organizes us in some semblance of
    order, binding some of us loosely,
baling others of us together like straw, but always there is a
    connection, albeit sometimes an
extremely loose one like a tendril that brushes against one, a
    lock of hair that falls over
the eye or a buzzing insect that is never too far away. And
    though the armature
that supports all these varied and indeed desperate initiatives
    has begun
to exhibit signs of metal fatigue it is nonetheless sound and
    beautiful in its capacity to perform
functions and imagine new ones when appropriate, the best
    model anyone has thought up
so far, like a poplar that bends and bends and is always capable
    of straightening itself
after the wind has gone; in short it is my home, and you are
    welcome in it
for as long as you wish to stay and abide by the rules. Still,
the doubling impulse that draws me toward it like some insane
    sexual attraction can
not be realized here. For that to take shape one would have to
    be able to conceive a linear
space independent of laws in which blunted gestures toward
    communication could advance or recede
without actually moving from the spot to which they are
    rooted; in other words, destiny could
happen all the time, vanish or repeat itself ad infinitum, and no
    one would be affected, one's
real interests being points that define us, the line, which is
    dimensionless and without desire.

Thus, all things would happen simultaneously and on the same
    plane, and existence, freed
from the chain of causality, could work on important projects
    unconnected to itself and so
conceive a new architecture that would be nowhere, a hunger
    for nothing, desire desiring itself,
play organized according to theology with a cut-off date,
    before large façades. And these
urges, if that's what they are, would exist already without
    propriety, without the need
or possibility of fulfillment, what the bass clarinet is to the
    orchestra, though of course we
would all get along very much as we do now, since human
    perfectibility would not
be sacrificed but on the contrary get promoted to the first
    desk, where it belongs,
and everybody would be free to draw his or her own
    conclusions and take them home like homework
provided the constellations remained inalterable, which is
    another question, and the
concept of beauty were abolished, which is another and
    possibly more important one. Anyway,
it looks like a nice day for all this, and I invite you to start
    revving up your VCR's;
who knows what may happen? In the meantime, look sharp,
    and sharply at what is around you; there is
always the possibility something may come of something, and
    that is our
fondest wish though it says here I'm not supposed to say so,
    not now, not
in this place of wood and sunlight, this stable or retiring room
    or whatever you want to call it.

Excuse me while I fart. There, that's better. I actually feel relieved.

Who knew at the time how froward they would be
later on, and in what circumstances we would be meeting
    again,
and how others with the names of heroes of boys' adventure
    novels would be replacing us

on the perilously steep escalator of destiny that only lurches
    upward,
ever unsatisfied, forever finding fault? Some of this crowd
were about right. But it can never stop raining. There are
    places you drive through
and people who come out to see what's going on, but in the
    end these are effects
merely. The truly vitiated look haggard and mean, whether
    they be socially
acceptable or no, and still the perquisite authority hasn't been
    distilled;
it is everyone's, for everyone to see. I will show you fear in a
    handful of specialists. Furthermore
the burliest male is but as a handmaiden to the suspicion of his
    own history:
he's got it right, OK? And so have a few others, while the
    waiting's been going on. But enough of
this self-congratulation in Aegean sunrises. Who are we, after
    all? And who needs profundity?
The moment I came down here I knew it was going to get
    better. There were autographs to sign,
and contracts, many of them in sextuplicate, and so I knew I
    was in for a good rest
after a long drive, and they'd leave me in peace, though not
    forget about me. Alas,
how sparsely furnished it all looks now. Chatterton's garret?
    And how much harder it is to pinpoint
the single, modestly important thing, now that we know its
    freight would be
long in coming, and much harder to decipher than any
entity before now. But of course! That's the solution! We know
    ourselves and everything
of the past. The one thing we don't know is how silly it's going
    to look in about five
minutes, like an eighteenth-century cherub atop a globe. You
    fuck me, I'll
fix you. You give me that, and I'll give you this. It's all so
    important yet so excruciatingly
banal, isn't it, darling? Then we'll have come home and there
    will be an end to it,

and they that have found it already shall have it taken away
    from them, and we who
never knew what a good thing we were on to shall be
    reproached and rewarded
with the viceroy's attention, though we must stand outside, I
    think. Fortify my ignorance
then, I shan't be doing anything to anybody but must not for
    this
reason stand alone, uninspired by hope. Three seasons shall
    pass before anybody gets up the nerve to jump,
by which time a perverse
order shall reign and those who have inspired us shall take their
    places in it
like latecomers ushered to their seats at the opera once the
    overture is finished. You can't
can it and sell it, that's for sure, but it *is* a commodity, and
    someday all
will be wiser for it. And the paradoxically strong sense of
    personal loss that overwhelms you
when you hear about the death of someone you barely knew
    will answer for it too: you'll
be exonerated and no one will ever make fun of you again, or
    turn aside
when your name is mentioned. Meanwhile you'll be slightly
    happy when they
see how much your standing in this rigid matriarchal society
    has been enhanced
by the little you do, trying to scrape out a living and keeping
    your sense of humor,
which is, assuredly, not always easy. Anyway, someone will
    care.
They'd better. And the funk take over. The generations collapse
    like floors
in a burning building, and it will all somehow be . . .
    appropriate. Er, yes. We is rich
and handsome, as it were. HOWEVER,
I'll face the world alone. Bad cats will want to eat me. Autos
will run over me. Dogs will chase me. Chickens, hawks, tigers,
    lions . . . Perhaps
I'd better ride up with you. You understand, of course.

I certainly don't want to live next to a taxidermist. Miss Gale, I
    may need you later.

Then in the car he proposed to me. In the back seat. We drank
    sacrificial wine.
It was so *good*. And underneath I was saying,
all men are rogues, but I guess I like them,
if that's what they are. Then we went out and a cloud like a
    magician's cape
covered the sun. I'll never forget that. And we walked on
awhile and I was trying to explain my embarrassing
tendency not to be able to distinguish things that happened to
    me years ago
from recent dreams. He was cool for a while after that. Men
never seem to know how much to erase, and afterward it's
    bedlam, greed and self-interest take over
to a point where they actually cancel each other out, and one
    is left
hungry for one's greed, at least it was something, and now,
    why no
one has anything left to be impatient about. It's like damp weather.

And everybody said no wonder. It's an hour to find you.
You, so belated in the past, your comments could never be
interpreted as part of history, or so you said, and that's what we
    thought.
I'm just a copier. You are the history, the book. In time I think
it'll get you straight and all peoples will see what we're up to.
    In the past they chided you:
no more. I'm sending for your things, your books and things,
    we'll go over
it again in the morning. First get a good night's sleep. There
    are people who think nothing of
writing out a check for the full amount and handing it to you.
    I mean we're talking
debts canceled, a link to the future, daybreak . . . Well I
    thought so too and
still I've had it with those who want to own you, as it were,
and give you nothing in return. Still, if it were possible to come
    to some agreement

or other, I think I'd be content, and they too. Here, it says in
    the bar
how much we're going to spend, and then we'll be equidistant
    from base camp and the
summit and have some voice in our lives and how much the
    future matters
to us, and to others as well. Boy, I'll say so. Meanwhile, do you
think they're going to kill us in cold blood? Naw, I don't think
    so, besides
it's too risky, and we're on this side of the great river, they
on the other. I'd like to thank you for what you just said, but I
    could never
find the words.

Oh, that's all right.

A soft rain,
a sudden shower. Why shouldn't it?
And of all the ones I like
this is the most promising. Here in the dry
it is, anyway. It likes us, saying, "We'll get you over
this one, then hand you back the tiller. The others
are all love and lovers, sometimes." We won't bite,
    though, having been deceived so often in the past. The fact
    that the
happy ending's only waiting your approval dooms it; you shall
    go off the deep end
once more and ultimately, and, not to put too fine a
    deconstruction on it, be redeemed only
in a distant future no one cares to look into. There's so much
    of it going round
now that no one wants to look farther than his or her pocket
    mirror. It's funny how certain natural
calamities bring people together at times, separate them at others.
    Rampant "me tooism"'s certainly
the order of the day, and such a tall order; one can view oneself
    framed, silhouetted, dead, and
still only think in terms of surfaces, boundaries; the very
    heavens
have lifted off for destinations unknown, and as we can sit

here, we do. It isn't uncold. Whence comes Iceland's beam?
    But suppose you know someone who's
got a vested interest, an urge to show you how your hostility is
    what's aborting
the final, suave wrap-up, with the guts to stand up and say so—
    then
aren't we uniting, and isn't something due
to come of it when the last tears stain the oak flooring, and the
    roasted swans, the pineapples,
are sent away untasted. How many of us does *that* make?
Two, surely, but there is something like flowers in the room,
    and that makes it
a magic number, confounding calculations, canceling reports,
bringing in other unknown elements that are a form of art, at
    least
as long as they stay that way. True, that puts us in one another's
    way; we can no longer
aim at that destination on the wall, that hill outside the window,
    that seemed to promise
indefinite relief, but at least, being boxed in, can thwart the
    unknown at home, swear
fidelity and probably mean it this time. And meanwhile the
    tottering parade of ancient red
double-decker London buses winds past the window like a shriek
of victory but in reality contradicting itself: no carnival could
    be this atrocious *and*
unfrequented, at least it seems so to me. And one fits exactly the
    space of the mind
opposite one; there is no
sequel and no blank pages. As far as I'm concerned it's a draw,
    and a decent one at that
if you keep your mind off it.

Voices of autumn in full, heavy summer;
algae spangling a pool. A lot remains to be done, doesn't it?
I haven't even begun to turn myself inside-out yet, and that
has to precede even an informal beginning. Try making up
    those childish itineraries we were once
so apt at, and you'll see. Even my diary has become an omen to
    me,

and I know how I'll have to go on writing it; it would be
   disappointed
otherwise. And those days we have to get through! Afternoons
   at the store,
and when bluish evening, the color of television
in a window high above the street, comes on, who has the
   strength to
judge it all according to a pre-existing set of criteria and then
   live with it,
let alone enjoy it and aim it at being a force for good, in one's
   life and that of those
we share, for a time, this earth with, and later on to judge the
   after-effect of those fruits of it
which may no longer exist except as examples and increasingly
   dim ones at that? Why,
it's enough to make you want to leave home, strike out on
   your own
at midnight: "Why Girls Leave Home," "The Trial of Mary
   Dugan": maybe these were the things
they were saying then in the theater or writing about in novels
   so that
people would *understand* and thereby save themselves a lot of
   trouble
and floundering. In the unprincipled mire we walk about in
   today, nobody bothers even
to warn you about the perils of white slavery (to cite an
   extreme example), but then again
nobody is forcing you to save yourself either. That would be
   uncouth. Yet it would be nice
to think that years afterward one might have a good laugh about it,
and that assurance is precisely what we lack today. The fact is
   that no one even cares
what's it all about. They see only shoe-leather
thinning into the future, and the inexorable dawn
shading into dusk, and know that's what they're made of, like it
or not. That's what everybody's made of,
and it comes as no shock to find out that the present is, after
   all, brittle
as glass in a burning conservatory. Listening to the dance
   music from outside

is all that matters. Really. Stockings are of secondary
    importance.

There was a strange, scorched taste to the soup,
I thought. Had you?

Otherwise who would believe us when we came
home to taste the soup, and cry a little, not wanting much?
Like little girls pretending to understand each other
when they talk like adults, we'd see that living
on this alternate rail was possible but not
eminently desirable, though definitely possible.

O in that winter what tore my thought was the shiny poem
I was about to read and recite, and write: a lacquered thing
with an even more exciting nimbus that spelt out possibilities
in all the tales we were going to be told, all the wrongs
inflicted on us and in turn by us on all those
around us, neither more nor less fortunate than we.

Trying to drum up business one begins explaining recklessly
one's family and the dates in one's house, the little
plum tree visible in the enclosure. The path one made
forcing oneself. And now these are out of date and exactly what is
required here. Let's pass on them without analyzing them,
and others who sang here, knowing justice mysterious, and out
    of the way,

the way a moth sings in the house. A letting go,
as finger by finger unclasps. But we told it the way we wanted
    it to go.
So what about your story? And the fires that made you, better
than you wanted, still not worth dying for? I placed an ad,
it was wrong of me, and how should I go?

There—it's over. And what a blessed relief. I have always loved the
sight of women sewing, and holly at the eaves, sometimes a
    look that
spears you through the darkness: you are the unaccountable
    one

but there are acres of us just now. And I thought I came off
　　looking lewd.
No, but with the dock ahead, and that man in pinstripes
and bowler. We knew there'd be repercussions, but they were soft
as cotton candy when they came, and respectful, like dreams
put away, like money in the bank.

Time was when weather seemed a release. Today it's screwed down
all the way, like a cap on a jar, yet it mirrors something
in each one of us, something we had been trying to find out
without much success as dogs came and went across
dull afternoons—the "dear, dead days" as someone called them.

It's there, but with a new intensity. Everything is landscaped
for one's greater peace of mind, the furnaces within banked
for greater authoritativeness. I would like to
come out on the plus side, *it* wants us to, and amid the
explosions of careless lovemaking I suppose that's possible.
What's the catch? No doubt it lies somewhere along the way

of overreacting to these minute meteorological changes,
a slight twist to the horizon's lip or the ghost
of a frown that could have seen anything, such as the V of a bird
disappearing desultorily into a cloud. And meanwhile
there are rooms to be put back in order.

How does one explain that by never looking back one is always
seeing backward, into the scarves, the times that never were,
and that placing one foot before the other is only a sign
to the unconscious guides to follow, and that one's destination
is the empty stockade, not this crowded landing? So it is when
　　children

forget to grow and they are suddenly looking at being older,
not recognizing much? Or when people decide to migrate
from the village that has held them all these years like a spot
and uncomplainingly releases them to fall back
into the dreams that are the very fabric of our maturing,

now that we've got one, assuming it's still there, on permanent
    loan?

The sound the water made
when I brushed my teeth seemed a good idea. Later the
    sources
became clear, as in a picture. There was nobody to go to that
    day.
Yet as long as the pins held, here was where I
would someday be—no kidding. And O I
held you through the long winter, held to you.

The numismatic triumphs, the snakes and ladders
of outrageous fortune were what finally put us across,
its message. And some days the wind does blow heavier
but it's with special understanding for our case, those inverted
    commas
without which we can't function it seems.

An odor of big bands in the night and one stands up,
free to go. If ever they
came looking for us, this is where we'd be. And who doesn't
    want to be right here?
Yes, the more I think about it. We're going to stay. We've
    elected to.
Pass the celery.

Then the travel came at him. You know what I mean.
A last chance to air the old mass. Going home, after so many
    promises
to consult the self before the next spin. It erodes. We all had a
    chance
at the city of faces moving around. Now it's humdrum
    detection
from a many-sided tower on which we interact,
perhaps. And this neck of the woods is picked over.
After a rain the slattern light spreads again
creating all endeavors like ditches that only spread
farther into the trees and eyesight as my wrenched narrative
    drips on, decays

while some sing of the heart and a few, in a home, of lasting walls
or winds, and live in and love the riddle that proposes us.

Also by seacoast moles the wave gives up the ship, slams
it against the slip. We are in more heartfelt times now that
vacancy defines itself, that true aether. Conversely the body lines
"evanish all, like vapours in the air," burnish the curve or cove
at certain times seen as majestic, or merely at rest, a timeless,
unwired mood from which good can fall. And chiefly does.
 Though I am aware
of a moaning under the door, a secret treaty, plans to shanghai
 the settled
order during the night when we are awake and cold, losing the
 thread.
This said, the bauble that peace sprouted, is
it another camp collectible, or are its strings somehow
drawn too taut in us? Then the next thing explodes,
like a cigar or a vase of flowers. Left in the rubbery wake one
 still keeps
meaning to be around both before and after, not during necessarily,
since there is no fruitful rest there, only a game of opposites posing
as right for the happy-to-be-blind and the tense modifiers,
grouping. All along that stand of trees you shed a path
adjacent to the end and some grazed there, mooring
large questions of how do you get off and what are we waiting
 for? Standing
like this? When all of spring is away? Who do you get to change it?

You take a guy who's never seen one before, a weather like this,
 and perforce he
will deduce brightnesses out of the pervading dullness we never
 knew were there;
it becomes a construction. So that the later glare of tidings
 seems almost "natural,"
and the agreement that hands closed on, a bargain, in that time
 and place.

Suddenly they all stopped talking about it. Yet I
can't get it out of my head. I just saw it here somewhere
late last evening. As a result, nobody thinks I'm normal, but I don't

care. Every answer may have been salted and put away just so
   as to spoil,
like a dissertation of some kind. A great deal of thinking went
   into it and out the other side.

But I did want to get back to the personal barbs. Why was I
   wailing for them?
Fact: people leave their doors open and don't even flush the toilet.
Fact: loving one another in these parts is more like gunboat
   diplomacy than it is
like a soap opera, and I, who don't care, always get caught in
   the middle.
I belong there anyway. I'm going to someplace from someplace,
   and think in these terms.
I'm like a corset string that gets laced up but never tied. I've tried
   to be kind and helpful,
I know I have, but this is about something else. It's about me.
   And so I am never
off the hook; I look at others and reflect their embarrassed,
   sheepish grin: all right,
can I go home now? But I know deep in my heart of hearts I
   never will, will never want to,
that is, because I've too much respect for the junk we call living
that keeps passing by. Still, I might be tempted
to love or something if the right person came along, or the
   time were right;
I know I would. But I can't be tempted, so far. I'm too pure,
   like the nature
of temptation itself, and meantime the fans stand back and
   wonder what to admonish
the players with, and I sit here empty-handed, my breast teeming
with unexplained desires and acrostics. I'll go on like this. Take
   my glasses off.
And he says to me, I'll vote for you. Our roads are poor. And
   he laughed and said it.

Others were paying for this call which is why in the first place
no string of dignity remained, no mention of how they would
   reopen

the clogged career of someone just starting out in life who
    finds himself injured
and cannot explain why. There is blood everywhere—no
    wound,
just the sign of bleeding. If one had thought not to count
and tabulate every moment and expose it to the litmus of living
    in some way
I can't understand, then it would be all right for those bald
    men at the beach and some could
redeem the morning pledge and saunter off distractedly into
    the football fields
of dusk, and leave others alone, and welcome death as a
    diversion and they in turn could write
this down. Lakes and raccoons and unspotted moons would be
    the result.
As it is, everyone now finds himself inferior: repeat, everyone.
There is unrest; the shadow of the ball carries over.
I am left to repeat standards that have no particular relevance
    for me. I write
on the sides of buildings and on the backs of vehicles, and
    still
no nail divides the splinter from its neighbor, no fish swims
    close to another.
I have seen it all, and I write, and I have seen nothing.

Draw up a map right now—all of the notches are there.
If we cared like this it would be all right, wouldn't it, so why
doesn't somebody do something? In addition to which God
    doesn't want us to be stupid
or overreact, else why these chains? *We don't have much call for
    those*. We can
slip into the forest with it, and be bait. I know I'd be taking off
    nothing
if I let you believe otherwise, but it's all I can do. The season is
    even rude
to finish us off, but there is something we have to do, weather
    permitting,
across the street before the king is murdered.
Anyway, it was the commandant's word against mine.

The incubus awoke from a long, refreshing sleep.
A lot of people think they have only to imagine a siren for it to
    exist,
that the truth in fairy tales is somehow going to say them. I tend
    to agree
with dumb people who intervene, and are lost; actors of a
    different weakness
who explain the traceries of fallen leaves as models for our
    burgeoning etiquette,
a system that doesn't let us off the hook as long as we are truth
    and know it,
the great swing of things. And of course it may yet turn up.

I couldn't believe he said it. But that's the way we lived. It
    existed.
I've been at this stand for years and I think I see how the wool
is pulled over our eyes gradually, so that each of us thinks of
    ourselves as falling asleep
before it happens, then wakes to a pang of guilt: was it that
    other me again?
Why did I take my mind off the roast, as it turned
hypnotically on its spit, and now it's charred beyond recognition?

The multiplication of everything ran on years back, she said,
until two scraps had been assembled. Then it was up to the
    death-rattle.
There was a great conflict at that time.
There are canisters of cartridges from that era which do little to
    dispel
the legend of our rabid ancestors. Hey,
they're yours as well as mine, buster.
Yet once the funeral herbs were strewn there was peace of a sort.
    The evergreen
canopy became an anagram of itself, telling us much
about how gold was hidden in the old places, and spirits that
    came forth, irritated,
from their resting place and pulled the magic latch-string, and
    the door flew open
and there were the wolf and Red Riding Hood in bed together,
    except that the wolf

was really Grandma. Whew! What a relief! They don't write
  them that way anymore,
because the past is overlay. What a city this is! In what rich
  though tepid layers you can
almost detect the outline of your head and then
you know it's time to read on. When crisis comes, with
  embraceable side-effects,
let's put a roof on the thing before it sidles, world-bound,
toward an unconvincing other world. I'm more someone else,
  taking dictation
from on high, in a purgatory of words, but I still think I shall
  be the same person when I get up
to leave, and then repeat the formulas that have come to us so
  many times
in the past ("It's softer"), so faithfully that we extend them
like a sill, and they have an end, though a potentially hazardous
  one,
though that's about all we can do about it. Every film is an
  abidance. We are merely agents, so
that if something wants to improve on us, that's fine, but we
  are always the last
to find out about it, and live up to that image of ourselves as it
  gets
projected on trees and vine-coated walls and vapors in the
  night sky: a distant
noise of celebration, forever off-limits. By evening the traffic
  has begun
again in earnest, color-coded. It's open: the bridge, that way.

HOTEL LAUTRÉAMONT

For Pierre

Light Turnouts

Dear ghost, what shelter
in the noonday crowd? I'm going to write
an hour, then read
what someone else has written.

You've no mansion for this to happen in.
But your adventures are like safe houses,
your knowing where to stop an adventure
of another order, like seizing the weather.

We too are embroiled in this scene of happening,
and when we speak the same phrase together:
"*We used to have one of those,*"
it matters like a shot in the dark.

One of us stays behind.
One of us advances on the bridge
as on a carpet. Life—it's marvelous—
follows and falls behind.

And Forgetting

When I last saw you, in a hurry to get back and stuff,
we wore tape measures and the kids could go to the movies.

I loomed in that background. The old man looked strangely at
 the sea.
Always feet come knocking at the door
and when it isn't that, it's something or other
melancholy. There is always someone who will find you
 disgusting.
I love to tear you away from most interests
with besotted relish, and we
talked to each other. Worked before, it'll
work this time.

Look for the strange number at number seven. You see
I need a reason to go down to the sea in ships
again. How does one do that? The old man
came back from looking at it his replies were facile.
Rubber snake or not, my most valued fuchsia
sputtered in the aquarium, at once all shoulders
began to support me. We were travelling in an inn.
You were going to make what design an apple?

Then the hotel people liked us so,
it could have been before a storm, I lie back
and let the wind come to me, and it does, something
I wouldn't have thought of. We can take our meals
beside the lake balustrade. Something either does or
will not win the evidence hidden in this case.
The plovers are all over—make that "lovers," after all
they got their degrees in law and medicine, no one will persist
in chasing them in back lots, the sanded way
I came through here once.

These days the old man often coincides with me; his remarks
have something playful and witty about them, though they do not
hold together. And I, I too have something to keep from him:
something no one must know about.

I'm sure they'll think we're ready now.
We aren't, you know. An icebox grew there once.
Hand me the chatter and I'll fill the plates with cookies,
for they can, they must, be passed.

The Large Studio

It's one thing to get them to admit it,
quite another to get soap in your eye.
As long as I can remember I have been cared for,
stricken, like that. No one seems to scold.

I have had so many identity crises
in the last fifty years you wouldn't believe it.
Suffice it to say I am well,
if you like peacock's feathers on pianos
and cars racing their motors,
waiting for dates who never get done with doing their hair.
There have been so many velocipedes, millipedes,
and other words that I'm token senseless.
Just bring me one more drop of the elixir:
that's all I ask.

But when you saw how many colors things come in
it was going to be a long rest of the day.
"Enjoy your afternoon," he said, and it was roses
that you never get enough of and they make you sick.

It was kind of a cable
from which depended seven-branched candelabra
and feathers on the pine trunks
in that witch wood where nobody was supposed to stay—
say, do you think I could? Smell the roses?
Live like it was time?

Lo, it is time.
He raised the horn to his lips.
Such an abundance of—do you mind if I stay,
stay overnight? For the plot of a morrow
is needed to sort out the pegs in, meanwhile enough of me
lasts to give us the old semblance of a staring, naked truth,
with drinks, that we wanted, right?
And because a gray dustman slips by
unnoticed, a thousand cathartic things begin to happen.
Only we know nothing of these. Nothing can take their place.

Today I squeezed a few more drops of color
hoping to blot you out, your face I mean, and then this
extraordinarily tall caller asked if this was something I usually did.
Do I work against the plait often?
And sure, his boots were the right size. I replaced
my little brush and with it the thought of your coming

to absent me after dust and bougainvillea had chimed.
The answer was a nut.

And then there are so many harridans all over
the wall one is encouraged not toward a strict accounting
of all that is taking place, and we have washed, we are nice
for now. And the bowsprit (a word
I have never understood) comes undone, comes all over me, washes
my pure identity from me—help! In the meantime your friend has tunnelled
even as far as us, and it gets to be cold and damp
because the days are no longer making sense, are coming unlocked
in the tin aviary where we pinned them, and no one

right now has any good to say about what temperature
clashes with what other kind statistic we were all against
when it came out but who remembers that now?
Who was even engaged when we first thought of that?

I'll bite your toes, see you in the morning.
Place the canopy on that old chest
allowing for a few grunts and drizzles, please,
and not another word of what you spoke to your father.

The Garden of False Civility

Where are you? Where you are is the one thing I love,
yet it always escapes me, like the lilacs in their leaves,
too busy for just one answer, one rejoinder.
The last time I see you is the first
commencing of our time to be together, as the light of the days
remains the same even as they grow shorter,
stepping into the harness of winter.

Between watching the paint dry and the grass grow
I have nothing too tragic in tow.

I have this melting elixir for you, front row
tickets for the concert to which all go.
I ought to
chasten my style, burnish my skin, to get that glow
that is all-important, so that some
may hear what I am saying as others disappear
in the confusion of unintelligible recorded announcements.
A great many things were taking place that day,

besides, it was not the taxpayers
who came up to me, who were important,
but other guests of the hotel
some might describe as dog-eared,
apoplectic. Measly is a good word to describe
the running between the incoming and the outgoing tide
as who in what narrow channels shall ever
afterwards remember the keen sightings of those times,
the reward and the pleasure.
Soon it was sliding out to sea
most naturally, as the place to be.

They never cared, nor came round again.
But in the tent in the big loss
it was all right too. Besides, we're not
serious, I should have added.

Autumn Telegram

Seen on a bench this morning: a man in a gray coat
and apple-green tie. He couldn't have been over fifty,
his mild eyes said, and yet there was something of the
    ruthlessness
of extreme old age about his bearing; I don't know what.
In the corner a policeman; next, sheaves of wheat
laid carefully like dolls on the denuded sward,
prompting me to wish of dreaming you again. After the station
we never made significant contact again. But it's all right,
isn't it, I mean the telling had to be it. There was such fire

in the way you put your finger against your nostril
as in some buried sagas erupts out at one sometimes: the power
that is under the earth, no I mean in it. And if all the
disappointed tourists hadn't got up and gone away, we would
> still
be in each other's reserve, aching, and that would be the same,
wouldn't it, as far as the illustrations and the index were
> concerned?

As it is I frequently get off before the stop that is mine
not out of modesty but a failure to keep the lines of
> communication
open within myself. And then, unexpectedly, I am shown a dog
and asked to summarize its position in a few short, angular
> adverbs
and tell them this is what they do, why we can't count
on anything unexpected. The waterfall is all around us,
we have been living in it, yet to find the hush material
is just what these daily exercises force on us. I mean
the scansions of tree to tree, of house to house, and how
almost every other one had something bright to add
to the morass of conversation: not much, just a raised eyebrow
or skirt. And we all take it in, even laughing in the right places,
which get to be few and far between. Still it is a way of saying,
a meaning that something has been done, a thing, and hearing
> always
comes afterward. And once you have heard, you know,
the margin can excuse you. We all go back to being attentive
then, and the right signals concur. It stops, and smarts.

Notes from the Air

A yak is a prehistoric cabbage: of that, at least, we may be sure.
But tell us, sages of the solarium, why is that light
still hidden back there, among house-plants and rubber
> sponges?
For surely the blessed moment arrived at midday

and now in mid-afternoon, lamps are lit,
for it is late in the season. And as it struggles now
and is ground down into day, complaints
are voiced at the edges of darkness: look, it says,

it has to be this way and no other. Time that one seizes
and takes along with one is running through the holes
like sand from a bag. And these sandy moments
accuse us, are just what our enemy ordered,

the surly one on his throne of impacted
gold. No matter if our tale be interesting
or not, whether children stop to listen and through the rent
veil of the air the immortal whistle is heard,

and screeches, songs not meant to be listened to.
It was some stranger's casual words, overheard in the
    wind-blown
street above the roar of the traffic and then swept
to the distant orbit where words hover: *alone*, it says,

*but you slept. And now everything is being redeemed,
even the square of barren grass that adjoins your doorstep,
too near for you to see.* But others, children and others, will
when the right time comes. Meanwhile we mingle, and not

because we have to, because some host or hostess
has suggested it, beyond the limits of polite
conversation. And we, they too, were conscious of having
known it, written on the flyleaf of a book presented as a gift

at Christmas 1882. No more trivia, please, but music
in all the spheres leading up to where the master
wants to talk to you, place his mouth over yours,
withdraw that human fishhook from the crystalline flesh

where it was melting, give you back your clothes, penknife,
twine. And where shall we go when we leave? What tree is bigger
than night that surrounds us, is full of more things,
fewer paths for the eye and fingers of frost for the mind,

fruits halved for our despairing instruction, winds
to suck us up? If only the boiler hadn't exploded one
could summon them, icicles out of the rain, chairs enough
for everyone to be seated in time for the lesson to begin.

Still Life with Stranger

Come on, Ulrich, the great octagon
of the sky is passing over us.
Soon the world will have moved on.
Your love affair, what is it
but a tempest in a teapot?

But such storms exude strange
resonance: the power of the Almighty
reduced to its infinitesimal root
hangs like the chant of bees,
the milky drooping leaves of the birch
on a windless autumn day—

Call these phenomena or pinpoints,
remote as the glittering trash of heaven,
yet the monstrous frame remains,
filling up with regret, with straw,
or on another level with the quick grace
of the singing, falling snow.

You are good at persuading
them to sing with you.
Above you, horses graze forgetting
daylight inside the barn.

Creeper dangles against rock-face.
Pointed roofs bear witness.
The whole cast of characters is imaginary
now, but up ahead, in shadow, the past waits.

Hotel Lautréamont

1

Research has shown that ballads were produced by all of society
working as a team. They didn't just happen. There was no
    guesswork.
The people, then, knew what they wanted and how to get it.
We see the results in works as diverse as "Windsor Forest" and
    "The Wife of Usher's Well."

Working as a team, they didn't just happen. There was no
    guesswork.
The horns of elfland swing past, and in a few seconds
We see the results in works as diverse as "Windsor Forest" and
    "The Wife of Usher's Well,"
or, on a more modern note, in the finale of the Sibelius violin
    concerto.

The horns of elfland swing past, and in a few seconds
The world, as we know it, sinks into dementia, proving
    narrative passé,
or in the finale of the Sibelius violin concerto.
Not to worry, many hands are making work light again.

The world, as we know it, sinks into dementia, proving
    narrative passé.
In any case the ruling was long overdue.
Not to worry, many hands are making work light again,
so we stay indoors. The quest was only another adventure.

2

In any case, the ruling was long overdue.
The people are beside themselves with rapture
so we stay indoors. The quest was only another adventure
and the solution problematic, at any rate far off in the future.

The people are beside themselves with rapture
yet no one thinks to question the source of so much collective
    euphoria,

and the solution: problematic, at any rate far off in the future.
The saxophone wails, the martini glass is drained.

Yet no one thinks to question the source of so much collective euphoria.
In troubled times one looked to the shaman or priest for comfort and counsel.
The saxophone wails, the martini glass is drained,
And night like black swansdown settles on the city.

In troubled times one looked to the shaman or priest for comfort and counsel.
Now, only the willing are fated to receive death as a reward,
and night like black swansdown settles on the city.
If we tried to leave, would being naked help us?

3

Now, only the willing are fated to receive death as a reward.
Children twist hula-hoops, imagining a door to the outside.
If we tried to leave, would being naked help us?
And what of older, lighter concerns? What of the river?

Children twist hula-hoops, imagining a door to the outside,
when all we think of is how much we can carry with us.
And what of older, lighter concerns? What of the river?
All the behemoths have filed through the maze of time.

When all we think of is how much we can carry with us
Small wonder that those at home sit, nervous, by the unlit grate.
All the behemoths have filed through the maze of time.
It remains for us to come to terms with *our* commonalty.

Small wonder that those at home sit nervous by the unlit grate.
It was their choice, after all, that spurred us to feats of the imagination.
It remains for us to come to terms with our commonalty
And in so doing deprive time of further hostages.

4

It was their choice, after all, that spurred us to feats of the
 imagination.
Now, silently as one mounts a stair we emerge into the open
and in so doing deprive time of further hostages,
to end the standoff that history long ago began.

Now, silently as one mounts a stair we emerge into the open
but it is shrouded, veiled: we must have made some ghastly
 error.
To end the standoff that history long ago began
Must we thrust ever onward, into perversity?

But it is shrouded, veiled: we must have made some ghastly
 error.
You mop your forehead with a rose, recommending its thorns.
Must we thrust ever onward, into perversity?
Only night knows for sure; the secret is safe with her.

You mop your forehead with a rose, recommending its thorns.
Research has shown that ballads were produced by all of
 society;
Only night knows for sure. The secret is safe with her:
the people, then, knew what they wanted and how to get it.

On the Empress's Mind

Let's make a bureaucracy.
First, we can have long lists of old things,
and new things repackaged as old ones.
We can have turrets, a guiding wall.
Soon the whole country will come to look over it.

Let us, by all means, have things in night light:
partly visible. The rudeness that poetry often brings
after decades of silence will help. Many
will be called to account. This means that laundries

in their age-old way will go on foundering. Is it any help
that motorbikes whiz up, to ask for directions
or colored jewelry, so that one can go about one's visit
a tad less troubled than before, lightly composed?

No one knows what it's about anymore.
Even in the beginning one had grave misgivings
but the enthusiasm of departure swept them away
in the green molestation of spring.
We were given false information on which
our lives were built, a pier
extending far out into a swollen river.
Now, even these straws are gone.

Tonight the party will be better than ever.
So many mystery guests. And the rain that sifts
through sobbing trees, that excited skiff . . .
Others have come and gone and wrought no damage.
Others have caught, or caused darkness, a long vent
in the original catastrophe no one has seen.
They have argued. Tonight will be different. Is it better for you?

The Phantom Agents

We need more data re our example, earth—how it would
    behave in a
crisis, under pressure,
or simply on a day no one had staked out for unrest
to erupt. What season would fit its lifestyle
most naturally? Who would the observers, the control group be?

For this we must seek the answer in decrepit cinemas
whose balconies were walled off decades ago: on the screen
(where, in posh suburbia, a woman waits),
under the seats, in the fuzz and ancient vomit and
    gumwrappers;
or in the lobby, where yellowing lobby cards announce
the advent of next week's Republic serial: names

of a certain importance once, names that float
in the past, like a drift of gnats on a summer evening.

Who in the world despises our work
as much as we do? I was against campaigning again,
then my phone started ringing off the hook. I tell you . . .
But to come back to us, sanded down to the finer grain
and beyond—this is what books teach you, but also
what we must do. Make a name, somehow,
in the wall of clouds behind the credits, like a
twenty-one-vehicle pileup on a fog-enclosed highway.
This is what it means to be off and running, off
one's nut as well. But in a few more years,
with time off for good behavior . . .

From Estuaries, from Casinos

It's almost two years now.
The theme was articulated, the brightness filled in.
And when we tell about it
no wave of recollection comes gushing back—
it's as though the war had never happened.
There's a smooth slightly concave space there instead:
not the ghost of a navel. There are pointless rounds to be
    made.

No one who saw you at work would ever believe that.
The memories you ground down, the smashed perfection:
Look, it's wilted, but the shape of a beautiful table remains.
There are other stories, too ambiguous even for our purposes,
but that's no matter. We'll use them and someday,
a name-day,
a great event will go unreported.

All that distance, you ask, to the sun?
Surely no one is going to remember to climb
where it insists, poking about
in an abstract of everyday phrases? People have better

things to do with their lives than count how many
bets have been lost, and we all know the birds were here once.
Here they totter and subside, even in surviving.

In history, the best bird catchers were brought before the king,
and he did something, though nobody knows when.
That was before you could have it all
by just turning on the tap, letting it run
in a fiery stream from house to garage—
and we sat back, content to let the letter of the thing notice us,
untroubled by the spirit, talking of the next gull to fly away
on the cement horizon, not quibbling, unspoken for.

We should all get back to the night that bore us
but since that is impossible a dream may be the only way:
dreams of school, of travel, continue to teach and unteach us
as always the heart flies a little away,
perhaps accompanying, perhaps not. Perhaps a familiar spirit,
possibly a stranger, a small enemy whose boiling point
hasn't yet been reached, and in that time
will our desire be fleshed out, at any rate
made clearer as the time comes
to examine it and draw the rasping conclusions?

And though I feel like a fish out of water I
recognize the workmen who proceed before me,
nailing the thing down.
Who asks anything of me?
I am available, my heart pinned in a trance
to the notice board, the stone
inside me ready to speak, if that is all that can save us.

And I think one way or perhaps two; it doesn't matter
as long as one can slip by, and easily
into the questioning but not miasmal dark.
Look, here is a stance—
shall you cover it, cape it? I
don't care he said, going down all those stairs
makes a boy of you. And I had what I want
only now I don't want it, not having it, and yet it defers

to some, is meat and peace and a wooden footbridge
ringing the town, drawing all in after it. And explaining the
    way to go.

After all this I think I
feel pretty euphoric. Bells chimed, the sky healed.
The great road unrolled its vast burden,
the climate came to the rescue—it always does—
and we were shaken as in a hat and distributed on the ground.
I wish I could tell the next thing. But in dreams I can't,
so will let this thing stand in for it, this me
I have become, this loving you either way.

Cop and Sweater

It's about this undulation thing,
how we were all beginners to get in on it when it began.
Once that had happened, there was another face on things:
trees no longer came to the door; the seasons
were always "forgetting" to include you in the list—
that sort of thing.

Now those homeless hirsutes we call men
are on our backs, there is no breath out of the kingdom.
Sometimes a plan will come
to take one of them away
but there are long pauses in which grass grows tall
above the elementary wall
behind which bricks, adders and valuable prizes are combined.
It is that we have no mind:
each of us has sampled so many of the others',
and now the concert is sick.
No rain to stay away from any more,
only a darkling yew
that lets pass a few
into the waiting cemetery
to mingle with the military
whose buttons are celebratory.

A man could smash through this, drain the Slough of
    Despond,
build individual habitats for bird and person,
suitable, and folly too.

I believe it already happened
in some oasis of desert sand
where they are only waiting to know now
what went on back here, so as to leave
and plant other destinies in the star-filled track
the moon makes on water. Then release
happiness to the wineries and rain barrels
where so much could have happened, and does,
even today! Peace to the fawns,
the tied-back curtains. This is the living,
and if we are to be more than music, the waving
shawls and fanlights of a greater possibility
than mine, than us. So we see always.
From the universal boutique each of us stumbles on.

Musica Reservata

Then I reached the field and I thought
this is not a joke not a book
but a poem about something—but what? Poems are such odd
    little jiggers.
This one scratches himself, gets up, then goes off to pee
in a corner of the room. Later looking quite
stylish in white jodhpurs against the winter
snow, and in his reluctance to talk to the utterly
discursive: "I will belove less than feared . . ."

He trotted up, he trotted down, he trotted all around the
    town.
Were his relatives jealous of him?
Still the tock-tock machinery lies half-embedded in sand.
Someone comes to the window, the wave is a gesture proving
    nothing,

and that nothing has receded. One gets caught
in servants like these and must lose the green leaves,
one by one, as an orchard is pilfered, and then, with luck,
nuggets do shine, the baited trap slides open.
We are here with our welfare intact.

Oh but another time, on the resistant edge of night
one thinks of the pranks things are.
What led the road that sped underfoot
to oases of disaster, or at least the unknown?
We are born, buried for a while, then spring up just as
everything is closing. Our desires are extremely simple:
a glass of purple milk, for example, or a dream
of being in a restaurant. Waiters encourage us, and squirrels.
There's no telling how much of us will get used.

My friend devises the cabbage horoscope
that points daily to sufficiency. He and all those others go
    home.
The walls of this room are like Mykonos, and sure enough,
green plumes toss in the breeze outside
that underscores the stillness of this place
we never quite have, or want. Yet it's wonderful, this
being; to point to a tree and say don't I know you from
    somewhere?
Sure, now I remember, it was in some landscape somewhere,
and we can all take off our hats.

At night when it's too cold
what does the rodent say to the glass shard?
What are any of us doing up? Oh but there's
a party, but it too was a dream. A group of boys
was singing my poetry, the music was an anonymous
fifteenth-century Burgundian anthem, it went something like this:

"This is not what you should hear,
but we are awake, and days
with donkey ears and packs negotiate
the narrow canyon trail that is
as white and silent as a dream,

that is, something *you* dreamed.
And resources slip away, or are pinned
under a ladder too heavy to lift.
Which is why you are here, but the mnemonics
of the ride are stirring."

That, at least, is my hope.

Susan

Flotsam, I told you, isn't the same as jetsam.
The latter is "cast overboard by the master,
to lighten the load in time of distress."
And as for lagan, it's very different, it's
"debris washed up from the sea, the right to possess such debris,"
or "goods thrown into the sea with a buoy attached
in order that they may be found again."

See what I mean? It's folk art,
as the shy scrolls around the oarlocks announce:
free booty. For everybody. For everybody on that wet strand,
anyway. Waves race to deliver the goods.
I want to get one of those big bags of music
before it's too late, before the sale ends
and we're left without even a fashion
to stand tiptoe on. Though that's when I'll find out
at last what my profession is,
staunch the energy hemorrhaging from my career,
and get back to work again. You know something?

You have the name of a street, that holds
wiles, incantations, thread, in memory of
the mess that made us. You're indigent
as an apple. There is nothing of substance here:
pink sky, gray buildings, white flowers,
a cup that lacks a base . . .

Are they annuals or perennials?
What does it mean to be a bush that grows
some of the year and then rests
until we decide to celebrate it
into trope? She said how quickly that poet followed too,
and after that the peninsula was stilled.

The King

> So have I heard and do in part believe it.
> —*Hamlet*

I

And you forgave the bastards
for a time
and even so their revenge amazes you.
Alarms wilt in our noon, the winding
roads mark the changing grades of the hills,
hovel and monastery fall.

At last night approached:
"Use me as you will, my properties
are yours; hallow or besmirch them."
How come no god sees
the tears that ooze from under
rusty eyelids? The road is
pitted and incorrect but it happens
to lie in territory that is ours.
We shall chase
the heavenly
bandit:

handlebars
of snow anchor the tole
steeple, so much
that is not ours, and the tale
besides, of bedouins

who broke out of silence as a river
assaults a dam.
                    These, our cold
possessions. The gods are never quite forgotten.

                    2

In June the plaited sheaves are still
undreamt of; the highest
prophecy is only a moment gathering
in a sibyl's throat like a tuck in a shirt.
In that moment, live some of
winter's peace. We can be seen
wearing our oldest clothes when it
shifts abruptly to darkness's excitement:
falling down with bears and our tears
cleanse the past, stiff architecture
too tired to mope, the actual thing,
hinge the story wrests from sleep,
lit in daybreak. And fools and
sages can read this, and it concerns them all.

But there where
the bend in the river is unseen,
watch out! And over all the
slopes we used to think of as our own
millennial rails have pierced
to the aquifers. No explanation
is offered, and none necessary.

The Whole Is Admirably Composed

In rainy night all the faces look like telephones.
Help me! I am in this street because I was
going someplace, and now, not to be there is here.
So billows pile up on the shore, I hear
the mountains, the tide of autumn pulls in
ever thicker like a blanket of tears, and

people go about their business, unconcerned
if with another. And to those whose loneliness
shouts envy in my face, I say I am here on this
last floor, room of sobs and of grieving.
It's better you know to actually live it
since always some unexpected detail intervenes:
how he came to your house long ago
on a forgotten afternoon filled with birds' wings
and the standard that stood then has crumpled
yet another has taken its place:

high up in the ivy where the water from the
falls disappears amid smooth boulders,
this renown, this envy. And most of all
the challenge sleep brings, how it coaxes
the dunce out of his lair, how meals are shared
and whispers passed around. Then the real boy
comes to you like a kite on wind that is flagging
through the needle hole of the hourglass—
as though this were the summit.

There is more to inconstancy than you will
want to hear, and meanwhile the streets have dried,
tears been put away until another time, and a smile
paints the easy vapor that rises from all
human activity. I see it is time to question trees,
thorns in hedges, again, the same blind investigation
that leads you from trap to trap before bargaining
to forget you. And this is only a bump
on the earth's surface, casting no shadow, until
the white and dark fruits of the far pledge be
wafted into view again, out of control, shimmering
in the dark that runs off and is collected
in oceans. And the map is again wiped clean.

By Forced Marches

the prodigal returns—to what mechanical
consternation, din of slaughtered cattle.
It was better in the wilderness—there at least
the mind wanders daintily as a stream meanders
through a meadow, for no apparent reason.
And one can catch snatches of the old cries
that were good before this place began
on a day some seventeen centuries ago.

We have reached the tip of a long breakwater
dividing the lake from the deeper and silenter ship channel.
A still-functioning beacon flashes there, proud
of its purpose and its reflection in the night.
There is nothing to do except observe the horizon,
the only one, that seems to want to sever itself
from the passing sky.

Now the links we had left behind
must be reassembled, since this is the land we came from.
It is no place for the squeamish. But as a finger triggers
a catapult, so is the task of the day discharged.

There were many of us at the stream's tip.
I squatted nearby trying to eavesdrop on the sailors'
conversations, to learn where they were going. Finally
one comes to me and says I can have the job if I want it.
Want it! and so in this prismatic whirlpool I am renewed
for a space of time that means nothing to me.

And there is dancing under the porches—so be it.
I am all I have. I am afraid. I am left alone.
Yet it is the way to a certain kind of satisfaction.
I kiss myself in the mirror. And children are kind,
the boardwalk serves as a colorful backdrop
to the caprices acted out, the pavanes and chaconnes
that greet the ear in fragments, melodious
ones it must be said. And the old sense of a fullness
is here, though only lightly sketched in.

Autumn on the Thruway

Say that my arm is hurting.
Say that there are too many buts in the sky today.
Say that we need each other off and on to see how it feels.

After which we'll promise to see to it, see that it
Doesn't happen this way again so that we may
Do something about it when it does happen.

Or that sincerity cover us with a cloak of shame
While our clothes are drying by the campfire this night
Of nights that means to go on and prepackage some of the
    original flame

In order to sell it so as to recoup some of the losses that
Started us on this path, repay the original investors.
How sweet then the bargain, the transaction. And you fear
    nothing

Notable, the skylight has been activated already.
Best to stay around admiring the new look on things.
Invent a new hat. Put on a growing season, staple the others

To the door hidden in the wilderness. And the losses be ours,
Not someone's in the sun, slut of some, weeping pointedly.
And the blinders—I have signed for them too.

Studies show it hanging in frost, in pajamas, up in the air
And a cerberus basks underneath, its own snowhole round
As an apple in belief. Water the tree in this area and it

Never expedites how much we were hoping to receive out of
What was promised originally, yes, traced on the tracing paper
Of some mood one day. We can never actually account for it

Or how lush its primitivism, in the beginning,
How steep the wall of its veil over face, or how
Far you had come, little

Spinner that that's all right now. How we come to be seen.
Yet we know we must pay

Not use up any money in between, for it

To become us, and then all lost, a second time
But in a time the merry neutral wisdom is gathered, to be
    sewed

Into the lining and you must cherish it there.
Never believe a false passport to the land of chocolate and bees'
Reasons and be forelost, freedom from a refuge
That took over once you began to get used to it. No, this
    other

Hand is the wish I bury and keep for you, really the only one
Beside me long, into a tense's dense conditions
And then you tear, tearing: O how long was it going to be
    for us

Until the scenery lay quiet like a beloved dog's head under the
    hand,

For what was moving to be moving, for it to have courted an
    aspirin
And lost face at the quarry edge. Hand me that theogony
And then get lost, don't read me my rights, please get out of
    here

Until I can think and then two more of us, for a day, come to
    where we two
Parted and it is on a day. I can't think
How it completes my thought but I never knew how that was
    going to begin.

Nor did it mean anything for anyone growing up then.
We were merely—"sentimental" about describes it, yet that can
    too be loving
In one's breath, provided other people also move around in it,

Disturbing it. It's no Volga but it's vast and dreary and it
    moves,
Keeps on moving. And so it is a show window at Christmas,
Brimming with lights, with more suggested memories than it
    could deal with, and we,

Well we help it along for our sakes, which is to say not very
    much.
We thought about it so often. How many figures I had
    rehearsed
In the garret where you could see your breath, whomping

My sides from the cold. Now, to have written it, merely,
Seems tepid, a kind of clashing conundrums thing, and
People walk out in the middle of it, rustling programs, tears
    spatter

The hateful embroidered lace, O why not tear off that Juliet
    cap and throw it
With the papers of dubious cleanliness, anything so
As to avoid the recrimination of a look that says you did just
    what you did,

No other, and how is it now for you. Stupid spruces tremble at
Stucco corners and why is this not to be attributed to the hand
Of some vengeful but well-meaning deity too? Why are we
    alone

Held responsible for the way everything gets to look, why are
    we admonished
Every time we walk out and see things starting to be the way
    again
They probably were in the near past, just yesterdays ago, when
    we haven't changed,

Only coarsened, merely from staying around a few too many
    seconds, an expression
That hardens while the photographer tries to focus on it, that's
    enough

For today, this day at least. And how much farther he tries to
    follow when you

Have passed under the willows' swinging garlands, past the
    sweep
Of the stream where you sink in up to the ankles, on to the
    drought and out,
And he says, what a fine time, why how much to be here,

Only you don't come round. Please send somebody to finish
Or our nails may be chipped, our locusts blighted, our
    hoarfrost dispelled by a breath
That who wants to enjoy the risk of? Not him. Not me,
    certainly,

Though what you ask for is not infrequently what you get.
Under an upturned cartwheel hat she looked up, so solemnly
    silly
That for a moment you had to forget to outtake her. And her
    drink needed replenishing.

So in the long run all of it takes us far from the sea of what we
    were as individuals
And more from the time when all that mattered, mattered as to
    a single
Individual too old for the part, though a pair. Now it's possible
    to see

How far apart we were on most issues, and the European cooks
    it differently,
Besides, and set against the plainness of American lives it melts
    like a wall and
Rivulets, runnels drain off it as though from a roof, rushing to
    join you

In the gutter, and where the growing begins askance
This time. No more frankness, it is apt to cloud, to
Give off steam in the time it takes to distinguish one accent
    from the truth.

So the lovely second theme is somewhat marred
By buried memories of revenge, and when the time comes to
Reinvent the initial phase, why, all but grinning stupidly, it hands

Its cards to another player and takes off in the direction of the pond.
Wait! But another's daring solution will never rescue twice the omen
That hankered for more polity, and beside us though we were of no mind

To reckon it into what we were being elaborated by. Myrtles fall,
Crape drapes. The spear
Is slowly lowered as for the last curtain.

You've got to decide what your name is going to be,
What to do about it. By what ring we are decoded. Tangles
Of snake-grass and more, though it wouldn't

Do to talk about it, would it? Why, since I have come home from school,
Why must I intend it? Who is the person who wants this? How many
Guests has he invited, where do they come from? Who isn't

In on the trail? Now his men have departed. They have been sent away. Does that
Mean they won't be back? Do we ever avoid our own reckoning, even
When the moist, mild sky smiles and the portcullis is up,

The drawbridge lowered, the road delighted to wind
Into a newly dapper landscape, pointedly new, and it runs away
With us, sweeps us up into something, some way to be

With pleasure and not be too long about it so the mood stays
But isn't fixed? If only I'd known what I was getting into
That day in Arizona, I'd have taken another detour, but you see

When you see gravel, you think roadbed, automatically,
    forgetting how little
It takes to set anybody off, buzzing into dreams. Old papers
    and
Memoirs. Feet under the desk. A tiny girl who smiles and is
    prepared.

What year was that? Who was in power then? By what
Sin have we been burned? And did the president point
His pointer at the blackboard to the word "articulate," and did

Those feet reiterate the premise, damp down through the ages,
    fresh, yes,
But so ancient, like an ague. Teeth chattering, all proceeded to
    the dump.
After all, it would be time soon.

After all, nobody knows how to make this any more. You can't
Find us in their lounges. Soon, soon, however, the overpass
    takes us home.
The leaves are spent, lying in a ditch. Girls gone. The music,
    the horses took off.

The Little Black Dress

All that we are trying most defiantly to unravel
is waiting, close to the path. Yes,
but the pace is both relaxed and insistent,
a swimming up from under. Your plan sounds fine.

I knew a brunette once in Omaha,
he said, and that struck us as news. He hadn't
been out of the truck long. On the dank ground the new
willow leaves lay, a reproof to him and us.
Why can't the clay bind us more firmly still,
until he can read,
get something out of these notations that arrive
every day, like letters, O not in the empty house.

Part of the Superstition

Help, when it came, came from an unexpected place.
It was so nice he couldn't sleep. Our rooms darken
with every new place of experience. All roses
admit this, and life stays on, fidgeting, their dream
disappointed, on the run, and it's your fault,
who never had the courage to know nothing and
    simultaneously
be attentive. That's where the secret comes in,
and, as you might expect, it's quite unhandy,
especially if you're in a coma. Now I don't want
to have to speak to you again; we're on the way down,
that much is assured, and leggy growth has to stop somewhere,
at least it did in my day. About what colors to buy:
this is something each dean and priest decides
for himself, and then they melt and turn into the jackpot,
which is a little disturbing. Don't squirm,
however, there are other houses on this road to peace
we can actually live in, as a snail its shell,
or bird pants. Then a calend grabs your hand
and tugs you into the future, and that's about all the space
there is left. Wipe your nose. Don't fudge
the horizon or it will come clattering down
on us like the earthquake at Lisbon, but always,
be brave. Yet these are old wives' tales,
in truth; nothing insists you believe in them
except as dreams, which permeate the background
of our day like colored raindrops, and so go away
before too long. Many have turned back
at this point; the trials, the trails, are thistles,
inherently unrewarding. Yet those who wish to play
say many are pleased to be in that day:
pleased, and not a little scared, but from where
will peace come if not from those beetling crags?

So many varied stimuli, and I
was nigh to frantic, as it may believe you,
and has for other hosts. Yet these passions, arrayed
like infantry, continue to absorb and confuse

by turns. No use shouting about waste, it was
a necessary corner in your apartment that couldn't be filled
by anything but its own besottedness. And we think, when we
do play, that a special aggravation
has sunk its beak in us like Prometheus' eagle,
yet all proceeds from an inability and desire to win
leading to narrow channels and bogus expectations.
Cut short the customary peroration:
its wings soar o'er us still, or will be, and we, we'll
have a hand in sorting them out, strand
by tinted strand, and be sure a life will arise swollen from this:
a vacant place in the story. My glory
when it comes will resemble yours in its feinting
and the way it orders waiters with soiled aprons around.
We can be back for much of it. Haste, arise;
a big thing is happening to everyone. We were so prudent
in our clothes back there it got forgotten, blurred
with the wet lawn. And when the president
looked out his window he saw it, and ran to tell the
    vice-president,
and so a compact was kept. I sure wish
it were possible to pole oneself more than a few feet off this
    shore,
but it seems to want us. And I can't explain how a muskrat
would ever know about such a thing, yet it did.

So there were times in between like the seasons
and the times between them when peaches fall,
and dancers sift across the stage like leaves,
and these are dark times. Only remember that the figure
worked deep into the fabric implodes there;
has a next, a resting place. It is from the multiplication
of similar wacko configurations that theses do arise
to attest the efficacy of this castor oil,
this medicine. And if why we want to go away
is as plain as the nose on your face, the buried village,
cut out of rose-petal limestone, is still standing. Haply
some faith trickles out of it, and is not lost
in the glittering grass, but persists to become a torrent,
then a turret, somewhere else. For there is a key,

and it leads to your door. Yet it is only repetition, something
the seasons like a lot. And as you get up to go you mutter,
and that's it!—the fortunate crisis that was always
going to stave us off, and explain so much
about car wrecks, and postage stamps and the like.
Farewell in the rain; it is surely lucky to know
as much as we do, and not to know as much
as we do. Or were taught was proper. Papers
will explain it, music it. That's a promise.

The Art of Speeding

And when some sidle awkwardly,
why, the grove is green again. There is more than enough
    catfood
for two, she said. And I think I belong in this prism.
Day means more than luck itself to me,
but I shall be forgotten
on a shore made monotonous by the inverted hulls of rowboats.
There is more than enough time for me,
sympathy too. I'm the cap and bells that don't belong.
A free-lance artist. The last and first of the romantics.

Sometimes a suppler season weaves pliant straws
into a crown for no one in particular.
This hiatus is my legacy:
a patterned map whose symmetries invite exploration
yet in the end repel the cold traveler, wrapped
in gray at the end of the mole.
He sees farther into the rising banister of the city's rage
and shuts out all ivory memories like pestilence.
Indeed he is the naked forager.

But when tomatoes are ripe and girls
don't mind, and the sun is civil again, then
look in your shoeboxes for sheaves of snapshots
that came over us and were here, wild as the wilderness.
We forgot who was talking to us on the quay.

It just might have been a distinguished stranger.
Now his visor keeps us from noticing
his general appearance, but genially we all say
how much we have loved this place, how gay
are the receipts. All we have to do is stay.

Yet more pictures are involved than the accountant
realizes, moaning over his headache: sometimes it agrees
with us to say we do. And then the game is darker;
no one pauses in the rain.

American Bar

We bake a dozen kinds of muffins every day
yet we are cold and disquieting at heart.
I fear for his sciatica, though
we were never lovers.
Let me memorialize this mattress, M.
le Comte, he will be decent
in this fog that emanates from everything
though the air is fresh and sunny. Thought
about wandering down to the river to have a
look at the water. It always has so much to say,
more than the upended rain barrel in its day
had. See the monkey in its cage.
Bright eyes are feasting again and again.

In the casual track of a zipper my penis
once got stuck, and it's been like that ever since:
feet stop where no snare lives, the best
is to die down and desist. Perhaps life is better
near the Arctic Circle, where the buildings are plain
and no trees sing. One can feel totally indoors.
The wireless plays a lanky tune;
there are spots on the wall from the moisture
you either keep out or keep in. I forget which,
and what a bird looks like. The winter night drones on
for centuries, and what keeps us at peace is actually

the sight of an empty cage
and a few children's drawings of it.

My, we have raced to be equivocally here
and have invented what sign? Off of what do we climb
to the lower level, what compact fleet of stairs
is nestled here? Or did we bowdlerize each other's delirium
in fear of having the last word, and it frightened *us* off the page?
In any case have a ripping good time. The boars
will be here around then, as you know.

From Palookaville

> "Death cancels all engagements."
> —Clifton Webb, in the movie *Laura*

The midgets stand on giants who stand on midgets
in Palookaville
that day of storm notwithstanding and it still takes one
on out to the "farther reaches" where boys play and maids bay
at the moon
in my Palookaville
where the stench of farts drenches outside irony with the dust
    of snow
where all is served up right
to blond kids in history books on the gothic outskirts
where everything gets unravelled just right
where you can see a coincidence coming for miles down the
    valley
along the trestle when the snow the femurs the cries
demur and act unwise
at a time when centers shatter in strict unison
when doubt is in the call of the fox
and the sunsets are like weddings

I came here of my own accord
from Djakarta
I'm as old as you are and dare to say so
but the falling liaisons spat out like miles of thread

are the lining of time's one easy lesson
the shocks deep and narrow like crevasses dog teams fly over
over and around
aiming no way to please
and it does in the arrested quickness of the visit, task—
even life is the least bit pejorative
but not the costumes the calendar
the trivia the painted trappings
to come undone
in your embrace and that's the word

You were sent for and that is all
no word on why some became
the anvil
and from here all that runs is dust
or consommé there was fear smeared again on the walk
and for two consecutive days
we go out on it it's pretty safe
so far
on the fifth day a bank fails there are great falls
and iodine in the little house
it smells more like an accord this time
and then there were birds you know too soft
this time for much
of an answer
and they came were there under steel arcades
the night brings its business along
stalls as though a feint saved the day one
other time and now it's horses all around for anybody that
    thinks
they've got a contusion or a monopoly
surely it was warm faces all round

The accents are distant as bells in that other hometown
the stories often gory
tell why please the accents and your own personal vignette
    came up
without a number and no one explained the cause
a dim musicale in some small room
folded under netting as though the crows stood by

to watch
under the felt cushion something impolite zoomed
it was suggested that we all carry away
our traces that we dispose of them "thoughtfully"
so as not to leave any bones of an argument around
for others mauling traces
in bushes
black ones riding with white snow a pure, defined drop
of atheism and it arches out too wide, too near the
    circumference
of the pier too much to say for what an old man did
on a recent day and what if it comes round
on a recent day and what if we all did
and who shoved the pace of the thermometer
on an outing who shamed the toaster
who is to say

Another Example

    Of our example, earth,
    we know the star-shaped universe:
    divisions,
             somewhere,
                        of July streets.
    Is it a bucket you sit in
              or on?
    How they led us past the fence
    The one horse was mortified.

    But it's unhealthy, you say
    we must have another example,
    just one.

    What's wanted is faces in windows
    screams that went away a long time ago.
    What says to recall them?

To be revived like paper ants
and then endure the long vacuum of pre-eternity
and still be allowed to buy something
on the station platform?

The train is turning away—
There are no familiar quotations.

Here, put some on a plate, he said. That's the way.

Avant de quitter ces lieux

They watch the blue snow.
It is the fifth act in someone else's life,
but here, on Midway Island, reefs and shoals interfere
with that notion. That nothing so compact
as the idea of a season is to be allowed
is the note, for today at least. It is Tuesday morning.
They sing a duet of farewell
to their little table, and to themselves as they were
when they sat at it. Noon intersects with fat birds
the rhythm of dishes in the cupboard. My love,
he seems to say, is this the way it is for you? Then we shall have
    to leave
these shabby surroundings for others, but first
I want to plant a kiss like a star
on your forehead. The ships are knocking together at the
    quayside,
the lanyards struck, there is more moving
than we were intended for, as we clear out
nodding to the caryatids we pass. Perhaps they will sing to us.

And in a summer house somewhere in Russia
a clematis soaks up the heat. One can think without breathing
of the blue snow that invades the fields, a curse some obscure
    ancestor
once let fall and now it's the custom, duly serenaded each
    season

before the apples rust
and the idea of winter takes over, to be followed in short order
by the real thing.
If all of us could lead lives of razoring things out of the
    newspaper,
filing them on pincushions . . . but no. There is the father
and morning to be dealt with, and after that the students
    arrive.
The rhythm is broken up among them.
That was a cold year, but not
the last. It will be remembered.

Why is it you always ask me this, and this:
is there no question behind the arras of how we now meet
seconding each other's projects, our emotions? Or is that too
    weak
as a question, though strong enough as an affirmation, so that
    we again go out
from each other. One shades one's eyes automatically, though
    the sky
is dark. "We have no place to go" (the fifteenth
major situation), and if God decrees we like each other,
    someday
we will meet on a stone up there, and all will not be well,
but that is useful. Great rivers run into each other and graves
have split open, the tyranny of dust plays well, there is
so little to notice. Besides we have always known each other.

Except for that it was automatically the century
before this one. Thus we are made aware of the continuity
of times that were, and time itself is revealed
not as a series of rooms but a single corridor
stretching into the truth: an alpine pasture, with a few goats
and, in the distance, a hovel. It is high noon. Dinorah,
who has lost her goat, sings the mad scene for which her life
has been a preparation, sings it out of daylight, out of the
    outcropping
of rock overhead, out of the edelweiss and cowslips.
Now it is the turn of the mountain god

but he refuses to play. The blue snow returns. Shopfronts are
   boarded up.

Still one should never be in a hurry to end, to contrast the ending
with the articulations that have gone before. True, these are
   merely space,
but one in which lives can take on a single and sparing
   sharpness
that is an education in itself. This is one life
as we thought it over, and there are other songs, some too true
   to mention,
others of little weight, optional, cut from most editions
but waiting silently in place where they are expected.
The story falls, mountains conspire, brooks hesitate,
the storm endures.

The White Shirt

Suddenly all is quiet again.
I want to talk about something.
It's not that easy. Pay no attention.

No amount of conservation affects
the wrinkled gourd. The dry shore.
A combustion engine
means it's not working.

Thing of the past,
you in your limits,
growing,
my working place.
The band is up.

But if it wasn't for changes,
where would we go? Just
having the illusion is enough.
But charge them for it;
serve immediately.

Baked Alaska

I

It will do. It's not
perfect, but it will do
until something better comes along.

It's not perfect.
It stinks. How are we
going to get out of having it
until something comes along, some ride
or other? That will return us
to the nominative case, shipshape and easy.

O but how long are you going to wait
for what you are waiting for, for
whatever is to come? Not
for long, you may be sure.
It may be here already.
Have you checked the mailbox today?

Sure I have, but listen.
I know what comes, comes.
I am prepared
to occupy my share of days,
knowing I can't have all of them. What is, is
coming over here to find you
missing, all or in part. Or you read me
one small item out of the newspaper
as though it would stand for today.
I refuse to open your box of crayons. Oh yes, I know
there may be something new in some combination
of styles, some gift in adding the addled
colors to our pate. But it's just too mush
for me. It isn't that I necessarily
set out on the trail of a new theory
that could liberate us from our shoes as we walked.
It's rather that the apartment comes to an end
in a small, pinched frown of shadow. He walked

through the wood, as a child. He will walk
on somebody's street in the days that come after.
He's noted as a problem child, an ignoramus;
therefore why can you not accept him in
your arms, girdled with silver and black
orchids, feed him everyday food?

Who says he likes cuttlebone?
But you get the idea, the idea
is to humor him for what vexations
may hatch from the stone attitude
that follows and clears the head, like a sneeze.
It's cozy to cuddle up to him,
not so much for warmth as that brains
are scarce, and two will have to do.
It takes two to tango,
it is written, and much
in the way of dragons' teeth after that,
and then the ad hoc population that arises
on stilts, ready to greet or destroy us, it
doesn't matter which, not quite yet, at least.

Then when the spent avenger
turns tail you know it had all to do with
you, that discharge of fortunes
out of firecrackers, like farts. And who's to say
you don't get the one that belongs to you?

But he speaks, always, in terms of perfection,
of what we were going to have
if only he hadn't gotten busy and done something about it,
    yea,
and turned us back into ourselves
with something missing. And as oarsmen
paddle a scull downstream with phenomenal speed,
so he, in his cape, queries:
Is the last one all right? I know
I keep speaking of the last one, but is it all right?
For only after an infinite series
has eluded us, does the portrait

of the boy make sense, and then such a triangular one:
he might have been a minaret, or a seagull.
He laid that on the car's radiator
and when you turned around it is gone.

II

Some time later, in Provence,
you waxed enthusiastic about the tail
piece in a book, gosh how they
don't make them like that in this century, any more.
They had a fiber then that doesn't exist now.
That's all you can do about it.
Sensing this, in the sopping diaspora, many a tanglefoot
waits, stars bloom at scalloped edges
of no thing, and it begins to
bleed, like a bomb or bordello.
The theme, unscathed,
with nothing to attach it to.

But like I was saying, probably some of us were encouraged
by a momentary freshness in the air
that proved attractive, once we had dwelt in
it, and bathed for many years
our temples in its essence. Listen, memory:
do this one thing for me
and I'll never ask you again for anything else:
just tell me how it began! What
were the weeds that got caught in the spokes
as it was starting up, the time the brakeshaft split
and about all the little monsters that were willing to sit
on the top of your tit, or index finger.
How in the end sunshine prevailed—
but what was that welling in between?
those bubbles
that proceeded from nowhere—surely there must be a source?
Because if there isn't it means that we haven't paid
for this ticket, and will be stopped at the exit-gate
and sent back on a return journey through ploughed fields
to not necessarily the starting place, that house

we can hardly remember, with the plangent
rose-patterned curtains.

And so in turn he who gets locked up is lost
too, and must watch a boat nudge the pier
outside his window, forever, and for aye,
and the nose, the throat will be stopped
by absolutely correct memories of what did
we think we were doing when it all began happening,
down the lanes, across vales, out into the open city street.

And those it chooses can always say
it's easy, once you learn it, like a language,
and can't be dislodged thereafter.
In all your attractive worldliness, do you consider
the items crossed off the shopping list,
never to breathe again until the day
of bereavement stands open and naked like a woman
on a front porch, and do those you hobnob
with have any say or leverage in the matter?
Surely it feels like a child's feet propel us along

until everyone can explain.
Hell, it's only a ladder: structure
brought us here, and will be here when we're
honeycombs emptied of bees, and can say
that's all there is to say, babe; make it a good one
for me.

III

And when the hectic
light leaches upward into rolls of dark cloud,
there will no longer be a contrast between thinking
and daily living. Light will be something even,
if remorseful, then. I say, swivel
your chair around, something cares, not the lamps purling
in the dark river, not the hot feet on the grass,
nor the cake emerging from the oven, nor the silver
trumpets on the sand: only a lining

that dictates the separation of this you from this some other,
and, in memorializing, drools. And if the hospice
gets over you this will be your magpie, this old hat,
when all is said, and done. No coffee, no rolls—
only a system of values, like the one printed
beside your height as it was measured as you grew
from child to urchin to young adult
and so on, back into the stitched wilderness
of sobs, sighs, songs, bells ringing, athirst
for whatever could be discerned in the glacier:
tale, or tragedy, or talc, that backlit
these choices before we learned to talk,
and so is a presence now, a posture like a chimney
that all men take to work with them
and that all see with our own eyes just
as the door is shutting, O shaft of light, O excellent, O irascible.

Private Syntax

The obligation I have assumed is an unprepossessing one.
I'll be glad to get back to the city of painted scenery

and horse-drawn carts, before resuming the march toward
new standards of equality. Rain washes in the chimney;

the immense task-force that drew us out into unwise
    confidences
repeats the crescendo in neon: this is about as sanguinary

as it gets, so why tremble on the edge? Leap, if you must,
only don't blame the processus for what you brought on
    yourself,

tarring others too with the brush of a rabid potential music
that cares for itself and dislikes oil-aureoled puddles

as much as it does human experimentation. Whose style
    degrades your

ruminating on it all until you think you've come up with
    something:

anything, don't share it. Don't be special, silly or civil.
In time grapes fatten. Waves accept one more chore, or shore,

and everything gets done, is distributed equally into your plan
of reducing the workload and actually making some money, for
    a change.

Not Now but in Forty-Five Minutes

Anyway, sleep came that day
not so that you'd notice
what was silhouetted against what—was it the pillow or the
    bags
over by that glass of water?
I mean we're not getting into androgyny?
You better believe it. Those towers say
the gift of day is wholesale
to men
under the awning, the annoyed shopkeeper's
gesture of putting something right
after you've touched it can be
believed

No it was an altogether more interesting case.
We often said throw out the baby with the bathwater
eavesdroppers seldom hear good of themselves
the plant stinks
lick honey through a cleft stick.
Other than that it is no premise to you
in time it will be calm be gay
stay away from others' questions
they will have you before time too
with the pilgrim's classic good taste
I'm spattered I am brunch

NOT NOW BUT IN FORTY-FIVE MINUTES

I know how to solve
you I love you
with that the cat
walked last into an open barrier
neither time nor spires were demeaning

I know I planned
it me to be
all over you
I thank a thousand dunces for this webbed, precious
gift of knowledge
to no man's height I am authorized
to stay here after the handcuffs
and the lard I am chilled
by the reflection
of you

and the stain stays
It was on the beautiful part
must now be read with it
I am all apple
to thank
you

No one knows what we do when we're apart
A veil veins the days of our separate living
when we're in trouble we're back in class
but now to do those tedious sums
requires having loved and in the course of it
shrugged
and if they came by that schoolhouse on such-and-such a day
everything would be normal from the dozing stove
to the pillar of milk on the door

and we should all get together afterward
put our other concerns
on the table
and we should all french kiss get elected
not to be trouble
to stand up in reason's roar

In Another Time

Actually it was because you stopped,
but there was no need to,
the forest wasn't too dark, and yet,
you stopped and then went on a little way
as though to embarrass the idea of stopping.
By then the everything
was involved in night:
cars were discharging patrons in front of theaters
where light swelled, then contracted
into tiny slivers. Then listened.

A kind of powdered suburban poetry fits
the description, and isn't
precisely it. There was no briskness,
yet things got quickly done.
The cartoon era of my early life
became the printed sheaves and look:
what's printed on this thing?
Who knows what it's going to be?
Meanwhile it gasps like a fish on a line.

It is no doubt a slicker portrait
than you could have wished, yet all
the major aspects are present:
there you bent down under the waterfall
as though to read little signs
in the moss and it all came to life
but quietly. There is no way to transcribe it.

Withered Compliments

Have a care lest
the jewelled words of others
force you to act, you too: "Delicious.
I love you. Goodbye." For in that autumn
after speech strange desires stir.

It is not enough
to have kept one's hands to oneself,

not enough to see them cheating
and take no action. It is not enough,
finally, to turn
and walk back to the house
where disappointed parents wait, not
enough to smile through abuse and gather them
into the big, hectic embrace.

These days there are other worries to assess.
How did that band of shrubbery grow so sharp
that the rest of the landscape is dim,
pleading ignorance? And the arborist has other
things on his mind, as does the land-surveyor.
If you too could see that far out to sea
your forces might crumble. They, though,
take it in stride, but that too might be a warning:
earth, air, tire, water,

let all stand, be around
as much as we wrap around them
at day's outer limits.
A kind of slow afternoon here, too.
The aftershock holds no surprises.

The Wind Talking

Faithful I keep coming over to address the issues,
the ills no man can stomach, or anything that *feels* warm,
less bumptious and froward perhaps, speeding,
on wounded calendar, and faithful you coming to me ouch
plans pleasure no person can resist, the time
to roll out of bed, run out the white door, into the sickness
of the apt. Approach. Wait—
too many trees are tied to this, for desire's
ambitions to become known. I'll say to you

how usually around you are and my coming frequently
fits. Young warriors are aghast—no one
had foreseen it. That just keeps making book, into play,
the play of the weather, where snowballs flew across the stage.
The cast was furious. Don't explain, there's nothing you can do
except stay out of harm's way, waiting, in a doorway—
I like you here, and by the woodpile, and think
it's after something, but no one came. And the door was
    slightly ajar,
too, it could be considered closed. Some welcome! Maybe
you are older and more spirited than I think, let's
have a try, go on, the crab missile told
how it was all just plain dust and guts. Any can hold him,
I've tried, and now you are back. The volume
of his chant extended me, to be with you, falling off, in the life.

Night promontories can be sticky there is a whole other suite
    of
glabrous thingamabobs adhering to the minutes of my vacuum.
Then to get down and crawl it, into the unimagined spaces
    that
were, it's true, there. I still address it. Like a lost man.
The oldest sewer in captivity. I can shrink it too,
and desperately bawling you knows no man's coming to lick it,
be beside it, extrapolate us on the ledge. We're caring.
Shoo, that's all-important now. Under the legs
of this chair I can see into the runnels. Midnight's near.
Let's doff with the clothes, lay on burlap
over granite. Ssh. He hears. The mouse's wits list
all somebody isn't going to tell us about the improbable
financial backing of the adventure just as it sinks. The lights
go out at sea. Try a waltz then.
The disease of timing's etched itself into the very skull
of the churl as plodding she shifts from Yule berries
to centerpiece, nothing more's in my craw.
How did I come over the last time? I'm all confused.
Besides, you got me when I was just out, and you were all
    going to say
I waited, plaited at the formal garage, all despair
and too tidy to come out. But I do. I'm like the

bashful bull, my bicycle has hindsight, my ass is clean,
I'm being raked over the coals by an uncertain
hand ceremoniously, the curtain's a riot, it could all

be badly blistered. Look, I have a vacuum cleaner.
In the janitor's hand some prurient
fun must be planned and I'll go where the washer decides me
into small dovecot openings that are for the birds. Please,
accept kindly the running board of my road
to you, the lucky dusk that was over Fifth Avenue. They
    chanted
variously, the lights separated into grave reminders.
Well I am coming up too and don't much like
your progress with the waves. Seems they are dividers,
or something, something that was cherished long before
you and the odious others came to think about it.
Come to think of it I know that man's name, but not his
    station, but I am
working on all those orders. If we have to come, he can come.

Meanwhile before the fire one putters and absorbs so much
of the floor it's like returning to a natural Elysium
one was meant never to have left. So long, it's so dry
in the dells that dust can't get accepted and we three
under the umbrella of stars shout down the well into the next
performance, which will be more varied.
I'm so glad the tocsin assimilated all the calls to order that
    must have
been found wanting under one odoriferous tree or another, it's
    all
the same, sample. My britches are wanting suspenders
and I too want, where it wanders, under regular
bridges and pavements. We seem to buy flowers
but are erased from death, it passes over
into the lovely material of the sky I get used to wearing.
The man I love is ready here in the faceless backrooms
under ground and by his shining, in the trees of heaven too,
a final note. Gorged and empty. Dissatisfied,
yet rolling in sleep's tresses as never, and in front of a junction
of light to lunar light, to folds of earth's sleep.

He's one to know. You'll all wear me out. I'm green and gray;
the current is voiceless and occasionally.

Joy

Think of it as some god-liberating whimsy
that heaven and the emperor's mice detain
in the province of boredom. The signor's wrath
is cold at these times, to nail the fizzle, explain
exactly what went wrong in clear, easy-to-understand
sentences. Besides, an imperfect embrace continues
from the past like an organ-point. So it was not you
in the original documents attributed to "I,"
and was no safer to pursue our advantage albeit
a mild one. The scene is classical;
the last twister corrodes into terror.

To be living on this scale. An old drum
collapses like ash. Seek it tomorrow
in the diversity of sleep,
the promised landscape.

Irresolutions on a Theme of La Rochefoucauld

"We are all strong enough to bear the misfortunes of others."

We leave out old regrets
that when they be found are almost blended
in the grass, shadows of apple stems
they might be or collages from another country.
We shall, at the steeps, commandeer all
that bed is good for, then sink into a platter of sleep.

Bringing water to the fountain, a hot day's
rest, and too soon is it excluded
to the delight of those sitting near us, who,
on the verge of bailing out, decided to approach

the argument again in a spirit of fairness this time
since we all have to cooperate, or else the earth
will get slightly out of kilter, its revolutions
a few seconds off, enough to produce climatic changes
in places you least think of—

One day the mice became suspicious. That was all
we needed to get going again, in plans
of luxurious travel this time—on foot, by plane
aching through the deserted night for its
imagined double, shot against the sunrise
with blips to read by, a miracle—

One should be filling out
the forms, but tension has lessened, though
we need to know we live in explosive times;
we can see our way around corners to where
we dressed the birds. They liked the clothes
we gave them, liked us, but still they
wanted to go home, not to a forest
or savannah, but to the place of captivity
they had always known, a cage somewhere inside a school.
So each day the predicament
emerges different, yet the same—you want
to have birds at your shoulders and wrists, to connive
with nature in her song, but something always
leaves you. Suddenly there are no more disappointments to be
    had
and the laziest are crowned and anointed for their efforts:
somewhere we see in this something which is shyly wrong,
some corner of the heart, bird-
haunted, by birdsong haunted, as though we two
were far away, and these others strangely near—
a paradise, if we had the facts to open it.

And when an elf
sits on a golf tee before you, and someone
behind you asks to play through: then, then
it doesn't matter much which of the old gypsy crones is
really a princess in disguise, with flowing

chocolate braids, and olive-dusted complexion! O may she
redress our wounds, and leave
connivance to us, where we shall find
it a suitable burial ground and all
will be as if we never had lied,
never hounded our mortal parents with persistent questions
and all shall be as though dawn came easily
any time. The mountains fall apart
in my hand as I hold you: there, three
are smoothed over already with
five more to come before a delicious breakfast,
and I try to cherish you.

A Call for Papers

It buttered no parsnips that it was raining
on some statues of older men. The call had gone out
and from all across the country, papers
kept blowing in. The little crazy guy converged
with a very interesting man who was right here
in an antique perspective:
The appetites were enormous, the provisions limitless.
Fifteen read their papers
last year at this time, the group said.
In the case of Boston-Cleveland or Hartford-Philadelphia
you don't get arrested for heavily kicking a sign.
But as daffodils and raindrop-preludes fall
from the symbol-laden heavens, you can be charged
for forgetting,
for ignoring the very basement of your and others'
ideas until they come at you like stray cats
and it isn't *their* fault. Remember that.

The scale descends
to a kind of landing, then descends some more.
Cooler heads prevailed
and something that the work was not resembling
gave you a distaste for discovery.

Whether I'm fooling around or not it is incumbent
on the brothels of history to raise up their sheets
and vote with a bean for or against capital punishment.
Don't you see
it's the only way to measure
the zebras moving to warn us,
reptiles in rep ties at the pass?
Carry on, crow.
Meanwhile sleep binds us lightly
so that we can easily slip away as the season
approaches on tortoise feet. Around the corner
of midnight, and a thousand miles away this morning?
What good are hygrometers, and what men need us
more than they need air or defense?

We'll see you at the end of the month! they cried.
Small waves broke as they re-formed
across the bay's lumpy waters
in time for this session and for the next
one and for the one after that.

Love's Old Sweet Song

Because if all of life is just a blip or some kind of exclamation
mark at the bottom of last week's weather (an almost
    snow-filled
field from which some weeds extrude; should we persist in
trying to find a home for these?), it means, doesn't it, that we're
allowed to backtrack to the slough we were backsliding into
anyway, and really learn about ourselves from it this time? I
    mean a
quagmire's a tidy place for pausing between highballs; there is
so much more to everything but this is a not inconsiderable
    prison
yard for getting that all-important exercise.
                                    Meantime, one
    comes
bearing an envelope that is fresh and blue; one salivates; even

if it's not a stay of execution but an order for the immediate
    putting-into-
effect of same, there's something to learn. It's not like two cats
ignoring each other in a basement areaway. By that I mean it
    was
going to lead up to something and then did, quite quickly.
    Better
than scanning hirsute sands for plumes announcing the arrival
of reinforcements; in those cases one invariably skips forward
    to a
time in the near future when everybody is happy again and an
    engagement
ring slips onto a ring finger of its own accord. But back,

I say, the heck with endings. I don't think I want to wear those
    socks.
On any other day of the week my attitude would elicit a few
    stares;
my value-judgments are like what they used to call an
    "overdressed"
woman, and it has come about that my shadow is invisible to
    me, but
I don't know this yet. The conventional wisdom is that we
desire what's unattainable (reclining clouds, distant factory
    chimneys)
for precisely that reason. No allowance is made for the
    goodness
that might be lurking therein, like love in a tongue-tied child
whose cheek one pinches as one passes along to bigger and better
disappointments. We never know what we could walk back to
    except
when we do go back, and then it's as if not knowing and
    knowing
were the same thing.   I long for more weather around us,
but it's just not going to happen till we're in the middle
of its happening and know the results without being able to see
    them.
The time for passing is past and none but an idiot would think
    otherwise.

Yet I see I shall be needing some appraisals, tall and lucky
totems foundered in taller grass.

Wild Boys of the Road

"Why, there's the well where the message fell apart:
its rusted chain gleams still. And there's the happy one,
so little she was excused from most occasions.
The blinkered sun circles it now, the last act,
noting how little its motions will be called on the carpet
(or it will fade the carpet), with the resulting freedom to act
like a knife, or a snake in the night. When it's all over
we say I could drink it now and then,
about three times a week. But the heavenly uproar
is heavier; storms mean business
in this day and age. The only viable
mode is to walk out; you'll find the slick streets keep time
with your advancing to what is really seen when it is sold.

"Fresh air will have noticed the pond waterfall, how
the trillium darted out from underneath but
had nothing to say, no excuse for being there,
though perhaps one for what was there before, as a henchman's
eyelids close just before the deep fact of one
sitter's enduring, to pass the test, and then
everything is all right; the sun seems to have shifted
its position, allowing gray skies, crazy boys to bloom
all over the place, and yet we are here, safe, unsleeping,
perjured to a man but that's
what gets removed I guess. You have to
return to the old. And age builds it shining new for you.
We have too many things to think about
not to notice the dull horseman's color of coming
back to check once again. Besides, the lilac
flavor of after-shave stood up, grew him a new one,
and all cattle, all sentries were dispersed from the yard.
It's hard being in an epic but harder still
to hold on to the thread as it whips like a kite-string,

and some of us do get our deposit back. But for the most part
there is only land and that is obvious,
too near the lunar chasm to be depended on
and too smart not to give us the slip
as the occasion warrants."

When all is said and done we avoid our friends
not from fear of us but from a holy desire
not to cause a commotion. Poor boy, you thought
to have sipped from the center would be such an easy, exact thing,
like kneeling in church. But you see now how the watchman
destroys whatever it is one happens to be made of, purloins
the bulging eyes of expectation, leaving
curious pebbles in their place, or better
yet, no things, nothing of which the touch
can be determined: strange, elliptical events
with no name for them in the glossary. How the vegetation
would take over now: we'd be stalled again, the bad
smell on the verge of happening once again, the tin
posy in the doorjamb as unconcerned as if this
were a hundred and fifty years ago. Something has got to stop,
yet I tell you the enemies are for us, shouting in our ears.
The leaves are too little at the top,
and the years, well they come to seem little too, little and nifty,
though I suppose not for long, and I seem to hear
something will wring us, wrench us from the extremes
of piety on the one hand and salacious diffidence on the other:
     just
enough for the sing-song to get along, as we were,
nice and easy for us, stone plinths with fringe of grass.

Le mensonge de Nina Petrovna

This slave brings me tea,
and happy, I sit for a moment, a spare
moment. Time under the tree passes,
and those things which I have left undone
find me out! O my spirit shall be

audited! and unknown readers
grasp the weight of my words
as their feathery hulls blow away
leaving the crabbed and sullen seed
behind. And how many of these shall grow?
Really I thought it was autonomous
as the birds' song, the vultures' sleep,
under crags to whom virtuous
dreams come and torture them awake:

all alone lest someone
approach too near, in a fever
that binds the edge of sleep
where it blurs to hysterical necessity,
in these hours I am someone.
A patch of damp cannot ever overcome
the hurricane that blows where it wishes,
and the Christmas tree ornaments may well be
dispersed, that look so perfect,
hanging together,
as must we all, to the distant cheering
of high-school students at a game
who mean no harm
but their kind words cannot save us

or quite leave us alone
as one hand of the clock homes
in on its chosen numeral.
Costumes and memorized poems are the order
of this night
as through an enormous pastry tube
clouds ooze around the stars, lest
(so brittle and unimportant are they)
the wherewithal be lacking
to bring earth into some semblance
of unity under the sky
that mocks us and will never
let us be entirely
all that we were someday to be.

Of Linnets and Dull Time

You said you don't want to know any more
than you do now, of every thing that might be
a person. It would be cheating. That is urgent.
If we are going to mean in so many ways
let them all be lopped off.
That way we'll know you're getting older.

I feel sorry for anyone that has to die.
The lines of what's expected
fan out like beaters. That's all,
I think. But I lose things, now.
The beautiful shape of the toilet interposed
a viability as the air-raid drill ended.
We've got to do something.
He may be up there now, trying to find us.
If you let me, I'll drive you back to the fairgrounds.

Korean Soap Opera

My sister and I don't seem to get along too well anymore.
She always has to have everything new in her house. Cherished
    ideals
don't suit her teal, rust and eggshell color scheme.
Of course, I was a buyer when she was still on the street
peddling the Communist Youth weekly. I have a degree
in marketing. Her boyfriend thinks I'm old-fashioned.
Well, I guess I do have an old-fashioned mentality.

What kind of a mentality
causes men to commit suicide in their air-conditioned glass
    boxes?
It has been a life of adjustments. I adjusted to the postwar
    boom
though it broke up my family. Some took their honor to the
    mountains,
to live on wood and water. But the investment years

wrought havoc with the landscape. Everything is modular now,
   even the trees.

Under the dizzying parabolas of the railroad bridge, where the thud
of laundry mallets used to resound, the swiftly flowing
current is like green cream, like baize unfit for fulling.
So old are the ways,
for lunch one might select a large smelly radish.
In the streets, as always, there is a smell of frying fish
no one notices. The rain cannot make up its mind.
Other people like it other ways.

I need to interact with postal employees, civil servants, that
   sort of thing.
Just being asleep isn't enough.
I must cry out against injustice in whatever position
sleep overtakes me. Only then will I have understood what the
   world
and servants mean by self-abolishment, the key, it is said,
to success. To stand and contemplate the sea
is to comprehend part of the package. What we need,
   therefore,
is market gardens bringing a sense of time with them,
of this time, honed to razor-sharpness. Yet the whole
scheme is invisible to any shareholder, and so the feeling
lessens, the idea that a composite portrait
may not be so important after all takes over like the shoulder
of a mill-wheel, slogging patiently under water, then back
to the zenith, where the watchword presumably is.
In schools they teach things like plus and minus
but not in the gorge, not in boiling mud.
Area residents were jolted to find what in essence
was a large swamp, pythons and all, in their communal front
   yard.
To me, this is insensate. I cannot stand the wind at my back
making of me nothing, to be handed
over, in turn, to this
man, this man. For though he weathered patiently
the name, the one that occurs to all of us, he went out

and came in, not in the best interests of abundance;
not, it seems, being anything but about to fall.

Here's a paradox for you: if the men are segregated
then why are the women not?
If the rich can survive dust-storms thanks to their red-and-gold
    liveried
postilions, then you are playing with an alphabet here: nothing
you invent can be a plenipotentiary,
turn itself inside-out, radiate
iron spokes at the mini-landscape, and so side with a
    population
of bears, who knows? Who knows how much there can be
of any one thing if another one stops existing? And the word
    you give to this
man, this man, is cold,
fossil fuel.

One snorts in the laundry, another
is broken beside the bed. A third is suspended
in a baobab for all the sins
no one ever knew, for sins of omission are like pearls
next to the sin of not knowing, and being excused
for it. So it all comes round
to individual responsibility and awareness,
that circus of dusty dramas, denuded forests and car
    dealerships, a place
where anything can and does happen, and hours and hours go
    by.

A Driftwood Altar

I'll tell you what it was like:
If you could afford it, you could probably have had it,
no questions asked. If it ran well, hugged the road well,
cupped your body like a loose-fitting suit, there was only
the down payment; the rest is future memories.
Of all those who came near him at this stage, only

a few can describe him with any certainty: a drifter
was the consensus, polite with old people,
indifferent to children, extremely interested in young adults,
but so far, why remember him? And few did,
that much is certain. I caught up with him
on a back porch in Culver City, exchanged the requisite
nod, shirt biting into the neck. How is it with you and some
who have no meaning, to whom nothing pertains,
yet the emptiness is always with you,
crowding out sadness, a drum
to which the pagan is alerted, glances are exchanged,
and someone, whom later no one can recall, slips out the side
    door?

In the bathroom there was considerable embarrassment.
One had taken off without notice, and in the sludge
that washes up on the beach are papers to be signed,
seals to be affixed. O why in this case bother a stranger, there are
enough of us to oversee the caring, the docketing; there is even
warmth on these chilly evenings of late winter, a no-season,
    remembering
how hot and sharp it was only a few seasons ago
when they wore their coats such-and-such a length
and cars drove by, even as they do now in certain
precincts where the roads are washed and small, trivet-shaped
    flowers
appear a moment and are gone, to appease the musk-god, most
    certainly,
and people spill out of lobbies and their greetings thicken like
    silt
in the runoff from a glacier and it is the standard attitudes
that are struck, there is no cry, no escape from them?
O certainly one of you must have known all this,
had it plotted for him ahead of time and said nothing: certainly
one of you runs down to the road with the news, or to get
    help, perhaps.

Then the idol winks and pirogues with their slanting
rows of oarsmen are seen departing backwards with undue
    haste.

It is time to think of spring and in pockets of not extreme
    despair
or under the threat of a ragged-looking but benevolent cloud,
    a thought
 occurs: we weren't always like this, something seemed to
    intervene
about halfway here; at any rate a great deal of action
scrapes what we are doing into shape, for the time being.
    Though I am lost
I can see other points on the island, remains of picnics nearer
than one had thought, and closer still the one who comes
to resolve it all, provided you sign a document
absolving others from their eternal responsibility, swearing
that you like this light, these birds, this rattling credo
as familiar as a banging shutter, and above all, promising not
just to go about your business but to do the thing, see it
    drained, emptied,
a box in which four seasons will again fit
just as they did once before fire took the sky
and airplanes in their spotted plumage were seen to waver, and
    sink, drifting
on the wind's tune that gets in cracks here, the same
old bore, the thing already learned.

For it is indecent to last long:
one shot of you aghast in the mirror is quite enough; fog
    mounts
gnarled roots of the trees and one could still
stop it in time. There has to be no story, although it is
bedtime and the nursery animals strike expectant, sympathetic
    poses.
And then in a quiet but tense moment the crossed
identities are revealed, the rightful heir stands in the doorway.
True, it is only a picture, but someone framed and hung it;
it is apposite. And when too many moods coincide, when all
    windows
give on destruction, its curfew anchors us
in logic, not reprehensible anymore, not even exemplary,
though emblematic, as some other person talking in an old car
    would be.

Poem at the New Year

Once, out on the water in the clear, early nineteenth-century
    twilight,
you asked time to suspend its flight. If wishes could beget
    more than sobs
that would be my wish for you, my darling, my angel. But other
principles prevail in this glum haven, don't they? If that's what
    it is.

Then the wind fell of its own accord.
We went out and saw that it had actually happened.
The season stood motionless, alert. How still the drop was
on the burr I know not. I come all
packaged and serene, yet I keep losing things,

I wonder about Australia. Is it anything like Canada?
Do pigeons flutter? Is there a strangeness there, to complete
the one in me? Or must I relearn my filing system?
Can we trust others to indict us
who see us only in the evening rush hour
and never stop to think? O I was so bright about you,
my song bird, once. Now, cattails immolated
in the frozen swamp are about all I have time for.
The days are so polarized. Yet time itself is off-center.
At least that's how it feels to me.

I know it as well as all the streets in the map of my imagined
industrial city. But it has its own way of slipping past.
There was never any fullness that was going to be;
you stood in line for things, and the soiled light was
impenitent. Spiky was one adjective that came to mind,

yet for all its raised or lowered levels I approach this canal.
Its time was right in winter. There was pipe smoke
in cafés and outside the great ashen bird
streamed from lettered display-windows, and waited
a little way off. Another chance. It never became a gesture.

Central Air

Not all the buds will open, this year or any year.
But the frame of the tree discovers this is how
what goes together gets woven together. Relief
is the thing here, the key
to all aspirations, including my own—what
do I mean, "including my own"?
Just that the shark gets tired after a few sips
of potential victims and dives off deep into
the underbelly of the sea. That signals are crossed.
That the fairies bloom in boxer shorts.

All right, but what about today,
the mystical leavening process that never occurs,
leaving us flat as crepes? How do I get
from there to here with only one side of me showing?
I can't take my pants off, that is a revolutionary
sin, akin to wiggling sideways. And this gum or
latex keeps me chained to it. There are so many floors
in this building I feel we shall never get down,
or that in the process I shall become a secret gourd
fit only for haruspication. Does that get indexed?

Anyhow, it's a downhill process.
Once that gets realized we can turn
into our parents, joining hands with them
just as the fatal drumroll is unsealed.
At that point a cat jumps out of the woodwork
to say it's all a mistake, how it'll await
your reaction as eagerly as fur takes on the aura of mist,
and goldfish turn away.

Too, some other peccadillo is missing,
which turns out to be a lucky coincidence
leading to an introduction to a memorialist
who has just turned the pages of a thrilling romance
in which a king is cuckolded and diamonds get turned into tears.
But that is all right that gets told about you;
it butters the toast, as they say in Peoria.

Yet you—here in this trattoria—
how did you get there?

Fifteen seconds ago I was no longer living.
But that's all right. You see it peps you up
to suddenly have a new book that you
are reading, happily, as print darts across pages

like larks across a field. Now, put it down.
There is someone here who says he or she knows you.

Everyone out of the house!
It was only a game of witch-tag, after all.
The spinach sky, reflected in the sea's
precise excremental tone, is what we have:
peeling posters in an old resort
announcing races on a certain July 25th.
Did we have to go? Here was more color, more options,
more reins to take, more flugel notes to be involved in.
There is nothing but business, and a businessman's
sand-colored suit, how he looked at you,
not quite sure how to take the grease-spots on your front,
yet unsure that a vacuum cleaner could remove them.
In time we just drifted apart,
and that says a lot—
says it above the drifting sound of the main, the leather
    breakers.
And in time we two are here.

Just as Jack had made sure that his friend Cordelia was out
and was preparing to ring the front doorbell a fleet
of blue and yellow airplanes, like frenzied butterflies,
attacked the outpost in the Falkland Islands where some
believe a secret is immured that shall save us.
But nobody ever came. Jack returned to the city where he now
    lectures.
As for Cordelia, it was all over in a few minutes—
she guessed that the gasp meant fiction, and proceeded
to take the necessary measures, and the sun was again wooed out
of the woods, happy to accept the throne if it

were offered, happy to retreat into senility if it were not:
it doesn't matter, it's just the way, the other way things happen,
that brings one regularly to the dentist's waiting room
with its large, appealing magazines. Meanwhile . . .

The Youth's Magic Horn

The gray person disputes the other's clothes-horse stature
    just send us some water maybe
herding him onto the escalator for a last roll
    and bitter, bitter is its taste

We don't pay contributors
    just send us some water maybe
We'll talk about the new flatness
    and bitter, bitter is its taste

I'll probably be sleeping with you sometime between now and
    next week
    just send us some water maybe
I haven't made a threat that the army hasn't carried out
    and bitter, bitter is its taste

Meaningless an April day hungers for its model a drawstring
    just send us some water maybe
Billboards empty of change rattle along beside
    and bitter, bitter is its taste

Somewhere between here and the Pacific the time got screwed
    up
    just send us some water maybe
but my spelling, as always, is excruciatingly correct
    and bitter, bitter is its taste

and I welcome intrusions like the sun
    just send us some water maybe
and all around us aquifers are depleted, the heat soars,
    and bitter, bitter is its taste.

First in dreams I questioned the casing of the gears the enigma
 presented
 You're a pain in the ass my beloved
The twa corbies belched and were gone, song veiled sky that
 day
 I have to stop in one mile

The century twitched and spewed gnomes from its folds
 You're a pain in the ass my beloved
The mule-gray pilgrim was seen departing
 I have to stop in one mile

I never knew the name for this brand of contumely
 You're a pain in the ass my beloved
Believe me I wanted to play the shores are still beautiful
 I have to stop in one mile

Here shall we sup and infest sleep for the night
 You're a pain in the ass my beloved
Morning will surprise us with winds like variable coins
 I have to stop in one mile

You're the truth in my cup, violet in the edge of memory
 You're a pain in the ass my beloved
Retrieve me at my dying moment so shall our hearts decay
 I have to stop in one mile

Remember the stone that sits beside you—
 You're a pain in the ass my beloved
Sometimes they come for you and forget
 I have to stop in one mile

Brute Image

 It's a question of altitude, or latitude,
 Probably. I see them leaving their offices.
 By seven they are turning smartly into the drive
 To spend the evening with small patterns and odd,

Oblique fixtures. Authentic what? Did I say,
Or more likely did you ask is there any
Deliverance from any of this? Why yes,
One boy says, one can step for a moment
Out into the hall. Spells bring some relief
And antique shrieking into the night
That was not here before, not like this.
This is only a stand-in for the more formal,
More serious side of it. There is partial symmetry here.
Later one protests: How did we get here
This way, unable to stop communicating?
And is it all right for the children to listen,
For the weeds slanting inward, for the cold mice
Until dawn? Now every yard has its tree,
Every heart its valentine, and only we
Don't know how to occupy the tent of night
So that what must come to pass shall pass.

Of Dreams and Dreaming

Tell me more about that long street. Actually we're
   overextended;
time is running out. While still all things to all people we
are no longer swimming in the pool left by the sunrise. No, a
forest has resumed the strict narration. One puts gloves on
to ward off something. What is it? And living by a chair
so close to a thermometer no one can count is business,
that is, it can't be put aside, and coming out to your guests,
to warn them, is the recreational side we love, that, and all
things, all producers of silence that let this hay
into the tunnel and came out the far side of sleep. Really,
your life is so fascinating. I don't get it. Neither do I—
I mean I was originally the fencing instructor here.
Now my head gets buried in the flour
of reading this translucent page as a vacuum mounts,
and so off to bed. Really it's too bad, though not calculated,
and can never be—Everests of tiny snow crystals would
have to be accounted for first, and that's not likely.

Meanwhile we live in the paperweight of swirling blizzards
and little toy buses painted vermilion like the sky
when it rises up reasonably to our defense in the half-hour
after sunrise or before sunset and likes to, it likes
the idea of museums. Then so much of us is fetched away.
Often you think you can see or even smell some part of it
before it too is put away, used and put away. But then these
so recent nights would be part of the elaborate past, that old
contraption, the one we were never sure about—

It is lively still, playing to packed houses.
What must the present-day analysts think, the ones who husk it
for what that's worth, then come to play games with us
as a consequence of their own dangerous behavior.
It was night over a mountain that seemed to be there, readily
and so useful we threw ourselves on the ground dank with
 animal
emotions and choked-out expletives: December first! The
 cocksucker
hasn't been around lately we see through gaps in the dead
or is it dormant vegetation. One of us has to go the whole way
 now:
shall we draw straws? Don't be ridiculous but don't look
either in the direction of the walrus, the caves of the sea
hold us, though we appear to you here on this simple street
asking so little. The third time it happened I thought I was
 seeing
it in a new light. Then the follow-up call came. Did I want it
delivered with the sheaves of my imagination, those other ones,
and if so what would I do with these lesions marking the
 enchanter's
space if he is off somewhere, bold song
if ever I sang one? Though this night I shall untune
the most insistent, entrenched breaths of purpose just so I can
 say you
can come to me, an attack like those told of in time to
an insane purpose that is what we call history; then it will be no
 nearer
to a resolution, by God; I have to cry out if this mess is what is
left at my doorstep. In the future we'll

have no time for backbiting conversations like this one.
Differences will be put aside. Aye, and rainbows too, slugs
of narrative even the best of us could follow to what ends
in wild weeds, here at the wind. An' if my daughter
bring it over to you there'll be no less use for a mouse
found in your castle and turned out into blind day, the
    passion
some think comes at night. And we're all over you.

Suddenly it was my time. I don't know whither the watchman
vanished. He told us of the night, then vanished.
The stars are purring in the little Mississippi runoff of the
pure, bulging sky. Ours to consider, no doubt. And what if
    when we pay
it off, in full, it still runs toward us, too badgered to think
to mention what other tales might have been in store, only the
    last men
took them away. These were never seen again. My toothache is
    subsiding
but I won't I guess be the ultimate one, the who-by-
    definition-saves
what one is after, cornflower that obliges us by never appearing
in the sole instant it is wanted, but is somewhere behind that
    house,
no, that other one. Besides, when in doubt you can strike a match.

Seasonal

    What does the lengthening season mean,
    the halo round a single note?
    Blunt words projected on a screen
    are what we mean, not what we wrote.

    The halo round a single note
    makes one look up. The careful blows
    are what we mean, not what we wrote.
    And what a lying writer knows

makes one look up. The careful blows
unclench a long-sought definition.
And what a lying writer knows
is pleasure, hallowed by attrition.

Unclench a long-sought definition:
what does the lengthening season mean?
Is pleasure hallowed by attrition
blunt words projected on a screen?

Kamarinskaya

And it was uniquely the weather, O *bombes-glacées* university!

Had they actually built something there?
It was whose turn to find out.
Tremendous lashings of cloud were pouring in, from over
    there, they said.
Mouths choked with news, though no news in particular,
blocked the corridor. Later aspects were discovered,
developed, and as always, they fanned out in twos and threes
or stood a little to one side to discuss whatever was being
    discussed.
The great moment paradigm had arrived for all of us.
Some of us reaped instant benefits. That very afternoon
we were five looking at the sea; the shore began its pitiless
    interrogation
and we were glad of the cleft that produced nothing and
    knowledge,
the freedom to wait.
                The dentist moon hovered by the wire: *Sure,
look in thy heart and write. But don't throw foreign articles.*
And after coming down from the plateau, the heights, we are
    amazed
at the power of the possibilities enfolded in each thing, but
    above all how long
they have lasted—longer than consciousness itself. We can go
    on building

and the structure, the shed that joins ours, will always be there,
kind, undermining. And the strength to be indeterminate
overtakes one. There are always laws, and people to break
    them; that's not the point.
What is is the majestic lineage that is merely nerve endings of
    the air, plus spice.
It's not often we get to point to something this way,
saying:

"It must be daring or I would not have done it,
not consciously; in my sleep perhaps. And yet there are tables
    near mine,
close enough to overhear, and all he says is Daddy brought you,
we must make it up. Make up anything you like. Steal it
from a magazine, no one will know the difference. Use its
    resonance
and throw the rest away, down the steep ravine into the dump.
That way the menace is erased. And the waitress asked sweetly
if there was anything else I would be needing and I said Swell,
it's the unpinning, the unrolling of the linoleum so soon, and I
who had dwelt in realm of fancy it was I who was coming too.
There was approval all around me
and a costly lamp-base where the seconds melted and in a
gash too deep for sleep I had plotted it already, I was being
    told;
the light and the fences had said it. I was being rushed from
    leaves to tall grass
not knowing whether I had made it or whether the others had,
    sure only of
one piece of information in the instant harbor: the one true
    way
to make a book and get out alive. Surely,
the bourbon sours have stopped; now will be the declaration
of the rest of the stairway, and then we'll see.
And it's true then a locomotive may pass through like an
    elephant and no
one raise their eyes. The time is past, she said.
But even this wan swan song looks like news to me—
there are so many others out and getting—
and whatever happens will be red and gold like a fire engine.

Now *he* said that *she* said that he didn't know where they put it
and *she* said that *he* said that the law was over soon, that in the
    interim of the land
not one of us was going to cry, but many, besides we'd see
what a disaster looked like, with the moon back there and
    people's lack
of attention." Then he got right out and said so. Did it. But
    the sheriff
and his men were there. Did that mean—? But a woman read
    the riot act.
Now all was song, and cleaving

to the spar, that precious one, thing
that always turns up, radiant, one for the books, you must tell
them about this, really. Did that mean we had been let out?
Listen, the password is like downtown, no peace
prohibited, we can get where we want now
and can't get to but the steep ride
is safe. What do you want with me anymore? True.

Elephant Visitors

Sweet Young Thing: "Why are you all down in the mouth?"
Testy Gent: "We're all in the business of getting older,
or so it seems; we're moving on. The daytime approach
can fail you. Sit on this moment,
pause on this deck. What if the earth fell on *you*?
But the dirty salad of lies, etc., about assassination
is approaching. Something has not been found."

Here, try the gloom in *this* room.
I think you'll find it more comfortable
now that the assassins have gone away.
Or got away. Take a week and shut off the engines.
But we do have to manage to stay here in the mountains, or at
    least
hover, in place. There are things I still haven't told you.
What is the state flower of Nova Scotia?

On whom do we depend
when we twist downward tangled in the parachute
and the ground is coming to greet us too quickly?
That's when you could use a newspaper,
but try and find one in the prairie. I was muffled
by the elegance of it all
but now I'll take one step if only to save myself,
yes, and others. Doctors

never tell you why these four-footed quadrupeds are friends,
if only foul-weather ones. There's a lot in envelopes,
and in a hole behind the house,
but if we think we're better in this instance,
give them something they WANT. Tasseled trees.
Until which time we sign off—wait, the lotus
wants to say something: it's MADE IN JAPAN.

The Great Bridge Game of Life

What with one thing and another they were all
too complicated. I was seen leaving.
Good grief, a frog. How funny that piece
of scaffolding flits against
yon crimson cloud, to their mutual betterment, actually.
Try saying that aloud. A nice military
mood and then where in the walk
I was mistaken and that took again.
We all fell over our numbers, if seeing
is to believing as the flat wave is on the stair.

No, scars. You forgot to pack
some. The world will live
without them and we must scurry to dream up
some other identical crisis. First it's men and
then it's me, that stayed nights
in a box, sometimes. Sometimes we were up and
sometimes we were down. It takes one of us to
reposition us and by that time danger has worn the day

down to its nub. It's best not to be
here. But if we linger after waters and cents
nothing is then too obtuse for the clime, the time
and all we travelled backward for: one good image,
the rest fenced off.

Do you think you're better for
all that clashing? The seesaw on the roof
in Zagreb disappeared, part of it.
There were no tonsils, no noodles in the paper that day.
One tries to keep oh so many
foreign things in mind but as mustard
seeps from a diary, the elegance had gone out of life.
Now there was nothing to repair.

The Departed Lustre

Oh I am oh so
oh so
Something is slightly wrong here,
a summer cold.

but I don't know what they're up to whether they're up to something else because

We made it fit years ago
made it fit in
an archetypal fit

and when it didn't go on
when it took root
the ship was obliged to leave for the islands—it doesn't matter
    which ones.
Where it's always too hot
and the spoons are slightly bent
and someone, always some other one, saves the day
though hell-bent for the lilacs,

heedless of the volcano's warning belch
yes, and the fires are put away for that day.

Yes, like a fish I enjoy swimming lessons.
Out into the cold with us, we have mastered all that the senses
can teach us now. Only our naked intelligence
stands somewhat apart
bowed under the bowing tree.

Such speed in the letter now—
how the pen races over words, underscoring
its happiness, and all the dots and curlicues
arise under a single heaven!
It means more to me than to it
and I am lightened by the passing cry of crows
blotted like jam in the sunsets
they have here,

as the swinging touch of the earth
deepens, leads to much

and the aurora stands tall on the nimbus

of what imaginable October could be

and the mucus of mountains hardens
each day, to my surprise. Erections
surprise us in gardens.
When the fatal beauty-sleep takes over
darkness imprisons the advocates who had the key,
showed it to you, pressed it into your hand
but it was like a dream you said
it could never outlast its moment so here
we are on the ground
and a child brings you another key
whiter than the last one
to unlock pinions, positions, bookcases

where the voice can dwell unsinging

There is so much to praise,
to hate,
one is grateful for the patterns,
the obscure, plain faces,
The capital "T" in "The."

Villanelle

As it unfolded and took on something of the aspect
of a garden in the rain, the acclaim with which others
greeted it scattered too, evaporated. Now who
is to say when battered night comes and you look
distractedly over your shoulder, whether the owners
of that night had the right to remove any of it
in strips and mask-shaped pieces, so that by morning
nothing of it remained except crescent
accents under cups? And they were seen as truly gone,
arch-fiends of emptiness, that it stayed
to lighten awhile? What if I told you that every
aspect of the cause had been pre-ordained, from
the brokers in wind-cheaters to the tumescent
ear of corn in its shock, and that no one, not one radio,
had ever been accused of inattentiveness to the
gradual unravelling of the scene?

This would have mattered bleakly to those, the growers,
who stay behind and amid bats and laburnum devise acrostic
governors whose motives shall be colorless and whose device,
strangely scrolled across a banner, translates
easily into Urdu as: "Let's put the boys' fire out."
No, there were sad others too, but let's hear it
in the rain-bejewelled jungle gym for the copers, the
coppers-out whose ears, the brass color of tubas, flare insanely
just a little as each new podium prank thunks
into place, like a hive of bees, questioning, unsure if the date
was last year's. And if so, deliver them a warning:
mornings are timely, sure no feet drag, and yet a weariness
as of a wolf's blasts the moment into shards. We were as good

as in bed, and all
we really wanted to know was the time on the other fellow's watch.
How hard he made it, and into what twosomes the grisly smile
delivered hands, prom-dates, catches in throats, the horrible
manliness for which time is an ascending ramp crowned by
    moonglow
made of hundreds of cigarette ends, and the return
to town is witchy, twin scotties on a leash.

How fast the others collected! Were we to be siphoned off
as casually as last year, pinned with a string? We who
were well off until a certain day, and now, loitering, the starlet
shakes her beads in contempt: no we had not even begun to
understand where the crime is, to what
succinctness of being we are summoned if it ever goes away!
The threads, at the back, seem to match an image our fathers
dribbled, but reversed, the image is Main Street,
Titusville, and there is no other home than these
pebbles, placid and revered. There are ghosts on the trail,
too, but until we have done with hopscotch, the little girl
crawls away and twin sinkers emerge like blobs
out of the twilight, there is no point to the crash, and no end.
The house is very revealing. She said it ought to. Oh my
first fears, leaders, never
turning over, never looking back, what is it on tomorrow's
agenda? What would you have done?

A Sedentary Existence

    Sometimes you overhear them discussing it:
the truth—that thing I thought I was telling.
What could it have been that I said?
To be more or less like other men and women
and then to not be at all—it's

    like writing a book that is both beautiful and disgusting.
Because we can't do it now. Yet this space
between me and what I had to say

is inspiring. There's a freshness
to the air; the crowds on Fifth Avenue
are pertinent, and the days up ahead,
still formless, unseen.

To be more or less unravelling
one's own kindness, noting
the look on others' faces, why
that's the ticket. It is all the expression
of today, and you know how we keep an eye on

today. It left on a speeding ship.

Erebus

I

Tonight we are going to try a different dish
some worried savior brought us:

a vanilla-flavored tragedy
on how the market closed.

Waving from a window: that's nice.
One hears the sheeted dead
braying in a box of pencils
by that curve in the creek,

and wonders how worse things can get.
Surely there are worse things

than reading, late at night, in bed.
I would like to write a Victorian novel

of terror about a crossing-sweeper's revenge
on life, somewhat in the vein of
Lady Audley's Secret. They can can you for that

or for drawing smoke in puffs the way
it does come out of chimneys only forget

about it. The truth isn't what's wanted.
Penguin races are. Yes but you knew someone
who once knew a penguin. That doesn't matter:

put it all in your book, what you were going
to say, and wake up with a shadow,

something less meaningful on the wall.

II

Too bad the way children
on their way to school get mislaid
and the market closes.

The honeyed wind claws at your throat.
I thought you were a fair-weather friend
but I find you here now, in tears,

begging me to give up that stratagem
I've fought a lifetime to perfect,

and I'd rather do it—for you—than bask on
the rampart of some accomplishment: always

no work, no tears, and if children
play this way, then it's all right.
I wasn't mistaken

except in dreams.

Then, Nordic champions come
to tell you how you failed
by a hair,

a breath. And you go on,
believing them. And you go on believing them

for what silver
night incurs in the pockets
of all those waiting desperately for a sequel.

But it comes round
to this: what is comic is no longer
fatuous, and you're the first to learn
about it and can keep silent about it
and make a killing. In the mean-
time your door is white as snow.

The Old Complex

As structures go, it wasn't such a bad one,
and it filled the space before the eye
with loving, sinister patches. A modest
eyesore. It reduced them to a sort of paste
wherein each finds his account, goes off
to live among the shore's bashed-in hulks.

Of course you have to actually take the medicine.
For it to work, I mean. Spending much time upstairs
now, I can regulate the solitude,
the rugged blade of anger, note
the occasional black steed. Evening warbles away.

You are free to go now, to go free.
Still, it would help if you'd stay one more day.
I press her hand, strange thing.

Where We Went for Lunch

I

The boss made it official.
Then a cherub came out and sassed us.
"Why do you listen to all this *chamber music*?
Why don't you ever listen to church music?"

Indeed, I thought I had always done so,
but now I had other things to worry about.
"Other things to worry about"—he keeps repeating that
    phrase
as though it were an escutcheon on a portcullis.
What manner of ridicule is this? Of course
there's nothing to worry about, except your response,
which is precisely what dissolves in music—you know the kind,
that keeps coming round again, like a customer
to a neighborhood bar, and some good exchanges
take place between a couple of fiddles, who then decide to walk
    home together.

Shit, if this were New York . . .
In the next episode he sees me with the eyes of a cat.
"You remembered . . . to bring . . . the gold stuff?"
Oh sure, but I'm not a catalog, nor
what's wanted here. I'm a Belgian
with lots of Belgian things to think about
such as newspapers and old shoes stuffed with same—say I
    think
I'll get out of here too. I don't know about you. This
cement sidewalk looks pretty steep to me, though it's broad . . .
(Hah, that part always fools them.) I say,
what if we took a turn through the thicket down there—
might clear our eyes out, *if you know what I mean*.

I do. But I keep returning to what is in dreams
for me, not certain I'm correct, that this place is suitable.
I think I'll lie on the shore, fighting with the sand,
for a little, if you don't mind. And then one of those parrots—

we might see one, eh? Oh he thinks he's Crusoe now.
So much for the general populace's idea of loneliness—
I thought they'd abandoned it years ago, but they still
like to keep up the pretense. "You think *you're* alone?"
No, I never said that, you are deliberately twisting my words,
but twist them you must, if you think you must.
Right now I'd like a long cool twist of something.

Sure, she goes out with *some* men.
But that don't mean you . . . Oh, hell,
there I go trying to make something of something
again. Time to pull in one's horns, me buckoes, if you
catch my drift. And if we don't? Then it will catch you, sure as
wavelets nibble little by little at the sandbar
they have no idea of covering completely in fewer minutes
than it takes to play an old 78 r.p.m. record, say,
make it nice this time, how about Dvorak's *Humoreske*?
I was just going to ask you about that word. They don't
make 'em any more. We don't have any in stock.
We are about a shout.

Why, when it comes time to saunter, why
we'll do that too. I was first desk at the Vienna *Musikverein*.
It was during the second Viennese school. Why do poets like
    to eat?
Why, you do something, you want people to know about it,
    it's as
simple as that, at least it seems so to me, but
I could be wrong, I have been in the past, and about more
    things
than you, Horatio. By the way, how's that bridge coming
    along?

II

When we sleep we see sweet things
and are wiser next day.
I forgot to play
yesterday. I'm all stiff today.

III

Seriously, what were we made to talk about? Just casters on a floor, that always leave something of a mark nevertheless. I will have to have my will read to you. That's as close to a tease as we ever get. This elevator just dropped seven floors and no one knew anything about it. Nobody thought they were going to die. Can you stand stupid people? Yes, me too, there's something so, well, *stupid* about them, they're like earthworms coming through a mound of dirt, you just have to love them. They're the ones with the passion. Now, there's something I'd like to have. Many's the time I've been chided for my presumed lack of it, and rightly too. Oh I know what I'd do if I had some, who I'd go over and see first. But if you can't have it you can't get it. That's where this thing called "intelligence" comes in. See, there's more to it than you thought—than *I* thought. If we can find our intelligence, and everybody has some, we can use it to make little stick figures out of Plasticine whose elbows we can bend, and then there is no expression more touching, my God I'm getting all crazy-eyed just thinking about it. We can make our own little race, and they have cars to fit. But I'm getting ahead of myself, my story, really. But I've told it to you. We can just look at each other and blink. Or not. We can just sleep together.

And when I was having lunch
I heard this voice singing
about the breath of other planets blowing.
I mean, who needs to be reminded?
I am at your doorstep after all,
sliding down the door, I pick up the knocker and replace it
    softly.
There seems nowhere to go,
nothing to do.

I can ask you out on some pretext,
only don't be lonely,
see?
There are enough unhappy people in this gyre.
But I was never one of them and now you will be too.

As Oft It Chanceth

You had but to look at a mound or nut
after the invention of perspective for it to become a rut.
Everybody was seeing and doing it.
That is why some few choose disorder
as scenery befitting the positive melancholy of their stance,
which means to get things done in a climate of awkwardness.
The perfidious sky tore past them,
its ribbons streaming revolt, and soon,
not right away, it would be time to go down to the street
to inhabit that walking shell of you
that by this time is all either of us knows of the other,
but it *is* something.

Pick up your room.
Your visitor is coming up the walk,
the door-chime sounds. Now if only in a second I could invent
the leagues of prosperous businessmen I mean to have
    commerce with; but no,
it is allegory still. The house on the hill,
the bramble bush, the neighbor, disappearing
along that appropriate perspective.
You believed it if it was convenient; otherwise
you may have believed it anyway, and it was all
shaken out, like clothes.

But in the room the guardians of same will have it
their way. And though this will never cause the temperature to
    change,
there are still others filling up the anteroom
with the breath of fog, with wishes not voiced
for a while, until it becomes obnoxious and incinerating not to
have them, in their way, as they crest down
on us. Anybody could've thought it up, but, funny,
no one ever did until that elaborate hour
wherein we go on seeing, and our order is taken.

Retablo

After it had jiggled down it came out OK.
Drugstores sold it. You to whom this awful mission has been
entrusted are barred, of course, from commenting
while it is held up in the courts
and none of your family or lawyers can, either,
which is unfortunate at a time
when such a lot depends on being supple and risky, the way
you always were, of course,
except that now it isn't quite enough, is it,
as was the case on certain days
gray and blustery, but otherwise quite undistinguished, quite
unmemorable. You had to choose.
Did I forget to mention that? It came with the package
and had to be peeled off and mailed back, but even that
foretaste of doom didn't rate a footnote, while other, less
notable and possibly less objectionable aspects dropped
out of the stone forehead, leaving it black,
something to be pitied, almost.

So much more came untied during the swinging
of the bell ropes and of course the maddening pandemonium
    of the bells
themselves—they get right inside your head—
that someone would invariably stop to ask, Hey what is this
redemption stuff anyway, all this talk about bonds and
    escrow—
wasn't it supposed to be on a more spiritual shelf
where presences of sages nod and fall on each other,
falling asleep all over each other,
and at noon the terriers run and die as though these
treehouses were meant for someone else who would fit them
    out
differently, all spare and nautical? Captain, you've got to tell
    me,
what is this insane voyage about? I haven't even bought a ticket
and besides am on dry land heading back to see my aunts and
    cousin, aw,
have a heart will you? And these garbage-flecked

shoals beyond the barrier reef, you can't tell me those orange-
haired floozies are sirens! Hell, I can hear 'em.
And *I'm* going nowhere, that's for damn sure, as I know you
know in this vacuum you label interest in other people's lives,
in seeing how they accomplish what they set out to do.

Probably the rain never got loose
for all you know, but it did, it was like cellophane noodles
    escaping
from a slashed envelope. I had a transparent raincoat to prove
    it,
but it wasn't enough, that wasn't enough, nothing was enough
    to be quiet
in the little schoolhouse, but it *was* enough to know the last
class was over many seasons ago. There was something learned
    once but
it had drained out through a ring of rust in the middle of the
    floor,
and besides the desk-captains never kept such good time
any more, but of course there was less to know in those days:
only a few harness-bells, and a heap of dust and straw.
Which reminds me: why are you shivering under that
    horse-blanket
when there's so much to be done by way of filing
the last perennials, each in its separate slipcase, and of not
    letting Jack get away.

He's got more to do; there's more to be done
than any of us ever dreamed of, whole pockets and mountains
of it, let into the side of a cloud hill.
Then the worrying starts, a fresh leak of pain
squirts through the tape and soon the bandage is loosened,
useless in the grass where I was standing all along, a picture
to myself. So the long rain waves drain;
there's a sense of compactness, or even nothing, though all the
    ships
have returned from Iceland, with stars, and with the scarves
    that sent them there.

A Mourning Forbidding Valediction

And who, when all is said and done,
Cares for thee like me? I know. *Thy* name
Is known to me, and if thou sufferest like a squall
That sirens rend, I'll be confident and of the other
Persuasion. Perfume that drenches like a pall
Is the old scent, and dear, true; its fame
Waxeth with the sun
And is not like, moreover, a lost brother.

When glory's steed pawed the ground,
Frozen and flinty the hour, yet for some
It was command out of the deepest basin, and who shall say
Which recombinant molecules have memorized the next rote
And when the reciters have fall'n, on a day
Stuck in time's craw, that merriment is a crumb
Unfit for sharing, only a sound
Like itself, endless fishy smell or zygote.

Nothing's here; the year
Is ripe, and frozen, all about me stand
Censors—veiled, tumescent husks who at the last
Come clean in the moulting of the season, and make no bones
About their city of origin. Them too, held fast
In Memory's drizzle, the Place St. Ferdinand
Negates, and surrounding highrises, mere
Chaff, or the power which breeds stones

And shall have much to say, come night-
Fall, and all around us awful blisters concur
In melting trusses, stalk the errant ptarmigan
Or deed no entry to fools and nimble savants beyond the moat
That weeps for times when the green cardigan
Of duckweed shrouded it, and, all exemplary, her
Nose protruded beyond the outline of the bight
Some saw beyond, and her raincoat.

To scrape the habit from our stand of being, and, once
It's accomplished, rescue it from shyness, out of a burrow

Of pleasure up toward greater mounds of pleasure, is to a name
What places are, and so be it
If trace elements are added and rules from the game
Subtracted little by little. Ergo,
Someone's won it. Dunce
Am I? So's your old man, you stupid shit.

Gallons and gallons of water slid over the weir
But since it was night, no one knew or cared. The owl,
For all his feathers, was a-cold. Peace lay in sections
On the raised edge of a circus ring, where sawdust
Conjures belly's emptiness and the recent elections
Are commented. Men prowl
Beside the recently abandoned pier
Sprung from any concept, from reckonings, crust

Of someone else's negligence, our cognizance.
O skate too far away, or else backpack, backtrack
Into the hay of an argument dimly seen, unscathed
Like time. The more marbles to our monument
The more the future won't be any less real to us, enswathed
In Hyperborean conundrums—that's as may be. To bushwhack
From here to Petaluma, then chance
Failed irrigation canals, faults, is my soul's sole integument.

I Found Their Advice

When you hear the language
(not the spirit of the language) it unfolds like a shelf
just to be equal with the level you have risen to.
A change takes place. No longer are steel leviathans erected
at points of entry to the city. The clouds have come down
to be a part of what they and we so long dreaded.

And we who cling in wonderment to a sheer surface
like chains of bubbles, we who talk and lecture,
know that it is half-past five, that what we were learning
has begun.

Who thought we weren't learning because we hadn't stopped
 learning,
know all learning is going. In the silence, the dear gray
crevices are scrutable as ever. But knowing
time as a blur comforts us, seals us
from inherited light, too fast and unsorted: who
knows what organic matter is contained there,
what difference to the environment?

The last fires are banked, the strip-search is less precise.
Now they just ask you what you're doing here,
or were doing here; it's not a ceremonial
but it doesn't jostle. The garden, the atrium are included
I'm afraid in the voice of praise, and the sleeping vines
machined for this feeling that has to leave:
willful, a chance for us.

French Opera

Hi. I'm Bob.
The long flight is over
and they have returned to the places
where they live in the ground.

The beloved past
is near, cautiously optimistic:
I've laid so much drawing over
the empty, original square, that it
almost ties figure
to ground, plot to decaying
character, last year with next.

I'm like a keeper of drawings:
they're fragile, lonely sometimes,
like best friends erected on the dark lace
of the sometime sonatas. Only let me not
checker my face with the derring-do of
having once been somewhere, of

having been brought down from the mountains
to testify in court, and gone back up again,
senseless, the stenographer reminds
us. We're trying to adhere
to it, to give you some money to tell her
you're here. In the responsory we could make
it go somewhere, round and round
the track if you wish, but do we
know where they teach? Do they sing?

In French opera, Charpentier's *Julien*,
for example, the problem is always the listener's:
trying to make sense of it all and feel sorry
for the characters and *still* keep faith
in ourselves and what others are doing, industriously,
nay, zealously, and the payoff
is always
in the next yard.

Still, no building collapses.
Reinforcements are on the way.
There is a whole lot of colored
imagery to sort out and sift away,
being careful not to get any of it
on one's clothes. There are forklifts
and fedoras. In short this *is* that
old chapel scene you once wanted to know
about, except that moving sands cover
the boards then as always.
You might wish to shift in your chair.

A Stifled Notation

No one ever oversleeps
until the time you are to improve your life, and then
what's one superstition more or less?
The lives, I guess. And it's best to be early

about things, not drink too much,
lest the pattern be seen in its undoing.
The judges march backward up the steps.

Well, you've solved this week's problem,
but the wind is wailing a little too enthusiastically
as the garden takes up the fugue at a point
where it's impossible to be lonesome and valid anymore.
The fishes swim, birds plod fustily
with heaven-dividing cries, until the whole world seems soaked
in the boredom of that sorrow you were promised,
but also
crazy with love and self-deception. Sometimes a charcoal sketch
of a refrigerator is supposed to be the edge.
How long you had no aim
for no other stream.

Haunted Stanzas

It has been raining on and off for a week now:
drip, drip. Already we are beginning to feel the effects of this,
as life slides insensibly onward. In one corner
a harpsichord is shelling peas. Watch out for rowboats!

When the new series of etudes was published it
caused quite a stir in the musical world.
Darkness was more perfect. Happiness no longer
was a thing to hold on to, but became a great curve,
listening instead. We don't know what pressures
you to behave as we do. We only do it out
of fear and love, meddling like
guardian angels with what does in fact concern us
a little.

Unbattered the storm plays, like a lion cub,
the bolts tremendous, and the basement is still coming apart.
I am less than enthused though a cautious display of
 differentiated

levels would be the appropriate note here. The thing done,
and the apron that came after.

I am not prepared to give up my life for a few drawings.
Nevertheless I want reassurance, as if this were the Mesozoic
    era and
people saw themselves differently as so much meat and
    whiskers.
I'm not sure I wouldn't have been enchanted
to have those advantages and see how women live when they're
    away
from men and don't have to think about it.

So the carpenter makes a list of
whatever *might* be needed and the ritual
gains in transparency from that.
Even the little piles of dust in the schoolyard had their say
and thought differently about it only they came to be in the
    end
what navigators had never asked for: the whole planisphere
pressed into one's hand like currants.

Who praises rigor?
The ones who have less to lose. Who live
in harm's way and poetry is as a vice to them. Never
mind, it is more meaningful that the settlers were unwearied,
as, given our best days, we all are. So I feel connected,
the car slithers forward, meanwhile

let me lick your shirt. I have an honest proposition to make
to you, one that I hope you'll find rewarding: turn
your back so as not to see the parade of prisoners escaping.
It'll do them good and it'll do you good. You have it in your
    power
to offer proof of the equations amid the alembics of the tower
where the gas flares and your nerves buzz. Well?

Shouldn't you be off and running? Until another day, then.
And he saddles his horse, which he called "Old Paint" (never

knew why, except that its rough exterior was somewhat
    suggestive of old paint)
and that was it. But I want to pray for you, whole
afternoons-worth, I do. But sometimes the sledge is honest. It
    bears us away.

Livelong Days

Feather in your cap? Not from heeding
the half-lit messages of other writers
you cherish and would like to forget.
I sat at my desk; the storm was brewing
on an April morning. The sun still shone
and the bud had blasted. There were shadows on the ground.
Yet I sat, not doing, not worrying whether we're living in it
    right.
And when her younger sister found out who I was,
why, that would take precedence. Certainly
we'd all be here a while longer
that would mean time to find out,
to test the fiddle's scrolled-up tensions
in case everything came out all right.

Those were the days for living in a sack,
a loose one for answering the door in.
The neighbors kept you up all night
with whispering and indecisions. It was time to
look into "Aunt Agatha's Tried and True Recipes" just to see
who was mulling it and if they could
somehow get back to you once the joint was cold.
Alas, these spoke only in terms appropriate to the occasion,
too much so, in fact. Where was the residue
of calm fear, the notices
to convene with the lawn chairs, that prompted inspection of
    other
recent ordinances? And the doormat wiggled like a ghost
in the draft under the door but there was quite a lot to be said

and none willing to go down, slog down if need be, the
    painted stair
whose ends were invisible
in this tide of sick summer light
wherever feet chose to take one, here
among the weeds and provisions, there in the rue,
and make chaff of all we built, all we had constructed against.

That is a way of being, it said. All right,
I won't argue, but show me the increment, fine as lint,
apparently, that tips it, festoons
a tree in the room, and finally delivers the book
to a publisher just as the door is closing. I won't envy it.
If I had the wings of an angel something, or everything,
would be slightly different, and you'd see: it would
come out in play. The differences that make us inexact now
    would
chase us into learning from that space, that pure longing
for the pauses just past, multiplying like mythologies, apples.

Quartet

Always

because I saw the most beautiful
name go down ahead of mine

I'm banished to an asteroid
perfect meld of soppy common sense
with somewhere a loose connection

only don't make me think it
always
I'm figuring out what went just before
with that which comes too late:

invitation to a pool party
where the hors-d'oeuvres are free

as well as the first drink but not
the later ones
this was pretty late in the season

for me I told a tired invisible guest
but one must invade new premises
scout new locations
from time to time I said he seemed
to agree

that my date hadn't been seen in some time
oh well I was trying to lose her suppose
we go upstairs and just have a look round
flash bulbs popping
I said
well anyway as it is baked so shall it endure

and the co-ordinated midriffs be here
at 10:30 sharp no one moves
before every hand is on stage I
think I know what that meant he said
there'd be no more coffee and doughnuts
before this smooth introduction I believe I'm
one of your friends of course he said make room for Miss Scott

I suppose it's idle of me to worry
how other people will take the cold
it belongs to each of us like a blanket
and like fear doesn't go away
though it does go away in the evening
and return in the morning
and each of us deals with it
like bowels or bladder like

it or not I said we is each
a machine for milling or sorting whatever
gets digested or eliminated there's no
planning to stop for a while
taking a brief vacation
taking in some theater or old film

it's useless because bad
we pronounced ourselves part of the
joint agreement

and indeed I just meant to come back for a moment
to make sure I hadn't left anything behind
and lo and behold I am the central protagonist
in this cabana and all that was
going to be hid from me is hid
and everything looks quite normal
and so I shall approve the document
there's no earthly reason not to
is there
I said and he said no it's all past in the weather

and no matter what private associations are
set in motion by this train of thought no
change can ever be the result
I saw where he was leading
and it was centuries before I could disentangle
my sense of what I thought was right from the legal
obligation to bind everything into a sheaf
to recognize myself on your mirror
when we both returned to the dark pond
agreeing it best to nourish the affection
with toasts and witty consolation

rather than undertake a new epic
that might get bogged down in production
anything rather than those covered wagons
converging on a new day and he said I'm with you
I can't understand what the cue cards
mean about it snowing outside the sanitarium
solarium and is it true I am to spend my entire life meddling
with someone else's desires and then piecing
everything together just before it all blows up and I can
say yes once I had the meaning of it it was pretty good
and now all can see the meaning in it and I have forgotten
it all but it all still seems pretty good I guess he said

And now I cannot remember how I would have had it. It is not a
conduit (confluence?) but a place. The place, of movement and an
order. The place of old order. But the tail end of the movement is
new. Driving us to say what we are thinking. It is so much like a
beach after all, where you stand and think of going no further.
And it is good when you get to no further. It is like a reason that
picks you up and places you where you always wanted to be. This
far. It is fair to be crossing, to have crossed. Then there is no
promise in the other. Here it is. Steel and air, a mottled presence,
small panacea and lucky for us. And then it got very cool.

Oeuvres Complètes

Everyone seemed pleased, even the then-invisible statisticians
who brought us to this pass. My barometer is working well;
a drop of milk in the scudding blue thinks so.
Maybe if I were shorter
the sky would stand up to greet me contemptuously
in that endearing way it sometimes has. My train is being
    flagged down.

Surely it's time to go where they want us to go.
I was never big on reading
though I enjoyed singing when I knew the words
which wasn't that often. And you, you sang with me
in the evenings for a while, and Minnie and Joe the goat joined
    in.

It was as impossible to enjoy the unseemliness of that present
as it was not to forget it, to cover it with showers
once spring had come. Once spring had come
the gigantic tail of a horse projected beyond the barn door.
The tail, I mean the tale, was beginning for us again
in ways too complicated to scrutinize, but we did come up
    with a set of questions.
Then the interviewer said that was all for that day.
The vice-president looked tired.

Back in my shack at low tide
I rehearsed the speech I would never have occasion to deliver.
Once I put pebbles in my mouth
though it lent no conviction to the list of wildflowers I was
    annotating.
I would say that on the whole it has been a good experience,
but I would also say that everything has been a good
    experience.
I touched needles, and learned how they were sharp.
Later I became a sharp dresser
having mastered the art of mix and match.
I think I'm going home now, to tea, it's sleepy:
just say maybe sir, ask the right gent
about it, he always gets it right
and then we're on the right track, which is always a relief,

isn't it? *But I have something to tell you.*
It was wrong of you to play this far, first; and when you had
    finished
you should not have raised your eyes to the sea that blinded us
through the open doors, even as you thought you had married it
and were obliged to. Or something. At this rate none of us will get our
sponge in time, while the river overflows with fish.
Be careful of that puddle.
If they knew we had indulged each other—but what earthly
use does anything have? Why are we here? I'll tell you:
it's so the little naked man can run out into the grass
that towers over him, sprayed with dewdrops,
to massacre the cold
and master the changed legions
whose breath never hurt
anything, but you are loved and it's your responsibility.

Just Wednesday

So it likes light and likes
to be teased about it—please
don't take me literally. That winter light

should be upon us soon in all its splendor—
I can see it now—and the likes of the haves
shall mingle with the have-nots, to some point
this time, we all hope, and the pride encoded
in the selection process that made us what we are,
that made our great religions fit us,
will be deployed, a map-like fan so you can
actually sit down

and find us where we came from. True, some
at first claimed they recognized it and later
admitted they didn't, as though the slow rise
of history were just some tune. That didn't prevent others
from really finishing the job, and in the process
turning up points of gold that are we say these
things we shall have, now. And the jolly
carpentered tune merely played along with all that
as an obbligato, but on a day
took up residence in its own strength.
A weary sense of triumph ensued but it was the reality
of creation. There were no two ways.

And so one emerged scalded with the apprehension of this,
that this was what it was like. You gave me a penny, I
gave you two copies of the same word that were to fit
you like rubber ears. Is it my fault if in the dust
of the sensation something got knowingly underscored, defaced,
a shame to all the nation?
After all, it suited when you set out dressed
in plum and Mama was to meet us at the midpoint
of the journey but she got taken away and an old
dressmaker's dummy draped in soiled lace was substituted
for the intricate knowledge at this juncture.
The grass grew looser but closer together,
the flowers husky and fierce as trees. On the spiffy
ground no wagers were taken and a few minutes'
absence is the bee's knees. It behooves

you to depart if the moon is cowled.
That homeless blanket you gave up—

you should have sent them both years ago. A few
cronies still gather there where the shore
was explained and now the waves
explain it with renewed mastery and suds. Almost
time for the watchman to tell it to the lamplighter
and I'll be switched, after all these years.

In My Way / On My Way

Pardon my appearance. I am old now,
though someday I shall be young again. Not, it's true, in the
    near future.
Yet one cherishes a hope
of being young before today's children are young grandparents,
before the gipsy camp of today has picked up and moved
into the invisible night, that sees,
and sees on and on like a ritual conscience
that bathes us, from whose dense curves we know
we shall never escape. We like it here as the trial begins,
the warming trend, more air, even the malicious smile in the
    prefecture garden—
would we like it as much *there*? No, for we only like what we
    already
know, what is familiar. Anything different
is to be our ruin, as who stands
on pillars and pediments of the city,
judging us mournfully, from whose cresting gaze is no
turning away, only peering back into the blackness of the pit of
    water of night.

Once I tried to wriggle free of the loose skein of people's
    suggestions
chirping my name. One can do that if one is rich. But for
    others a bad
supposition comes of it, there is more death and pain at the end,
so that one is better off out of the house, sleeping in the open
where chiggers infest the lilacs, and a sullen toad sits,
steeped in self-contemplation. By glory I had

better know before too long what the verdict is. As I said I was
    changing
to more comfortable clothing when the alarm bell sounded.
Which is why I am you, why we too
never quite seem to escape each other's shadow.
Perhaps drinking has something to do with it
and the colored disc of a beach umbrella, put up long ago
    against the sun.

Yet even where things go wrong there is more
drumming, more clatter than seems normal. There is a remnant
    of energy
no one can account for, and though I try
to despise my own ways along with others, I can't help placing
things in the proper light. I am to exult
in the stacks of cloud banks, each silently yearning
for the upper ether and curving its back, and in the way all things
seem to have of shaping up before the deaf man comes.
O in a way it is spiritual to be out from under these
dead packages of the air that only inhibit
further learning and borders, as though these too came to see
    the sea
and having done so, returned
to selfish buildings enclosed by walls. Their conceit
was never again to be quite as apt as that time that is
    remembered
but no more, on a quilted sea of pylons and terminal anxiety
far from the rich robe, imagined and unimagined, as far as the
    pole
is from us. As around the pond, several rods away, the liquid
performance starts and repeats, endlessly.
We live now in *that* dust
but no one shakes it, no finish is yet prized, prized and
    forgotten.

As when we bumble, maintaining steadfastly that there is no
    life in the truth of us,
no bearings in the grass, and who cares anyway, why the salt
on his fingertip is life enough for us under the present
    circumstances,

something always focuses attention on all we have done since
    school,
how we were naked, and fell, and those
coming up behind dutifully picked us up and presented us as
    evidence
and the court in a major shift decided to hear the arguments
and all was sadness, it was decreed, for a while,
till pregnant pauses were abandoned, and miniskirts returned,
    and with them
a longing for a future of fashionable choices,
dotted earthworks in the comforting desert,
various fruits to assuage thirst
and the almost maniacal voice of your leader
reminding us of practical solutions so out of date they were all
    but forgotten.

Far from fear of crowds stumbling,
what ought to incite you is a new hunger for all the angles of
    whatever
day this is, placed against the sandstone of undoubted
approval from many different quarters.
True, all that we hurled
returns to visit, and true too that the bayoneted
clock recovers, that composure is a gift
that sometimes the gods bestow, and sometimes not; their
    reasons in the one
as in the other case remaining inscrutable even to apple-
scented mornings where the light seems newly washed, the
    gnarled trees in the prime
of youth, and the little house more sensible than ever before
as a boat passes, acquiescing to
the open, the shore, the listless waves that distract us
out of prurience and melancholy, every time. Yet something
    waits.
I can hear the toad crooning. It's almost time for intermission.
The guest register awaits signing. It's another, someone's,
    voyage.

No Good at Names

We've been out here long enough.
The past recedes like an exaggeratedly long shadow
into what is prescient, and new—
what I originally came to do research on.
I have my notes, thank you. The train is waiting
in the little enclosed yard. My only duty
now is to thank all those who put up with me
and trusted me so long. It must have seemed
like a long process. My thanks are due, too,
to others with whom I never came in contact,
who may not have been alive, but
somehow we were in apposition, and as my pen
strikes out on its own, it is chiefly those others
I wish to remember. In a word, *merci*.

And at random stages of the journey he sees
what we were meant to see: underwear on a clothesline,
flying leaves, patches of dirty snow. It's true no one
ever tests you on these things, that nothing would have been
    different
if you hadn't seen them all, yet by emerging
they have become part of the picture, so vast and energetic
it gets seen by nobody. Later, in the station,
you greet a small group of close and not-so-close friends,
sparring about would the bargain have been different
if it had happened in something resembling a time-frame,
or a landscape, even a landscape one has only heard about.
And you show each other your clothes, smiling shyly,
and talk about the after-effects of the medication
everyone's taking these days, and it seems to have made
a difference, brought out the leaves in the public squares.

Great travel writing has to be manufactured this way
for the desert's glitter to sink back into something tractable
and frozen antennae to balk at the day's closing prices.
A moment of horrible witchcraft isn't too much to be swallowed
for the land to become whole, and people wise
in the way that suits them.

Film Noir

Just the washing of the floors
under him was cause for hope. If there was a flaw
in something precious, it meant one or more persons
had been inducted already. When they heard about it
it would come to seem as though the rich background
was you, your space. It lent you
a furious dignity that you breezed right through.
No more apples on the dashboard,
this is cheating the real thing, earnest
with life and self-assurance. And when you died
they remembered you chiefly. It was two
lights on a rowboat, a half-mile off shore
as the evening breeze drew nigh, cementing relationships.
And it seemed as though they always heard you, loud you,
that otherwise nobody remembered except conveniently.

When the inevitable abrupt change arrived
I looked to you for reflected confirmation of what
was happening to me, and unfortunately got it.
The afternoon windows released their secrets in a flood
as though no one had ever had any. In the downpour
distinct noses and adam's-apples could be determined
in a mounting hush of congratulation soon to be
shattered by a train's ear-piercing whistle:
the doors slid shut, there was nothing to do except wait
for another train, yet this one still stayed at the platform.
Too bad suicide is discouraged
in certain modern climates and situations; it makes
for such a neat ending; nevertheless we will brush on,
clinging to separate ideas as though they made a pattern.
And all shall be insulted
at the end where the going gets sticky
beyond any apology, beyond dried beans and casual sex,
    beyond even
the neighbor's girl in a schoolyard, half a century ago
when things still seemed pretty modern
and underlying motives were the same
though not the dark, intricate working out of them.

Say we just landed, like strangers in a hole:
what manner of manners is to be cut out of us, what sails
trimmed for the descent
into the matter of the sun.
Are Americans sexier, she breathed, or what is it
that gives their nudes a subliminal variation
on this often rehearsed enterprise, until we can see
into it, arranging differences? And that moan
you heard was just idle gossip, someone running around
to instruct the clerks of our compassion
in rules, rhetoric or some other tell-tale destiny
if we are about to get it right again.

But on the curb of the residential street
where wind thrives and the locals
shrug off any connection to the scenery, back where it was bad,
the same dichotomy obtains. We and they.
It's not much more simple than that.
And as I approach the master switch
for instructions, there are little smiles of recognition
everywhere, in the curdled clouds, on the reluctant shore,
to tell us it's safe to go home.

I hope they can come.
They can sleep under my bed.

In Vain, Therefore

    the jetsam sighs,
    flooding the front hall,
    with the fragile violence etched
    on the captain's forehead:

    some got off at the next-to-last stop;
    others, less fortunate
    were lost on the trail,
    pines and mist carrying over
    until the exit wicket

displaced all thoughts of a former, human time.
We, it was reasoned,
led lewd lives, belong with the bears.

A very few carry enough energy to
create a kinetic bonding arrangement.
These are the so-called sad ones
eating alone in restaurants,
drying their hair . . .

The dandelions are dead and the mud
of summer. They
tell of roasted meats, be oblivion
but a decade away
and the waterfall, unused,
is ruined, it is ruined, is not to stand.

The Beer Drinkers

Think of it as something that is happening
or something that is merely in the way, unnamed
until we call a meeting, go over it, eat it.
And then of course so much more of it is found
than was really necessary. Look at this season.
Trees are shiny, trapped in prisms. Umbrellas
are a new, raw color. The temperature's
not what it's supposed to be yet. Look. Enjoy.
Your house comes clattering down around you
like beads from a string. That's
nice. Each has its strength, its subliminal magic
and knows just how to keep out of the way
until the time for its expression is scratched
into the rude stone. How it will be forever.

You couldn't do that young. Now,
you set about what is going, and already
find it refreshed. And what of the new year?
It had an air of finality to it when last seen

but weathers wash so many of what we are, it
seems lame at last, then crowded into the omnibus
with all the fates, and furies, and us
of course, and the folks from home. How we
managed it yet again is a tale
for the newspapers by now, but how
the wariness of the telling could so
stock a nursery is something that continues
to baffle authorities. And all the colors
put up for sale, were they meant to
go by us two, and what is the change.

They have this tremendous power
in their doing, these Americans, and next you
know a coin extracted from a pouch
will be seen to be the real truth serum,
only you cannot get away just now
and in the autumn the roads freeze over.
And then of course he added distance
and rightness to them, and they came
apart amazed, and he was in someone else's camp
but could write to you. And you were embarrassed
in a bathrobe and it shut them all up.
He was only dying to air these anemones as a truth
and the truth shot all over him
and he came, and of course that one fact annihilated him.
Time for toasts now, darling? I think
rather, and hope I shall see him long
one of these evenings before the new snow starts.

That You Tell

The cannons waved summer goodbye
and the long arcs of breathing took up where they left off:
speechless. An old jalopy with wobbly wheels was seen to limp
into an abandoned filling station. Autumn sticks
in your throat; you must have a reason for doing anything now,
such as looking in a place you were sure

they weren't. Then you find something. Money jingles,
brightness is for a second. Then the cars, crows and cows walk away.

In sixteen years it hadn't been like this . . . this
symphonic stretch. How room had been created
before the notion of what was to go in it actually existed,
and yet by becoming, it did. And already had a history.
You, you were in it too. It started to curl back on us
like a sheet at night, and the choices were somehow limited,
the instructions far from complete. You must go down
to the shore of the steeply flowing river and assuage
whatever they call gods there. Then the reflected shimmer
    waxes bright
again. This is the prologue. The irises are dark
and prudent, and I like my male-pattern baldness. Far at sea
porpoises and businessmen are asleep
taking us farther than can be imagined, to the floor above.

I knelt and listened. There was nothing unusual,
no appearance of impropriety. Meals were prepared again,
the summer's sheaf raided, rains drowned the meadows
    pell-mell
under the eyes of peasants. Is what I'm being singled
out for, to tell of this, while the main population
of truants escapes over nearby hills? If so, so be it:
I've taken my stand and am pretty much prepared
to let it wear me out. Nor does the crucible of what we said
out of turn return to urge a new complacency, quiet
between the paws of the sphinx, nor does anything electrical
    have to interfere.
I know the air itself is noxious. I must breathe it
for those who can't; only let the nodes be protected from
    themselves
that in some joyous valley, far from here, picnicking
can occur under the vines, and the
tiniest constituents be sorted and drained, and approved.

The opposition has its way
always. See that neon fence? It spells out too much common sense,
which is a good thing, in the sense that memory is voided.

Afterwards, the monoliths grow untended;
something strange and seedy in the sky though centralization
has finally been realized after how many decades
of struggle and one may live
in these little homes, with their gardens, and all
be complete for a few more years. But I think the stealth
is a parasite hidden in it somewhere, that soon
other towns and banks discourage newcomers and there is a
    shortage
of the most vital commodities and even time
has almost run short. Now, tell it to your teachers,
kids, how well off we were and what you were going to write
in your essay about the conversion. What is vast is also hollow,
ragged with age, riddled with false modesty and complaints
from divers sources, including death. It seems
the truth was about something else, various and vicious, or it
    was
these very elements but mostly
a protracted span. And when it was over, that was the truth:
a nest of eggs still hidden, the false flight of a bird.

A Hole in Your Sock

A man walks at a city
as though veering off somewhere.
They extend arms, touch hands.
This is how it is done, every day.

My phone is tapped.
I wish to call the police.
Not, not obviously, part of the
"proceedings,"
the message takes control smoothly.

We contemplate the shells of crustaceans
long dead, waiting for the Bronze Age to end.
We go farther, fare worse.
And they gave us our little raincoat back.

Then the government gets into the act
and the others crowd in and out.
That was something, sainthood
of a sort. You have to take it.

They simply . . . die. And that's it.
When we come back
in fortuitous weather
the charm has multiplied beyond the sky,

is ever so contemporary,
as an ingredient should be.
The class marshals, boring thespians
have walked on. A teardrop
stands in the middle air.

This future does us good.

And Socializing

Back from his breakfast, thirty-five years ago,
he stumbles, finds in the sun a nod that's new.
Which is not to say we are any better off than a second ago.
These days, by turns solemn and skittish, our days,
belong to someone who once was here. More we cannot say.

Yet a vague pathos urges them in our direction.
"Wait a moment," it says, "perhaps a compromise
could be reached, who knows?" But we are in the departure
mode. All along the autumn, the hunters'
red coats star the rubbery and decaying foliage:

"It looks as though it's been through a lot."
So that when we say we *are* sorry, that was just
a little growing accomplished too fast, no one hears us.
The time for trumpets is here, has just passed. Gosh,
and I was getting up to answer the door, and by the time

I got there no one was there. Oh, well,
there's no use crying over spilled peanuts.
But I want the one I love to be aware
that we are all cowards, not just me, and just so
we have our normal victory in the time that ordinary

arriving brought, and rooting about
enthusiastically in search of cohorts;
and when none are definitively there, why, it has grown cooler
and we can talk this over endlessly, under the vine,
quaff the abstract moonlight.

Revisionist Horn Concerto

What more clouds are there to say
how it all matters to us? Buttons, strings, bits of fluff:
it's all there, the vocabulary of displaced images,
so that if its message doesn't add up to much, whose
fault is it? I can imagine casting the answer correctly
but it doesn't work, there's no question implied
in those gorgeous, plaited ravellings. Only a little
is known about them, and nothing about their hometowns,
backgrounds, etc. Really nothing more than a masterful
way of dealing with silence, of leaving it there, and then
being off on some expedition. So nothing
works. But there is nothing there that can harm us.

Don't be afraid to let it hurt you, dance it
under morning's wire, ponder anew the shuffle between the
    infinite
time bomb of the Nile and today's shoelaces. Besides, these
    periods
have a way of elapsing, and the so-called healing process.
Does anybody care, anymore, where it went? Or whose sleep
it interrupted with a unique dissonance
of its own devising? They were always photographing
the cash register, some men came in and said it should be this way.
From now on you're in the proverbial fix. Yet what was promised

was equal to what was subtracted, while periods of socializing
in the yard made up for how the money was spent. It wasn't until
years later that someone got around to noticing the bald,
comic error that had been hidden there in the first place
to equate it with life's beginning. By then it was in full sail,
swinging on the gate of how much longer we
have to lean out of the railroad car, swaying, singing.
The foul mouth should be caked with mud and weeds by now.
But we're not going to let a little thing like that
spoil this surprise birthday, are we?
In addition to which the pole
still turns, in dreams, like the enormous wheel
of a rickshaw, viewed from up close, now
dipping into the mud and chaos, now rising like a sigh, a lark
on the mend, to remind us that all is well, or should be,
or will be shortly, given the interest in its shadow.

The Woman the Lion Was Supposed to Defend

And sometimes when you want it to it won't:
the space around a yodel grows deafening,
then vomits into the orchestra pit.

Yet all of this was waiting for me,
to hug me into accepting what I thought
I was losing, barrel of light down the stairs.

You know when we leave home for a short time
we can never be sure what that place will be
when we get back—some yellow tenant gibbering

in place, or, more likely the furniture
will be a shade blacker. And of course it's
up to you to find out—it's *your* problem.

Which is why I so precisely intuit
the edge of all you gave to hold back:
precisely the forlorn edge of the road

that slices through much of time and ourselves.
Don't butter it—the trees
will be officious; the frog on his own time,

a bored meter-reader. And if we can't get off the bus
why then we'll adore that patch of leopard-gray
where the schoolchildren would have assembled.

And if I had gotten laid—or mislaid—
somewhere in the cosmos, there was always an ancient
truth to speak about it. How quietly everything

conducts to this day past, urges, without pressing,
nature's monuments on us, and before you know it
we have dreamed the spectrum again. Some days

are for washing ("*this* is the way we wash our clothes"),
others for sneaking about, eating. The patchwork girl
was heard singing in her studio. For a few weeks

after I got off I was like one possessed—couldn't
find the proper forms. The silence was terrible.
But after being battered by weather and coasts,

something creamy slips in, a wedge
more or less of the temper that compounded you,
drafted you, waited for you to fall, oversaw.

The sledge of ice melts in spring sun—
more water to weep over. Soon the first picnics . . .
But they led to the black cove

pirates used to drown each other in. What was
contracted for is now scaffolding, steeped in blue.
We have ways to keep in touch with you.

Harbor Activities

The prospect: roofs and more roofs.
Look for a street-guide too:
anything that will attract a name.

But it doesn't mean that the getting-together
of the newborn
casts the *Lumpen* in a definitive shape
like a rafter. The clots,
cloth slits, upended
breezes could be imagined by no human wizard.
The stalls they take down argue
impenetrably. That's good. In a month's time
when the bicycle's eye scrutinizes
this landscape, we'll be vapid and know how.
Every hand has a player;
every player a new hand.

Casting for consciousness like an angler,
you make them stop to admire you.
What greater form, better force, than this?

This spreading out over the page
of someone's newspaper at breakfast?
A small thing nevertheless,

for piano left-hand,
for piano four-hands.
Later, we take the train.

It Must Be Sophisticated

There are attics in old houses
where doubt lingers as to the corrosive
effect of night-blindness: namely,
are its victims directly linkable to a chain
of events happening elsewhere? If so,
we should shrug off resemblances

to our line of work. What was said around
the house had undue influence on one of several
shapely witnesses. And, as dames do,
she started talking to any and every
interlocutor out of harm's way. One day
you wake up and they've skipped. Or was it

always empty like this? It's hard
to remember a time when it wasn't. Maybe
your memory's playing tricks on you? Maybe
there never was such a person as Lisa Martins?
Maybe it's all over when you stand up
to walk the last mile in Enna Jettick shoes,

and they draw the blind quickly to forget you.
Once forgotten you're as good as dead,
anyway. And who would help you now?
You might as well be trapped at the bottom of a well
in the Sahara. They don't know you're alive,
or that your life was anything but exemplary

when it came time for you to live.
The fashionable present keeps queening it
over the slightly dishonorable past. Your
bridesmaids are scattered on the wind.
You don't feel like having lunch. Maybe
a walk, and a cup of tea later?

We'll see you at the end of the month!
they cried. Now it keeps ticking,
there must be a mystery down there,
darn it. I'll find it if it takes all night
and then some other sleuth can solve it.
I was only hired as a go-between. My tour is ended,

and if I've a piece of advice for you, it's
check out the rafters, the mouldings.
You can't tell who might have bargained
for clemency in your absence, leaving you holding

the bag when you got back, restless,
ready to start school, but the vagrant air's black,

what with the negative promise of spring.
The boys are still rehearsing their parts
they haven't been over, and really
it's none of my business. Said the table to the chair.
I was confined here. That's all I know,
truthfully. During the amnesty I walked

out through the open gate. The streets were full of people,
running back and forth, talking disjointedly. I was
supposed to be somewhere else, but no one knew it.
In the confusion I returned home.
Now the newshounds pester us daily.
What was I born for? More experiments?

Why are they fighting over a fuse? It doesn't
seem to be harmless like those people are listening to over there;
at the same time, everyone's a suspect in the new
climate and country. The wind turns a page
of the old tome, then another and another; soon
it's riffling through them too fast to stop.

There's nothing in it anyway. Time to move on
to another frontier beyond the transparent frieze
of foliage, guns, barges, to where he began.
Sure, dem days is gone forever, but it's the attention span
that's really gone. Back when they'd send for you
once they got a house built, it was clever

to hedge your bets and produce a fraternal twin
made of bedclothes with a mop for a wig
while you scaled the wall on a rope ladder
to be the next new thing that thinks
and cautions others not to. Far from the
inner city of conflicting attitudes, one fled with one's

holy illusions intact, one's misconceptions too, until the whole
mindset took on a largely symbolic

look, an indifferent jewel, toy
of the weather, of successive washes of light.
I can hardly believe I'm here
in this tiny republic carved out of several conflicting

principalities. It's enough, perhaps, that I was questioned
at the edge of my performance. That now I'm safe
from my own sang-froid and scores of others,
that mere forgetfulness can save up to fifty-three lives,
that they can share your power and go on glancing
upward. Because after all we were the three

original ones, the president, vice-president and treasurer
of our class. And were formed to repay
what obscure debt and be summarily
taken out of school and handed over to our parents.
It's what matters then, and after. No one
says you have to live up to principles; indeed, what are they?

What difference does it make which one came too close
in the richly darkened theater, if all
they were after was to coax you into the light,
watch you blink a minute, and then pass on, they too,
to the larger arenas, each in the wind,
in the sand, the reeds, growing? Because even if it doesn't

punish you exactly, the thing has been
lived through, the experience sealed.
O what book shall I read
now? for they are all of them new, and used,
when I write my name on the flyleaf. Look,
here is another one unread, not written. Time for you to
    choose.

Alborada

My friend, how are you?
I write with my mouth full
of crumbs in this waning summer city
as ruby grains sink majestically
to the bottom of day and others float
up past them, into something that speaks of cloud.
Do we all know we're aspected—
frightened, rather, while what comes as a ghost
continues as street life, pausing
to hitch a stocking, rambunctious, reproved,
all over the partings?
O if it were the thickness of a book,
laminated, or worse, into the meaning of chapters
that overlay one another like a horse's blankets.
But what shoots up, will.

Another day he likened it to the roar
of Paris traffic, how expensive it all seemed at first;
later, a sparrow. Besides they all get out of their cars,
stoop, and notice. Then the first one's
risen, in men's eyes. Her bathing suit
took first prize but I have to say climate never
nourished luck more, nor came out as an extraordinary
pencilled thing draped across rooftops
for all to see, till they saw, and the resultant gold-rush
landed us in the pokey. Here, as ever, some
are believers. Top-notch achievers.
In this way one gets to do it
and become one's self. Never
again did the small matter of a raised
skylight's hasp sicken the winter, the kitten.

By evening only the thought rained.

How to Continue

Oh there once was a woman
and she kept a shop
selling trinkets to tourists
not far from a dock
who came to see what life could be
far back on the island.

And it was always a party there
always different but very nice
New friends to give you advice
or fall in love with you which is nice
and each grew so perfectly from the other
it was a marvel of poetry
and irony

And in this unsafe quarter
much was scary and dirty
but no one seemed to mind
very much
the parties went on from house to house
There were friends and lovers galore
all around the store
There was moonshine in winter
and starshine in summer
and everybody was happy to have discovered
what they discovered

And then one day the ship sailed away
There were no more dreamers just sleepers
in heavy attitudes on the dock
moving as if they knew how
among the trinkets and the souvenirs
the random shops of modern furniture
and a gale came and said
it is time to take all of you away
from the tops of the trees to the little houses
on little paths so startled

HOW TO CONTINUE

And when it became time to go
they none of them would leave without the other
for they said we are all one here
and if one of us goes the other will not go
and the wind whispered it to the stars
the people all got up to go
and looked back on love

AND THE STARS
WERE SHINING

For Anne Dunn

Token Resistance

As one turns to one in a dream
smiling like a bell that has just
stopped tolling, holds out a book,
and speaks: "All the vulgarity

of time, from the Stone Age
to our present, with its noodle parlors
and token resistance, is as a life
to the life that is given you. Wear it,"

so must one descend from checkered heights
that are our friends, needlessly
rehearsing what we will say
as a common light bathes us,

a common fiction reverberates as we pass
to the celebration. Originally
we weren't going to leave home. But made bold
somehow by the rain we put our best foot forward.

Now it's years after that. It
isn't possible to be young anymore.
Yet the tree treats me like a brute friend;
my own shoes have scarred the walk I've taken.

Spring Cries

Our worst fears are realized.
Then a string of successes, or failures, follows.
She pleads with us to stay: "Stay,
just for a minute, can't you?"

We are expelled into the dust of our decisions.
Knowing it would be this way hasn't
made any of it easier to understand, or bear.
May is raving. Its recapitulations

exhaust the soil. Across the marsh
some bird misses its mark, walks back, sheepish, cheeping.
The isthmus is gilded white. People are returning
to the bight: adult swimmers, all of them.

The Mandrill on the Turnpike

It's an art, knowing who to put with what,
and then, while expectations drool, make off with the lodestar,
wrapped in a calico handkerchief, in your back pocket. All
    right,
who's got it? Don't look at *me*, I'm
waiting for my date, she's already fifteen minutes late.
Listen, wiseguy—but the next instant, traffic drowns us
like a field of hay.   Now it's no longer so important
about getting home, finishing the job—
see, the lodestar had a kind of impact
for you, but only if you knew about it. Otherwise,
not to worry, the clock strikes ten, the evening's off and
    running.

Then, while every thing and body are getting sorted out,
the—well, *you* know, what I call the subjunctive creeps
    back in,
sits up, begs for a vision,
or a cookie. Meanwhile where's the bird?
Probably laying eggs or performing some other natural
    function. Why,
am I my brother's keeper, my brother the spy?

You and Mrs. Molesworth know more than you're letting
    on.
"I came here from Clapham,
searching for a whitewashed cottage in which things were dear
    to me
many a summer. We had our first innocent
conversation here, Jack. Just don't lie to me—

I hate it when people lie to me. They
can do anything else to me, really. Well, anything
within reason, of course."

Why it was let for a song, and that seasons ago.

About to Move

And the bellybuttons all danced around
and the ironing board ambled back to the starting gate
and meaningless violence flew helplessly overhead
which was too much for the stair
Better to get in bed they cry
since Zeus the evil one has fixed his beady eye on us
and will never come to help us

But out of that a red song grew
in waves overwhelming field and orchard
Do not go back it said for if there is one less of you
at the time of counting it will go bad with you
and even so, many hairy bodies got up and left

Now if there was one thing that could save the situation
it was the cow on its little swatch of land
I give my milk so that others will not dry up
it said and gladly offer my services to the forces of peace and
    niceness
but what really does grow under that tree

By now it had all become a question of saving face
Many at the party thought so
that these were just indifferent conditions
that had existed before in the past from time to time
so nobody got to find out about the king of hearts
said the woman glancing off her shovel The snow continued
to descend in rows this rubble that is like life infested with death
only do not go there the time should not be anymore

I have read many prophetic books and I can tell you
now to listen and endure

And first the goat arose and circled halfway around the ilex tree
and after that
several gazed from their windows
to observe the chaos harvesting itself
laying itself in neat rows before the circled wagons
and it was then that many left the painted cities
saying we can remember those colors it is enough
and we can go back tragically but what would be the point
and the laconic ones disappeared first
and the others backtracked and soon all was well enough

Ghost Riders of the Moon

Today I would leave it just as it is.
The pocket comb—"dirty as a comb," the French say,
yet not so dirty, surely not in the spiritual sense
some intuit; the razor, lying at an angle
to the erect toothbrush, like an alligator stalking
a *bayadère*; the singular effect of all things
being themselves, that is, stark mad

   with no apologies to the world or the ether,
and then the crumbling realization that a halt
has been called. That the stair treads
conspired in it. That the boiling oil
hunched above the rim of its vessel, and just sat there.
That there were no apologies to be made, ever
again, no alibis for the articles returned to the store,
just a standoff, placid, eternal. And one can admire
again the coatings of things, without prejudice
or innuendo, and the kernels be discreetly
disposed of—well, spat out. Such

   objects as my endurance picks out
like a searchlight have gone the extra mile

too, like schoolchildren, and are seated now
in attentive rows, waiting trimly for these words to flood
distraught corners of silences. We collected
them after all for their unique
indifference to each other and to the circus
that houses us all, and for their collectibility—
that, and their tendency to fall apart.

The Love Scenes

After ten years, my lamp
expired. At first I thought
there wasn't going to be any more this.
In the convenience store of spring

I met someone who knew someone I loved
by the dairy case. All ribbons parted
on a veil of musicks, wherein
unwitting orangutans gambled for socks,

and the tasseled enemy was routed.
Up in one corner a plaid puff of smoke
warned mere pleasures away. We
were getting on famously—like

"houses on fire," I believe the expression
is. At midterm I received permission
to go down to the city. There,
in shambles and not much else, my love

waited. It was all too blissful not
to take in, a grand purgatorial
romance of kittens in a basket.
And with that we are asked to be pure,

to wash our hands of stones and seashells—
my poster plastered everywhere.
When two people meet, the folds can fall
where they may. Leaves say it's OK.

Just What's There

Haven't you arrived yet?
A sleepiness of doing dissolved my one
scruple: I lay on the concrete belvedere section
belabored by sun.   Nuts convened in the chancel,
a posse wheezed by in some oater: Chapter I, etc.

In the past I was bitten.
Now I believe.
Nothing is better than nothing at all.
Winter. Mice sleep peacefully in their dormers.

The old wagon gets through;
the parcel of contraband is noted:
a brace of ibex horns,
a scale worshipfully sung at the celesta.
We know nothing about anything.
The wind pours through us as through a bag
of horse chestnuts. Speak.

The orderly disappeared down the hall.
For a long time a sound of ferns rallied, then
nothing, only dumb snapshots of unknown corners
in strange cities. The tedious process
of fitting endings to stories.
Ground review. An obscurantist's trick.

Once you've wheedled as many as are there
at a given time, there's a certainty of dawn
in the not-much-else-colored sky. A phone booth
pivots daintily in air. O crawl back to the peach
ladder. A comic-book racetrack breathes somewhere.

A pianola was offered:
astonishment on the third floor.
The nice whore mended her ways.
The breathing came fast and thick.
The ushers will please take their seats.

Title Search

Voices of Spring. Vienna Bonbons.
Morning Papers. Visiting Firemen. Mourning Polka.
Symphonie en ut dièse majeur. Fog-soaked Extremities.
Agrippa. Agrippine. Nelly and All. The Day
the Coast Came to Our House.

Hocus Focus. Unnatural Dreams. The Book of Five-Dollar
  Poems.
Oaks and Craters. Robert, a Rhapsody. Cecilia Valdés.
The Jewish Child. Mandarin Sorcerers. The Reader's Digest
Book of Posh Assignations. The Penguin Book of Thwarted
  Lovers.
The American Screwball Comedy.

Scenes of Clerical Life. Incan Overtures. The House on 42nd
  Street.
The Man in Between. The Man on the Box. The Motor Car.

Rue des Acacias. Elm Street and After.
The Little Red Church. The Hotel District.
I'll Eat a Mexican. The Heritage of Froth.
The Trojan Comedy. Water to the Fountain. Memoirs of a
  Hermit Crab.

The Ostrich Succession. Exit Pursued by a Turkey.
In the Pound. The Artist's Life. On the Beautiful Blue Danube.
Less Is Roar. The Bicyclist. The Father.

Free Nail Polish

Cool enough. Granted,
she has beautiful legs, you know.
Men's thoughts are continually drawn behind
the apron of her success,
or to the tank top of her access
to the secrets of the great and philosophic,

of the most polite spirits
that invest these semitropic airs.

I need a tragic future to invest in.
Getting no support from others, I—
wait, here it comes along the rails,
a slow train from Podunk, the ironed faces
of the passengers at each window expressing something precise
but nothing in particular.

Yes, the mooing woods around this station are
partly extreme,
and wire fences are deep within
some parts of them. We know not
what they're for, nor why we snore
at a bug's trajectory
over the wallpaper's lilac lozenges.

Till the Bus Starts

> "This heart is useless. I must have another."
> —*The Bride of Frankenstein*

I like napping in transit.
What I ought to do
just sits there. I like
summer—does it like me?
So much cursory wind
with things on its mind—
"No time to worry about it
now," it—she—says.

In short I like many
dividers of the days
that come near to eavesdrop on our thoughts.
What about gliders?
These, yes, I like these too.

And greened copper things
like things out of the thirties.
I must have one—no,
make that a dozen, all wrapped
fresh, at my address.

And were it but a foozle
schlepping round my ankles
by golly I'd give it the same
treatment all those guys,
years, gave me. You can't fasten
a suspender stud and not know about it,
how awful they looked,
and when they returned home under trees
nobody said
anything, nobody wanted it.

Still, I'll go
out in my way, waiting
for yet another vehicle.
It seems strange I read this page before, no,
this whole short story. And what
sirens sing to me now,
cover me with buttons?

The Ridiculous Translator's Hopes

Gracious exterior, but the rooms are small and mean
and so papered over with secrets that even their shape
is uncertain, but it is the shape of the past:
no love, no extra credit, not even civility
from those shades. Do they even see you?

They were so anxious for you to be there,
once, in the playground of what was happening to them.
Messages were bright then, hats undoffed,
manners fresh and cool, like a seasonable day
in early spring. The glancing

rivulets in the gutters struck a note that was a trifle flint-like,
though, and the birds were wary, warier than usual.

It took a man with a cane to magnetize
all those invisible and partly visible crosscurrents,
reluctant, downright sullen, or ones that hadn't yet had the
    time
to reflect on what was being set up here: a point,
no more nor less. Instead of trying to kiss you,
I too felt sucked into the ambient animal-revenge scene:
By twos and threes the animals returned, to their cages,
and sat obediently while the trainer barked orders at them.
They, it seemed, had nothing to lose. Nor in all the
    whitewashed domain
of the present past tense was anyone privy to the secrets
that now make us strong, or tall, and vulnerable
as a bride left waiting at the church, inching backward
to the cliff's edge as the photographer gets ready to smile.

The Story of Next Week

Yes, but right reason dictates . . . Yes, but the wolf is at the
    door,
nor shall our finding be indexed.
Yes, but life is a circus, a passing show
wherein each may drop his reflection
and so contradict the purpose of a maelstrom:
the urge, the thrust.
And if what others do
finally seems good to you? Why,
the very civility that gilded it
is flaking. Passivity itself's a hurdle.

So, lost with the unclaimed lottery junk,
uninventoried, you are an heir to anything.
Brightness of purpose counts: Centesimal
victorious flunkeys seemed to grab its tail
yet it defied them with invention.

Stand up, and the rain
will be cold at first in your pockets.
Later, by chance, you'll discover supper
in the sparkling, empty tavern.
A nice, white bed awaits you;
your passport's in there too.

A Hundred Albums

Acts have been cleaned up.
In the latest compromise
the hip audience mostly understands.
Unpleasantness, strange blips arise,
the nine-bathroom garage.
But where are we to begin again,
and what *are* we compared to Thee,
as two men scuffle in a checkout line
and a child bends
into the light, her knowledge of innocence
as a death now, name in the register
a gloved hand signs?

For what have we been rescued, if not
to see these and other things
that have no love for us?

For relishing something once done
in secret, and you lose footing further on,
out of the frame,

and everything that proves dimensionless is haggard.

He was something, wasn't he?
Until everyone has been let in and found sleep
we go his way, profiting
from the glances we get, the attentions to
special mores that are side-splitting.
And no caretaker comes to mulch us

once the ground is frozen,
no pike stabs the secret surface of earth
in time for a vigil of all you see.

The rose in the planetarium
asks for calm QUIET PLEASE can't you
see the door is leaking embers from that last, crucial light
we'd just stopped by for, like a mug of hot wine,
but it is soup that is being dashed in your face.
Then one day he sat down and wrote that line
that is so beautiful everybody wants to hum it
on this hillside, shoulders locked swaying to
its rhythm and the Master will come forward then,
the being no creation has seen,
perfect as a crowing cock in a ballad
most will have foretold, alas.
What wretch hasn't taught me that?

A Waltz Dream

She wasn't having one of her strange headaches tonight.
Whose fault is it? For a long time I thought it was mine,
blamed myself for every minor variation in the major upheaval.
Then . . .

It may have been the grass praying
for renewal, even though it meant their death,
the individual blades, and, as though psychic,
a white light hovered just above the lake's layer
like a photograph of ectoplasm.

Those are all fakes, aren't they?
In slow-moving traffic a man acts like he's going to be hit
by the stream of cars coming at him from both directions.
Like a cookie cutter, a steamroller lops the view off.

There are nine sisters, nine deafening knocks on the door,
nine busboys to be bussed—er, tipped. And in the thievery

of my own dreams I can see the square like a crystal,
the only imaginary thing we were meant to have,
now soiled, turned under
like a frayed shirt collar
a mother stitches for her son who's away at school,
mindful he may not care, may wear
another's scarlet and sulfur raiment
just so he take part in the academy fun.

And later, after the twister, slowly
we mixed drinks of the sort
that may be slopped only on script girls, like lemonade.
Who knows what the world's got up its sleeve
next brunch, as long as you will be a part of me and all what I
    am doing?

Falls to the Floor, Comes to the Door

That arrival, a foretaste of which appalls some,
assumed its rightful place as a statistic. "I don't suppose
    you . . ."
"No," I snapped, "nor at the opera, with the slush outside.
It seems to me a mildewed brick has been planted in my path
that wasn't there when I last looked . . . *but when was that?*
Why keep the charade up, if it matters so little,
like a tiny window or a bit of missing veneer?"
Then I get my hopes up.
So much gets sorted out in coming,
like the spring cleaning you always dreamed of.
What, me? It's as though an elf on a charger commanded
me to lie on my back, under the tree whose trunk
is swelling, becoming the world, it may be.
And I have galaxies to turn out, into the street,
in knickers, anywhere, so long as they be going . . .

One reads how another one's kinsman
has inherited a vast estate in Scotland.
The things that happen to other people! Surely

it was only a minute ago I caught you in a lapsed prayer
that was answered, you said it yourself. I, from this shelf
whence I see no land, not even space, can yet recall
how the ducks danced under their umbrella.
The past was peaches then.

The Lounge

That it was a relief to him, my lord
who pestered me, with lint, with secrets,
always others' secrets, you knew
already. Two caitiffs were severed
from the trial, like a gordian knot.
That you knew too.

It is so hearty in this lounge.
Some bogus tint tampers
with the prairie sky in the mural,
makes it fresh, immediate, wrong
for these immaculate circumstances.

Then it's back to the old school, wagers,
brothels soon to come. It could have been settled
way back when so simply. But then there would have been no
    plot,
no peg to hang a dress on
of gauze the filmiest.

You, I suppose, wanted it this way
because we all want it this way.
Thus the story never gets sugar-coated,
protrudes like a bayonet from a shawl.

If there were others, they never came to see
what the disturbance was about. In fact there was
no disturbance, nothing to slide a hand along,
only postscripts and self-mutilation
the old way: cash and carry,
no refunds.

The Improvement

Is that where it happens?
Only yesterday when I came back, I had this
diaphanous disaffection for this room, for spaces,
for the whole sky and whatever lies beyond.
I felt the eggplant, then the rhubarb.
Nothing seems strong enough for
this life to manage, that sees beyond
into particles forming some kind of entity—
so we get dressed kindly, crazy at the moment.
A life of afterwords begins.

We never live long enough in our lives
to know what today is like.
Shards, smiling beaches,
abandon us somehow even as we converse with them.
And the leopard is transparent, like iced tea.

I wake up, my face pressed
in the dewy mess of a dream. It mattered,
because of the dream, and because dreams are by nature sad
even when there's a lot of exclaiming and beating
as there was in this one. I want the openness
of the dream turned inside out, exploded
into pieces of meaning by its own unasked questions,
beyond the calculations of heaven. Then the larkspur
would don its own disproportionate weight,
and trees return to the starting gate.
See, our lips bend.

"The Favor of a Reply

is requested." That's where it began—
something like an engagement, with collusion
in its footsteps following. Like the slanted look
in the eyes of old portrait photographs—the three-quarters
view is more than sufficient to tell the ambition,
the dread.

There's some reality, too, some entertainment
here. Did you see where the couch rests
after dinner, the clearing up, the
white skirts around the house?
No one ever made it up but no one
made it sound better.

They dragged you out after that.
It wasn't until the leaves were partly rusted,
clashing with the fresh green, that a cover-up
was admitted. By then it was time to get new clothes,
new coals—to adjust. And some are still coping,

the mist still seems to cause them to blush
though it's only an illusion. After sex
there's nothing, only a reason,
a table of wearied books. A piece of lace
hung high up in the sky.

A Held Thing

Then he sort of lobbed it
over the fence if you know what I mean.

I do know what you mean
but I shall not tell anyone
about it until all your meaning
is clear to me, that is until it becomes clarity
that sucks us out of the void and across the orchard.

A HELD THING

When I was a little teenager
I heard the far-off voices and imagined
them to be cries painted on a canvas.
Each had its own color, or a more vivid
approximation of that color, waiting
to be invited in for tea, or anything,
patted on the head.

I must haul myself down from there—
underbrush too thick with communion.
We've a million reasons for eccentric behavior
or even outright madness—you have only to choose one
and follow it to its logical conclusion.
Say you are sitting in that orchard,
mending or praying—the overhead rush
will make you think of a dog, and in time
wonder whatever happened to that dog.

Okay for starters but the colors
are more bleak and heavy now
but that's all right because more rounded,
human, like a statistic in mourning
for the body it used to represent
back in the good old days.

Now that you've come this far
it makes sense to take stock of you
in the mirror. Seams straight? "Seems"
they are. But you must get off the hood
of that car, or the bonnet, whatever the English call it,
for it to be happening, falling days and days
in dumb amaze. Happening like a city
of little explosions that protects
you wherever you go. And we need that protection—
It's colors, just like the ones were at the beginning.

Strange Things Happen at Night

Without thinking too much about it,
prepare to go out into the city of your dreams.
Now, look up. At first they cannot see you.
Later, the adjustment will be made.
Your boyfriend sips bark tea.

The number should've turned up by now.
Perhaps the driving rain impedes it,
the recession. In any case there are two too many of us here.
We must double up, or die.

And that might be a practical if remote solution.
It's not every day you get to bicycle past the ribbons
of people, watch the grand hotels
for some event thought imminent—not lost.

If ever I was going to turn up your volume—
but this isn't about living, is it?
Or is it? I mean, many suppers in the seven modes
or grades, as many as can be made to last
once the bosses and their beagles have passed through.

World's End

Sometimes it's more time than we care to be,
with the others. Sometimes it's interesting.
I can only tell you how to stop things happening.

Life is legendary. We're very bullish
on life. Dogs and other lives
convince us life is dog-cheap.

The future is a ghost. The past,
it says here, is an automated manikin.
Not death, one of his plenipotentiaries.

Sea in my regards,
this life is lit
with all the sleep it can absorb.

I used to shuffle a lot. Someday
with luck, I'll make it to the newsstand
and buy some cherries, greet old friends.

Ice Cream in America

All of us getting our licks
and then some: the proud with the small,
those who fell off the canvas
and reappeared downstream.

. . . always forgets her pills, reverses herself, takes some.
The hen thinks chicks,
the man in the moon, profile: a piece
of the undoctored action.

We wake up, admire the day,
let our shoes take us where they will.
The weather's glorious:
a real shine.

Fill your cap with nuts.

Works on Paper I

Life in Japan is one of the most famous with all these
chairpeople and night stalls brewing
around a contradiction,
but the fowler knows his business takes him elsewhere,
telephoning, with more time to awake in the crystal pageant
of perplexed symmetries. Doomed because of it?
I never get hangovers until late afternoon

and then it's like a souvenir, an arrangement.
An old Dutch taxi takes us down to the sea
where other passengers are trying to change their reservations,
but the great flummoxed geodesic dome won't let them.

What will he do with it?
You're looking at an empire that has lost its clangor.
You get there by dying.

I tell particularly a thousand pounds of dust I saw
interspersed between the benign mountain-shapes
on the outskirts,
and how everyone was reasonably free to change. After all,
we make no effort to distinguish ourselves.
Those who wish to remain naked are coaxed out of laughter
with tea and nobody's nose is to the grindstone
anymore, I bet, and you can figure out these shivering trees.
But the owner of the bookstore knew that the flea was blown
    out of all proportion,
with September steps to go down in passing
before the tremendous dogs are unleashed.

Local Time

    What can we do,
                except
    clasp, unclasp the hand that never is ours,
    much as it wants to be? Under a gray skylight
    the eclipse burns still, there are lilies, perfection
    arrives, and then the tines
    unearth fewer embers. Can it be time to go?

    Models, when they undress,
    misread the configuration even
    while confessing to no version:
    the heated or the clad. Tight boy,
    you reminded me of dragonflies skulking,
    of aromatic fires peaking,

and neither of us gets to know the other.
Next thing you know it's winter.
The skylight, now aproned with white,
is our bare harvest.

But there is good in reappearing:
the flames' roar, beaker of scotch, the old way
things were probably supposed to be all along anyway.

Well, Yes, Actually

To whom it may concern: Listen up.
About a year and a half ago a young man was in my office.
This young man,
whose name was Michael,
was the friend of another young man I already knew, Frederick
    by name.
Well, the upshot of it was, Michael,
who had pulled himself up by his bootstraps, wanted
to know the secret of things already not so secret,
like: Water, does it seem swollen, or how much does it weigh
when all the water molecules have been withdrawn,
and to whom does one address oneself after the correct
    answers have been passed around?
I told him, as best I could,
indeed, as I have told others in the past, that such soft
mechanisms, such software, can't be regulated, and if it could,
no one would want any answers. Well, he just sits there,
dumb. Then, as the call of the crow renews itself
across valleys and pastures, in the island at night,
the answer speaks in him too. Only it can't, he realizes right
    away,
ever be repeated. Or someone would pull nettles in
    exasperation,
slapping them all over the place, and then what devil-may-care
attitudes it pleases you to ration out will be flat as paper,
flatter than shadows peeled off of pavement. But I digress.

In this town, near this tree, a school rose proud and tall
once, and from a distance many were seen going in and out
    of it
as the bell sounded the hour from its red, hacienda-like tower.
And sure, mutts wandered in and out too,
and radish sellers. Well, one
man, a rustler to all appearances, wasn't happy
with the school and all its appurtenances: desks, faucets,
blackboard erasers and such. He thought it was a pity
that some come to learn and enjoy, while others plait
their tresses idly, in cool shadow, and read no book
and add no sum, the while the milk sours
happily, in the shade. And children from out of town would
    come
and look down at the others, and they too would fall to
    quarreling
until the teacher summons all, and says,
"Blessed children, my children. I would have it no other way
but this." And the man thinks, if that's what they teach you in
    school,
maybe I should go back to school. For I'm a loner, I warrant,
and loners never learn, though they may know the one thing
nobody else knows, or, by the same token, needs.
And a shadow fell across the fields
of radishes: This was the real, the genuine article,
and all other speculation had been slightly but sadly displaced.

And they thought about it. The teacher thinks about it to this
    day,
wondering where she went wrong,
why the prisms no longer irradiate electric colors
and the Bunsen burners cause no retorts to fume
and gurgle over, over the long desks that were.
These are the apples of my crying,
she says, the ones they never brought me, and I,
I am too distressed to dream.
Well, don't you think Michael and Frederick heard about it
and were the first to offer their condolences? But first
they swept all the chalk bits into a neat pile
and dedicated it to the stranger, and to the teacher they offered

the product of Pomona's blissful yearnings,
who dances alone all day by the sea, inebriated,
yet loves us as only a modern spirit can.
And they propped the door open
with a wedge-shaped piece of wood, so that it stayed open all
    the time.

My Gold Chain

Under the big Greenaway hat, the Diva,
diamonds aslant . . . Heavy trains hiss past, whiffing
the stench of Petersburg's canals, and the station
men's room thereof. What is it, spring? I can't

help being a little European. At times. After all.
I had no say in the matter.
He hollered at me later,
"Be gone, your phantasies, sun-dried hopes

simmered to a tisane of forgetfulness, forgetfulness
in May, when everything is beginning, or would be
if it weren't so shy. But check it out next week,
the meat that bleeds on newsprint

of the butchers' scales. But by then you may not need it,
in which case, why ask me? I'm only a doryman after all . . ."
Wind enters the slim curtains.
It was all right to be like this.

Nobody ever asked me to be a bridesmaid,
so maybe I'm a bride? The things you think of telling,
only you can't, you know, tell a leaf from a silver
chewing-gum wrapper. Things we mustn't know

but nothing we can't know. His song's over, I
better get ready to go on. Tell your readers
to write me, I love their questions, only it gets
so dark sometimes, you just want to stand and shake.

Footfalls

O did he see something yesterday?
I cannot begin to say.

*Something fell
on the floor.*

A rice danger you have whipped up for us.
Congratulations, too, on the weather,
though I know you had nothing to do with that:
exhilarating, a bit flinty,
as a lock gets lost in a wash of wind.

When I've already stopped to do things, he
hasn't been able to insult you yet. Our love affair,
like dinnerware, lasted about a year,
then went away. My car's still in the rut,
but who could have foretold these greennesses,
the girl with the aigrette
who didn't barely want to sleep there?
But when we all came out, the day
assumed the role of host, did what was necessary.
Above the architecture were
tinseled outcroppings, a space in between.
In short it was marvelous, the young master was mad to
    have us,
but until such time as the thorny legal angles
can be worked out, joy must stay
imprisoned in the air around us, like humidity.

Today there were no tassels.
Funny, I'd gotten used to them,
and to the bells on your toes.
There's a story in that,
she said. I'll tell you later.
Two have already been supportive.

Weather and Turtles

The rain fell with startling regularity.
Sections of understanding were imposed
on the lake—a likable but needy reservoir—
and on that great instrument, the street.

Okay, but can we have a little luster,
here, please, a little texture? It's like a weekly occurrence,
this laughing at the limbs of people
who march by you, intent on shopping
or seeing the world—whatever, so long
as it has nothing to do with you, frantic dimwit
on your nightmarish carousel of doubt, who sees
and yet proclaims, and sees on, but no one
can stop the demented *danse macabre*
ensuing from soda fountains, shoestores, penny arcades
buried in a stratum of light like cheese.

It's the old dumb-show thing now.
I see, I read, I nap.
Thankfully the chimaera never came near me,
relaxing in its cave.

Sometimes in Places

And patient, exacting
no confirmations from those who know him,
the poet lies down under the vast sky,
dreaming of the sea. For poetry, he
now realizes, is cleverer than he.

So where to go, what to be in?
For as the robin builds a nest,
so each day weaves a bower of itself
to offer to the world. I am standing
here listening, but no one word proves the truth,
though several do. And we shall acclimate

towns, cities, sunsets, to our desire, O
accidental mandarin, and the purple
velvet of plenty dominate
our dreams, for a while, and then we shall
nod to the post, and be off again.

Day falls of its own weight.
And basing your luck on that,
you too enter the skirmish
of ghosts and dragons, and so are blessed
with deafness to the clamor of surviving
frogs' catcalls. Forgot your lunch,
was it? No, I thought you had one.
No, that was mine.

William Byrd

With the precision of one who fights, slowly, the shadow of the battering ram of absolute knowledge behind him, in a barrel-vaulted, hallowed space . . .

The gnomes' contumely notwithstanding, it was a red-letter day, really for all concerned, and then the tide poured in. It is fatal to forget this nugget of charm even as one flounders knee-deep in it, smashing at gulls, cries, the wind . . .

Art-deco priestesses summon from distinct alcoves brains made for discerning timekeeping ordeals. The little pennants that flutter ominously from the rigging of ships cannot help but evoke a charred red entity, staircase landing for some. Blue is the cobalt at which we point our belts, energetically, soulfully.

Tied in some neurosis competition, I was happy to see you as a little girl at your birthday party so many years ago, changed, and with a glove for each tear-starred hour of the day. It was graceful then to be back-bending, to half-turn as the obsessed host comes into one's line of vision, from a nameless spree, polite and indifferent, most indifferent to his politeness and that of others. For we live in a three-channeled creekbed and there are no balloon-offenses leaving from here.

I thought you had drilled the dendrite of your extra keeping into my forehead by now, flesh the texture of a reed.

And you know, the skunk family approved it too, including old Grandpa skunk. But which does not take us very far from wars and their canons. The chipped, dried paint managed to signal enthusiasm. There was beginning to be in the world like a low cloud of birds circling. The higher you direct our gaze the less it sees the struggle at your feet, out of which a victor will emerge, and yes the orphans play with us often on the sand until one by one they get adopted. Which is why the angles are all acute ones and it's colder than the inside of a pocketbook.

Suddenly, shambling
she comes up to me, a thing partly of architecture,
of how it would like to be the basis for *all* partaking,
communicating, and is in arrears because of some
dumb thing over your head. Oh well. The misery of others
is a sad thing to behold but one must contemplate as well the
    gathering
that goes on, in bits, in pits, whatever is exposed at low tide.
The brief diamond that you dangled . . . And then all want
    to come to see, tremendous
crowds overwhelm the dock, which threatens to collapse under
    their weight, but
they want to see, they *get* to see. At first it's like some
phenomenon's unbirthing, then a cold star, but always an
    alphabet among whose
letters are interlaced much affection and dying.

Hold my stinger as a stranger and I will be presently.
I haven't filled out the forms.
I can see heaths and coasts;
in them we become magic and empty again.

Assertiveness Training

I like the integrity of what you have to say,
drama or dream. What is credibility
without assertiveness, endurance without skepticism?
And the abrupt thrust of your bearing
at me under a low-hanging branch.
What shall any of these do without skeletons
as ideas? I hear the tango beginning,
the waltz that is loss. Crossed logs in the chimney . . .

Without aggressiveness, hope, I couldn't conquer any of it.
There'd be no piece of it to bring back to you,
saying, "This is me." A lie
among others we're exposed to. And when the needle finally
    swung
it was wrapped in rags, in pitch blackness.
I escaped from the dream of living
into a fairy tale with no happy ending, no ending at all,
only bedtime to live ever after.

You could climb a fence amid barberries
and never see the departing smile on the swan's face.
Only your need will be redeemed
when you dwell again among us, much misunderstood.
For now your glass prayer encases both of us.

Like a Sentence

How little we know,
and when we know it!

It was prettily said that "No man
hath an abundance of cows on the plain, nor shards
in his cupboard." Wait! I think I know who said that! It
    was . . .

Never mind, dears, the afternoon
will fold you up, along with preoccupations

that now seem so important, until only a child
running around on a unicycle occupies center stage.
Then what will you make of walls? And I fear you
will have to come up with something,

be it a terraced gambit above the sea
or gossip overheard in the marketplace.
For you see, it becomes you to be chastened:
for the old to envy the young,
and for youth to fear not getting older,
where the paths through the elms, the carnivals, begin.

And it was said of Gyges that his ring
attracted those who saw him not,
just as those who wandered through him were aware
only of a certain stillness, such as precedes an earache,
while lumberjacks in headbands came down to see what all the
    fuss was about,
whether it was something they could be part of
sans affront to self-esteem.
And those temple hyenas who had seen enough,
nostrils aflare, fur backing up in the breeze,
were no place you could count on,
having taken a proverbial powder
as rifle butts received another notch.

I, meanwhile . . . I was going to say I had squandered spring
when summer came along and took it from me
like a terrier a lady has asked one to hold for a moment
while she adjusts her stocking in the mirror of a weighing
    machine.
But here it is winter, and wrong
to speak of other seasons as though they exist.
Time has only an agenda
in the wallet at his back, while we
who think we know where we are going unfazed
end up in brilliant woods, nourished more than we can know
by the unexpectedness of ice and stars
and crackling tears. We'll just have to make a go of it,
a run for it. And should the smell of baking cookies appease

one or the other of the olfactory senses, climb down
into this wagonload of prisoners.

The meter will be screamingly clear then,
the rhythms unbounced, for though we came
to life as to a school, we must leave it without graduating
even as an ominous wind puffs out the sails
of proud feluccas who don't know where they're headed,
only that a motion is etched there, shaking to be free.

Two Pieces

I

Edith and Julian
waiting, awaited by others
in the hills, yes.

But by what unobstructed parade
ground do I reach that hill?
For it is
      simple to say
the coordinates when they greet you,
not like getting on with life,
not the street.

II

When the cauldron is
tipped, whatever
is in it flows outward
like the mouth of a river
taking out its dentures.

No obit, more socks.
And a stray whoosis
that knew your name once

now sits on the floor.
Now no aftershocks.
The horse's mane tears—

The Friendly City

Unless you put it away
he can never play with it again,
the marimba, and you know what that means.

Our city bemoans us, or does it
only seem to? Showers that come in shifts,
light poles guarded in air,
the dry cackle of trees in the Botanical Gardens?

Was it for this suburban marketplace
you wrote, and are writing still
in that wire-bound notebook?
Things like: "Man cannot stand what he has become
but he loves to lap up his own vomit"?

In that case the city will probably stay around
for most of the day. It likes your sleeping sound,
not the bad silence of the others
who are even now clogging its approaches,
giving the place a bad name.

Oh if it was a name he wanted
why didn't somebody say something?
We could have found him one so easily
like "Elector of Brandenburg,"
and the city could have seen its reflection
finally, a ducal palace, upended.

The Desperate Hours

The man, someone's uncle, went down
to where the barrier said to him why
do you disturb a corner of the universe
that is yours that had been yours
before either of us was invented?

He said truly I did not know I snore.
He said truly I invented a hoof medication.

But these are tangible, lazy things—
what about the uncertain, pallid ones
they gave you at birth to play with?
Why did not the city centers
come to be called what is this town?

He said I never saw any but chaste cheeks reflected
in her armor. The tower leans
O more desperately than it has done
these twenty centuries past.
Why is it my dungheap, my rosary?

And in this true saying all are warehoused,
the flatirons, the jib, even the two horses
not paying any real attention.

But it is your watch fob,
your crenellated bow window, bent
indeed like a bow, that's why they call them that,
your small town, your farm of about forty acres
outside it. Your wart. Your five-year diary.
Your intention to have made this once it had passed.

The Decline of the West

O Oswald, O Spengler, this is very sad to find!
My attic, my children
ignore me for the violet-banded sky.
There are no clean platters in the cupboard
and the milkman's horse tiptoes by, as though
afraid to wake us.

What! Our culture in its dotage!
Yet this very poem refutes it,
springing up out of the collective unconscious
like a weasel through a grating.
I could point to other extremities, both on land
and at sea, where the waves will gnash your stark theories
like a person eating a peanut. Say, though,
that we are not exceptional,
that, like the curve of a breast above a bodice,
our parabolas seek and find the light, returning
from not too far away. Ditto the hours
we've squandered: daisies, coins of light.

In the end he hammered out
what it was not wanted we should know.
For that we should be grateful,
and for that patch of a red ridinghood
caught in brambles against the snow.

His book, I saw it somewhere and I bought it.
I never read it for it seemed too long.
His theory though, I fought it
though it spritzes my song,
and now the skateboard stops
impeccably. We are where we exchanged
positions. O who could taste the crust of this love?

The Archipelago

Well, folks, and how
about a run for the sister islands?
You can see them from where you stand—
will you barter vision for the sinking feeling
of lumps of clay?
                The daffodils
were out in force, as were, improbably, the nasturtiums,
which come along much later, as a rule. But so help me,
there they were.
                She said, may I offer you some?
His tangling so flummoxed him,
all he said was "Boats along the way."

Really, there are so many kinds of everything
it halts you when you think about it,
which is all the time, really—oh, not *consciously*,
that would be a waste, but in sly corners,
like a rabbit sitting up straight, waiting for what?
We can study drawing and arithmetic, and the signs
are still far away, like a painted sign
fading on the side of a building. Oh, there is so much to know.
If only we weren't old-fashioned, and could swallow
one word like a pill, and it would branch out thoughtfully
to all the other words, like the sun following behind the cloud
    shadow
on a hummock, and our basket would be full,
too ripe for the undoing, yet too spare for sleep,
and the temperature would be exactly right.

Miserere! Instead I am browsed on by endless students,
clumps of them, receding to this horizon and the next one—
all the islands have felt it,

have had their rest disturbed by the knocking knees of foals,
by kites' shrieking. And to think I could have had it
for the undoing of it,
                snug in the tree house, my plans

open to the world's casual inspection, like an unzipped fly—
but tell us, you must have had more experiences than that?

Oh the cross-hatched rain, fanning out from my crow's-feet,
the angry sea that always calms down,
the argument that ended in a smile.
These are tracks that lovers' feet fit.
But at the end they flag you down.

Gummed Reinforcements

Insane, trapped together in a . . .
How would you like one?
Growing up is what it is,
leaning into the wind, without a cent.

We had the most beautiful childhood
and lunch—that's even better.
I only paid $4.75 for mine.
An embarrassment, considering
it would be an embarrassment for me too.

Then he frolicked and said, whatever happens
happens in a dream,
eleven, twelve, fifteen times a day.
Sometimes when you are away
it happens at night,
all night.

Children we had lost once
know how to keep repeating the piece
they learned, knew the way back to us,
us, as grave robbers, of an old candy store
with a cake as centerpiece: a wild,
fragile one. Therefore read this:
a sun, mild as any, with diamond-tipped consequences
somewhere. An atmosphere of brooding, perhaps . . .

Yes! And the cake was square!
How did you guess? And all along, a
stork was creeping up the stair
to its bower, injured by the furniture
and last-minute preparations. Nobody
came to sign its register.
There was no one in the large drum
a canker folded over, looking
at you real mean-like.

And I and the dream are still only acquaintances
after all this time, a century, it seems,
from Arkansas. Did the goats get milked in time
for your hand to graze it? Was the squall over then?

Those who paint the heavenly porch
put a damper on all our ideas, extreme creations
like love. You heard me, ladies—
past and pure truth, swaying,
light out over the land.

The crowd of robbers doesn't go away.
It would rather be sunset, if that were inexorable
enough. But it's not. Count the pigeons, the people,
townspeople, running fast in all directions.
Sign here for the blanket of furze, please.

Spotlight on America

I must proceed unflustered.
I should have shopped around.
After all, comparison shopping is what this place's
all about. I think. These are very crisp.

Nothing like a big stranger in the dark
"to concentrate the mind," as Dr. Johnson said.
Venetian blinds are for keeping close watch on—
there goes another one!

And if there is no peace in declarations
they may become ornaments. After all, superstitions
did once, and aren't they very like history,
even the same thing as?

Back then when someone said "Pigs in a blanket,"
these shifting animals in nordic drapery
would coalesce. Today, other pieces of statuary
from far and near, near and far,

are hastening toward the whirlpool of history.
Well, let them try it. And if a few old pros
want it, let them try it too. Let this frangible
passing moment be the last to know, as usual.

What Do You Call It When

The fire betokened it
as a woman means many things
in this deck—
that's why unsavory characters

He knew that out of hiding
the fire would burn fast at last
providing the smooth yet crinkled edge
so much flatness requires

that from savannas
the kitchen landscape may begin:
amazed quinces
the drink on the corner
so everything would be a red or a blue sign

Crowders-out of old age
assassins of youth
gentlemen walking:
the trustees of this enterprise.

It is not difficult to single out one pearl in a bushel of them. What's needed is to set us back on the track, having gently peed, and that for some orpheum other than ourselves. Some shelter that is not us.

They laughed and began to dance in a ring, heads bobbing, ankles sweeping, the same old private dance that is remorse for not having blossomed sooner and the poison of this day, under vines, to correct that stance.

Fairs and cupolas notwithstanding it is a tray of cameos to be brushed past, the invisible seizure, as when crowds don't find what they are looking for.

So I came at last to you for the comedy of it, and in this I have no regrets, only silences, secrets, and the mask that was sent me long ago. I repeat it in paragraphs in these parts and am not ready to go home yet.

Pleasure Boats

Wash it again
and yet again.
The equation drifts.

Wallowing in penguins,
she was wallowing in penguins.

With fiendish cleverness
the foreground closes in.

The four-leaf clover loses.

Pretty Questions

The two parks interfaced,
of summer earth,
of shroud and color,
red hope.

Are you growing up to write your novel now?
He'd been waiting on tables for several years,
lost without a stinger.
Should travel agents travel less?
The girls can never be free of the volcanoes' might.

Anybody not having any?
See, it was like tar between the boards,
outlines, though without force or purpose—
just things to drag
along, carry along, to meet a fee
with. And the damage
during the minute was requested:
that it was over last night
before quitting was necessary,
in a certain way that I was going to tell you about.

They came at me with ice-cream implements.
You read it first here.

Why you are all blue,
your shoes are too,
so is the barrel of space that encloses us.
Maybe everything is.
We should want it to be.
Help. I have to go to the bathroom.
Why, there's your difference, of course,
your having to come down
from the park, gorse-scented,
and the pleasing treetops.
Not much of this was ever mine
but some of it had to be for

me to invest it with a shine.
Go on. I'll go on doing that
if we can stay together, play together.

The two mountains *were* all mine.
They are yours now.
That is, you can have them if you want them
and the day that comes with them.

Pathless Wanderings

Whereas I, efficacious ruin,
in former times a ladder, no quarter
gave to the bullies as they were emptying out
of school, in the time of roses.
It seems I grew exceeding tall.
There was something wrong with most men.

Women, however, were overcome with sympathy
where the last lawn tennis had been.
In my sleep I shared tears and bread
with my loving companions. We were three,
stamped with the bravura of those times.

I can tell you not one swatch matters now.
The tide has come in once too often.
We kneel to say our prayers
to an enormous kettledrum. The reeds' stance
perfects the searchlight's curving grasp,
sleeps behind things.

Which is what we all . . .
Then when I saw the ball descending
and felt the air crisped for the packaging of me
I did what others before you have done:
appeared to you as a raven in a dream
that washed away all landscapes, now and to come.

Too bad the birds don't like their bath.
I like it cheaper,
and to have the exact change,
teeth for this meat.

On First Listening to Schreker's
Der Schatzgräber

The woman with the confused soul keeps calling.
Was gibt es? Now that you're in Honolulu you've got to live it up
no matter what kind of grub they throw at you
on Main Street. O but my past is operatic
you see, the glitter, wink and shimmer,
all are in my bones. The hegemony of irrational
behavior always leaves the by-then-very-determined hoplites
    astonished,
they moan in groves. Or do you prefer

the sea? How about this empty, gravel-encrusted courtyard?
The sea please. A time of increased understanding.
Such things as male bonding didn't exist.
En revanche, ponytails were something small horses wore.
Asses in gear, we frisked in salt-air sunlight. Obviously a whole
    lot
aren't going to exist today; we should be thankful for it
and pick up our rooms, for tonight the night will be bright,
fewer of us than can stand it will be chosen,
examined, tossed cruelly into corners like rag dolls
missing one or more limbs. Say, then,
what did you want when you came here?
Was it to subvert our cunning, our lust,
and turn them back on us, reflections in a chipped pocket
    mirror?
And if so why then utilize us
as indicators? Our auras are unsafe,
or so we think, so we have been taught. And those who graze
    them
invariably come to grief.

But that's just what life's about, isn't it?
So your coming sped our just deserts.
One is off with a nerd in a pothole somewhere.
And we can have, have, I say,
whatever surplus barriers come our way.
But be brief. What remains to be quizzed will be spelled out
    for us
in the epilogue, in the unheated crawl space under the eaves.
The time of the fool approaches. And an aureole is running.

Dinosaur Country

So, with a bath and tin words,
the stranger settled in. Just so,
the evening idlers—lorikeets, back-
scratcher vendors, declined to take cognizance.

Everyone waits for the BIG day
that happened billions of years ago
or is definitely tomorrow—take your pick—
while fending off tunnel vision in the race
for the sauna. The new purple bath towels
are here!

But what if on a subtle
sky-ridden day some scum comes up to you and sez:
"Jeez! Can't anybody take a joke anymore?
I was only asking after the missus and those ten
dear, dim orphans whistled for the fur to fly.
Now I'm on an island in a self-engrossed river
with the selected essays of Addison and Steele
and enough K rations to last till Michaelmas
and its daisies, which, incidentally,
bloom only for me."

I'd thought no one knew about the pact between me and
    Junior.

But a woman getting off a bus twisted her ankle and shouted:
"For the last time! My dwelling place is no longer your oven
no matter how much you fancy its delicately frosted petits fours."

And then there was the time
when you just joked coming
up to me, laid your wrist on
my shoulder and whispered the news about
the Romans: They'd won again,
and, what was more to the point, done so
in an era that surpassed the age of the dinosaurs
by as much as this minute moment of pleasure
scoffs at you for the taking, and you flash your sweatshirt
for everyone in the country to see, and hold on to.
Yes, there are shadows still, but
cheap compared to the price you'd pay for not gainsaying
that sail swooping toward you, for not getting even
with the white-haired acrobats.

Leeward

Up, up it rises,
the penumbra,
for all to see.

Heaven is open—
make no mistake.
That row of books
just slid over by itself,
and a guy, a tubby guy,
came to look at it, sneer,
snicker, be off again—only,
ouch! There are other strands
in that equation, he sees now, not
too late. The green spoilage,
all other things being equal,
may be contained.

Only wear your shirt right.
Wash it again
and yet again.
The bear is still around
whose hide you sold,
wondering why children fear him.
Is it too much to ask
safe conduct, yes, for him too
in the travesty of night
we all must wear
for a while?

Paraph

I have to sign my name
to this paragraph. Writing pieces you can't use up
till the bus starts. I feel like a beer,
buxom brew.

One felt secure, reading
the edge of a newspaper.
More schools come out. An overload.
Destiny and the comics. Two can't play
as one. In the box outside
the golf course hasn't disappeared.

Spot watering of test areas
guarantees a mediocre result. We can dance
to it.

We can't read around the edge, the rim
is whiter before we were done.
Check this out. A situation
in which no situations appear.

And the code is locked in your throat.
We should be leaving or
the bird will chide us,
no chime break.

Not Planning a Trip Back

And the ignorance on your hands is August,
is white August. Breathe but on a stone
and a common wish-fulfillment is put in reverse.
All these dinners you paid too much for—
not worth writing about? Then the astral walk
resumes. Men are playthings. I've been
notified before.

Or pause before a bush in August,
and the trepidation that is natural in men
takes root here too, is bigger than before
but not so just. Take a boat ride.

I give to strangers—make that, I grieve to strangers,
asking no rebuttal, no rebuke. The jackass
is off his rocker again. How pliant the gold of the stars
is! We stare and stay, then part anyway.
There's a reason for this, but it's shut up
in a tomb, somewhere.

Oh the wind whips through here sometimes.
Gosh, does it? Can't these feuds
ever be removed, like lace panties?
Can't we stare down the stair
that's coming to get us? If we had the right look
everything could be secular, and easy.
But the soul isn't engaged in trade.
It's woven of sleep and the weather
of sleep. Forgets what there is to hide.

Myrtle

How funny your name would be
if you could follow it back to where
the first person thought of saying it,
naming himself that, or maybe

some other persons thought of it
and named that person. It would
be like following a river to its source,
which would be impossible. Rivers have no source.
They just automatically appear at a place
where they get wider, and soon a real
river comes along, with fish and debris,
regal as you please, and someone
has already given it a name: St. Benno
(saints are popular for this purpose) or, or
some other name, the name of his
long-lost girlfriend, who comes
at long last to impersonate that river,
on a stage, her voice clanking
like its bed, her clothing of sand
and pasted paper, a piece of real technology,
while all along she is thinking, I can
do what I want to do. But I want to stay here.

Man in Lurex

It's only a matter of days now.
The luster on the child's eye says so.
Be back before morning she says.
O return! Return so that my enemies may see me
lolling in the grape arbor.

Once we've given our brother a breather
where is the hill that will take us down?
He loved the formal: sonatas and knot gardens
and more manner than one had anticipated:
alienating, idled.

Down farther: the economics of doubt,
this carapace, gives pause to some.
For us it is the very concept, the scent
of home. As snowshoes are meant for snow.

In the Meantime, Darling

The time is for going out
and across.
One woke up and wished he was dead.

There is for everyone a solemn feeling
unless you put it away.
Go on adumbrating he said.

Go on listening because
eavesdropping is the only way to write.
O so you're doing a handbook again.

Thought I'd ankle over.
Then the sea rushed past.
Hurricane Charlie and his sister
sure were glad to see us.

At times there is a daze
with a diamond-like purity.
These and others could be sent for later.

It's not the food in his mouth.
He'd hear others could become
and just drift away.

Pterodactyls still haunt
the ethnic ballpark.
It's better this way,
just inside this window
as night approaches.

Just for Starters

Charges about this unhappiness:
They would run out and stay a minute,
exhibit the requisite stinginess,
roll up in a blanket.

That's how they and she looked to you and me.
But of course we were vendors of a sort,
tied to no actual drift, and so
when it became poorer and spoons were put up for sale
we stood in our back alleys, chagrin
painted brilliantly on our faces.

I don't know what got me to write this poem
or any other (I mean, why does one write?),
unless you spoke to me in my dream
and I replied to your waking
and the affair of sleeping and waking began.

No matter how hard I try
I can't get back on the tricycle.
Look, a fish is coming to save us.
A sail nods gallantly in our direction.
Maybe unimportance isn't such a bad thing after all.

Bromeliads

In my original philosophy for the age of gink
it felt like a harp was being plucked.
How not to respond to those suggestions, if that's what they are,
like little breezes lifting grass and leaves,
as a delta of mattering fans out from
a point like a minimal encounter.

That's how I faced up and got far away
from the lucky island and arrived at this place of crossings
where no two things occupy the same outline

in both space and time. It's as if the people
who brought you up were to abandon you in your best
 interests
so as to bring on a crisis of enlightenment—
and then jump up from behind furniture and out of closets
screaming, "Surprise! Surprise!" But it's not clear
just who ages in the process. I look ever closer
into the mirror, into the poured grain of its surface, until
 another I
seems to have turned brusquely to face me, ready
to reply at last to those questions put long ago . . .

Will we achieve anything? Not likely.
But as starlings occur in patterns, and in pairs, it
seems that *does* mean something and you shouldn't stay
in your cave until this century is forgotten.
Who'd pay the photographer then?
Did I tell you your prints are ready,
that you look as reckless as an enchanter emeritus
and weary as the first gables of spring?

Commercial Break

Take care of values. The rest is shopping,
raiding the islands
for what little coral they possess.

Tell me . . . You opted for the shrimp cocktail.
I have no more
sand in my shoes. The witch squints at the fire.

Sicilian Bird

The perfume climbs into my tree.
It is given to red-haired sprites:
words that music expresses
almost amply.   The symphony at the station
then, and all over people trying to hear it
and others trying to get away. A "trying"
situation, perhaps, yet no one is worse off than before.

Horses slog through dirt—hell,
it's normal for 'em.

And that summer cottage we rented once—remember
how the bugs came in through the screens, and
all was not as it was supposed to be?
Nowadays people have cars for things like that,
to carry them away, I mean,
I suppose.   And wherever man sets his giant foot
petals spring up, and artificial torsos,
dressmaker's dummies. And an ancient photograph
and an ancient phonograph, that carols

in mist. Pardon. The landlord locked us out.

Mutt and Jeff

> But what he does, the river,
> Nobody knows.
>   —Hölderlin, "The Ister"

Actually the intent of
the polish remained well after
the soup was nailed down. Remnants to cherish:
the sunset tie old Mrs. Lessing gave me,
a fragment of someone's snowball.

And you see, things work for me,
kind of, though there's always more to be done.
But man has known that ever since the days
of the Nile. We get exported
and must scrabble around for a while
in some dusty square, until
a poster fragment reveals the intended clue.
We must leave at once for Wabash.

And sure enough, by the train side the blue-
uniformed bicycle messenger kept up easily
and handed me the parcel.
"Ere the days of his pilgrimage vanish,"
I must reflect on exactly what it was he did:
how lithe his arm was, and how he faded
in a coppice the moment the yarn was done.

Still, the goldfish bowl remains
after all these years like an image
reflected on water. It was not a bad thing
to have done what I have done,
though I can imagine better ones, but still
it amounted to more than anyone ever thought
it would. The mouse eyes me admiringly
from behind his chair; the one or two cats
pass gravely over or under my leg from time to time.
The point is there's no bitterness,
not here, nor behind the scenes.

My sudden fruiting into the war
is like a dream now, a dream palace
written for children and others, ogres.
She was braining my boss.
The day bounced green off its boards.
There's nothing to return, really:
Gumballs rattled in the dispenser, I saw
my chance for a siesta and took it
as bluebottles kept a respectful distance.

Coventry

*There was one who was put out of his house
and another that played by a pond*
of a lateness growing,

one that scalded his hand.

And now, he said, please deny there was ever a house.
But there was one and you were my mirror in it.
These lines almost convey the comfort of it,
how all things fitted together in their way.
But it was funny and we left it—
her address, her red dress.

Just stay out in the country a lot.
You have no house. The trees stand tentless,
the marmoreal floors sweating . . .
A delusion too.

Good thing. Good luck.
You'd have to stay in Coventry.
But I'm already there, I protested.
Besides, doesn't any leaf or train want me
for what I'll have stopped doing when I'm there,
truly there? Yet who am I to keep anything,
any person waiting? So we diverged
as we approached the city.

My way was along straight boulevards
that became avenues, with barrels of trash burning
at each corner. The sky was dark but the blue light in it
kept my courage up, until the watch spring
broke. Someone had wound it too tight, you see.
Then I could only giggle at the odd bricks,
corners of tenements, buildings to be leased.
I fainted, honey.

And I never saw you again
except once walking fast

across the Victorian station
lit by holiday flares
yet strangely dumb and rumorless
like all the sleep and games that jammed us here.

And the Stars Were Shining

I

It was the solstice, and it was jumping on you like a friendly
   dog.
The stars were still out in the field,
and the child prostitutes plied their trade,
the only happy ones, having learned how unhappiness sticks
and will not risk being traded in for a song or a balloon.
Christmas decorations were getting crumpled in offices
by staffers slumped at their video terminals,
and dismay articulated otherness in orphan asylums
where the coffee percolates eternally, and God is not light
but God, as mysterious to Himself as we are to Him.

Say that on some other day garlands disbanded
in the fresh feel of some sea air,
that curious gulls coasted from great distances
to make sure nothing was getting more than its share
of pebbles, and the leaky faucet suddenly stopped dripping:
It was day, after all. One of those things like a length of sleep
like a woman's stocking, that you lay flat
and it becomes a unit of your life and—this is where it
gets complicated—of so many others' lives as well
that there is no point in trying to make out, even less read,
the superimposed scripts in which the changes of the decades
were rung, endlessly, like invading kelp, and
whatever it takes to be a simp is likely not what saved you
in time to get here, changing buses twice, and after,
when they sent you to your corner to lick
your wounds you found you liked licking
so much you added it to your repertory of insane gestures,

confident that sleep would punish those outside
even as it rescued you from the puzzle of the dance,
some old fire, thought extinguished, that now
blazes in the stove, and in an instant we realize we are free
to go and return indefinitely. Is that

what you meant by lasting? Oh, sure,
hedgerows are in it too, and the doves there and insects
and treed raccoons that eye one with frank disapproval:
"You unmitigated disaster, you!" I was pleased to discover
one could flatten or otherwise compress it, its Tom
Tiddler's ground having induced only a subcoma, a place
where grown men drink screwdrivers and giggle at the melee
that would certainly have resulted if someone, some prince
    regent or sheriff,
hadn't been in charge, while the long day moped
and opened the fan of its grievances, harassment
being the only one that stands out in the blur now, after such
    distance.

The steed returned home alone, requiting all previous loves.

II

To have been robbed of a downturn
today, I have drunk some water,
rollicked in the texture of a late,
unfinished sonata,
sinking into snow,
falling forward in the oratory,
violent as the wolf's cue and anything
you take from that side of the ledger
only beware of boredom, boredom-as-spell.

Then, slipping into the gentle jacket of
my having to know why everybody passes me,
how I cursed that heir, braided that subway
of signals seen only from behind,
the old rug and its mug—all were madness for me,
yet only dust. And as I undid its much-stitched

frogs, a near melancholy approached
from across the lake—little slivers
of sense unbent, that were right about it all
in their way, though I unlatched these tears,
bleached for the occasion.
                        The stairs knew
it was under them, but by the same token couldn't
    acknowledge
the enormous debt lifted from the mountain's brow.

And the same foreman, the same teacups jingle still,
following a localized pattern,
uncovering what till now has been everyone's pill.

III

The nude thing was taken around
to various ambassadorial residences.

And on the day he had come home
to see her, her in the maze of
sandwiches some artisan proposed,
he was like a bee in summer.

Remember the reflexive mode, the soul
can live with that, or live behind
it he said, to no avail. The last
breasts caught up.

And in morning like sugar she gave her head
to the toll-places the mind suggests.

IV

words like so many tiny wheels
—Joubert

divide the answer among them
on the façade of the spinning jenny as it
approaches improbably,
a toxic avenger . . .

Later amid the hay of reasons
we sort out a sparse claim.
Was it to be thirty he dressed her
in black-and-white checkers of gingham,

or,

perforce, did the lad go athirst
thinking no doubt too late of the spines,
pelage of mingled hairs and spines,
when all would have meant protection
for him from the main highway, the chief.

        A porch

rattles in the near, clear distance.
There was never any insistence on a name,
though we all have one. Funny, isn't it?
Yours is Guy. I like "Guy," "Fanny" too,
and they grow up and have problems same as us—
kind of puts us out into the middle of the golf course
of the universe, where not too much ever happens,
except growing up, hook by hook,
year after tethered year.
And in the basement, that book,
just another thing to fear.

      v

The problem
would have to have had so many other things wrong with it
to remain remonstrably a problem that we would have had to
  float,
it to its bottle of capers, I to my mound of gin,
for the others to see us and pretend not to notice.

That would have been the bonanza, the great volcano,
but as they say in Cheyenne, "Ain't some weekends no
more than sister days of the week when it comes to volleyball
and dimity shrouds," and aquarelles are for the masses

to live off of, when food and conversation run out.
I know because I was a kid with a banana,
but that's for eternity only. All other gaps open out
in the mind of the possessed. I'll be glad to

repeat what I said in court, but send
no lawyers after me, no *papier bleu*, if you please . . .
And the spider shinnied down the thread it was making as it
    did so,
curious about what other alarming event could be occupying
    this same moment,
and when he got there, well, it was too late. Death
makes no excuses and, by the same token, exacts none.
The race
is to the fit, and it's a great day for the race,
the human race, yes, but also the tent race,
and my husband is as a cored apple to me:
beautiful, sometimes, and in and out of the dark.

We cared less for each other
than any two people on earth, but the point is we cared.
Don't tell the scotties we didn't.
They wouldn't believe you anyway—it's just
that my mind is full of eyes, days like this.

VI

A silly place to have landed,
I think, but we are here.
The door to the dressing room is ajar.
A tremendous fight is going on in there.
Later, they'll ask and you'll say you heard nothing
out of the ordinary, now, not that day.
Madame had gone out . . .

So bring the scenery with you.
Midwife to gargoyles, as if all or something
were appropriate, you circle the time inside you,
plant an asterisk next to a kiss,
and it was going to be okay again, and the love

of which much was made settles closer, is a paw
against a wrist. Hasn't finished yet,

though the bread-and-butter machine continues to churn out
faxes, each grisette has something different
about her forehead, is as a poinsettia
in the breeze of Rockefeller Center. I don't like
a glacier telling me to hurry up, the ride down is precipitous.
Then a smile broke out on the ocean face:
We had arrived in time for the late lunch.
The dogs were instructed not to devour us.
And so much that in the past
was kept in flavors of ice-cream sodas now jumps
into one's path. We'll have to
take note of that for tonight's return trip,
though silver sleighbells pamper us,
hint that we'll get to see the Snow Queen
after all, at long last, obscuring the fact
that somebody *was* running along the courtyard.

Then the janitor wasn't screwy, the mickey
he was to have been slipped was stuck in heavy traffic,
and all those conversations about carbon dioxide
were a smokescreen too. How brittle it all was,
in the way abstractions have, and yet how
much it mattered for those children: It was their
funeral, and they should have had a say in its undoing
by the lighthouse's repeated lunges.
He claimed it was to read Sir Walter Scott by.

No one ever questions *him*. That asparagus-like mien
wasn't made to encourage dolts and stutterers.
Yet I think a clue is back here
behind the sofa, where lost bunnies whimper
and press together. He *had* been a seafarer,
who knew where his last hamburger
had come from, and whose cursive signature adorned
the polished bullet. In a little while peace
would establish itself, welcome foreigners and venture capital,
and tides rush in to destroy

what little progress in unleashing the sense of things
I and my classmates had made. We were still
at the beginning of the alphabet, chanting things like "Tomes
will open to disgorge intuiting of our altered dates,
we stepchildren, who had no place to go, and nowhere
to be late, and brash breezes
play with our buoys. Still, a little consideration
might have helped, at that point." And time will be as precise
as a small table with a cordless telephone on it, next to a television.

VII

Rummaging through some old poems
for ideas—surely I must have had some
once? Some people have an idea a day,
others millions, still others are condemned
to spend their life inside an idea, like a
bubble chamber. And these are probably
the suspicious ones. Anyway, in poems
are no ideas. No ideas in things, either—
her name is Wichita.

Later with candles coming to the
celebration, it occurred to me how
all this helps—if it wasn't here
we'd be like lifeguards looking for prey.
Look, one of them stops me. "Your
candle, sir?" Dammit, I know there was something
I was supposed to remember, and now I'm lost.
"Oh no you're not, the smile on that big
bird's beak should be enough to let you in
on the secret, and more." He's here to help,
the whole darn nation is, even as
tidal waves suck at its precipices and high-speed
dust storms dement its populace. One
will say he's seen an anchor in the sky—
why am I telling you this? It's just that the light,
violet, impacted, made a difference
for a moment
back there.

The bug-black German
heels and back areas, the long tilted
cloaks for sale, the others—yes,
they're still here?
Something must be done about it
before it does it itself. You know
what that will be like. The white tables with their
roses are so beautiful. It doesn't matter if the corn is faded.

VIII

I've never really done this before.
See, I couldn't do it. Does this
make a difference to you, my soul's
windshield wiper? See, I can try again.

Now, try to expose it.
We'll look back and it won't seem
so long ago. This late in Dec.
you go from day to night in 32 minutes,
the peonies ajar—

That which I polished
as a child stands up to me.
A peashooter blows away
the soldiers.

I have seldom encountered more libidinousness
on the road to the tracks. My shanty
looks okay to me now, I can live with it
if not in it,
who had the prescience—the prescience of mind
to buy a part of New York
while it was still a logo on someone's umbrella,
a rococo convict from the Laocoön tableau.
Those snakes get worse each season
the deaf man said
and he had reason
on his side, they were strangling his kid
and goat even as we talked in the parched

weather that was obscurely damp and white.
Next swamp we'll do better,
tidy up things, the davenport
that got thrown out, the kerosene lamp
you wanted for your henhouse. The stoves,
so many of them. The refrigerator:
Eskimos really do need them
to keep their food from freezing
you said to the teacher, and my eye
is dry, all the riddles come undone.

Hot, swift choices
over the lake in May.
The old gray mare.
Violets blossomed loudly
like a swear word in an empty tank.
The fish mostly had gone home
the admiral repeated falling into
his habitual stammer—whenever he came
to the words "iron blow" it happened for him,
poor rich man, who despised the stall tickets
once he recovered from the rage
of being within us again.

And whether it was smoke on a balcony
or idle laurels that seem to creep
out of his books in the library
we were chastened—"by the experience"
and so went to bed and never read again.
It was glorious standing up in the various rain
to keep clear of the teeth but that changed nothing
fast like a fast game of checkers.
The kind of cry that can't be heard

yet others outside might know of
soon as the mist was sucked
up through a tube and the platonic curve
returned for various dignitaries to perch on
like members of the Foreign Legion or the French Academy.
Androgynous truths never shattered anyone's

complacency on Broadway even though they use thermal down
now (I thought it had been outlawed)—
beckoning though maybe not at you
as you come to evaluate
all the leaning together.

And the store models are free
for the asking—aye, that's just it,
"for the asking." What isn't? And who
can make that chirp
sound round in the eye of the traveling salesman—
taller than might have been expected, than Mont Blanc—
who sees the talisman perishing amid lichees
while others gape and walk back toward
Washington Square.

If I had night I would feed it to you
but I have something much better—the desire to run
away for president, with you
in my back seat. And whether butter
brings a smell of gas with it or the Beefeaters
look bloated, all is of some concern to us—
we didn't need to be separated before you knit that
sweater as a plenary indulgence: shimmering
with only pastel colors like a life lived
near sunlight exclusively, like a page turner's
romance with the page and the soloist.

It breaks into thunder:
thought that comes to you,
a safe haven from the shipping.
Lo, a low hill welcomes those who wish
to climb its flanks, to its summit
just over the near horizon, blue and cream,
the colors of my navy she said, I'll bet yours
are similar too. That was why I had to play
my gray cape, the lost card

no one is ever conscious of having.
And if we had something for the stew,

some salt or something, why that could go in too
as long as land could still be sighted
to the left, a silver crow's nest in which all
lost objects, blue Christmas tree ornaments, arise
and sing the national anthem of Hungary
and the river garments come together with a clap
to shield those who never previously wore them
and the gold tooth extracted from a brooch
join in the general clamor
of do-gooders—the common sort of folk
all over us like a coat of burrs.

Once the bear knew he headed back to his cave.

Winter wasn't clear yet
but all the days of the year were tumbling out of its crevices,
the chic ones and the special-interest ones,
and those with no name upon them.
Everything looked slight
which was all right.

Then the magician entered his chamber.
Too bad there are no more willows
but we'll satisfy his bent commands anyway,
have a party in the dark,
throw love away, go neck in the park,
fill out each form in sextuplicate—then let the storm
be not far behind, the old graves and swords
of winter erupt out of turn. It won't be bad
for us. You see, the penguins have stayed away too long,
ditto the flamingos. I think I can make it all
come together, but for that
there must be a modicum of silence.
Your ear's just the place for it.

IX

New technology approaches the bridge.
The weir, ah the weir, combing the falls,
like the beautiful white hair of a princess.

In the oxidation tank he thinks
of fish, how strange they can get the oxygen
they need from the water, and then when it goes blank—
why, pouf! And you realized the past suffered
from housemaid's knee, and that when the present
came along, why no one would speak up,
and it just moved in, with pets . . .
For the medium future I had thought striped stockings
and a kind of beard like a haze, seen only
on certain ancient sun deities who walked
absorbed in fields, as children groused
and crocuses sputtered the unbelievable word.

Right, it's definitely our situation.
We can come out of it but not simply leave it.
It will die of having so many things in it,
like a barrel choked with leaves. Yet sooner or later,
you know, one is dipped in it
and spotted lawns, greatcoats emerge.
The cistern really was built
by the workmen while you were away.
It's alive and containing.
And so many horticulturalists sway,
inebriated with the hardiness
of the ranunculus, the gladiolus.
Even so, he asked us to leave him
alone, at night, wanted to think
or something, about love or something,
something that turned him on.

Only later when we came to bask
in his friendship, did that marine eye astonish us:
Out over so much plains, such doo-wop wind,
you'd think it wouldn't spell "ceremonial" to him.
But he merely shaved the numbers off, dawn removed
the fingerprints, and why I am with you
and these several elves, no one can piece together:
not Great-aunt Josephine or her mortician boyfriend,
not the robbers of the "School of Night" drawing.

And we shifted, you and I, causing the rowboat to take on
    water.
Strange, how a few decibels can make your day.

                              x

Of course some of us were more risible—then.
Stopping by an apartmentful of freeloaders
on a snowy evening, I was asked about the *other
mysteries*, and, forced to prevaricate, noted
that time was setting in.

As one gets peeled away from life
and distant waterspouts put their kibosh on the horizon,
just one message makes it through the triple filters:
Go easy. Your chums on this shore have
worked long and hard on the inclined-plane thing;
if you haven't any suggestions (and you haven't),
let them continue to think it was sorcery
that was lacking. The fact that no directional
arrows pointed the way to the mother lode
proves their greenery to them, and they begin
to reason: "The kitchen's not such a bad place,
if it's sinks you're after. Sure, Caruso was singing
somewhere behind the padlocked velvet door,
but if we stay—no, linger—here, the problem
will reverse itself. Tom and Jerrys all around."

As for the ritual endowment
so prized by the Coca-Cola girl, that only arrived later
to prove its wetness and wildness non-fatal
just before the sun came out and caked it.

We sure live in a bizarre and furious
galaxy, but now it's up to us to make it
into an environment for maps to sidle up to,
as trustingly as leeches. Heck, put *us*
on the map, while you're at it.
That way we can smoke a cigarette, and stay and sway,
shooting the breeze with night and her swift promontories.

XI

> But in the soul of man there are innumerable infinities.
> —Thomas Traherne

There is still another thing I have to do.
I've never been able to do this
and I have this announcement to make
over all the streets, all the years we have been difficult
leading to this. This icon. That walks and jabbers
fortuitously or not. Bells splinter the ice
and I am away, on a trip somewhere. Kansas.
It doesn't matter for me
and matters so old for you, sobs distant as tractors.
We are the people we came to see
or might as well be, bringing cabbages as gifts,
talking nonstop, barbed wire stringing the trees,
cigar smoke bellowing.

It was all the same to us,
we came in and out,
were thoughtful as strawberries, and the great athlete
    overturned us,
made us obsolete. Now that was a day I can trace
with a little mental calisthenics
and find I know what I was doing, to whom
I spoke, the kings, carriages, it was all there.
And my knowing derives no comfort
from that parallel shelving of events.
No kind of nexus. As if the doll herself knew
what you weren't supposed to know, and survived the fall
from the attic window to incriminate you,
just before the draft swept her into the furnace.
The burning is beginning again.

But there are a giant two of us,
the remnant, or product, or a complex
bristling-up-around, then a feigning of disinterest
in a corner of the room, and the fuse ignites
the furniture with blue. It's earth-shattering, they say,
as long as you contain it,

and you have to, can. The brain-alarm is being recalled
but the message exists even with no words to inflict it,
no stanzas to be cherished. For we end
as we are forgiven, with chords the bird promised
caught in our throats, O sweetest song,
color of berries, that I lied for and extended
improbably a little distance from the given grave.

XII

A late glimmer read into it
what is not to be intuited,
only pressed, like a hand or pants,
as the sea presses against rock
for lack of anything better
to do—surrounded by buddies
taking a breather, it was always thus with you,
you who come close enough to me:
Oh, you've often found
clues in the garden where the hornets
and the robins make their nests;
clues on the stairway, in the vestry
and the garage with its enormous drums.
Say something that will strengthen me,
let me sip all the colas of the world
before I dive off this reef, into
that region of ferns and bubbles that awaits us,
where all are not so bright, but a few are.
These we clasp to us, our bodies' tattoos
seeking psychiatric help, and the earth
guzzles and slurps rhythmically.
A dog would like you for it,
but here no voice says to come all the way in.

Here are holdings,
taking name in the urban dusk
that grazed you just now. Have you brought the lesson?
Good, I was sure of it. But can no longer
go out past the doorman. Here, take this basket of iced cookies
anyway. And he jubilates. Everything is in time for him,

eating in the capacity, along with the French
and motorcycle community, is what the headphones told us.
And when we no longer have each other to look at
these buzz and resonate still. From what dark pitcher
or mirror I brought you, from Duluth, and minus
astral influences, you are grateful, and for wrappings in general.
It is time to feast
so soon again.

Slow crows still rally round that puncture mark
in a Danish heaven where a sawhorse delivers
the belated aspirin and spools are wound
in the interests of a greater clarity than this:
Soon, all will be hidden,
like a stage behind a red velvet curtain,
and this mole on your shoulder—no need to ask
it its name. In the brisk concealment
that has become general everything thrives:
bushes, lampposts, motels at the edge of airports
whose blue lights guide the descending vehicle
to a safe berth in soon-to-be night,
as wharves welcome their vessels, however frumpy
they may seem, with open arms.
And I think it says a lot about us, about
our welcoming, that days don't disturb themselves
or think too much about it, or manage
the disheveled trace that was to have been our signature.
We're too cagey for that in any case,
wouldn't be fooled by the most elaborately duplicated passport,
bill of lading. It's as though we've come refreshed
from another planet, and spied immediately what was lacking
      in this one:
an orange, fresh linens, ink, a pen.

Still, the hothouse beckons.
I've told you before how afraid this makes me,
but I think we can handle it together,
and this is as good a place as any
to unseal my last surprise: you, as you go,
diffident, indifferent, but with the sky for an awning

for as many days as it pleases it to cover you.
That's what I meant by "get a handle," and as I say it,
both surface and subtext subside quintessentially
and the dead-letter office dissolves in the blue acquiescence of
    spring.

XIII

You get hungry,
you eat hot.
Home's a cold delivery destination.
The emphatic nose puts it on hold.
Clubs are full.
I kind of like the all-night dust-up
though I'm sworn to secrecy,
with or without a cat.

I let so many people go by me
I sort of long for one of them, any
one, to turn back toward me,
forget these tears. As children we played at being grownups.
Now there's trouble brewing on the horizon.

So—if you want to come with me,
or just pull at my sleeve, let them make that discovery.
Summer won't end in your lap,
nor are the stars more casual than usual.
Peace, quiet, a dictionary—it was so important,
yet at the end nobody had any time for any of it.
It was as if all of it had never happened,
my shoelaces were untied, and—am I forgetting anything?

CAN YOU HEAR, BIRD

For Harry Mathews and Marie Chaix

[Three poems published in *Can You Hear, Bird* are omitted here because they duplicate poems (in two instances under different titles) that had been included in *And the Stars Were Shining*: "Andante Mysterioso," "Heavenly Arts Polka" (published as "Sicilian Bird" and "A Waltz Dream," respectively, in *And the Stars Were Shining*), and "Like a Sentence."]

A Day at the Gate

A loose and dispiriting
wind took over from the grinding of traffic.
Clouds from the distillery
blotted out the sky. Ocarina sales plummeted.

Believe you me it was a situation
Aladdin's lamp might have ameliorated. And where was I?
Among architecture, magazines, recycled fish,
waiting for the wear and tear
to show up on my chart. Good luck,

bonne chance. Remember me to the zithers
and their friends, the ondes martenot.
Only I say: What comes this way withers
automatically. And the fog, drastically.

As one mercurial teardrop glozes
an empire's classified documents, so
other softnesses decline the angles
of the waiting. Tall, pissed-off,
dressed in this day's clothes,
holding its umbrella, he half turned away
with a shooshing sound. Said he needed us.
Said the sky shall be kelly green tonight.

A New Octagon

Over a cup of flaming tea, the ogre assessed
my chances. Nothing in this blue vault belongs
where you put it; therefore are you the dupe
of its nonchalance. Try to wriggle free, remembering

what the great collector said: Serenity is a mild bridle
lending dignity to any occasion. The best truss
is the severest, but your village
ends where mine begins. Angry little houses litigate;

the roof leaks. Present your wrist for stamping
as you go out into the northwestern territories, otherwise
we'll see whose absence becomes it.
Daughters Tiffany and Brittany concurred. There

isn't much in the way of agony impeding the astral
path you seek. On with the
ways and
the variance sequestered by others.

A Poem of Unrest

Men duly understand the river of life,
misconstruing it, as it widens and its cities grow
dark and denser, always farther away.

And of course that remote denseness suits
us, as lambs and clover might have
if things had been built to order differently.

But since I don't understand myself, only segments
of myself that misunderstand each other, there's no
reason for you to want to, no way you could

even if we both wanted it. Do those towers even exist?
We must look at it that way, along those lines
so the thought can erect itself, like plywood battlements.

A Waking Dream

And the failing panopticon? That happened before,
when my uncle was in his bathrobe, on vacation.
Leastways, folks *said* it was a vacation . . .

Are you referring to your Uncle Obadiah,
the one that spent twenty years in the drunk-tank

and could whistle all the latest hits when sprung?
No one ever cared to talk much about it, it seemed a little *too*
peculiar, and he, he had forgotten the art
of knowing how far to go too far.

Just so. When driven, he would materialize in a Palm Beach suit
and Panama hat with tiny rainbow holes in it.
That was someone who knew how to keep up appearances
until he had exhausted them. Some of the railroad crew
got to know him at times, and could never figure out how he knew
exactly when a storm would hit. And when its anthracitic orgasm
erupted, we were out in the salley gardens mending coils
from the last big one. Such is my recollection. And vipers
would pause to notice. Meanwhile he was acting more and more

like a candidate. Then the wave of beach chairs crashed over us
and there was nothing more to be said for it. The case was closed,
it was "history," he liked to say, as though that were a topic
he could expand on if he chose, but it was more likely
to be night, and no one could extricate it properly.

Yet I had been told of an estimate.
That's what we don't know! If only I could get my senses
back in the right order, and had time to ponder this old message,
I could have the sluice-gates opened in a jiffy. As it is,
they're probably more than a little rusty, and do we know,
really know, as chasm-dwellers are said
to know, which way is upstream?

Abe's Collision

So much energy deployed
in circumnavigating the seer's collisions!
Don't do it yet,
it hasn't happened.
There is something in it.

And if we were a guidepost,
life would come along one day,

verify its balance, then leave
straight into the flustered ballooning of branches,
hands on the long ramp
leading to the restaurant with its coffee.

Sure, it's time we merged.
There are no others to do it
for us, we think we're nice.
That's why we've got to do it.
It takes balls to do it
and a heavy-duty sucker across the way.

A snake will unplug the drain.
The slate will light up and read itself.

Allotted Spree

How the past filled its designated space
with every kind of drollery, so there
were not just the things one knew about.

It's the secret of my gospel, it can never
be gone for too long or get too fancy.
Everybody wants to own a share in it!
This, too, is impossible.

I saw a woman in red move, come out from behind the brush.
I saw ten milky-white puppy dogs who chanted at me:

"You're a handful." I saw the spire of St. Diana's
prick and light up the sky. Those were gnashed doldrums.

Down where the last coitus happened,
another, a new madman in a cloak and hat,
was rising with the moon. They don't let you off
for these little things. Try imagining it.

Yes but against the sofa of your captivating lens
your appetites are wizard, dear. Let's give them all
a chance. On to the starboard
list of the apartment, to the gemstone-crusted tankard.

Angels (you

know who you are), come back
when you've aged a little, when the outdoors
is an attractive curiosity no longer.
Don't get me wrong, I *like* your waving
turquoise mittens extantly. I must polish
my speech, having spent a life
watching old Steffi Duna movies, and being warned
about the consequences. It seems I should pass;
there's only one essay question, and it can be about anything
you like. Yet I hesitate, like a spermatozoid
that's lost its way and doesn't dare ask directions—
they'd club it if it did. Once you're en route
it doesn't matter if you know, besides, anyway.

Conversely the winter circuit closes down
until some time in spring, but more likely forever.
Signs of rot and corruption are everywhere
and are even copied by the fashion-conscious.
I must sugar my hair. And my factotum?

You said there was one more in your party.
No one is in a hurry.
Suddenly the day is crocus-sweet.

Anxiety and Hardwood Floors

Only a breath of this region
spindles me off and growing, yes, again.
How fine to be late in the season
where the hopeless hide their fetters
in chains of golden hair. Its air

wants nothing to do with any of us. Yet if I am
the strong man at the post office, as the clock's nine
o'clock tells me I am, why it will go better for the all
of us in here. This living
room he taunts me with. But everybody can see the
sun, abashed and unashamed, pummeling through the rusted
curtains. Pass me that box of gin,
will you?

At First I Thought I Wouldn't Say Anything About It

but then I thought keeping quiet about it might appear even
    ruder.
At first I thought I had died and gone to heaven
but that scapegrace the unruly sun informed me otherwise.

I am in my heavyset pants and find this occupation of
    beekeeper charming
though I have yet to meet my first bee.
We don't know if I get to keep the hat and veil.

"Too hot," he said. "Too hot for everything!"
He so caring, so mundane. ". . . to have you on board."
Bulgarian choirs everywhere stood up and sang the song of the
    rent.
It was lovely. Now I shall take a short vacation,
proof that I am needed here. Nobody wants my two cents

anymore, I believe. To some it was like skating in summer.
A small turret perched over the lake. It exploded.
That's the way I feel about people taking me out
to some nice repast, and afterwards you go home and
go over everything that was stated. I prefer flowers and
   breathing.

At Liberty and Cranberry

The car bounds forward eagerly, and for a moment
it's like Madrid: a taste of cinnamon and something
almost too unimportant to mention. A sense of morning
without any of the particulars that morning is,
that it inhabits, all of them, individually.
And yes we invited the fish
over again to tell about high school and yes
he came apologetically and mentioned sodomy parenthetically
until we all played cards and it was time to go.

Everybody realized
there had been such a beautiful evening.

Yet if I want to take you on my lap
and be romantic—well, or use the word "romantic"
several times and bring up the faded question
of sentiment and sentimentality, like faded lips
on a post, I'm allowed to be only monastic and neat,

while the cute are always with us,
are all around us, out on the bay, the river,
like a miniature armada
with an ad on every sail.
Go back through here, it says,
you didn't come up this way, but through here
you'll find it's very nice.

And, unruffled, we do.

Atonal Music

The hamlet stroked its reflection in a
plum—it wasn't crooning now, not for generic
supplies, anyway. They are lowering hoops
from houses, the whole thing's very much up in the air.
I twiddle my thumbs in a doorway, look
out from time to time. It's fine to reminisce,
but no one really cares about your childhood,
not even you. It's not even that, or a past,
but an aesthetic remoteness blossoming profusely
but vaguely around what *does*
stand out here and there: a window square, a bone
left by an intrepid dog. You own
them but may not appreciate them—they're
too mortal for that, for you.

I woke in the night to hear a runnel
coursing down my mansard—damn!
I'd left the trapdoor ratcheted. It all
smears me, like scenery. I can
only be ambient.

They observed me once, you know.

Awful Effects of Two Comets

There will not always be a step
to the undoing of the rightness you now so justly feel

in the edge of Hong Kong where it's all right to buy spirits. The
canal crowd threw fetters at him.
Then there will not always be a stair
to punish the unborn and the boy who said he'd rather

do it on another day. There is a chair,
its arms rubbed almost bare from excess living.
There is a fan I think over there.

Otherwise we make no money off them.
They're not worth importing, only to smoke
the tips of and then the whole magazine
goes up, to some surprise and cheers
on the part of petite nudist pedestrians

who can make nothing rise,
not even your eyes, which, seriously, I love
staring at and making love to:
I, a merchant from over the hill
with hunger and a big cow to fill.

. . . *by an Earthquake*

A hears by chance a familiar name, and the name involves a riddle of the past.

B, in love with A, receives an unsigned letter in which the writer states that she is the mistress of A and begs B not to take him away from her.

B, compelled by circumstances to be a companion of A in an isolated place, alters her rosy views of love and marriage when she discovers, through A, the selfishness of men.

A, an intruder in a strange house, is discovered; he flees through the nearest door into a windowless closet and is trapped by a spring lock.

A is so content with what he has that any impulse toward enterprise is throttled.

A solves an important mystery when falling plaster reveals the place where some old love letters are concealed.

A-4, missing food from his larder, half believes it was taken by a "ghost."

A, a crook, seeks unlawful gain by selling A-8 an object, X, which A-8 already owns.

A sees a stranger, A-5, stealthily remove papers, X, from the pocket of another stranger, A-8, who is asleep. A follows A-5.

A sends an infernal machine, X, to his enemy, A-3, and it falls into the hands of A's friend, A-2.

Angela tells Philip of her husband's enlarged prostate, and asks
   for money.
Philip, ignorant of her request, has the money placed in an
   escrow account.
A discovers that his pal, W, is a girl masquerading as a boy.
A, discovering that W is a girl masquerading as a boy, keeps
   the knowledge to himself and does his utmost to save the
   masquerader from annoying experiences.
A, giving ten years of his life to a miserly uncle, U, in exchange
   for a college education, loses his ambition and enterprise.

A, undergoing a strange experience among a people weirdly
   deluded, discovers the secret of the delusion from Herschel,
   one of the victims who has died. By means of information
   obtained from the notebook, A succeeds in rescuing the
   other victims of the delusion.
A dies of psychic shock.
Albert has a dream, or an unusual experience, psychic or
   otherwise, which enables him to conquer a serious character
   weakness and become successful in his new narrative, "Boris
   Karloff."

Silver coins from the Mojave Desert turn up in the possession
   of a sinister jeweler.
Three musicians wager that one will win the affections of the
   local kapellmeister's wife; the losers must drown themselves
   in a nearby stream.
Ardis, caught in a trap and held powerless under a huge
   burning glass, is saved by an eclipse of the sun.
Kent has a dream so vivid that it seems a part of his waking
   experience. A and A-2 meet with a tragic adventure, and
   A-2 is killed.
Elvira, seeking to unravel the mystery of a strange house in the
   hills, is caught in an electrical storm. During the storm the
   house vanishes and the site on which it stood becomes a
   lake.
Alphonse has a wound, a terrible psychic wound, an invisible
   psychic wound, which causes pain in flesh and tissue which,
   otherwise, are perfectly healthy and normal.
A has a dream which he conceives to be an actual experience.

Jenny, homeward bound, drives and drives, and is still driving, no nearer to her home than she was when she first started.

Petronius B. Furlong's friend, Morgan Windhover, receives a wound from which he dies.

Thirteen guests, unknown to one another, gather in a spooky house to hear Toe reading Buster's will.

Buster has left everything to Lydia, a beautiful Siamese girl poet of whom no one has heard.

Lassie and Rex tussle together politely; Lassie, wounded, is forced to limp home.

In the Mexican gold rush a city planner is found imprisoned by outlaws in a crude cage of sticks.

More people flow over the dam and more is learned about the missing electric cactus.

Too many passengers have piled onto a cable car in San Francisco; the conductor is obliged to push some of them off.

Maddalena, because of certain revelations she has received, firmly resolves that she will not carry out an enterprise that had formerly been dear to her heart.

Fog enters into the shaft of a coal mine in Wales.

A violent wind blows the fog around.

Two miners, Shawn and Hillary, are pursued by fumes.

Perhaps Emily's datebook holds the clue to the mystery of the seven swans under the upas tree.

Jarvis seeks to manage Emily's dress shop and place it on a paying basis. Jarvis's bibulous friend, Emily, influences Jarvis to take to drink, scoffing at the doctor who has forbidden Jarvis to indulge in spirituous liquors.

Jarvis, because of a disturbing experience, is compelled to turn against his friend, Emily.

A ham has his double, "Donnie," take his place in an important enterprise.

Jarvis loses his small fortune in trying to help a friend.

Lodovico's friend, Ambrosius, goes insane from eating the berries of a strange plant, and makes a murderous attack on Lodovico.

"New narrative" is judged seditious. Hogs from all over go squealing down the street.

Ambrosius, suffering misfortune, seeks happiness in the companionship of Joe, and in playing golf.
Arthur, in a city street, has a glimpse of Cathy, a strange woman who has caused him to become involved in a puzzling mystery.
Cathy, walking in the street, sees Arthur, a stranger, weeping.
Cathy abandons Arthur after he loses his money and is injured and sent to a hospital.
Arthur, married to Beatrice, is haunted by memories of a former sweetheart, Cornelia, a heartless coquette whom Alvin loves.

Sauntering in a park on a fine day in spring, Tricia and Plotinus encounter a little girl grabbing a rabbit by its ears. As they remonstrate with her, the girl is transformed into a mature woman who regrets her feverish act.
Running up to the girl, Alvin stumbles and loses his coins.
In a nearby dell, two murderers are plotting to execute a third.
Beatrice loved Alvin before he married.
B, second wife of A, discovers that B-3, A's first wife, was unfaithful.
B, wife of A, dons the mask and costume of B-3, A's paramour, and meets A as B-3; his memory returns and he forgets B-3, and goes back to B.
A discovers the "Hortensius," a lost dialogue of Cicero, and returns it to the crevice where it lay.
Ambrose marries Phyllis, a nice girl from another town.
Donnie and Charlene are among the guests invited to the window.
No one remembers old Everett, who is left to shrivel in a tower.
Pellegrino, a rough frontiersman in a rough frontier camp, undertakes to care for an orphan.
Ildebrando constructs a concealed trap, and a person near to him, Gwen, falls into the trap and cannot escape.

By Guess and by Gosh

Even so, we have forgotten their graves.
I swear to you I will not beat one drum in your absence.

And the beasts of night will not forget their crimes,
nor the others their roly-polyness.

It was in a garage where tire irons jangled in the breeze
to the accompaniment of flyswatters functioning
that we first heard of that Phoenician sailor
and how when the tide was out he would pretend to be
the Flying Dutchman on one of his infrequent shore leaves
to garner a spouse. But he was all red with jewels—
not rubies, cheap gems. And his incisors struck fear
in the hearts of the entourage. Nevertheless, many
were the maidens who considered him an option,
though they always ended by rejecting it. Some said it was his
    breath,
others, the driven cornsilk of his hair. Perhaps
it was the lack of something called "personable,"
though I think I don't even want to know what that is, I'll
    follow
my heart over warm oceans of Chinese lounge music
until the day the badger coughs up that secret,
though first we must discover the emetic,
the one I told you about.

Confused minions swarmed on the quarterdeck.
No one was giving orders anymore. In fact it was quite a while
since any had been issued. Who's in charge here?
Can't anyone stop the player piano before it rolls us
in the trough of a tidal wave? How did we get to be so many?
I wonder what's playing at the local movie theater.
Some Hitchcock or other, for there are many fanciers
in these unsightly parts. And who would want mothers
for supper?

Can You Hear, Bird

And for all the days it doesn't happen
something does happen,
solid and nutritional like a wrapped steak
tossed on a counter. At first I couldn't believe the thirst;

soon, so soon, it becomes average and airy,
a fixture. Precept to be toyed with.
The road started to get rough with me.
A mere 800 feet away the car wept
on its blocks
and little Peter came and looked around and went away.

It was kind of a mistake and he went away.

It was a kind mistake, breezes over dashboard.
Twin violins sew
a fine seam;
a paw slips over the face of the clock,
laggards and dudgeons in between.

All I meant to suggest was the negative of what has
been done surges and slops against fifth-floor windows
in the time it takes to anchor a tricycle.
And we full of such courtesy,
blind to the days and it seems their systems the night,
teetering on a board's edge;
sure and the unrolled film fans out
in suns like a dolphin or a skate's wing.
After all who blubbered the truth
It wasn't I

Cantilever

I knew we should have stopped back there
by the pudding station
but the pudding people were so—well—
full of themselves.

The Sphinx didn't want us to come this far
even though we answered her questions
and threw in a bonus answer: "As honey is to the jaguar."

And we so well all along too—

Coming up is the world's longest single cantilever span.
I am numb with thrips.

Chapter II, Book 35

He was a soldier or a Shaker. At least he was doing *something*,
going somewhere. Often, in the evenings, he'd rant about
   Mark Twain,
how that wasn't his real name, and was he hiding something?
If so, then why call himself a humorist?
We began to tire of his ravings, but (as so often happens)
it was just at that point that a salient character trait
revealed itself, or rather, manifested itself within him.
It was one of those goofy days in August
when all men (and some women) dream of chocolate sodas.
He confessed he'd had one for lunch,
then took us out to the street to show us the whir and dazzle
of living in some other city, where so much that is different
   goes on.
I guess he was inspired by Lahore. Said it came to him
in his dreams every night. And little by little
we felt ourselves being transported there. Not that we wanted
to be there, far from that. But we were either too timid
or unaware to urge him otherwise. Then he mentioned
   Timbuktu.
Said he'd actually been there, that the sidewalks were pink
and the huts made of mother-of-pearl, not mud, as is
   commonly
supposed. Said he'd had the best venison and apple tart
in his life there.
               Well, we were accompanying him in the daze

that usually surrounded him, when we began to think about
    ourselves:
When *was* the last time we had done so? And the stranger
    shifted shape
again (he was now wearing a Zouave's culottes), and asked us
would we want to *live* in Djibouti, or Providence, or Lyon,
    now that
we'd seen them, and we chorused (like frogs), Oh no, we
want to live in New York, not that the other places aren't as
    splendid
and interesting as you say. It's just that New York
feels more like home to us. It's ugly, it's dirty, the people are
    rude
(kind and rude), and every surface has a fine film of filth
on it that behooves slobs like us, and will in time turn to
    diamonds,
just like the mother-of-pearl shacks in Timbuktu. And he said,
You know I was wrong about Mark Twain. It was his real
    name,
and he was a humorist, a genuine American humorist for the
    ages.

Chronic Symbiosis

These things can be arranged, he said.
Besides, glitter has become reasonable again.
Hadn't you heard? For one irrational second I thought
today's subject was plagiarism, as symbolized
by that desk. But no, it's joy
in never knowing, in having once known,
and in its still not being too late to know.
Yes, but I know now that I knew
long ago when children
around me grew. Some I liked, others
probably not as much. And from that the road to living sped
ever onward, brambles in its hair, dark patches
under the trees where no moon was. Which means I guess
I can summon all objects from their shelves,

sucked with us into the vacuum-cleaner bag
the open road is. Quick, tell me a story

that I may repeat it with minor variations
and the job be over. Rakes and shovels lean beside
the open door this evening with a special luster
all their own, that they can't know. And I,

I was spirited away by a handsome enchanter
to a medium-sized city not twenty miles from here
and live my life as I can hear and smell it. No grouch
am I, yet hardly an earth-mother either. That's
what befalls most of us plagiarists. We write steadily
away in a barn, with straw and barn swallows for company,
mindless of inspiration or imagination. We have everything
we need for today. We can feed it to crows.

Collected Places

When you come on,
    I respond more sweetly.
But the key is laced in
    a travesty,
much like the dead man's cane.

For generations I went to bed because I was asleep.
Something overt about the silence
and how we traded its futures
for chameleons, shenanigans.
I feel as though I just woke up,

which of course I just did,
my head at your thigh.
Is there any place known to the coast,
I mean *this* one, that rides
us so severely, yanking the bridle,
digging its stirrups in, that will leave
a pine forest and jam in the holes in the sieve

of my memory, when the adders have slept?
Order it then open,
longitude stricken from the record.

And where is the dismal mouse
that will affront me for so little?
There is retching in the sky,
a blue pencil box
for the sores we own and still wear,
a nodding as of rabbits, or storks.

And the head is still miles away.

I fear you cannot read this.
I shall make amends
in some other book, but not today,
not until the horseless carriage is reinvented
in the free land of our screams
and the remainder can be calculated
exactly, morning and confrontational cliffs,
a place you want to hear.

Coming Down from New York

The harshness isn't intentional.
It's the dark side of these frightful enterprises
that would otherwise leave us washed by the sun
in extravagant attitudes, situations
only the insufficiently trained ought to try.

Dangerous Moonlight

Of course you will. It happens even after you're dead.
Or, in some cases, the results are positive, but the verdict
negative. "In such a muddle," you said, and "all muddled up."
I wish I could help but I've a million things to do

and restoring your peace of mind isn't one of them. There goes
   my phone . . .

The professor's opinion on all this was: "Well, he leaps around,
   doesn't he, your little surgeon-poet. Seems to lead an agitated
      life
on the surface, but if you really listen to him you find he's got
   everything down pat. Knows where his bread is buttered, and
      his ass.
I could open a drawer of rhetorical footnotes, translated from
   the Japanese or Old Church Slavonic, if I felt like it, and in
      there'd
be something that rhymes with him and his coziness, his
   following the trail
all the way back to its point of origin. Plus his lively
   friendliness, which
coexists, numinously I grant, with a desire to inflict harm.

There is a poetry in mere existence,
the kind that shopkeepers and people walking along the street
   lead,
you know, and evenness, that fills them up to whatever brim
is there, and stays, transient, all the days of their lives.
Such enharmonics are not for your poet-person. He sees, and
   breeds:
Otherwise the game isn't worth the candle to him. He'd as
   soon rhyme breeze
with breathes, as walk over to that fire hydrant in the grass
to examine it, see what it's made of, make sure it's not an idea
   in some
philosopher's mind, that will bruise and cloud over once that
   mind's
removed, leaving but a dubious trace of itself, like a ring of
   puffball dust . . ."

Suppose we grant its power of conserving to listening,
so it's really a full-fledged element in the creative process.
Well, others have done just that from time immemorial,
when women wore tall cones on their heads with sails attached
   to them.

But, as mattering ages, it hardens into something smooth like
    good luck,
no longer kinetic. Then you can listen all you want
at palace doors, creaky vents . . .

This imploring process is twofold. First, let's not forget its root
in implosive. That's something it's got up its sleeve.
Did you ever see an anarchist without his round bomb?
And then the someone that's got to be implored,
how does he fit in? I'll tell you: like a wedge that was
    subtracted
from a wheel of cheese, and is replaced, so that it fits perfectly;
no one can see where the cut was. Well, that's
poetic argument for you. It stands on its own ("The cheese
    stands alone"),
but can at the drop of a speculation be seen again as a part,
a vital one, of the mucus cloud that is generalized human
    thought aimed at
a quarrel or a rebus in the lining. And that's the way
we get old with poetry. Comes a time when no one has a
    notion
of anything else, and the odor of fried brains contends
with the damp of vacant ancestral halls, to their mutual
betterment, actually. Here, hand me that cod . . .

Debit Night

We were coming down from the city the city is where you come when you don't want to listen or be excused from listening. It is a hard hat out and some days "stiletto" heels—but who told you about hat we don't know about hat too much or about how "hat" grows. Coming down we passed through a former violet producing center. Around World War I there were maybe a hundred violet farms in this region of New York state conducive to violets. It is a very labor intensive thing now there are no longer any except one or two. Up until the end of World War II it was the fashion for ladies to wear bunches of violets but then it changed. Now no one had any use for them. Now everyone likes violets I don't see. Yes but you don't see anybody wearing them or buying any. Some even think of them as weeds. Nevertheless the former violet business has left its trace in place-names here such as Violet Lane and Violet Hill. They are beautiful aren't they until you stop to think that violets could be weeds and of a reason why nobody buys them anymore. Yes but I will still think the

names

A sandbox sometimes had weeds growing in it including one that looked like a dandelion only it was tall and thrifty. Always was the sand more beautiful after the rain when there was a dried wet crust on top with pebblelike pores starring its surface. But mostly it was out of sight. There was not a window of the house where it wasn't around the corner so naturally it is seen less and thus gets worn into the mind like a crease in a road map that has been folded up the wrong way too many times.

Jana prefers the city. Says there's more light in it, or the light gets divided up by the streets more so a little goes a long way. Light is something that should not be wasted so as to produce its maximum effect as it is even on some boulevards where it stretches out too much, too wide and too long into the future. This is true but in the country it gets more soaked up in the bushes and buildings so a little more is always required and a little more is all there is. In the city you can eavesdrop on brick walls and this is called "repointing." What comes up in the inevitable ensuing conversation is sure funny but doesn't look ahead to the future of philosophy or decide how life should ultimately be lived. There is no conversation even about half-serious things like the theater. Instead everybody makes a unique little mess like a child shitting in its pants that's proud of it. The auto horns scare everything near away anyhow. The place pivots; this has already been patented. You can go down to sleep by the river or in a movie. See that boat? It's real.

So after we had done the chores and brought back living to the house there was something on its mind like a ball of yarn. Yes, a ball of yarn is what is there as I wanted to say. Say, stay anyway will you? I might. I've got things to do. Yes, but this is one of them. That's true. But I still have things to do I might go. Oh no you're not. Oh no? Okay then I really will stay because I want to really. Really she said? Then I will show you this dried crust of bread which is the truth, you must never forget it. Oh I never will I said it's what I wanted all along. How many acres do you want? Oh I never sought them they always came to me until quite recently. Indeed? Well here comes another one it's green or black. It must be yours she said. You played the mandrake right. Yes well here comes another and a whole lot of them. By George she said we should have been ready for them, but that's the way

it is you can't be and you are. Think of World War I, it's green and black and surely there was less daylight around then, more fog and boats on the East River with people lining up to go on them. Yes it was a premonition of these our times she said and so I conjure you, don't go around telling what you know to people, you are likely to get it back. Then peace, of a sort? The high-minded sun combs the tallest man-made structures on earth and then you get a little peace and some darkness down in the lobbies where everything begins to happen. No one in his handsome and enduring stable. Just having to endure is like going for the jugular but it should be a caravanserai. The problem is to get over what is being endured but hasn't been and to make for the middle distance, after the teacups and primulas but before philosophy and "last things," where thighs shine astride dim neighboring curbs and strangers greet you convulsively. These are more last things, I think, to think about

all along along what I wanted all along

Do Husbands Matter?

Let's get this going again. It might work. To ask pardon . . .

These days I am much on the cliffs. I like cliffs. They lead to

a nice breeze . . .

Forests of fire hatch the soupstone factory.
When they get infected they tend to gyrate,
sometimes a lot.

Trees come to stand in for the scenery that's missing.
Well, and what might that be? Well, trees of course. The
    occasional shrub.
The windjammer's jammed again. Solemn, small porticoes.
Stone steps leading down into the ground. Potatoes.
And you don't even know them.

Did it seem perfect then?

The townside, sea of troubles, value, money.
Dr. Driscoll will be here soon
with his decoder. Meanwhile, everybody
just stand still. If yawl
don't move it will summon the laser legs.
In a matter of hours we can be on the high seas
where marriages are consummated
and amazon drummers croon
and we encounter the order of the day.

At last, we can split hairs.

I needn't remind you how much of the mirror-ball is in this, nor
how such states are very much the exception to the general
    rule of not interfering.
Even then the interpersonal
has been around, hedges its bets
as though this were a matter of some gravity,
though no one can stake it out, or even know

very well what it happens to be.
This much I could hesitantly aver
and turn into a saga, that melts next day
like an iceberg towed into tropical waters.
That's an unusual boat: wearied-seeming,
caught in the cleft of a dream,
or is it something you just wear, like diaries
on special occasions, while welcomes are wearing out
and tall men have come to eat
mattress-insides, this time.

O the woman lay in the longboat.

Sometimes it comes from even farther back.

Dull Mauve

Twenty miles away, in the colder
waters of the Atlantic, you gaze longingly
toward the coast. Didn't you once love someone
there? Yes, but it was only a cat, and I,
a manatee, what could I do? There are no rewards
in this world for pissing your life away, even
if it means you get to see forgotten icebergs
of decades ago peeling off from the mass
to dive under the surface, raising a
mountain of seething glass before they lunge back up
to start the unknown perilous journey
to the desolate horizon.

                              That was the way
I thought of each day when I was young, a sloughing-off,
both suicidal and imbued with a certain ritual grace.
Later, there were so many protagonists
one got quite lost, as in a forest of doppelgängers.
Many things were going on. And the moon, poised
on the ridge like an enormous, smooth grapefruit, understood
the importance of each and wasn't going
to make one's task any easier, though we loved her.

Eternity Sings the Blues

Music lovers everywhere
endorse it—just thought I'd let
you know it's National Frivolity Week
again. Will they ever get done
with these things? Stop commercializing 'em?

Music and worry—the two most terrible
things a man can know. How about
women? Strangely, they come off better
just by observing things. This hundred-year-old
inkstone is evidence enough of that. How so?

But music, played by a gifted child,
is just about the finest thing anywhere.
Puts me in mind of a cigar
I smoked in a picket line once. They all thought
the boss hired me to do it. Now I ask you.
But I kept on smoking. The point is, when you spot
worry, you have to move straight in through
the flanks it invariably leaves unprotected.
I am cussed now,
more worse than ever, yet I never
bequeathed an orange to an orphan,
or padlocks to a mechanic. I had too much
to do, too much fun getting out of there
into another house of which I remember little.
Oh the places I've lived. Airplanes to London,
and then it was hard not to uproot the rancid
stalk of romanticism, so I left it there
as an experiment. Soon the fairies was buzzing
round my head. I got out of there *real* fast.

Why do these dreams of worry plague you?
You seem like such a comfortable man.
Aye, I am that, but I'm also terrible
in the northeast. Wasn't it D. W. Griffith
who said, "You don't know what it's like to have a big nose"?
And so we dream some of the same dreams,

him and me together—of kitchens, and bushes outside 'em,
and a woman who hides behind a tree,
waiting for the keyboard of her youth to unravel
in unsightly seams over the pavement.
Absolutely nothing he or she does
escapes my vigilant attention. But if you'll wait here
I'll go over and see what that car wants.
Oh stop that—now you really are
learning to be boring. Soon no one will want you
except for the occasional syphilitic barmaid,
and then what will your urine tests prove?
Better a spotted record than a tarnished silver thread
I always tells them. It's true, nobody will unveil me.
I've slept with my feet in the spittoon, with only
a pair of chopsticks for a pillow.
I've been deferred. And all because some runt
of a chameleon put a curse on me once, mixing me
up with his oafish brother-in-law.
Is that any way to begin a life?
And long after my Enoch Arden–like return
to the world of discos and lemon groves, his words
return to haunt me still: Avast,
ye pantyhose-wearing, portmanteau-carrying,
bleached-out denizen! Return to the sea that vomited you
on its shore one fatal August afternoon. Begone!

So must I carry this paddle
forever, until I find a sucker who'll buy it
for less than I paid for it. So runs this carousel
we call life.

Yet for those not snookered
by it, a fatal balm mollifies
susceptibility to drafts, and mild
allergies, or are they transgressions in disguise?
Better to sleep on the docks
than in the linen closet of privilege, always
wondering what it was that woke you—I've known
that routine too, like a serial killer
with nothing on his mind, who couldn't make eye contact

with you for all the gold in Scotland Yard.
You think of yourselves as having lived
a life of amused tolerance, woozy
with doubts, at times, but buoyed by your
delusion that all this, guarded moments and all,
is part of some life-affirming élan vital. Well,
I'm here to tell you you're as doomed as the hoariest
chink or octoroon, or the "anthropophagi,
and men whose heads do grow beneath their shoulders."
Would anyone like this oar? The special ends tomorrow.

Often over the bluff-infested coasts a warm
zephyr breathes. We forget about memorizing
our parts and retreat to the dressing room,
silly with relief and grief. What! Was it for this
I squeezed the tubes of paint
on your pristine palette, and is it
that I am going to be rewarded by something
other than a fatal sting? And the lads
and lassies assure you that such is the case, that
in any event no one ever escapes the swimming pool
without being shriveled to a prunelike consistency.
O beaters, how did you find my forest?
What will you do if I stay here
just for the hell of it? In any case
it's getting late, cat burglars are astir, and something
smokelike in the wind. I'll be
off now, the tide is running, the ship
writhing in the roads, and I must finish
my diary by midnight, or be fated
to continue this life into the next. O
brothers, sisters, friends, catamites—
it's been a long and intelligent journey, hasn't it?
If I ever found myself here again I'd do something
about fixing the holes in the landscape
and healing the sick, though there's about
as much chance of that as finding a used lottery ticket in a
   dungheap.
Tell you what—
you continue on the road to House Beautiful

and I'll strain my eyes in their sockets looking
for a single white wave of a hand in the distance
as my train speeds by. I was told not to get
into any of this, not to talk about where I
came from, or my mission here, but I'm tempted
to share a few secrets with you, though I guess I won't.

Remember me to those assholes the judge
and the bailiff. Speak kindly of me to gossip columnists,
praising the achievements I was once noted for, that are
sprouting like Roquefort, or a zinc tree. OK,
worry, I'll catch up to you in a minute, once I've
dusted off my shoes and finished adulating myself,
adoring my stretched reflection in the funhouse mirror,
and stopped handing out tracts that look like Chinese
takeout menus. I'm both bogus
and bold. Not to put too fine a point on it.

Fascicle

No one ever had to face such turmoil
in these days of riots and student demonstrations.
Don't bet on it. "No one the governor recruits
ever passes muster," she said. "And painted rooms are bonny."

Nevertheless, I opened my attaché case.
"It's enough to fluster
Hercule Poirot or Inspector Javert. Why,
it almost seems as if we are arriving

in a port of Cyprus, the damaged
storm in ruins, past the mole
and the breakwater to the incredible piles
of volcanic tuff no one esteems, if indeed

we're here. Let's see, my flotation mask
is in order, ditto my Cypriot currency (dinars,

no doubt—isn't everybody?). My cocktail and ticket
are perfect. Not so the drops of sweat beading my

headband, but no one cares what you look like—
it's appearances that count. But here in this
cultural demimonde I've been banished to, they'll seize on
    anything:
earrings, a trace of luster on the broad swath

of evening, signed by a renowned couturier. If it weren't
for living, that is being alongside almost everything
that happens and hearing thirdhand about the rest, we'd all
have rotted at our moorings eons ago, sunk to the mucky

bottom of this cretinous ocean. Say, did he tell you the one
about the flea and the cabdriver picking his nose,
or has he saved you for more august reunions,
under a turtle moon, its starched sheaves heaving? In truth

he knew not to what saint to address himself
when the last panhandler buzzed into view.
That were a churring time." Beats me, I mean
why we're not to make more of it, if you

know what I mean . . .

Five O'Clock Shadow

I

Don't just stand there, Kiki.
You're onstage. They're all looking at you.

"Along life's weary path I glide . . ."

Leda, when it came time
to consider the swan's suggestion, humbled
her braces, brought success to heel.

Tell her half the story.

Then weeping on these shoals,
like an enchantress extruded
in bar light, overturned the fashion
shoot, brought dumb heterodoxy
out into the open:

"For seven years I twisted the splint
till the pain grew more or less correct.
I should die in the right page."

II

Another time we were digging a fire trench.
Along came a fireball,
stopped, asked the time of day
and went politely on his way.

In the house they looked out:
Yet another hour had come;
the alcoves were deep with remembrance,
remembered piety. A woman offered fruit
mechanically. It's just like the games of my day
which no one can authenticate anymore:
How many times do you kick the can?
How long must you remain blindfolded?
And we knew the flag was a friend,
forgotten ceremony, nailed to the floor,
climbing, tooth by tooth.

From the Observatory

When they had climbed the Valley of Thieves
and rested at the aleatory base camp
a horseshoe moon began to pierce the curtain of dreams.

It seemed there was something wrong with everything.
The greenhouse was ethereal and too far away.

A gnat ignited the harbor; it rose up gold and sloppy,
with too many seals to think about. The basement
was a dirigible. The Home Counties bristled at suggestions
of voyeurism and venery: "Was it for this you came?
To watch us writhe and cringe? Are you happy,
knowing the palace janissaries have subdued us?"

The cult of personality issued conflicting commands
that managed to puddle every surface.
It's like it was before the flood: Nothing
is dry enough or wet enough. What's needed is a sense
of invitation, to this or some other domed picnic.
But since we're here, we might as well memorize the rules
for future reference. All other details
are as the exterior of this wall that reared us: ancient,
trapped in an understanding of the present, where submarines
gather, and eavesdroppers ply their trade.

                                    And the riddle
unknotted itself; the second agreeable ordeal began.

Fuckin' Sarcophagi

And when they had mounted it on the flatbed,
the dogfish requested a commuter's ticket. I'm no longer
    feeling
any of it. Generations of toppled heads
have come home to roost in my priory.
The smell of doughnuts frying offers them minimal
support.

All those years with the tree's rings growing around me,
the leaves in my face, branches obstructing others,
have learned me how one deaf animal forgets another
in the rush to light. And there on the threshold it forgets
its name, its very purpose. And allows septic deviance
to whittle away at the formatted intertext.
It's as well the hygrometer was swallowed

by a tusked creature, as we never came here at all.
All those suds on the porch and the front walk
only meant that baby likes to blow soap bubbles
when not involved in anything more strenuous,
such as teething. She sees through the holes in my coat
imaginable dapper Dans who one day will become part and parcel
of the AstroTurf.

When I wonder weather it's over between us, ever over,
why, a shy spiral announces your cue:
You too are to have nothing to do
for the next five hours.
Look, I've packed lunch . . .

Betimes the *bêtises* fall where they may.

Getting Back In

Melodies of the past, fibers, tangled tracings . . .
Getting back in is the easy part.
Being stuck in today isn't.

What is this "today" you speak of so incessantly?

It's where the rubber meets the road and they discuss
in one long fawning kiss. It's the posse's
new poster child. It's . . . My system was downloaded
but bogus retorts are still coming out of it.
It's pleasures and palaces. A commitment.

This is where the road tires and all vehicles
instinctively lean toward some breakdown lane
or other but there aren't any. The police,
of course, are aware of this but don't let on.

I see where someone was put in prison just for dreaming.
Sixteen long years. And when they let them out,

they go back to it. It's as natural for them as copper moths
or striped cabanas in the rain forest. You do have got to
give credit to the organizers, though. Without them this whole thing
would be as chaotic as a clambake. And us with no spirits,
no place left to land. No airport wants us.
And if we get juiced and relax everybody wants us
for purposes of synchronicity. A single item is too many,
but a pair is just fine, they say.

Well, I've had it with the 'burbs.
From where I sit I can see hundreds of freight cars,
some of them painted bright colors, but mostly
they are of a dark sort of color.
It's so lissom, the light! Rabbits everywhere . . .

Gladys Palmer

Do not go into Hawaii.
Even the price tags are afraid.
A bunch of wetsuits slapped a utility pole.
Something like a pupil
accosted me across from the mill.
The new wave of hijackings
resembles the others only in intensity. Otherwise, forget it.

We sanded the floors
and invited the ocean in.
The yellow pages promised free ginseng,
and a glorious spring morning
eloped with a tired, dirty afternoon from the end of winter.
Bubbles issued from people's mouths
before the solons could do anything about it.
It was foul to be afoot then, or a trick knee.

The man and the woman wondered:
Shit, what *about* the lost amulet?
What about it? Closer than the side

of this week's truncheon, communicable
as today's newspaper, yet everybody
got a piece to take home: The difference was significant.
I told the truth (it's best), but unfortunately I *was* the truth.
Come along, we'll forget till tomorrow
feet over these smooth pebbles, the prisoner's
last question.

Hegel

Like a coffee table, the chair slides
across the polished floor—its aides have brushed its sides
again. How it shines! Hugs are interspersed with kisses;
the scrofulous interfaces with the electric clock.
It certainly is midnight
and for once it was early.

She said she had "dishpan hands"—no one
quite understood what she was talking about, yet issues
were skirted, no questions raised. Now when a peacock
stares out of the barnyard, no one mistakes it for a Christmas-
    tree ornament,
goes up to it and says, I liked you better in felt,
or was it at the Rangoon racetrack? But a bird
always has the last word.

I Saw No Need

I saw no need to paint the sky,
to cheer the runners passing by,
to let the lovely forest bleed.
I saw no need.

I saw no need to argue writs
with one who in a courtroom sits.
I saw the folly princes breed,
who saw no need.

I SAW NO NEED

I saw no need to cancel love—
Heavens, what was I thinking of?
I cannot read what others read.
I see no need.

I know the earth is out of whack.
I pine for boys whose name is Jack
who never pause to spill their seed.
They see no need.

And when visible day is done
all start to run. Stand up
to it. They stand up to you.
Hey, you never know.

I came upon a birch tree once,
a softly swaying silver dunce
in whose black branches mist had spread,
and gazed, and left it there for dead.

I saw no need t'explain myself
as others have concerning pelf.
This ditty bland seduces me.
Enough! I'll leave it by the tree,
the idling birch.

I saw no need to go to church
yet wearily I there did lurch
from time to time, and in the end
I felt its body like a friend.

Soon I forgot my mission's itch
and at the same time ceased to bitch.
Ineffable beauty where are you
I said I'm coming for you

and even if we don't match up
eventually we'll catch up
one to the other, comparing notes
or jotting down our favorite quotes.

All passion's spent; the evening dew
comes transitorily into view.
Tomorrow it will evaporate
and morning tigers seal its fate.

So, when it comes to choosing sides,
You be the one who's using guides.
Refreshed, I'll to my perch return
and leave these cherries in the urn.

I, Too

Happy thoughts weren't made to last,
but it is their compactness that eludes us.

The built-in obsolescence of every nanny, every pram,
is a force from God that issues from us.

How could we not like it, watching it emanate
like a breath of witch hazel
or a grayish-purple shroud?

Something has got to be done to the way we feel
before we get completely numb, like a colossus
floundering in its own wake.

See these hands?
Really we must make it up to them
or they'll take credit for everything we've accomplished
which they will anyway.

And what's-his-face can sit on his porch burping
uninterruptedly—propriety isn't hardy in this zone,
but that's not his problem. In fact
he doesn't have a problem. We, who see
around corners, into strongboxes, must wear
the guilt of our glancing. It's another appurtenance,
like a birdhouse or dishwasher, that we came to terms with

eons ago, when a tsunami of slime collided
with our pink stucco skyscraper. We know so much we've
kept it all in. That may be changing.

In an Inchoate Place

I

Is there another person you would like me to invite?
I shall, you know,
if only for the exquisite confusion it causes in you,
like a rope of starfish, tonight.

Opinion is divided on the merits of the majority of the guests.
The siblings are standardized but substandard:
red tadpoles lisping.

II

They are all free to come and go as they please
through the vanilla-flavored venetian blinds.

In Old Oklahoma

A tad triste I too found it,
along with other November matters that need not
concern us here. But what's wrong with here? Suffice it
to say baroque street gangs were breaking up

thanks to the same principles that oversaw their gestation.
A meaningless scuffle or shuffle ensued.
One wondered which stamps were licked, what tea poured
from on high as negative celebration

of all that is lost to us now, and all that is to come—
mysterious hybrids, most likely, veined purple pods

growing out of control to no one's detriment—I insist
on that. And then it rained fat rabbits—I

should have listened to my dog. In all,
another pleasant institution, like so many
pavilions that asterisk the harbor rim.
In all my life it was my twentieth birthday,

she came over; the night is all stuttering
orange flares and fig-colored queries
in the margin—it starts like this. It's breathless
and out of hope, a quartet for someone

semantics will never graze, nor the idling,
puny zephyrs, the last saviors one thinks of
looking to. Old Mother Hubbard knew nothing of pain
that flows as fondly as conversation among acquaintances,

and as discreetly.

Limited Liability

And one wants to know everything about everything.
Such is my decision, though I will abide by others,
that goes without saying. Still, I fell off the sandbar
walking back toward shore, and that was a time of sorrow,
even of great sorrow, for myself and many others.
No, make that a few others. Whatever I was
trying to do automatically broke the hearts
of those in the seats on either side of mine.
It was wild like weather, yet you couldn't just live in it,
you had to drool, your facial muscles had to twitch,
at least some of them. About the time the thought
of living in England occurs, and one succeeds in eating a
little asparagus and custard, the old guard revives its dug-in
positions. You knew about these. They were like lace and
    spring,

they went away but they never really did. They require a
    context
of mourning, and public relations. If a cock is being sucked
at a certain moment, it will not jiggle the seismograph,
    provoke regret
from one who is esteemed and dry, but rather break out
    disjunctedly
in another hemisphere, and people will start reasoning
from there on. The kid was only a gas-station attendant;
he couldn't have been more than seventeen or eighteen, yet the
    evening
wind begins promptly to blow, the morbid goddesses sing
that a brooch came undone and pricked one's finger, all
    silently:
so much for revanchisme. "But of course." And like it says
    here,
cooperation is part of the school of things, only don't get too
    close
to overboard, and be burned by the musing that sets in then.
Is that why cows live in clusters, why the foxglove
covers for the hay, and all gets done in a day like it was
supposed to, only there are no more feet to bathe?
I confess I was leery
the first time she told her story
but having heard it enough I can never get enough of what it
    was determined
should never be shielded from the rain or its attendant wetness;
by the same token they are always with us. Once I started
to count the ways I was indebted to the moose and its house
of night, some old saw had me battling again, kicking up moss
and letting it settle along with other debris. No
one saw me when I came here; I swear it. You can have a
    handle
on me now, only don't abuse it
too much yet. The sky popped out of the oven
like a tin of blueberry muffins, and there's so much to say.
Only I don't feel I'm dry enough. Yet. Take ten,
there's a good caddy. Go do someone's bidding,
then meet me under the larch when the storm crackles. I'll tell
    you then.

Love in Boots

Our first assignment was to make a square,
a place for living and carping in,
where the Sphinx could panhandle and maids desist,
if they cared to.

It seems my plan was too perfect!
People ended up hating it and the lives they lived in.
Back to the bogs! But the way was cut off,
or no one quite remembered it. *It should be here,
somewhere* . . .

In these demotic times one is grateful for a variety
of sundries: footprints on the prow of a ship,
or a wolf taking the trouble to cross over and tell you
he's engaged. Sunny things, the fins and buttons of childhood,

passing through grace and beyond it.
One finds there is time, after all, to wind the clock.
Yet no one noticed it had stopped. Would it make
the afternoon editions, blowing like mold across the blue
canyons we call our trellis, causing alembics to burst
in carnival sheds? What *about* next time? Could we eliminate it
from the list of essentials taxpayers pray for,
then shrink from, noticing it reflected in the rain barrel
when all the other dimensions remain quietly on hold?

Perhaps, on some more sophisticated planet,
these things tow the gravity they require,
and people are no match for them, don't even envy
or imagine them. Everything proceeds from a simple
gesture that never goes out of style. Yoo hoo. Look, it's Clara
and Amos. Aren't they simply divine? But it *is* getting late,

and I have to get up and chop wood tomorrow. Oh, if you're
    looking
for a timetable, it's there, in that train, that's now
two feet away, now one, but will never obstruct
or demolish us. Thank heaven for Zeno's paradox!

Love's Stratagem

The comparison says enough, really, nay is eloquent on the
 subject
of Paris furs, how she descended the avenue
wondering what was wrong, or warm. The best comparison
I can give you is two heads. His head literally exploded,
mine felt like a grape that prudent fingers leave on the bunch
to cloud over and legally pass out of the picture.

Yet his face it resembles a fig.
Where can I find seeds in heaven? I want to take some back to
 earth with me
and plant them if it's illegal. Imagine the surprised cackling!
My bedsores have healed! I just hit a hole in one!
My Labrador just had twins, and I don't know where to
 register them!
I replaced a file with a file

so asps wouldn't eat it. Now that we are out in the fun you
 must run
farther than any salmon bringing milt home to meet the missus.
Only say, if we are categorically united,
how many rooms does that make? Does one count the
 bathroom
or the patio, if it's enclosed? (*We'll have to make a run for it,
 don't
let on you know anything about Sheba.*) Er, where was I?

I know. I can see it now that the fog has evaporated
and taken most of the town with it. Come to think of it,
why did we settle here? Did God ordain it? Why couldn't we
 have
gone on just hanging around the window seat, head out the
 window,
eyes drooping, tongue lolling? Or were we meant to discover

the boiling point of Minnesota, the town in Nebraska?

Many Are Dissatisfied

yet the wind from Seattle blows over and over,
against the facing page and against the anthill.
You would wonder at all the crumbs
that have been dropped, lest you find your way
through this tangled story of ours,
and at how the gentlemen fliers cursed us
as mere entertainers, made us put our wallets away.

There was nothing they wouldn't do to make us comfortable,
short of approving our lifestyle.
Which is why I fester on the porch,
a Hun without a regiment, till the great pretender
comes to knock us over.
It was so gray and mild,
the evening we played air hockey, that I could hardly
condone your singing. You thought about your neighbor's come,
listlessly, as a child with a slinky badgers cardoons,
while in the great specialist's plaid-paneled waiting room
the air has gone mad.

My question to you now is: How
do we escape the fat boy, in lemon overalls,
twenty stories high, with feet two blocks in diameter?
I guess it was just that spring
emptied like an Egyptian sewer into the street,
fringing our losses before the bad time that went away.
Or is it all declamation—the wanting
to sue nature for the tide's infirmities,
sliding off into a lather,
mouthing the old pulchritude a house has?

Military Pastoral

Hello, Blubberface. You can come in now.
No, I didn't say *now*. What are you, My Man Godfrey?
Now go out and come in gently. What

had we asked you to bring? Or was it only
to show off reentering a different way?

In any case my apples are blasted.
This tin screen grates on my ear.
Asked back, over the tides and mangrove hummocks
of last year at this exact same time—
kind of makes you feel younger, doesn't it, buttocks,
if you're really in the mood for improvement?
But my pale army subsists on what it can scrounge
from the larders of thrifty *paysannes*.
All around me I see only hope and dopiness
etched against a sky of ferule tan, of so much incongruity
they fall slap in the middle of village streets.

And when I, vanguard of mortality, review my troops
it's as if the moisture had evaporated from the air.
I say one, two, twelve times. Only the thrush hears
and appreciates the humor of the saga, but of course
the cat already has its eye on her. We only learn from books,
I suppose, and partly hidden tattoos that tell of sunken treasure
and other boundless efforts that are required of no man.
Might as well unpack the laurels—they're starting to arrive.

My Name Is Dimitri

I am going to be your host tonight.
Do you wish the fiddle or the fish?
The hen with ivory sauce is very fine, very light.
An experience unlike any other pushes you

toward what holy extremities? To a margin of uncertainty
where not just drinks are muddled and an old frump
of a past straddles you. Uncertainty polishes the china
to a mirrorlike daze.

A World War I soldier wants to say Thank you,
Fuck you, from all the trenches his heart is bleeding

from, from the aghast question and the problem of novelty
to the tip of sores that ends this peninsula
back where it began, where the pilgrims trod.

There is so much in Warsaw—
too many restaurants, too few connections
that would otherwise make things interesting.
We have nothing to cling to, only torn memories

of a station between stations that wasn't
the one that was supposed to be there. An altar of roses
climbed halfway up the stadium which was full of misfits
with no store to come home to. Still, there was the bus,

a place beyond all others, curdled in the neat sky.
An insane child wishes the grass whipped less
at the bends where the posts are. The merger of innocents
matters less than the hum of interim authority and the screech
    of descants

that take you by surprise as they tide you over.
Goodnight. The windscreen is heavy with imagery
in entranced colors like the plumes of a canary
or lyrebird. Keep the rats out of that granary

and all will be well for a century, but if the mailman
leaves me no mail it will be a vast appointed mistake,
vast as a throne room in an old castle by the sea,
as Thuringia. The moss grew for me, and there
the matter rested, in salt pits and other geographical refuse.
Besides, they were coming over the ridge,
would save us, and then we'd see what we would see—
despondent daughters of the Hellespont, fickle as creation
and the lives that extend it down to this trough.

My Philosophy of Life

Just when I thought there wasn't room enough
for another thought in my head, I had this great idea—
call it a philosophy of life, if you will. Briefly,
it involved living the way philosophers live,
according to a set of principles. OK, but which ones?

That was the hardest part, I admit, but I had a
kind of dark foreknowledge of what it would be like.
Everything, from eating watermelon or going to the bathroom
or just standing on a subway platform, lost in thought
for a few minutes, or worrying about rain forests,
would be affected, or more precisely, inflected
by my new attitude. I wouldn't be preachy,
or worry about children and old people, except
in the general way prescribed by our clockwork universe.
Instead I'd sort of let things be what they are
while injecting them with the serum of the new moral climate
I thought I'd stumbled into, as a stranger
accidentally presses against a panel and a bookcase slides back,
revealing a winding staircase with greenish light
somewhere down below, and he automatically steps inside
and the bookcase slides shut, as is customary on such
    occasions.
At once a fragrance overwhelms him—not saffron, not lavender,
but something in between. He thinks of cushions, like the one
his uncle's Boston bull terrier used to lie on watching him
quizzically, pointed ear-tips folded over. And then the great rush
is on. Not a single idea emerges from it. It's enough
to disgust you with thought. But then you remember
    something William James
wrote in some book of his you never read—it was fine, it had
    the fineness,
the powder of life dusted over it, by chance, of course, yet still
    looking
for evidence of fingerprints. Someone had handled it
even before he formulated it, though the thought was his and
    his alone.

It's fine, in summer, to visit the seashore.
There are lots of little trips to be made.
A grove of fledgling aspens welcomes the traveler. Nearby
are the public toilets where weary pilgrims have carved
their names and addresses, and perhaps messages as well,
messages to the world, as they sat
and thought about what they'd do after using the toilet
and washing their hands at the sink, prior to stepping out
into the open again. Had they been coaxed in by principles,
and were their words philosophy, of however crude a sort?
I confess I can move no farther along this train of thought—
something's blocking it. Something I'm
not big enough to see over. Or maybe I'm frankly scared.
What was the matter with how I acted before?
But maybe I can come up with a compromise—I'll let
things be what they are, sort of. In the autumn I'll put up
    jellies
and preserves, against the winter cold and futility,
and that will be a human thing, and intelligent as well.
I won't be embarrassed by my friends' dumb remarks,
or even my own, though admittedly that's the hardest part,
as when you are in a crowded theater and something you say
riles the spectator in front of you, who doesn't even like the
    idea
of two people near him talking together. Well he's
got to be flushed out so the hunters can have a crack at him—
this thing works both ways, you know. You can't always
be worrying about others and keeping track of yourself
at the same time. That would be abusive, and about as much
    fun
as attending the wedding of two people you don't know.
Still, there's a lot of fun to be had in the gaps between ideas.
That's what they're made for! Now I want you to go out there
and enjoy yourself, and yes, enjoy your philosophy of life, too.
They don't come along every day. Look out! There's a big
    one . . .

Nice Morning Blues

The promised "great getaway" turned out to be
shorter than anyone could have foretold. It was,
in its way, perfect. We looked down from a terrace
to the sea. Beneath its surface was another terrace,
and under that a different sea
of a color hitherto unimagined. And beneath that, the old campus
that had formerly stood there exhibited its perfection:
mitered slabs of stone in pale, meatlike tones
that put dentistry to shame.

How was I to know, leaving the garage,
that one of us would never meet the other again?
Yet round after round of schnapps was served
and that did seem to be a good thing.
There was an enormous choice of tempting salads—

And so it goes, visit followed visit
in a distressed but pristine season.
The crabapple blossoms were a deeper pink;
girls wore them on their skirts. There was always more
to do, with a promise of love in the evening.
And yes, nothing came of it. Nothing produced nothing.
We were saddest on the most luxurious perch,
or so it seems. Then sadness wanders away
like a child getting lost. What is there left to do?

No Earthly Reason

There are additional reasons having to do with security
for why we cannot extend to you this funding
unless you are prepared to keep an open mind,
fondle your pet discreetly.

"It has warm legs and a furry complexion," you said.

That's just fine. I keep my hat screwed to my head.
So, good. The pencil and pens in my pocket
that some make fun of are as lemon verbena to my ears.
If the tide-racked coasts rememorate it
no great moment attaches to it
(truth's medicine ball by itself)
but we want you to remain in this sanatorium,
out of harm's way, for at least a spell.

I could think of no earthly reason to give him my dress,
but I did it. He took it, walked off with it too.
And now the palms in the government palace courtyard
are busy filing their report. We're in it too—
about how many times I wash, how dreams come to me,
what brand of athletic shoes I buy. It makes me angry,
but my anger is as a doll is to a child:
insignificant in comparison to myself,
but occupying its secret corner anyway.

It would be nice if it was very dark
and only a little rent of light on the floor. I need your help.
Offer me sweet unguents. I'll tell you the same.

But in the parlor many floors below
the jury has already voted, using beans
kept for this purpose in a large glass canister.
We should know the verdict before long
he says coming closer his breath a fuzz on the sleeper's
    window.
It would be nice if a vulture could have some of this meat
but we have already tried justice in the streets.
It doesn't work. It would be better to run for your lives, and
    yet
I always linger. Behind a tree. I capture a great big bonus.

No Longer Very Clear

It is true that I can no longer remember very well
the time when we first began to know each other.
However, I do remember very well
the first time we met. You walked in sunlight,
holding a daisy. You said, "Children make unreliable witnesses."

Now, so long after that time,
I keep the spirit of it throbbing still.
The ideas are still the same, and they expand
to fill vast, antique cubes.

My daughter was reading one just the other day.
She said, "How like pellucid statues, Daddy. Or like a . . .
an engine."

In this house of blues the cold creeps stealthily upon us.
I do not dare to do what I fantasize doing.
With time the blue congeals into roomlike purple
that takes the shape of alcoves, landings . . .
Everything is like something else.
I should have waited before I learned this.

Obedience School

Let us leave the obedience school.
The door is open. Outside the sun is shining.
Why do you hesitate? Why do you hold back?

If there were some warts on the obedience school
we should have known about it before this.
You don't learn the cancan at obedience school.

Yup. But the parkway night is festering.
Besides, there are so many trained-dog acts now
nobody wants any competition.

That's why I bought Flossie the ticket
back to Puyallup. Her ladies-in-waiting
were flouting the scent of incense smoldering;

her high heels provoked "zounds!" of acclaim
from the wrong kind of gent-customer
we want no truck with.

And when the old school shudders
in a sudden ray of March sun,
accusers and behoovers alike will be believed;

behemoths and mammoths struggle and give up
in the aquarium dawn. Then a run on the feedstores
ensues. Causes are given up for lost. The queen's pony

capers on its hind legs, quite as if narcissism
were going out of style. Poor children! Why, it broke their heart,
but Dad's with them now. Dad can conquer this thing.

Ode to John Keats

From a dark land of figs
and morello cherries and plum jam
and lettered building blocks, the gold horn
extends its welcome to red paper fish.

The king has but one eye
but it is as round
as a dinner plate and sees
what others haven't the knack of,
except sages. Bursts of something
in midafternoon have flooded
the treasuries, roofed the spires
with stagnant dignity. One must
carry out these orders, or die
in the equation that links us.
Waiting for a bus requires more stamina,
or lurking under a weeping beech.

Of a Particular Stranger

My country is but scrubland,
plaguey country. From its opposite shore
I can see you sitting, surrounded by nursemaids
and rolled umbrellas. O it's not quitting
on us, my dear, only making a marginal note.
The time of tomes vast as valleys
hasn't approached us yet. Just wounded vets
doing the desert shuffle, a can of sperm
in one hand, a chilled beer in the other.

And I, I walk into the wrong room,
well-rounded, keeping my patience together.
A bat flies out over the tarmac.
We shouldn't have wasted so much hesitancy
on ourselves, it's for others, makes 'em feel genuine
and wanted. They start to like us,
then they *really* like us, it's too late
for them to cancel. They start to forget us,
then positively dislike us, as though we'd tampered
with their mnemonic machinery. An angel in brocade
witnesses this, copies it down.

By afternoon's end we were soaked
in a thrilling downpour that promised much
in the way of freshness, clamor. Writing, I
overshot the page into the sandtrap
of bucolic enthusiasm. You always rescue me
from such occasions, bind me to my own quiddity
and bookmarks. After all, there are a lot of books
to be read, lots of pages in this warehouse.

Operators Are Standing By

In some of the stores they sell a cheese rinse
for disturbed or depressed hair. You add whiskey
to it at the last moment. Now that

it's nearly Christmas, we could buy
such things, you and I, and take them with us,
though it seems like
only yesterday I hit that Halloween homerun.
It backed up and kind of flowed back
into my side I think, creating a "strawberry
jar" effect. There was nothing Arvin
or I could do about it.

Determining everyone is a bigshot
is sometimes all he cares about.
I've slept on the ground with him,
and deep in a birchbark canoe.
Once there was two of him.
At school no one could tell us apart
until we smiled, or his big laugh came unbuttoned.
Fatally, venery has taken its toll
of him these last years. I can't
get near him without being reminded of Venus,
or the hunt. I come in six different packages,
from the "jewel case" to Wrigley's spearmint.
In the time of friendly moose
droppings I followed them to the Shedd Aquarium.
No one was selling tickets that day.
I wandered in and out of the fish tanks,
stopping occasionally to leave a handprint
on the plate glass for the benefit of some fish or other.

Others Shied Away

> The Autumn seems to cry for thee,
> Best lover of the Autumn-days!
> —Susan Coolidge

And they have cooler armchairs.
They have an imaginary tunnel down there.
It can be the color of your choosing. With bridges, splayed
so wide of the mark, you wonder how they thought of
    crossing.

It can't be over.
I haven't taken my final exam
nor received the notice
to do so. The halls for my oratory
haven't been built yet. They'll be nice and new,
with buff-colored dolphins dangling from the ceiling.
The world will see something of my art in this,
though I had nothing to do with the actual building, and turn
    away,
admiring me and their clothes—so appropriate!
How did we know how the moon was going to be today,
what drinks to serve after driving fifty miles through parched
    savannas?
Yet does it all come miraculously to life?
Or is it the solitary crank who's right,
the unofficial historian? He never hazards an opinion,
yet stays by the door like a porter, pose
that fools no one. It seems none of us has begun to digest
the meal of all our lives. There's nothing left to do but count
    the rooms—
nine, all told.

I told you when I set out for
the market town, the saddlebags would be full
of gold and silver coinage, just for you;
coffers would bulge, orchards
overflow their walls with blue fruit.
Every day would be a cocktail party, all day long.
Now the tunnel seems withered.
We must return to the sparse blessings
that place our shoes on this winter path;
nothing can stay outdoors all the time—
there must be intervals for books and fire
and endless conversation that means very little
unless we'd prefer to have it some other way,
little girl, blinking at the autumn's rough practice,
crude language, distemper—wound into a ball for you.

Palindrome

In the days of French film and infanticide
and red flannel hash, words we kept for trading
up, which were later lost, other lost words,
angry at being snubbed for so many years,
surrounded us like owls in a boathouse. "To whom
are we indebted for the honorable occasion?" Words
no dictionary ever knew, or acknowledged having known,
like "spludge" or "parentitis." But then, what can we do,
there are so many, like zillions of bats
emerging from a cave at sunset, feeling the cool air
thread deliciously down their membranes. Yet they too
can get us in trouble. And it's fun to play along,
ears cocked for no special din, until the thud
of morning commences, and a child appears,
etched on the air of my room.

Penthesilea

No more odes, the good doctor said.
Come in with something distressing. Aw,
we said, the silted lakes are obedient already.
That is to say, a run on cash at the banks
that will never be mismatched or compensated.

The nice person sat and drank tea. You know
how it is when you find a café space
that is yours ideally, that snakes eternally
past a bit of ecstatic burnt blue from the street
around the corner. A place where nettles lean enthusiastically
like acrobats or stoats. O much as we
love you you can't come in.

But I did something before I died,
like bringing the wind into the house with the wood,
making it sit far off over there, in the thin corner.
The red furniture grew up.

Suddenly it was the rush hour, and we were on our hands and
    knees
trying to find the magnifying glass
that speaks in measured terms of these deliria,
and tying on one's skates,
half a century from the grouches of home.

Plain as Day

with all its accoutrements
(of course)—intact, impervious
to air, sand, and time—the three fatal
sisters with nary a thought
in their heads except where to cut it—
and it goes out, like a candle or a father
to buy a pack of cigarettes. You knew
this. WE all knew it. It's the old

weather shuffle behind a different
sun veil—shot, diapered
the way they always want it.

It never snows on Tuesday—far
be it from me to suggest otherwise, only
there *is* this difference, this little difference
that won't go away,
that's been waiting since before the office opened.
What shall I tell it?

Those that are taken leave no footprint
on the air, no smile
on the soused sky.
It's another kind of smile
speeding toward us like an express train
we'll never see. Please put out the light,
the ashes, when you leave.

Same in Texas or Louisiana. Meaning
no mail for you today, and would you please call back?
It's urgent. Well, *was*. I've been waiting hours
on a bench next to a fugitive general.

"Be sure of retail," he says. "The life insurance
building, the pickle garden. Heaven knows they
attack our radar too, swoop down on us like bats
and the mystery illness."

Are you Big Bang?

Point Lookout

The object of the game is, after all, not to die but to grow into
    easeful death, winning. Forty shopkeepers sinned and for
    this they were betrayed.

He seems not to have understood the rules of perspective.

We have the technology to tame the edges.
For this we must become hedgehogs again, blindly
    entertaining all the
philosophy of light.
It goes nice and easy like a drink, or remark in a salon.
All this time we were wishing, we
wished to hazard an accomplishment or two.
Come, I'll play you an old comedy
of the bartered bear and soothsayer, no ways to be out of
    doors, no
thing on the milky plain, the wind dropped. Soft
from my curlicue she bounces around.
The animal traces hovered and steamed. The soft shell of a
    particle
twists itself off from the name, stands defiant, budged.

We mourn those who do briefly paddle.

Poor Knights of Windsor

Say it was any day.
A knock on the door, a neoclassic cannonball flies past.
The hall is done up in scarlet; something more powerful
than just plain good taste is obviously at work here.

I agree to share your game with you.
We saunter on the terrace (Emerson
said a man should "saunter"). We eat some trail mix.
Gosh, what a limited bunch of things to do there is.

Anything that can be done with stale bread
will sometime be done. The English like to
twist it and dip it in something till it hardens: the result
is called "Poor Knights of Windsor."
It's some kind of savory.

They don't have those much anymore,
and we, why we never had them.
That applies to most things. Not plumbing, though—
if anything we have too much of that.

But those knights,
having to stand by a checkered cloth, pretending
it was OK by them, this really not much more than a scrap,
like the rarebit the hunter's wife tosses him when he comes
    home late,
his game bag empty
his fun exhausted
ready for a round of Monopoly—

Does the heraldry impose itself,
trickling on the forehead
for all to see?
Do brands ultimately matter?
Are the lasses more froward? The lads
bent over backward? What is this thing
you wanted me to see? Oh, a shovel. You might have said so.
And the way back is polluted, the spears
almost indecent.

Quick Question

We took to the lake
in small boats.
The once-in-a-lifetime flood
was approaching on dainty, centipede legs.
Something about the gestalt
told me not to release this comment to the wire services
before the various motivations were rehashed.

This was the next day.
Only a few empty cans met the gaze.
"Sprinkle it!" the children advised.
"Oil quickly becomes rancid."
Matter of taste, he thought.
Or matter of boobs.

Sometimes an old woman is coming to get you
through the boughs that were her home.
It's enough if the summer night light
can chasten, the tree-barbs sustain you
on their perjured breath.
There's no returning to haggle,
then. The sea is like pale green linoleum
and all the grenadiers have returned to Sicily.

Detraining, one thinks: This house was always haunted
by porcupines, which is as it should be.
Waiting for people to get down to business,
put their cards on the table, can be such a random act, like a
    minuet
of gnats against a blistered sky.
That is something to stare at: neither squat,
nor a tenement. A block of some often-penetrated material,
a liquid of another density, crawling along like honey
to greet its forebears—

better to leave ribbons of sand behind.
The journey becomes you, but is its way of becoming,
valid until the gold pinprick

comes to a head further along further night?
Shall we embark tomorrow,
when a favorable wind rustles the sheets?

Reverie and Caprice

It seems very unlikely that my wishes will
be accomplished "in the name of the Lord."
Couldn't He have foreseen this? What is this?
Tragic mealtime preparations
beneath a paper-bag colored sun that wants
to cast no light. And pockets
or strips of difference, fresh from the paper shredder.
How much cleaner would it be now,
O my works, if to be left alone
had been the original thrust, not this
woven screen, like wicker or billowing fabric,
tense but loosely dwelling
in the hostile night from which we took directions.

And after we climbed
a certain distance it was only a boy
in a suit with his bird. Unidentified youths
set off after him and were never seen again.
The banyan tree loomed large, and nothing came of it,
only a preposterous jelly made of shards
of boiled facts and unkept promises. Promises
that were never intended to be kept—she had a saying:
"Never stay in the pantry
while the mill is operating." Pure, putrescent poetry.
All along you were trying to make me give up the other.

Safe Conduct

The coast is clear. Bring me my scallop shell of quiet,
my spear of burning gold. I am definitely setting out tonight,
unless someone calls, to immerse myself in the Great Lore,

which I should have been doing all along. Never mind,
it can wait, it's been around long enough. I am afraid
it might involve cutting a swath through the fruited jungle.

That was the other thing about him: how many times
he avoided using the word "eclipse." It was as though
he bore his personal darkness with him, furled
like an umbrella, but ready to snap to attention
at the fall of a wombat's tear. It would be sufficient

to engulf us for centuries, thanks. The innocence
of his position, as laid out by him, before God and the elders,
drew delighted applause from the sparse crowd at the racetrack.
"And if we come home with you tonight," one beribboned lady
  caroled,
"will you tell us about Midas and the seltzer bottle? Pretty
  please?"

I am annoyed before each investigation
that will definitively clear my name. A toad watches me
from a lily pad, its lidded eyes plunged in despair.
"Was it for this I tamed you, brought you up from mere
  pollywog
to outstanding frog prince? Alas, the mists
that gather now are of the old kind, from the Iron Age,
and every instrument you practiced then
is being fine-tuned for tonight's one-person recital."

Salon de Thé

Some time before you wore that belt
on a boat, with a tree branch covering half the Caucasus,
I asked if she knew the *Caucasian Sketches*
of Ippolitov-Ivanov—"It's like looking at a distant aviary."
Yes, and the chords are like bullets
that can reach halfway to Siberia.
Very committed they are, and faithful
to their idea of the troops.

The troops need no notion
but a path through the rocks always helps,
like dessert and laundry. Oh, if you were going to change your
    shirt,
but I like this one. It's time to buy a new one.
Does my lemon-zest-patterned tie please you? Oh, I implore
    you,
no talking on the phone after 9 p.m.

Then the ladies got busy,
hung rugs on the metal clothesline and walloped them,
a good afternoon. Your sister was waiting on the shore
to tell me it was time to get to my job as busboy
at the Cloak and Dagger Tearoom. Makes me squeamish
just to imagine it. And it *was* a hard time,
but in summer, at least, you could dress cheaply
and look just like the rich kids
in their darkened limos.

I'll hear no more about it.
The bank messenger wants Fuzzy to stay away from me,
and all along I thought we were playing for apples,
but the reward money came as gourds, plastic-colored ones.
The kittens showed some restraint
and the shade was lowered as it is every Doomsday.

See How You Like My Shoes

Two twisted dry turds on the sidewalk;
the weather one's gray dropcloth.
What town is this?
The weather has a choke hold on foreseeing
what happens to it.
Heck there is nothing but the alike
except persons are not. Things are
like institutions. Stumbling from perjured
personhood, all seem alike
but the fugitive person has got things

his sisters (in Olympic
statehood) haven't got: to mimic
two legs like a dog is out
and times three sheet music in the door
is to planting. They really resist,
soaringly. The salesman head
is two whole shoes, and that be
the graveyard by the flame talking,
earnest ouch spelled by night.

The great symphony fell down before it could be revived.
On this oceloted tree they still think and wonder
how the person caved in
yet remained so spick-and-span a presence
all during the end-of-century doldrums
someone forgot in the telling.
They was many of same left out.
Many felt left out
their beat repealing to the besotted orbs
left out in the rain. Yet I am this person,
you. I like to titter.

Sleepers Awake

Cervantes was asleep when he wrote *Don Quixote*.
Joyce slept during the Wandering Rocks section of *Ulysses*.
Homer nodded and occasionally slept during the greater part of the *Iliad*; he was awake however when he wrote the *Odyssey*.
Proust snored his way through *The Captive*, as have legions of his readers after him.
Melville was asleep at the wheel for much of *Moby Dick*.
Fitzgerald slept through *Tender Is the Night*, which is perhaps not so surprising,
but the fact that Mann slumbered on the very slopes of *The Magic Mountain* is quite extraordinary—that he wrote it, even more so.
Kafka, of course, never slept, even while not writing or on bank holidays.

No one knows too much about George Eliot's writing habits—
my guess is she would sleep a few minutes, wake up and
write something, then pop back to sleep again.
Lew Wallace's forty winks came, incredibly, during the chariot
race in *Ben Hur*.
Emily Dickinson slept on her cold, narrow bed in Amherst.
When she awoke there would be a new poem inscribed by Jack
Frost on the windowpane; outside, glass foliage chimed.
Good old Walt snored as he wrote and, like so many of us,
insisted he didn't.
Maugham snored on the Riviera.
Agatha Christie slept daintily, as a woman sleeps, which is why
her novels are like tea sandwiches—artistic, for the most
part.
I sleep when I cannot avoid it; my writing and sleeping are
constantly improving.

I have other things to say, but shall not detain you much.
Never go out in a boat with an author—they cannot tell when
they are over water.
Birds make poor role models.
A philosopher should be shown the door, but don't, under any
circumstances, try it.
Slaves make good servants.
Brushing the teeth may not always improve the appearance.
Store clean rags in old pillow cases.
Feed a dog only when he barks.
Flush tea leaves down the toilet, coffee grounds down the sink.
Beware of anonymous letters—you may have written them, in a
wordless implosion of sleep.

Something Too Chinese

    for me now.
    And I thought how strange, one is always
    crying after this and that,
    against all odds.

As in the sex game, shimmering
like a peach—the *impératrice*
measures your guns, the townspeople
shuffle around, the one who will be the hero
is still viper-thin, and green
as hope. We all need a change of scene,
she said, a change of air—

try the sea. It is good for some persons.
A closet works best for me
with a view of an abandoned apple tree,
a wedge of porch. *Here, take these—*
running with the hare, I'll be back instanter,
before you can observe you, wipe the grime
and tears from the mirrored clock
over and against time.
These are mere cavils.

Swaying, the Apt Traveler Exited My House

It's so easy to be attractive when
you're young, even if not particularly favored by nature,
even if nerdy, spotted, and pacific,
even in the wrong clothes, rumpled with anxiety
like a maze, even if without interests
from the wrong side of the street.

Standing with one's bother,
wiping off the strictures of dark, demented doubt,
one believes what one lives in.
The air freshens the rooms.

I float from the dormer down
to the brick path darkened by the lawn sprinkler.
It seems I was inside once.

Oh I'm careless to tell the advantage of that pact
with truth I made as I undress.
The truth is it would have gotten to me
after five or six seasons of that sort of thing.
But it wasn't to be. Baby blushed anew at the air's demands,
and the pine tree fell over on the back porch, causing it to
    cave in.
That wasn't in my list of grievances though.
In fact there was never any list;
I coped by coping, living out life shred by shred
until a magma caught up with me. In the broken alley
one passed strollers and people pushing them. One comet
    caught my eye
but it was too late, too late to praise she always says.
My pants were wet
and someone is coming up the road, some zombie
or other.
This tune I never asked for
is a different one, a furious clarion
shrilling a hornet's nest of replies.
The others will be older, other rapists
than the ones that were put down.

It would be time to plan an escape.
This is difficult in a hotel.
There are bands of bullies waiting to frisk
you, and on the esplanade the scenario doesn't get much
    better:
Even the little girl with the balloon is planning to annex half of
    Western civilization,
and the ticket-of-leave man has his eye on the colored bastions
we plummet over, seeking release in the sea, the sea!
Two dolphins like two colons in a sentence
are rinsing me now,
pouring me out from myself.
I feel as though I'll never be big enough
to efface scars as an adult ideally should—
wait, though! I'm coming to the corner where
pockets of jasmine and lavender inhale—
Be my scope limited, it's something

just to have been in the intimacy of all the stories
down the stairway to where it ends, to have worn
linen and passed as a man in suits.
I'll tell that one too
though you don't want to hear it,
though it's as old as the hills,
though displeasure is now rage, I'll canvass
for funds for it, not giving up,
not showing myself up this time,
too close to Mother and the difficult calm,
to the overextended fruit of this day,
this dream.

Taxi in the Glen

You throw matches on the floor.
I collect antique lard cans.

"You know, some day there'll be an interest
in these, though it will peak, like the tide,
in infinite relief, and be back next day.
But somebody will surely remember them—
the succinct red of that metal.
Then we drink everything in, avidly,
yet we are not thirsty. Some mechanism declines
our auroras, and so must it even be
until the day of waking up and not finding out.
I'll be a spruce-god by then, but you, you
should still be savoring the advantages
of belated puberty."
      And I'll dress you in grass
and sing to you, a song where the words are the music
and the music has no point. Let me chafe your nipple, I . . .

And time will be happy. *Quiet, runt.*
The world's most astonishing plant couldn't
faze you, nor the fat ogres beyond the icehouse.
Lilies and sweet peas think you're swell.

I even have a nephew who is about
to invite you to the cotillion in Baltimore,
after taking a few more readings, and say,
wasn't it cool the way the alive came up to you,
all combustible, dreadful with tears,
and capped your burning oil well?

You've got friends
out there, more than you know,
but time is running short and we have to do something about it.
How about a nice whistle, something Grandma
can use on her back porch. Or a subscription
to *Reader's Digest* and the black methane-haunted city.
In any case it will be a peaceful interlude
when you get around to it—limning storm clouds
with the rigor one knows of old
of you—and caution an angered bluebottle
to calm his romantic hopes.

The Blot People

Something's not right. There were vibrations,
"vibes," a moment ago. A bush rubbed its bark against the sky.
The miserable thicket smelt of firecrackers

and I found everything in more or less the same order
when I got home. Still, it's hard to remember
what the order was after the first few things: a tie, a sofa,
a sheet of paper artfully placed so as to point to
who might have moved it in my ripe absence:
the bruised, alien thing, but familiar
as a smile on the face of anyone.

A few coat hangers jingled slightly
in the breeze from the closet. Someone was here.
Someone may triumph over the other one.
The family returns from the sea
with dogs and radios and fishing rods.

Old fishermen greet them in the ruddy glow
of lamps. The prisoner, an Uncle Joe,
returns after a great distance—so many miles,
so many hours tethered into days
that built the long log road from here to the east.

The Captive Sense

Nothing I'd ever want to own,
this feudal inequity transmits
its haze through the computer's
silent convulsions.

I'd wager there's life in the old bird yet—
the château of shaving cream is the most refreshing
thing to come along since tires in the theater.
When I arrive in the morning can I send it
collect, on the half shell? No? Not my fault?

I'm not going to tell you about regularity and anything,
me, Moses on my little raft. When it comes time
to rescue me, they will. Even four thousand years are
"like an evening gone." Some prosperity spurts
from its core, the core of waiting.
How could it be otherwise? Colored fountains in the night,
playing to dulcimers who dream of crocodiles?

My wish kept me captive, growing in it
till I fitted it exactly. And now the soothsayers can take over.

The movie dream was corny anyway, something
with spear carriers and a woman spinning flax
in a hovel by the sea, how great waves carried her along
to this pleasant plateau we are pleased to think of as
the present, conniving with something eldritch behind there
that takes me back. Never knew my heart could be so yearny.

From Hollyhock House to the Hollywood Hotel
the ill-lit Undine evolves, sashays even.
Who could have known the future would be such a big bunch,
and our share in it so meticulously outlined?
Not fiends, surely. But not friends, either.

The Confronters

Which of the incredible lies will prove true?
Ah, you ask me things
I wish I could not even ask myself.

A fire burns in a fireplace.
Cups are on a sill.

A man is working. He moves along. There is so
much to learn, so many teachers.

A dog howls from a roof.
Is it a wolf? Someone wants it to be.

In short there are these topics.
In winter and in summer there were.
The other seasons mediate
and end up having more topics.

"Hives with no bees," you said.
Which is how I remember them
through a bloodred transparent curtain, that looked
like rubber.

The various inequalities are parceled out,
now. There are suburban subdivisions
with no shards of land left on them.
Impatient dawns arrive.

The Desolate Beauty Parlor on Beach Avenue

So much has impaired here
as well as getting here. It's where
we used to trade personals, then divide up
the aptly named "spoils." You know the kind of crud
I mean. Zombie set-tos,
the kind of thing.

It was impossible to locate hell or heaven
standing in the basement, inspecting
which pipes might have led to upstairs.
And the little pines off the street—
so sweet, but no sweeter
than what's been taken down in the interim.
I wonder where people hang their laundry nowadays,
who's for sale.

Then I saw it over Cannibal Beach—
a big baboon of a moon wafting this way
and that across the silken heather. It gave me
the widdershins. I'm still counting.
But the nice octagon trainer—*he* offered something
in the way of comfort, that eyeglasses can choose to go
and fit if they're so inclined. I'm talking
product now, and the new productivity
that comes from it. No one can afford
to ignore it anymore. Sure, sheep
bawl at their station, mad at having voted,
at being voided. But another way of sexy being
has been unveiled, and disturbed. I almost think
they won't be able to fix it, but it's so new—

Wait for the end, though. It's a small, arched close
built to contain ragged passions, and emptied
of them at present. The dale sweeps down
the sober dawn. Every face shows signs
of extreme concentration. Now *that's*

the way I'd like to behold you. For always.
For when the clipper blows astray and the
cheap shot is parted.

The Faint of Heart

were always right
about things like chansons de geste
and why they couldn't, at the time, be bothered.
Huon de Bordeaux was a highly important person
at least in Bordeaux which is an important French city,
that smells better than Perth Amboy but worse than
    Newton-le-Willows.
As has been pointed out
by myself and by other researchers, the object of the game
is to sit on a cold rattle.

I love the broad avenues of Washington, D.C.,
all leading toward—what? What is it they are escaping from?
Who in this great city cares anything about these data
that are the wellspring of truth? Torches emblazon the field
in front of the White House, which is where our president sits,
and Congress, when it is in session. Have I omitted anybody?
No, only the man who summons the president's taxi
who is too unimportant to figure in your list.
What about that dray horse's withers? Ah,
I shall have to begin again,
to start all over again from the beginning. Nomenclature
being its own reward.

And the fang? It's pleasant-looking and practical.
The board of surveyors is ours.
I trust in and admire it.
The Bureau of Mines belongs to all of us
in this dang-blasted country. Each of us has a share in
    tomorrow.
The light on that ilex

reminds me of an old school-chum of mine. None of us,
you see, was ever divested of anything,
which is why we're running riot now, in the alphabet-coded
    streets
and others named in memory of hydrangeas and vernal
    blushes.
And he said, "Varnish the floor!"
Winter is coming and it's going to be spectacular.
The squirrels and woolly caterpillars told me so.

In time the review squads appeared.
They carried Gatlings and were dressed in plum-colored
    eighteenth-century uniforms.
The mood was sour. I offered to chase a member of the enemy
but it wasn't going down well. Then *you* appeared, covered
with rubies, and it was decided we should "get down."
Secaucus had looked better. The snow on the reeds—

Soon the president joined us. He was worried but polite.
The daughters in their simple white frocks came out on the
    White House lawn
and had a very nice chat. They said it was an allegory
or oligarchy, and to roll with the punches. Better
alive and upbraided than rocked in the cradle of the deep,
someone said. But that's what I'm trying to oppose—
how you been?

The Green Mummies

Avuncular and teeming, the kind luggage
hosed down the original site. Who is ready
last, but I kind of get a kick
out of what-the-heck's surface optimism.
He doesn't believe in sex—that's *one* point
in his favor—but knows all the standard
Antonio stories and has told them to the Ladies'
Auxiliary in Loophole. You see, all his life
he wanted to be a trainer, or *something*, maggots

even. But fate's crow-like wing
had other plans for him. We were meant to have slept
during the time we were awake and learning; conversely,
as air-raid wardens we made good Michelin men—the tummy
always in repose, the chin barely protected by a ruff
of sneering blight. But it's time

you took that old comforter off. Adam and Eve
on a raft could say good day here, laughter in the
loved opus sounding. Yet wan derision only
watches, won't come forward. Next year is electric;
this one only divides and serves us, bathes us,
as we know how. Better pickled moray
than a jungle diorama, full of who-knows-what quirks
and surfaces. Yet I like him; his white hat
fell off and landed in the sound. Mortified,
he herded us into the vestibule; we had brought
the wrong kind of medlars.

The Latvian

Knowing John, it might have been.
Then again, maybe *you* know him—
food on his dried-up puss,
handsome for a day, a stunning
figure.

Why any of this bothers me, *I'll* never
know. My place is down here, with you
pagans and sun-worshippers, to whom
we turn when all else is exhausted, as, in fact,
it usually is. Then smiles break out
on rain-stippled streets, plaid plastic hats
and flowers appear. It's enough
to put the "cow" back in "macabre."

And we weave together the lesson
of today, me holding the ball of yarn,

you at your embroidery hoop.
Relief comes on strong. It pits
man against ghost, neighbor to neighbor,
falling down as the fur flies.

Who knew if the embassy had tickets,
or if they would even sell one?
By that time it was half past nine:
too late to dust the refrigerated air,
too early for the hockey scores.
Yet if I infiltrate this page of music,
like a violinist inflating Mozart, the seams,
the dear themes, come true.
We are all a falling in love.
Let's leave it that way.

The Military Base

Now, in summer, the handiwork of spring
is all around us. What did we think those
tendrils were for, except to go on growing
some more, and then collapse, totally
disinterested. "Uninterested" is probably
what I should say, but they seem to like it here.
At any rate, their secret says so,
like a B-flat clarinet under the arches
of some grove.

The house took a direct hit
but it didn't matter; the next moment
it was intact, though transparent.
No injuries were reported.
There were no reports of looting
or insane buggery behind altars.

The Peace Plan

These are the eyes I have stared out—
the others' suit them. Not to cry,
though. I brought the wind
and a pharmacist with me. You know, nuts and bolts.

Once on Lake Ontario
the swan heaped up her cries, the wind then
knew what to do, came in at a right angle,
the lake stoppered, parceled, traduced made it all seem plainer
as plain things can seem.

Then a licensed party might be drawn
she thinks. The horse, sheepish in his manger, shifts
from foot to foot—when was I last shod?
Will all these old differences unmake me at last,
or do I have to wait for a peach to blow?

A white-headed sage
remarks your angst, walks on
to the corner of Tilsit and Mulberry
whence he is abruptly inducted into heaven.

To what uncheer
has this oasis brought us?
Have some pagan robbers bought us
without our knowing? Then stealth
will be my cry, season after season, even
as the virgins on the porch circle round, take up a collection
of obliging smiles.

The Penitent

What are these apples doing here?
I thought I told you never to bring them inside.

And that wedding cake—what does it think it is?
Promises? Was it for this I sublet the apartment,

consecrated myself to a life of prudery
and banal satisfaction? I could have sold my life

story to a famous writer. But by then
it would have been over. Too much to write about isn't a good
   thing.

He recognized me! The famous man
knew my name! He held my hand

a second. I'd do that for someone.
The library is too fast tonight,

there's some spoilage in the lagoon, but everyone
is looking forward to your coming of age,

to the diamond stickpin and the hat.
Yet others carp,

seek annoyance, complain of the shadow,
as though 'twere always dusky night,

but your face looks good in the bathroom mirror.
I like your air freshener, your after-shave—

Say, what is it you do to look and smell so good?
Methinks some of it might come off on me

in the forest, with the cool sky
ambient with rubbings.

The Problem of Anxiety

  Fifty years have passed
  since I started living in those dark towns
  I was telling you about.
  Well, not much has changed. I still can't figure out
  how to get from the post office to the swings in the park.

Apple trees blossom in the cold, not from conviction,
and my hair is the color of dandelion fluff.

Suppose this poem were about you—would *you*
put in the things I've carefully left out:
descriptions of pain, and sex, and how shiftily
people behave toward each other? Naw, that's
all in some book it seems. For you
I've saved the descriptions of chicken sandwiches,
and the glass eye that stares at me in amazement
from the bronze mantel, and will never be appeased.

The Sea

We carry our anxiety about the land with us
when we leave the land to travel overseas.
She shouts: "This is the dimmest
thing you ever did! In all time
was never such lurching, so much rubbing of the chin."

It's true: I'd have deserted the land of my forefathers
a dozen times before if I'd thought
I could get away with it.
And a triangular shadow whose apex is my toe
comes to tell me of my rights, warning me
of perjury, in some books the most serious crime of all.

Even the crinkled stars in the meadow
cannot look the other way, forcing me
into my constrained idea of myself.
I must go out with the light, and some day
someone will see through and love me.
I look down at these asters, unsteady,
unsure of what to grab. The tuneless sing to me.

The Shocker

What would I learn? That this vale
of sudden diphtheria matters less than a string.
That nudism equals terror.

My universities, you let me graduate
into a world riddled with solemn put-puts,
echoing across a bay in south Jersey,
fresh from delivering funnel cakes, a local specialty.
The brambles of the surf tangle
with the rafters of the beach. The Sea of Tranquillity.
You'll always get a kind of hum. No use
doffing those earmuffs. Besides it's not cold enough
to be wearing them. Amazed
people will look at you like you're crazed.
Now, all I wanted was to be back at the table
in my little laboratory, observing water spots on a plate,
trying to tune the old crystal set
to KDKA.

Here the weather is tethered to no air.
The eyes in the head in the house
look out over a spotty landscape of bilious green chest hair.
I believe I am the Man from Nowhere. I'm expected.
The taxi karma circled the pebbled drive and departed
through the great iron gates, which clanged shut.
You see I have to stay here. I *am* expected.
Yes well we'll pursue that over cocktails
and lunch.

They were destined to meet one more time,
briefly. Is that a hand on my sleeve . . .

The Waiting Ceremony

The binding clause—
it concerns us,
behooves us to behoove it.

Yet I'm so far away
(I'm not far away) . . .

Eighty-eight keys on a piano—
how do they know that?
I mean, *know* that? Oh, sure,
I know how they know it.
Excuse me for living.

Once in a while
the fun gets taken out
of what wasn't supposed to be fun.
That's the boiling point, what
they mean by one.

I get a stiff neck watching.
But then it seems old cereals (or serials)
are the part-time joke—like this rubber of bridge,
with all the bridges receding into the distance, brought
to their time of rightness. I would stress
the very white side of a house. Go on,
give it away, give it to a child
or some tax-free person.
(Nothing bumptious about that.)

We hold all the ends
of the story, like the four corners of a sheet,
resuming and resuming. We are the thick.
And the thin.

The Walkways

> To know how to walk in the night, to have
> a goal, to reach it in the darkness, the shadows.
> —Joubert

The man behind you spoke to the tracery
as it killed him. The witches' envoy
brought a tusk to the guest of honor.

It was covered with vapid inscriptions about not
exhuming the past until the day
when smoke rises from a hole in the ground
alarming no tots, but then a journey like a cipher
elaborates its undoing. To have knitted scarlet
earnests in the epistolary novel of my Russian phrase book
and cloned them to a besmirched integrity
was my plan all along. There was no need to get your
balls in an uproar. Now, during one of the violinist's durable
encores the horse is teed off again, galloping toward the
    horizon
with the frail buggy and its precious cargo (two terrified
jeunes filles) in tow; the violet ribbon comes undone
and precious antique letters pepper the landscape
of early spring with plangent, mourning-dove complaints.

Why did you never write me? I bled for centuries
from that tiny puncture wound. One day I woke up whole
and it was all unreal, though I could hear the music
of your fingertips sliding over vellum, the scenery.
Meanwhile I had been getting stronger every day
without anyone's suspecting it, myself least of all.
When I finally stood up my head towered above the hills
and brass gates, terrorizing the little folk
beneath, who raced like ants in all directions.
Now I was past caring. Those feverish gifts
from many Christmases ago ceased to implore
or annoy. I eyed them wanly. Only a picture of a barefoot girl
sitting on a fence rang a distant bell, and that sullenly,
too deeply buried in today's growth
to answer my clear call.

I understand by this that you are taking over.
Wait—here is the key. Now that Lord Chesterfield has joined
    us
you'll need it to unlock conversations, great ones,
as a great wind is great. I am lucky to have come so far, only so
    far,
though the pantheon receives us all. Such is its way.
To be roofed and slavish, and then unstitched by apes,

is all a fellow needs, these modern days, unkempt, mourning
beside a gate, forever undecided,
like a partially opened umbrella.

The Water Carrier

I did not, then,
or later, pull my finger out of the hole
and make us as comfortable as possible.

While driving down East Raven Street
baroque and proud,
extend my hand to the nearest of you,
only the nearest.

Our decisions were made in filing-card days.
Now, someone else emotes.
Was it—? The oh-so-long summer,
gravel in one's boots—then, at night,
lettuces.

But continuing along
then, as now, soul-kissed
the powers, one after the other
into a haunting new day.

By the dried-out concrete pier
another was watching,
slowly, spilling his beans
into the pants, or porridge, of the night thing.

Then there were only a few of us orphans
who laugh, and shout,
lingering by the manure pile

who do daylong things.

Theme

If I were a piano shawl
a porch on someone's house
flooding the suave timbre . . .

Then forty, he,
a unique monsieur—
and yet he never wanted to look into it.

"Have you forgotten your little Kiki?"
Smoke from the horses' nostrils
wreathed the pump by the well.

The stink of snow
was everywhere. Too bad it looks
so good.

O beautiful and true
thou that glitterest
, in storms,

starting to discuss gardening. I don't
want to throw cold water
on this.

That music has changed my life
a lot, since I made the
mistake of learning it.

Another passionless day. The peach
forms a stain
at the end of the line.

Learn to lock love enjoy:
"The dream I dreamed
was not denied me;

hence my love is mad—
a castle's satin walls
folded in blood."

The deputy returned
the peashooter. I have learned
to plait wasps

into a bronze necropolis.
The ticket and the water
only endure, as one can

in the right circumstances,
mon cher Tommy. I think the theme
created itself somewhere

around here and cannot find itself.

Three Dusks

I think it's nice of me
to admire this coastline
of small houses:

firm outlines.
How the drainpipes sag
in the eves,

reserved for the bounciest
critter.

Ouch! Was that a new flavor?

•

Anyway, they come and go.
No point in trying to stop 'em
or say hello: They'd misinterpret

this as a sign of greed
on your part. I know;
that's why I ripped up the goalposts.

•

No one ought to know
what I was thought to know
for many years, among cherries
and without. The victor wears a stovepipe hat.

Your mucilaginous narratives come from somewhere:
I *know* that. I urge you to use your influence
with the young prince. He's headstrong,
and a bit difficult, besides, at times.
You're a perfect size 7,
you know. Yes, I know.

But what comes out of me
strolls back into dark.
It were not good
to show much of me,
only what red
neon can understand,
whisper to a little brother.

There were tens of thousands of cabbages
in the field.
Now, what one wanted was a little broth
with butter in it.

The cranes have flown far from their perch . . .

Today's Academicians

Again, what forces the critic to bury his
agenda in interleaving textualities and so
bring the past face-to-face with his present

isn't naughty, but it *is* both silly and wrong.
The past will have to get by on sheer pluck
or charm, entirely consistent with its ten-
dency to nullify and romanticize things. The
way a pain begins. The flying squirrels of
this particular rain forest mope in flight;
the audience has already done what it can for
them; and the pure light of their endeavor
bespeaks the modesty of the program: "mere?"
anarchy. That the men with spotted suits
and ties get down to it is one more nail in
their coffin. These portly curmudgeons dig-
nify no endeavor and are also about as "right"
as the weather ever gets. All in my time.
More meteor magic. Seems like.

Touching, the Similarities

Surely it was the same blank wall of twenty years ago.
How the past identified with every kind of collectible,
so there were not just the things we knew about.
The girl in white ran across the little bridge scattering pigeons
this way and that, there was no contenting them.
A little house poked up from under the vines.

Have a few beers at the Topple Inn,
throw a few darts at the board, put
someone's eye out, spend the rest of your life
under a pall. Granted, it must have been easy.

The similarities must have been monstrous then,
yet the obtuse angle of evening is mum on the subject.

Tower of Darkness

I cannot remain outside any longer
in the cold and pervasive rain.
I grab my crotch wishing for a ball of light
in the shaggy interior other people have.
I shall go away without fetching a grain
from the earth,
            compact,
                        with the climbing design
we knew and hated so well, and when it was our turn
to die we just gave up, mumbling some excuse.

Do you often go to see them?
They can't have much cause
to journey here, yet their footprints,
foreclosed by snow . . .

It was the barker whose patter started it
well before we were awake, into the dawn
that grizzles, now, a fright
                        to be wished, to be read,
unlike the old healing that will come again in time.

Tremendous Outpouring

According to most of these people, a good "ladle"
is hard to get—mothers of such things, the cousins, added on,
splashing and crying. I brushed him. Let others watch
the espaliered proof, the tapered belfry. The human gust.

Little things like that—would I
like to request it? No.
In the cold night, spun out of the past,
the names. Frost. An obscure petulance fattens the rafters
overhead, bulges the curtains. The cigarette boat
goes out. The urban brewery
coincided with the jingle in my pants
to chill those ways.

Tuesday Evening

She plundered the fun in his hair.
The others were let go.
There was a wet star on the stair.
Upstairs it had decided to snow.

Not everyone gets off at this stop
the turtlelike conductor said.
If you'd like to hear those beans hop
it could be arranged in your head.

Now from every side, cheerleaders
and their disc-eyed boyfriends come.
The latter put up bird feeders.
Birds alight on them and are dumb

with anticipation of the meal.
The punishment is not due
in our time said the wise old eel.
Its overture is still distant in the blue

sign of a vacant factory. You'll know
when it starts up. Darn! That's what I thought
it would be, I said. Isn't there a hoe
somewhere to root these weeds out?

Or a chair on a blanket
of a manor house in time
and shouldn't we somehow thank it
for the perfection of the climb?

Straight over roads, in culottes
the marching women go. Why besmirch
that casket, choose fleshpots
over a stand of young birch?

The veranda failed to make an impression,
ditto the lavaliere.

Potted ferns have become my obsession,
waltzing under the chandelier.

No one weeps to me anymore.
Then up and spake greengrocer Fred:
"Time and love are a whore
and after the news there is bed

to take to. Don't you agree?
It's lonely to believe, but it's half
the fun. Here, take a pee
on me, but over there by that calf."

The things we thought of naming
are crystals now. You can see from the porte cochere
now a small business flaming,
now the besotted rind of some pear.

It all seems ages ago—that time
of not being able to choose
or think of a rhyme
for "so many books to peruse

until the body is done." A chicken
might pass by and never notice
us standing pale as a mannequin,
clutching a fistful of myosotis

as though this would matter some day to some lover
when the time was ripe and our mooring
had been sliced. Then it would be time to rediscover
a plashing that would seem more alluring

for being ancient. You see, the past
never happened. Nothing can survive long in its heady
embrace. Our memories are a simulcast
of lost conventions, already

drowning in their sleep. In some such
wise we outgrew ourselves, lianas

over lichen. Forasmuch
as sweetness comes to the nicotianas

only at evening, your arrangement is overbred,
threadbare. You may want to think about this
a little. Down in their pavilion, whose overfed
airs waft lightly, naughtily, Dad and Sis

are waving, calling your name, over
and over again. But it's like a wall of veil
tipped in. We can dance only alone. Rover
senses an advantage—it's the Airedale

from the next block again. To keep even the peace
sounds extraneous, now. How many senses
do we need? Our motives predecease
our cashing them in. Fences

will be happy to relieve you of that icon
for a small consideration. And you,
what about you? Slowly unraveling, the chaconne
sizes us up: right pew,

wrong church. O if ever the devil
comes to claim his due, let it be after
the touching ceremony, yet before the revel
becomes frenzied, and ambitions turn to laughter.

Resist, friends, that last day's dying.
The melodious mode obtains. Always
remember that. At trying
moments, practice the art of paraphrase.

Just because someone hands you something of value
don't imagine you're in it for the money.
You can always tell a gal-pal you
prefer the snakeroot's scented hegemony.

Or go for a walk. It counts too.
In my charming madness I dress plainer

than when they used to mispronounce you,
but what's correct streetwear in N'Djamena

clashes in the old upstate classroom.
Come, we're weak enough to share a posset,
divide with the boys another hecatomb.
All other rodomontades are strictly bullshit.

Such are the passwords that tired Aeneas
wept for outside the potting shed,
when, face pressed to the pane, he sought Linnaeus'
sage advice. And the farm turned over a new leaf instead.

We can't resist; we're all thumbs, it seems,
when it comes to grasping mantras.
The oxen are waiting for us downstream; academe's
no place for botanizing; the tantra's

closed to us. Song and voice, piano and flowers,
abduct us to their plateau.
Look—becalmed, a horse devours
buttercups in the ruts by an old château.

If this is about being regal, it must be Japan
has assented. Let's take the vaporetto
to where it goes. A sea cucumber of marzipan
promises decorum. The boatman quaffs Amaretto.

Well, and this is the way I've always done it. A fricative
voice from this valley wants to think so. Those jars of ointment
are still untouched. Were patients always so uncommunicative?
Even Jeremy? He's late for his appointment,

and I must go down an inclined plane
to the city's anthill, with only dissolved rage
for company. And should some perdurable chatelaine
gain control over the police, must we summon the archimage

to bandage the hurt? Only a little moisture
remains at the tip of the tongue, a pro forma

signal of engagement. Before the great rupture,
still a duo, we sang the "Casta Diva" from *Norma*

on Sunday morning. Now all's retrograde;
the new openness cloys. Pencils are to sharpen,
yet I keep mine dull. My cockade
is tarnished, my dress puny, my shoes of cordovan

behind the bed. Sometimes I like to ride in a carriage,
over dales and downs. My fiancée is a lacrosse player.
When the moon is full one's in the mood for marriage,
amiable for a while. But the village soothsayer

warned us against it, of dreary days to come
unless we interacted on a vast scale. And who can predict
furtive new developments? Because we'd swum
the Hellespont long ago, in our youth, we assumed the verdict

would be sealed by now. And you know, only anonymous
lovers seem to make it to the altar. The rest are branded
with a time and place, and rarely know each other. The
    eponymous
host of the Bridge and Barrel, a moralist, was openhanded,

yet nothing could bar the tear from one blue eye. He'd chattered
vainly till now. So I assumed the aggressor's fate.
Behind the door crockery clattered
mysteriously, the beadle was stunned, the boilerplate

contract wilted in the intense heat
of the deluged afternoon. Even when the tumbrel
arrived, it seemed it would have to wait
for the century to catch up. Meanwhile, in the adumbral

hall not a whistle could be heard, no screams, no catcalls,
unless you counted the willows' sobbing.
Evening came on boisterous. Pirouettes and pratfalls
were executed before an admiring crowd. Demons were
    hobnobbing

with whatever entered on skis. To have proffered
only this was sublimely sufficient. But what of cattails
loosing seeds on the air like milkweed? A scoffer'd
not turn away, just this once, for what prevails

is most certainly what will be current
years from now: celadon pods with opal juices
oozing from them. Fruits of the sand, blackcurrant
and bayberry, and a crowd of mild smiles, a burnoose's

wandering cord. When needed to combat flatulence,
the correct pills turn up in pairs. I mistook embroidery
in the stair carpet for something else, the doll's petulance
for a sign from the heavens. The whole darn menagerie

is after me now; I have strength for but one curtain call,
and that a swift one. But will the critics
recite my reasons? Luckily a landfall
materialized in the nick of time. Luckily my desire wasn't great.
   Politics

overwhelms us all. In seasons of strife we compose palinodes
against the breakers, retracting what was lithe
in our believing. By evening, its heresy implodes
under an August moon; repercussions writhe

in a context of mangroves. Perfervid scroungers
invade the Catalog Fulfillment Center, diverting the sick
   energy
in our wake into easeful light, and day. A few loungers
on the mezzanine are puzzled, but most are not. The ambient
   lethargy

incises its monogram on the walls of bathhouses, in wooden
tunnels: To wit, man plays a role in his conspiracy,
ergo, he cannot be a victim. After a sudden
denouement, the climate again turns bland; its apostasy

was too minute to register on God's barometer.
Only an occasional letter to the *Times*

hinted that a change might have occurred.
Otherwise it was *beau fixe* on the speedometer

as it raced toward clayey lands with windmills
and similar giddy appurtenances. From far,
from night and morning, innovations arrive in schools,
    whippoorwills
are calling. The Circolo Italiano welcomes new adherents, a
    streetcar

bearing members of the Supreme Court floats in the sky like a
    zeppelin.
It was all over in a trance. Now it's the fiction
weighs us down, an iron corset. Adrenaline
is channeled into new, virtuoso ways, wherein constriction

is viewed as normal, soothing as an antimacassar.
Better to live in a fictive aura, I say, than putter
in one's garden forever, praying to NASA
at dusk, as in Millet's *Angelus*, closing a shutter

on substantive dreaming. That, after all, is where we're
at. It is time for the rebuilding of melody
on a grand scale. Reread Shakespeare; a fakir here
and there won't sabotage the kernel of parody

baked into the airiest ontological *mille feuilles*, nor change that
    gold
back into straw. The medicine men knew what they were doing
    when
they lanced boils with direct imaging. Charm gained a foothold,
then exploded into bronze deities. No matter, the regimen

practiced by the ancients, i.e., inhaling
dust and air near a body of water, is still around to restore
lost fossils of wit to their living, vibrant selves, unveiling
a menu both familiar and alluring. Before

quitting this backdrop of a Renaissance piazza, open
your body and mind to all comers. They are both factory and
    garden
to the happy few, thunderstorms to some, a dull weapon
though fierce, to others. And as attitudes harden,

the lost light stares as a man in pajamas
crosses the ravaged street. All this decision-making entails
sophomoric stunts and impatience. From the Bahamas
to Torquay stretches the dun pilgrimage. Cocktails

infiltrate it, but the man knows he must go
just so far and stop, that his beloved will have forgotten
him by then. He must choose the stars or the snow,
a naked stick figure. All the rotten

things that can befall a man with a comb and toothbrush
already happened to him, leagues ago. And there is no ending
it. Yet the past is profitless slush,
same as the present. Tomorrow is on hold, pending,

and great lizards infiltrate the Dalmatian-spotted
sky. Was it for this you gave yourself up
to some cause or other, that has now trickled away, dotted
with colored pom-poms? Only a final hiccup

sits on the step, awaiting orders. You were wrong about
    language,
see. Its arrows are raining down like ejected porcupine
quills. An archer (Robin Hood, for instance) could gauge
the correct distance between identical hummocks. Which is fine

with me, except I don't think anybody's going to notice
the directive that brought you here. Best to marshal the
secondary promptings and forget the awful journey before
    rigor mortis
sets in. You mean it hasn't? Right. Then I'm still in the
    Marshalsea,

my dependency shall never cease! And there's a kind of
    happiness,
though a bitter one, in that. I'm going to cash in my chips
and quit while I'm winning. The loveliness
of statues of statesmen survives, a barcarole drips

from their sagging jaws, graphic as springtime.
In twos and threes, peasants
vanish behind yon ridge. The celestial pantomime
engulfs them slowly. The pheasants

of our kingdom aren't as plump as yours. No matter.
I'll wager a microclimate's responsible. And did your sister
ever loan you those three bucks? No, the regatta
closed down while we were still ogling its pinnaces, and a twister

slashed through at that precise moment, there was nowhere
to hide, in the confusion we got separated.
Now I must arise and go where
the flying fishes play, and poppies perplex the cultivated

plain. Go ahead, I'll keep an eye on things, you can breathe
easy. It's what I had in mind: a sail printed all over
with musical staves. I would unsheathe
love's whippet and embrace us all, even if Rover

never growled again. "Springs, when they happen, happen
    elsewhere.
A certain sexiness . . ." ventured the prince. But where, oh
    where, is the nectar
that makes babes of us? Our printout's in disrepair,
the parterres are fading, and the projector

is spinning out of control. Half a hundred youths
could sustain us, swimming in the moat
with reeds to breathe through. The emptied booths
by the front gate are cheerless indeed. A stoat

swept by me on the waters, halfway to refurbished oblivion,
but my antennae suggest nothing apposite

to formalize his trajectory. A safe-conduct from the Bolivian
chargé d'affaires flutters in the breeze of my room. In the
   windows opposite,

a massacre is reflected. Is it meant as codicil,
or mere free-form tangling? Anyway, night is serendipitous
again; swallows clutter my windowsill;
bats are executing stately arabesques. A precipitous

slide into belief must have occurred recently, but left no earnest
of its passing. A videotape of sports bloopers
keeps unreeling, determined to rescue its syllabus from the furnace
of eternity; airheads are treated roughly. One of those Victorian
   peasoupers

is equalizing everything, titmouse and pterodactyl
alike. When it will be the fashion again we'll have trochees
galore. Even the bellicose double-dactyl
will flourish for a time, in Okefenokees

of subjectivity. Lakes will overflow, bargain
counters shrivel to nothing, the Great Bear look away, brittle
talismans explode at dormer windows. The degradation Ruskin
warned against is back, a heap of frozen spittle.

We see one thing next to another. In time they get
   superimposed
and then who looks silly? Not us, as you might think, but the
   curve
we are plotted on, head to head, a parabola in the throes
of vomiting its formula, piqued by the sullen verve

of day, while night is siphoned off again. And as wolverines
prefer Michigan, so this civil branch of holly is nailed to your
   door, lest you
fear my coming, or any uncivil declaiming, or submarines
in the bay that spreads out before us, or any gumshoe.

We'll party when the millennium gets closer. Meanwhile
I wanted to mention your feet. A dowser

could locate your contentedness zone. But where have you
    been while
folk dancing broke out, and colorful piñatas, waking Bowser

in his kennel, rendering the last victuals
in the larder unappetizing? Yet those feet shall impose the glory
of my slogans on the unsuspecting world that belittles
them now, but shall whistle them *con amore*

anon. That doesn't mean "peace at any price,"
but a shaking-down of old, purblind principles
that were always getting in the way. Self-sacrifice
will be on the agenda, a lowering of expectations, a ban on
    municipal

iron fences and picnics. Man must return to his earth,
experience its seasons, frosts, its labyrinthine
processes, the spectacle of continual rebirth
in one's own time. Only then will the sunshine

each weekday lodges in its quiver expand till the vernal
equinox rounds it off, then subtracts a little more each day,
though always leaving a little, even in hyperboreal climes where
    eternal
ice floes fringe the latitudes. On a beautiful day in May

you might forget this, but there it is, always creeping up on
    you.
Permit me then for the umpteenth time to reiterate
that basking in the sun like an otter or curlew
isn't the whole story. Tomorrow may obliterate

your projects and belongings, casting a shadow longer than the
    equator
into your private sector, to wit, your plan to take a Hovercraft
across the lagoon and have lunch there, leaving the waiter
a handsome tip. For though your garrison be fully staffed,

the near future, like an overcrowded howdah,
trumpets its imminent arrival, opens the floodgate

of a thousand teeming minor ills, spoiling the chowder
and marching society's annual gymkhana, letting in smog to
   asphyxiate

palms and eucalyptuses. One paddles in the backwash of the
   present,
laughing at its doodles, unpinning its robes,
smoothing its ribbons, and lo and behold an unpleasant
emu is blocking the path; its one good eye probes

your premises and tacit understandings, and the outing
is postponed till another day. Or you could be reclining
on a rock, like Fra Diavolo, and have it sneak up on you, spouting
praise for the way the city looks after a shower, divining

its outer shallows from the number of storm windows
taken down and stashed away, for it has the shape of a sonata—
bent, unyielding. And, once it's laid out in windrows,
open to the difficult past, that of a fish on a platter.

Expect no malice from it and freshets
will foam, gathering strength as they leapfrog the mountain.
But a quieter realism plumbs the essence of ponds, as nitwits
worship the machine-tooled elegies of the fountain,

that wets its basin and the nearby grass. In a moment the
   dustmen
will be here, and in the time remaining it behooves
me to insist again on the lust men
invent, then cherish. But since my mistress disapproves,

I'll toe the line. And should you ask me why, sir,
I'll say it's because one's sex drives are like compulsive
   handwashing:
better early on in life than late. Yet I'm still spry, sir,
though perhaps no longer as dashing

as in times gone by, and can wolf down the elemental
in one gulp—its "How different one feels after doing
   something:

calm, and in a calm way almost tragic; in any case far from the
   unwholesome
figure we cut in the reveries of others, a rum thing

not fit to be seen in public with." Yet it is this ominous
   bedouin
whose contours blur when someone glimpses
us, and is what we are remembered as, for no one can see our
   genuine
side falling to pieces all down our declamatory gestures. They
   treat pimps as

equals, ignoring all shortcomings save ours. And of course, no
   commerce
is possible between these two noncommunicating vessels of our
   being. As urushiol
is to poison ivy, so is our own positive self-image the obverse
of all that will ever be said and thought about us, the vitriol

we gargle with in the morning, just as others do. This impasse
does, however, have an escape clause written into it: planned
enhancements, they call it. So that if one *is* knocked flat on his
   ass
by vile opprobrium, he need only consult his pocket mirror:
   The sand

will seem to flow upward through the hourglass; one is pickled
in one's own humors, yet the dismantled ideal
rescued from youth is still pulsing, viable, having trickled
from the retort of self-consciousness into the frosted vial

of everyone's individual consciousness noting it's the same
as all the others, with one vital difference: It belongs to no one.
Thus a few may climb several steps above the crowd, achieve
   fame
and personal fulfillment in a flaring instant, sing songs to one

more beloved than the rest, yet still cherish the charm and
   quirkiness
that entangle all individuals in the racemes

of an ever-expanding Sargasso Sea whose murkiness
comes at last to seem exemplary. So, between two extremes

hidden in blue distance, the dimensionless
regions of the self do have their day. We like this, that,
and the other; have our doubts about certain things; enjoy
    pretension less
than we did when we were young; are not above throwing out
    a caveat

or two; and in a word are comfortable in the saddle
reality offers to each of her children, simultaneously
convincing each of us we're superior, that no one else could
    straddle
her mount as elegantly as we. And when, all extraneously,

the truth erupts, and we find we are but one of an army of
    supernumeraries
raising spears to salute the final duet
between our ego and the endlessly branching itineraries
of our *semblables*, a robed celebrant is already lifting the cruet

of salve to anoint the whole syndrome. And it's their proper
perspective that finally gets clamped onto things and us,
    including
our attitudes, hopes, half-baked ambitions, psychoses:
    everything an eavesdropper
already knows about us, along with the clothes we wear and
    the brooding

interiors we inhabit. It's getting late; the pageant
oozes forward, act four is yet to come, and so is dusk.
Still, ripeness must soon be intuited; a coolant
freeze the tragic act under construction. Let's husk

the ear of its plenitude, forget additional worries,
let Mom and apple pie go down the tubes, if indeed
that's their resolve. For, satisfying as it is to fling a pot, once
    the slurry's

reached the proper consistency, better still is it to join the
    stampede

away from it once it's finished. Which, as of now,
it is. Wait a minute! You told us eternal flux
was the ordering principle here, and in the next breath you
    disavow
open-endedness. What kind of clucks

do you take us for, anyway? Everyone knows that once
    something's finished,
decay sets in. But we were going to outwit all that. So
where's your panacea now? The snake oil? Smoke and mirrors?
    Diminished
expectations can never supplant the still-moist, half-hesitant
    tableau

we thought to be included in, and to pursue
our private interests and destinies in, till doomsday. Well, I
never said my system was foolproof. You did too! I did not.
    Did too!
Did not. Did too. Did not. Did too. Hell, I

only said let's wait awhile and see what happens, maybe
something will, and if it doesn't, well, our personal
investment in the thing hasn't been that enormous, you crybaby;
we can still emerge unscathed. These are exceptional

times, after all. And all along I thought I was pointed
in the right direction, that if I just kept my seat
I'd get to a destination. I knew the instructions were
    disjointed,
garbled, but imagined we'd eventually make up the lost time.
    Yet one deadbeat

can pollute a whole universe. The sensuous green mounds
I'd been anticipating are nowhere to be seen. Instead, a dull
urban waste reveals itself, vistas of broken masonry, out of
    bounds
to the ordinary time traveler. How, then, did he lull

us, me and the others, into signing on for the trip?
By exposing himself, and pretending
not to see. Solar wind sandpapers the airstrip,
while only a few hundred yards away, bending

hostesses coddle stranded voyagers with canapés
and rum punch. To have had this in the early stage,
not the earliest, but the one right after the days
began to shorten imperceptibly! And one's rage

was a good thing, good for oneself and even
for others, at that critical juncture. Dryness
of the mouth was seldom a problem. Winking asides would
    leaven
the dullest textbook. Your highness

knows all this, yet if she will but indulge
my wobbling fancies a bit longer, I'll . . . Where was I? Oh,
    and then
a great hurricane came, and took away the leaves. The bulge
in the calceolaria bush was gone. By all the gods, when

next I saw him, he was gay, gay as any jackanapes. Is
this really what you had in mind, I asked.
But he merely smiled and replied, "None of your biz,"
and walked out onto the little peninsula and basked

as though he meant it. And in a funny kind of way, the nifty
feeling of those years has returned. I can't explain it,
but perhaps it means that once you're over fifty
you're rid of a lot of decibels. You've got a tiger; so unchain it

and then see what explanations they give. Walk through
your foot to the place behind it, the air
will frizz your whiskers. You're still young enough to talk
    through
the night, among friends, the way you used to do somewhere.

An alphabet is forming words. We who watch them
never imagine pronouncing them, and another opportunity

is missed. You must be awake to snatch them—
them, and the scent they give off with impunity.

We all tagged along, and in the end there was nothing
to see—nothing and a lot. A lot in terms of contour, texture,
world. That sort of thing. The real fun and its clothing.
You can forget that. Next, you're

planning a brief trip. Perhaps a visit to Paul Bunyan
and Babe, the blue ox. There's time now. Piranhas
dream, at peace with themselves and with the floating world. A
    grunion
slips nervously past. The heat, the stillness are oppressive.
    Iguanas . . .

Twilight Park

Surely the lodger hadn't returned yet.
He had, but she hadn't heard him.
He was waiting five steps below the landing:
a black cloth in one black-gloved hand,
a band of light from the streetlamp like masking tape
across his eyes. He wanted to write something that would *sell*,
and this seemed the only way.
                            Desperate are the remedies
when one is broke, and no longer all that young or handsome.

Attention, secondary characters, and that means you,
Edith Fernandez: The snow is no longer pallid enough
to sum up your footfalls. One is ever so impatient;
now the tape falls, now carnival music
bashes in the front door. One can never be wholly
right, or wrong: catsup or ketchup? We must reread this.
The ending is considered particularly fine.

Umpteen

In this childhood you can
sort of tell by manners, like tomatoes,
who looked to be—may be—

like cute monsters who don't go away
but are never any trouble,
but what's *behind* it, this anything?

Is anything behind what we say
when we are not alone, not too far apart,
otherwise constricted?

Like a novel read on shipboard
or an old play with complicated stage directions
that may never have been carried out.

Perhaps the snow scene was too difficult,
the bison stampede too compromising.
We wake and are physical, the morning and

a thousand nerve endings are chiding,
clamoring . . . and all for what?
These files have nothing on you.

What the Plants Say

Don't cry it's lentil soup!
Kind doll rush us away
to a situation where the hay is mortgaged.
It was in fact time for a roll in the hay
so beautifully reflected in the color Polaroid
in the estate agent's window, but it
wasn't time to go. And she channels us
out over the silver plain's mush—
no wonder everybody wanted Karelia,
chiggers and all, and then it *was*
time, time for dusk.

If only one outrageous jeweler thought it
why then it must be true. A Cadillac
with a platinum pretzel hood ornament—
why not! You and all
you're taking me to must be true,
and silent, bodacious. That's the way
I like 'em—mystery girls
with buttermilk braids and a microchip of plain
caring, over the deserted wall.
So much rubbish! or trash . . .

Well, the bird flew down the well
and that was the last ointment anyone wanted.
For sure we got to go. Now's
the time, Ida.

When All Her Neighbors Came

the most beautiful combination appeared
on the game board. Normally we don't do these things
to each other. There's always a little kissing,
ha ha. Of that you may be sure. Yes, but mostly
they don't go round together, tethered to a median
that takes itself for the Judgment. Well I can't be
picking apples and playing the piano simultaneously,
now, can I? A withered little bird applauds. Some day,
it says, you may go back to the glasshouse and fiddle
what we all were taught, from day one. Your ale-colored
shirt is only an onus. Inside the others are dry.

The "give and take" of the other schools
isn't what I had in mind, thank you. A snake,
perfect in its horror, is. And the bondsmen drift off,
the decision buried in papers for a century or two,
and we, why then we are too, frugal of spirit,
reacting to the latest news. This lady of costmary
is the essential spoon. We may live more patently,
more expectantly, now.

Where It Was Decided We Should Be Taken

Your name here invisible as a headache
starts it off again and we are rolling
helplessly between the trees—we should
have seen it coming, but not many
are able to do just that. So we
dusted off our knees it was nice
to hear from you again over so many moons
with stars in them and now it has
become time for you to become comfortable again
which is not romantic as hydrangeas
aren't romantic until you imagine
a shed for them to be in
to be in the darkness like lilies, overspending
their light it seems, always on the carpet
for something, on the incoming tide
that many faces surround.
                                  Say it was
in some burrow you could hear planes overhead
but nothing was nasty this time, everybody
wanted to contribute to a general effort
which was being made

by a general on the other side of Kit Carson country.
Did I tell you about my hobby? It's—
Well, we can talk about my dreams if you wish.
I had a good one the other night
when everything was still
and in the morning I awoke with a red nightcap
on, really a dunce cap, of which
no one has ever seen one. I have a friend who
wants to collect them for a certain room in a
castle. But he can't.
There aren't any.

Another day I was out with Miss Peevish
paying calls, it seems like nobody's home anymore
and you have to walk so far to leave a card
over a stile and then a frog's in the

middle of the path—"Confrontational,"
she murmured. If only they asked *one*.
Cakes are optional, and credit.
They moved closer toward the sphere
of the lighthouse, the overcoat slid off,
revealing—in some way the boy gets in the way
all the time. Reason and habit
have beaten a path he's always circumnavigating,
but *this*! No one would ever—

These accents let us down
gently onto the torso of a wood
where birdcatchers yodel and bobwhites cheep.
It's not going very far, it's like going to the door
after the salesmen have slid into the universal pit.
And when one goes out it's time to go too,
as though Mother and the piano had never exited
and those china knobs you never put away.
Feed the horse on brambles the moon
is coming

Woman Leaning

However it may come back to you
it'll seem all right. At first.
Till the ones who do the realizing
realize, and call you to their office
at one in the morning.

I said fix the radiator.
These gray grapes are spread out before us
in a feast situation. Yet who can explain
why we should banquet here?

Then, in she plops—
a soloist trained to lead us
out of the briar patch of history,
trap that was always here.

And we, we listen. That's obvious.
There was more said in the tent,
but what I remember only has to do with paddling.
Then, inexplicably, we're safe.

No one loves us for it, yet
they can dictate to us now
from a striped sofa that was years in the making.
And what they tell us to write makes no difference
but is enough light for us to see by.
Everyone jumped over the fence safely.

All that was left was a book under a weeping
willow, in whose table of contents the glottal insistence
of the stream was repeated endlessly, like tears
for our benefit, if we should ever get to know them.

Yes, Dr. Grenzmer. How May I Be of Assistance to You? What! You Say the Patient Has Escaped?

We were staying at the Golden Something-or-Other.
Anyway, what does it matter now?
The boats have rolled up their colored sails.
The city is like a hinge. In the morning its glass
girders are flushed with light that gets drained
in the afternoon, but then something funny happens:
The westward-looking buildings reflect the sun's
rays more fiercely than they are projected.
They become a rival sunset in the east. That's heresy,
or at any rate bigamy. Tall buildings
"to suckle fools and chronicle small beer"; such is my story,
but I'm glad to be having this chance to tell it to you
even though we are in a silent movie and can speak only words
painted with milk. Yet someone comes to care about them:
There is always someone to care, somewhere,

but the sheriff vandalizes the day they return.
I didn't let you dream about it.

It is for this I am being punished
by reforms harder than the ones in Congress.
They have rules to go by, sins to atone for:
I, I have only weightlessness
and a vague feeling that I should be spending my time
doing other things—sweeping the apartment,
washing out a child's mouth with soap.

It was nugatory. They fed us delicacies
while we waited for the order of quilts to arrive—
or was it kilts? Joshua had this haunted feeling
he'd never finalized it at the start, when all
should have been beginning, but instead was pleased to slosh
    around
in mid-harbor. Anyway, there *were* invoices. Of that
he was almost certain. And a number of young girls
came and stood around the tree in which he was sitting—
were *they* the ones who had placed orders for the kilts?
Or were they mere raisin fanciers? "You'll see
when the weather gets dry and yellow the raisins
will form all by themselves, alone on the branches,
and no one will care. And those that like to eat them
real fast out of boxes won't have a clue
as to why that old horse-collar is draped over a branch
of the weeping willow, causing it to weep (that is,
bestir its leaves) even harder. Some people somewhere are
    prepared
for a few things to happen, but that's not counting us or our
immediate families. An apple-green boxcar slithers along
a distant railway, yearning for something
unnameable at the end of the canyon. Not
a handful of raisins, probably, but you catch my drift."

Soon all was drift. They had a feeling
they had better go inside, yet none could make a move
in that direction. All remained transfixed. "Tell them,"
the skald continued, "but only if they ask,
how this situation came about. We'll see then
what jury will convict me, just because I feel like a woman
trapped in a man's body, but only a little—not enough

to want to wear a skirt, but enough
to make me feel like putting on a kilt, and even then
only in Scotland, if I should be so lucky
as to find myself there some day." Tremors
stirred the little band; there was obvious sympathy
for his plight, mingled with something more acidulous,
like pickling spices. And all the girls turned away
to weep, but were changed to ivy
and stuff like that. Why am I telling you this?
To assuage my conscience, perhaps, hoping the bad dreams
will go away, or at least become more liberally mixed
with the good, for none are totally good
or bad, just like the people who keep walking into them,
and the scenery, familiar or obvious though it be.

Besides, I've raised one major issue—
at least credit me with that. It will be a long time
before this turns to nothing, and in the meantime
we can sit upon the ground, and tell sad stories
of the lives of pets, as the ground freezes and thaws
many times—it is past caring. And what goes on within us
will be inscribed by the dancing needle on our chart,
for others to consult and be derived from.
I thought it would all end casually on a bank
of flowers, but alas, a real bank was growing out of it
with tellers and guards. Who liked the flowers.

Yesterday, for Instance

No longer available is the hare
with milky fur grazing on the clover of memory.
O beautiful basketballs! How far stretch the docks,
farther than my bonny sailor is from me.

The pigeons shift. The sky is syrup and pink gold.
I can no longer lie. I must tell it "like it is."
But where is the raincoat that will hustle me
to the forest crossing? For it is a convenience

to know and to learn, and haply no good is in me.
I must claw the ground for grace. These poor root-systems
are in faith no better. I must see about clobbering
the backstairs monster on his toes, let him cover

my rail of defense with dandelion slips. Then I'll be off
into who knows whose trouble that the boarded-up sign
couldn't spell. And then after years and years
I'm back—but it's like two seconds on a conductor's watch.

He patronized me, and all I could say was, "Wow,
this is goofy!" And he liked me in it, with the croquet tresses.
And the buccaneer said it was too soon,
that we'd find out in the grass trap, which is why

I echoed. Even children couldn't pay attention
to all of it, and all of it is most certainly
where we are. No more candied lies. I'll come out as the movie
trailer ends. I promise the sun was a switch, or tickler.

You Dropped Something

So what if it's brackish my love
today's junk mail is full of arms for you
the erotic weavings of slumlord
hermits and piss-elegant diatribes:
No more waving for you
at least for the time being
which is anybody's stable

The lost nights thatched with regrets
shingled with antinomian heresy and hedged
about with ifs ands and buts
are nobody's dream cycle to you
the arena of matches and pups

and further slide
into romantic chaos

Say they're not keeping track anymore
that the wounded demoiselle is hopping
mad and more coal barges
have arrived on the harbor's
slippery surface

Say then that they're not well again
Jumping through hoops to train
myself to attract attention was always
sometimes my endeavor to attract
smart eyes

You that go out and go in
through memory's many castles
are you single or just alone this evening
castrati belch forth some
air thought to be unfit
for today's goads and geodes

She'll be coming round the house
and faster too; some press goodies
overlooked in the mad rush to prepubescent freedom
whose minds got mismatched

Throw many more daggers at the stone
It's ancient after all
how many comic strips do you invoke
what tarheels
in fashionable disarray
more strokes this morning

You come to the end of the row
you could switch over or begin a new one
at the wrong end and work back to the previous beginning
Do we really want to see it turn out all right
Are the guns trained on her
quarterdeck what about the ketch

And you do really go in

It's a passably elegant solution
for what was only land office before
ancient miles of wind picking
the harrow clean

All standing around
just to welcome you
you and your pie-eyed souvenir chest
and the bride you brought from back east
nailed to the sun

You, My Academy

Maybe untwine my breath, like.
Remove the cast-off castanets from my chest hair.
That's better. I can see more in the distance.
I won't be giving this up any time soon,

yet commerce no longer functions the way it used to
in the days gone by. Small businesses
are beginning to go the way of the peacherino,
following the Pied Piper and his rats
into the cavity beneath the hill. Even big business
is foreign to itself, knows not what it dreams,
or wants. If it glances into the mirror
at times, it sees only a blank, supplemental wall.
Profit-taking is an unheard-of concept.

Only muddled enjoyment perceives that a crossover
took place in the recent past. Huddled shapes
of the homeless, hidden under dirty quilts,
are the one sign of that baleful trajectory
that left the street full of cannonballs like horse manure.
Enjoyment becomes a rare earth amid such strata,
something the landlady was going to tell you
but you were too quick for her on the landing.
It's diffused now in the racing forms.

Fiona and Ilona, just back from Riga,
can't understand what's the fuss. "Weren't there
seventeen-story G-men back when, too? Anyway, the kids
haven't turned litmus pink—*or have they?*
What manner of golfer stands to reap anything
from this desperate situation?"
Ask a situationist, lady, I'm here for the free canapés
and the gin.

Bituminous ballocks thrash the sand spread outside.
It were time for the library, and to ferret out
who killed the sexton. "Not I," says the dung beetle,
"Nor I," the worm. But one of you surprised him in
the few seconds he went to get his pants. And my theory
is all but erected—an imposing pyramid
of squashes, eggplants, artichokes, leeks, celery, et al.
Is it too late to absorb that?

That's why screeds were written—for dictionaries
to read them, and then come to conclusions
that would have been startling once, maybe thirty-five years
    ago,
but now no longer have power to shock, or even charm
as butterflies laughed to us in childhood,
and the creamy sails on the marsh filled with the light and the
    wind.

It must be light and bright as a brazier
down where you are now. Are you going to fax us any fun?
I was just sitting on the toilet, dreaming a ruse
to make you factions obey, and here you ring my doorbell
and hand me a large box wrapped like a harlequin—
Is it full of dishes? Are you going to be my "wee one"
once the attorneys have sailed back?

Or do we lose each other in the desolate glens
it seems the world is largely composed of?
Is that where your pointed toe is leading?
I'd jump off buildings for you, scale circus tents,
though I know it's not exactly what you had in mind.

How about suburbia? "A sad pavane
for these distracted times." How about the Everglades,
then? A mangrove is a wondrous thing
that never stops growing, unlike
our pencil-thin projects for reaping dividends
once the troglodytes have had their way with us,
and been assimilated by us. That won't be for centuries,
but time's caprice is a wild card, compressing lives
into a space of weeks or months, if need be,
sometimes.
    And sometimes
when my horse looks at me, it's a great treat,
or a great fright. Animals are about the last to listen
as you read from the Book of Hours—they get frisky
with listening, and the natural beauty of everything
wants it so—cut up for lenses to devour,
or vague and transparent as a subpoena when a tractor
stops to give us a lift to the nearest menstruating sun.

You Would Have Thought

Meanwhile, back in
soulless America, people are having fun
as usual.

A bird visits a birdbath.
A young girl takes a refresher course
in polyhistory. My mega-units are straining
at the leash of spring.
The annual race is on—

white flowers in someone's hair.
He comes in waltzing on empty airs,

mulling the blue notes of your case.
The leash is elastic and receptive
but I fear I am too wrapped up in cloudlets
of my own making this time.

In the other time it was rain dripping
from a tree to a house to the ground—
each thing helping itself and another thing
along a little. That would be inconceivable
these days of receptive answers and aggressive querying.

The routine is all too familiar,

the stone path wearying.

Young People

Slowly he is eating the stars—
they are like the spines of books to him,
but don't throw two ladies or locations at him.

He called this Nomad's Land.
Yet it was clean and serious. Not, it is true,
cheerful. Not by any means. Yet the old men

in pajamas made a leisurely appearance.
Good times were on the phonograph.
Surely somebody can be his wife,

surely there are strong husbands for such women,
who keep a rifle in the broom closet
and never ask for i.d. Their colors:

those of a saffron strand at evening
in disappointed August. We rise with the swifts,
never to know what cut us loose.

WAKEFULNESS

For Jim and Dara

Wakefulness

An immodest little white wine, some scattered seraphs,
recollections of the Fall—tell me,
has anyone made a spongier representation, chased
fewer demons out of the parking lot
where we all held hands?

Little by little the idea of the true way returned to me.
I was touched by your care,
reduced to fawning excuses.
Everything was spotless in the little house of our desire,
the clock ticked on and on, happy about
being apprenticed to eternity. A gavotte of dust-motes
came to replace my seeing. Everything was as though
it had happened long ago
in ancient peach-colored funny papers
wherein the law of true opposites was ordained
casually. Then the book opened by itself
and read to us: "You pack of liars,
of course tempted by the crossroads, but I like each
and every one of you with a peculiar sapphire intensity.
Look, here is where I failed at first.
The client leaves. History goes on and on,
rolling distractedly on these shores. Each day, dawn
condenses like a very large star, bakes no bread,
shoes the faithless. How convenient if it's a dream."

In the next sleeping car was madness.
An urgent languor installed itself
as far as the cabbage-hemmed horizons. And if I put a little
bit of myself in this time, stoppered the liquor that is our
  selves'
truant exchanges, brandished my intentions
for once? But only I get
something out of this memory.
A kindly gnome
of fear perched on my dashboard once, but we had all been
  instructed

to ignore the conditions of the chase. Here, it
seems to grow lighter with each passing century. No matter
    how you twist it,
life stays frozen in the headlights.
Funny, none of us heard the roar.

Baltimore

Two were alive. One came round the corner
clipclopping. Three were the saddest snow ever seen in Prairie
    City.

Take this, metamorphosis. And this. And this. And this.
If I'd needed your company,
I'd have curled up long before in the clock of weeds,
with only a skywriter to read by.
I'd have laved the preface
to the World's Collected Anthologies,
licked the henbane-flavored lozenge
and more. I'm presuming,
I know. And there are wide floodplains spotted with children,
investing everything in everything.
And I'm too shy to throw away.

Palindrome of Evening

In other places where it was found
necessary for there to be buttons, expectations were naturally
    higher, and higher,
and higher.
Here,
a sow's purse translates into a silk ear, and communications
are jammed.
No one takes hold any more.
Look, the flower has escaped from its trellis,
the bear goes down into the lake.

In my second house rare footage
of metempsychosis plays endlessly, like a tune
variously tooted.
I often feel I'm a buyer,
but the painted carnival head reasons otherwise,
badgers me. There is no release in sight,
in the works, down the pike.
Horrified spectators jam the football field;
it was like night and day.
We can't go back to the restaurant;
the roof is snatched away.

What *were* expectations back then?
Do we know how high the astronauts carried us,
let us fall, bouncing for what seemed an eternity,
until all was well again?
I've got my cool
in these pants, keeping it for you.

Cousin Sarah's Knitting

You keep asking me that four times.
Why trust me I think.
There is, in fact, nobody here.

Nobody in the past.
Nobody to turn to for advice.
A yellow flagpole rears thoughtfully.
Now if you were that nice.

He was pulled from space,
as from a shark. After they examined him
they let him go. What does that prove?

And called him Old Hickory.
As in hickory. No there were
at that time none living

out of a sideshow at the edge of a forest
and were mistreated in proportion,
with understanding, so they all grew

into the shade and for once it seemed
about right. Oh, call down to me.
It seemed about right.

Then there was something of a letdown.
Patrol boats converged
but it was decided that the . . .

and could continue its voyage
upriver
to the point where it tails off

and then there was a large misunderstanding.
It was misunderstanding, mudsliding
from the side where the thing was let in.

And it was all goose, let me tell you,
braised goose. From which a longing in the original
loins came forward to mark you.

So many brave skippers,
such a long time at sea. But I was going
to remind you of this new story

I can't remember, of the two chums meeting in the overfed
    waste land and it supported them. And one got
off at the front. The other wandered for days and daze, and by
    the time nobody remembered it it was summer again
and wandered around defensively. Sure the organ meat
was pumping and somebody's boy came up to the correct
thing at the well head. Sure as you can claim Dixie your tax
    accountant
wandered over the remaining riviera, all to be blue again. And
    the rascals . . .
and I was going to say keep it. You can keep it.
Granted she has no reputation, an eye

here, another clovered savior here, they pretend to us, and it
   was time for the firemobile too.

Last Night I Dreamed I Was in Bucharest

seeking to convince the supreme Jester
that I am indeed the man in those commercials.
Simultaneously it peaked in Bolivia, the moon,
I mean. Then we were walking over what seemed to be
heather, or was called that. The downtown riot
of free speech occurred. Plastered to its muzzle,
Randy the dog's decoding apparatus went astray.
By then it was afternoon in much of the world;
iced tea was served on vast terraces
overlooking a crumbling sea. You can't juggle
four toddlers. Three is enough. Out of the beckoning
sea they arrived, in white ruffles with black coin-dots
attached; the lawn was closer to a farm
this time; it mouthed "Farm." Will vacuumed the whole of
   space
as far as the mind-your-own-business wire stretched, that is,
from Cadiz to Enterprise, Alaska. We thought we had seen a
   few new
adjectives, but nobody was too sure. They might have been
gerunds, or bunches of breakfast . . .

Added Poignancy

What could I tell you? I couldn't tell you any other way.
We, meanwhile, have witnessed changes, and now change
floods in from every angle. Stop me if you've heard this one,
but if you haven't, just go about your business. I'll catch up
   with you
at the exit. Who are the Blands? The second change was
   perhaps nothing more than

the possibility of changes, one by one, side by side, until the
    whole
canyon was carpeted with them. Nice. Summer, it said,
ever rested my mind. Something occurs everywhere then,
an immediate engagement with the atmosphere
we'd like to have around, but it was big, then, and obvious,
and oh, this is for your pains. No, really. Take it. I insist.

He thought if he lived amid leaves
everything would surface again, by which he meant, balance out,
only look what this random memory's done to him!
He eats no more, neither does he sleep. A permanent bell tone
seems to create his hearing at each moment of his elevator. Obey.
    We're
in for it. There are no two ways about it. Wait—
did I say two ways? That's it! We'll fix his wagon with too many
    ways—
so it'll be lopsided, with no judges to pay, and we can all go home.
Sweetheart? I fancy you now—

Hence it ends up with a scenario of them all getting paid,
the bums, and walking out into the eternal twilight
with gurus and girlfriends on their arms, one for each fist.
I like that way about it. I'm making believe
it never happened, that we got this way
merely by having been here forever. Millions of languages
became extinct, and not because there was nothing left to say
    in them,
but because it was all said too well, with
nary a dewdrop on the moment of glottal expulsion.
But now I've got to go put out the signs on the chairs
so folks'll know when to stop, and where, really, only a poodle
separates us from this life and the next.
It will take us longer to get from here to there.
And the cigar band is ecstatic,
stunning in its mauve and gold obsolescence,
an erratic bloom on sheer night, faintly deleterious . . .

Quarry

I was lying, lying down,
reading the last plays of Shakespeare.
A brat came to me, eyes squealing,
excitement its thing. Until I put two and two together

I never crossed the inlet
or realized what tributary meant.
O we all have fine times

in the spring she said.

No one needs to know pretty much
about that attitude I suppose,
yet there are riders, and puzzles, and soon,
baking at the long end of day
a poor cloud measures its shadow,
the intent of all those gone away.

Laughing Gravy

The crisis has just passed.
Uh oh, here it comes again,
looking for someone to blame itself on, you, I . . .

All these people coming in . . .
The last time we necked
I noticed this lobe on your ear.
Please, tell me we may begin.

All the wolves in the wolf factory paused
at noon, for a moment of silence.

From Such Commotion

The dress code is casual, the atmosphere relaxed
in the licensed quarters of our city;
young couples graciously stopping beneath umbrellas
in the street . . .

And this is not a thing that matters:
walks on grass, through flaring Adirondack chairs.
You caught me napping said the belle-lettriste.

No, perhaps it's not that, that's the point. You've
been in to see these?
And we should have decided to go there, gone for a second time.
Yes, well, they're working on it, et cetera, etc.

The summer capital exits past us, we have to
sell product. It "fell through" the European system,
now it's time for avatars. At four in the morning
the art demonstrations begin, psalteries jingle, the whole damn
    ocean
is there, up for review, for us. It's just

that we don't understand. It's my negative capability acting up
again. Well, I'm within my rights.
It's like apples and pears, or oranges and lemons,
what I always say.

From nests as admirable as these, wallpaper islands,
the vivid flow reverses. That's in-house.
And we go as far
with them as possible, suffer stupid reverses, get plastered,

the goateed scorpion insists.
And it was while waiting for the drying to happen that we all
    got lost.
Please, he insisted, there's more to the point than two doors, O
    I know
it I said, I can't be damned to travel

any time. You should have pointed the way to me while I can,
while it's still light, otherwise what will all your gnashing
    accomplish,
the oatmeal? Please. Now just go away. It's
raining, the sun is shining, braver outdoors. Can we come
    listen to that.

Moderately

> . . . and as the last will come a sort of moderato part, (which some is of multiple motions, quick, slow, hampered, expressive, popular, and peopled speech . . .)
>
> —Stefan Wolpe

The fox brooding and the old people smelling
and the tiebreaker—why did I not think of that?
Why have doubts upon me come? Why
this worldliness?
And I remember no longer at the age of sixteen,
and at the age of seventeen great rollers
eating into night, I uncared for,
stopping among the weeds along the way. Phantom
harvesters hovered. And the great, dry creekbed was a sea
of gravel and stones, the willows were capsized ships,
and none of it was for now.

There is a draught
in the room
and all along the room a sight that is like living
and looking out over a situation. The periods danced in a
    sentence,
and it was my way, the one I chose, even if I didn't choose it,
or like it; was all a coming on,
downpour,
marooned on slopes.

And then the burst of it.
He knew what the world's going to be like I think,
so why the explosions? And caught in the draught,

one fell from darkness, two fell from darkness,
yet another. Maybe that's dust a very fine kind of dust and I
    eat it,
it goes on thrumming, seated in the back row of the orchestra,
men masturbating here and there and like I said the clock
is tremendous,
wider than any minute hand or hour hand.

And sheepish it fell out of books:
the land of painful blisses,
the man who stubbed his toe.
All around us pain came sledding in,
and am I like this today, tomorrow, and two
tickets please, the boy and the ruffian come undone,
he was in the park, it was the salutary last person
to hoodwink you and all is well.

There were times a kind of cream was on the jagged borders
or suchlike events and carnivals, and you sat, smiling,
the tongue unleashed from its surroundings. Why was I never
    here?
Why such playacting? Didn't I ever realize the kernels *are*
    deep-seated,
that everyman will overrun his banks just like an errant stream,
and cardboard principles be jostled? O who
mentioned this session? What is the matter with truth and paying
and all over the paisley fields dominoes are braying,
a matter of luck, or chance, it seems? Who broke the next dish?

Why is that man crying,
what does he mean to do? Impertinent, in person,
what does he mean to do,
if these capers are not unusual
and bricks merge with sand, the unusual
at its best as usual, and can't we give up? What
would be the point of continuing? I can't smoke this weed,
I give it back, we are all blessed, commensurates within
a star where many things fit, too many, or not too many,
    whatever
it says about you, whatever saves.

Alive at Every Passage

Roll up your sleeves,
                             another day has ended. I am not a part of
    the vine
that was going to put me through school
but instead got sidetracked and wandered over the brink of an
    abyss
while we were having a good time
in full view of the nearest mountains. *Mon trésor*, she said, this
    is where I
disappear for a few moments, I want you to be brave.
Sure, nothing like a date in bed,
waking after midnight to the blank TV screen
that wants us all to listen to its cute life and someday
    understand
what rhomboids the earth took
on its way down to get us,
that we must be happy and sad forever after. No I don't think
it was in your best interests nor do I shave with an old-
    fashioned straight-edge,
you dolt. But I was coming to that,
doing the mystifying. So if he says not to be aloha, not again,
well gee in this old-fashioned bar, however will the runts learn
    from their again imploded
hair balls how straight everything is.

The rest, as they say, as they say, is history:
I captured a barracuda, it was midnight in the old steeple, the
    clans casually
moved on us, leggings barely jerked out of the ditch. It was
    folly
to be noticed, then, astir on the perhaps more urgent
surface of what becomes one, indeed comes to become one
through impossible rain and the sly glee of mirrored
    xylophones.
Say only it was one for the books,
and we, we did belong, though not to anything anybody'd
    recognize
as civil, or even territory. I need to subscribe,

now, history will carry me along and as gently leave me
here, in the cave, the enormous well-being
of which we may not speak.

The Burden of the Park

Each is truly a unique piece,
you said, or, perhaps, each
is a truly unique piece.
I sniff the difference.
It's like dust in an old house,
or the water thereof. Then you come
to an exciting part.
The bandit affianced
to the blind man's daughter. The mangel-wurzels
that come out of every door, salute the traveler
and are gone. Or the more melting pace of strolling players,
each with a collapsed sweetie on his arm, each
tidy as one's idea of everything under the sun is tidy.
And the wolverines
return, with their coach, and night,
the black bat night, is blacker than any bat.

Just so you know, this is the falling-off place,
for the water, where damsels stroll and uncles
know a good thing when they see one.
The park is all over.
It isn't a knee injury, or a postage stamp on Mars.
It is all of the above, and some other things too:
a nameless morning in May fielded by taut observers.
An inner tube on a couch.

Then we floated down the Great Array river, each
in our inner tube, each one a different color:
Mine was lime green, yours was pistachio.
And the current murmured to us mind your back
for another day. Are
you so sure we haven't passed the goalposts yet? Won't

you reconsider? Remount me to my source? Egad,
Trixie, the water can speak! Like a boy
it speaks, and I'm not so sure how little all this is,
how much fuss shouldn't be made about it. When another boy comes
to the edge of the falls, and calls, for it is late,
won't we be sorry for not having invented this one,
letting him fall by the wayside? Then, sure enough, waves
of heather recuse the bearers of false witness, they fly like ribbons
on the stiff breeze, telling of us: We once made
some mistake, it seems, and now we are to be judged, except
it isn't so bad, someone tells me you'll be let off the hook,
we will all be able to go home, sojourn and smile again, be racked
with insidious giggles like guilt. Meantime, jugglers swarm over the volcano's
stiff sides. We believe it to be Land's End, that it's
six o'clock, and the razor fish have gone home.

Once, on Mannahatta's bleak shore,
I trolled for spunkfish, but caught naught, nothing save
a rubber plunger or two. It was awful,
at that time. Now everything is cheerful.
I wonder, does it make a difference?
Are sailors waving
from the deck of their distraught ship? We aren't
envious though, life being so full of
so many little commotions, it's up to
whoever to grab his (or hers). The violin slices life up
into manageable hunks, and the fiddler knows not
who he is moving, or cares why people should be moved;
his mind is on the end, the extraordinary onus of finishing
what's set out for him. Do you imagine him better off than you?
My feet were numb, I ask him only, how do you carry this from here to over there?
Is there a flat barge? How many feet does a centipede have?
(Answer in tomorrow's edition.) I heard the weeping cranes,
telling how time was running out. It was Belgian,

they thought. Nobody burns the midnight oil for *this*,
yet I think I shall be a scholar someday, all the same.
The hours suit me. And the rubber corsages the girls wear
in and out of class. Sure, I'll turn out to be a nerd, and have to sit
in the corner, but that's part of the exciting adventure. I know things
are different and the same. Now if only I could tell you . . .

The period of my rest is ended.
I shall negotiate the fall, then go crying
back to you all. In those years peace came and went, our
    father's car changed
with the seasons, all around us was fighting and the excitement
    of spring.
Now, funnily enough, it's over. I shan't mind the vacant
    premise
that vexed me once. I know it's all too true. And the hooligan
ogles a calla lily: Maybe only the fingertips are exciting,
it thinks, disposing of another bushelful of ripe nostalgia.
Maybe it's too late,
maybe they came today.

At the Station

Renewed by everything, I thought
I was a ghost. All we've got in the back seat are doors.

I was just thinking
it was time to go back, pick up the pieces,
place them on a stand. You are nearer
to the high-school orchestra.
Youth plays absorbed.
If it had its own way, we'd be
outside. The decision is HERE!

Already they're taking it down,
distributing the various parts to places built in the ground

just for them. Next, we'd be tiptoeing
up and down the station platform. Look,
I've brought you a box of candied chestnuts, for the great
    voyage
into the technical dream you will learn to read.
For us, it is enough that the grass grows
sideways into the loam,
and that the wind is curious, silent tonight.

Another Kind of Afternoon

Remotely the unnamed keeps up with me.
It must be quite a time
since the last dignitaries visited with you.
Yes, and I'm about out of breath

for all the quiet cells we kept company in.
Must be a zillion years—
Look, here comes one of them.
I know I just met the czar's brother

in a book report. Soon it was time to return home,
past the midpoint, skipping-place.
Fierce, how that cloud suffocates
the sun, then is gracious for a while

but we can't go back there
due to the clamor, it's just as well
that they roll about
on the grass, young ones, old ones, the deer,

the pointer. And when you've imbibed as much
of the hurt as likes you, it's time for tag,
game that rolls down through our lives
over and over. You get what you have

to ask for, which turns out to be enough
to divide with the haphazard, rather ragged

assembly.
> We didn't go near the
windmill again for years, it was as though it had crumbled

in the imagination. Pretty soon six-pointed
purple stars stabbed us awake, and my goodness . . .

Tangled Star

A cup drips air,
peanuts fester. A wallaby streaks for the light,
suspenders down, indeed his pantleg is falling.
A ghost train appears over the snow-shrouded moor,
shoving us into silence. I decline the irregular verbs
of which our life is composed, but I cannot sing.
It stirs in the pencil box.
The ruler is too close for that.
Wind chimes grate against the door,
as though we never had one. Electricity
is named for the first time.

There are tensions. I suggest we try them out,
but the New England steeple looks sourly at us,
all coffins to the wind.

Alas, we are forbidden to worship the tensions,
even to play with them. If the next moon provides the addition,
the hearse its hamper of ham sandwiches, why then we will go,
as I told you we must. We are forever outdoors,
saving people's lives. The cattails get to see so much of us
that their contempt breeds civility, and the swamp
comes to seem right. Why hadn't it seemed so all along?
Now that it has gophers to chew on
we can imagine a less festive, more brackish
raison d'être of it. But we like it that our play be long,
and too many overseers crowd the hutch.
It is definitely time to move on.

Yet I had thought all of this was a party.
It is, but only in its duration, that sweeps us
down the stairs and over the side of a hill
where baubles float, and you get to interrogate that special
    someone.
In a flash, more finches, blue jays and fronds appear,
bronzed with a special effect of light, that says
it only to outdoors. To imagine what lies outside it
you would have to be a king or confidence man. And alas,
we have other plans for you. You are to come to see us
this evening, in the confusion of evening, to test our reflexes,
to speak to the dressmaker's dummy, and derive of it what
    comfort you can.
Your horoscope says so. What sign are you? Aw, Libra
with Pisces rising. Then I command you back to the cold

that you like so much, even though I had second thoughts
about it and everything. Can't you see the bear's paw
prints? They are elusively alive, held up by the trainer's
hoop, to be an example
to the ferocious wilderness. Here, take these herbs.

So many things, so many role models.
Their eagerness dances in the firelight.
We can't just say no to them, they have to live us
too. And in places where the water has ebbed the sky is
    midnight blue,
like ink spreading from a nib. They're all here, the catchers,
umpires, men in blue flannel suits, women
with a trace of tears like re-embroidered lace,
dusty with diamonds, seams in place. There is the mother;
she calls to the son. The tortoise and the hare
have come to tolerate us. Out on the lagoon
macaws are coughing. It is important to respect our situation.
One of them tries to get back to "normal,"
but the place is too exaggerated. Madame Nola is here.
And the bishop's children. And silly Irmgard.
And Rodney's commando. The teacher's pet. The cigar baron.
Marshal Tito. The young Eleanor Roosevelt.

Deeply Incised

If this is July, why does it look like August?
Sadly growing up into the real world
I don't even ask these questions *myself.*
Why are the shutters drawn
over that restaurant?
The moon's backwash is like a deeply incised
hairnet against the stadium.
Bats drool into the gutter.

If everybody is so intent on illustrating what they *know*,
why is the ant syllabus closed?

Tropical Sex

Yes, making a point of using it
makes a point, and otherwise all is but fish scales
and fish delivery—the clear-eyed blue trough of song
in whose pit I stumbled. O Lord,
help me to get over it. That's better, for a minute
there I thought I was a goner
and now I brushed up this interesting world
of lutanists and lunacy, and afterlife
not unlike the one we were used to—
Gosh, it's so thrilling,
everyone is so nice,
one had almost forgotten chiggers existed,
and bedpans, and dumb ugly coffers
like the one we lived in.
But that is only a sign now.

Be warned. A slight distance.

Or picture an insect struggling.
But it's going to be all right, I tell you.
We can live in The Heights and conjecture interestingly
about how life is made, how a man is paid

after all the contracts and ledgers are signed, blotted
in the sun. And surely one can stagger then,
get up and stagger to the nearest public telephone
and make slurping sounds at an invisible opponent: gone,
    warned
away, washed away. This siding came in with a crumpled
building already on it. Now only frogs can compute
the earth-sign that led gradually to dementia and panic.
The storage place is over there. I can see thistles
out of the corners of my eyes. It must be we are waiting

on another's aggression, handmaidens to the very plot
that would destroy us. We can
manage a giggle or handshake, but in the end the ink seeps
    through
and the person who did this wants very much to believe it,
has put himself inside us for this purpose. O chilblains,
weather vanes in the aching March wind,
did you want this ending? For this to happen
even as we were sitting all nice inside
the house, and by its hearth, and the brutal call
of the scarecrow fell like a hush over everything?
My friend thinks so—tell *her*
the bad news: "up to our ears in debt," playing a little
on the tidal lawn, abashed by our failure
to keep track of the consequences as they happened, and now
    a little
girl goes out to the squirrel. Hey, kid,
can I see your—
            Sorry, time's up.
We get to place a small white stone here at the crossroads;
it can be any one you like. Remember to vote. The clothesline
    has fallen
to the enemy somewhere. Yet the awnings are still prim and
    conspiratorial.
My chapter met and discussed you. Any number can play, the
    fleet's in,
and with the recyclables, our starched T-shirt.

The Friend at Midnight

Keeping in mind that all things break,
the valedictorian urged his future plans on us:
Don't give up. It's too soon. Things break. Yes, they fail
or they are anchored up ahead, but no one can see that far.
As he was speaking, the sun set. The grove grew silent. There
are more of us taking ourselves seriously now than ever,
one thought. We may never realize about our lives
till it's too late, and a man with a dog comes to shoot us.
I like to think though that everything is its own reward,
that liars such as we were made to last forever,
and each morning has a special chime of its own.

Thus we were pitted against the friend who came at midnight
and wanted to replace us with a song. We resisted furiously:
There was too much food on his table, the night was too black,
while all around us shrinking bands of outsiders
entered into negotiations with his darkness. It
seems to omit us, his reasoning, or in the well of time
we may be overdrawn, and cosmetics come to put a good face
    on us,
asking, why this magic wind, so many angles
against the river's prism and the burnt blue sky?
To which one answers, nothing is adrift
for long. Perhaps we will be overtaken
even in our happiness, and waves of passion drown us.
Now, wasn't that easy? A moment's breath and everyone
has gone inside to ponder the matter further.
Outside, children toboggan endlessly.

Stung by Something

but my advice is—be comfortable.
Wear a smock, with fractals. Be native!
You'll find people are more interested in your story,
and they will, too. Revisit

the recurrent tragedy of life.
Make sure it has its priorities straight.
Then—ziff! Jump off the end of a dock.
Color a monsoon yours, to do business and pleasure with.

With Smokey, everywhere seemed like pastime.
Girls in their girdles wandered up
amazed—they had never seen so many cheekbones.
The irises on the dump bloomed surlier that year—

too many tin cans. But you and I were deriding
ourselves, therefore it couldn't be over yet
and the past never happened here. Pounding
on his front door, one day or other,

the jasper eggs somehow knew my name.
It was all over, in fits. The tree-house
curtains were drawn, laughter strangely spattered the mist,
stippled the tenement wiring. Oh it's been gone

too long, tragedy again visits the dying shires,
tells one to hang in, it's over the top
with you. *Looks like
we've been invited to a party.* Treason peppered

the masts of my little skiff. Help! And then
an eternity of silence. Bores
shifted on the upper floors, there are not
enough spider-crabs, spiders of the sea,

for this embroidered doormat to clinch the departure bell.
Surely all's well—
we'd have heard about it otherwise. Strangers tell
this in shifts, for a little pleasure, a brittle hour.

The Last Romantic

Not to stumble, to get to tell you something simple
about the way the grass was being waves, how we broke
the world after we made it. Then it was a thorn-bearing
>   crescent.
Now you must be funny. Paranoid gigolos and candy,
lots of it, over the airways, in fact how could you,
you knew he was coming today. Well, better to squash
it once and for all. I was a fool for coconuts, I said
coconuts. Nobody believes me anymore, they think I've been
let out, but I haven't, I'm still locked up, and lovelorn.
Pretty please promise me a dish of scrolls.
After that one nip everything will be nasty and then it will be
>   romantic.

They pass him with muffin heads down along the winter beach.
So many characters. They told him there were too many
>   characters
in your novel, that the plot was still complicated, but still
they keep coming on, there must have been a leak, wait, it's
>   not even that,
there are just too many people out there. Well I suppose it
>   seems
so to you, who are not normal, but if you could see
it all from the outside you'd find how many are glued
to your coattails, and not too many, never less than enough,
and that includes children. My stars well I
never counted on all this being here. No, and neither
did your daddy, and it's quiet in the city,
too quiet, except for the largest vans and convertibles, and
>   these
are safely filed under "European"—we can let everything go,
>   really,
and then come back and look at it and pick it up.

Well it sure was farther the way
you always insist on taking us, me and one other person, but in
fine it was not a great distance, only a matter of some blocks
in one ward of the city. Say, I had a great

idea and now it's gone off and become useless.
So may I someday, sitting at play in my little unknown
    courtyard.
So may we all, while cats whine and grapes mature
and a prickly dust of unknown origin seems to rise upward
    from the seats.

Shadows in the Street

She bit the bridge. A photograph can stomach it. I'll be in
some time in the middle of July. Now the best time
of the year is around now, none can gainsay August
and Mr. Random's tooth running in the street, he liked to say
    hi, it was just
him running, which is a bit awkward. A diagonal lipstick
chased him across the street. From there on in it was just damn
    melancholy,
no anchovies, nothing in particular, nothing to say. If so why,
    why do it,
says Peter, who fought hard for the post, fought it and won,
and why we are here, in the middle of a secondary terrain, mad
    and absorbed
by life, by the truth, as always.

But the nice part
I was going to say is fenced out. Take to the hills then. There
    goes
one petal, the tree is falling apart, zounds I can do almost
    nothing
while the hills come and separate us, plant us in tomorrow
or until the last dish is unearthed.

Out crept a third one.
Savannas that have been dangerous, now no one remembered,
the evil shifting of feet denounced the lady travelling salesman
to our liposuction expert. A single afternoon cooking at the
    stove
and all is more or less gone over, too bad

the futile Molotov cocktail exploded
but in any case in another land, with more furniture than we
 expected.
So we said, grant us this, it shall be done in another kingdom
as in the king's den. Don't let the roof fall in!
I was kind of sidelined by the barber pole
but explained practically about the dark petal, that it was good
and we were appearing in its time, and shall be heaven, about
 time, about
that point. Rockets lifted. Read me. There is no point to all this
 listless
hive. He took off in a manner that betokened bats
when it was over and they came over. It's time, now, some are
 good and alone,
lost up unto the rest. They can go and cancel
around it's too moot to be played at. They are, for the rest
 unsavory,
thyme in the corral, three jumps from last school
the patio ignited, sworn to safe-conduct, like bread out of a
 school
conducted at last to here.

The Earth-Tone Madonna

What were you telling him about,
and why were veins implanted in the marsh
where everyone looks? Today
is the first day of spring, I think.
Sailing near us on a monocle,
the spray tapped and jiggled,
forever like a lifeboat.

And true some were found perjured
in cornshocks, there was no meat left that day,
no edge one could run around on.
There were peepers in the loose chaos called
oblivion, and not much else on the table.
Miss—er—Jones, what is the order of events?

I think not sir she cabled
from a vantage point in Toronto where all ships
and trains have their terminus. And if it's Wednesday?
Then man the egrets, the snowplow is coming
to rest where all of us have our workshops on
and it will be a tough call to divide up the rope
and Saturday.

There was no hope in the statue
of the saint, eyeballs collapsed, sloping forward
like a scythe, and yet we came to know
how he was doing, and appreciated a chat
at his knees. Now this was only the fourth time
any had done so. So we squeegeed
the happy-face off home plate, and bunches
of aristocrats all around us applauded
what came to seem fair, and in time
were whisked away—the ox in his pumps,
forgotten for daydreaming, the tangled marl
of old Sol's beard. Everything was decimated,
which was devastating, yet we went on
living, along the row we had been set down in
and soon we had reached the end. A conniving quiver
set compass needles skittering, prize lists
fairly glittering. And I looked to thee
to see what a retroactive spouse might be
yet we got lost somehow in the confusion
attendant on the formal victory. We were back
home, in fact, but no one thought to look
for us there. We were let out to pasture
in the shade, and six more volumes dovetailed.
The first part of the novel was now complete,
a hundred years in the making, yet its style
seemed chaste, if not downright lackluster, in the best sense,
as many terriers were starting to run,

yappingly. If there was a space for us
in all this fireside, it got debunked. We were kept waiting
right up until the announced departure,

and so became part of humanity. Part and parcel, I was going
   to say.

In the dim
eclectic din, beaters waited.
Let's handsel it, love, O my love, I said.

Dear Sir or Madam

After only a week of taking your pills
I confess I am seized with a boundless energy:
My plate fills up even as I scarf vegetable fragments
from the lucent blue around us. My firmament,

as I see it, was never this impartial.
The body's discomfiture, bodies of moonlit beggars,
sex in all its strangeness: Everything conspires
to hide the mess of inner living, raze
the skyscraper of inching desire.

Kill the grandchildren, leave a trail
of paper over the long interesting paths in the wood.
Transgress. In a word, be other than yourself
in turning into your love-soaked opposite. Plant
his parterre with antlers, burping
statue of when-was-the-last-time-you-saw Eros;

go get a job in the monument industry.

The Laughter of Dead Men

Candid jeremiads drizzle from his lips,
the store looks as if it isn't locked today.
A gauzy syllabus happens, smoke is stencilled
on the moss-green highway.

This is what we invented the suburbs for,
so we could look back at the lovable dishonest city,
tears clogging our arteries.

The nausea and pain we released to float in the sky.
The dead men are summoning our smiles and indifference.
We climb the brilliant ladder toward their appetites,
homophobes, hermaphrodites, clinging together like socks
hanging out to dry on a glaring day in winter.

You could have told me all about that
but of course preferred not to,
so fearful of the first-person singular
and all the singular adventures it implies.

Discordant Data
for Mark Ford

Still in spring, my coat
travels with the pack, unbuttoned as they.

The weather report is useless. So,
sigh and begin again the letter.

"This is the first time in weeks
I've had to communicate with you. It all

falls, in balls of fire. I guess the
North Dakota landscape doesn't do much for you. Have you

no conscience, or conscious, conscious conscience?
May I remind you that every sentence, everywhere,

ends with a period? A disclaimer of sorts?"
He thought we'd gotten to the middle of the grass.

His glass fire hydrants can have no end.
Oh it was just an idea;

there, don't rail. The posse is coming
by for drinks, we can skip enslavement today.

Concentrate, instead, on this day's canonicity.
It has to be from somewhere,

right? Many prisoners have left downtown, the old man
assents. He was tremendous and bald. Liked a practical joke

now and again. Look, the white rain is writing on the wall
of his saloon. Could be he was over the hill,

we'd assumed, but the flapping in the net's too
strong for that. Don't you agree? Have you

had any further ideas on the subject? Yes, you
could well afford to give up a few.

Bogus Inspections

The things that were in the drawer were dispersed a long time
 ago.
Some were wetted by snow. Others were dry but could not
 refract the light.
On the harbor's side a frazzled touch obtained.
Peace of mind fell through a grating in the sidewalk
where it lay visible for a few hours

and then it went away. Anyway, what can I tell you?
Not the things you want to hear, I suppose.
Nor can your interest deflect my moodiness. I shovel all the
 things you want to hear
into a wheelbarrow and leave it on your front step.
Perhaps some of it will reflect on me, on you, hell,
who knows what will jump out of it?
Some other passports were issued. Pilgrims
with scrip and staffs lined the stairwell and the near reaches of
 the street

in the moony swell that always seems to take over there, at a
    certain point
when I'm far from you. That's the message of it all—
of life, even.

You say you shied away from every event
in our small house. Yet at the end it turned sociable;
there was a breeze in the flags that they noticed
and one felt like running toward some inescapable doom, just
    for the fun of it.

Some were on vacation, a busman's holiday
they called it, and would have it no other way. Gradually my
    hands readjusted
to the stitchery in the tablecloth. If it was going to be *this* way,
    why
not pass the wine around again. Hoist up your stocking
to where the emerald stickpin has pierced it, a joy
for all to see. Say, I suddenly realized I want
to be you along for the ride. Why not? And the breeze
is cool.

You see, in your pharmacopeia of battered notions
just the right things prevail. A man is his house. Two naked
    girls
are in tubetops. Fun to see. A lazy susan spins round again:
What has it brought you this time?
Are there going to be summer suckers?
What'll be the big surprise?

Good news. The universe has been challenged again
by a schoolboy in South Orange. And oh yes,
long division has come out on top.

To see you the way you go this way
is to know the marvelous state of tulips in this our parkway.
What goes around comes around. The medicine dropper
    approached the sky.
This will soon cure *that*.
So wonderful you could see us again.

Floatingly

Kill the white beaches, the hotel, bugs!
The crumbs on a table sang this song to insulate themselves,
but the chickens merely pecked harder. We do, we don't, we
    do, we do mean
to vacuum these crumbs, unless someday an idiot boy
pass through the wood on his way to the ballpark,
tossing his cap unassumingly, for what is, in fact, a gesture?
It is only a gesture. So, sure, morons
can be on your side of the spleen fence: It's only gurus
matter to outsiders, after all, the lame girl said.

She spoke, and I averred:
No one who has known this beach can undo the righteousness
    that begat it
out of sand, close to a fence.
By the same token, one needs two tin cans.

And let the browsers beware, she famously
ad-libbed, for chickens are like jurists in at least one sense:
Neither is wanted when the old line undulates,
shrieking its core across water.

No saffron impediment to evening's fine-sanded
elliptical body,

for the presence of a mote is always singular.
Towheaded ideas learn from and are transformed by them.
We have only too much lettuce, lettuce to give away.
Our fronds shall not know us
nor apocryphal lectures train us to eye the side aisles.

Tenebrae

  For a little snow you get your asking price:
the Ace of Wounds, star of tubs, brushfires
from there to here like an afterthought,

and this suddenly not all that you willed it to be.
We marched in different directions.
Once a week there's a very big field day.

Plant two skyscrapers. Then the moat will be less
unexpected. It's coming round to you again;
indeed, it dances. And in this starting to be something

something disappears, but a shine prevails.
And they don't pay attention,
and they don't pay attention, that's all I can say.

See what the prisoners of war are all about.
How close are you? Rocks seep into the night
and the clay gets the attention it deserves.

We build and build our shadow-pulpit,
then seize morning when it comes,
in chirrupy stride: names of the lost ships,

lasting until today, until nostalgia sets in. We're home
in what passes for a city in America (are the streets

laughing at us?). We can't drive yet,
or even walk.
And one is given the run of the land.

Outside My Window the Japanese . . .

Outside my window the Japanese driving range
shivers in its mesh veils, skinny bride
of soon-to-be-spring, ravenous, rapturous. Why is it here?
A puzzle. And what was it doing before, then? An earlier
puzzle. I like how it wraps itself
in not-quite wind—
                sure enough,
the time is up. What else do you have in your hand?
Open your hand, please. My elder seraph

just woke up, is banging the coffee-pot lid
into place. See! the coffee flows
crazily to its nest, the doldrums are awake,
jumping up and down on tiptoe, night-blindness ended.

And from where *you* stand,
how many possible equations does it spell out?

My hair's just snoring back.
The coprophagic earth yields another of its
minute reasons, turns to a quivering mush,
recovers, staggers to its feet, touches the sky
with its yardstick, walks back to the place of received,
enthusiastic entities. Another year . . . And if we had known
    last spring
what the buildings knew then, what defeat, it would have
    turned to mud
all the same in us, waved us down the escalator,
past the counter with free samples of fudge, to where the
    hostess stands.
This was never my idea, shards, she says. This
is where the anonymous donors carved their initials in my
    book,
to be a puzzle for jaycees to come, as a nesting-ground
is to an island. Oh, we'd waddle
often, there, stepping in and out of the boat
as though nobody knew what time it was, or cared
which lid the horizon was. We'd get to know
each other in time, and till then it was all a camp meeting, hail-
fellow-well-met, and the barstools
reflected the ceiling's gummy polish, to the starboard
where purple kings sit, and it was too late for today,
the newspapers had already been printed, telling their tale
along avenues, husks of driftwood
washed ashore again and again, speechless, spun out of control.
What a gorgeous sunset, cigarette case, how tellingly
the coiled rope is modelled, what perfume
in that sound of thunder, invisible! And you wonder
why I came back? Perhaps *this* will refresh your memory,
skateboard, roller skates, the binomial theorem picked out in

brutish, swabbed gasps. All the way to the escape clause
he kept insisting he'd done nothing wrong, and then—pouf!—
   it was
curtains for him and us, excepting these splinters
of our perpetual remainder, reminder
of all those days to come, and those others, so far back
in the mothering past.

Any Other Time

A couple of shivers of attitude
ago the ship coasted out of sight
to its life in rain.

More morbid mongrels munching
and the news from over there clouds
the hockey pageant's desperate coda,
that shakes with the glitter of edges, of the steep
vocabulary that's coming . . .

All around us fires
are trained at the center, neatest thing
that ever happened. I'll bye-bye you
in blue
if it's the last thing we do.

So we say: Someone had an urge, a whim,
and lightning began there. On all
roads we merely trespass, finding a level,
store-bought thing. Like buying a grapefruit
and having it displayed. Yes and we have teas,
boots for the sore, beds for the weary,
a whole warehouse full of notions,

and this. Makes you kinda comfy.
The less said the more we'll shut up about it—
on the cusp, actually.

Probably Based on a Dream

Like you've done it before—
Are you working hard? Hello? Mrs. Grizzli?
      Only the happy few know what keeps us
from ballooning into our strength. And when we try
    to capture wisps from the rocket,
sinking in the hay, there are those who tell you
    to come again another day,
that the past is soiled and forgotten. Yet neither
    you nor I know what happens in the thud
of cannon threatening to take off with the wild ducks
    thunderously, and you, if I'm not
mistaken, were around here once, once too often
    the landlady tells me. Quick! Where is
your whoop? How unexpectedly have we arrived? In a brusque
  mountain
    workshop where tankas are forged, and the truth comes
unsliced, like bread, the captains and the pageants err and
  repeat;
    for nothing all along was it?
But someday, I know, my idol will slip me a pill
    for as long as bunkers repeat themselves. Alyssa?

Shovel the maps into the diving helmet.
The press cuttings have come to grief;
wind slaps the high buildings.
You too know Kokomo, O unpreceded one.

The Village of Sleep

Why, we must dye it then—

Would I like to stay here indefinitely?
We have trees to prune, cryptograms to decode,
it was all a blind running into the light—
She couldn't say the word for "fish." Nor are his genes undone
by what oafish submarines remain. Aye, sir,

Captain Nemo, sir, we've spotted the junk
in the roads up ahead. What! That spasm I created for my own
    diversion, now
it's clearly emerging out of the octopus drool that so long
    enshrouded it,
while I, a nether spur to its district railway, am overrun with
coughing doubt for the duration, yet here I must stand,
a seeming enigma. Outside, life prattles on merrily,
like an embroidered towel, and would probably be too weak to
    object
if we decided to postpone the picnic until November.
I hear you; the arches under the embankment
are part of what I'm all about. I too was weaned from excess
in some silvery age now lost in a blizzard of envelopes.
How frostily jingle the harness bells!
It's all we can do to keep up with the dunce's velocipede,

while in a neutral corner of the quarry
the same binge of history is conning men's eyes
into dogged superstition. So we must make sport of it,
reel in our catch while yet there's time, but droplets
are exploding in the gutter. The gambling ship ferried us away
past larkspur, past concertinas, and the old name became
    visible again,
briefly, on the building's dusty façade. I

thought we'd lost you. No,
I'm still here.
Do you want to jump out a shy window?
Little by little one took in the foxes' keening:
It's all right, it's sober,
they chortled. This was just a plant,
it counts only for the next time,
and we in beach goggles, brilliant suspenders . . . The party
    beast
in me says let's abandon, cooler heads say dive,
dive like a frog while famous night is coming on
like the blistered exterior of a sigh.

In My Head

I walk out over the moors, the hills, the sand valleys.
My head is listless. The wind is scrubbing the stars.
Yet I don't detonate. There is too much land behind me.

Birds sang it once, then not so much anymore.
I am striving to be late, and to kiss a fish.
It would be a greater one who came back
to the ghost frontier.

She wrote on this.

They all taste pretty much the same,
cut flowers, as I was semen in someone's mouth, an avalanche
    of whorls.
What next for me? Not to be the first one there.

And the wind rattles its scarecrow bones in the living
room, the spring came apart in disorder,
all over the rug. The landsman, he must care,
came too, the others joying his renewal, his removal
as in an old dump truck on the fortieth mile of the road.

Seafaring, the faring, and pickling,
so many admonitions to the Great Lout
who watches over us. He must have approved. In the dimness . . .

The Spacious Firmament

Say that this is a street therefore people walk down it.
I stand holding a bunch of keys,
burn up my motto, read Kleist in November.
Can it be that I cannibalize others' lives,
the lives of others' words?
Or am I simply going back to where I came from,
not too long ago, to excuse whoever took my place
when I was gone? Sudden indecision,

dear reddish flowers—I am about a comma in space.
I neither go nor return unfazed.
In short I am this comedy you wrote for me to star in.

Yes she waits, time out, time in,
for me to get the wail, whale of a wail, off my chest.
Yes the coddling circuits
that baited
the time giveaway
are standing all over me too like foxglove angels,
drawing in their breath, giving us what we bargained for—
no crossing, chumps at the end of the market
where needle soldiers ferreted us out,
wished us well, taking a piss at a private hall about
a mile down the road,
coming in during the week.
They had put their kilts on first.
Pull you out of my wool,
toiling as the will
bends us to ends and now is no more.

That force going under,
it kind of makes it stand out
and for me too the trees in this room
we bide our time in, happy as in a nursery,
till the times dictate otherwise. Oh, he was a grown man,
scrofulous it's true, but neither piebald nor land-proud.
A great equator did him in, the fullness of time
waited at the end of my hall, cobbled quodlibets,
procession toward a context. Capitalist
actions forced it into a runoff.
Model villages provide all sorts of
plumbing. Cherry blossoms cascade
in spring, don't last long.
I think we shall be moving to
the dance baths on the river, river that is ripe,
right for explication, as you do plaster it with the wasps
just coming into being, no names yet.
Twenty years ago my dance professor
reinterpreted it, we'll have it on the ground soon

he said coming back, my hand blotted with crystals, your
    breath calls.
No, something to lug up behind the office at noon.

Proximity

It was great to see you the other day
at the carnival. My enchiladas were delicious,

and I hope that yours were too.
I wanted to fulfill your dream of me

in some suitable way. Giving away my new gloves,
for instance, or putting a box around all that's wrong with us.

But these gutta-percha lamps do not whisper on our behalf.
Now sometimes in the evenings, I am lonely

with dread. A rambunctious wind fills the pine
at my doorstep, the woodbine is enchanted,

and I must be off before the clock strikes
whatever hour it is intent on.

Do not leave me in this wilderness!
Or, if you do, pay me to stay behind.

Going Away Any Time Soon

I'll see you in my dreams she said
then they let the gate down
unplugged the coffee
It was time for my annual cure at Wiesbaden

What good are rules anyway
They apply only to themselves and other rules
This rule rules out this other one

GOING AWAY ANY TIME SOON

The rule of glass, sleek and dark
was poring over my auto-autobiography
like an intensely private person
with hazelnut eyes

When it came time to invent, invest someone or something
you look to the urgent fallen petals
each imbibing its share of life's mystery
as a cat sips and turns away and sips some more

Little mystery are you good for anything?
No she says I came out in time for school
then went back inside to resist sleep
that is still coming as all my absent years are coming

The slower time speaks the less majestic its tower
the fewer bats warbling to interrupt
whatever domestic tasks we believe we have set ourselves
in a truth that is mostly underground

The settled rhythm revives ancient purposes
What did I think going out
and never a tiny random note creeps back in
but all alone a star weeps, watches in the drizzle

and the four magicians fell down.
One took a train to Pennsylvania.

One abstracted his gold hair
picked up a cushion and said

And how is it with you back where you are now?
How many worms to a dozen
How long how many of the others cheat seeing
elbows at this windowsill serious as bunting

on a cloudy day
Which of the antique manners has changed?
For as yet morning is a long way off
Puckered mists trash the hill ecstatic as lozenges

Like America

People are buying store-dolls.
I wonder if that's forbidden too.
Does it mean one isn't to lead one's life?

Today, a day that makes very little sense,
like America,
in clear disarray
everything's getting worse.
Besides, who are we not to endorse it?

And these shattered ornaments to truth
almost grew up to me.
The sun and the yard
paused over a thousand times,
unable to explain the arch that is daylight.

And the tribes that were before
this panicked band announced it was quitting
saw the crocuses too. They were purple and awful.

It's almost leaking to say it.
But how much longer could I go on not missing the point?

New Constructions

Boy I can remember when February
gave out and it was all "no quarter"—the sect of the
levellers passed over and was as night and fire
and more peace. He returned in an hour.
Perpetually flummoxed doorkeepers trying to kill
the men who did the migration proceedings
on the evening news
were backed up all the way to the Arctic Circle.

The aunts were out in zones
of cozy brilliance I

noticed with teapots to their names
like birthing, and they could do Finland then.
It was a kind of parenting. I notice they
doubled our salaries. It was all over
by 6 p.m.

Many causes later he came
in and hurt himself. I
saw a lot of cherry bombs. Is this the place
where one foregathers?
If so, what are all the urchins doing?
Oh she warned it's just to the end of the block
where knee-high tulips pucker and all is reassuring
as they'd rather not have you believe. Does
that clear everything up? Well I think so well I
would like to see the proof of the invitation:
a hand print. I'm so sorry these are inexcusable.
I'll dust myself up, or off;
meanwhile in the clearing they are pouring something.
Do you think you could be kind to come in

and matter where the horse esteems mechanized shortcuts?
Say rather he came in and hurt himself,
and now the bagpipers have nothing left to mourn,
the day just wheezes and goes down a funnel
counterclockwise. It was all just a fit
to have made you start bolt upright
on the steppe terns parted from
with little glovelike cries
awaiting the refrigerator that was to have us all
on its digital menu.
Wait, there are extenuating circumstances
and I myself am just a bum;
whatever came in with the weather
and dematerialized in the corners of the room, just so
am I to myself and others around.
But how do you justify

the crank silhouetted against the sky?
That's just it, I don't; it is all leftovers

and why am I crying
when the boats pass
in the narrow ship channel
with corduroy undies for all the years
I took off from Mrs. Bacon's
and the way they came flooding back at me
like complaints in a gyroscope
or an armillary of vexations.
Then she proposed take this needle
and thread it for the two
messages you have missed.

I'll not start another reptile war;
I look to the end of the komodo dragons thundering
    overhead.
Otherwise I sleep under the eaves; the cabbages
keep me company at evening, and are all
the society anyone wants. And Yes,
I keep up the sewing, the round robin
of Lettergate wherever a spare postal employer
taxes us with unlived puns: *There*
do we stop and pitch camp,
and I'll tell you it's not going to get easier,
only harder.
With that they

took off, just a bundle
of stems to make a totem with.
I sit on the site over and over,
let it absorb hard doing,
piecemeal reconciliations, laundry
marks rubbed out in the wash, seasonal
hares and conviviality and the rest,
the rest.

Whiteout

More and more obviously, the trainer won't handle things
his way, or ours—beats me how cute everything *used* to be.
We stood poised in a circle, and
some note of admiration bloomed and faded.
The cow was coming to ask our forgiveness
for the blue flax. Then everybody segued into a canon,
more ships were lost, more men at sea, the carload of opals
bringing bad luck from Anatolia. And in a wash,
it was gone. No more having to pick up one's room,
one's socks.

Luckily there is an umpire who sees that
behavior is coded, that it all shakes down into the mesh
where the train never minded, that there is still fun out on the
     horizon.
The blues—did we mention that?
And the energy that was coming to unsex all but the lifeless on
     Mars,
the initiated, grasping at handlebars.

A French Stamp

Of handedness and the Brothers Handedness,
too often that tale had been told by Yore,
fifth-century scribe. He liked inking in details.

If one is a cigarette lighter
that's lonely, which is lonely. Or a tricycle
coasting in gales, there is a secret satisfaction

fins emulate. Here, keep my scalp,
I'm seeing a pattern here, divestiture of some knave.
It was likely to be our last onus, this plaid scarecrow
out of a Braille encyclopedia. Hurry with the milk,
be here. Fortune placed tots in escrow. Good to monitor 'em,

go with the feed. In Manhattan merely
two minutes to two, moonlit torso returns. Sheesh.
Some abbey's got him. Let Fido lick
last year's olive branch. I'm outta here.
I told you, no way, it's dorsal.

One Man's Poem

John came into town at night
and the clock was striking.
The damn boat leaked. Well, I . . .
It *was* pretty unusual.

Never mind, hand me that eyesore.
He came to see a tailor.
More about it I do not know
out on the canal.

The twins schlepped raisins and plums,
my dogbeat, for as far as we forgotten
come together to make sense
by midnight's shattered drum.

There was more walking around and talking.
Then all got into a car and drove away.
Its tail was silver red, and a
banjo stood on end in the car.

The waves of freshman and sophomore grief
slide by me somehow.
We are old and dated
and cannot of our lives make any sense.

It was in the way he put it to me,
muddied or on a rock
at the center of a field puts us to shame.
There is more than the spirit jabs,

under the little hollow birds creep
   and are asked forgiveness. Some are afraid
   that they will fly away.
   By morning all is shot to hell.

The Pathetic Fallacy

A cautionary mister,
the thaumaturge poked holes in my trope.
I said what are you doing that for.
His theorem wasn't too complicated,

just complicated enough. In brief,
this was it. The governor should peel
no more shadow apples, and about teatime
it was as if the lemon of Descartes
had risen to full prominence on the opulent skyline.

There were children in drawers, and others trying to shovel
    them out.
In a word, shopping had never been so tenuous,

but it seems *we* had let the cat out of the bag, in spurts.
Often, from that balcony
I'd interrogate the jutting profile of night
for what few psalms or coins it might
in other circumstances have been tempted to shower down
on the feeble heathen oppressor, and my wife.

Always you get the same bedizened answer back.
It was like something else, or it wasn't,
and if it wasn't going to be as much, why,
it might as well be less, for all anyone'd care.
And the ditches brought it home dramatically
to the horizon, socked the airport in.

We, we are only mad clouds,
a dauphin's reach from civilization,

with its perfumed citadels, its quotas. What did that
mean you were going to do to *me*?
Why, in another land and time we'd be situated, separate
from each other and the ooze of life. But here, within
the palisade of brambles it only comes often enough to what
can be sloughed off quickly, with the least amount of fuss.
For the ebony cage claims its constituents

as all were going away, thankful the affair had ended.

From Old Notebooks

As rain cobbles itself
    together, puts an expectant face
on things, we lived those
greasy times. Sordid
with excess rapture, blue
as a cow's face. We came out of it pretty well
    at the end.

Worth looking up, these tepid old
    things

could still jiggle
a thug's arms, thrum the upholstery's
lilacs. Warehouses make like
marauding castles in the heat, I am always steep
when being remembered.
                  Ash on a coed's face,
this barren step planted in Thieves' Row, more where
your mother muddled all things. And if it be not,
where is its funnel—pass the luster,
please, something's abiding: love-in-a-storm,
it says.

Many Colors

There is a chastening to it,
a hymnlike hemline.
Hyperbole in another disguise.

Dainty foresters walk through it.

On the splashed polyester walls
a tooth fairy held court. And that was like mud gravy,
a sop to the reigning *idées reçues*.
It's all too—
charming.
It makes you want to scream
and hug your neighbor like he was your best friend.

I'm over my head with it.
Suddenly there was a travelling salesman with balls,
like an ant on V-J day.

And easing through the night we felt scoops
of clay like tired ice cream.
Here, here's your vigil. Now get it out of here. One of us—
Gus the plumber—is entranced.

Of course you could let them come to you
as if you'd asked, and don't blame it on me
when they get silted up to the snow line.
A master craftsman is coming to stay with you, to save you.

Yes and my horse knew all about this
but wasn't letting on
until the time you and I got over the fix on his importance he
    had,
only to discover another's hip-huggers in the brown dust
under the mailbox.

And we all came quietly.

In what axis I've heard you ringing—
there is no time to do that.
This is no time to do that.
The passion police are on your case
and we'll get back to picking winners anon, at eventide,
asunder.

Go blow. Tremble. Decipher. Mix and match.
Maybe. We'll see.

Autumn in the Long Avenue

I see and hear the wind.
It is unreceived. Clouds flee backwards.
I think myself into a stupor.

Once upon a time everybody was here.
Then the pellets started to go.
They move and move little,
like my brother or childhood,
or a little schoolhouse
near the zoo, boarded up with directions
to some other telltale structure, crusted
with scaffolding like frosting on winter's cake,
to tell you, go through, go through now,
die and formally die.

Yet autumn stays sequestered
and likes it. In that period
some people still came to visit, with nothing
on their minds, no reason, not even liking you.
A lot of autos stormed the site
of the one pine's expiration, breathing, asking
for you. Some said you had gone,
but you were hiding under the porch, stung
with remorse. Now this person
comes and says have you seen the shed,
it gives me goose bumps, and I, stuck as always on

which word should be the first, but comes out
in no particular order, volunteer my notes on the
time we sat with woodpeckers on the
various counterpane and had a swig—
when you were, I mean, on the fence,
just inside, talking the way people in dreams
talk to those who are awake, subverting the last
ditch of defense in time for what
takes it away . . .

The light of late afternoon
chiseled the sea and barracks, but who
was keeping count? There were more tourists
than usual that day, the town seemed to run away from them
as we approached them, wondering what was wrong, what was
    the matter
with the bland corpses they had come to see name
something we ourselves couldn't see for being in it
as mute pedestrians moved to adjourn it.
I've seen it before, I've seen it in the street:
These various resolutions fade in and out,
plaiting a track on the texture of day,
a legacy of distant effort, wispy
and traditional, like dads and moms coming off
the assembly line. But they never get that right.
I just said goodbye.

Snow

As a fish spoils
in a time of truce, so these galoshes go
hopping over sidewalk and snowbank, not really knowing
to whose destiny we are being summoned
or what happens after that.

As time spoils,
it may have known what it was doing
but decided not to do anything about it, so everything is lost,

wrapped in a landfill. It could be caviar
or the New York *Daily News*.

After all, *I* come next,
he said, am a cruel object like all the torsos
you unbuttoned all over your previous life, scant in comparison
to this one, and I said, go ahead and quit clowning
if you like that game, but

leave me beside myself,
like a kid next to a lamppost. Okay, what gain
in not replying? What capitalist system do you think this is?
    Surely
it's late capitalism, by which I mean not to go
yet and peace undermines

the uproar we all made
about it, and you are positively put on hold
again. I like the mouse in this turmoil, not exactly purring
adroitly, not seeming to conjugate the
avalanche of fear.

Now when Norsemen
(or some substitute) tumble out of the north, sifting
down over our busy, shuttered, dignified street with hints of
    the Azores,
there's no untangling the knots we put there before
and paused to identify

as the four winds rushed
in and purified the place of partnerships,
fanning overhead, a-bristle with doodads, chafing at every
    chime
from every earnest steeple, coughing too much.
The little guy was

impatient, was serious,
every time a blow fell adjured another conspirator,
and so, when it got quite dark we became an outing, another

quilting-bee disaster. And if it tried too far
there was always salt to rub

in wounds to be licked.

Within the Hour

The tea is too hot.
The curtain in the window blew around.
Rind rotting on brown chairs.
In the valley of bartenders the one-eyed stooge is king.

What I'm doing now is write.
That's the real stuff.
It doesn't work!
I got a card from him yesterday I could ask Dick.

What is the fresh approach?
Your mini body coming unto me, unshelled
as peace pavanes no one undertakes,
not without a woofing in the chest-o-ciser,

two strokes and it's gone.
You owed the fresh kind.
Why yes. Remember
me? Remember me
in any case.

The Dong with the Luminous Nose
(a cento)

Within a windowed niche of that high hall
I wake and feel the fell of dark, not day.
I shall rush out as I am, and walk the street
Hard by yon wood, now smiling as in scorn.
The lights begin to twinkle from the rocks

From camp to camp, through the foul womb of night.
Come, Shepherd, and again renew the quest.
And birds sit brooding in the snow.

Continuous as the stars that shine,
When all men were asleep the snow came flying
Near where the dirty Thames does flow
Through caverns measureless to man,
Where thou shalt see the red-gilled fishes leap
And a lovely Monkey with lollipop paws
Where the remote Bermudas ride.

Softly, in the dusk, a woman is singing to me:
This is the cock that crowed in the morn.
Who'll be the parson?
Beppo! That beard of yours becomes you not!
A gentle answer did the old Man make:
Farewell, ungrateful traitor,
Bright as a seedsman's packet
Where the quiet-coloured end of evening smiles.

Obscurest night involved the sky
And brickdust Moll had screamed through half a street:
"Look in my face; my name is Might-have-been,
Sylvan historian, who canst thus express
Every night and alle,
The happy highways where I went
To the hills of Chankly Bore!"

Where are you going to, my pretty maid?
These lovers fled away into the storm
And it's O dear, what can the matter be?
For the wind is in the palm-trees, and the temple bells they say:
Lay your sleeping head, my love,
On the wide level of a mountain's head,
Thoughtless as monarch oaks, that shade the plain,
In autumn, on the skirts of Bagley Wood.
A ship is floating in the harbour now,
Heavy as frost, and deep almost as life!

Come On, Dear

It was another era, almost another century,
I was going to say. The saint wept quietly
in her ebony pew. It was the thing to do.
Then garlands of laughter, studded with cloves and lemons,
joined the standing figures with their distant nimbi.
Inexplicably, all was well for a time.

Soon, discordant echoes reined in the heyday:
It was love, after all,
that everybody was talking about
and nobody gave a shit for.
But why am I telling *you* about all this, who wrote the book,
who stamped his initials in the fairway
for all blokes to see? And if it only came
down to this smidgen, would apes and penguins be any wiser
for all the tunnels of love we shuffled through,
scared by skeletons, by bats, at every turning
of our loose-leafed trajectory through shallow water?

Only when the iodine sunset
bleeds again against red day, will all children
get permission to go out where the grass is short,
where the absent-minded postman leaves earnests of his passing
from this day to the next, where the eaves are clipped
close to the houses. Five days from the last clerestory
your ambiance drained into the pockmarked shutters.
Obviously the jig was up. What's that? Whose jig? O I can see
    clear
ahead into the flying; the poor don't talk much about it,
but her apron is ambrosial with trellised stars,
her stance stares down even the most unquiet,
and on days like this you ride free.
There was such numismatics in his pocket
as only jitterbugs in cyberspace could conjugate
while from fate's awning the diamond drip descended, bigger
than both of us, big as all outdoors.

Gentle Reader

Abruptly, unassertively, the year starts,
as freeways close and roofs collapse,
and all kinds of incidents give nervure to the map:
a stitch in time, a local hero here,
boys falling in tune with the ageless argument.

So out of the turquoise turmoil a name
implodes like a star, having made its point.
And the seasons, welcome as you know,
are seen packing it in. Maybe add some rust
at a crucial jointure, no? But who am I
to be telling you your business. Next, young and beautiful,
emerging from a door, casting your essence
along the face of today's precipice, you see "there's no
    tomorrow,"
only avatars waiting in the wings, more or less patiently.
This is what it takes for you to do what's best,
covering all the exits.

Oh, there is a danger there?
Who would have thought it in today's heat?
But on the other hand, why just be standing
while its morose page rolls over,
an encumbrance to all, not just ourselves?
And when twilight licks appreciatively at the sky,
your answer will be there in the circuitry,
not bypassed. For you to hold,
to genuflect with.

A shadow of a flagon crossed your face:
The cease-fire is improving?
And in this starting to be in something, what had the older
children been doing? Taking lessons still to be paid for,
impinging on what comes next. Comes now.

Soon there is something to be said for everything,
he said, whiplash, whippets; why even my identity
is strange to me now, a curiosity. When someone comes later,

who will I be talking with? The erroneous vision
made no mention of this. Its conquering agenda is complete,
and we, of course, are incomplete, destined to ourselves
and its fitful version of eternity:
the one with chapter titles.
More worldliness to celebrate. And yet, someone
will take it from you, needy thing.

Homecoming

Weather drips quietly through the skeins
in my diary. What surly elision is this?

Who faxed the folks news of my homecoming,
even unto the platform number? The majestic parlor car
slides neatly into its berth, the doors fly open,
and it's Jean and Marcy and all the kids, waving pink plastic
    pinwheels,
chomping on popcorn. Ngarrrh. You know I adore ceremony,
even while refusing to stand on it, but this, this is too inane.
And the cold anonymity of the station takes over,
reins in the crowds that were sifting to the furthest exits. No
    one is here.
Now I know why I've always hated the tango, yet loved the
    intimacy
secreted in its curls. And for this to continue, we've got to
get together, renew old saws, let old grudges ride . . .

Later I'm posting this to you.
I just thought of you, you see, as indeed I do
several million times a day. I need your disapproval,
can't live without your churlish ways.

GIRLS ON THE RUN

To Eugene, Rosanne, and Joseph

Girls on the Run
after Henry Darger

I

A great plane flew across the sun,
and the girls ran along the ground.
The sun shone on Mr. McPlaster's face, it was green like an
  elephant's.

Let's get out of here, Judy said.
They're getting closer, I can't stand it.
But you know, our fashions are in fashion
only briefly, then they go out
and stay that way for a long time. Then they come back in
for a while. Then, in maybe a million years, they go out of
  fashion
and stay there.
Laure and Tidbit agreed,
with the proviso that after that everyone would become fashion
again for a few hours. Write it now, Tidbit said,
before they get back. And, quivering, I took the pen.

Drink the beautiful tea
before you slop sewage over the horizon, the Principal
  directed.
OK, it's calm now, but it wasn't two minutes ago. What do you
  want me to do, said Henry,
I am no longer your serf,
and if I was I wouldn't do your bidding. That is enough, sir.
You think you can lord it over every last dish of oatmeal
on this planet, Henry said. But wait till my ambition
comes a cropper, whatever that means, or bursts into feathered
  bloom
and burns on the shore. Then the kiddies dancing sidewise
declared it a treat, and the ice-cream gnomes slurped their last
  that day.

Inside, in the twilit nest of evening,
something was coming undone. Dimples could feel it,
surging over her shoulder like a wave of energy. And then—
it was gone. No one had witnessed it but herself.
And so Dimples took off for the city, which was near and
    wholesome.
There, with her sister Larissa, she planned the big blue boat
that future generations will live in, and thank us for. It twitched
at its steely moorings, and seemed to say: Live, like life, with
    me.

Let the birds wash over them, Laure said, for what use are
    earmuffs
in a snowstorm, except to call attention to distant tots
who have strayed. And now the big Mother warms them,
accepts them, for the nervous predicates they are. Far from the
    beach-fiend's
howling, their adventure nurses itself back
to something like health. On the fifth day it takes a little
    blancmange
and stands up, only to fall back into a hammock.
I told you it was coming, cried Dimples, but look out,
Another big one is on the way!
And they all ran, and got out, and that was that for that day.

II

Hungeringly, Tidbit approached the crone who held the bowl,
. . . drank the honey. It had good things about it.
Now, pretty as a moment,
Tidbit's housecoat sniffed the undecipherable,
the knowable past. They were anxious
to get back to work. Diane was looking relaxed.
Then, some say, Pete said
it was the afternoon backing up again, inexorable
with dreams, looking for garbage to pick a fight with.
"My goodness! Do you suppose his blowhole's . . . ?"

Sometime later they returned with Pete and the others,
he all excited, certain he had spotted a fuse this time.

Rags the mutt licked and yelped. "Oh, get down!"
But Rags seemed to be on to something. "And if they come
through the alfalfa this time, we'll have a nice idea
of where they are, of who these men are. If they abrade
the abandoned silo, no one will be wiser. Look, their pastel
tent, and flags made from the same substance, waving *dehors*—
I've got to get an angle on this, a firm tack of some kind."
Willingly, the flood washed over the day
and so much that was complicated, from the past:
the tiny doggy door Rags had made with a T-square,
surplus sequins.
     And if they don't want to play
according to our rules, what then? "Why, then
we'll come up with something, like the sink-drain.
Anyway, this is all just an excuse for you to leave your posts,
toying with anagrams, while the real message
is being written in the stars. To go ahead,
it says, but be watchful for scouts
in the corn shocks. This close to Halloween there are lots of
 little bumps
around, and tea cosies to shroud them. Beware one last time;
but as the spirit of going is to go, I can't
control you, advise you much longer. Just keep on
persevering, and then we'll know what we have done matters
 most to us."
     With that, the sticks uprooted the tent.
A thousand passions came unleashed,
but fortunately for the girls, none of them were around to
 witness it—
they were off in a cage with the canaries.
       Now, though,
when it came time to vote for who the deed was done
by, the others mattered too. It was just their pot luck.

Oh well, Laure offered, we were going to close down that
 shaftway
anyway, and the subway came close: It was Mother and her
 veering
playthings again, torn between the impossible alternatives of
 existing

and saying no to menace. To everyone's surprise the bus
    stopped.
Our stalwart little band of angels got on it, and were taken for
    a ride
into the next chapter, a dim place of curlicues and bas-reliefs.
If I had a handle, Laure thought.

III

Out in Michigan, or was it Minnesota, though, time had
    stopped
to see what it could see, which wasn't much. A recent hooligan
    scare had blighted the landscape,
lowering the temperature by several degrees. "Having
to pee ruins my crinoline relentlessly,
because it comes only ecstatically."
But the wounded cow knew otherwise.
                                        She was at least sixty,
had many skins covering her own, regal one. So then they all
    cry,
at sea. The lawnmower is emitting sparks again,
one doesn't know how many, or how much faster it will have
    to go
to meet us at the Denizens' by six o'clock. We'd have been
    better
off letting the prisoners stage their own war. Now I don't know
so much, and with Aunt Jennie at my side we could release
a few more bombs and not know it.
                                    Everywhere in the tangled
    schist
someone was living, it seemed to say, this is my doing;
whoever shall come afterward is a delusion. And I went round
the corner to say, Well it sure looks like an improvement—hey,
why don't you tie your shoes, and then your bonnet will be
    picture-perfect?

No, only getting away
has any value to her: A stone's throw is better than a mile
since one will have to be up again much later, and this way
saves time. How often did you let your mother say,

How did you get your Sundays packed away? And yet it's
   always treasonable
to be in the middle. H'm, there are objections to that,
just as I thought. This might help. Yes. But the color
of this paint is too fabulous, I'd asked for something
   fragmented
like sea-spray. In that case we cannot be of service to you.
   Farewell.

Now I had walked the terrible byways for what seemed like too
   long.
Now another was following, insensately.
Would there be foodstuffs on the steps? How did that ladder
   point into nowhere?
"Shuffle, you miser!" Just so, Shuffle said,
I don't want to be around when the gang erupts
into centuries of inviolate privilege, and cisterns tumble down
the side of the slope, and all is gone more or less naturally to
   hell.
To which Dimples replied, Why not? Why not just give
   yourself, one time,
to the floods of human resources that are our day?
Because I don't want to live at an angle to the blokes who
   micromanage
our territory, that's all. Oh, who do you mean? Why, the red-
   trimmed zebras,
Shuffle said, that people thinks is the cutest damn things in
   town
until the victory bonfire on the square, and then there's more
   racing
and chasing than you can shake a banjo-string at,
and it'll have muddled you over by the time the war has crested.

He sat, eating a cheese sandwich, wondering if it would be his
   last,
fiddled and sank away.
                          And as far as the wires
could stretch, into the inevitable jerk-kingdom, the little girl
crawled on her hands and feet. That was no jack-in-the-box
back there, that was the real thing.

Yes, Stuart Hofnagel, they came to you, they'd expected big
   things
of you back in Arkadelphia, and now you were a soured loner
   like anybody.
Old town, you seem to remember otherwise.
That was you backing into love, wasn't it? So we all came and
   were glad that day.
That was all a fine day for us. Happiness, that we loved you so
   much;
phony energy, because we were happy.
Yet the town held back, rinsing her skirts
in the dour brook that fled the sawmill, just before four
   o'clock.
None of us slaves knew any different, having been nursed into
   solitude the night before last.
Certainly, if someone knocks on the open door
we will be pleasant, and look after the stranger just as if he
   were one of our own.
That's the way we were made. We can't help it. Conversely,
if a friend obtrudes his thinking into this plan of ours,
we shall deny all knowledge of him. It happens this way in the
   wilderness.
Plus the pot is full of old oddments. The rhubarb stains on
   Peggy's frock
almost—but not quite—match its rickrack trim.
That's where the human aspect comes in.
Some were born to play with, to think constantly about it, with
   a nod,
not much more, to the future and what its executives might
   have in store.
We aren't easily intimidated.
And yet we are always frightened,
frightened that this will come to pass
and we all unable to do anything about it, in case it ever does.
So we appeal to you, sun, on this broad day.
You were ever a helpmate in times of great churning, and
   fatigue.
You make us forget how serious we are
and we dance in the lightning of your rhythm like demented
   souls

on a hospital spree. If only,
when the horse crawls up your back, you had known to make
    more of it.
But the climate is military, and yet one can't see too far ahead.
Better a storehouse of pearls than this battered shoehorn
of wood, yet it can cause everything to take place and change
    for you.

IV

Dearest, we had waited for this star,
the marriage couldn't take place without it. A louse
drags its lonely way up to the end of a porcupine quill, expires,
and can we have heard anything? I mean the paced breathing
    just outdoors,
and then inside, it's just squalid and quiet,
nothing more. I have a bowl of cherry syrup.

These halls, when the rush of spring is echoing, far ahead,
collapse into tendrils, their décor foreseen
since the dawn of history. One can walk across them, and time
    suddenly
seems funny, stops, is dead, or mute. And prisoners come
    begging
for a primrose, or a shaft of sunlight, and the all-seeing sees
    them
and averts his gaze until tomorrow. Thus, our doom, ringing
    with half-realized
fantasies, is a promise of a new beginning on another
    continent.
Only, we must get out of here. A man stands by a cactus,
    counting
the flecks of rage as they pass by, and you are in another suit,
abashed, a dapper salesman today. And the volley of the
    shooting gallery
vies with the welter of jarred complacencies, multiple over
    time,
if time wishes: "*Lacrimoso*, our sport is behind us!
Lacrimoso, we can't get anything done!
Lacrimoso, the bear has gone after the honey!

Lacrimoso, the honey drips incessantly
from the bough of a tree."

Worse, it was traditional to feel this way.

V

Just as a good pianist will adjust the piano stool
before his recital, by turning the knobs on either side of it
until he feels he is at a proper distance from the keyboard,
so did our friends plan their day. Sometimes, after a leisurely
    breakfast,
they would get to work immediately, cutting, gluing, stitching
as the model came entrancingly into view. Other days it was
    more of a pain,
or more elaborate. Persnickety Peggy was frequently at the
    heart of things,
her strength often an inspiration to the others, though offset
    by her tendency to brawl
and generally make a nuisance of herself. The other girls took
    this in stride,
though. Little by little the house was rising
where only sky had hung before, and it seemed like good news,
a good berth. That was before Tommy took over
and ruined everything. But I am getting ahead of my story.

Sometimes to wake up in the morning was enough. They
    began feeling better.
Lecture plans were discussed, and a gleaming white envelope,
    shocking in its purity
as the dawn, would be sealed by two or three of them. There,
that's better, no one would say, and that's how they got down
    to business.
On rainy days they would stay indoors
watching the chase of drops on the pane, realizing, a little
    half-frugally,
how it would be impossible to ever go outside. Moss drips on
    moss;
the more interesting-smelling exhibits have been packed away.

Or was there a terminus, sadly, deep underground? This, only
 children can know,
and some adults who have turned the steep corner into
 childhood.
Plums are ripening,
the pitcher of sangria darkens and deepens. So it was ever this
 way,
until it was past time to become "normal" again. Tell it to the
 neutered pets
that day! Already the verandas are awash with trouble, and
 color, the darts seldom miss their mark.
Heidi and Peter dissolve in the crystal furnace;
something says it's too late to change, now better to let it come
 toward
us, then we will see what it is made of.
To have had a son back there . . .
But the unthinkable is common knowledge now. We must let
 down a ladder
so the others may attach their boats to it, and in that way we
 shall be saved.
Only I think we're . . . It's all coming nearer.

VI

Nov. 7. Returned again to the exhibition. How strange it is that
 when we
least imagine we are enjoying themselves, a shaft of reason will
 bedazzle
us. Then it's up to us, or at any rate them, to think ourselves
 out of the
muddle and in so doing turn up whole again on the shore,
 impeached by a
sigh, so that the whole balcony of spectators goes whizzing
 past, out of
control, on a collision course with destiny and the bridesmaids'
 sobbing.
Of course, we listened, then whistled, and nobody answered, at
 least it
seemed nobody did. The silence was so intense there might
 have been a

sound moving around in it, but we knew nothing of that. Then we came
to. The pictures are so nice on the walls, it seems one might destroy
something by even looking at them; the tendency is to ignore by walking
around the partition into a small, cramped space that is flooded with
daylight. And what if we asked for another spoonful? Look, it's down
there, down at the bottom of the well, and we are no wiser for it, if
anybody asked. Which they don't. By common consent,
including ours, we are ignored and given the cold shoulder to. OK, so it's
all until another day, and we can see quite clearly into the needle whose thread is
waving slowly back and forth like a caterpillar, accomplishing its end.
So may it be until the end that is eternity.

VII

The thread ended up on the floor,
where threads go.
It became a permanent thing, like silver—
every time you polish it, a little goes away.
Then the ducks arrived, it was raining.
Such a lot of going around and doing!
Sometimes they were in sordid sexual situations;
at others, a smidgen of fun would intrude on our day
which exists to be intruded on, anyway.
Its value, to us, is incommensurate
with, let's say, the concept of duration, which kills,
surely as a serpent hiding behind a stump.
Our phrase books began to feel useless—for once
you have learned a language, what is there to do but forget it?
An illustration changes us.

These were cloistered. They stayed
with us that winter, then went on awhile.

Soon they were back. It was partially time to go out in the
    opening.
Some enjoyed it.
Then, if they were true,
the blue rabbit heaped bones upon them. There was no going
    back,
now, though, some did go back. Those who did
didn't get very far. The others came out a little ahead,
I think . . . I'm not sure.

Look, this is what I am, what I'm made of.
Am I then to usurp the rose
that blows on time's pediment, wrapping all wisps in a kind of
    bundle
of awe? But the sundial smiled in the rain, the stile
beckoned, the sign said it was three miles. In the lane the
    parson's
ambulance pestered gold pigtails, who were in for a shock
when the fox returned smiling, fanning his great tail in the
    comet
of the lighthouses the sausages were so concerned about.
Did the game of stealing please any? Here, on the other side,
    they were in sync,
their bowls of muesli crooning to the sidelong bats of evening,
    and then they were let out
to smoke a cigarette in the meadow. No one knew how many
tried to escape, or how many were successful. You had to read
    it
in the evening's news, and by then sea-cows were weary.
They taxed themselves out of existence. Our raft capsized
and they opined the day was bright with promise, though shut
    off
from what really happened. It was time for golf.

This was that day's learning.

Finally when Angela could retrieve her moorings they sent the
    tide out,
but it came back next day, increasingly bizarre.

Bunny and Philip weren't sure they wanted to see more. "But
you must,"
Angela urged, breathing a little faster. Then they all wanted to
know why it goes on
all the time, and the preacher answered it was due to bats. In
the silos. Oh,
I thought you wanted to know, Philip said. We do, but other
than you there are two
pails formally, and no one can figure out what is inside. Indeed?
Well I'll
take the plunge, Philip volunteered. He was always a brave
little kid.
Now it was this side of sunset again. Nobody knew which was
in error: the stove, or its corset.
After which the elm buds chanced a summer intrusion
and all the nifty year was almost gone. Well isn't that a
catastrophe, Aunt Clara gurgled,
or are some of you please going to take it outside? Aw, but it's
raining, someone grumbled,
why can't we stay inside and have school?
Yes but the quitter must go far out into the bogs. It's time for
the badgers to nest
and who is that coming over the hill this time? It's
Spider, Angela suggested.

But as for leaving you all without a tale to tell, I would be daft,
nay derelict, not to insist on where the others have gone. Isn't
there a place
to stop, that we'll all know about when we come to it?
Yes there is, she said, we'll just all have to back down
into the gloom, and bait our hooks with peanut butter.
Which is what they did
and so they left home that day.

VIII

"All aboard! If there's one thing I hate it's a loner,"
Uncle Philip said, or someone who's beside himself. Please,
Uncle,

can't we go out today? Aw, shut up, Philip said. Now there
 were two bald uncles
who lived in the nearby swamp. One of them knew Shuffle.
 And he said:
If it's to play in, why not. But if it's just to play over and
 around
then I don't see why you need to, and indeed shall expend
 every effort
to see that you don't. But if the mirror
refract any of this, then boy you can be sure you can go.
And in a little while the mirror reflected all of them
back at each other. This was exceptional. Those getting up to
 leave were stayed
in their rubber boots, and those arriving were perplexed and
 pleasured. Why, isn't
it a rebus, Aunt Clara wondered, and Tootles agreed that it
 was.
From a distant patch of loam the speck started arriving, bigger
with each hulking gasp. Why doesn't the foreman go, someone
 wondered, it's
part of his job description, and the others can go anyway, if
 they want to. So all
got to be sensitized. And in the large gap for brooding that
 was created
some of the saner heads got wind of the passing football
and were mortified into a decision. Sun shovel it in,
there's no more room for today, and you can go. I said you can
 go.
Oh, the man said, not understanding, and a third time they
 shouted at him:
You can go.
And he betook himself on his two legs.

Under frozen mounds of yak butter the graffiti have their day,
 and are elaborate,
some say. Nobody wants to go there. Yes, she said, we will
 swim
there if necessary. The arroz con pollo can take us
and do with us what we will. Just as I thought I had found a
 solution

to this and other present error, the knitting needles collapsed.
Never bathe or shave on a cloudy day, Uncle Margaret
    cautioned. The twins were in limbo
over this but we steered the car carefully, permanently
toward them and they too were saved. Hey,
we put it all aside for a rainy day, and this is one, and this is just
    superior,
Dave asserted. And all we've got to do is roll over
and the dream will be over. Not so fast, Aunt Clara indicated,
    the gum
trees are a-rattle. The stealth of the horizon
nears us. That cat is asleep. And who shall take the dinner pail
    out
to the sodden farmhands, and just leave? Be it us,
that will be all OK. And in two strokes it was done. And they
    came and cancelled
the signature, so that everything was as it had been before. The
    militia capsized
and died from eating a certain kind of mold. Now the sentry
    wanes,
sinks and dies of its own weight. All the marbles have rolled
    inside the house.

IX

And now everyone must sleep.
The kiddies are silent for a while.

and yes, singly or in pairs,
they come down to the water's edge, to drink their fill. The
    wide-eyed pansies gaze
immutably. Rev up the old flivver, we'll be disparate for a time
and then we'll see, the mice will see. Why all the fuss?
You know you came here just for this, this kiss, on the face, the
    dog said.
Where are you starting to go? Are my pants too wide?
What if someone else on the other side of the globe
told you this, would he fall off? Would I?
That's why they say stand clear.
You can never do yourself favors enough, in the rosebush

from which man never extricates himself. I see,
someone said. Does it matter about being alone? No it's
    important
but not that important. I see, this person said. But then what if
    I am
no longer alone? What then? Two of you can board as long as
    one stays on the lookout,
the relaxed policeman said. He brought a sandwich down the
    street
and placed it on the curb, he was so nice. We didn't expect the
    birches
to explode just then. The sound traveled over the neighboring
    hills
down to the makeshift waterfront, lugubrious in the darkening
    air.
It's the cold
again he said. Every time I forget something, whenever
    anything is in motion
again, this happens, and I am not prepared for it. I'm plum
    scared.
Then you should go out,
your dress will be as morning to the cows,
she said. And he did and it was.

By and by Allen told us of a scheme
to rescue Pliable, if the latter consented, which surely he
    would,
and it would all seem as if it had never been.
But it would have, we'd know that, and ever after, as adults,
wandering the velveteen streets, we'd come upon someone
    who would have known someone
who wasn't all there and we'd be back at square one in the love
    market
and oceans of tremors would have been discovered. A word
would issue from a crack in the pavement, and it was up to
    Jane and the detective to decide
whether they'd heard it. If they hadn't, fine.
Otherwise it's down to the station
to sort everything out in the middle of the night, and not
    taken to too kindly

either. Drunks passed back and forth. Jane
was titillated but squeamish. She thought of asking Cupid
if the seams of her stockings were straight, but Pliable
    intervened strenuously,
arguing that no two people can take love into their own hands.
    Oh. Excuse me. Bye bye. I'm
outta here. No, said Jane, you don't
understand, he means to be nice. He's a sheep, really. Yes but I
    don't see
how that affects me, and anyway I'm not interested. Oh, please,
    you must be,

she agitated, just for a little while as we perch
on this twig that must be the end of the world for us. Jolly
    good,
Pliable thought, it's me or you, now or never and here
    comes—

I awoke from the dream. A big boom
was passing over my head. I could see clear up the mizzen, if
    that counts,
any more, your honor, I just want to say I respects
all what is good, and don't come here any more, I won't. That
    is good.
We'll take off and be back pronto. Don't
answer the telephone until dawn. Supposing they come and
want to ask you and we are gone, or in the middle of
    something? That's OK but don't
be gone too long. We'll come too.

I'm no expert but I see a problem here.
The fisheries have come undone, as the headlong race to the
    pole
has made alarmingly evident. As I say, I can speak only for
    myself,
but as soon as I got here the rules became different.
They didn't apply to me any more, or to anyone else except a
    distant runt,
almost invisible in its litter. So how was

I to know who to stand up to, when to turn abrasive, when all
    things nestled,
equidistant, all hearts were charming, and it was good to be
    natural and sincere?
True, we had much to worry about,
other things to think about, but when has mankind had the
    leisure
to distract himself from these and other unassailable syllogisms?
So the truth just washed up on the shore,
a bundle of nerves, not resembling much of anything
we cared to remember. Was polite, stoical,
and anything else to deflect attention from its seething
    ambiguity.
It was time to come back, back into the flower-bedecked
    house.
A stunning moment of certainty survived
briefly, then it too was washed away in the rising flood,
tortured, unambitious.
School was over,
not just for that day but forever and for seasons to come.
The reason was that the truth was just average
on the iniquity scale, and nobody wanted to get involved.

x

Often a strange desire:
we hear you
you hear me
we can hear you
you make my period rounder.
You are the center of the universe
a tuber time invents.
We were all passing the fumes
of the car,
green sky explains
more tomorrow
under whatever sun they send up
to be worshipped,
imbibed,
glee from head to toe.

It will not do
and it's true I do
we had to have summer.
We were too baked.
Some of us got up to go,
the others stayed behind
in what position one wants to know.
Larry Sue said bye bye.
The sets of vigorous twins left by the walkway.
This is a nice place we're in.
Then it all comes to nothing walking
have you a care where we're walking.

Often a strange desire
mingles cats and near-greatness
that you all left startled standing. There are no more heaters
    understandably.
A pipe is needed, pleasant moments.
Heaven knows the place of our desires—
it is here somewhere, over there
or under this.
We must add up as many to the total
as is possible. To the passing fine day
were added the rudiments of music.
I too a cruel one I gave some
of my substance to the wind
and then it returned it I came ashore.
I am overly satisfied with the present-day facility.
Are you Pam's nursery arrangement.
No four of them insisted count the dogs. Count the dogs!
Count the dogs as furniture
as otherwise there will be no chairs.
No warrant out for his arrest I see no
other way I came down the stairs in darkness
to what is here.
In darkness we live sensibly perhaps satisfied with too much.
But when daylight wanes we take aim
at a larger quadrant. There are people in the store.
There is a sale of fine foods and beaded hair products.
So notice this gun lest you withdraw altogether from chiming.

He was infinitely dark and creepy
but at a point leaving for the sun state it is hard not to get off
not to leave this train that takes us with it as long as we want it
    to go.
I was looking at a book he created, glued and spliced.
Next the decorations are kablooey, old potted bricks.
He took a couple of puffs.
Plastic star removal continues.
Our reporter took an immigration ride, the dented land
    seemed there. By all
accounts something was "obtuse."
We must have spent half on vegetables the fertilizer crop was
    good.
Old Mr. Jenkins liked to play around with himself in that way.
The place has to
be there I had to recognize it.
Do you like clams Emily no not raw steamed.
Those look softer. I still like 'em.
Instead of letting it be area in all those big air bubbles—
rubber.
They were so . . . impatient.

After I jiggled it back and forth the finish started coming off in
    my hand.
Oh it's a song something to sing.
In my head we sang under
the vanilla tree
where breasts are stacked loosely.
Why should American tourists interrogate the town hall.
The justices file in file their brief their file
soon it is time to go to bed for dinner.
The obelisk hobbled over. "Do you know which way
to the basilica?" he marveled.
Such tall spruces and so many of them!
I had foreseen everything but this
in this place of spruces whether they be right
or not they have a right to be here
I guess or I try not to think it.
It is a nursery ditty grave or gay.
It seems to say

how much longer will my spruces be on tap?
How many more years of availability?
Wisely the spruces contented themselves with rustling.
It was just like a kitchen with the blue gas burning
in a special flame for all to see.
So all grew. The tainted fir-trees
fell over and were loam. All were.
We can see enough on this side to convince us of the merit of
    that other.
But if a tank wishes to convince us we cannot contradict that.
So all grew, more and more, into the bower of empowerment,
and all were pursued by what happened this time
so as not to be puzzled by what happened next on the long
    pier
of time reaching to the vanishing point.

Some were cold, some were near, some were clear.
Some were like lighthouses out of which startled gulls flew
to change something in the colored environment of sky
before retracing their steps to the dome.
Some of them were having kittens that night;
it changed something for everybody
and not enough to come out on top, oh well
the seer said my pastry is here.
I shall dispose of myself as I will
and I shall not come back
and no one will notice not ever not even the dimpled sun
as it coasts majestically by these geese
that come up short. In good time
I shall return for I have other things to do other fish to fry
he said but in the meantime it will look as though I'm not
    coming back
or returning. The woods resounded with campers' cries,
they are bringing something back, back to the deck
with them. "You see I should never have gone away,"
the seer remarked, now I can not ever
as long as accounts not be settled and the ride over the corn is
    over.
It seemed as though shale were about to break off the Old
    Man of the Mountain.

The holidays mystify me I cannot grow
as long as that path undulates in front of me,
and that crow ululates devaluating me
within the radius of this embroidery frame for ever and ever,
where "pie are square" and nobody knows how many.
Ssh, you are loud.
The seer teeters on the bench near the pool.
It is all just about over.
A fine man with coal nostrils
he was just about ready for this fix
when April surprised us with mistrials.
The man gone again, triumphant
in his absence
and with some remainder of light, of permanency
sliding toward day. I feel

that this is a letter being delivered to me, haply at dusk before
     night's purple
wrinkles have shifted the scenery, perhaps dolorously into
     death and the storm-
tinged future of lying and social regret. Don't stand, I might
     see you there,
she said. Helpless but doomed,

he countered good-humoredly. And these are our intuitions!

XI

First the cellos rebelled. Then a broader breaking-out erupted
nearer to home. All the girls were paralyzed (for a minute)
but Jenny Wren came to release them from the spell
Tom Cat had caused. They ran away, glad for that day.
Until Bruin came home and lay with his big amazing paws
on the hooked rug and it was time to go again. Goodbye,
Bruin said. I'll see you in the piece of country next door
which is exactly what happened, behind the tattered gate.
Then it was almost time to go fishing again. Here they paused,
wondering whether any of them had seen the big flash in the
     sky.
They decided to go no further. The tree dropped its seeds

into the birdbath. Alas the long wall, for all under this spell
will be ungrown some day, and are still here
to kiss the stair. Never mind, they said,
we'll all be here to cheer you on, and then they didn't mind.
Some had come unconvinced about the importance
of this daydream in which they were all entombed. Hark, one
   said, it smells like ice
or night here. Another agreed. They looked down on the
   procession
of sad children imagining they'd been forgotten about, and one
   stood in strength
on a tire rim and blew a whistle to the others. Zounds, it's our
   escape
one said. Here in the city repugnant with dust, Pliable's house
   was on fire
and nobody knew to stop it. I'll wager it was arson, Kitty said,
and others fervently agreed. He was coming back with a big
   sack
on his back, filled with plunder, perhaps, but there was no time
   to think of roses.
They had all walked for the day. Tonight's
question mark loomed in the agate sky, pointing them toward
   dewdrops
and madness. Are you listening, one of them said,
or just insane. Look, this pulley works,
we'll unscrew the pears from the plate, and put them back
   again,
and no one will ever know the difference. So they set to work,
   with a right good will,
saw and hammer in hand, and little by little the thing took
   shape.

It was the exact replica of a house
Tim had seen in his travels. Be it blue,
or red, I'll have it, Pliable said. Yes but you must go out
into the wind, one said, it's not that easy to see. I'll
wager I see it, he said. In fact she had achieved her level.
Ten million visitors are anticipated
next season, and as for the future, who knows
what it holds? They let down the bar

and each traveler was safely enclosed for the night.
It couldn't have been that anyone was coming to have it
or Bill the barrel would have known. For which everyone
was thankful, and induced into sleep, but
with a terrifying roar the house exploded again.
Now let me sink into my minutest crevices
if ever I give up a latchkey again! Yet girls and boys rolled
on together, the end was not in sight,
nor was it a division yet. Thanks, the cowboy yells are most
    gratifying.
But all wondered if it wasn't divided
from itself, and if more sleep hadn't built up on the other side.

XII

Other dreams.
Judy the petulant watered her flowers
from a sprinkling can, and the rose hurtled into bloom.
My message is it's all right to go on, it said.
Sure enough daisies and yellowbirds paired off in the peace of
    the moment,
which is to be lasting, but someone unearthed the old saw
on the gravel beach. "We can't use this." No but we'll go over
    the top
and down into the wrinkle on the other side, you'll see.
So they did what was natural and becoming, and all were
    satisfied
and rewarded. And some
shall be excused, and others have to go and wait on the border
    for it,
if we can believe the poets who wrote all this down many
    decades ago.
And we should come nearer, it's warmer,
if we want to, only on that other side
which seems so far away from us, but alas is too near
almost to count. With that the hedgerow winked
good-humoredly, and they stand, they stand
unimpressed but interested perhaps
even today, and that's the gist of it.

Dream lover, won't you come to me?
Dream lover, won't you be my darling?
It's not too late or too early.
Dream lover, won't you kiss me and hold me?
Dream lover, won't you miss me and mold me?
See, it was better that the chickens gulped concrete
commas to be able to rinse backwards.
Otherwise the driveling idiots would be maligned
and come to feel transparent.
Dream lover, are you apparent?
I only wish the awful bushel of shins would go away.
My accountant says it's time to harvest the burrs
where the asphalt beaches tame shrieks and the byword is love.

Yet, more and more blobs are in favor of love.
The tax district can't annul it.
The ivy wants to get strenuous.
The old ladies in the tower dream and curse
whoever put them out to pasture with geraniums.

It is too my house.

And they tracked the Canadian trappers far into the mist,
it was gone over with a horsehair comb, brisk
in the seasoned twilight, from which other squall
daffodils and the girls depended. See, it's me.

Briefly the dolls rested on the sink.
If the contest was over, nowhere
had not been told so. Time's evening relish,
hole of the great world, came to ice over
in morning-glory privies where no starlight is,
no autograph sessions, no costume contest.

New creatures fly past, out of the starting gate forever. The
    pink boomerang returns
to home base, flutters, settles in the dust.
Our therapist has been with us for five years.
Some pretty desolate pairing
has gone on in the interval; none of us are satisfied

with that just yet. He scooted down the wind
just in time for us. Omigosh, that means he's here.

Yes, a majestic crash is heading our way.
You and the girls must learn to prize it
while the water buffalo behaves and all is asunder
on the grass, between the chairs, under the apple blossoms.
And what does this have to do with me?
You'd better water your garden again under the circumstances,
look at them till they come down the street,
forming a parade, taut, hangdog. We can run away
at some point? The blue is
materializing and no one will ever know the outcome any
    more.
No, I mean no one will ever know the outcome,
the sails they took to get here, over fields, marshes,
the salt hay slipping, the season reviving
its forecasts. The sea air is like sludge.
We'll go out and rest in snowbanks while the nightingale titters
and crumbs fall down an airshaft, disappearing forever from
    view.

If they had heifers on Mars, bub, this would be
all it is like and it would be peaceful in time for mom to go
    home,
but as it is, we'll have to settle for Siena. As you
can see, the hands of the oversize clock are at 5:30;
the plastrons will be here soon. I forgot
they were coming. I have a handkerchief in this sandwich. Oh,
    give me
that. The goddam house is haunted,
and you're goofy too. I was only practicing my wail
thought the witch. This really is unfortunate.
Same goes for all the centuries we wafted over to get here,
only to be left in the lurch, far from the nearest poltroon
    garage,
on a deck dipping roguishly into the foam of the sound.
We should all plan to go back there together
into the room, and count who's there first. By
golly I think she's right. Yes, and you would too,

if a cannonball was your uncle. Yipes,
the general said.

XIII

And some were vortices
of blue, and yellow.
These, wherever the waves grazed, laughingly,
were slower. Then good General Metuchen said, It
has come to my attention some of you are not letting your
   streamers out.
Please, bear in mind, streamers must be released and parties
   accompany them,
such is my desire. O,
sir, the landgrave said, we cannot do it. Why? Well, we just
   can't,
that's all. Then I command you to do it. So the plains
   re-echoed
with indecision that day, and it was a day like the first.

I dream too much, Metuchen swirled, and in the gasps in his
   doublet
many live fish pirouetted and stank.
Now it was Phoebe's turn to complain: "Whoever thinks he
can outwit the sun is in for a rude awakening. For her parents
are always turning up in the strangest places,
such as the top of a bluff or at a pencil fair,
when fountain pens are the color of crayons dipped in the
   watercolor that was used in the landscape.
We acknowledge it and go on living. This
pen is for you because you're about twenty-four."
Glory how the running of the teams was acknowledged
that day! For they forgot to drain the swamp,
but in doing so created new, higher ground
for kids to live on.
And there was talk of acknowledging it since yesterday:
"It positively shimmers."

Yet how ephemeral are the repercussions, this valley of branches,
when we come to take our place in the parade,

piddling in the foreground, "some in rags,
some in jags, and some in velvet gown," as the saying is,
like that little old Rhode Island lady no one has talked to since
    last November.
I break the silence, it shatters my lips, fronds
come all over me, I am besotted
at least twice this year. Who will lock up their numbers, who'll
    know
exactly how much we were valued at? Shucks,
the most contented among us are aware of that;
you other buggers can go now. Even with dense night
pouring over us? For how did you expect us to get out
once we got in, or was it a secret for those in authority
to bottle up within us? You did the right thing,
that's for sure. Now it's time to surrender, or be riven asunder,
    garroted, eviscerated
by the actual time of the explosion. They had some nerve
telling us to come over at such and such an hour. I'm sure
    they'll be sorry
once they've been told about it.
Yes, for this is the season of flares, Farmer Jones will sew a
    patch on it
until we're delivered. O is it like onions then?
Can it be invisible? But the skunks were swaggering among us
    but this time
it was all a fever, a coming apart at the hinges
glowworms had appeared at, several summers back, before the
    big naked
cloud pushed rudely into the foreground, and they all sank into
    apathy,
puzzled by this latest evidence of villainy in the ranks.

How strange it all seems lost! How white it then was! Page
    torn from a notebook . . .
for the end that doesn't come any more.

We so enjoyed having salt to sprinkle on the meat,
until it seemed none of us could be a worker or welfare recipient.
Cashing in on the laughs in the alley,

Melinda strums a thighbone guitar, the rest are off in the distance.
Daytime drowsiness, dizziness, headache, nausea, stomach upset, vomiting, diarrhea, lightheadedness, muscle
aches and dry mouth may occur
so long as we are in unreasoning variation to one another,
which might be repaired by dawn's unsealing the tips
of tall buildings, so they sway to and fro,
in time with the maker's rhythm. He had a plan
but it was too late to use it.

XIV

Heightened with a sense of mysterious confusion, or completion,
the books in the library give off an odor of display, are about allegorical whale-catching,
or about the roads each of us takes, that cross over each other
from here until the end, whichever arrives first.
Yes, Shuffle, he and I many times asked ourselves that,
breaking the theme up
into slivers
that the king melds together, driving in his carriage out of the straight gate
into the taxis of City Hall. Best not to let them guess
what is in your hand. Varmints tell the truth
you may want to sip in later days, which is part of the story, an important one,
as is listening to the telegraph
wires, and how we can never listen to nor quite escape the sound
that brings us
to this place of feasting. Again, you've
got to be something without grapes,
and no one knows where it can lead to.
The truant officer plays with a doily,
outside, in the street. Playground noise smears the crowd,
bewitches those who had brought along questions, placating questions of faith,

so that when it's all gone a lorn dog's skin
comes quickly up the path, loping into the light of what was
    done.
My dears, doesn't it all seem a little suspicious to you that we
    are here,
unable to throw the volleyball into the adjoining courtyard?
Fred the truant officer smiled and turned sheepishly.
It made less difference now,
its fluency was less tortured. So he spoke, and drifted away
out of the girls' thoughts, all but a few of them.

Trevor his dog came, half jumping.
The oblique flute sounded its note of resin.
In time, he said, we all go under the fluted covers
of this great world, with its spiral dissonances,
and then we can see, on the other side,
what rascals are up to. What games the malevolent play.
Only then we are distanced, and can relax in the great
cradle of earth's two cents, for what it's worth,
and can recline, looking upward to the great here and there,
even as it falls short at our feet.

I'll go you one better, Fred chimed in, here's a diver,
let's call her Josephine, who dives and dives, further and
    downward,
all our lives' span, to the basis of that bridge.
Does that make her any more coquettish than we are? More
    sure-footed?
No but and here's what I was going to say
all along, must we recast ourselves in the image of the ocean floor:
To wit, are we not shipshape entities? Have we not corollas?
O the moon shines bright on the birdbath
as on a summer's stream, and we pass slowly from view,
borne by the tide's single-mindedness, and come to seem happy
as birds frolic, words wuther, and the contented are at peace
    again.

Whoa, Trevor responded, these dances of life—
always pissing, and shitting, and waking up in the great
    grapefruit

as in a trundle bed, breathless following how it goes, leads
to the great here and there.
Let's take my toes, if you insist. What I said
no one now remembers. Oh, but I do, Josephine said brightly.

We were talking about thingamabobs, and how one sheep's antler
can subdue dispassionate multitudes with its glint.
But is that all that brought us together? What about sex?
Yes, he remembers quietly, we too were part of the line.
Then why have sidled against this puzzle-wall for miles and miles?
Do you think it can speak to us?
Or are we, as was said of the others, just slush?

Hold it, I have an idea, Fred groaned. Now some of you, five
  at least, must go over in that little shack.
I'll follow with the tidal waves, and we'll see what happens next.

It was agreed for that day they would separate into two groups,
the lovers and learners side by side with the vexed and disinherited.
If only his plan had worked better—
but we must learn to read, "and that ain't easy," Trevor summarized.
Oh for a pen, for a blotter,
for a more regulated environment. Tired, the girls lay down to
  sleep amid the rocks.
It was just play, they dreamed,
tomorrow will be another day, and different.
For after taking off from the spring, the squirrels
touch earth again and die. Much that is lovely
may be voiced then, though not exclusively. The mad neighbor
pursues a fish; desperate, islands collapse,
and it's all vertigo now on the railroad. Yes, chained
to a post, I might have agreed with that. But now, the bees
come. See how fast they come,
suspecting the glad harbor holds opals for them.
But the wish for truth is denied. A twinkly Christmas tree

rushes over the sand, and whether the scale is practiced for the
    benefit of many,
or whether it voices a portent of shooting stars to come
is not known. I'll write you from that solemn coast,
but you must promise never to remember me, never speak of me,
until we are found at last behind the bathroom door, with the
    broom.

XV

Fred began to get chills: It sure was his mission, he averred,
to get everyone out before the avalanche came down.
But it was equally certain the girls' light chatter had dispersed
the whaling ships to wherever. In tints of prune, or lilac, these
    arrived
to chase the gloom of our arrival. Now, some of them were still
    in short pants.
But all that mattered was that they take off their clothes
in innocence, miming sleep, and be none too particular.
"The chime irritates me, I'll lose the thread
if I follow it much further," Trevor whispered. And where
should we go for relief, we who have never had any, have never
    felt
what it means to go without pangs, unless momentarily
    forgotten,
by the bridge, in sunlight's vale? It's because there are pairs of
    everything, that we miss the
chink in the stair where memory was supposed to reside.
    Indeed,
she was there until recently, until this morning; no one could say
why she went away.

The consignment of leeches hadn't arrived yet.

I was whispering, where were you?
I know, I was close by, but dared not speak. Try surrendering,
but not often. A loved one may be driving home
into the forest and then this—it's enough to make you ache
with hunger at a banquet.

The men never learned to love much. There was both hunger
    and sadness
at their feasting, the rocks wave over the airstrip, the hyenas of
    sleep redescend,
the leeches brace themselves for one last fetid leap into
    thanksgiving
there where loam signals the synod's pallid approach. It was a
    little too unresonant.
Still, they'd imagined they'd be saved
all this time, so why take a different tack now?
So marl oozed through the bookshelves
and a yellow wind turned the trailer park to dust.
Strange glyphs seemed to advise one to consign oneself to
    temporary oblivion;
we were very expressive in words, and in feeling. The
    mastodon broke his chain
and wanted to be petted, or at least encouraged, and tall lupine
clambered up the pesky wall, infesting projects with smug
    I-told-you-so's
in case any of us were still rattling around inside the domed
    hut's emptiness.
I like it here, but why should anybody else? It was my spasm
    that brought this on,
now I'll sink or swim in it. The latter, preferably,
but Damian still reached for Emily's shoelaces,
as the lich-gate came unhooked. It was still laughing like a
    lunatic
several hours later when reinforcements arrived at the stockade
just as General Forester's nerves were giving out, and a thin
    gruel
was being served to the men in the guise of supper. "I'll not
    swallow this!"
But you must, otherwise the story would have no turning,
and blind sockets gaze at streaks the plow left
in sunburnt earth, for only some are permitted to be happy,
surmised Emily, and that means none of us
at the present time. Sure enough, Trevor leaped on the
    horizon,
causing cheerfulness to jump-start the stubborn little band of
    marauders. When they awoke,

as from a dream, only a mauve magician was occupying the
   premises,
and he too pretended not to notice anything was amiss. This
   was too much for
Laure. She pushed impatiently past the guards, on the pretext
of bringing Trevor his bowl and saucer, secretly
counting up the number of clothespins that still lay scattered
   around the tent threshold.
This marks the moment

when everything must be summed up or there will no longer
   be a way past the mercenaries.
You see we all thought the ride would be lovely
and worth the trip, which it was, but now we cannot go
   anywhere
having already been everywhere. No, do you
understand how realistic it all is? Bear-baiting was considered a
   privilege
in those days. Then I have one piece of advice for you: Go easy
on the imperatives, for night is coming, than which there will
   be none bigger.

Sure enough, suds coursed down the boulder's slate face,
moonflowers danced, and it was all here and in a jiffy,
the present, made up like a cadaver, but more tastefully,
   though not too
much so. A raft descended the millrace
and Lou jumped off at the prearranged moment,
to the astonishment of many, but survived to yodel another
   day.
We listened to some semiclassical music, and someone got the
   idea of hooking up
the car's old engine to the plaster sheep on the hill.
The effect was startling; moths buzzed in the light
from its extraordinary vibrations. Fifteen years passed in this
   way.
When it was over no one had the courage to come out into the
   daylight,
or knew there was any. I fell asleep

on a sandhill, and dreamed this, and gave it to you, and you
    thanked me, solemnly,
but we were not permitted to associate, only to correspond,
    and you came out
to me again, and we wished one another good afternoon, and
    then went away
again into the fog-lit embrasure. Not that we didn't have good
    reason
to do whatever we did, but the question never came up again.
Where was I? Back in the explorer's cottage, with the
    thundering sea
bathing the rafters, not sure how many of us were to have gone
    out to meet
the pack of returning travelers. Some stayed behind. Others felt
    it a breach of dignity
to have gone. Still others put a good face on it, and were in
    turn
kissed by blue bats, and the coroner caught up on his sleep.
    "Forty winks!
That's all they allowed me!" And grumbling, he too left the
    shift.
For wasn't that what the Creator had in mind? That we should
    all muck about
helplessly, for a few minutes, and then stand back
to look at what a small difference we had made merely by
    observing crusty silence and then speaking up briefly?
Sure as canvasbacks are part of nature, we could not have
    observed it
another way, or brought our chairs back to where the laundry
    was spread out, effectively drying.

XVI

Dolores . . . you wisteria . . .
Destined to be destined
Like a lilac I am coming on your shoe.
Uncle Margaret was dull-witted.
He had tried the various positions.
The tame suburban landscape excited him.
He had met his match.

Dimples replaced the mollusk with shoe-therapy.
Sun burning his way through that flower . . .

Since Labor Day hardly any curls were outside
on the ladies' heads, the ones who sold jelly-bean screwdrivers
    inside.
Uncle Margaret's wren ranch was getting on his nerves just
    now.
Why, I'll wager some of them even wear raccoon coats
on shopping tours to East Testicle, he thundered. But what
    does showing off prove,
except to stop it, right here and now?
                                            Aw, don't
be such a grouch, Dimples curdled, but then suddenly the
    plain was awash with
ocher sediment; testaments to the superiority of life overflowed
    the trap;
all around us were boondoggles and poverty parades.
Which is it to be? Shall I spoil you
a little, or can we just go back to being peacemakers
in love, and in our time? Broken clocks
sound the hour in forty different cities at once, and in this, I
    was right,
I told you so, Jane's warlock said. But in other things I am less
    right,
like wanting to go in to town the fast way.
Yes you surely are right:
Some dream, some faint away, others are dragged up in
    morning's consciousness
like breakers from overseas. The shore patrol, ditchdiggers
    clawing,
and the mostly interesting ephemera of dawn, then a big one,
then a not so big one, then another one, then quite a small
    one,
then another big one followed by two middle-sized ones. For
    whom
are these? Day struts and stammers
on our headlands, so it seems, half-threatening to be off into
    night
as all collapses, leaving the players in fearful jeopardy,

but as time goes on they begin to forget their bruises,
settling down into the seats of the jalopy of day.

What if someone called back to you
from a distance? What would that sound like? What would you
    think? Does anyone
care any more about it's being night? "We think
night is fine, it enables one to get over the headaches of day
and so survive until day returns,
a limpet in his arms, one blue eye poking out from the vellum
    of his matted hair."
So what is important,
if the universe decides not to challenge us, and even
    breakwaters fall asleep?
Why, the old, seminal
undertow, that's what. The nor'easter will be out in force
    tomorrow,
an insane force in an otherwise docile universe.
Why beat about the bush? One of us knows the truth, and she
    isn't telling.
And so they betook themselves to the Carolinas.

Now he was the daughter or granddaughter of somebody
    famous,
folks for miles around knew that. But no one could say what
    she was up to,
she was far too clever for that. "Look, Uncle Wilmer," she'd say
    sometimes.
"The dark forest is my kitty. Just feel how soft it is!"
Let chunky Ida have that, Uncle thought, but he said nothing.
The tides were still active, one coming in
as another was going out, and one's thinking got caught
in these shifts, too positive some days, too blank the next,
and it all did matter somehow, though it didn't seem to
compute at any given moment. Pink shrouds fell on the pansy
    jamboree,
mocking the circular nature of events with its own kind of
    back-to-the-beginning
free fall. A few pansies got drowned. Yet this was as nothing to
    the terrible

muttering of the distant cavalry, like an express train coming to
    exhaust itself on the shore,
and over and over the same note was struck. Go back! This is a
    place too far.
In any case you ought to reconsider the places back there,
teeming with sandalwood and bees. You think you know it
but you don't, there are inner coasts to be discovered, sat on,
whittled to a point more dangerous than Father Time's tuning
    fork,
if you but knew. In the minute
before the terrible tide turns there's time enough to go back
if you are engaged, shoes slushy with sand.
Go, do as I say.
                    Uncle Bert chided the fens at Mr.
McPlaster's side, and they stretched away into the hyacinth
    distance, meek enough,
or so it was thought, for the time being. Then everything
    began to explode
in a geyser of impatience that crested at where the nearest
    cloud-scraps had been.
"Now that's funny,
he was here only a moment ago. I thought I saw him go up,
    and out." The flies
on the flypaper said they hadn't seen him; birds whistled
    unconsciously
at a shadow-bulge in the grass that could have been almost
    anything
except the two principal survivors, who were nowhere to be
    found
on a fine day, with the red mailbox standing near, as always, *if
    you know what I mean.*
This is where we break for lunch.
Those who want to go back to the base camp can do so. I
    swear
I've never seen a more ornery bunch, though civic-minded
at heart, I suppose, but there's a great gap between their
    intentions
and the harvest moon that seems to belie mediocre aspirations
even as it secretly promotes them, waxes as it wanes
into delirium tremens, and other missed opportunities

too numerous to scramble for, in disbelief's fomented ocean.
Oh my there were a lot of them
then, some as had names, and these were brought to the front
    of the group,
with Ida, who seemed to be their leader.
Roll back this pokey late-morning sense of being extra,
she was begged. Bring us all to your birch tree.

XVII

After a few rounds of this the leader fell silent.

Well, what did you want me to do,
arrest the perpetrators?
What would we have seen?
Ida and the rest imaged the tambourine. They were never to start.
In fact as they got older, wasps reminded them continually
of their delicate condition; they never amounted to much
and were called up for screening. Well sir, sure as your nose
heads north, an' they were caught out in the singing sands
a hundred miles from home. And decimated.

You see the mouse was in between the papers.
There was a limit to what any fool could do.
Our faces were wiped clean, we wept for the goodness
that is earth, and in autumn comes to fondle us
with new, rich, more mature colors, just as the sun is going
    down
and down and down for the last time. Night did not recognize
    us
or our claims, but the night season is good
for all and sundry, to children especially, and plays a game
    without brains.
In the utopian schemes there was nothing left. Some
    resolutions
perhaps? Maybe a little freedom for play? That was all right,
but time was up, which was the same as if there was no way,
no bemused situation to chortle at, no lava
on the red earth's rim, which is running down to meet the land
    and the sea

in a way that deviates. O say is there any more,
truly? Can we have something? No, the machinery is ugly and
    preserved in dust.
There were no two ways to have it. All came undone
from Brigitte's shorts, and this was supposed to be the way
    home,
even. But not anything mattered any more, not even to the
    shirts
some children wore then, out of sight until the last tide
    destroys us.
The envy of the age sweeps over us, tidying us into pits of
    darkness
that men shall understand, and forgive their promises
to those who had forgotten them, lauding all future
    dust-storms
as long as the king will stay alive on the road.
Bird-feeders introduced a new element of sashaying
nobody picked up on, and the direction all were taking was
    done to death
most slovenly. Where the girls' shorts
had been, only a minus sign stood.
So the bad angels went away, and other creatures returned.

XVIII

Did you read that book I was telling you about? Ach, it
    concerns puberty.
Do you suffer, child? That is fundamentally inaccurate.
Your talents are warehoused now. In another time they would
    spring forth
with the red beacons of spring, prepared to do battle with
    rocks.
In a tenderer meridian
their phalanxes would cripple the overseers, bonk.
The guides would unleash their elastic trains.
So much sorrow, yet quite a lot of laughter. "I say,
Does the train run on Sundays?" We, quite a lot of us, were
    mired east of here
and could feel the valley's separateness and shortcomings.
    When it came time to repeat

the scene, Dennis was numb with fear.
His velvet tread was steadfast on the stair. The fall had occurred
to someone nice this time, tatters of milk on the stone.
Preserve us all from horseradish
but if the saints won't let us in, blast us
into nether pandemonium, for that will be where their compacted truths hibernate.

See, they need to have a story line. Sexy. So it appears.
The seven colors are remanded. We should have put aside our differences.
We are refracted. They never learn to drive.
They never slide much
these days,
what with the cartwheel hats, and all the underachievers.
It's a big scare. The Lollipop Mountains are an entertainment mogul.
She said. But—
they are under orders. When the balls came on Fred was over with the bears. He started.
They all did waiting for something coherent to happen.
Then it was all over.
The ball-juice had expired
in the lobby, as though something were promised me that came out like an anteater,
poked around, went back in.

Slush and feathers. The hippo trod on a pine needle, they all sank back into relief.
Everywhere we go is something to eat
and fat disappointment, tears in the rain. Somebody is coming over the radio.
A lull.

XIX

He complicated everything by dying. He wouldn't hear
of it. Fate was two valleys away. Wind slithered over the
sandbar. Two women caught the train

from the new town. More elaborate buildings betokened sly
    adjustments
in the retinue of the living, underground. Aphasia leaked,
a sprinkle of diamond confetti, over confused lands and places,
the places we had ignored when we went through them the last
    time
when you were there for me.
                              I pointed the ladder to the ceiling.
It seemed we could join there.
The pre-Columbian bats were in ferment, just at that period.
The ladder shrinks in living water
whereas in your time the fiction we would otherwise be
    without
stays and stays and finally comes to seem permanent,
all along. It was almost twenty to six,
they churred. Slim weasels stirred behind the chink,
the oxymoron got his rocks off, there was hell to pay, but pay it
    they did,
after which the streets absorbed the laughter and lust that had
    been the morning
as Pamela was at last captured.

XX

A virtual rout ensued. Tell me, can you tell it any
different where you come from? I know the highlights are
    blurred
now, the witnesses less than forthcoming,
but fences are down, and we can travel where it was never
    supposed
anyone could go, to highlands of the spirit that refresh and
    punish
the blame we were supposed to ingest, until they leave that off,
    too.
A ton of regret is supplied and it never needs any replenishing,
as long as we citizens still stomp the earth, favor it with our
    occasional
attention and pull up stakes each night. But I'm not too sure
    what boils at the center of the earth.

I'll go along with what you say. We must isolate the moment
from its comperes, look behind it,
and if possible draw the appropriate conclusions from its
    appearance of unease
while the nurses are still on the grounds. The fat clock ticks.
    It's time to repair
to the orchard, or just to repair.

When it was all over, a sheep emerged from inside the house.
A cheer went up, for it was recognized that these are lousy
    times
to be living in, yet we do live in them:
We are the case.
And seven times seven ages later it would still be the truth in
    appearances,
festive, eternal, misconstrued. Does anyone still want to play?

It was only inevitable, after all,
what shoes they could muster. So they made bold. Prudence
    won the spelling bee with "cotoneaster."
Harry wanted to believe. Prodding succeeds. So does
    popularity. Pierre thought it might too.
Lochinvar believed. All systems became taut. This is only what
    they did do.

They danced, and became meaningful to each other. It was
    cosmic time,
tasting of grit. If this is a mutual admiration society,
why not? We were, after all, going to pull our town out of the
    encampment. The proud similarities
twinkle. Coming back to our doorstep, it was in the vegetables'
    vocabulary
and nobody had noticed. Nobody, that is, except Swann.
Anyway, it overshoots the mark, as a log a waterfall.
Each gemstone blooms out of corruption, and somebody
    knows it.
But if that is the case, who knows it? Bookcases wouldn't give
    you the time of day.
Time wasted in beehives is about right. And extraneous
    moraines,

coming from the kitchen to be all over the map of the United
    States,
and Canada, whose states are affectionately known as
    "provinces."
Aye, to be brought up in the provinces equals an old Dodge or
    De Soto,
and who is coming back to get us, after all? Looks lonesome,
I mean. Where's the energy needed to strike?

Come, it's silver, children, the unbearable letdown
has gone under the hill to bide its time. Centuries shall pass
    away this way.
When we wake up it will be over. The motor will have started
    up,
and peas have been planted in Wyoming. Time grabs us
again, it's terrible, for a little while. And then it becomes more
    and more like this
in its way. Then time broke off
discussions, they were shunted to Sheboygan, some mystery
    wolf came to the appointment
instead, there were further negotiations, a child lay dying, there
    was more other
to be sad over, the whistle charged doom, its impact
was tremendous, light exploded all over the football field, the
    nails were there,
pus of the sun, brooding, help, it looks more doctrinaire, than
    we can handle, I mean,
and goes on and on, not just changing in the fire
from the attic bathroom. Kids came over, it wasn't right to put
    the blame on anyone,
can you see, it should have gotten by all right, but it didn't,
    that's what "hopeless"
is all about, where I come from, oh you shan't, shall you, shut
    up, the dish, over
what I am doing is all broke out, the cattails
again, more underwear, trees implored, then lunch, for crying
    out loud,
and more of the same, ideal limits, a good spanking. Call your
    jewels up, it seems the only way.

Who am I to be horsing around? You are someone. Rats. A tan
    umbrella
coasted.

Weary, the dogs broke off the game.

It was just dandy where you were standing.
It was like everywhere. It was just average.

XXI

When more and more people come to you, you know
what they are saying, and you know how to deal with them.
Many were the whiskers that applied that day,
and many the salvage operations bent on rejecting them.
If you have some ointment it would be good to use it
now. Otherwise the opportunity may never again present itself.
I know you mean well, Hopeful murmured. Talkative was
starting to tell one of his stories again, and smiling,
Hopeful silently abetted it. He knew the old boy was feeling
    his oats,
which was fine with him, as he too was feeling good. Talkative,
    you old so-
and-so, he volunteered. Then his father-in-law blew up. The
    Overall Boys, fishing poles in hand,
charged into nether regions.
Susie never thought she'd see the day when so much surplus
    was at stake,
and she alone, outdoors, waiting for the postman's red bicycle
for what seemed like ages. He explained that it was a routine
    assassination,
that that was what had delayed him. Crestfallen, Susie hardly
    dared look up
into the eyes of her man, a breeze was blowing, it was snowing.
    The droplets made diagonal streaks in the air
where pterodactyls had been. It was time for an exodus of
    sorts;
Paul picked up the legend
                    where it had been broken off: "No

blame accrues to those who were left behind, unless, haply,
   they were climbing
the wall to get a better view of the stars, in which case the
   next-to-last
must pay a tribute, and so on. It can be anything, old money,
a calico scarf, whatever has soiled the hand of the donor by
   staying
to wear out its welcome. O in time it will shrivel.
What is it to imagine something you had forgotten once, is it
inventing, or more of a restoration from ancient mounds that
   were probably there?
You that can tell all, tell this."

At first Talkative was reluctant to speak, then the words fell
like spring rain from his lips, all was as it had been before,
with no two dancers in step, and a bright, really bright light
   exploded
above the barn. A horse wanders away
and is abruptly inducted into the carousel,
eyes flying, mane askew. There is no end to the dance,
even death pales in comparison, and at the same time we are
   forced to
take into account the likelihood of the moment's behaving
   badly, the eventual cost
to our side in terms of dignity, compromised integrity. Twelve
   princesses
stepped ashore, no one knew them, they too seemed not to
   know where they were.
"In what region . . ." one began timidly, then the whole flock
   took off
like a shout, leaving the beleaguered ground to fend for itself.
"There were picture books at that time,
and dreams woven in and out of them. But one was not to
   notice,
only to go on behaving. And at the end, when everything was
   added up,
we probably owed them a penny. It's enough to make you
   weep.
But skies are gilded and armored, we shall put a brave face

"on it for a time, then school will be over, and sublime rest
flow from the uncorked flask like a prodigious perfume,
or sleep, a potent but dangerous brew,
a new assignment. Then we can get out of hock,
redeem Daddy's dear old coupons." He broke off, not wanting
    to bestir
the others, who had in fact ceased to hear, so monotonous
was the noise of his voice, like rain that flails the spears of vetch
in Maytime, to reap a tiny investment.
So we faced the new day,
like a pilgrim who sees the end of his journey deferred forever.
Who could predict where we would be led, to what
extremes of aloneness? Yet the horizon is civil.

A struggle ensued and the driver fell out of the vehicle.
And what did the old lady do then?
"She gave them some broth, without any bread, and . . .
    and . . ."

All are like soup.

So if it pleases you to come
out we all await thy pleasure, Stuart Hofnagel.
Who was with Young Topless? It seemed then an abyss was
    forming,
a new set of lagoons. More than look past it
one cannot, for more
than that is denied us.
So have I heard it said in old kingdoms, it said.
Larkspur towering over miniature turrets. The bandoleer was
    shot to hell.

The spa looked closed. So,
if you are in the market for a steeple, I commend this one
rigorously. It was not given to human divination to exhume it
like the comet, but to pause briefly, the blind
man's praise will cook itself. A giant paw
over the moon. Melons bloomed in corners. Shrimp blew away
to be fecund elsewhere, next year.
In time it will be your caesura too, but we mustn't

think of that. We caregivers especially. We must forget,
while others only live, peer into circles of living embroidery.
    The geese
will jump for you again, anon. Then it's no business. They
    closed
the place, the food court, they all
have gone away, it's restless, and mighty, as an ark
to the storm, yet the letter
of the law is obeyed, and sometimes the spirit
in forgotten tales of the seekers—O who were they?
Mary Ann, and Jimmy—no, but who were they?
Who have as their mantles on the snow
and we shall never reach land
before dark, yet who knows what advises them,
discreet in the mayhem? And then it's bright in the defining
    pallor of their day.
Does this clinch anything? We were cautioned once, told not
    to venture out—
yet I'd offer this much, this leaf, to thee.
Somewhere, darkness churns and answers are riveting,
taking on a fresh look, a twist. A carousel is burning.
The wide avenue smiles.

YOUR NAME HERE

For Pierre Martory
1920–1998

This Room

The room I entered was a dream of this room.
Surely all those feet on the sofa were mine.
The oval portrait
of a dog was me at an early age.
Something shimmers, something is hushed up.

We had macaroni for lunch every day
except Sunday, when a small quail was induced
to be served to us. Why do I tell you these things?
You are not even here.

If You Said You Would Come with Me

In town it was very urban but in the country cows were covering the hills. The clouds were near and very moist. I was walking along the pavement with Anna, enjoying the scattered scenery. Suddenly a sound like a deep bell came from behind us. We both turned to look. "It's the words you spoke in the past, coming back to haunt you," Anna explained. "They always do, you know."

Indeed I did. Many times this deep bell-like tone had intruded itself on my thoughts, scrambling them at first, then rearranging them in apple-pie order. "Two crows," the voice seemed to say, "were sitting on a sundial in the God-given sunlight. Then one flew away."

"Yes . . . *and then?*" I wanted to ask, but I kept silent. We turned into a courtyard and walked up several flights of stairs to the roof, where a party was in progress. "This is my friend Hans," Anna said by way of introduction. No one paid much attention and several guests moved away to the balustrade to admire the view of orchards and vineyards, approaching their autumn glory. One of the women however came to greet us in a friendly manner. I was wondering if this was a "harvest home," a phrase I had often heard but never understood.

"Welcome to my home . . . well, to our home," the woman said gaily. "As you can see, the grapes are being harvested." It seemed she could read my mind. "They say this year's vintage will be a mediocre one, but the sight is lovely, nonetheless. Don't you agree, Mr. . . ."

"Hans," I replied curtly. The prospect was indeed a lovely one, but I wanted to leave. Making some excuse I guided Anna by the elbow toward the stairs and we left.

"That wasn't polite of you," she said dryly.

"Honey, I've had enough of people who can read your mind. When I want it done I'll go to a mind reader."

"I happen to be one and I can tell you what you're thinking is false. Listen to what the big bell says: 'We are all strangers on our own turf, in our own time.' You should have paid attention. Now adjustments will have to be made."

A Linnet

It crossed the road so as to avoid having to greet me. "Poor thing but mine own," I said, "without a song the day would never end." Warily the thing approached. I pitied its stupidity so much that huge tears began to well up in my eyes, falling to the hard ground with a plop. "I don't need a welcome like that," it said. "I was ready for you. All the ladybugs and the buzzing flies and the alligators know about you and your tricks. Poor, cheap thing. Go away, and take your song with you."

Night had fallen without my realizing it. Several hours must have passed while I stood there, mulling the grass and possible replies to the hapless creature. A mason still stood at the top of a ladder repairing the tiles in a roof, by the light of the moon. But there was no moon. Yet I could see his armpits, hair gushing from them, and the tricks of the trade with which he was so bent on fixing that wall.

The Bobinski Brothers

"Her name is Liz, and I need her in my biz," I hummed wantonly. A band of clouds all slanted in the same direction drifted across the hairline horizon like a tribe of adults and children, all hastening toward some unknown destination. A crisp pounding. Done to your mother what? Are now the . . . And so you understand it, she . . . I. Once you get past the moralizing a new winter twilight creeps into place. And a lot of guys just kind of live through it? Ossified soup, mortised sloop. Woody has the staff to do nothing. You never know what. That's what I think. Like two notes of music we slid apart, far from one another's protective jealousy. The old cat, sunning herself, had no problem with that. Nor did the diaphanous trains of fairies that sagged down from a sky that suggested they had never been anywhere, least of all there. At the time we had a good laugh over it. But it did hurt. It still does. That's what I think, he slapped.

Not You Again

Thought I'd write you this poem. Yes,
I know you don't need it. No,
you don't have to thank me for it. Just
want to kind of get it off my chest
and drop it in the peanut dust.

You came at me and that was something.
I was more than a match for you, you
were a match for me, we undid the clasps
in our shirtings, it was a semblance of all right.

Then the untimely muse got wind of it.
Picked it up, hauled it over there.
The bandy-legged man was watching
all this time. ". . . to have Betty back on board."

Now it's time for love-twenty.
Assume your places on the shuffleboard.
You, Sam, must make a purple prayer
out of origami and stuff it. If you've
puked it's already too late.

I see all behind me small canyons, drifting,
filling up with the space of drifting.
The chair in the attic is up to no good.

Then you took me and held me like I was a child
or a prize. For a moment there I thought I knew you,
but you backed away, wiping your specs, "Oh,
excuse . . ." It's okay,
will come another time

when stupendous seabirds are carilloning out over the Atlantic,
when the charging fire engine adjusts its orange petticoats
after knocking down the old man the girl picks up.
Now it's too late, the books are closed, the salmon
no longer spewing. Just so you know.

Terminal

Didn't you get my card?
We none of us, you see, knew we were coming
until the bus was actually pulling out of the terminal.
I gazed a little sadly at the rubber of my shoes'
soles, finding it wanting.

I got kind of frenzied after the waiting
had stopped, but now am cool as a suburban garden
in some lost city. When it came time for my speech
I could think of nothing, of course.
I gave a little talk about the onion—how its flavor
inspires us, its shape informs our architecture.
There were so many other things I wanted to say, too,
but, dandified, I couldn't strut,
couldn't sit down for all the spit and polish.
Now it's your turn to say something about the wall
in the garden. It can be anything.

Merrily We Live

Sometimes the drums would actually let us play
between beats, and that was nice. Before closing time.
By then the clown's anus
would get all chewed up by the donkey
that hated having a tail pinned on it,
which was perhaps understandable. The three-legged midgets
ran around, they enjoyed hearing us play so much,
and the saxophone had something to say
about all this, but only to itself.

Clusters of pollen blot out the magnolia blossoms this year
and that's about all there is to it. Like I said,
it's pretty much like last year, except for Brooke.
She was determined to get a job in the city. When last heard
    from
she had found one, playing a sonata of Beethoven's (one
of the easier ones) in the window of a department store
downtown somewhere, and then that closed, the whole city
    did,
tighter'n a drum. So we have only our trapezoidal reflections
to look at in its blue glass sides, and perhaps admire—
oh, why can't this be some other day? The children all came over
(we thought they were midgets at first) and wanted
to be told stories to, but mostly to be held.
John I think did the right thing by shoveling them under the
    carpet.

And then there were the loose wickets
after the storm, and that made croquet impossible.
Hailstones the size of medicine balls were rolling down the
    slope anyway
right toward our doorstep. Most of them melted before they
    got there, but one,
a particularly noxious one, actually got in the house and left its
    smell,
a smell of violets, in fact, all over the hall carpet,
which didn't cancel one's rage at breaking and entering,
of all crimes the most serious, don't you fear?

I've got to finish this. Father will be after me.
Oh, and did the red rubber balls ever arrive? We could do
 something
with them, I just have to figure out what.
Today a stoat came to tea
and that was so nice it almost made me cry—
look, the tears in the mirror are still streaming down my face
as if there were no tomorrow. But there is one, I fear,
a nice big one. Well, so long,
and don't touch any breasts, at least until I get there.

Brand Loyalty

"Father, you're destroying the collectibles!"

"You are mistaken. I'm enjoying them! The green magenta finish on this one reminds me of the piano shawl in our flat in Harbin—only greener, as though slits of light were coming through its slits."

"At least we have the lilacs."

How he would get a little too creative, God and I both know. He's spent the morning chiding the waterspout, clearly amazed as it drew increasingly closer. "I've had it with natural phenomena. They never know when to draw the line. At least we have some sense, and we're natural phenomena too, for goodness sakes."

I wouldn't let it get to me. On the other hand, the waterspout or whatever you call it *is* getting to us. It touched down, back there, and only a moment ago it was in front of us. I suggest we sidle along the sand.

The deuce you say! On the other hand, if you really think so.

We could offer it tea and cookies, but in a moment it'll be too late for anything but palsied brooding on the tired theme of retribution. Like I said, they build them stronger and stronger until it's encoded in them. They can't help putting their best foot forward, and where does that leave us! After all, a little peace was all we were after.

If only you'd read up on the subject like you said you were going to.

Yes, well we can't alarm our surroundings too much, even as they torture us. That way we'd only slip out of pain and not see the exciting denouement. And what a sweet-tempered morning it was. Put aside our notions of the intrepid, the universe is paying a courtesy call, God has us on hold, and there's not much we can do except spin like dervishes, human tops. Hair climbing upward to a point, a kind of spire, and all I'd done was brush down the sides.

Can we do it that way now?

Not exactly. The village is walking toward us, we are becoming its walls and graffiti-sprayed cement bathrooms, its general store, the tipsy taxi driver. If I told you where we were going it wouldn't be a surprise anymore, and yet it would . . .

Sounds like my friend Casper, the girl said.

Rain in the Soup

Raindrops fall on the treetops. A rainy day.
Yes, it's that kind of a day. Some human suffering.
A number of malcontents. If Mr. Soup
will stay in his bowl, I'll blow on him.
Elsewhere stockings are being darned.
The darning egg is as big as a house.

All this less-than-great happiness
may be doing good to life somewhere else,

off in the bayou. Maybe. But we see it
from the top, like a triangular dome,
so it looks okay to us.

Unicyclists are out in force,
leading to the Next Interesting Thing
that's sure to be gone by the time you and I get there.
I don't count ivy climbing a chimney,
that's reached the top and is waving around, senselessly.

I'd like to push a raft down the beach,
wade into the water waist-deep, and get on it.
But clearly, nothing in this world was made for me.
It's sixes and sevens, the chimes go out
into the city and accomplish something valid.
I can stand to stand here, standing it, that's all.
Good day Mrs. Smith. Your daughter is as cute as anything.

Bloodfits

As inevitable as a barking dog, second-hand music
drifts down five flights of stairs and out into the street,
adjusting seams, checking makeup in pocket mirror.

Inside the camera obscura, jovial as ever,
dentists make all the money. I didn't know that then.
Children came out to tell me, in measured tones,
how cheap the seaside is, how the salt air reddens cheeks.

Violently dented by storms, the new silhouettes
last only a few washings.
Put your glasses on and read the label. Hold that bat.
He'd sooner break rank than wind.
He's bought himself a shirt the color of Sam Rayburn Lake,
muddled ocher by stumps and land practices. Picnicking
    prisoners
never fail to enjoy the musk that drifts off it
in ever-thickening waves,

triggering bloody nostalgia
for a hypotenuse that never was.

Implicit Fog

We began adulating
what we were staring at
too:

I was following the paths in the music.
Might as well have been patting myself dry
under a toadstool.

Winter came on neck and neck
with spring, somehow.
The two got tangled up for reasons
best known to themselves.
By the time it was over
summer had ended

with a quiet, driven day
out under the trees
in folding chairs:
troops ejected from a local bar.

It got lovely and then a little hirsute.

Dream Sequence (Untitled)

Yes, she chopped down a big tree.
We could all breathe easier again.

It wasn't the hole in the landscape
that gladdened us, it was the invitation to the weather
to drop in anytime.

Which it did, in proportion to our not growing interested
    in it.

After a third mishap we decided
to throw in meaning. No dice.
Our tapestry still kept on reviving itself
athwart the scary shore. You could look into it
and see fog that had been dead for years,
cheerful hellos uttered centuries ago.
Worse, we were going somewhere;
this was no longer the bush leagues, but a cantata
nature had ordered from the celestial caterer,
and now it was being delivered.

There were only a few false notes; these mattered less
than a cat in a cathedral. Suddenly we were all singing
our diaries of vengeance, or fawning thank-you notes, or
    whatever.
The hotel billed us by the hour
but for some reason the telegraph wires weren't included
in the final reckoning. Too, the water-tower had disappeared
as though deleted by a child's blue eraser.

It was then that the nets of chiming
explained what we had needed to know years ago:
that a step in the wrong direction is the keyhole
to today's busy horizon, like hay, that seems to know where it's
    moving when it's moving.

What Is Written

What is written on the paper
on the table by the bed? Is there something there
or was that from another last night?

Why is that bird ignoring us,
pausing in mid-flight, to take another direction?
Is it feelings of guilt about the spool

it dropped on the bank of a stream,
into which it eventually rolled? Dark spool,
moving oceanward now—what other fate could have been
    yours?
You could have lived in a drawer
for many years, imprisoned, a ward of the state. Now you are
    free
to call the shots pretty much as they come.
Poor, bald thing.

Caravaggio and His Followers

You are my most favorite artist. Though I know
very little about your work. Some of your followers I know:
Mattia Preti, who toiled so hard to so little
effect (though it was enough). Luca Giordano, involved
with some of the darkest reds ever painted, and lucent greens,
thought he had discovered the secret of the foxgloves.
But it was too late. They had already disappeared
because they had been planted in some other place.
Someone sent some bread up
along with a flask of wine, to cheer him up,
but the old, old secret of the foxgloves, never
to be divined, won't ever go away.

I say, if you were toting hay up the side of a stack
of it, that might be Italian. Or then again, not.
We have these things in Iowa,
too, and in the untrained reaches of the eyelid
hung out, at evening, over next to nothing. What was it she
    had said,
back there, at the beginning? "The flowers
of the lady next door are beginning to take flight,
and what will poor Robin do then?" It's true, they were
    blasting off
every two seconds like missiles from a launching pad, and
    nobody wept, or even cared.
Look out of the window, sometimes, though, and you'll see

where the difference has been made. The song of the
    shrubbery
can't drown out the mystery of what we are made of,
of how we go along, first interested by one thing and then
    another
until we come to a wide avenue whose median
is crowded with trees whose madly peeling bark is the color of
    a roan,
perhaps, or an Irish setter. One can wait on the curb for the rest
of one's life, for all anyone cares, or one can cross
when the light changes to green, as in the sapphire folds
of a shot-silk bodice Luca Giordano might have bothered with.
Now it's life. But, as Henny Penny said to Turkey Lurkey,
    something
is hovering over us, wanting to destroy us, but waiting,
though for what, nobody knows.

In the night of the museum, though, some whisper like stars
when the guards have gone home, talking freely to one
    another.
"Why did that man stare, and stare? All afternoon it seemed he
    stared
at me, though he obviously saw nothing. Only a fragment of a
    vision
of a lost love, next to a pool. I couldn't deal with it
much longer, but luckily I didn't have to. The experience
is ending. The time for standing to one side is near
now, very near."

Industrial Collage

We are constantly running checks.
Quantity control is our concern here, you see.
No batch is allowed to leave the premises
without at least a superficial glance along the tops
of the crates. For who knows how much magic
may be imprisoned there?

Likewise, when the product reaches the market
we like to kind of keep an eye on things there too.
Complaints about the magic
have dwindled to a mere trickle in recent years.
Still you never know if some guy's going to get funny
and tamper with the equation, causing
apocalyptic sighs to break out in the streets,
barking dogs, skidding vehicles, and the whole consignment
of ruthless consequences. That is why we keep a team of
    experts
on hand, always awake, alert for the slightest thread of disorder
on someone's pants. In spring these incidents can double,
    quadruple, even.
Everything wants to be let out of its box come April or May
and we have to test-drive the final result before it's been
    gummed
into the album dark farces regulate. Someone, then, must be
    constantly
on duty, as well as a relief contingent, for this starry mass
to continue revolving.

Like an apple on the ground
it looks at you. The neighborhood police were kind,
arrested a miscreant, though he was never brought to trial,
which is normal for this type of event.
Meanwhile spring edges inexorably into summer,
where, paradoxically, there is more activity but less to show for it.
The merry-go-rounds begin turning in the carnivals of August.
Best to leave prison till winter, once the honor system has
    broken down.
A stalemate could pollute new beginnings.
November tells it best, in a whisper almost,
so that there is surprisingly little letdown,
only this new background, a finer needle to thread.

Frogs and Gospels

> How does one interpret, on this late branch, the unexpected?
> —James Tate, "The Horseshoe"

A chance balloon drew these settlers nigh.
It was the year of green honey that sprouts
between the toes of the seated god. "None
can explain it further." No explanations,
not from me.

I sat in the bakery, rumpled, unshaved,
pondering a theorem. What you said the hotel was.
Someone else's towel approached me in the laundry.
"Ouch was what I said." This has been more than I know of,
brimming with indifference, some American in Europe.

He let me off at the corner of some strange country.
The signs were in English. No one cared if
you knew the rubbish was filth.
He carried me from the room in which people were sitting.
They always think they know better, even as they confess
their ignorance blindly, to the first stranger they know.
I see, it's a market garden, or was
some seasons ago. In this dark stubble I abide.

A messenger came with tidings. I'm sorry,
I've had enough tidings.
Giddy with surprise, he crawled upward
toward where I was toasting myself.
A male muse I suppose. I've listened to that
before, too. All I want is to be let out
to travel on the gravel. You still don't
get it, this is a seat. All right, I want my seat,
I said.

That's no easy manner. The blond moon came untied,
drifted through blue-black wisps
of a woodpile somewhere. Must I follow her too?

Must I follow her too?

Whatever it says you must do.
You had calm days in store, now they have come undone.
Worries stretch before you into the distance.
Perhaps distance is what you had,
once, and must now drink. Only forty years ago
early skyscrapers arched their backs, waiting to be fed.
And still the feeling comes on.

Weekend

Swan filets and straw wine,
an emphatic look to the driveway
whose golf clubs are scattered feelingly.

You can undress and sit down
on the corduroy doormat blowing
and when the Weird Sisters come calling
pretend to be talking to yourself.

Trouble is they don't come calling,
suffering as they do from terminal agoraphobia.
A frog juts from a pinecone.

My goodness was that you back there?
You sure know
how to give a feller a good scare.
I'd thought it was just bats
dripping tar on the heads of the guests and the footmen.
You see so little live action in this town
and then everybody wants to cooperate
or celebrate, sort of. I can do that too.
Always. Have a good time.
Something might come out in group therapy:
your velvet soul as I just realized it.
Please come back. I liked you so much.

Thistles, dandelions, what do we care?

Get Me Rewrite

The
ghoulish
resonance
of
a
cello
resonates in a neighbor's cabana.

What do I know of this?
I
am
sitting
on a pile of dirt in a neighbor's back yard.
Was there something else to do?

Long ago we crept for candy
through the neighbor's gutter
but found only candy wrappers
of an unknown species: "Sycamores,"
"Chocolate Spit," "Slate-Gray Fluids,"
"Anamorphic Portraits of Old Goriot."

The way a piece of candy seems to flutter
in the prismatic light above a clothesline, stops,
removes all its clothes.
There was a bucket
of water
to wash in,
fingerposts pointing the way to the next phenomenon:
sugar falling gently on strawberries, snow on a pile of red eggs.

None of us was really satisfied,
but none of us wanted to go away, either.
The shadows of an industrial park loomed below us,
the brass sky above.
"Get off your duff," Reuel commanded.
(He was our commander.)
"You are like the poet Lenz, who ran from house to forest

to rosy firmament and back
and nobody ever saw his legs move."

Ah,
it is good
to be back
in the muck.

Invasive Procedures

> I flee from those who are gifted with understanding, fearing that all
> their great and illuminating invasions of my being still won't satisfy me.
> —Robert Walser, "The One of Fairy Tales"

Massachusetts rests its feet
in Rhode Island,
as crows rest in cowslips
and cows slip in crowshit.

I may have been called upon to write
a poem different from this one.
OK, let's go. I want to please everybody
and this is my song:

In Beethoven Street I handed you a melon.
Round and pronged it was, and full of secret juice.
You, in turn, handed me over to the police
who thought (correctly) that I was the spy
they had been looking for these past seven months.

They led me down to their station, you need to know,
where they questioned me for days on end.
But my answers were always questions, and so they let me go,
exasperated by their inability to answer.
I was a free man!
I walked up Rilke Street
chattering a little hymn to myself.
It went something like this:

"Beware the monsters, but take care
that you are not yourself one.
Time is kind to them
and will take care of you,
asleep on your grandmother's couch, sipping cherry juice."

How did the pigs get through the window screens at night?
By morning it was all over.
I had never sung to you, you never coaxed me to
from your balcony, and all trains run into night
that collects them like paper streamers, and lays them in a
    drawer.

Unable to leave the sight of you
I draw little crow's feet in my notebook, in the sunlight
that comes at the end of a sudden day of tears
waiting to be reconciled to the fascinating madness of the
    dark.

My mistress' hands are nothing like these,
collecting silken cords for a day when the wet wind plunges
through colossal apertures.

Suddenly I was out of hope. I crawled out on the ledge.
The air there was frank and pure,
not like the frayed December night.

Paperwork

Waste time on these riddles?
Because what would I lecture on then?
The master that comes after, after all,
brushes them aside or burns them.
Am I therefore not very strong?
Will my arch be built, strung along the sand
within sight of olive trees? No,
I am cut of plainer cloth, but it dazzles me
in the evening by the moonlight.

L'heureuse, they called her.
Day after day she gazed at the blue gazing globe
in her sunlit garden, saying nothing.
Noticing this, the old stump said nothing too.
Finally it couldn't stand it any longer:
"Can't you *be* something? You have the required manners
and your dress is a shifting of pea-green shot with sea-foam."

I know I shall one day come to the reason
for manners and intercourse with persons.
Therefore I launch my hat on this peg.
Here, there are two of us. Take two.

Turning and turning in the demented sky,
the sugar-mill gushes forth poems and plainer twists.
It can't account for the roses in our furnace.
A motherly chimp leads us away
to a table overflowing with silverware and crystal,
crystal smudgepots so the old man could see through tears:

He is the one you ought to have invited.

The History of My Life

Once upon a time there were two brothers.
Then there was only one: myself.

I grew up fast, before learning to drive,
even. There was I: a stinking adult.

I thought of developing interests
someone might take an interest in. No soap.

I became very weepy for what had seemed
like the pleasant early years. As I aged

increasingly, I also grew more charitable
with regard to my thoughts and ideas,

thinking them at least as good as the next man's.
Then a great devouring cloud

came and loitered on the horizon, drinking
it up, for what seemed like months or years.

Toy Symphony

> Palms and fiery plants populate the glorious levels of the
> unrecognizable mountains.
> —Valéry, *Alphabet*

Out on the terrace the projector had begun
making a shuttling sound like that of land crabs.
On Thursdays, Miss Marple burped, picking up her knitting
again, it's always Boston Blackie or the Saint—
the one who was a detective
who came from far across the sea
to rescue the likes of you and me
from a horde of ill-favored seducers.

Well, let's get on with it
since we must. Work, it's true
suctions off the joy. Autumn's density moves down
though no one in his right mind would wish for spring—
winter's match is enough. The widening spaces
between the days.

I sip the sap of fools.
Another time I found some pretty rags
in the downtown district. They'd make nice slipcovers,
my wife thought, if they could be cleaned up.
I don't hold with that.
Why not leave everything exposed, out in the cold
till the next great drought of this century?
I say it mills me down,

and everything is hand selected here: the cheeses,
oranges wrapped in pale blue tissue paper

with the oak-leaf pattern, letting their tint through
as it was meant to be, not according to the calculations
of some wounded genius, before he limped off
to the woods.

The stair of autumn is to climb
backward perhaps, into a cab.

Memories of Imperialism

Dewey took Manila
and soon after invented the decimal system
that keeps libraries from collapsing even unto this day.
A lot of mothers immediately started naming their male
    offspring "Dewey,"
which made him queasy. He was already having second
    thoughts about imperialism.
In his dreams he saw library books with milky numbers
on their spines floating in Manila Bay.
Soon even words like "vanilla" or "mantilla" would cause him
    to vomit.
The sight of a manila envelope precipitated him
into his study, where all day, with the blinds drawn,
he would press fingers against temples, muttering "What have
    I done?"
all the while. Then, gradually, he began feeling a bit better.
The world hadn't ended. He'd go for walks in his old
    neighborhood,
marveling at the changes there, or at the lack of them. "If
    one is
to go down in history, it is better to do so for two things
rather than one," he would stammer, none too meaningfully.

One day his wife took him aside
in her boudoir, pulling the black lace mantilla from her head
and across her bare breasts until his head was entangled in it.
"Honey, what am I supposed to say?" "Say nothing, you big
    boob.

Just be glad you got away with it and are famous." "Speaking of
boobs . . ." "Now you're getting the idea. Go file those
   books
on those shelves over there. Come back only when you're
   finished."

To this day schoolchildren wonder about his latter career
as a happy pedant, always nice with children, thoughtful
toward their parents. He wore a gray ceramic suit
walking his dog, a "bouledogue," he would point out.
People would peer at him from behind shutters, watchfully,
hoping no new calamities would break out, or indeed
that nothing more would happen, ever, that history had ended.
Yet it hadn't, as the admiral himself
would have been the first to acknowledge.

Strange Occupations

Once after school, hobbling from place to place,
I remember you liked the dry kind of cookies
with only a little sugar to flavor them.

I remember that you liked Wheatena.
You were the only person I knew who did.
Don't you remember how we used to fish for kelp?
Got to the town with the relaxed, suburban name,
remembering how trees were green there,
greener than a sudden embarrassed lawn in April.
How we would like to live there,
and not in a different life, either. We sweltered
along in our union suits, past signs marked "Answer"
and "Repent," and tried both, and other things.

Then—surprise! Velvet daylight
came along to back us up, providing the courage
that was always ours, had we but
known how to access it downstairs.

We used to crawl to so many events together: a symphony
of hogs in a lilac tree, and other, possibly more splendid,
things until the eyelid withdrew.

Now I can sample your shorts.
So much more is there for us now—
runnels that threaten to drown the indifferent one
who sticks his toe in them.
Much, much more light.

To whose office shall we go tomorrow?
I'd like to hear the new recording of clavier
variations. Oh, help us someone!
Put out the night and the fire, whose backdraft
is even now humming her old song of antipathies.

Full Tilt

Disturbing news emanates from the wind tunnel:
He's gone, who never lacked for champions,
killed by daylight saving time, or a terrible syllabus accident.

The dead leaves, maple or aspen, are a sign of life.
Let's leave things as they are,
drying in the sun, soaking up the sweetness
that's in everything.

This is what taking chances was all about, and look where it's
    led us!
To the root, it seems of human misery.
Misery, get up, get down. Your hair is a mess
and your dress a fright. Yet your curdled armpits
speak to us. Sometimes it's better to have nothing to say
when you are telling about what happened today.
It was so much, after all, that morbid agenda.

Now, why not investigate the way
all this can end up being pretty? Not just the whore

who waits on the corner till the last sliver of taxi is gone,
to be repackaged next night in a department store window
so you can pretend you bought it? I'm up here, Louise,
we're all up here, waiting for you to step up to home plate
and bat us a cool one. Oh, but
I was supposed to be in the station an hour ago.
That's the way it gets illustrated:
the four of you in Cincinnati, waving across the plain
to us, the lemon in hot pursuit, leading to student unrest.

We don't have to worry about that now—
tomorrow or the day after will be just as good.
The fraternity has already waited an eternity. Only coaxing the
    stars
out could produce the fruit you need to have in your stocking
    or shorts.

Then this scene too faded away like a fable.

The File on Thelma Jordan

Coldly, we put away the cabin flatware.
Tomorrow, a transport strike. Damaged vacations will result.
What the fuck, we're already in one and have somehow
got to make it what with the living, you know,
the sport and recreation around. Pious reflexes too.
So now about the apple? You know, what about it?
Vague chintzes all around, her hair caught in the door.

It seemed time when the bus came for Jacques in Vienna
that the other Boston terriers would be having their day too,
but no such luck—the sapphire eyes of one, confused,
were just about it. You could go away, too.

A poseur held up a scroll which, predictably, cascaded to the
    floor.
Something about an annual charity bazaar. We'd forgotten
it again, in the garden, this year. Why must things emerge

before you've finished wisecracking about them. What
does it all mean? In what rut were you born? I've got to
fix the baby's things. I'm on my way to the garret. Don't come.
I assure you everything is under control. It's of no importance.
Stop it. I said it's not that important. What's not important?
What couldn't be under the blue sails dripping
as they develop, develop their theories about us,
haunting the ether with memories of clay? We haven't a stitch
to wear. Rumson's is having a sale. I thought I'd
got out of that one. Oh no? A car is having its way with her,
carrying us down to the beach, against our will, as if by magic.
The chorus of foresters raises their muskets in a silent
gesture of solidarity with the departed. There, I thought
I'd finish this story before making another mistake and now it's
happening. Oh, dear! Grace, fetch some ketchup, will you?
Now, there it's all better. As I was saying . . .

Strangers salute you in the street,
brave marquis of many years. What are thy wishes?
A shore dinner would be nice, perhaps on the boat launch
where we could feel for mussels afterwards. I like that,
reminds me of an encyclopedia I once read in an afternoon.
Oh yes, well, there were always a lot of stories
about how you played and who won. Nobody set much
store by any of them, but now you two men are like bricks
in a chimney, nobody is going to separate you or carry you off
or stand by you much longer, once the office closes.
Did it? It's five o'clock and there are no roses . . .

I thought I'd followed that street to the end
but it was only the end of the beginning, the rest was
    transparent
and needle-pure. "Best have a look at it." The sun goes down
with a plop in these parts, like an egg falling on a counter,
and who is there to count the endless waterfowl, water ouzels,
beavers with otters on their backs? I'll take that chessboard.
I mean I want it back now. But the tanks
rolling in the city hinted at another scenario,
another worst-case one. Listen to the pretty snowflakes.
Oh, I love you so much in such a little time.

It seems a shame we have to go on living. I mean,
we could get more loving into it. I'm not quitting.
I mean, I am but I'm not a quitter.
Whoever said you were? Climb up that cello and try to get
    some rest.
In the morning I've got to see the accountant.

So it goes, in the old country as well as in the new.
Pelicans startle us, then some reason for living gapes
in the wall of a building that once housed a bookstore
and is now for sale. The unlikeliest bidders come and go,
pandering to the lower orders shall I say
and the unguents who made all this possible. Let's give them a
    hand . . .

Hey, you don't think there's any more
over the horizon? I'm not sure I could stand it if there was,
I mean their faces. Oh, they'll all be home for Christmas
sometime, I'm sure. Why don't you take a little trip
to an aching village? You look tired. Are you OK?
It was just my brother calling from Wichita. He says the
    downtown's on fire.
Well if I was you I wouldn't go there.
No, I have no intention of doing so.
Now, about those missing "fish" cards, did your nanny
take it into her head to "hide" them in her workbasket
or did Sheila abscond with them?

I'm not saying the boys isn't responsible.

It was two of them to one of us in one box.
After the team finished cheering the fridge opened by itself,
    violently,
as one thinks of spring tempests tearing into trees,
mindless of viaducts below. People are wearing hound's-tooth
    more.
That's one way you can sense the change
in the average person's deportment. I'm trying to unpack
these worthless drachmas so as to get the twins off to school,
Hey, some of those could turn out to be valuable.

Says who, and besides it's raining in the next street and all
  around town.
Finny creatures lurch by. We must try frying the endive
next time. In the meantime my noggin will sport a red golfing
  cap
in case there's anyone around to see, which at this hour is unlikely,
I admit, but I intend to have the old niblicks at the ready
just in case, and it's sure foul out. Don't jolt that.
It pertains to me. It's a stuffed raven given to my great-
  grandfather by
Edgar Allan Poe himself. Said he was finished with it. It had
  cost him a poem,
though, a great one. Want to hear . . .

Two for the Road

Did you want it plain or frosted? (Plain vanilla or busted?)

I bet you've been writing again. She reached under her skirt. Why don't you let a person see it? Naw, it's no good. Just some chilblains that got lodged in my fingertips. Who said so? I'll tell you if it's any good or not, if you'll stop covering it with your hand.

For Pete's sake—

We had forgotten that it was noon, the hour when the ravens emerge from the door beside the huge clock face and march around it, then back inside to the showers. Oh, where were you going to say let's perform it?

I thought it was evident from my liquor finish steel.

Oh right, you can certainly have your cocktail, it's my shake, my fair shake. Dust-colored hydrangeas fell out of the pitcher onto the patio. Darned if someone doesn't like it this way and always knows it's going to happen like this when it does. But let me read to you from my peaceful new story:

"Then the cinnamon tigers arose and there was peace for maybe a quarter of a century. But you know how things always turn out. The dust bowl slid in through the French doors. Maria? it said. Would you mind just coming over here and standing for a moment. Take my place. It'll only be for a minute. I must go see how the lemmings are doing. And that is how she soiled herself and brought eternal night upon our shy little country."

Heartache

Sometimes a dangerous slice-of-life
like stepping off a board-game
into a frantic lagoon

drags the truth from the bathroom, where it has been hiding.
"Do whatever you like to improve the situation,
and—good luck," it added, like a barber adding an extra plop
    of lather

to a stupefied customer's face. "When they let you out
I'll be waiting for you." It had been that way ever since a girl
    with braids
teased him about getting too short. Yeah, and I'll bet they have

places for people like you too. Trouble is, I don't know of any.
The years whirled quickly by, an upward spiral
toward what ghastly ascendency? He didn't know. He cried.

One November the police chief came calling.
He had secretly been collecting all the bright kids
in the universe, popping them into a big bag

which he lugged home with him. No one was too sure what
    happened
after that. The kids were past caring; they had the run
of the house after all. Was it so much better outside?

Snow lashed the windowpanes as though punishing them
for having the property of being seen through. The little town
grew quieter. No one missed the kids. They had been too
   bright

for that to happen. Night sprang out of the dense cold
like an infuriated ocelot with her cub that someone had been
   trying
to steal, or so it pretended. The frightened townspeople sped
   away.

There was no longer any room on the sidewalk
for anything but "v's" drawn in pink chalk, the way a child
draws a seagull. Down at the tavern the neon glowed a
   comforting

red. "All beer on tap," it said, and
"Booths for Ladies."

The Fortune Cookie Crumbles

You have a kind and gentle nature. Not overly
challenged more than once. The "small things" matter
once you've replaced the dish on the shelf
and moved very convincingly toward the door.
"Just dying for attention," you've been around
the block yourself a few times, paid the bills
and furniture. You were a tulip
in some past life, it says here. You have "two lips,"
as winy and luscious as a Chevy
in your dad's garage.

On a sorry note, your correspondent
notes that you have a tendency to fly off to Europe
at the slightest provocation. Must mean you're getting old,
or "devoid of charm" is maybe what it says.

It is likely that a viable present can be brokered.
Your past is all used up now, anyway.

The lilies love you more than ever
now, it seems. I love you too, but my brow
is furrowed.

I mean, what am I going to tell my shoe?

Onion Skin

In the end it was their tales of warring stampedes
that finished us off. We could not go them one better
and they knew it, and put our head on a stamp.

"Then I should have some pain, too?"

Redeemed Area

Do you know where you live? Probably.
Abner is getting too old to drive but won't admit it.
The other day he got in his car to go buy some cough drops
of a kind they don't make anymore. And the drugstore
has been incorporated into a mall about seven miles away
with only about half the stores rented. There are three
other malls within a four-mile area. All the houses
are owned by the same guy, who's been renting
them out to college students for years, so they are virtually
    uninhabitable.
A smell of vitriol and socks pervades the area
like an open sewer in a souk. Anyway the cough drops
(a new brand) tasted pretty good—like catnip
or an orange slice that has lain on a girl's behind.

That's the electrician calling now—
nobody else would call before 7 A.M. Now we'll have some

electricity in the place. I'll start by plugging in
the Christmas tree lights. They were what made the whole thing
go up in sparks the last time. Next, the light
by the dictionary stand, so I can look some words up.
Then probably the toaster. A nice slice

of toast would really hit the spot now. I'm afraid it's all over
between us, though. Make nice, like you really cared,
I'll change my chemise, and we can dance around the room
like demented dogs, eager for a handout or they don't
know what. Gradually, everything will return to normal, I
promise you that. There'll be things for you to write about
in your diary, a fur coat for me, a lavish shoe tree for that other.

Make that two slices. I can see you only through a vegetal murk
not unlike coral, if it were semi-liquid, or a transparent milkshake.
I have adjusted the lamp,
morning's at seven,
the tarnish has fallen from the metallic embroidery, the walls have fallen,
the country's pulse is racing. Parents are weeping,
the schools have closed.

All the fuss has put me in a good mood,
O great sun.

Variations on "La Folia"

Now another one who said it is gone,
killing all the wonderful suspense, desired or not.
Shut the window. It's chilly in here.
Yes, I know it's only open a crack.

It's "all moon and no stars" again,
and I cast no shadow.

It's not a good thing.
There aren't that many seats.

I remember when Clement Attlee was world premier.
There was more austerity then but less things to get done.
The amniotic valley still holds memories of those
kids who have sway, some blue-violet,
some only an outline. It was what he meant by austerity,
I think. There was a man named Silhouette once,
renowned for his stinginess.

As I think about it the more it gets lighter and brighter.
I had asked for it monogrammed.
A hurricane blasted the triple-mud sundae
into the room where I like to write sometimes in the
    afternoons.
There was no dealing with the gangsters then.
They all had disappeared.

My dog, green pussy, came along with my bowl of grape-nuts.
I let out an unaccustomed howl
yet no hoosegow gaped.
I was wholly on my own.

Hollyhocks strangled the windmill's blades
till it stopped to ask for more, for directions
where it was going, which obviously was nowhere.
Cormorants clove the air. Men had poured oil
on their eggs to prevent them from hatching
so as not to reduce the fish population,
though the fish had never asked for that. Far from
it. They believed in the equality of the species,
that a pesky bird was worth no more and no less than a dumb
    fish.
Man, again, is the interloper here. He takes whatever he
    chooses
from the dish life holds out, then acts surprised
a century or two later when the world has spun out of control,
and wakes up scratching his head, wondering what happened.

We should all be so lucky as to get hit by the meteor
of an idea once in our lives. It would save a lot of
 hand-wringing
and bells tolling in the undersea cathedral,
a noise to drive one mad, past the brink of human decency.
Please don't tell me it all adds up in the end.
I'm sick of that one.

De Senectute

Whatever charms is alien.
Throw it back in the water, makes no difference.
I was amazed at your absence, child,

from the chapel's round window.
You forgot, you see.
And me, sometimes.

There is true worth strapped away in there.
Fifty is young today. So's eighty. Depends
on which side you're looking at it from.

And she leans toward purple colas,
returns with salt on her tunic's hem.
Too crazed to cry. In which she resembles

all of us. I'm not going to the benefit.
I hate charity. But it's the greatest
of the three. Can't help it, I'm an old boa

constrictor. I feel about life much as you do:
as a diary from many years ago. We thought we'd caught
something in March, some kind of flu,

but it lasted even until now,
though no one remembers it. You will,
upon opening your garage door, stumble

on some unpleasant evidence of the neighbor's dog's
recent passage. Is there anything you can do?
No. Later on in spring, when the robins

are nesting, something will splat on your car's windshield
or windscreen. Again, it profits not
to go looking for causes and effects

in a froth of rage whipped up
by someone else. August with its cooling showers
from the hose invites us to take a breather.

Yes, a breather is what we've longed for,
can get no closer to
than the rain barrel, its surface of dust and

fruitflies. Well, back to work
again. It is the one thing that won't be
denied that won't save us. Pensively, the watch crystal's

warning us to be off, ere another hour strikes.
Oh, I love you so much in such a little time
it seems a shame to have to go on living.

Yet another hour protrudes. The imps
have all become children. Well, wish them away.
The pyramid's gravitas

will never manifest itself with them around.
The wolf took up a broom and swept the walk
up to the front door, and seemed to

want to be petted for its efforts.
The hell with that. The empty corral
is on the point of coming into being, a "perfect"

circle, brand new as you please.
Somebody, someone in authority, said it was all a joke,
so we packed up and went home that day.

The Gods of Fairness

The failure to see God is not a problem
God has a problem with. Sure, he could see us
if he had a hankering to do so, but that's
not the point. The point is his concern
for us and for biscuits. For the loaf
of bread that turns in the night sky over Stockholm.

Not there, over *there*. And I yelled them
what I had told them before. The affair is no one's business.
The peeing man seemed not to notice either.
We came up the strand with carbuncles
and chessmen fetched from the wreck. Finally the surplus buzz
did notice, and it was fatal to our project.
We just gave up then and there, some of us dying, others walking
wearily but contentedly away. God had had his little joke,
but who was to say it wasn't ours? Nobody, apparently,
which could be why the subject was never raised
in discussion groups in old houses along the harbor,
some of them practically falling into it.
Yet still they chatter a little ruefully: "I know
your grace's preference." There are times
when I even think I can read his mind,
coated with seed-pearls and diamonds.
There they are, for the taking. Take them away.
Deposit them in whatever suburban bank you choose.
Hurry, before he changes his mind—again.

But all they did was lean on their shovels, dreaming
of spring planting, and the marvelous harvests to come.

Who Knows What Constitutes a Life

Really? Uncle Pedro is coming
with his entire entourage? They want
to take over the whole top floor?

They say they'll be arriving soon? Day
after tomorrow? Not in a century,
I bet. These things are like dreams
of things that are real. And they really exist
beyond the breezeway, where no man has ever been.

How, then, can we be confident
they are solid and peaceful, like chimeras?
The shit list is long
and extends far back into the last century.
If we admit them *now* . . .

I was just standing on the landing
and a rush of air whooshed by me
on its way to the attic. I caught the scent
of Uncle Pedro's discreet *eau de toilette*
(notes of lily-of-the-valley and wild hickory bark)
but to conclude that I am involved in this,
or that any of it is my affair, is, well,
downright dour. I am off on my own again,
will return in an hour
to see if the house has burned down
or the calf given birth to calflets.

Sacred and Profane Dances

If all you want is kittens,
come back later. At dusk. No later.
The kittens will be in by then.

"What if I said I want no kittens,
just a big fat you?" The Motorway City,
Leeds, has more of them, more varieties.
And I said I just couldn't. Mime the dialogue
any faster. They're taking rollcall now.

With all the spontaneity of a sarabande
he wakes up, showers, puts on a tie,

jumps in his Dodge and drives to work.
Here there are other, secret choices.
He cannot look at them. He must needs leave this place,
office, whatever. The beavers look at him endangered
from their saw-palmetto-shrouded photomural.
No matter, he's driving to this special house.

Word gets out. He makes a U-turn
and is soon speeding along a numbered highway
out in the country somewhere. "How did it get so itchy?
So late?" They bind him to the trash
and escort him up the ramp, to the sacrificial slab.
Oh? Well, if that's the way things work out,
more power to 'em. Being is only a way of being.
When in doubt, fast forward, I always say.

Now that it's Christmas and Mother
there must be an explanation for the shadows,
the gaps in the grass of the downs
over there. "Ssh. Don't think."

And I was all for a descent into a churn
in my diving helmet. Funny the way things work out.

I said, it's funny the way things work out.

Here We Go Looby

Where is that tricycle, man?
You know I set much store by it
since there is nothing else in the world right now.

Here is the church and here is the steeple
and the vast hill that recedes under them
down to the squirrel's nest. He has to have one,

you know. She wrote letters and crushed them
under her pillow. Years later they turned up

in the mill race floating quietly, secretively,
near the shore. I'll

get up and get one. No,
you won't. This is strictly the governor's business,
who held hands with Miles Standish, or Priscilla—
a tectonic unrest made less awkward
by the distribution of the braille mail and disposing
of table scraps. Sometimes one gets caught in a pail,
"in pailed." And the doily scissors scallop your tootsies
as though primitive man had lived this way all along,
just waiting for you to show up and be astonished.

In truth sir you are a jaybird.
But just come with us and everything will work out fine,
I'm sure. Oh no you don't, that's the way you got me the last
    time,
you bastard and I let them punish me for it. Gentlemen,
we've a problem here. On the one hand I don't want to appear
    too harsh,
but his lackadaisicalness is truly unconscionable—I—I
just don't have a word for it.

Now I want the flower girls to appear stage left.
The peacocks and our mother will take care of everything else.
I am unperched, dispossessed, and this is the helpful truth of it,
the holy harp I keep harping on.
If they had wanted it another way they would have arranged it

that way. It would be cruel to dwell much longer in their
    collective memory
and I'm ready for a shower. Oh, just one thing—
did that guy ever tell you where my tricycle is, or the light
    switch?
It was all a drawing on canvas, you see. This way no one gets
    hurt,
and a few of us learn something.

Avenue Mozart

Some of these houses are startlingly old.
Other, newer ones seem old too.
Only when a line of trees ends in something
Does it resemble the model of progress glimpsed once
in a bottle as a boy. Our references have all aged a little
as we were looking at them, not noticing.
Now there's something perverse in every yellow leaf,
every cat loafing, even the stick leaning against the door.
I'd like to get out of these clothes . . . "Later."

And a full moon of oxymorons swings up over the ridgepoles
with their chimneys. It's light enough to read by.
But nobody feels like reading now.

Life Is a Dream

A talent for self-realization
will get you only as far as the vacant lot
next to the lumber yard, where they have rollcall.
My name begins with an A,
so is one of the first to be read off.
I am wondering where to stand—could that group of three
or four others be the beginning of the line?

Before I have the chance to find out, a rodent-like
man pushes at my shoulders. "It's *that* way," he hisses.
"Didn't they teach you *anything* at school? That a photograph
of *anything* can be real, or maybe not? The corner of the stove,
a cloud of midges at dusk-time."

I know I'll have a chance to learn more
later on. Waiting is what's called for, meanwhile.
It's true that life can be anything, but certain things
definitely aren't it. This gloved hand,
for instance, that glides
so securely into mine, as though it intends to stay.

Vowels

Instant insufficiency edged eerily over our oasis.
Under us, awed angry Airedales adjusted.
The octet closes with a signing-on in shipyards.
Through naked fingers of the rain
Easter week, and during the winter the valleys
are like yeast. This much I divined, walking,
then turned my back on the mighty fragment of yesterday.

Everything was at peace with everybody. A dark stone
   glistened.

Beverly of Graustark

It's wind, it's sleeting.
It's real adventure. It hasn't happened yet.

It's time to break for lunch—
half a bean sandwich. Yours isn't here yet,
you asked for black bread on bacon.

The perp is becoming abusive,
and I would like a chiller, wind
in my pants, my long taffeta gown,
to take me anywhere from any place
before this insane excursion is finished. Please—
the seamstress is inside down below.

The president of Slavonia is on the wire:
We'll have to go ahead with the order for flatbed trucks
now stretching far into the offended distance.
Stop! Some other way may be found—
That's what you think, sister.

The day extracts, in a loosely confining way,
what these pills signified,
and what they were supposed to absorb before your seconds
   arrived

and now it's too late to include the meeting.
It would only baffle the establishment.

Yes but what I am hearing is from plazas of wailing
tilting back into the bland exposure of it,
the idle secret. It was again a lunch of sandwiches,
but truth will perforate. As sadly as I'm
in your line of vision, Venice is closed,
another browser sidles in
through a snow of ecstatic fleas,
what my alma mater is all about I think I once said.
Photographs of members enjoin us through the back seat
on a spring day once; green grass and toilets
spooled on a little anticipation.

"Nelly"—that's all I needed and we're off again, down foul
    alleys
ending in meticulous squares, and none of us knew the
    outcome yet.
We could see the blue ice-slick clear through the Turkish
    uniform,
and the bowling alleys ended out in the garden as is right
and proper.

Poor Beverly—they never gave her (him?) a chance
to prove herself in the journals of the East End
before being summoned to that rocky principality
from which no bulletins ever issue—only brickbats
and the occasional red herring press release: "Collapsed
felt underdrawers are invading the season, counsels
Léopoldine from Phalsbourg, but don't
dare disguise those shoulder pads yet. Instead, why not
think rotting horseflesh this year? Some beaux even prefer it
to the spritzed violets so common underfoot
these days of walking back to the starting gate
where everything began, inconceivably it seems, in light—"
a fiery bazaar no one needs to talk too much about anymore
till the next in the round of visits happens.

It's incredible though how few latent oblivions have been
   canceled—
we're back on track at least as far as
late returns are concerned. Most of them are in.
A few hotel ghosts wander stiffly, wondering if catarrh
can ever be cathartic, and if there's any afterlife, and if so,
whether it's near as the next room, or the closet even,
which might just be preferable to daytime's sloping agendas,
the roof at night, the rent, and the violet pallor flooding us
   now always.

The Pearl Fishers

And he would say, "You ought to write him and thank him for
   it," and I'd
say, "Yes, I'm going to when I have the time." Of course I had
   intended
to, but the project aged. It was slightly too dry. I'll begin
   again, I'll
thank him. And so I did, in my own way. I forgot him and his
   seven journeys
to success. We became as one—a stilt. A single stilt isn't of
   much use,
and that's how I thanked him—by reminding him from time to
   time,
as the salt ball rolled toward the glacier.

It melted and did not. Wait, you can't get up. There's A.I. sauce

on her slipcover. Informality be damned, he said. Whenever I
   come here I
like to take two lumps instead of three. Unfortunately you can't
   have either,
we're out of everything I said. The sun smiled wanly on the
   Cimmerian landscape,
which stirred. It seemed as if it was at last about to take an
   interest

in rubber goods,
piles of filth,
gossamer undies,
potted hyacinths,
stumps no tree would own up to,
casinos rattling till three in the morning.

I'm sorry, Mrs. Swan-toe,
we meant not to disturb and then this waterfall
rushed over the island, as I'm sure you noticed. By the time it
    had passed
fully, except for the occasional unavoidable runnel,
no one could remember how to count.

It was a Royal Accident.
You can't rely on those,
they always win.

They Don't Just Go Away, Either

In Scandinavia, where snow falls frequently
in winter, then lies around for quite some time,
lucky cousins were living in a time-vault of sorts.
No purchase on the ground floor, but through a funnel-shaped
    drain
one could catch glimpses, every so often, of the peach-colored
firmament. It's so terrific! It's purer than you think,
too, not that that need unduly concern us.

Father sat in his living room
off the main parlor, working at his table. We never knew
exactly what he did. We kids would amuse ourselves
with games like Authors and Old Maid, until Mamma abruptly
withdrew the lamp, and we all sat shivering in the dark for a while.
Soon it was time to go to bed. We groped our way up
non-existent flights of stairs to the attic funnel.
Everything is so peaceful in here I can dream of more kinds
of things at once. But what if the dreams were prophetic?

Stumbling down an alley, screaming, forehead bathed in blood
or ossified like an old tree root that can barely speak, and when
    it can,
says things like: "Do you know your horse is on fire?"

Many winters were passed in this way.
I cannot say I feel any wiser for it.
Instead my brain feels like a face freshly shaved
by the barber. I rub it with satisfaction,
giving him a good tip on the way out.
More fanciful patterns await us further along
in our destiny, I tell him, and he agrees; anything
to be rid of me and on to the next customer.
Outside, in the street, a length of silk unspools beautifully,
rejoicing in its doom.

Father, I can go no farther, the lamp blinds me
and the man behind me keeps whispering things in my ear
I'd prefer not to be able to understand . . .
Yet you must, my child, for the sake of the cousins
and the rabbit who await us in the dooryard.

Conventional Wisdom

Although I have known you for a long time
it seems as though we hardly know each other at all.
It was as a rehearsal for coming to be in time
that leaves are aslant. Take another look
for the cookie hoarded in armpits up till now,
the pointed stare.

When the satchel came undone I was running around
the corner please, sure as a clock's breath
in the allées, digging. Heaven sent this pinprick.
It was another time to be riding around in.
Alright I said I can take care of myself.
Then depth spun its wheels. I was sliding on gravel somewhere.
Take a look around you for your personal belongings

before getting on this bus. Not one but three old ladies came
    along.
The flustered caddy spoke for the local cesspool contractor
    when he said
man the trailer I thought I belonged here but what
the hey, said in wartime the beets were too much spinach.
Now I can unclog you be patient.
A girl in the apse wondered why the cymbals
were drained of vowels in these perplexing times.
Have you ever read Rimbaud's Les Voyelles No I haven't I said.
It's too much like the class room in here. Now if we replaced
    the air
with cobwebs wouldn't they all march in correctly
to the triangle's tune? Sure, the major is bound to be pissed off
but all that counts is our air conditioner. In a jiffy
the dock was rehabbed. The colonel grabbed Mavis and Iris.
It's dumb overhead. I know this but please,
let's resolve our differences in gentlemanly fashion. What'll it
be, swords or soldier beetles. My is there a difference?
Mayhap only in dreams where you bottle it and sell it.

And the can fell off the radiator.
Althea's glazed look came true. It was deep blue in the palaces
of revolt. Something extraordinary was happening
all the time. The due date kept flashing past

the diamond slot in fishnet pumps and a shadow,
the shadow of the lunge on the bridge,
of monsters congealing above the town,
and of a lost slip with my name on it in the cradle of the ages.

And Again, March Is Almost Here

If I were a tree you'd say
I was lost by a highway.
Death overflows the ditches
in which life confined it
and will be that way for some time.

I saw the alchemist drown
in his turquoise at seven
and elsewhere saw the less spiritual side.
God, how it gets me down.

Then furtively a bailiff came
as though to take my measurements
for a new suit. "Here, I don't need this . . .
brine." I was cluttered for the day.

A Mrs. came out of her house
being as I was on the road to say
look for the heather that is father
to the salt hay down the road.

I guess I only confused
my eager willingness to understand
just about anything that was offered.
Alas, it wasn't much.

There were few requests for employment
and those seemed old and pallid
as though faxed by a squid one day last March.
Now, a year has gone by. Not quite

a year though, as I
was going to say.
They offered me Bluebeard.
So much that was unacceptable

that day and all the forests to come.
Though bathed in sleep and aromatic
persons, other stimuli come to the aid
of the hairs of one's neck:

a lad on a bicycle, once,
beautiful as the crescent moon;
enjoyable as a book in a long set of books
who asks you this secret again.

A Descent into the Maelstrom

Hell no, the creators weren't anguished,
just determined to keep you dangling
above the maelstrom a few more seconds.
Then it was as if everything that was going to happen
had. Here, walk into my living room,
put on these sandals, you must be tired.
You've come a long way since the evening news
put a half-nelson on both of us. Here,
drink this sugared tea.

It was as though my childhood were beginning again,
with bills to pay, defective homework to be done,
and the rain getting in, wanting to play, it seemed,
like a cat. A great big cat loves me, I guess.
I was down in the swamp tuning my viola,
and naturally everybody comes by then to ask you for a favor,
or, more rarely, to offer to do one for you.
I guess they think nobody ever goes outdoors.
Me, I can't understand it. It's the dicey ones
can't, the car waxers, the dictators. Then say hello to him
by all means, though I guarantee he won't know what you're
    saying.

Sonatine Mélancolique

Then I walked on a ways.
It became apparent that the journey (for
such it was) was far from unavoidable.
A twig skewered my sock
and I looked up at the oak tree's strapless trunk,
hoping to escape from what seemed a parable,
from which escape is never possible.

I know *that*. But there is still time for surprises
like the time you looked at me and smiled
just as the sledge was dragging us past a bunker
scented with antique urine. In short

it is here that I shall found a colony
and call it God.

The wasps that night had never been loonier,
making reading impossible. I put down my volume
of *Little Dorrit*, and gnats flung themselves even closer
with propositions. "Hey, how'd you like to be rid of that guy
and us too? All you need do is push a button
and a mandarin somewhere on the other side of the world
will stagger for a moment, seeing his life transpire
before him: that first bowl of gruel, graduation day
at mandarin school, and later on doubts and remorse,
a flummoxed present that seeps into the past,
making a whole life seem regrettable." No,
I cannot condone your offer, the thick answer is for later.
Meanwhile I shall try to pacify my eyeballs
with the mist leaking from the ceiling.

That proved sufficient, caressing the knocker,
a goblin's face, that drew us back a hundred years
even as it gazed at us in surprise, speechless
as a field of daisies, to a time when we too were out of step
and the whole sentient world offered to bathe us—
pale bluster, flubbing today again and again.

Stanzas Before Time

Quietly as if it could be
otherwise, the ocean turns
and slinks back into her panties.

Reefs must know something of this,
and all the incurious red fish
that float ditsily in schools,

wondering which school is best.
I'd take you for a drive
in my flivver, Miss Ocean, honest, if I could.

A Postcard from Pontevedra

Just how I feel
I feel today.

The witch stirred the soup
with a magic spoon.

She said, "We can make this happen.
We can never make this happen?"

Excuse me? I was waking up
at the Maison Duck you see.

People are walking past me,
faster and faster—it seems they are running toward something.

Call me old-fashioned. No, don't,
on second thought. We'll call an ambulance

instead. I was waking up with this humming in my ears—
sound of the sea, of a basket of nettles.

It's O.K. to ride, to not go along. I'm not sure
where Pontevedra is. If I was I'd have to ask myself

so many other questions, ones you never
taste in the brightness of your day,

though they answer me
like the risen sea.

A Suit

> The audience was scattered forever, and the story left untold.
> —from the film *Careful*, by Guy Maddin

Maybe it only looks bedraggled.
Let's take it up to the fifth floor and see.

One can look quite far in that light, into the corners
of experiences we never knew we had, that is to say most of
   them.

But the city is new. The new apartment building, now vacant,
circles like a moth that as yet has no idea
it's trapped in a spider's web, that the indelible
will soon come to pass. For a few moments now
we can drink tea and talk of the famous doll collection
in the museum of a small European spa.
Shadows on the tent alert us: Breathing isn't going to be as
   easy
as we'd thought once. Mr. Cheeseworth is always so right
in his calculations, yet when one comes to believe him, where
   is he?

It has been a life of qualification and delay.
Yet we knew we were on the right track; something surged in us,
telling us otherwise, that we'd arrive too early at the airport
or something about the drips on the taxi in the dusk.
We doctored it all up,
and I think I have an explanation for the manna
that falls softly as pollen, and tastes like coconut or some other
unaccountable sherbet. It seems clothes never do fit.

Yes, I could have told you that some time ago.

Crossroads in the Past

That night the wind stirred in the forsythia bushes,
but it was a wrong one, blowing in the wrong direction.
"That's silly. How can there be a wrong direction?
'It bloweth where it listeth,' as you know, just as we do
when we make love or do something else there are no rules for."

I tell you, something went wrong there a while back.
Just don't ask me what it was. Pretend I've dropped the
   subject.

No, now you've got me interested, I want to know
exactly what seems wrong to you, how something could

seem wrong to you. In what way do things get to be wrong?
I'm sitting here dialing my cellphone
with one hand, digging at some obscure pebbles with my
    shovel
with the other. And then something like braids will stand out,

on horsehair cushions. That armchair is really too lugubrious.
We've got to change all the furniture, fumigate the house,
talk our relationship back to its beginnings. Say, you know
that's probably what's wrong—the beginnings concept, I mean.
I aver there are no beginnings, though there were perhaps
    some
sometime. We'd stopped, to look at the poster the movie theater

had placed freestanding on the sidewalk. The lobby cards
drew us in. It was afternoon, we found ourselves
sitting at the end of a row in the balcony; the theater was
    unexpectedly
crowded. That was the day we first realized we didn't fully
know our names, yours or mine, and we left quietly
amid the gray snow falling. Twilight had already set in.

The Water Inspector

Scramble the "Believer" buttons. Silence the chickens. We have more important things, like intelligence. We say so many cruel things in a lifetime, and yet. In a whorehouse, young, I obfuscated. Destiny was this and that, no it was *about* this and that. Do you see what I'm saying? Nobody needs the whole truth.

Even so we exact repetition. The beat goes on. Terribly surprised about the report, about your father's death, but these things happen. Often the dead are found next day, alive but shaken, wondering what it was that happened to them, trembling beneath a cellar door. And we too wonder what happens when the sky as we know it cracks in two. Beetle voices serenade us. The earth and its fountains can't do enough for us, yet we remember, shaken too, like in the old days.

We were reading and there came a knock at the door. The water inspector, we thought, and of course no one was there. Stung, and stung again. So we proceed, always on course, always begging the stars to tell us what happened, whether we were clean really, were we on course. Always the silence says yes, you can go home now, round up your playmates, head for the nearest wooded area if you think that will help.

I was once surprised but lay and brooded, my life at my back now, my discourse like weeds far out on a lake. It must have come to me, it always does, part of my profound business.

I think in the think tank, always elegant in my thinking, far away. Far from what I consider. Once it was all grace in the lifting. Awkward, yes, and not a little disconcerting.

Cinéma Vérité

Be kind to your web-footed friends, I murmur to myself half anxiously, hurrying to the movies. After all, a duck *may* be somebody's uncle. Or niece. I am lost. I ask directions of a horse-faced policeman who gives no satisfying reply. Or is it? "Somewhere up there . . . You'll be sure to find it," he offers. I'd like to wipe the smug expression off his cheeks. Or is it a kindly and beatific smile? I continue along what I think is my way and come to a grassy riviera, a few rusted hotels browsing among smug new ones. A large red and yellow plastic sign says, "Cinema."

Those rocks have a basalt look about them. I was here before once. I can tell by the way the breeze scurries by, patting my cheek as it does so. O solemn breeze! You are the one thing I wanted to have happen to me, the only thing that matters in this concrete canyon of years, so why can't I get close to you?

Already you have made off with the chickens I was taking to the cinema, planning to have them for dinner later. Now I shall go hungry, for you and for them, telling my adventures to anyone who will listen, outside on the slippery alabaster stairs. Or in the roomful of people?

The Old House in the Country

The walls are whitish. Is it cold enough in here? No,
it's the statuary I came to see. And the gizzards, you wanted the gizzards
too? No, it was buzzards
I'd mentioned in my letter of introduction, which you seem to have lost,
but I was reminded too of ancient blizzards
that used to infest these parts. Ah, but gizzards
breed sapience, there can be no other way.
Allow me to pass in front of you
while I keep you waiting in the draft that is colder
than the room it besmirches.

Now we can see eye to eye, and it is a good thing.
I would not have thought it easy to set off the smoke alarms
had we been closer together.

"*Now* is the time for escape, you fool."

Don't you see it another way
back in the ridges that bore you, that nature knitted for you?
I don't know, but something keeps getting in the way
of our orderly patrolling of these rooms.
I suppose it's that I want to go back, really . . .

And so you shall, on the 7:19. Meanwhile examine this bronze.
I'll get Biddy to set out the tea-things
and that will save us some time.

Autumn Basement

I lost my notes, or they were useless. Luckily
I had scribbled down this number on the baggage claim.
The countess remarked, and with reason, that they
only hold you up if you appear to have been dipped
in aspic. Alas, such was my case. Two hedgerows

    further and I'd have made it. Now a rag chairperson gives me
        the runaround,
thinks we met once on a breakwater—
I say, a glass of tea would clash with the silence
of the conundrums, keeping your clatter from me,
safe from me, that is. Would you—er—mind?

So each gets immobilized with a diamond stickpin
under the barrel vault that was invented at just about that
        time—
notice its groin—and there'll be capers with rabbit for supper
again. I don't know how much longer I can stand August,
though September was always his favorite month, and here
it comes with a packet of unscented breeze.
Yet it always seems that salt should be savory,
the embers more at ease. The moving picture lights, and
        having lit
perfects a new way out of the shimmering maze. Pity we can't
lingo here forever, but no one lives forever,
or so I've been told.

Hang-Up Call

Preposterous. That was the word she used,
one much admired for its overtones of thrift and conviction.
I let her go where she wanted with it.
After all, *I* wasn't there to hear it,
looking somewhat dazed amid the regatta
and its ships—or are they one and the same?
Every restful person pauses here

to ask me a question. I have a few ideas
but they wouldn't interest you by a country mile,
not by a million of 'em. Some day I'll have to release my antidote
for disappearing ink (hint: it contains mummy)
and a few other of the brilliant ideas
I've managed to put aside in this old life of mine,
but until that day comes I see no reason to get excited—
hey, wait, *you* were the one who was asking *me*!
That's antenna-dust sparkling on the shoulder
of your silk patchwork bolero. I wasn't even going
to be part of this, remember? I never signed on.
All I remember is press gangs working the bars in Bristol
and waking up on a heap of moldy straw
with a lump the size of a duck's egg on my cranium
and a taste of iodine in my mouth.

But it wasn't me we were going to discuss, remember?
As far as I'm concerned there have been no arguments;
ergo, I have never lost or won any.
Now give me my pants and money and let me go
back and join the others. They're crying, you know.

Lost Profile

I had a voice once,
braid falling over the front
of my forehead-house and down the sides.
No need for cream separators here
someone said. My guide took it as a compliment.
Anyway, we got here. Somehow. Now the question

is losing relevance since water is everywhere,
like a transparent mine. I lost my voice a long time ago.
Voices of children ripple endlessly,
endorsing new products. The lizard-god explodes.

The lady on the next bar-stool
but one didn't seem to understand

you when you spoke of "old dark house" movies—
she thought there must be an old dark house somewhere
and you wanted to take her there.
Still, my arrival flabbergasted her,
since it suggested you had no such thing in mind,
at least for the present.

And today I am a mad Chinese monk
chasing after his temple. Which way did it go?
Around that corner of bushes? Or was there ever
a temple? It seemed more and more likely
that it was a figment of your imagination, a figment
perhaps like many another, only a little more underripe.
Undeterred, I chase it in the madness of the gathering dusk
that crashes into ponds, trees, scared bridges.
It had to have been back here somewhere—

As if the air were pure lightning
and the earth, its consort, benevolent thunder,
I can stand and finally breathe.

Light shrinks from the edges of my fingernails
and armpits. This is a page that got bound in the diary
by mistake. It seems we were so happy once, just for a minute.
Then the sky got clouded, no one was happy or unhappy
forever, and the dream of the oppressor had come true.

How Dangerous

Like a summer kangaroo, each of us is a part
of the sun in its tumbling commotion. Like us
it made no move to right things, basking where the spent
    stream
trickled into the painted grotto.

Yes, and the snow-covered steppe, part of the same opera,
stretched into dimness, awaiting the tenor's aria
of hopelessness. Yet no shadow fell across any of it.

It might have been real. Perhaps it was. Stranger tales
have been spun by travelers in unreassuring inns
while the last embers collapse one into the other, waking
no riposte. "It was at a garrison in central Tadzhikistan."
And then sort of get used to it, and then not be there.

Each noted with pleasure that the other had aged,
realizing as well that new scenery would have to be sent for
and transported thousands of miles over narrow-gauge
    railroads—

a fountain in a park, a comforting school interior,
a happy hospital—and that, yes, it would be worth waiting for.

Humble Pie

Various flavors recite us.
Meanwhile the inevitable Caspar David Friedrich painting
of a ship pointing somehow upward has slipped in like fog,
surrounding us with vowels of regret
for the things we did not do
rising like a great shout above the barrel.

I was going to say I kissed you once
when you were asleep, and that you took no notice.

Since that day I have been as a traveler
who scurries to and fro among nettles, never sure
of where he wants to end up, a Wandering Jew
with attitude.

All this time the sun had its eye on us
as it was going down. Finally, when it hit the horizon,
it had something to say. Something like pick up your two
    weeks' salary
on your way out
and don't ever let me catch you on *this* planet again.

Fine, but on what token shore
are we to be misted? We all have to end up somewhere
    together.
Might as well be in last week's parish newsletter
or in the elbows of a nubian concubine.
I mean, we *are* right, somehow right, which is the same
thing only more so. Sticks and tokens
are my hymn to the sun that has gone,
never to return, it seems,
though.

More Hocketing

The fear was that they would not come.
The sea is getting rougher.
There is a different language singing from the wall.
No singing from the wall.

The fear was that they would come.
Here, have one of these.
Have this one. No, have this one.
To have followed an adage
almost from the beginning of life, through
suburban pleats and undergrowth shrugged
off like underwear on a dinner plate.

Then to emerge fast
into where it's taken you:

no more figs, pretzels. Breakfast's
run out of steam.

And the last car has left.
Let those who never denatured another's remark
swim in wit now. Let the curtains fall
where they may. They are only in distress today.

We have further inversions, like father
and his children sewed up for a day.
Like the feathers you enjoy, the mail
you enjoy receiving.

You have successfully undermined the mountain that threatens
    us.
Now, panthers prowl the streets.

I took a streetcar that turned into a bus toward the end.
God rewarded me with chirping yellow fuzzballs.

I intended a sonnet that turned out a letter
when Rose crossed the road with her nose
and her father is doing better.

I always like it when somebody explodes out of a bush
to congratulate me on my recent success
for which I'm only partly responsible:
The siblings helped, they prevented it from melting
so high among the Alps you'd have thought it stayed frozen
always. Apparently not. Now we might have a riot
if everybody would calm down for a second.

A shadow-person conducted me along a road
to a little house where I was fed and absconded
with the clock on the wall. I told them I was mortal
and they seemed to let me go. Yet no one heard me.
I was as dust one takes a glove to,
a white one, then tosses in disgust, leaving it lie
in all the trickling creases you absorbed
in childhood, loving it. Two doors went away.

We were alone at last, as they say.
These winters can button you up.
They say Canada geese mate for life, or
till one of them dies, whichever is shorter.

Amnesia Goes to the Ball

In the avuncular waiting rooms they begin handing out the handouts. For some reason my name isn't on the list. But I receive my handout anyway—somebody obviously recognized me and knew I should get one. I open it without much enthusiasm. When was it I last received a manual for regular sex? There isn't much distinction in it, nor does it totally lack distinction. I rearrange my orange suit. Modular sex was what it actually says. This starts me off on a new train of ideas, complete with gambling and smoking lounges. I am not to capitalize on this moment. It is already particularized.

So always going down into new things. It's as though the clouds somehow don't matter—yet look at them! Was anything so enormously real ever explained away before? And who is history anyway? Does it have a bum?

I have to finish this or pretend it isn't written. The Sheriff of Heck is coming over and you know what that means. Ocarina blasts building up the fake festive restiveness, yet you and I know what a gardenia is. You even owned one once. After the boring compliments there will be time enough to say what is to be said. Then I'll go home, feeling better if not exactly okay, and probably lie at your side. We'll phone the neighbors and have them in.

Railroaded

Job on the hills . . .
Is that wrong too?
To tell the truth I hardly heard her

what with the wind whistling through the pinecone.
Tell us more about your experience.
That's what really interests our readers.
You know, times when you were down and out

and depressed, like everybody.
When you got up from the table hungry
and didn't eat for a week after that.

Or places with names to which you've fastened a special
    resonance:
Florence, Florida. Women (and I'm sure there were many)
with whom you spent the night in silken sheets,

or guys (the ones with dicks), I'll wager
there were a few of those too.
Now add salt to the cauldron
of lies and wishes—oversalt,

in fact, or the end result will be downright bland.
I can picture this happening in a kitchen
below some stairs . . .

Darn, I can't help it if there was no room
for my girlfriend's shoes, her vast collection
of pocketbooks with scotties on them.
There never were enough closets,

you see, to go around. We kept things spread out
all over the house. If someone wanted something
he knew where to look for it
and it would probably be there
just as in our time the moon is probably there
where you last looked for it, in one of its phases.

The sun was glorious too
and the marigolds.
Hand me my pickaxe. I think I just overstayed my welcome.
An alarm just went off, some place deep inside.
The wallpaper of my bedroom has been destroyed.
No more angelfish for a while, at least. Too bad.

Honored Guest

Accept these nice things we have no use for:
polished twilight, mix of clouds and sun,
minnows in a stream. There may come a time
we'll need them. They're yours forever,
or another dream leaves you thirsty,
waking. You can't see the table
or the bread. How about a clean, unopened letter
and the smell of toast?

School is closed today—it's thundering.
The calendar has backed up or been reversed
so the days have no least common denominator.
Anyway, it was fun, trying to figure out
who you were, what it was that led you to us.
Was it the smell of camphor? Or an ad
in an out-of-state newspaper, seeking news
of someone who disappeared long ago?
He was in uniform, and leaned against a car,
smiling at a girl who seemed to shade her eyes from him.
Can it be? Candace, was it you? There's no way
she'll look our way again.

What can I tell you? Everything's been locked up
for the night, I couldn't get it for you
if I wanted to. But there must be some way—
it's drizzling, the lamps along the path are weeping,
wanting to show you this tremendous thing,
boxed in forever, always getting closer.

Our Leader Is Dreaming

Up there our leader is dreaming again.
Down here, timid streets unfold their agendas;
propose, gingerly, a walk out into the night
to view the night sky. What else
is there, you might say, and you'd be right.

Still, someone must be calling the shots. I can hear them
from afar, tapping out some name
in Morse code, making pigeons blink.

Today is still open. I think I'll take some time off,
try to smash this losing streak, until—

It's our founder. He wants to know why you didn't disconnect
his spelling. I said you were off shooting mugwumps
as each emerged, tentatively, from the booby hatch
and hustled back in. Right, but he says you've
let your tennis game go to hell, and he still can't spell
the words the sky proposes to him. Your shelter
isn't taking calls, he says. Instead a curious epiphany
pilots us back to the shoals where a lone telephone booth was
    last sighted
amid shark-infested eddies. Sparrows are OK,
though, no one wants to kill or eat them. Same goes for carrot
    tops.
Tell him we've a few gross of those left, too. As for
    ammunition,
you can't have fuel *and* ammunition. You can have soup, or
    shoes.

So it was that I departed the caldera, leaving my oboe behind
as security. Its sweet voice haunts me still.
I think I brought you the bloom this time,
will let you know after the last guests have gone. The clouds
    vanished,
and my headache miraculously thinned,
as on the milk train to Thuringia Falls. To think we could have
once trusted each other, but it's all the same to me. I love me,
and you anyhow.

   So the great brazen hump saw us, gazed out over the
       landscape.

Last Legs

My nephew—you remember him—
tongue along a dusty fence.
And I the day's coordinates.
That's what an impression I am.

He was slow to back into the sea,
which ran to meet him, pushing him
on to dry land. Dry land was his place,
after all. He lives there to this day,
with all the hammocks, gramophones,
double old-fashioned glasses, macaques
and expired magazine subscriptions that constitute
a life for some. His framed diploma
from some Methodist medical school,
from which his name is mysteriously absent.
The gold seals are impressive.

By land or sea or foam
I'll get there someday, though—
a particular slice of the past
whose perfume intoxicates, imbibes me
and nobody notices. The sled I was going to take
only it wouldn't fit in my footlocker.
Besides, the tramp steamer was heading for Bahia
or some such.

Lemurs and Pharisees

And of course one does run on too long,
but whose fault is it? At five dollars
a blip, who's counting? One could, I suppose,
relax one's discourse, not enough
to frighten it, but to have something cold
in the hand, to cool the palm; the words might
then unspool in a different mode, shadow
of an intention behind the screen

before the lights go up and the generals
sidle on for another confab. "It was *you*
who got us involved in this Dreyfus business." "Liar!"
Let's take a commercial break here,
my head is cobwebby from all the facts
that got stuffed into it this afternoon.

In no way am I the island I was yesterday.
Children and small pets rejoice around my ankles;
yellow ribbons come down from the tree trunks.
This is *my* day! Anybody doesn't realize it
is a goddam chameleon or a yes man! Yes, sir,
we'd noticed your singular pallor, singular
even for you. Ambulances have been summoned,
are rumbling across the delta at this moment,
I'd wager. Meanwhile, if there's anything we can do
to make you comfortable for two or three minutes . . .

The heath is ablaze again. Our longest hose
won't come to within four miles of it.
Don't you realize what this means for us,
for our families, our ancestors? The page,
summoned, duly arrived with the wilted asters
someone had mistakenly ordered. It's a variation
on our habitual not-being-able-to-keep-a-straight-face
    withdrawal,
turning our back on the smoke and blood-red fumes
we already knew were there, plunging out of hedgerows
so dense not even a titmouse could get through.
Never were we to be invited back again, I mean
no one asked me back again. The others sinned too, each
in her different way, and I have the photographs to prove it,
faded to the ultima thule of legibility.
Next time, you write this.

The Underwriters

Sir Joshua Lipton drank this tea
and liked it well enough to start selling it
to a few buddies, from the deck of his yacht.

It spread around the world, became a global
kind of thing. Today everybody knows its story,
and we must be careful not to offend our sponsors,
to humor their slightest whims, no matter how insane
they may seem to us at the time. Like the time one of them
wanted all the infants in the burg aged five or under
to be brought before him, wearing rose-colored sashes,
in order that he might read the Book of Job to them all day.
There were, as you may imagine, many tears shed,
flowing and flopping about, but in the end the old geezer
(the sponsor, not Job) was satisfied, and sank into a sleep more
    delicate
than any the world had ever known. You see what it's like here—
it's a madhouse, Sir, and I am planning to flee the first time
an occasion presents himself, say as a bag of laundry,
or the cargo of a muffin truck. Meanwhile, the "sands"
of time, as they call them, are slipping by with scarcely a
    whisper
except for the most lynx-eyed among us. We'll make do,

another day, shopping and such, bringing the meat home at night
all roseate and gleaming, ready for the frying pan.
Our names will be read off a rollcall we won't hear—
how could we? We're not even born yet—the stars will perform
    their dance
privately, for us, and the pictures in the great black book
that opens at night will enchant us with their yellow harmonies.
We'll manage to get back, someday, to the tie siding where the
    idea
of all this began, frustrated and a little hungry, but eager
to hear each other's tales of what went on in the interim
of our long lives, what the tea leaves said
and whether it turned out that way. I'll brush your bangs
a little, you'll lean against my hip for comfort.

Pale Siblings

Cheerio. Nothing on the shore
today. Far out to sea, some eczema
mimicking sunlight and shadow, with but temporary success.

Was it for wandering that I have been punished?
Or was it another plot of the siblings,
always anxious to torment, to twist my hair
into witches' brooms, with no inherent power?

Remember they love you like powder
in the air, and it wouldn't take them long at all.
Twenty-five years ago it was different. Please
be patient. Your term too will arrive.

See, he's a very good friend for you, you know that.
You just don't want to sit in a pile of ashes all day long,
licking the milk from your chin. Do you? Then get up
off your ass, stride into the melting twilight,
see the sights of the city. More grass
there than you'd expected, you can bet.

So I wandered fleecy as a cloud and one day an old shepherd crossed my path, looking very wise with his crook. How much use do you get out of that thing, I asked him. Depends, he replied. Sometimes one of 'em doesn't go astray for months on end. Other times I've got my hands full with them running around in all directions, laughing at me. *At me!* Well, I never would have taken on this job, this added responsibility, rather, if being thanked was all I'd had on my mind. Yes, I said, but how do you avoid it when someone's really grateful, and graceful, and you're fading away like you're doing now, your rainbow cap a cigar-store Indian's wooden feather headdress, and all your daughters frantic with glee or misapprehension as you slide by, close to them though they can't see you? Oh, I've learned to cope shall we say, and leave it at that. Yes, I said, by all means, let's.

Nobody Is Going Anywhere

I don't really understand why you object
to any of this. Personally I am above suspicion.
I live in a crawlup where the mice are rotted,
where midnight tunes absolve the bricklayers
and the ceiling abounds in God's sense.

Something more three-dimensional must be breathed
into action. But go slow, the falling threads
speak to life only as through a haze of difficulty.
The porch is loaded, a question-mark
swings like an earring at the base of your cheek:
stubborn, anxious plain. Air and ice,
those unrelenting fatheads, seem always to be saying,
"This is where we will be living from now on."

In the courtyard a plane tree glistens.

The ship is already far from here, like a ghost ship.
The core of the sermon is always distance, landscape
waiting to be considered, maybe loved a little
eventually. And I do, I do.

Poem on Several Occasions

In truth there is room for disquiet
in the wake of the admonitory hiss that accompanies
me wherever I go, to the dentist and back
or sometimes a squeak of approval
will eavesdrop on what I just said,
or even a tiny quiver of applause
will blur in the middle distance, causing
even more distant dogs to bark.

I like to watch the stars giggle and nibble
my hand as I hold it out in a trusting gesture,
like Goethe indicating some Italian hills his companions
might otherwise have overlooked. "I tell you,

it's all in the seasons, or the seasoning, Wolfgang—
otherwise all your inventions might as well have
washed up on a distant strand." That's right,
blame *me* for the ethics issue. Meanwhile can't you
see that children, young adolescents really, are waking
under apple trees, picking up their bookbags listlessly
and traipsing down the road that presumably leads to school?
There they'll read about what we—you and I—have said
to each other on important occasions.

No one will be any wiser. Twenty scarlet nuns
came in and led them off in the direction
of the forest, whence issues a medley of big-band
tunes by forgotten composers from the turn of the century.
Now another century is turning. Will it be pretty or depressed?
What have you to say for that jacket you're wearing, those
    baggy
pants the color of scarlet elm-leaves?

It will turn out to be a popular color in the new century.
They will call it "white."

Slumberer

        Bug-eyed at the possibilities
she slumbers.
I mean there were more of us on anthrax
than not.

        Out of the coal bin
lumbers
our governor. He hasn't been getting too much sleep of late.
Something puzzles him. I know—it's the seepage
of ink in the dairy trough. It bothers him, I now know.

Our way,
that way and in.

Besides, it's elsewhere.
Adventurous.
Wind your way to
the floor.

Noggins were getting a workout,
and all we wanted was the way to the zoo.
We wanted to free the flamingos
but they took off and flew right over our heads,
almost grazing them.
I thought I was going to get knocked down.
Then a kind zoo attendant came over. "It's natural,"
he explained, "at your age (cough, cough), to want to do
    something
for these pests, or pets, but it's really better to do nothing
for them or anybody. See, they're used to a certain profundity
and get all riled when it's disturbed
even by a well-intentioned impulse such as yours, *especially*
if it's well intentioned. Such, I fear,
is the essence of the tragi-comic. But who could live without
    it?"

You may well ask, you
who have never done a lick of work save clang metal gates in
    people's pusses.
Point taken, though. We live in an old soup of the tragi-comic.
Werewolves circle us, wishing they were us.
We, on the other hand, wish only that we were somewhere else.
Now are you going to let us into the cage, or what?

Swiftly it was done. A swarm of passenger pigeons whooshed
    past,
some of them dropping like mayflies, for they were after all
    extinct,
only some of them hadn't heard about it yet. Other rarae aves
were nowhere to be seen, though the label on the cage
indicated otherwise. But it was old and rusted,
like the cage itself. Hey, does anybody take care of this place?
It's like a ghost-zoo.

Aye, and so it is, my son.
You've only just noticed? Well, we come up with some pretty
extraordinary things down this way—smouldering peat-bog
    golf courses
with skeleton golfers, hoping for that hole in one
that comes all too regularly.

We have academies for the undistinguished
with long waiting lists, and subscriptions to the opera,
only you wouldn't want to hear any of 'em, not if I was you.
Our pre-schoolers are famished, and the grade school is full of
    microbes.
I could carry you on my back,
I suppose, across the smouldering turf to the nineteenth hole
where we could wet whistles with some sake and dim sum,
only I wouldn't advise you to stay around much after sunset.
Oh, not that anything funny goes on. Nothing ever does,
in fact. It's just a wide, loose kind of feeling
that refocuses you on yourself like a truant lens
in some aged Kodak, and you see all you can or ever wanted to
    be,
laid out on the gravel littoral, drying in the sun,
as if there wasn't enough to stink up the place as it is.

Well, I'll be paying my respects to your missus,
who, no offense, knows me better than she may have let on.
But who cares? Life is a carnival,
I think. Besides, it's elsewhere.

Night started to shrivel as he departed.
We were wondering what on earth we were doing here, and how
to extricate ourselves, should we ever really want to.

Pot Luck

You always leave me where we left off.
You bring me every little thing,
which is probably a mistake.

You shaved my canary once.
I am anxious to be out by the speedway.
At least, almost nothing happens there.
I was drugged by a cat once
on the edge of Lake Lucerne. Woke
feeling like a businessman without portfolio.
Wait, here goes a new one. He'll examine the fork
to see if it's rooted. Well, it is. In danger.
In the past, which is much the same thing.

So we dance the bolero in times like these.
I believe I am slimmer than my last bathing suit.
Tommy sat on the step, looking so cute. It was
run for your lives, now or never. Now
I don't feel so much better. I had dropped off the letter
at the office, thinking it would be quicker.
Perhaps the editor never got it. I enjoy playing
the glass harmonica, am slender and look half my age.
Catcher in the Rye is my all-time favorite book.

And how about you? Do you, too, come out here
with your family on Saturday afternoons, hoping
for a little rest and relaxation, far
from the city and its desks? Here they have daffodils.
Look, there is one over there by the city.
They have a name for it. "Detroit."

And all the time I thought I was being a pest
someone was desperately in love with me.
The person sickened and apparently died
in a hospital far away. Now I have no one,
no friends to gripe with or call coaxing names to.
I was definitely born at the wrong time
or in the wrong city. Pot-luck dinners were shared.
I thought I had gone to hell. Too bad I woke up in time.

Short-Term Memory

A few things came to observe me:
a terrible explosion,
flowers, dustiness in the boroughs,
planners plagued by increasingly goofy proposals.

I could have pretended not to be in.
Instead I came to the door in shirtsleeves,
extending a hand to the vexed guests. "What about those
   Orioles,
this terribly warm weather we've been having?" Truthfully,
I was suffering from the heat and didn't know it.
It was enough just then to perceive life as a sandbar,
or a mirage of one, that the tide is frantically
trying to erase so as to cover its tracks.

Broken discoveries invaded my short-term memory,
but not so you'd notice. Continuing the polite
palaver I asked after the health of this one and that one,
how little Lois was doing in school, what Howie was up to
in his treehouse. It was as though no one cared.
Or had seen me. They shuffled aimlessly away
to come alive later no doubt in some sex sequence,
while here leaves are browning before the end of summer
and the groundskeeper waits.

What about your immortal soul?
I may have lost it, just this once, but other chapters
will arrive, bright as a child's watercolor,
and you'd want to be around me.

Vendanges

A tall building in the fifteenth arrondissement faded away slowly and then completely vanished. Toward November the weather grew very bitter. No one knew why or even noticed. I forgot to tell you your hat looked perky.

A new way of falling asleep has been discovered. Senior citizens snoop around to impose that sleep. You awake feeling refreshed but something has changed. Perhaps it's the children singing too much. Sophie shouldn't have taken them to the concert. I pleaded with her at the time, to no avail. Also, they have the run of the yard. Someone else might want to use it, or have it be empty. All the chairs were sat on in one night.

And I was pale and restless. The actors walked with me to the cabins. I knew that someone was about to lose or destroy my life's work, or invention. Yet something urged calm on me.

There is an occasional friend left, yes. Married men, hand to mouth. I went down to the exhibition. We came back and listened to some records. Strange, I hadn't noticed the lava pouring. But it's there, she said, every night of the year, like a river. I guess I notice things less now than I used to,

when I was young.

And the arbitrariness of so much of it, like sheep's wool from a carding comb. You can't afford to be vigilant, she said. You must stay this way, always, open and vulnerable. Like a body cavity. Then if you are noticed it will be too late to file the architectural pants. We must, as you say, keep in touch. Not to be noticed. If it was for this I was born, I murmured under my breath. What have I been doing around here, all this month? Waiting for the repairman, I suppose.

Where were you when the last droplets dribbled? Fastening my garter belt to my panty hose. The whole thing was over in less time than you could say Jack Robinson and we were back at base camp, one little thing after another gone wrong, yet on the whole life is spiritual. Still, it is time to pull up stakes. Probably we'll meet a hooded stranger on the path who will point out a direction for us to take, and that will be okay too, interesting even if it's boring.

I remember the world of cherry blossoms looking up at the sun and wondering, what have I done to deserve this or anything else?

Small City

Small city where I lived for some years in total darkness,
whose pale terminology took over
my varied instincts for right and wrong.
Sometimes in the long evenings one would stop talking,
then, if the topic was, say, shoes
the others would mouth their assent. I cannot go in or out
of doors to this day without recalling your vocabulary
of dirty words that no longer count. I mean they are clean
    now.
The working dead pitch in at seven.

A new table had taken your hands.
You should move into it, dining space,
letting the wine of your spit wander over and muzzle
the hollow square of guards out in the square.
One was always missing, or so it seemed,
but they had ingenious ways of disguising it,
like a pretty girl in a shawl was sent to the doctor's
to reclaim some suds, and nobody noticed her by the
time we'd realized she was gone. The antlers over the vitrine
however grew clammy and trembled—
no doubt at the thought of some sport
infinitely postponed, or curtailed.
Yet we followed where her eyes led dancing, wild topic.
Find hordes! Or else it was all over in the suburbs
whose furious light beat like an ornery orrery.
The band marched in and played the doctor symphony
while we were talking amongst ourselves. What to do next?
There was bread in the breadbox
but all the shoe stores were closed.

We like our pixillated selves
in that tertiary period, yet always
a vague dissatisfaction gnawed at our tripes.
There was mewing between the thunderclaps.
We were sure we wouldn't get out alive,
yet we always did, somehow. Someone must have told on us,
    though,

for we were made to stand in the basement
as the hours oozed through the window grill.
We knew we could catch up
someday when foam would caress the weir
and black-eyed susans stumbled.

It is not a happy place to be
until after the rain has ended.

Vintage Masquerade

That article I'd meant to read—
you saw it first, a while ago, in some magazine,
perused it and forgot its major tenets.
Only the ghost of its prose rhythms served you,
like water at the base of a log
some minnow undermines.

So they never came for us in the suburbs
of what city we were living in at that time.
We lived undisturbed, in the manner of the great dead writers:
metallic coffee in the morning, then work until almost noon
with a couple of poached eggs on rye toast then, then more
of the same till afternoon shadows lengthened, and it was time
to go for a long walk and play ambush. Stealthily we'd return,
sampling the largesse of unknown ancestors,
admiring the way those rocks look on business trips,
blush that suffuses the whole earth. Tell me,
can you remember any of this? I, who put it all down,
I cannot, and so let the living choose my books
at the rental library, evening's salad from the greengrocer's.

If there is more to remember, I gift you with it
because of the eternal person you were sometimes, and the
    loveliness
of your being, shaken clear of you like duck feathers.

To Good People Who Should Be Going Somewhere Else

Apricots: "Oh, there won't be any again this year."
—Flaubert, *Dictionary of Received Ideas*

Many couldn't stop being in love with you,
and that in a decade. In the pileup every noble
impulse is disgraced, every overture rebuffed,
no matter how insincere. A wall of plums towers
over the effort at tilling. Usually they paint it up
so you can see it in the haze. Not today.

A freckled girl misunderstands me and laughs,
as though I were part of her explanation.
"You see, the boys drive right through you.
And I thought *I* was invisible." Hon, it's your hat,
not your fault, that evening headlines tilt at.
Everywhere is a great fuss, though there were parishes
of tranquillity only last week. They decided to change things
just because things ought to change, or else because they do,
    anyway.
Peace in the distance is merely a metallic whine,
the fruit concurs. And now very seldom.

Another Aardvark

I cannot recommend your curls too highly—
that is, I cannot recommend them. Sometimes
I wish I could, whenas in silks
you go, past the cat's dish
and on into the living room. I wish
there was some way to add a story-line, or patter,
melody, whatever you want to call it,
but there just isn't. Something greater
than us approaches, calls down to us:
Has he left the building? Is the theater empty,
really empty, its rows of red velvet seats
devoid of a single guest, or ghost?

There was a party last night but I didn't go,
couldn't stand the ruckus, the questions
people put to you: How do you like living
in your new house? Fine. I moved there twenty-five
years ago, but it all still seems new to me,
the sink especially. Then you spend a lot of time
in the bathroom? No, it was my books I was talking about,
my treasured library. I don't see how anyone can read
too many books, do you? Am I delusional? Is it a forest
that's approaching, with its format of shadows,
wind among its grasses? And all this time
I thought you were asleep. I took a long walk.
Ended up next door. Ed had been hitting the sneaky pete
again. And I have things to do, walks to shovel,
before the next train, and the grain
that is sure to follow in its wake.

Has to Be Somewhere

Having escaped the first box,
I wandered into a fenced-off arena
from which the distance, peach-blue, could be ascertained:

convenient for my adventures
at this period of my life. Yet I wriggled farther into an
    indeterminate space
that was actually a mood, or many moods, one overlaying
    another
like gift wrap.

This is actually what was supposed to take place:
a duet of duelling cuckoos, at the close of which the winner
gets to stand next to me for the photo-op.

Alas, things went terribly wrong.
For I can now claim no space as rightfully mine
and must stand at the edge of the crowd like a ghost
for an unforeseeable length of time.

All this because I meant to be polite to someone.
We had met in the desert, you see, and he wished for a warm place
that wasn't the desert, and I said, "Why not try my hometown?
It's warm in winter. Sometimes."

Days later at the hotel bar I learned his real name
and his reason for wanting to trail me to my so-called hometown,
where I had never felt at home, yet never dreamed
of wishing for another. He said our great-great-grandmothers had been friends
in France, in the time of Marie de Médicis. "In any case
you can't let me down now, now that I've tracked you here
and seen how you actually live."

Was that meant to be a compliment? I suppose not,
yet something in his bright-eyed delivery made me imagine
I'd found a new long-lost friend. "Let's go visit the post office,"
I proposed, and he eagerly assented. Walking the narrow streets
I would never again recognize, I got this wistful feeling,
like a long, slow song sung from the tip of a distant tower.
I'd been rejected again, yet how? Nothing had really happened.
My friend was looking straight ahead, not saying anything.

"Is this the place you wanted to come to?
It's not much, I know. Terrazzo floor, frosted panes, a bit of brass
handle here and there, like a handle on a bedpost."

"What's that supposed to mean," he said, and sighed.
"Tomorrow I must be in Ottawa.
I'd hoped to spend the whole day with you, but now it's getting dark
and my bus will be leaving shortly." How could he do this to me?
Easily enough, apparently. "But what about Marie de Médicis?"
I stammered, as the mist broke and then reformed its ranks.

"Shucks, there's not much you can do in Ottawa on a
    Tuesday."
"That's what you think," came the curt reply. Now all is
    darkness.

The Don's Bequest

It's often more crazy like this
as I slide the wooden greyhounds along
their respective slots, ever in pursuit of the elusive hare
or is it a note of music, a particularly silvery one
heard only once, in the bow of a ship
what seems like ages ago?

In any case they are
dispiritingly spirited in quest of the elusive eidolon,
waft of breeze—was that laughter?—trimmed wick, whatever.
And we all know the race ends soon,
soon enough to be over.

So I spray this collection of days and hours
from the fat old album with a mist of Florida water,
something to bring them down
and to their senses simultaneously.
That's all I get for my pains—a glimpse
of beard through the judas peephole as it slides back,
then shut. The barren February street still assumes
a fleeting charm, known only to itself.
At least I never met anybody who was familiar with it,
knew its surname.

It's time to make my bequest to the land
we all landed on, and will be leaving at some point
in a hot-air balloon painted voluminous colors. I said
we could keep some of the currants, you didn't have to hog the
    whole bushel.
And so it goes, earth crunching underfoot,

interesting thoughts flowing through the head, the scalp in
    heaven.
When I see a cabinful of these wanderers I want to shout,
    though.
Why can't you all go back to chafing and wondering?
Yes, that's what we all do best.

Strange Cinema

In sooth, I come here sadly,
not trembling, not against my will,
hoping you will set the record straight.
You can, you know, in a minute
if the wind is right and no felon intervenes.

And we sit and you tell me how crazy I am.
I shall petition the other board members
but am afraid nothing will ever come right.
It has been going on too long for this to happen,
yet it was right to go, to go on as it did,
even if there was a strangeness in the rightness
that no one can now see. They see the night
in its undress, plaits unplaited, brushed,
the sound of the surf churning on distant rocks,
can think only about how heavenly it would have been
if it had all happened later or differently.

Now, according to some sources,
new retrofitting trends are a commodity,
along with silence, and sweetness.
Doucement, doucement . . .

And when the sweetness is adjusted,
why, we'll know more than some do now.
That is all I can offer you,
my lost, my loved one.

A Star Belched

On she danced, but had forgotten
how fancy it all was, how plain too.
Outside the silver motel they greeted her:
"Lotta traffic today." But she made no semblant
of hearing. "I say, he's big sir."
And on and on. The basement held no magic for her

nor for us anymore. It was as though we had come home
to dine on a single lamb chop, and it was gone.
The rain peered in the window
and directed its gaze succinctly at the linoleum.
All passion had been drained from the deep.
They might as well write it on blackboards.
Yet I was having too good a time to stop thinking yet.

Overhead the manager rushed. Now don't pull
my sweater away like that. Yet in time manure produces
    cherries
the clerk murmured. So we all forgot to compare these groans
to the ones suffering had caused, back in the vengeful night.
The moment I stare I kiss you.

When Pressed

Why has the sailor come in
too late? What star waters the garden?

You do intelligent things
at the first juxtaposition.
Luck is the composite of all these forces.
By then experience itself has been outlasted.
The grass shrivels.

It seems they came to lunch, through mist, on a Sunday many
    years ago.

On a sandwich plate was a letter, written in ivy,
casting doubt on the bearer,
your great-uncle.

They lingered, and fell apart.
We grew up impeccably, caught in the vise of sleep,
frequently taken advantage of.

Return me to that sense which I don't know.
Encased in a world, not seeing anything wrong
with how it grew, not getting better.
The juxtaposition happens again, farther along this time with a
  rueful elegance.
The painters have whitewashed the building,
our roof looks sleepy. And they, the witnesses inside,
they had heard something of this.

We keep on extricating, not certain the patch is over
or what it included up till now.
Is someone slap-happy? Are all parades uncertain, rinsed
of cloud, like a tree in a tear.
Note that the box has been "discontinued."

The Impure

Your story . . . most enjoyable.
I sat down and read it through from
beginning to end at one sitting,
whatever it is. Reams and reams of it.

White ambulances chase each other through the mist
and the fish swim by, too haughty
to have an opinion on anything.

These timed-release capsules work very well
but how could anyone know that? We are where
we began. This gray October day

that no one could have imagined, save Mama and Papa
sitting on their porch, having doubts about the weather.
When they go inside
it will all be over.

Casting about for some impurities
in your rock-crystal speech, I was struck by a tone
only mute dragonflies can keep up for long.

Then I thought about your brother Ben,
gone so long in the far land.
Would he return with the car,
with garlands flowing from its fenders,
to utter the word "drizzle"? Oh, Ben,
we liked you so much for such a long time.
Then you became insufferable to us
in just a few moments, for no reason. And now
we think we like you, Ben.

Crowd Conditions

Across the frontier, imperfect sympathies are twinkling,
a petite suite of lights in the gaga sky.
Most of the important things had to be obliterated
for this to happen. Does that interest you, *ma jolie?*
Something else would have happened in any case,
more to your liking, perhaps. Yet we can't undo the sexual posture
that comes with everything, a free gift.

Now the blades are shifting in the forest.
The ocean sighs, finding the process of striking the shore
interminable and intolerable. Let's pretend it's back when we
    were young
and cheap, and nobody followed us. Well,
that's not entirely true: The poodle followed us
home from school sometimes. Men in limousines followed us
at a discreet distance, the back seat banked with roses.

But as we got older one couldn't take a step
without creating crowd conditions. Men dressed like reporters
in coats and hats with visors, and yes, old ladies too,
crooning about the loss they supposed we shared with them.

Forget it. It all comes undone sooner or later.
The vetch goes on growing, wondering
whether it grew any more today.
Such, my friends, is life, wondered the president.

Enjoys Watching Foreign Films

To stay here forever. To lie down.
Lord, let us leave these petty shacks
of masonite, this angular scrub-forest,
speaking incessantly of the love of man
for woman, of woman for man, of man
for man, of woman for both woman and man,
and journey to some antique pergola
whose orange lozenges cast the light of reason
on these appalled, formal faces.

And if we size up all that
crushed fabric that lies across the river,
pretending to no dream, no appetite, why then I
will become the accuser of the race in myself. I cannot outrun
the gibbets at the New York City limits,
but perhaps things are better off this way.
You can see clear into the checkered chevrons
of a child's eyes, thirsting for grace
with the other millions. O don't give up, just
pretend it's Monopoly we're playing,
and I've just landed in your hotel.

Fade In

Continually detouring among the mountains,
some got lost, bathed in freshets.
Others stumbled onto the fringes of a large city
just as revolt was breaking out. Tourists, they were told,
should not try to escape, but enjoy the genuine hospitality
of the country, its superior hotels, some with rooms facing the
    ocean,
all provided with the latest in fitness equipment.
"Sure, try to put a good face on it, make nice with the natives
staring at us. I wonder when the bars open, or if they do."

Back at the Hotel Frisson the mood was one
of subdued reproach, such as a tardy guest feels, even
after apologies have been made and accepted.
Metallic fronds brushed against the catwalks.
Every so often a child would come, always silent,
with simple gifts in her hands, like a rabbit eraser.

This couldn't quite compare with real life though,
as we thought we had experienced it in the past,
even the very recent past. The monsoon, striking at five,
just as elaborate drinks were at last being served,
canceled civility, forcing huge residents to flee.

Over at the Mutts'

Funny, it says "hidden drive." *Look where you're going!*
I do, yet no drive emerges. Later on, maybe.

Tune in next week. My midair flight: live, awkward being.
Like the console radio says, none too consolingly,
you are your own hair and father.

Don't ever live close to a canal. The noise of fish
is ear-splitting. When the barometer plunges it takes you with
    it.

I don't mind heat so much, though.
It's the barometric pressure against my zinc-lined stomach
that makes me come on all funny. Hey, can I come over?

She's gone and stitched the lining to his dinner pail
filled it with nail polish remover
and left for the station. Next train isn't till forty-eight hours
from now. That's all right, I'll wait. Where does it go?
Oh, lots of places that have plums and wolverines in them,
but it's the jacket of your report card that interests me now.
Let me see it.

Why is it they always run out of party favors?
Here, I'll look for some more, on the ground.
The forest wind-chimes are favorable tonight
and the horehound drops toothsome.

She was dancing in the next part of her living.
Yes, she danced, and it didn't matter to her,
though others admired her gaze, her step, her hair's moist
    highlights.

I brought you over to make something out of myself.
I'm sorry. I should have left you at home, between the bookends.
Oh, but it's all right! Really! This afterlife has been a learning
    experience.
I am gradually turning to chalk, taking both of us with them,
and it'll be all right in the morning too. I guarantee it.

Pastilles for the Voyage

If it is spring it matters a little,
or not. Some are running down
to get into their cars, shoving
old ladies out of the way. I say,
dude, it made more sense a while ago
when we was on the grass. Tell it to the Ages,
that's what they're there for. You know,

miscellaneous record-keeping, and the like,
the starving of fools
and transformation of opera singers
into the characters they're supposed to be onstage.
Here comes Tosca, chattering with Isolde
about some vivacious bird's egg winter left behind.

I turn the corner into my street
and see them all, all the things that have mattered
to me during my long life: the dung-beetle
who was convinced he could tap dance; the grocer's boy
(he hasn't changed much in eighty years, nor have I);
and the amorphous crowd in black T-shirts with names like
slumlords or slumgullion spattered over them. O my friends
(for I have no other), the beginning of fermentation is *here*,
right on this sidewalk or whatever you call it.
We know, they say, and keep going.
If only I could get the tears out of my eyes it would be raining
   now.
I must try the new, fluid approach.

Of the Light

That watery light, so undervalued
except when evaluated, which never happens
much, perhaps even not at all—I intend to conserve it
somehow, in a book, in a dish, even at night,
like an insect in a light bulb.

Yes, day may just be breaking. The importance isn't there
but in the beautiful flights of the trees
accepting their own flaccid destiny,
or the tightrope of seasons.
We get scared when we look at them up close
but the king doesn't mind. He has the tides to worry about,

and how fitting is the new mood of contentment
and how long it will wear thin.

I looked forward to seeing you so much
I have dragged the king from his lair: There,
take that, you old wizard. Wizard enough, he replies,
but this isn't going to save us from the light
of breakfast, or mend the hole in your stocking.
"Now wait"—and yet another day has consumed itself,
brisk with passion and grief, crisp as an illustration in a
     magazine
from the thirties, when we and this light were all that mattered.

Your Name Here

But how can I be in this bar and also be a recluse?
The colony of ants was marching toward me, stretching
far into the distance, where they were as small as ants.
Their leader held up a twig as big as a poplar.
It was obviously supposed to be for me.
But he couldn't say it, with a poplar in his mandibles.
Well, let's forget that scene and turn to one in Paris.
Ants are walking down the Champs-Elysées
in the snow, in twos and threes, conversing,
revealing a sociability one never supposed them as having.
The larger ones have almost reached the allegorical statues
of French cities (is it?) on the Place de la Concorde.
"You see, I told you he was going to bolt.
Now he just sits in his attic
ordering copious *plats* from a nearby restaurant
as though God had meant him to be quiet."
"While you are like a portrait of Mme de Staël by Overbeck,
that is to say a little serious and washed out.
Remember you can come to me anytime
with what is bothering you, just don't ask for money.
Day and night my home, my hearth are open to you,
you great big adorable one, you."

The bar was unexpectedly comfortable.
I thought about staying. There was an alarm clock on it.

Patrons were invited to guess the time (the clock was always
    wrong).
More cheerful citizenry crowded in, singing the Marseillaise,
congratulating each other for the wrong reasons, like the color
of their socks, and taking swigs from a communal jug.
"I just love it when he gets this way,
which happens in the middle of August, when summer is on its
    way
out, and autumn is still just a glint in its eye,
a chronicle of hoar-frost foretold."
"Yes and he was going to buy all the candy bars in the machine
but something happened, the walls caved in (who knew
the river had risen rapidly?) and one by one people were swept
    away
calling endearing things to each other, using pet names.
'Achilles, meet Angus.'" Then it all happened so quickly I
guess I never knew where we were going, where the pavement
was taking us.

Things got real quiet in the oubliette.
I was still reading *Jean-Christophe*. I'll never finish the darn
    thing.
Now is the time for you to go out into the light
and congratulate whoever is left in our city. People who
    survived
the eclipse. But I was totally taken with you, always have been.
Light a candle in my wreath, I'll be yours forever and will kiss
    you.

UNCOLLECTED POEMS

Hoboken
(A collage made from Roget's Thesaurus)

Excitation, excitation of feeling,
Excitement, mental excitement,
Heart interest [slang], sensationalism,
Yellow journalism, melodrama, irritation,
Etc. (resentment) 900; passion, thrill, etc.
(State of excitability) 825.2-5.

Work *or* operate on *or* upon.
Stir, set astir, stir up, stir the blood.
Fillup, give a fillip.
Illumine.
Illuminate; fire, set on fire; inflame.
Apply the torch, fire, *or* warm the blood.
Fan, fan into a flame, fan the fire *or* flame.
Blow the coals, stir the embers, feed the fire, add fuel to the fire.

Change color, turn color,
Mantle; whiten, pale, turn pale; darken, turn black in the face,
    look black *or* blue;
Turn red, blush, flush, crimson, glow, warm.

Voice of the charmer, flattering tongue, unctuousness,
    mealymouthedness, etc.,
Humor, soothe, pet, coquet, slaver, beslaver,
beslubber, beplaster, pat on the back, puff.
Fool to the top of one's bent.
Do one proud, pull one's leg, sawder, soft-sawder, soft-
Soap, butter, honey, jolly, blarney, lay
It on, lay it on thick [all coll.]; lay it
On with a trowel, string, string along,
Honeyfogle [U.S.], oil, soap, [all slang];
Make things pleasant, gild the pill.

What is the use of running when you are
On the wrong road—J. Ray. *Mentus gratissimus error*—A most
    pleasant apprehension.—Horace.

One goes to the right, the other to the left; both err, but in
    different ways.—Horace.   Who errs and mends, to God him-
Self commends.—Cervantes.   To err is human to forgive
Divine.—Pope.   Errors is worse than ignorance.—P. J. Bailey.

Will-o'-the-wisp.

Off the track; on a false scent,
On the wrong scent *or*
Trail, up the wrong tree; at cross pur-
Poses.

Intense darkness, pitch-darkness, Cimmerian darkness,
Stygian darkness, Egyptian darkness, monte, reversi,
Squeezers, old maid, beggar-my-neighbor, goat, hearts, patience.

Dull, dullsome, dull as dish water.
"The face
That launched a thousand ships."
Wind-swept, bleak, raw, exposed,
The storm is up and all is on the hazard,
Rainy, showery, pluvious.

Avant-courier, *avant-coureur* or *avant courrier*,
Disentangle.
Vice-sultan, vice-caliph, vice-queen,
Bitter as gall.
Liqueur, cordial, sweet wine, punch,
Beanstalk.
"Leave not a rack behind."
All moonshine, all stuff and nonsense, all tommyrot,
"Thick as autumnal leaves that strow the brooks in
    Vallambrosa."
Bags, barrels, tons, flock,
In one's stead.
Prolocutrice *or* prolocutrix,
Accept the stewardship of the Chiltern hundreds.
View with disfavor, view with dark *or* jaundiced eyes,
Loblolly pine.
Ineptitude, inaptitude,

"As like as eggs,"
Swim *or* go with the stream.
Myrtle, turtledove, Cupid's bow,
Cupid's dart; love token etc. 902-5,
Bewitch, enrapture, inflame with love, carry away, turn the head.
Once in a blue moon [coll.],
Once in a coon's age [coll.],
Continually, incessantly, without ceasing, at all times, ever and anon;
Every day, every hour, every moment,
Daily, hourly, etc.
Daily and hourly, night and day, day and night, morning, noon and night,
Hour after hour, day after day, month after month, year after year,
Day in day out, month in month out, year in year out;
Perpetually, always etc. 112.5; invariably etc. 16.7.
Wander etc. from the truth,
Be in the wrong, be in the wrong box,
Bark up the wrong tree, back the wrong horse,
Aim at a pigeon and kill a crow,
Take *or* get the wrong sow by the ear,
The wrong pig by the tail, *or* the wrong bull by the horns,
Put the saddle on the wrong horse, count one's chickens before they are hatched,
Reckon without one's host, misbelieve, sin,
By special favor, yes, by all means.

I refuse! By no manner of means! I will not! Far be it from me!
Not if I can help it! I won't! Like fun I will!
Count me out! You have another guess coming! Catch me!

Volunteer, come forward, be a candidate,
Barkis is willin'.

Don't! Don't do that! Enough!
No more of that! That will never do! Leave off! Hands off!
Keep off! Keep off the grass! Hold! Stop! etc.
Refusal, refusing, declining, etc.

Leave alone, leave it to me,
Leave the door open, open the door to.
Open the floodgates, give the reins to etc. (allow freedom).

Above par.
Best, very best, choice, select.
Picked, elect, prime, capital, of the first water.
First-rate. First-class. First-chop.
Top-hole. Bang-up. Tiptop.
Top-notch. A 1, A one *or* number 1.
Crack, gilt-edge *or* gilt-edged.

Good, superb, super, superfine, exquisite,
High-wrought, precious, worth-its-weight-in-gold.

Worth a king's ransom,
Precious as the apple of the eye.

Good as gold,
Priceless, beyond price.

Invaluable, inestimable, rare.
Exceptional, extraordinary.

Beau idéal

Chevalier sans peur et sans reproche

Undeformed

Beyond all praise, *sans peur et sans reproche*

Clean, clean as a whistle, completely (etc.)

Koh-i-noor

Corker, trump [both slang]

Black tulip

Cygne noir, black swan

Admirable Crichton, Bayard, Roland, Sidney

Parasol.

Choice, best etc.

Standard, pattern, mirror etc. (prototype) 22

Call It "Untitled"

One day he said to me,
"I'm staying with you but you go with me."
Question: what am I going to do about it?
Life, even at its most festive, barely ingratiates.
Or days are amphibious, like expatriates,
like a cage of bengalis:
interesting enclosed original phenomenon.

Then take a snapshot of yourself.
"It wants only a note of citrus
to lunge from the potential we have all had
sometimes, or at one time or another
into the potent everyday real
you inhale through difficulty."

Question: what am I going to do about it?
Throw good money after bad?
Imagine sleep as a terror one can never remember?
If it lied, who would know?
That we live it
as we do
means nothing in front of us.

Life's little mysteries:
loitering on the edge of dream,

cool grass systems the pliant brain
instructed are ever as complex
as we imagined, then willed, them.

1992

Le singe d'une nuit d'été

In the eighteenth century, many avenues of expression were
    open to monkeys.
They could become doctors, judges, astronomers, painters,
Consulted by other monkeys of superior rank and lesser
    understanding.
It was the period of *singerie*, an enclosed monkeydom
Neither inviting nor refusing respect or ridicule,
Where they could lead lives neither more nor less fortunate
    than our own,
And look forward, from peaceful deathbeds, to coming muzzle
    to muzzle
With that supreme being, the creator monkey.

Today one sees them mainly behind bars, unclothed,
Masturbating, to the delight of children and their parents, or
    searching, a little anxiously, for fleas.
Occasionally you encounter that anachronism, the Italian organ
    grinder, who provides the music—well, music of a sort—
And lets the monkey, dressed in a soiled uniform like that of a
    bellhop in some seedy hotel, do the actual begging.
And then your eyes meet, yours and the monkey's, and it's not
    a pleasant sensation,
That look of pity, animosity, wariness, and just a trace,
Too slight to register on one's emotional litmus, of love.

1992

Fruit and Tea

Let it come back to this: no child's reason to intuit
anything but innocence can withstand same; conversely
the child is the irreducible lump all our most serious
fantasies become when we have moved on to become older:
no argument there. So it's a matter of bopping
back and forth between two reflecting yet mutually
unrecognizable emitters, and of living the life
reserved for those who have never thought things out clearly.

Only do not be deceived yet: some spells are for the mild
wintry calm of the present, when shoppers mail letters
and buses slide peacefully from view. To be told that
there's a sale of things for older people at so-and-so's
department store "spoils" us as children are thought
or said to be spoiled, by rattling this cage of dice
so frantically our peace comes to be seen as grounded,
that constant vibration is the medium and condition
of life, even of our peace.
                            (More stones grow
at the edge of hope's chasm than can ever be affixed
to the envelope of changing its subject to new and green
days-after-tomorrow, but we like the feeling of being
envied, anyway for a while.) If someone set out to tell you
this was all true you wouldn't believe them, but you can buy
the option and not feel traduced by it, nay, play along
with it for as long as roads care for the raw magenta
of the sunset reflected in their ruts; too, the playful
amphibian forms of this reptile hope are sometimes remote
and sometimes overbearing, so that if one can negotiate
its crawl-space and come out on the other side of enforced
leisure in one piece there's a good chance it will
all sidle down the train with the flung coffee-grounds,
     tea-leaves
and other assorted glop that makes of these same
moments a tent in which all
power is entertained; its consequences

carried to their logical extremes. To mope
is human; I mope, therefore I am. It requires
but a candle-flame to read it (the hour)
while with little expense and no fuss the darkness ends
then happily; the tossing, the turning, subside.

1992

Two Norwegian Moods

Norway

Some of the finest and most spectacular scenery in the world is along the Norwegian coast that frames villages like this one at water's edge. Norway is the northernmost country in Europe. Countless fjords, giant oceanic fingers, touch deeply into nearly all regions of the country. The Gulf Stream keeps most of the coastal areas fairly warm, with mild winters.

Aprikoskake

Cream margarine; add sugar gradually. Cream mixture until almost white. Add eggs and beat. Sift flour with baking powder and add alternately with milk; add apricots. Mix until apricots are evenly distributed in batter. Pour into two greased and floured loaf pans. Bake at 350 degrees until cake tests done. Yield: 24 servings.

1993

Tahiti Trot

We close in on ourselves,
then yelp that the world is awry.

If one person could see his (or her)
reflection outlined in the mirror

the last knot would come untied,
the great ship slip into the depths
of the Atlantic Ocean. Who told you
to say that? Why have you come here?

We need more people like you
to tell us what we're not like. True,
aging would get lost in the process.
We'd be sitting on the grass like young

idiots, involved in some personal spell
when the boiler exploded. You'd say,
"I can't get over that hat," and I,
pretending not to understand, would say,
   "Can I get you anything?"

1993

Tin Steamboat

Run water from a tap into one of the pipes
at the back end of the boat until it comes out of the other pipe;
this fills the boiler. Put the boat
on the water. Then, using the wax pellets
and wick provided, make a candle in the "spoon,"
light it, and place it in the boat
so the flame is heating the water in the boiler.

The water expands and pushes out of the back
thus propelling the boat. A vacuum is then
created in the boiler which sucks in more water.
This starts a cycle
pushing water out of one pipe
and sucking it in the other one.

When making the candle ensure that the wick overhangs the edge
of the "spoon" so that it does not gutter in the melted wax.

When the bag of wax runs out
use wax and wick cut from a normal candle.

Warning: This boat is not a toy
and is not suitable for unsupervised children.

1995

My Favorite Dress

Go ahead, plant that tree.
In early full autumn a former discreetness
stands out, one thing is a little different from the rest,
my shackles, meter maid who brought me
toast, a battledore, some raffish sayings: We tat you
on a blond cushion. The waist *was* overdue.

Someone inscribes his name in the log of erotic nightmares,
with recumbent orange cattle. Funny,
he thought he liked climbing trees. Ah,
the seed of man was ever a divisor, and
we are in it for the long haul.
He has lit the gas, you know.

1996

Yes, I Have Been Reading

Yes, I have been reading your book, I think not now,
not longest, sights overcome. Sure you jabber and prate,
just as surely as I laugh, risible. Then storms come,
we cannot see, less without each other's breathing.
I read your book. It was jaunty

and I so far from all living, what recipe
did I give myself, for the spatial breathing and what to know
    about it, dear
diviners of clear water!
It adds down to this. Nether-node of sap
at the tree's base. I merely buy
milk.
And by the ten days it courses over from the Lakes, telling bloom
cast as a shadow on that prison, road
that was telling right from the beginning.

Here too. Here too,
the one who will cope, cluster and bangs,
shortribs, be their way allover.
She brought too much,
those crazy initials

in a flash the star man-made out on the slump
it falls into—
in their way fitfully channeling into entropy, yet,
all in their way, the noose clings.
If I had been let out of the legging sooner
for my name to be made dust, my stations brought back to
    where the
patient crowds ring, and then it must have us.
I like your book.
I am ringing off the hook, must have more, tartan and sawdust,
the plan for beginners,
and old house, old oak, the door is drawn,
space enountered, satellite dish
waits, is elaborate in boring folds
at river's mouth,
fish came to these times generous
here too. The lazy
labyrinth encircles our day plastic perfumes and pages
cut from catalogs. The ends bend.
Are cryptic references. Dancing overseas
highlights the caution to be places on these altogether different
and sultry conditions.

1996

Often in Sorting Out

the new production
you are overwhelmed by the sameness of speech:
come, on, blow, sprint, death.
You have made a hideous blunder
the size of Manitoba, an aging actress visits
you and returns refreshed to the land
of desiccated ladders and café tables
where her husband waits. Kudos to you, Bob,
it was really underestimated what you have done.
As for me, the wolves are kinder this year
and I think I can breathe. Which is not to say all—
but you get what I mean. Under the covers
a shirt and a razor strop

which is not to say decay,
only the radical view of nothing from a rear car window
slopes down to me dramatically.
It was easy when there were five of us,
Now, days of the week and meal times
are a concern. I have just built this jiffy doghouse.

Strutting in the rain
alone (not to say we are alone) bridges toward composure.
Damn. I'll have to get it out for you—
the car, buried in blossoms, isn't what I meant.
The lean-to with its sullen taxpayer is.
There is a warrant out for my arrest, I—

1996

The Dissolving Bride

Well, let's see.
It's about process and debunking.
I left it in Tennessee.

There you had it. I
wasn't too nonplussed,
yet concerned that some of my colleagues might
wise up to the strategies which had brought us all
to this pass. This portal,

burning like an axe,
in real time, something crisper than just the old
etc. She licked my hand. The night was starry.

1996

Shadows on the Street

plunge into distress. The same calling uproar, whoa in another
    time.
She bit the bridge. A photograph can stomach it. I'll be in
sometime in the middle of July. Now the best time
of the year is around now, none can gainsay August
and Mr Random's tooth running in the street, he liked to say
    hi, it was just
him running, which is a bit awkward. A diagonal lipstick
chased him across the street. From there on in it was just damn
    melancholy,
no anchovies, nothing in particular, nothing to say. If so why,
    why do it,
so says Peter, who fought hard for the post, fought it and won
and why we are here, in the middle of a secondary terrain, mad
    and absorbed
by life, by the truth, as always.

But the nice part
I was going to say Is fenced out. Take to the hills then. There
    goes
one petal, the tree is falling apart, zounds I can do almost
    nothing
while the hills come and separate us, plant us in tomorrow
or until the last dish is unearthed.

Out crept a third one.
Savannas that have been dangerous, now no one remembered
the evil shifting of feet denounced the lady traveling salesman
to our liposuction expert. A single afternoon cooking at the
    stove
and all is more or less gone over, too bad
the futile Molotov cocktail exploded
but in any case in another land, with more furniture than we
    expected.
So we said, grant us this, it shall be done in another kingdom
as in the king's den. Don't let the roof fall in!
I was kind of sidelined by the barber pole
but explained practically about the dark petal, that was good
and we were coming in its time, and shall be heaven, about
    time, about
that point. Rockets lifted. Read me. There is no point to all this
    listless
hive. He took off in a manner that betokened bats
when it was over and they came over. It's time, now, some are
    good and alone,
lost up unto the rest. They can go and cancel
around it's too moot to be played at. They are, for the rest
    unsavory,
thyme in the corral, three jumps from last school
the patio ignited, sworn to safe conduct, like bread out of a
    school
conducted at last to here.

1996

Media Runner

Am I to be allowed to go back?
By nightfall they're breathless with eavesdropping.
As usual, the light between your toes stands up
and backs clumsily off stage.

Is the night chilly and dark?
The night is chilly but not dark.

My anti-growth hormones are working overtime, I think.
They just came in and announced it.

After I cut myself shaving
the key jammed in the lock. There are mitigating circumstances.
I would like to enter them too.

Yes, they sell these everywhere. How much by the gross?
A lot, man. Of course if you bought them individually
they would be even more expensive.
How could we even begin to justify

his pants to the ruptured miner? April lip-gloss
is tearing again. In the back alleys, a perfumed rabble
welcomes generous bankers to the hold. If we just keep on
we'll come to the horizon and see over it

into the land of something. Why, did you endorse
this? Where did all these come from? Who put them here?
The point is, he knew all that
and didn't care. It didn't stop him from leaving, paintbrush

in claw while the jury of owls,
his peers, dumbed down. A stump calls, wheezingly,
from the black brush. An itch goes away.
You don't feel it.

1997

The Hailstorm in Belgrade, May 24th, 1937

and they can't all be prayer too.
Before the close of the century
how many things will exist?
(The little schoolfriend.)
I hate them and I ate them

and in southern Poland
the novice crosses the tundra—quick,

a camera! These bells, tolling the sound of fuguish
growth
and no aftermath, in the cider, the cellar. And we came
round

this place of storage
shuttered and unlike

1997

Victrola floribunda

I am always shaking deliquescent bonbons
out of my hat. Is that a hat-trick?
I have never known what "hat-trick" means,
though I am sure there are many who do
and many more who do not.

1998

The Green Dress

It ached to cross the Crimea
in all its fabled fabledness.
Alas, only a few yurt-workers
looked up, and then down again
at the lamentable work at their feet

We wore it in the night, a light chop
of a lake ripple only a little plumper
than the rest. Then all was silence
and bad feeling again. The prefect stood up
from his mohair chair, a sign
we were to hit the rose-paths again.

I found a pretext
to fall behind the others, and plucked a rose,
milk-pink—a Maréchale Niel no doubt.
All alarms went off, the gates shot up

Automatically, trapping me and my friends.
We began to run, helter skelter, through angel-wings
of the mounted sprinklers, that coat the lawn with vast
arcs of tribulation, *sans* regret

It couldn't have been more than a few hours
when we had regrouped at a café on the village square.
The dress, we were to understand, had saved us, nay
terrorized our inquisitors, who chased us from the precincts.
It was dark with water spots now, a lovely thing.
"If you could just send . . ." she said.
But I cut her off. "Did he ask for it?"

1999

Hierarchy of the Unexpected

There is still something I'd like to explain,
yet can't be sure I'm ready yet.
Beside, we've done pretty well with the non-sequiturs,
and they by us, don't you think? Next time
I recognise one I'll call you, but will you hear me?
Will I suddenly find myself alone in some glade or dell
(it scarcely matters which) from which I'll have a time
extricating myself? Let's not waste time worrying
about needless necessities, though. I've packed a hamper
of dog food, there should be a star tonight
if we're lucky, which as you know we seldom are,
and yet the violence of the race still pursues
us benevolently. What's that, a shirt
you've got there? All is ready, I think, for this major tryst
that was going to be the last one, yet I see a whole lot of little
woolly ones marching straight over the hill to where the horizon
would be if we could ever catch it, make it spit out its name.
Oh it can be horrible out there sometimes.

Then there's the obscure holiday
we hadn't counted on. I was already dressed for work
trying to fasten my celluloid collar to my unforgiving,

slightly tattered shirt, and lo, a letter in pink ink
is deposited by a wavelet at my very door. Needs
must I read it. Well, we missed the first bus,
but another's soon arriving, there will probably be more
empty seats, though we'll arrive just as twilight is hinting
at encroaching at some point in the not too distant future.
At least the bills are paid. Yes! scream all those aboard.
I know I've left something behind—my sense of displacement
perhaps. Yet no mood will be shattered if we are diplomatic, for
   once.
The inheritors of those woods and groves won't oppress us,
and there'll be a chance for sleep and some grub. You'll see.

1999

Welcome to Entropy

No more absenteeism. It didn't go away. It just melted, in the
   sunlight.

Picnics and circuses, once in demand in ancient Rome,
have abated also. In their place stands stillness,
the stillness of a still street with a still tree
halfway down its block. Moon goes by, strutting
but still still. How does it work?

A walk around the block is the answer to most things
you live for and long for in paradise.

The sheep stand very still,
like ice sculptures.

This man is in for a very big surprise.
When he was young his father herded petunias,
lots of them, blue and white, scraping the street
as they fluttered past the newsboy. By not erasing this initial
   ecstasy
he has missed meeting many who might have become his
   friends,

helping him do things, helping him wash the car.
Now in the snowy dusk they don't see him
either. It's as if ten minutes had just passed.

You wake from the dream you hardly had time for
though it seemed several centuries were entangled
in it, struggling to be free of the curling iron,
old and bent, getting up from a park bench
to interrupt the unbroken breeze.

1999

Invitation to a Wooing

Still no this morning,
and still it rains again, a dry, crumbly sort of rain.
Outside of that, everything is more or less normal.
Factory hands are seen to enter the gate,
lunchpails in hand. A thin strip of what is probably blue
secretly alters the horizon.

Someone must be punished for this carelessness.
Though I believe in the abolition of all punishment
we must concentrate, for once, on getting the thing right.
Otherwise this hole in time will come to seem a fragment
of a dream that never happened. We can't have that. Think how
    stunned
the birds would be to learn they had never existed in that
    split-second
that is praying to you now, clawing from the light.

The old man and his boss took to it,
that is they took a gun with them, and a dog
over the hill to chase down the lost birds. None were to be
    seen.
This confirmed the old guy's expectations,
but naturally he refused to say anything about it.
Tamped some wadding in his gun. The thing blew up,

his face was all bloody. The dog took off over the nearby hill
and was never seen again

unless the dog seen lurking near the courthouse
a couple of weeks later was that one.
By that time the birds had come back, the pigeons, at any rate,
and were roosting proud as you please
on the doric pediments and the statue of General Ebenezer
    what's-his-name.

The horizon was a little bluer then, like tea.

1999

These Symptoms I Know So Well

In autumn things swell, books or leaves.
Out of the molting pumice of summer, the leaves
give over and are taken, wondering what happened to them
all along, yet we are docile, a woven environment
exists for us in twos or threes. Aching, we lay aside
the book of summer, winter's ruts are still ahead.
In the behind-the-scenes splashing, one or more of us
is overheard, and the chill gets lost. Darkness doesn't bring it.
We are far though from the swan's webbed feet,
and equally far too from a titanium ladder leaning against a wall.
Shall we topple it? More likely are we to scrabble
for a little heat, temperateness in darkness. The loon fixes
us with its stare then. To cross the street
with it and others in tow, nevertheless each of us earns the sigh
he began with. Lovers and meticulous birds answer this call,
run and are one. The river's gaze absolves us,
I mean absorbs us, and you have not done yet, the apples'
blaze undermines the trees, all along, upon
that shore, spoons knocking against the gutter's edge.

This is worse than that other time.
Yet I am freely coming to understand it,

it makes sense to me in ways other, more certain overtures
    didn't,
and now it's too late for the light, save in unexpected kingdoms
whose grass shall entail us, follow where we have gone
in massive understatement, whispers of wine, the close cordial
not involved in setting any of this to rights,
for you dream, and cheat. I've plucked pears
for you, look what it says here.
We cannot, ever, yield up that privilege,
it says here, not stay rowing,
back into the time of something else I was about to do
and get paid for it. Lock up your casement, lovers,
for night, noble night, the bearer of shadows, is coming.

2000

Vauban

About a year ago around lunch time
I still carry this small picture of you
etched to my forehead. In storms and ripples
it bides my face secure. In the garden
I was transformed into a lump. I
took out one of those gray things but it didn't
bristle anymore. Suddenly the world had turned to mush.

Three summers before she wrote me that she was a very
    dedicated person
I already knew that. What I wanted to know was if
she could stand up to the savor of daily conditions,
fail with the planet's whirl, and somehow arrive
back in your own backyard without missing a beat.
Well, there were excuses. A whole doll's house full of them.
No place for Mother to go, except behind the faux fringed drapes
that cost a year's ransom we should have been spending on
    other things
like how to get his feet out of the closet.

Then, suddenly at breakfast last year
she appeared. "Take something along with you"
had for decades been her battle cry, and so it was now with us;
we took the oblong witch and her cackling consort back into
    the living room
where they belonged, ready to sort out the three rival poets
until evening's chaconne arrived and we bled into rivulets of
    darkness.

2000

Greased Lightning

I

Reading this folderol
sewers flooded the drains
short-circuited the marble furniture
the truth exploded into jigsaw shapes

A man comes after
What do you want, he says
Nothing we're only waiting here
waiting for the last crisis

In a thousand years harebells will bloom.

II

The guide got excited
had never seen a hot-air balloon before.
"Please, may I touch?"
It should unload all its sorrow, all cares

into the next room
dim with the mirrored bureau
in whose drawers stockings sleep.

I practiced my piccolo all day
and far into the night

No one caused me to inquire
My letterbox is empty from A to Z.

Next blouse we'll have to undo the quagmire
but that won't be for a long time
till Tuesday.
Look, the rain is shaking the tree-branch now
in anger
All the pets have run away.
It is my coronation day.

This particular ladder
picked out in wired diamonds
against the febrile darkness
your so-so clasp
takes me for another
I must needs go indoors

tie a feather to my forehead and oh sob.

2000

A Leap in Time

And when do we get to the threadbare house,
with the man-in-the-moon chimney
and the melon slices on the roof,
with you, as an experiment?

Its shadows are of powdered mummy.

He did all you asked of him,
even what you only hoped he'd do,
and seemed never to have thought of doing
anything else. He anticipated your desires,
created them, even, so as to be able
to satisfy them with silence.
Now he's gone.

I played with him decorously
as a boy plays with a girl, consciously
doing good and sewing the fragments.

From this no little torment has come.
Can't we return to the threadbare house
even though it's dark and gone away?
My brother didn't want me to tell about living
in a magazine. He's like that.

We may move in some day.
But me—I've got to shove off.
Can't stand the uncertainty
of being on a plain with no mountains in the offing.
That's what I tell *him*, anyway.
I keep my reasons to myself.

But then some morning when the post office is ablaze
voilà—he's the champ. The one you really came to see.
Male fragrances are in the offing,
a smell of soup in the stairs.
These burnish me so I can live right.

But living the old way was the only right way,
wasn't it? Didn't I get that idea from you?
Now crystals are dissolving, taking us with them.

2000

Befuddled

Ah, the farts
we used to let back then.
Flatulence was a kind of way
of life, I guess.

Sitting around doing nothing
was another one.
It's a burden, all right,

in an elegant apartment
overlooking the Seine.

The pilgrim's stare
pierces you like a sharpened goose quill.
You look down along a day,
alack,
these spoons still recognize us
but the groundhog has gone under his hill.

Now there will be no one to play with
when we come out in groups, after four,
until evening's parachute settles on us
like a pinkish-gray mushroom.
You must empty your pockets
of everything, including sand
and screw-fragments. Now I think
it's going better, but uphill.
We must join the orchestra.

Could travel posters have been
more delirious? Colors of breadfruit and ice cubes,
salt and bourbon. A railroad trestle
in a faintly "cubistic" style
so you can see the other train approaching
from its bed of spruces . . .

The rain livens things up, at last.
Downtown is perky, though overbuilt
off the face of the planet.
Here is where a sea serpent unrolls
and devours the city.
Miraculously we are all inside its belly
in a cathedral
with windows aglint—it must be Christmas
if you say so.

(I didn't.) Jerking away
from the land is all that's possible
for us for the time being.

I like you in lacquer.
You are going to have to love me in gypsum.
But the pointed roofs under their dusting
of talc have not made it to the frontier.

We sit beside a stone and grieve for them.

2000

A Lot of Catching Up to Do

Dark days, lit by a falling flame
from time to time. A door stands open
or not. It's much the same.
Only the top layer is of any importance;
the rest, why the rest is immanent,
that's all.

It hurts only when you think about it.

To my friends in the rough:
When all the toys were swept out of the attic
only a bluish pitcher remained,
as though marking time. Shadow of wing in the air,
the dream nevertheless wanted to be congratulated for its
    condolences.
It took off prudently, however.

Then there were many napkins, many knives in the Seine.

2000

The Lyricist

So I was bewildered, OK?

Around here we keep the toilets flushed
and look out the window over the kitchen sink
at redstarts. "This is New England, dear.

It's pure. There are churches. Walking along the road
a girl comes. She could be a duchess
or a goose person. It doesn't much matter
in the state we are in. Awkward, yes, and not a little
   disconcerting."

And the driveway behind the satin drapes
glides to its destination.
That evening when you sat with all those people and were
   happy,
other forces were at work. In the flume
was gesturing, shouts.
We cannot hear what we are supposed to know.

But I'd also be happy just in a life of crime.
The key is sticky with the blood of other wives.
He looked so displeased
and now it's all over, isn't it?

The spinning out or at,
telephone switchboard of the Grand Hotel.
Great looms the shadow of the shuttle.

Anglefish bloom in aquaria.

2000

CHRONOLOGY

NOTE ON THE TEXTS

NOTES

INDEX OF TITLES AND FIRST LINES

Chronology

1927   John Lawrence Ashbery is born July 28 in Rochester, New York, the first son of Helen Lawrence and Chester Frederick Ashbery. (Father, b. 1891, is the son of Henry Ashbery, a fruit farmer, and Elizabeth Koehler Ashbery. Mother, b. 1893, is the daughter of Henry Lawrence, a professor of physics at the University of Rochester, and Adelaide Seeley Lawrence; before her marriage to Chester Ashbery, she worked as a biology teacher.) The Ashberys live on a farm near the village of Sodus, thirty miles east of Rochester.

1930   Over the next four years, John lives often with his maternal grandparents in Rochester, where he attends school. Spends summers in the Lawrence cottage in Pultneyville on the shore of Lake Ontario, six miles from Sodus.

1931   Brother Richard is born March 12.

1933   Sees first film, *The Three Little Pigs*, with maternal grandmother (as later described in his poem "The Lonedale Operator"), sparking lifelong interest in movies (which influences his writing and is cultivated particularly with classmate Bob Hunter at Harvard, Elliott Stein in Paris, Richard Roud in Europe and New York, and eventually with filmmaker Guy Maddin).

1934   Upon retirement of Henry Lawrence from University of Rochester, John returns to parents' house on farm. Maternal grandparents move permanently to Pultneyville. John attends schools in Sodus for the next nine years and spends his summers and weekends mainly in Pultneyville.

1936   Begins piano lessons, which he continues until 1943. Reads about landmark Surrealism exhibition at the Museum of Modern Art in New York in *Life* magazine; decides to become a surrealist painter.

1938   Attends art classes at Rochester's Memorial Art Gallery with brother Richard, after Sodus school stops teaching art. (Art classes continue until 1942.) Father drives boys to lessons, also delivering eggs from the farm to a restaurant where they often have dinner after class; favorite art teacher is Rebecca Cook.

1940	Richard dies of leukemia.
1941	John becomes finalist in national *Quiz Kids* radio competition and travels to Chicago with mother and maternal grandmother for radio broadcast in December.
1942	Sees Walt Disney's *Fantasia*, which marks the beginning of a serious lifelong interest in classical music; gets first phonograph and starts collecting records.
1943	Enters *Time* magazine's high school competition on current affairs and wins Louis Untermeyer's *Modern British and American Poetry* anthology; becomes interested in modern poetry, particularly the work of W. H. Auden. Boards at exclusive Deerfield Academy in Massachusetts; Karin Roffman's research for her biography of Ashbery has revealed that a friend of his mother's arranged for a scholarship and his parents paid the remaining tuition. Publishes poems in school newspaper, *The Deerfield Scroll*. While at Deerfield, continues painting (which he will abandon at Harvard) and acts in school productions of *The Man Who Came to Dinner* and *Arsenic and Old Lace* (continuing childhood interest in theater, which persists throughout his life and includes occasional performances in plays and films).
1944	Makes first trip to New York City in December; visits the Museum of Modern Art and the Gotham Book Mart and sees Broadway musical *Carmen Jones*.
1945	Roommate at Deerfield appropriates two Ashbery poems, "Seasonal" ("Though we seek always the known absolute") and "Lost Cove," and submits them to *Poetry* magazine under pseudonym Joel Michael Symington; they are published in the November issue. Ashbery enters Harvard in July. Takes classes in English literature. Reads poetry of F. T. Prince, Nicholas Moore, and Delmore Schwartz. Takes poetry writing class taught by Theodore Spencer; Robert Creeley and John Hawkes are classmates. Meets Barbara Zimmerman (later, as Barbara Epstein, a founding editor of the *New York Review of Books*).
1946	Reads poetry of Marianne Moore, Wallace Stevens, Elizabeth Bishop, and other modern American poets.
1947	Meets Kenneth Koch. Publishes six poems in *The Harvard Advocate* and is elected to its board; fellow editors include

	Koch, Robert Bly, and Donald Hall. Attends Harvard reading by Auden.
1948	Writes sestina "The Painter" and "Some Trees," the earliest poems included in his first full collection, *Some Trees* (1956). Publishes four poems in *Harvard Advocate*, including "Song from a Play," from *Everyman: a Masque*, his first play. One of his collages, made with a classmate, is used on cover of *Harvard Advocate*'s November issue. (Pursues interest in visual and literary collage sporadically throughout the years, particularly with encouragement from Joe Brainard during the early 1970s, with works exhibited and published; his earliest known collage poem is "'controls'" from 1952.) Meets Auden after a reading at Harvard.
1949	Takes class on poetry of Wallace Stevens with F. O. Matthiessen. Is elected class poet. Publishes two poems in *Harvard Advocate* and two in *Furioso*. Meets Frank O'Hara. Writes honors essay on poetry of Auden. Graduates from Harvard and moves to New York, partly because of encouragement of Kenneth Koch, who introduces him to Jane Freilicher and Larry Rivers. Works a summer job in Literature Department at Brooklyn Public Library. Begins MA in English Literature at Columbia in September. Lives on West 12th Street in Greenwich Village. Reads novels of Elizabeth Bowen, Henry Green, Ronald Firbank, and Ivy Compton-Burnett. Writes "The Picture of Little J. A. in a Prospect of Flowers," "The Mythological Poet," and "Illustration." Meets artist Nell Blaine and playwright Arnold Weinstein.
1950	Plays leading role (with Freilicher and Rivers) in Rudy Burckhardt's film *Mounting Tension*, the first of several involvements with Burckhardt's projects. Writes play *The Heroes*. Publishes two poems in *Poetry New York*. Writer's block lasting some eighteen months begins in June. Moves to another apartment on 12th Street, where O'Hara visits in December.
1951	With sets and costumes designed by Harvard classmate Edward Gorey, and music for flute and piano composed by Frank O'Hara, *Everyman: a Masque* is performed on the inaugural bill of Poets' Theatre in Cambridge. Ashbery completes MA at Columbia, writing thesis on three novels of Henry Green. "The Picture of Little J.A. in a Prospect of

	Flowers" published in *Partisan Review* by poetry editor Delmore Schwartz. Is introduced to the writings of Raymond Roussel by Kenneth Koch. Begins working in the Publicity Department of Oxford University Press in October. Meets James Schuyler at opening of a Larry Rivers exhibition at Tibor de Nagy Gallery in New York City.
1952	Attends New Year's Day concert of John Cage's "Music of Changes" with O'Hara, and is impressed by Cage's use of the aleatory; as a result of this experience, starts writing poetry again. With Freilicher, O'Hara, and Schuyler makes short film *Presenting Jane*, written by Schuyler and filmed by Harrison Starr; in car on the trip back to Manhattan from the Hamptons on Long Island, begins writing the novel *A Nest of Ninnies* with Schuyler. Meets artist Fairfield Porter, who paints the first of several portraits of him and encourages him to paint again. Is one of three winners of 92nd Street Y's Discovery Prize, judged by John Malcolm Brinnin. *The Heroes* is produced in August by the Living Theatre at Cherry Lane Theatre, on bill with Alfred Jarry's *Ubu Roi*; the production closes after only three performances when the New York Fire Department declares the theater unsafe.
1953	*Turandot and Other Poems* is published by Tibor de Nagy Gallery, with four drawings by Jane Freilicher, part of a series of chapbooks by the young poets who were friends of the gallery's artists (who illustrated the books) and who would come to be known as the "New York School"; this is the first of many collaborative projects with artists such as Alex Katz, Joan Mitchell, Jane Hammond, Archie Rand, and Trevor Winkfield.
1954	Leaves Oxford University Press and, after a brief stint at the Council for Financial Aid to Education, takes position as copywriter at McGraw-Hill Book Company. Publishes first translation from French (a poem by Robert Cordier) in *Folder*; published translations will include works by Roussel, de Chirico, Mallarmé, Reverdy, Rimbaud, and others. Grandfather dies.
1955	Ashbery publishes four poems in *Poetry*—his first to appear there since the "Symington" poems were published without his knowledge ten years earlier—and four more in *Quarterly Review of Literature*. Placed on waiting list for Fulbright fellowship to study in France. Submits manuscript of *Some Trees* for Yale Younger Poets prize, but is rejected by first

readers. Writes *The Compromise, or Queen of Caribou*, a theatrical parody of silent films, which is performed the following year by Poets' Theatre, starring Frank O'Hara. Travels to Mexico with Jane Freilicher and Joe Hazan (but does not visit Guadalajara, the city described at length in poem "The Instruction Manual" in *Some Trees*). Learns on his return that he has been granted a Fulbright fellowship and that *Some Trees* has won the Yale Younger Poets prize. (Auden, judge of the prize, had decided not to give it that year because of the low standard of the entries; his partner, Chester Kallman, knowing that both Ashbery and Frank O'Hara had submitted manuscripts that Auden hadn't seen, advises the young poets to send copies directly to Auden's summer residence in Ischia. Auden then awards the prize to Ashbery.) Leaves for France in September. After a month in Paris, travels to Montpellier, where he spends one of the coldest winters on record there.

1956   *Some Trees*, with a preface by Auden, is published by Yale University Press and receives admiring review by Frank O'Hara in *Poetry* ("Faultless music, originality of perception —Mr. Ashbery has written the most beautiful first book to appear in America since [Wallace Stevens's] *Harmonium*"). Ashbery makes several trips from Montpellier to Paris, and in March meets Pierre Martory in a bar on rue du Cherche-Midi. A month later, meets Harry Mathews. Spends two weeks in London, where he meets F. T. Prince, and visits Italy (Milan, Venice, Rome) for the first time in July. Returns briefly to U.S., visits family and writes "Idaho," one of his early experiments with literary collage, using material from the English novel *Soundings*, by A. Hamilton Gibbs, which he found at his parents' home (he had already published "Hoboken: A Collage Made from Roget's *Thesaurus*," written during his tenure at Oxford University Press, probably in 1953, in *Semi-Colon*, magazine published by Tibor de Nagy). Moves to Paris for the second year of his Fulbright, sharing with Pierre a *chambre de bonne* (literally "maid's room," a small room on the top floor of an apartment building) on rue Spontini. Teaches courses on American literature and American education at the University of Rennes. Visits Kenneth Koch and his wife, Janice, in Florence in December.

1957   Publishes new poems and a review of Gertrude Stein's *Stanzas in Meditation* in *Poetry*. Writes "'How Much Longer Will I Be Able to Inhabit the Divine Sepulcher . . . ;"

"'They Dream Only of America,'" and "A Last World." Takes boat trip along Adriatic coast to Greece with Pierre. Returns to New York City in September and takes courses in French literature at New York University. Meets Thomas B. Hess, editor of *ArtNews*, and writes reviews for the magazine; the first is published in October, beginning a long career of writing about art. Decides to write doctoral thesis on the work of Raymond Roussel, partly as a means of returning to Paris.

1958 Returns in June to Paris to begin research on Roussel. Continues experimenting with techniques of cut-up and collage in his writing. Moves with Pierre into apartment owned by Harry Mathews near Porte de Vanves in the 14th arrondissement. Lives on money earned from translation work. Publishes, in Alfredo Rizzardi's anthology *Poesia Americana del Dopoguerra* (Milan: Schwartz), the first of many translations of his poems into other languages.

1959 Through efforts of Donald Barthelme and Thomas Hess, wins Longview Foundation award for "'How Much Longer Will I Be Able to Inhabit the Divine Sepulcher . . .'" and "April Fool's Day," published in *Big Table*. Takes trip to Munich, Vienna (where he sees Parmigianino's *Self-Portrait in a Convex Mirror*), and Italy with Pierre; visits Arnold Weinstein in Florence. Meets French painter Jean Hélion.

1960 Is appointed art critic of the European edition of the *New York Herald Tribune*. Travels in Spain with Frank O'Hara, who is scouting for material to exhibit at the Museum of Modern Art. With Harry Mathews, Kenneth Koch, and James Schuyler, founds the little magazine *Locus Solus*, named after a novel by Roussel; travels to Majorca with Mathews to oversee printing of first issue.

1961 Moves to apartment on rue d'Assas with Pierre. Is asked by John Hollander, an editor of the poetry list at Wesleyan University Press, if he has a second collection ready; sends off the manuscript of *The Tennis Court Oath*. Through Hélion, meets English painters Anne Dunn and Rodrigo Moynihan.

1962 Publishes *The Tennis Court Oath* (Wesleyan University Press) to generally hostile reviews. Publishes "Re-establishing Raymond Roussel" in *Portfolio and ArtNews Annual*. *Locus Solus* folds.

1963	Ashbery returns to America for the first time in five years. Meets many young poets and painters, including David Shapiro, Tony Towle, and Joe Brainard, at a party in his honor hosted by Frank O'Hara. Gives a reading at the Living Theatre. Meets Alex Katz. Begins work on his longest poem to date, "The Skaters."
1964	Founds *Art and Literature: An International Review* with Anne Dunn, Rodrigo Moynihan, and Sonia Orwell. Travels around Italy and Morocco with Jane Freilicher, Joe Hazan, and Larry and Clarice Rivers. Returns to America twice, first in summer, when he reads "The Skaters" for the first time at Washington Square Art Gallery, an event organized by Ruth Kligman, then for his father's funeral in December. Begins work on "Fragment." Publishes "Les versions scéniques d'*Impressions d'Afrique* et de *Locus Solus*," an account of the dramatization and staging of Roussel's two novels, in review *Bizarre*.
1965	Gives reading at U.S. embassy in London in June. Meets English poet Lee Harwood. The family farm near Sodus is sold; deterioration of his mother's health prompts return to New York City, where he accepts job as executive editor at *ArtNews* and sublets Gramercy Park apartment of painter Esteban Vicente and his wife Harriet. Is welcomed back with a party given by Andy Warhol at his studio, The Factory. Publication of *John Ashbery and Kenneth Koch: A Conversation*.
1966	Collaborates with Joe Brainard on episode of *C Comics*. Moves to apartment on East 95th Street (in a house owned by painters Giorgio Cavallon and his wife, Linda Lindeberg). Publication by Holt, Rinehart and Winston of *Rivers and Mountains*, which is nominated for a National Book Award. Frank O'Hara dies.
1967	*Selected Poems* is brought out in Britain by Jonathan Cape. Guggenheim Foundation awards Ashbery a fellowship. Premiere of Eric Salzman's musical setting of "Europe" as *Foxes and Hedgehogs: Verses and Cantos*, performed under the auspices of the Juilliard School of Music and conducted by Dennis Russell Davies (and later by Pierre Boulez in London), the first of many musical treatments of his work by a variety of composers, including Elliott Carter, Roger

Reynolds, Ned Rorem, Joan Tower, Christian Wolff, and Charles Wuorinen. *Art and Literature* publishes its final issue.

1968　Ashbery delivers lecture "The Invisible Avant-Garde" at Yale School of Art. Travels in Europe from October to December on Guggenheim fellowship; stays with Pierre in Paris, and goes with mother to Switzerland and Italy.

1969　Publication of novel *A Nest of Ninnies*, written with James Schuyler and begun seventeen years earlier; Auden predicts it is "destined to become a minor classic," and it is republished several times, ultimately by Dalkey Archive in 2008. Publication by Black Sparrow Press of *Fragment* with illustrations by Alex Katz. Ashbery meets painter Trevor Winkfield. Receives American Academy and Institute of Arts and Letters Award in Literature, and a National Endowment for the Arts publication award.

1970　Publishes *The Double Dream of Spring* (E. P. Dutton). Through Elaine de Kooning, meets her former Carnegie Mellon students Aladar Marberger and Barbara Schwartz, whom she helps establish in New York's art world. Meets David Kermani. Moves to West 25th Street.

1971　Is published in Penguin Modern Poets series (in volume with Lee Harwood and Tom Raworth), edited by Nikos Stangos. At invitation of Ann Lauterbach, director of Institute of Contemporary Arts' literature program, goes to London with David Kermani to give reading in June; meets Anthony Howell. Makes brief trip to Paris.

1972　Publishes *Three Poems* (Viking), which wins Shelley Memorial Award from the Poetry Society of America in 1973. Is invited to read at Poetry International in London in June; his mother accompanies him. After *ArtNews* is sold and almost all staff fired, accepts a job teaching creative writing at Brooklyn College (CUNY) and co-directing its MFA program. Travels to Iran, where he joins David and attends Shiraz Arts Festival (Merce Cunningham and John Cage also attend); writes article about festival with David for *Saturday Review*. Moves into building on West 22nd Street in Chelsea, where he lives for many years in a series of apartments. Meets Douglas Crase.

1973　Spends February at Fine Arts Work Center in Provincetown and begins "Self-Portrait in a Convex Mirror," which he finishes in April. Is awarded second Guggenheim fellowship, which allows him to postpone taking up post at Brooklyn College until 1974. Meets James Tate at Amherst.

1974 Begins teaching at Brooklyn College; students will include Ed Barrett, Star Black, and John Yau. Travels by bus around New England and writes *The Vermont Notebook*. Receives Frank O'Hara Prize from Modern Poetry Association for "Self-Portrait in a Convex Mirror" and four other poems published in *Poetry*.

1975 Publishes *Self-Portrait in a Convex Mirror* (Viking) and *The Vermont Notebook* (Black Sparrow), with illustrations by Joe Brainard.

1976 *Self-Portrait in a Convex Mirror* wins the Pulitzer Prize, the National Book Award, and the National Book Critics Circle Award—the first time all three major American prizes are given to the same book. From this point onward, Ashbery is increasingly seen as one of the most important poets of his generation; numerous academic essays praising his work are published by influential critics such as Harold Bloom, Marjorie Perloff, and Helen Vendler. Awarded many prizes, he is frequently asked to give readings, and his work is translated into many languages. Subsequent trade volumes are published simultaneously in Britain (by Carcanet) and the U.S. Ashbery composes "Pyrography" for the catalogue of "America 1976," an exhibition of paintings of American landscapes sponsored by the U.S. Department of Interior commemorating America's bicentennial. Begins four years serving as poetry editor of *Partisan Review*. Publication of Kermani's *John Ashbery: A Comprehensive Bibliography*, which includes listings of his art writings and documents his involvement with various art forms and creative activities.

1977 Publication by Viking of *Houseboat Days*, which becomes a finalist for the National Book Critics Circle Award. Ashbery receives Levinson Prize from *Poetry* magazine and a lifetime achievement award from the Friends of the Rochester Public Library, the first of many such honors.

1978 Becomes art critic for *New York* magazine. Influenced by Elliott Carter's *Duo for Violin and Piano*, composes "Litany," a long poem in two columns that he will later record and occasionally perform with Ann Lauterbach. Publishes

	Three Plays with Kenward Elmslie's Z Press. Receives Composer/Librettist grant with Elliott Carter from the National Endowment for the Arts, which will result in *Syringa*. Purchases house in Hudson, New York.
1979	Invited by James Cummins to be Elliston Poet-in-Residence at University of Cincinnati, and begins acquiring furnishings for Hudson house while there. Publishes *As We Know* (Viking). Begins dividing time between Hudson house and New York apartment. Is named Phi Beta Kappa Poet at Harvard University. Receives honorary DLitt from Southampton College of Long Island University and Rockefeller Foundation grant in playwriting. Columbia University Press publishes David Shapiro's *John Ashbery: An Introduction to the Poetry*, the first book-length study of his work.
1980	Ashbery is named Distinguished Professor by Brooklyn College. Accepts job as art critic for *Newsweek* (splits the year with Mark Stevens, with each working six months). Is elected member of the American Academy and Institute of Arts and Letters. Participates in USIA–sponsored trip to Poland with Susan Sontag and others; meets Piotr Sommer, editor of *Literatura na Swiecie*, who will translate and publish work by and about him.
1981	Publishes *Shadow Train* (Viking), which is named a finalist for National Book Award.
1982	In the spring, a near-fatal spinal epidural abscess causes paralysis and requires neurosurgery, which results in impairment. Is elected Fellow of the Academy of American Poets.
1983	Is elected member of the American Academy of Arts and Sciences. Receives Jerome J. Shestack Poetry Award from *American Poetry Review*, the New York City Mayor's Award of Honor for Arts and Culture, and the Charles Flint Kellogg Award in Arts and Letters from Bard College. Is interviewed by Peter Stitt for *Paris Review*. Meets Rosanne Wasserman and Eugene Richie.
1984	In January, makes first visit to Berlin as guest of Literaturhaus at invitation of Walter Höllerer. Publishes *A Wave* (Viking), which becomes finalist for both National Book Critics Circle and Los Angeles Times Book Awards, and receives the Bollingen Prize in Poetry (Yale University) and the Lenore Marshall/*The Nation* Poetry Prize.

1985	*Selected Poems* is published by Viking and becomes a finalist for the Los Angeles Times Book Award. Ashbery is awarded a five-year MacArthur fellowship, enabling him to give up teaching post at Brooklyn College and position as art critic for *Newsweek*. Receives Wallace Stevens fellowship from Yale University's Timothy Dwight College.
1986	Meets Mark Ford in New York. Receives Commonwealth Award in Literature from Modern Language Association. Harvard University arranges to acquire his literary manuscripts and correspondence.
1987	Publication by Viking of *April Galleons*, which is a finalist for National Book Critics Circle Award. Mother dies. Ashbery begins work on his longest poem, *Flow Chart*. Receives Golden Plate Award from American Academy of Achievement.
1988	Artist Siah Armajani incorporates commissioned prose poem [untitled: "And now I cannot remember . . ."] into his Irene Hixon Whitney Bridge, commissioned by the Walker Art Center in Minneapolis (Minnesota). Is selected by David Lehman to edit the inaugural volume of annual series *The Best American Poetry*. Elected chancellor of the Academy of American Poets, a position he holds until 1999.
1989	Travels to Japan with David in spring; meets Tomoyuki Iino. Publication by Knopf of selected art writings, *Reported Sightings: Art Chronicles 1957–1987*, edited by David Bergman. Receives Creative Arts Award in Poetry from Brandeis University. Delivers Charles Eliot Norton Lectures at Harvard on the work of six favorite writers: John Clare, Thomas Lovell Beddoes, Raymond Roussel, John Wheelwright, David Schubert, and Laura Riding.
1990	In the spring, finishes Norton lectures at Harvard and takes USIA–sponsored trip to Yugoslavia, Sweden, and Soviet Union; David accompanies him. Is appointed Charles P. Stevenson, Jr., Professor of Languages and Literature at Bard College, a position he will hold until 2008; students will include David Gruber, Arlo Haskell, Khalil Huffman, and Stuart Krimko.
1991	Publishes *Flow Chart* (Knopf). Receives Horst Bienek Prize for Poetry from the Bavarian Academy of Fine Arts.
1992	Publishes *Hotel Lautréamont* (Knopf), which is a finalist for the Pulitzer Prize. Receives the Accademia Nazionale dei

Lincei's Antonio Feltrinelli International Prize for Poetry, and the Ruth Lilly Poetry Prize from the Poetry Foundation. Visits Australia with David and renews his friendship with Australian poet and editor John Tranter.

1993　Is named Chevalier de l'Ordre des Arts et des Lettres by French Ministry of Education and Culture; the award is presented by French minister of culture Jack Lang during a reception at Harry Mathews's Paris apartment.

1994　Publishes *And the Stars Were Shining* (Farrar, Straus and Giroux). *The Landscape Is Behind the Door*, a collection of poems by Pierre Martory translated by Ashbery, is published by Sheep Meadow Press. Receives honorary DLitt from the University of Rochester. Short works by twelve leading American composers based on his poem "No Longer Very Clear" are performed at Lincoln Center.

1995　Publication by Farrar, Straus and Giroux of *Can You Hear, Bird*. Ashbery receives the Poetry Society of America's Robert Frost Medal, and (for the second time) *American Poetry Review*'s Jerome J. Shestack Prize. With David, takes second trip to Japan.

1996　Becomes first English-language winner of the Grand Prix de Biennales Internationales. Receives Silver Medal of the City of Paris, recognizing publication of *Quelqu'un que vous avez déjà vu*, a volume of his poems translated by Anne Talvaz and Pierre Martory.

1997　Publishes *The Mooring of Starting Out: The First Five Books of Poetry* (Ecco), which is awarded the Bingham Poetry Prize by the *Boston Review*. Receives Gold Medal for Poetry from the American Academy of Arts and Letters.

1998　Publishes *Wakefulness* (Farrar, Straus and Giroux). Establishes Flow Chart Foundation with David, James Tate, and Dara Wier. Pierre Martory dies.

1999　Publishes *Girls on the Run* (Farrar, Straus and Giroux), a long poem inspired by the paintings of Henry Darger.

2000　Publishes *Your Name Here* (Farrar, Straus and Giroux) and *Other Traditions* (Harvard University Press), revised versions of his Charles Eliot Norton Lectures of 1989–90 edited by Rosanne Wasserman. Receives Walt Whitman Citation of Merit from New York State Writers Institute and is named

	New York State's Poet Laureate, a position he will hold until 2002.
2001	Publication by Michael Gizzi's Qua Books of *As Umbrellas Follow Rain*. Receives an honorary DLitt from Harvard University, Harvard University's Signet Society Medal for Achievement in the Arts, and the Wallace Stevens Award from the Academy of American Poets.
2002	Is Visiting Fellow at University of Pennsylvania's Kelly Writers House (and again in 2013). Publishes *Chinese Whispers* (Farrar, Straus and Giroux). Named Officier de la Légion d'Honneur (France). Travels to Europe with David in September to participate in events marking his seventy-fifth birthday at the Pompidou Center in Paris (the first public multimedia program incorporating aspects of his involvement with music and the visual arts with poetry, organized by Olivier Brossard and Omar Berrada) and the Tate Modern in London. At the suggestion of Nicholas Jenkins of Stanford University, the Flow Chart Foundation sets up Ashbery Resource Center in 2002, conceptualized by Micaela Morrissette, Olivier Brossard, and David to deal with bibliographic and domestic archives.
2003	Pace University awards him an honorary DLitt Publication of *John Ashbery in Conversation with Mark Ford*, a book-length interview.
2004	Publication by the University of Michigan Press of *Selected Prose*, edited by Eugene Richie.
2005	Karin Roffman invites Ashbery to speak to a class she teaches at Bard College, leading in subsequent years to her involvement with projects relating to the Hudson house and his biography. Publication by Ecco of *Where Shall I Wander*, which is finalist for a National Book Award.
2006	In March, via John Yau and Michael Silverblatt, Ashbery begins correspondence with filmmaker Guy Maddin, whose work he has long admired. The Italian Accademia Nazionale dei Lincei elects Ashbery to a foreign membership. The New School hosts a three-day international John Ashbery Festival (organized by David Lehman), and the New York City Council declares April 7 John Ashbery Day. The University of Massachusetts at Amherst devotes its annual Juniper literary festival to the celebration of the fiftieth anniversary of the publication of *Some Trees*. Meets Adam Fitzgerald.

2007   Publication by Ecco of *A Worldly Country* and *Notes from the Air: Selected Later Poems*, which wins International Griffin Poetry Prize. *Haunted House*, his translation of a text by Pierre Reverdy, is published by John Yau's Black Square Editions. Ashbery performs the role of narrator in one of the "live" productions of Guy Maddin's film *Brand upon the Brain!* in New York. Is named first Poet Laureate of mtvU television network. Bard College hosts weekend celebration of his eightieth birthday, organized by Ann Lauterbach; among other tributes in various countries, *Conjunctions* publishes special birthday anthology.

2008   Publication by Sheep Meadow Press and Carcanet of *The Landscapist*, his translations of Pierre Martory's poetry, edited by Rosanne Wasserman and Eugene Richie, which is a finalist for a National Book Critics Circle Award and a Poetry Book Society Recommended Translation (U.K.). Ashbery receives honorary DLitt from Yale University. "A Dream of This Room," a symposium on Ashbery's "Created Spaces," edited by Micaela Morrissette, is published in *Rain Taxi*'s online edition. First solo exhibition of Ashbery's collages, made from 1948 to 2008, held at New York's Tibor de Nagy Gallery (other solo and group shows will follow in later years). Library of America publishes his *Collected Poems 1956–1987*, the first volume in that series by a living poet.

2009   At invitation of Deborah Landau, begins annual series of "Conversations" in graduate writing program at New York University, which continue through the spring semester of 2017. Receives Harvard Arts Medal and *Paris Review*'s Hadada Award. Harvard Film Archive presents programs examining reciprocal influences between film and his work. Is awarded special international Premio Napoli prize, in conjunction with publication of *Un mondo che non può essere migliore; Poesie scelte 1956–2007*, a selection translated by Damiano Abeni and Moira Egan. Publishes *Planisphere*, designed by Jeff Clark (Ecco). Ava Lehrer organizes Ashbery's research materials on Raymond Roussel, which become important components of ongoing international Roussel exhibitions and renewed scholarly interest.

2010   Begins collaboration with Guy Maddin that develops into Maddin's 2015 feature film *The Forbidden Room* and his 2016 interactive film project *Seances*. International conference "John Ashbery in Paris," organized by Olivier Brossard and colleagues, held in Paris. Receives Brooklyn Book Festival's "BoBi" award. First translation of his controversial 1962 volume *The Tennis Court Oath* published in Spanish (by Julio Mas Alcaraz), which garners much attention (also translated into French by Olivier Brossard in 2015).

2011 Publishes translation of Rimbaud's *Illuminations* (Norton), which becomes finalist for Oxford-Weidenfeld Translation Prize. Inducted into New York State Writers Hall of Fame. Awarded Medal of Honor from New York University's Center for French Civilization and Culture, and National Book Foundation's Medal for Distinguished Contribution to American Letters. Named one of Equality Forum's "Icons" for LGBT History Month, and an honoree on the "*Out* 100" LGBT annual list (*Out* magazine).

2012 Receives a National Humanities Medal, presented by President Obama at the White House. The New School, under Robert Polito's direction, begins multi-semester interdisciplinary project to document Ashbery's Created Spaces, particularly his Hudson house (the project is later sponsored by the Poetry Foundation in 2014, and further developed by Karin Roffman at Yale University Library's Digital Humanities Lab, from 2016, going online in 2017). Receives honorary DLitt from Middlebury College/Bread Loaf School of English. Publishes *Quick Question* (Ecco).

2013 Receives New York City Literary Honor in Poetry. Exhibition "John Ashbery Collects," based on his Hudson house, held at Loretta Howard Gallery in New York City, co-curated by Emily Skillings and Adam Fitzgerald. Smithsonian Institution's National Portrait Gallery commissions poem "Hand with a Picture" for catalogue of 2014–15 exhibition "Face Value: Portraiture in the Age of Abstraction" (which includes Fairfield Porter's 1952 portrait of him, with argyle socks). Begins collaboration with artist/poet Kenneth Goldsmith on "Jeanne Moreau" series of rugs.

2014 *Collected French Translations*, edited by Rosanne Wasserman and Eugene Richie, published as two-volume set (poetry and prose, by Farrar, Straus and Giroux), named finalist for Pegasus Award for Poetry Criticism (Poetry Foundation) and the poetry volume selected as Recommended Translation by Poetry Book Society (U.K.). Awarded Medal of Honor for Achievement in Literature by National Arts Club. Begins consulting with poet and scholar Farnoosh

Fathi on a new edition of poems by Joan Murray (1917–1942), whose work he has long championed.

2015 Publishes *Breezeway* (Ecco). Two-person exhibition of new collages with Guy Maddin at Tibor de Nagy Gallery. Pioneer Works (Red Hook, Brooklyn, New York) hosts celebration of Ashbery, organized by Ben Lerner, with Monica de la Torre, Geoffrey G. O'Brien, and John Yau.

2016 Steve Cosson's experimental theater group The Civilians creates *Rimbaud in New York*, commissioned by the Brooklyn Academy of Music (BAM) and The Poetry Foundation, inspired by Ashbery's translation of *Illuminations*. Is one of four honorees at New York City benefit to celebrate *The Harvard Advocate*'s 150th anniversary. Begins collaborating with filmmaker Michael Almereyda on *The Lonedale Operator*, exploring the relationship between Ashbery's experience of film and his poetry, completed in late 2017. Gives readings at Columbia and Yale Universities. Publishes *Commotion of the Birds* (Ecco). Exhibits new collages at Tibor de Nagy Gallery in New York (December 15–January 28, 2017).

2017 With curator Antonio Sergio Bessa, begins planning fall 2018 exhibition of his collages at Pratt Institute's Manhattan campus. Gives reading at Princeton University with screenwriter and director Jim Jarmusch (via Skype). *The Songs We Know Best: John Ashbery's Early Life* by Karin Roffman is published by Farrar, Straus and Giroux. In recognition of his contributions to Roussel studies over many decades, receives first Raymond Roussel Society Medal in program at Instituto Cervantes (NYC). Library of America publishes his *Collected Poems 1991–2000*. His ninetieth birthday is marked by various tributes, including the annual "Read and Feed" festival at Basilica Hudson, organized by Jeffrey Lependorf. Publishes new poems in *The New Yorker*, *The Nation*, and *LitMag*. Participates in selection of images, editorial, and layout work with Mark Polizzotti and John Yau for *They Knew What They Wanted*, a book about his collages to be published in early 2018 by Rizzoli. Continues making collages, writing poems, and working with Karin Roffman on next volume of his biography until September 1. On September 3, dies peacefully, of natural causes, at his home in Hudson, New York, aged 90.

Note on the Texts

This volume contains seven volumes of poetry by John Ashbery: *Flow Chart* (1991), *Hotel Lautréamont* (1992), *And the Stars Were Shining* (1994), *Can You Hear, Bird* (1995), *Wakefulness* (1998), *Girls on the Run* (1999), and *Your Name Here* (2000). It also collects twenty-five poems published during the same years but not included in those seven volumes, along with a collage-poem from ca. 1954 that was not included in this book's companion volume, *Collected Poems 1956–1987*.

The order is based on the chronological publication of Ashbery's books by his American trade publishers. (These books were all published in the United Kingdom by Carcanet Press.) The arrangement of the poems does not account for the publication of Ashbery poems in limited editions brought out by small presses or as separate broadsides. All poems in such limited-edition books or broadsides are included in the present volume, either under the heading of the American trade-publisher collection in which they later appeared or, in the case of the poem "*Victrola floribunda*," in the section devoted to Ashbery's previously uncollected poems.

Ashbery does not significantly revise his poems once they are published in book form, though in a few instances, there have been small emendations (such as a change in punctuation) when his poems have been reprinted—as in his *Notes from the Air: Selected Later Poems* (New York: Ecco, 2007, hereafter referred to as *NFA*).

The texts printed here are taken from their first American book publications. The list below provides information about the seven books of Ashbery's poetry gathered here, along with the uncollected poems he has chosen to include in the present volume:

Flow Chart (New York: Knopf, 1991). The text printed here is that of the Knopf first edition, with the addition of thirty-eight lines between "other mooted toys" at 66.22 and "or motion at a stranger" at 68.29. After working on the poem for more than seven months, Ashbery completed a first typescript draft of *Flow Chart* on July 28, 1988, his sixty-first birthday. The text of this typescript was then retyped on a word processor, as part of an ongoing revision process spread across successive typescript drafts and page proofs. On page 41 of the word-processor typescript, there is a handwritten instruction to "insert p. 33 of ms. here" (referring to the page containing the thirty-eight lines mentioned above), but this instruction was not followed by the typist, and neither the next typescript draft nor the page proofs for the Knopf edition contain the missing lines. The omitted passage was discovered by John Shoptaw and published in his monograph *On the Outside Looking Out: John Ashbery's Poetry* (Cambridge, MA: Harvard University Press, 1994). At Ashbery's request, these lines are restored in this edition. The text of these lines is taken from Ashbery's first typescript draft of *Flow Chart*, currently at Houghton Library, Harvard University. Section V of *Flow Chart* was later included in *NFA*.

Hotel Lautréamont (New York: Knopf, 1992). Poems in *NFA*: "Light Turnouts," "Autumn Telegram," "Notes from the Air," "Still Life with Stranger," "Hotel Lautréamont," "On the Empress's Mind," "The Phantom Agents," "From Estuaries, from Casinos," "Autumn on the Thruway," "The Little Black Dress," "*Avant de quitter ces lieux*," "In Another Time," "*Le mensonge de Nina Petrovna*," "Korean Soap Opera," "A Driftwood Altar," "The Youth's Magic Horn," "Seasonal," "Kamarinskaya," "Elephant Visitors," "Retablo," "Quartet," "[And now I cannot remember . . .]," "Just Wednesday," "In My Way / On My Way," "No Good at Names," "In Vain, Therefore," "A Hole in Your Sock," "How to Continue."

And the Stars Were Shining (New York: Farrar, Straus and Giroux, 1994). Poems in *NFA*: "Token Resistance," "The Mandrill on the Turnpike," "About to Move," "Ghost Riders of the Moon," "The Love Scenes," "Well, Yes, Actually," "Myrtle," "Mutt and Jeff," "Coventry," "And the Stars Were Shining."

Can You Hear, Bird (New York: Farrar, Straus and Giroux, 1995). Three poems in the 1995 edition are not included here at Ashbery's request, because they had been published in *And the Stars Were Shining*: "Andante Misterioso" (as "Sicilian Bird"), "Heavenly Arts Polka" (as "A Waltz Dream"), and "Like a Sentence." Poems in *NFA*: "A Poem of Unrest," "A Waking Dream," "At First I Thought I Wouldn't Say Anything About It," ". . . by an Earthquake," "By Guess and by Gosh," "Can You Hear, Bird," "Cantilever," "Chapter II, Book 35," "Dangerous Moonlight," "Debit Night," "Dull Mauve," "My Philosophy of Life," "No Longer Very Clear," "Operators Are Standing By," "Plain as Day," "Sleepers Awake," "The Faint of Heart," "The Green Mummies," "The Military Base," "The Problem of Anxiety," "Today's Academicians," "Tuesday Evening (excerpt)," "Yes, Dr. Genzmer, How May I Be of Assistance to You? What! You Say the Patient Has Escaped?" "You Would Have Thought."

Wakefulness (New York: Farrar, Straus and Giroux, 1998). Poems in *NFA*: "Wakefulness," "Baltimore," "Cousin Sarah's Knitting," "Last Night I Dreamed I Was in Bucharest," "Added Poignancy," "Laughing Gravy," "From Such Commotion," "Alive at Every Passage,"

"The Burden of the Park," "Dear Sir or Madam," "Discordant Data," "Outside My Window the Japanese . . . ," "Probably Based on a Dream," "Proximity," "Like America," "Snow," "The Dong with the Luminous Nose," "Come On, Dear," "Homecoming."
Girls on the Run (New York: Farrar, Straus and Giroux, 1999). Sections I, II, III, VIII, IX, and XXI were reprinted in *NFA*.
Your Name Here (New York: Farrar, Straus and Giroux, 2000). Poems in *NFA*: "This Room," "If You Said You Would Come with Me," "A Linnet," "The Bobinski Brothers," "Merrily We Live," "Caravaggio and His Followers," "Industrial Collage," "The History of My Life," "Memories of Imperialism," "Heartache," "Redeemed Area," "They Don't Just Go Away, Either," "Sonatine Mélancolique," "Stanzas Before Time," "A Suit," "Crossroads in the Past," "How Dangerous," "Lemurs and Pharisees," "The Underwriters," "Vendanges," "Has to Be Somewhere," "Strange Cinema," "Fade In," "Pastilles for the Voyage," "Your Name Here."

UNCOLLECTED POEMS

Hoboken: *Semi-colon* 1:3 (n.d., ca. 1954).
Call It "Untitled": *Mudfish* 6 (1992).
Le singe d'une nuit d'été: Poetry International (Rotterdam, Holland, 1992).
Fruit and Tea: *New York Review of Books*, August 13, 1992.
Two Norwegian Moods: *Mudfish* 7 (1993).
Tahiti Trot: *Poetry* 162:3 (June 1993).
Tin Steamboat: *Mudfish* 8 (1995).
My Favorite Dress: *Salt* 8 (1996).
Yes, I Have Been Reading: *Denver Quarterly* 31:1 (Summer 1996).
Often in Sorting Out: *Café Review* (Fall 1996).
The Dissolving Bride: *Café Review* (Fall 1996).
Shadows on the Street: *Salt* 9 (1996).
Media Runner: *Sophisticated Brat* (1997).
The Hailstorm in Belgrade, May 24th, 1937: *Tongues* (1997).
Victrola floribunda: Dorothea Tanning, *Another Language of Flowers* (New York: George Braziller, 1998).
The Green Dress: *Bard Papers* (1999).
Hierarchy of the Unexpected: *London Review of Books*, September 30, 1999.
Welcome to Entropy: *Stand* 1:4 (December 1999).
Invitation to a Wooing: *TLS*, December 10, 1999.
These Symptoms I Know So Well: *Verse* 16:3 (2000).
Vauban: *Colorado Review* 27:1 (Spring 2000).
Greased Lightning: *Combo* 6 (Spring 2000).

A Leap in Time: *Gay and Lesbian Review* 7:3 (Summer 2000).
Befuddled: *Kenyon Review* 22:3–4 (Summer–Fall 2000).
A Lot of Catching Up to Do: *Columbia* 33 (Winter 2000).
The Lyricist: *Columbia* (Winter 2000).

On the following pages, a stanza break occurs at the bottom of the page (not including pages in which the break is evident because of the regular stanzaic structure of the poem): 7, 65, 66, 68, 74, 123, 183, 205, 222, 227, 228, 232, 233, 241, 244, 246, 249, 250, 252, 253, 261, 270, 292, 294, 296, 302, 305, 306, 315, 324, 332, 336, 337, 339, 341, 346, 351, 353, 358, 368, 371, 385, 386, 387, 390, 391, 393, 400, 405, 409, 413, 423, 428, 430, 436, 442, 451, 456, 457, 467, 469, 471, 474, 477, 482, 485, 486, 490, 497, 504, 513, 515, 516, 523, 526, 532, 534, 535, 537, 542, 543, 548, 556, 560, 566, 570, 578, 583, 584, 587, 599, 603, 621, 626, 629, 639, 643, 651, 657, 660, 662, 665, 666, 667, 670, 675, 677, 680, 681, 689, 690, 693, 695, 705, 706, 708, 716, 717, 718, 721, 725, 726, 731, 736, 743, 744, 747, 749, 750, 752, 753, 761, 762, 763.

This volume presents the texts of the original printings chosen for inclusion here, but it does not attempt to reproduce nontextual features of their typographic design. The texts are presented without change, except for the correction of typographical errors. Spelling, punctuation, and capitalization are often expressive features and are not altered, even when inconsistent or irregular. The following is a list of typographical errors corrected, cited by page and line number: 68.9, off the; 500.28, time.; 520.4, eucalpytuses.; 705.14, Casper; 714.33, others'.

Notes

In the notes below, the reference numbers denote page and line of this volume (the line count includes headings). No note is made for material included in standard desk-reference books such as Webster's Collegiate, Biographical, and Geographical dictionaries. Quotations from Shakespeare are keyed to *The Riverside Shakespeare* (Boston: Houghton Mifflin, 1974), edited by G. Blakemore Evans. References to the Bible have been keyed to the King James Version. For references to other studies and further biographical background than is contained in the Chronology, see Mark Ford, *John Ashbery in Conversation with Mark Ford* (London: Between the Lines, 2003), the Flow Chart Foundation's website (www.flowchartfoundation.org), and Karin Roffman, *The Songs We Know Best: John Ashbery's Early Life* (New York: Farrar, Straus and Giroux, 2017).

FLOW CHART

4.23–24 our hope for years to come] From the hymn "Our God, Our Help in Ages Past" (1719), with words by the English hymnist Isaac Watts (1674–1748).

11.19–21 "*when such a destin'd wretch . . . on board*"] From "The Castaway" (1799), lines 3–4, by the English poet William Cowper (1731–1800).

12.12–13 "*And I in greater depths than he,*"] Cf. the last lines of "The Castaway": "But I beneath a rougher sea, / And whelm'd in deeper gulfs than he."

19.39 *bon gré mal gré*] French: like it or not.

25.36 all time had in the wallet at his back.] See Shakespeare, *Troilus and Cressida*, III.iii.145: "Time hath, my lord, a wallet at his back."

26.34 hunger *de tous les jours*] Everyday hunger.

27.17 Little Nell] Orphan heroine of Charles Dickens's novel *The Old Curiosity Shop* (1840–41).

31.4–5 Full many a flower . . . waste its fragrance] Cf. "Elegy Written in a Country Churchyard" (1750) by the English poet Thomas Gray (1716–1771), lines 55–56: "Full many a flow'r is born to blush unseen, / And waste its sweetness on the desert air."

31.39 "Queen Mab"] Long poem (1813) by the English poet Percy Bysshe Shelley (1792–1822).

33.5 they managed to save Hitler's brain] A reference to the cult movie *They*

791

Saved Hitler's Brain, directed by David Bradley (1920–1997), released in 1967 as an expanded version of the 1963 film *Madmen of Mandoras*.

34.26–27 *meliora probant, deteriora / sequuntur*] Latin: sanction the better way, follow the worse, phrase cited by Edgar Allan Poe in the essay "The Philosophy of Furniture" (1840); cf. Ovid, *Metamorphoses* 7.20: "Video meliora, proboque, deteriora sequor" ("I see better things, and approve, but I follow worse").

42.27 "the devil's beauty,"] The beauty of youth.

49.8 Holophane] Prismatic glass reflector, a light fixture named for its manufacturer.

54.2 *and roam at will, timeless*] From "Tinian" (c. 1801–6), draft of a hymn by the German poet Friedrich Hölderlin (1770–1843), in Richard Sieburth's translation ("Und lustzuwandeln, zeitlos").

54.26 *dans un bois solitaire*] French: In a lonely wood, the title of an arietta (K.308/295b) composed by Wolfgang Amadeus Mozart in 1777–78, with words by the French writer Antoine Houdar de la Motte (1672–1731).

56.22 Clapham Common] A park in south London.

57.10 old chromo] A chromolithograph.

57.31 Osiris] God of the underworld in Egyptian myth.

66.2 "no habitation unless one linger."] The third-to-last line of Hölderlin's poem "Der Ister" (c. 1803), in Sieburth's translation ("Unwirthbar wär es, ohne Weile").

79.2–3 *fons et origo, nemine dissentiente.*] Latin: the source and origin, no one dissenting.

87.15 Mélisande] Character in the play *Pelléas et Mélisande* (1893) by the Belgian poet and playwright Maurice Maeterlinck (1862–1949) and in the opera (1902) based on it by Claude Debussy (1862–1918).

94.28–29 *O / don fatale*] Italian: O fatal gift, title of mezzo-soprano aria sung by Princess Eboli in *Don Carlo* (1867), opera by Giuseppe Verdi (1813–1901).

105.23 *attelage*] French: harness.

109.13–14 "Whatever things men are doing . . . page."] "Quicquid agunt homines nostri farrago libelli": Juvenal, *Satires* 1.85–86, in the translation from Latin given in "On the Periodical Essayists" (1819), essay by the English writer William Hazlitt (1778–1830).

110.9 Hebe] Greek goddess of youth.

115.3 Lost Dutchman Mine] Legendary lost gold mine in the Superstition Mountains of Arizona, named for the German immigrant Jacob Waltz (c. 1810–1891), who is said to have died without revealing the mine's location.

121.18 *cum frumentum*] Latin: since grain.

122.27 Sezession Vienna] The Vienna Secession was an aestheticist movement in art, architecture, and design founded in 1897 by a group of Austrian artists and architects, most notably Gustav Klimt (1862–1918), its first president.

123.31 *facture*] French: workmanship.

127.16 *ouvreuse*] French: usherette in a cinema.

129.36 the lost chord] Title of popular song (1877) composed by English composer Arthur Sullivan (1842–1900) while his brother was dying, a setting of a poem (1858) by the English poet Adelaide Anne Procter (1825–1864).

135.8 *gare*] French: train station.

135.37 Paganini] Niccolò Paganini (1782–1840), virtuoso Italian violinist and composer.

138.1–2 are they gone, the old familiar faces?] Cf. the repeated line in "The Old Familiar Faces" (1798) by English essayist, critic, and poet Charles Lamb (1775–1834): "All, all are gone, the old familiar faces."

139.1 *durch ein ander*] German: confused.

141.16 Alvin and the chipmunks] The Chipmunks (later Alvin and the Chipmunks) were featured on a series of novelty records beginning with "The Chipmunk Song" (1958); the three high-pitched voices were sung by Ross Bagdasarian Jr. (billed as David Seville) and speeded up in playback. The characters became the basis of comic books, several television series, and animated films.

141.25 just lay down in a boat and slept, Lady-of-Shalott style] See "The Lady of Shalott" (1832), part IV, by Alfred, Lord Tennyson (1809–1892): "It was the closing of the day: / She loos'd the chain, and down she lay; / The broad stream bore her far away, / The Lady of Shalott."

142.8–10 Carthage . . . animal's hide] According to legend, the ancient city of Carthage in North Africa was founded by the Tyrian queen Dido. See Virgil's *Aeneid*, bk. I, lines 442–46, for the Tyrians' purchase of as much land as could be enclosed by a bull's hide, which was cut into strips to increase the area.

144.17–18 like Leda her swan] In Greek mythology, Leda was raped by Zeus after he came to her in the guise of a swan.

146.5 Mercury slew Argus for vulgar reasons] In Greek and Roman mythology, Mercury (Hermes) charmed the hundred-eyed giant Argus to sleep, then killed him, on a mission from Zeus. Argus was guarding Io, a young priestess beloved of Zeus, whom he had transformed into a heifer in an unsuccessful attempt to dispel Hera's jealousy.

150.11 I hear America snowing.] Cf. Walt Whitman, "I Hear America Singing" (1855).

153.11–12 bunches of grapes . . . shrug at] Cf. Aesop's fable "The Fox and the Grapes," where a fox leaps to grab some grapes but cannot reach them, then claims not to have wanted them because they are unripe and sour.

160.31 *rêves*] French: dreams.

162.31 Malone] Edmond Malone (1741–1812), Irish Shakespearean scholar and editor.

163.6 Kjerulf] Halfdan Kjerulf (1815–1868), Norwegian composer.

168.20 hold that tiger?] Repeated phrase from "Tiger Rag," first recorded as an instrumental in 1917 by the Original Dixieland Jass Band.

169.15–17 be one of those . . . lost.] See Henry James's "The Art of Fiction" (1884): "Try to be one of the people on whom nothing is lost!"

171.12–13 "Unwillingly, . . . shore."] From Virgil, *Aeneid*, bk. 6, l. 460: "Invitus, regina, tuo de litore cessi."

180.37 *trouvaille*] French: lucky find.

184.22 *procès verbal*] In French law, a written statement pertaining to the facts of a criminal case.

186.3–5 "the swan-winged horses . . . manes,"] From a song in *The Bride's Tragedy* (1822), II.i.32–33, a verse drama not intended to be staged, by the English poet Thomas Lovell Beddoes (1803–1849).

187.19–20 *But there were dreams to sell, ill didst thou buy:*] Beddoes, "Dream-Pedlary" (1829–30), lines 20–21.

188.26 "out of hell's murky haze, heaven's blue hall,"] Beddoes, "Dream-Pedlary", lines 31–32.

189.3 *Dreaming a dream to prize*] Beddoes, "Dream-Pedlary", line 24.

190.5–7 chopping-block sounds . . . Mary Stuart and Lady Jane Grey] Two women who were beheaded in sixteenth-century England: Mary I of Scotland (1542–1587), the Roman Catholic rival of Elizabeth I known as Mary, Queen of Scots, and Lady Jane Grey (1537–1554), nominal queen for nine days installed in an unsuccessful attempt to prevent the accession of Mary Tudor, a Catholic, to the throne.

190.15–16 *We nightingales . . . so listen to us:*] Thomas Lovell Beddoes, from *Death's Jest-Book* (1829–49), III.iii.319–20.

190.25 Tim the ostler] Character in the poem "The Highwayman" (1906) by the English poet Alfred Noyes (1880–1958).

190.37 minnesinger] Twelfth- or thirteenth-century German poet-musician.

192.33 *Improvvisatore!*] Performer of improvised oral poetry popular in Italy from the fourteenth to the nineteenth centuries.

NOTES 795

195.1–2 *La Fille mal gardée* is my favorite piece of music?] The ballet *La Fille mal gardée* ("The poorly guarded girl"), choreographed by the French dancer Jean Dauberval (1742–1806), was first performed in 1789 and accompanied by popular French airs and dance music. In 1828 French composer Ferdinand Hérold (1791–1833) provided a new score, with his own music and selections from operas by Rossini and Donizetti; in 1864 it was staged in Berlin with music by the German composer Peter Ludwig Hertel (1817–1899).

196.15 We're interested in the language,] Here begins a double sestina that derives its twelve end-words from the double sestina "The Complaint of Lisa" (1870) by the English poet Algernon Charles Swinburne (1837–1909).

196.37 *culte du moi*] French: cult of the self. *Le Culte du moi* (1888–91) was a trilogy of novels by the French writer and politician Maurice Barrès (1862–1923).

198.3 James VI of Scotland] Also James I of England (1566–1625).

203.37 *voyage d'affaires*] French: business trip.

211.12–13 I will show you fear in a handful of specialists] Cf. T. S. Eliot's *The Waste Land* (1922), line 30: "I will show you fear in a handful of dust."

211.26 Chatterton's garret] The attic in London where the young, impoverished English poet Thomas Chatterton (1752–1770) committed suicide.

216.18–19 "Why Girls Leave Home," "The Trial of Mary Dugan"] *Why Girls Leave Home* (1904), stage melodrama by the American playwright Fred Summerfield, filmed in 1913 starring Bessie Learn and in 1921 starring Anna Q. Nilsson; *The Trial of Mary Dugan* (1927), stage melodrama by the American playwright Bayard Veiller (1869–1943), filmed in 1929 starring Norma Shearer and in 1941 starring Laraine Day.

218.13 the "dear, dead days," as someone called them.] The American journalist and poet Henry Austin (1858–1912), in the poem "Bohemian Days," collected in *Vagabond Verses* (1890). The phrase was later used by the American cartoonist Charles Addams (1912–1988) for the title of *Dear Dead Days: A Family Album* (1959).

219.11–12 the snakes and ladders of outrageous fortune] Cf. Shakespeare, *Hamlet*, III.i.57, "The slings and arrows of outrageous fortune." Snakes and Ladders is a board game.

220.6 "evanish all, like vapours in the air,"] From the closet drama *The Tragedy of Darius* (1603) by the English poet and courtier William Alexander (c. 1567–1640).

HOTEL LAUTRÉAMONT

225.1 LAUTRÉAMONT] Comte de Lautréamont was the pseudonym of the Uruguayan-born French writer Isidore Ducasse (1846–1870), author of *Les Chants de Maldoror* (1868–70) and *Poésies* (1870).

228.2 go down to the sea in ships] Psalms 107:23.

235.7 "Windsor Forest"] Traditional ballad collected in *The English and Scottish Popular Ballads*, edited by Francis Child.

235.14–15 Sibelius violin concerto] Violin Concerto in D minor, op. 47 (1904, revised 1905) by the Finnish composer Jean Sibelius (1865–1957).

238.33 Republic serial] A film issued by Republic Studios, whose serial releases included *The Lone Ranger* (1938), *The Adventures of Captain Marvel* (1941), and *Captain America* (1944).

242.1–2 Slough of Despond] A deep bog into which the protagonist of John Bunyan's *The Pilgrim's Progress* (1678) sinks under the weight of his sins.

242.19 *Musica Reservata*] Style of a cappella music developed in the second half of the sixteenth century in Italy and southern Germany.

255.24 the earthquake at Lisbon] The earthquake, tsunami, and great fire of November 1, 1755, destroyed most of the city of Lisbon and killed an estimated sixty thousand people.

256.5 Prometheus' eagle] In Greek mythology, Zeus punished Prometheus for giving fire to mankind by having him chained to a rock and having an eagle tear at his liver each day.

258.29 and no trees sing.] Cf. John Keats's poem "La Belle Dame Sans Merci" (1819), lines 4 and 48: "and no birds sing."

259.11–12 "Death cancels all engagements." . . . movie *Laura*] The epigraph is from the novel *Zuleika Dobson* (1911) by the English novelist, essayist, and caricaturist Max Beerbohm (1872–1956), not from *Laura* (1944), a film noir directed by the Austrian-American film director Otto Preminger (1905–1982). In *Laura* Clifton Webb (1889–1966) plays Waldo Lydecker, an acerbic columnist and radio commentator.

262.8 Avant de quitter ces lieux] French: Before leaving these places, a baritone aria from *Faust* (1859), opera by the French composer Charles Gounod (1818–1893), act 2, sung by Valentin.

263.32–33 Dinorah, who has lost her goat, sings the mad scene] In *Dinorah* (1859), by the German-born composer Giacomo Meyerbeer (1791–1864), the eponymous heroine is mad for much of the opera, throughout which she searches for Bellah, her lost goat. During her mad scene in act 2, she sings the aria "Ombre légère qui suis mes pas" ("Nimble shadow that follows my steps"), known as the Shadow Song.

279.20 *Love's Old Sweet Song*] Victorian parlor song (1884) by the Irish composer James Lynam Molloy (1837–1909), with words by the English lyricist Graham Clifton Bingham (1859–1913).

281.3   *Wild Boys of the Road*] Film (1933) about teenage hobos directed by William Wellman (1896–1975), starring Frankie Darro (1917–1976) and Rochelle Hudson (1916–1972).

282.30   Le mensonge de Nina Petrovna] French film (*The Lie of Nina Petrovna*, 1937) directed by Russian-born director Viktor Tourjansky (1891–1976), a remake of a 1929 German film.

292.5   *The Youth's Magic Horn*] A collection of anonymous German folk poems set to music by Gustav Mahler (1860–1911).

293.4   the twa corbies] The two crows, the title of an anonymous Scottish ballad.

297.9   *Kamarinskaya*] Orchestral work (1848) by Mikhail Glinka (1804–1857) based on Russian folk songs.

297.10   bombes-glacées] Plural of "*bombe-glacée*," an ice cream dessert with a spherical shape.

297.27–28   look in thy heart and write.] Cf. *Astrophil and Stella* (1591), sonnet 1, line 14, by the English poet, courtier, and soldier Sir Philip Sidney (1554–1586).

305.11   Erebus] The underworld in Greek mythology.

305.26–27   in the vein of Lady Audley's Secret] Best-selling novel (1862) by the English novelist and editor Mary Elizabeth Braddon (1837–1915), about a woman who attempts to kill her first husband and abandons her child.

309.16   Dvorak's *Humoreske*?] Cycle of piano pieces (1894) by the Czech composer Antonín Dvořák (1841–1904), of which the best known is no. 7 in G-flat major.

309.21   Vienna *Musikverein*] Concert hall in Vienna, home to the Vienna Philharmonic orchestra.

309.22   second Viennese school] Group of composers based in Vienna in the first decades of the twentieth century, including Arnold Schoenberg (1874–1951), Alban Berg (1885–1935), and Anton Webern (1883–1945).

312.1   Retablo] A Mexican devotional painting, often in the folk art tradition.

314.1   *A Mourning Forbidding Valediction*] Cf. the title of the poem "A Valediction Forbidding Mourning" (1611–12?) by the English poet and clergyman John Donne (1572–1631).

315.8–9   The owl . . . was a-cold.] John Keats, "The Eve of St. Agnes" (1819), line 2.

317.10   Charpentier's *Julien*] The opera *Julien, ou La vie du poète* (Julien, or the Life of the Poet, 1913), by the French composer Gustave Charpentier (1860–1956).

324.11 Oeuvres Complètes] French: Complete Works.

340.13 "*this* is the way we wash our clothes"] From the nursery rhyme "Here We Go Round the Mulberry Bush."

342.12 Enna Jettick] Company that manufactured "sensible" women's shoes.

345.1 *Alborada*] Spanish term for an aubade, as in Maurice Ravel's composition "Alborada del Gracioso" (1905).

AND THE STARS WERE SHINING

349.1–2 AND THE STARS WERE SHINING] Aria ("E lucevan le stele") from act 3 of Puccini's opera *Tosca* (1900), sung by Cavaradossi.

352.27 am I my brother's keeper] Cain's response in Genesis 4:9 when God asks where his brother Abel is, after Cain has murdered him.

354.19 *bayadère*] French: Indian dancing girl.

357.2–3 Voices of Spring. Vienna Bonbons. Morning Papers.] Orchestral waltzes by Johann Strauss (1804–1849).

357.4 *Symphonie en ut dièse majeur.*] French: Symphony in C-sharp major.

357.9 Cecilia Valdés.] Novel (1839) by the Cuban writer Cirilo Villaverde (1812–1894).

357.14 Scenes of Clerical Life.] Book of short stories (1858) by George Eliot (pen name of English writer Mary Ann Evans, 1818–1890).

358.17–18 "This heart . . . *The Bride of Frankenstein*] From *Bride of Frankenstein* (1935), film directed by English director James Whale (1889–1957) and starring Boris Karloff (stage name of the English actor William Henry Pratt, 1887–1969) as Frankenstein's monster. The line is spoken in the laboratory by Dr. Frankenstein, played by the English actor Colin Clive (1900–1937), after the beating of an isolated human heart, stimulated by an electric current, comes to a stop.

368.10 We must double up, or die.] Cf. "We must love one another or die," line from "September 1, 1939" (1939) by the English poet W. H. Auden (1907–1973).

373.1 Pomona's] Roman goddess of fruits.

373.8 Greenaway hat] Hat of the kind worn in illustrations to the children's stories of Kate Greenaway (1846–1901).

376.14 *William Byrd*] English composer (1539/40 or 1542–1623).

379.11 Gyges . . . his ring] The ring of Gyges, described in book 2 of Plato's *Republic*, enabled its owner to become invisible.

379.31–32 Time . . . wallet at his back] See note 25.36.

NOTES 799

383.1 *The Decline of the West*] Historical study (1918–22) by German historical philosopher Oswald Spengler (1880–1936), which argued that Western civilization was in a state of decay.

383.2 O Oswald, O Spengler, this is very sad to find!] Cf. "A Toccata of Galuppi's" (1855) by the English poet Robert Browning (1812–1889), which opens "Oh Galuppi, Baldassaro, this is very sad to find!"

384.29 *Miserere!*] Latin: Have pity.

386.30 "to concentrate the mind," as Dr. Johnson said.] In *The Life of Samuel Johnson* (1791), James Boswell (1740–1795) records Samuel Johnson (1709–1784) making the remark: "Depend upon it, sir, when a man knows he is to be hanged in a fortnight, it concentrates his mind wonderfully."

391.5–6 *Schreker's* Der Schatzgräber] Opera (The Treasure Hunter, 1920) by the Austrian composer Franz Schreker (1878–1934).

391.8 *Was gibt es?*] German: What's the matter?

391.19 *En revanche*] French: On the other hand.

392.27 Addison and Steele] The English essayists Joseph Addison (1672–1719) and Richard Steele (1672–1729), co-founders of the influential periodical *The Spectator*.

392.28 K rations] Packages of processed food distributed to U.S. military personnel during World War II, consisting of breakfast, lunch, and dinner packets.

397.1 *In the Meantime, Darling*] Film comedy (1944) directed by Otto Preminger, starring Jeanne Crain (1925–2003) and Frank Latimore (1925–1998).

400.23 *Mutt and Jeff*] Popular newspaper comic strip, 1907–83, created by the American cartoonist Bud Fisher (1885–1954).

400.24–26 "But what he does . . . *"The Ister"*] These lines from Hölderlin's "Der Ister" are taken from Richard Sieburth's translation.

401.12 "Ere the days of his pilgrimage vanish,"] "How Pleasant to Know Mr. Lear" (1871), line 31, by the English poet and artist Edward Lear (1812–1888).

405.28 Joubert] Joseph Joubert (1754–1824), French essayist. The epigraph (1803) to this section is taken from Paul Auster's translation in *The Notebooks of Joseph Joubert* (1983).

407.6 *papier bleu*] French: court paper.

409.18 No ideas in things, either—] Cf. William Carlos Williams, *Paterson*, Book I (1927): "No ideas but in things."

410.30 Laocoön tableau] In Greek myth, Laocoön was a priest of Apollo at Troy who warned the Trojans not to touch the wooden horse sent by the Greeks as a gift. He and his sons were killed by two huge serpents, which was interpreted by the Trojans as a sign of the gods' disapproval of Laocoön's advice.

The incident is the subject of one of the most famous of ancient sculptures, excavated in Rome in 1506.

415.6–7 Stopping by an apartmentful . . . evening] Cf. the title of Robert Frost's poem "Stopping by Woods on a Snowy Evening" (1923).

415.21 Caruso] Italian opera singer Enrico Caruso (1873–1921).

415.24 Tom and Jerrys] Cocktail made with brandy, rum, eggs, and milk.

416.2–3 But in the soul of man . . . Traherne] From *Centuries of Meditations* (first published posthumously in 1908) by the English poet and clergyman Thomas Traherne (1636–1674).

CAN YOU HEAR, BIRD

427.18 Steffi Duna] Hungarian-born dancer and stage and movie actor (1919–1992); her films included the short *La Cucaracha* (1934), *Anthony Adverse* (1936), and *Waterloo Bridge* (1940).

427.29 *I must sugar my hair.*] See the song of the Mock Turtle and the Gryphon in Lewis Carroll's *Alice's Adventures in Wonderland* (1865): "'Tis the voice of the Lobster: I heard him declare, / 'You have baked me too brown, I must sugar my hair.'"

432.19–20 "Boris Karloff."] See note 358.17–18.

435.8 That Phoenician sailor] The drowned figure on an imaginary Tarot card in T. S. Eliot's *The Waste Land*, corresponding with the drowned "Phlebas the Phoenician" later in the poem.

435.10 the Flying Dutchman] Spectral captain of a legendary ghost ship said to be doomed to sail the oceans forever; among the many adaptations of the legend is Richard Wagner's 1843 opera.

440.25 *Dangerous Moonlight*] British film (1941; released in the U.S. as *Suicide Squadron*) directed by the Irish director Brian Desmond Hurst (1895–1986), starring the Austrian-born British actor Anton Walbrook (1896–1967) as a Polish concert pianist who flies with an RAF fighter squadron during World War II, and the English actor Sally Gray (1915–2006) as his wife, a journalist.

442.13–14 "The cheese stands alone"] From the children's song "The Farmer in the Dell."

447.34 D. W. Griffith] American film director (1875–1948) whose films include *The Birth of a Nation* (1915) and *Intolerance* (1916).

448.20 Enoch Arden–like return] In "Enoch Arden" (1864), poem by British poet Alfred, Lord Tennyson (1809–1892), a shipwrecked sailor returns home after ten years to find his wife married to another man.

449.6 élan vital.] Term used by the French philosopher Henri Bergson (1859–1941) to denote a creative principle or life force inherent in all living organisms.

NOTES 801

449.8–9 "anthropophagi . . . shoulders."] Shakespeare, *Othello*, I.iii.144–45.

449.39 House Beautiful] Palace in Bunyan's *The Pilgrim's Progress* where Christian stops to rest on his pilgrimage to the Celestial City.

450.24 Hercule Poirot or Inspector Javert.] Fictional Belgian detective who appeared in many novels and stories by the English writer Agatha Christie (1890–1976); police inspector in Victor Hugo's *Les Misérables* (1862).

451.26 Leda] See note 144.17–18.

454.14 *bêtises*] French: stupidities.

462.34 Zeno's paradox!] The famous paradox of the Greek philosopher (c. 490–430 B.C.E.), which demonstrated that Achilles could never overtake a tortoise in a running race.

463.1 *Love's Stratagem*] Title of a short film (1909) directed by the American director and actor Harry Solter (1873–1920).

464.32 My Man Godfrey] Film (1937) directed by Gregory La Cava (1892–1952), a screwball comedy starring William Powell (1892–1984) and Carole Lombard (1908–1942).

465.10 *paysannes*] French: rustic women.

474.22 Shedd Aquarium] Public aquarium in Chicago.

474.28–30 The Autumn seems to cry . . . Coolidge] Susan Coolidge was the pen name of the American children's author, poet, and editor Sarah Chauncey Woolsey (1835–1905). The lines are taken from her poem "Helen."

476.17 Penthesilea] In Greek mythology, an Amazonian queen who fought for the Trojans, the subject of a verse tragedy (1807) by the German writer Heinrich von Kleist (1777–1811).

479.7–8 Emerson . . . should "saunter"] See the journal entry, June 8, 1838, of American philosopher and essayist Ralph Waldo Emerson (1803–1882): "A man must have aunts & cousins, must buy carrots & turnips, must have barn & woodshed, must go to market & to the blacksmith's shop, must saunter & sleep & be inferior & silly."

481.29 Safe Conduct] Title of memoir (1931) by the Russian writer Boris Pasternak (1890–1960).

481.30 Give me my scallop shell of quiet] From the first line of the anonymous poem "The Passionate Man's Pilgrimage" (1604), often ascribed to Sir Walter Raleigh.

481.31 my spear of burning gold.] Cf. William Blake's poetic preface to *Milton* (1808), now commonly known as "Jerusalem": "Bring me my Bow of burning gold: / Bring me my Arrows of desire: / Bring me my Spear: O clouds unfold!"

482.14 Midas] In Greek mythology, King Midas of Phrygia was granted his wish that everything he touched be turned to gold.

482.25 Salon de Thé] French: Tea Room.

482.28–29 *Caucasian Sketches* of Ippolitov-Ivanov] Two orchestral suites (1894, 1896) by the Russian composer Mikhail Ippolitov-Ivanov (1859–1935).

484.21 Sleepers Awake] The English title for the hymn "Wachet auf, ruft uns die Stimme" (1599) by the German clergyman Philipp Nicolai (1556–1608), the basis for a cantata (BWV 140; 1731) by Johann Sebastian Bach. It is also the title of a prose work (1946) by the American poet Kenneth Patchen (1911–1972).

485.4–5 chariot race in *Ben Hur*] Famous set piece in *Ben-Hur: A Tale of the Christ* (1880), best-selling novel by American writer Lew Wallace (1827–1905).

485.9 Good old Walt] Walt Whitman.

485.11 Maugham] English writer W. Somerset Maugham (1874–1965), whose novels include *Of Human Bondage* (1915) and *The Moon and Sixpence* (1919).

486.2 *impératrice*] French: empress.

490.19 "like an evening gone."] From Isaac Watts's hymn "Our God, Our Help in Ages Past."

491.1 Hollyhock House to the Hollywood Hotel] Building at 4800 Hollywood Boulevard in Hollywood designed by American architect Frank Lloyd Wright (1867–1959); fashionable hotel at 1160 North Vermont Avenue, torn down in 1956.

491.2 Undine] A water sprite in Germanic mythology, the subject of a novella (1811) by the German writer Friedrich Heinrich Karl de la Motte Fouqué (1777–1843), which was adapted into several operas, ballets, and a silent movie (1916).

493.6 chansons de geste] French medieval epics, including the thirteenth-century *Huon de Bordeaux* (493.8), named for its protagonist.

494.11 Gatlings] A forerunner of the machine gun patented in the United States in 1862, named for its inventor, Richard Gatling (1818–1903).

494.22 rocked in the cradle of the deep] Title of a popular poem (1831) by the American educator and activist Emma Hart Willard (1787–1870).

500.10 Sea of Tranquillity.] Lunar basin that was the site of the first manned moon landing, July 20, 1969.

500.18 KDKA] Pittsburgh-based radio station.

501.29 Joubert] See note 405.28.

502.13 *jeunes filles*] French: young girls.

502.32 Lord Chesterfield] Philip Dormer Stanhope, 4th Earl of Chesterfield (1694–1773), English politician, diplomat, and author, known for a posthumously published collection of letters to his son, offering advice on manners and worldly advancement.

507.9–10   "mere"? / anarchy.] See W. B. Yeats's "The Second Coming" (1920), line 4, "Mere anarchy is loosed upon the world."

513.2   the "Casta Diva" from *Norma*] Aria from act 1 of *Norma* (1831), opera by the Italian composer Vincenzo Bellini (1801–1835).

515.2   *beau fixe*] French: set fair.

515.16–17   praying . . . Millet's *Angelus*] *The Angelus* (1859), painting by the French artist Jean-François Millet (1814–1875), shows two peasants praying over a basket of potatoes at dusk.

516.32   Marshalsea] London debtors' prison.

518.19   Ruskin] John Ruskin (1819–1900), English art critic and social commentator.

520.11   Fra Diavolo] The bandit title character of a comic opera (1830) by the French composer Daniel Auber (1782–1871).

522.18   *semblables*] French: counterparts.

525.7–8   Paul Bunyan and Babe, the blue ox.] In American folklore, a giant lumberjack of superhuman strength and his animal companion.

528.23   Kit Carson] Christopher "Kit" Carson (1809–1868), American frontiersman and soldier, who fought the Spanish in California, fought with the Union in New Mexico during the Civil War, and conducted a campaign against the Navajo. Fictionalized versions of Carson's career appeared in dime novels, comic books, and movies.

528.34   Miss Peevish] Cf. Miss Peevish Scornful, subject of a poem by the English poet John Clare (1793–1864).

530.27   "to suckle fools and chronicle small beer"] Shakespeare, *Othello*, II.i.160.

WAKEFULNESS

542.27   sow's purse . . . silk ear] Cf. the proverbial saying "You can't make a silk purse out of a sow's ear."

549.11   Stefan Wolpe] German-Jewish composer (1902–1972) who fled Germany in 1933 and eventually settled in the United States. The quotation is taken from Wolpe's description of the fourth movement of his *Piece for Oboe, Cello, Piano and Percussion* (1954).

557.37   Marshal Tito.] Josip Tito (1892–1980), leader of Yugoslavia from 1945 to 1980.

575.1   Captain Nemo] Captain of the submarine the *Nautilus* in *Twenty*

Thousand Leagues Under the Sea (1870), novel by the French writer Jules Verne (1828–1905).

576.22   The Spacious Firmament] Cf. the title of Joseph Addison's poem "The Spacious Firmament on High" (1712).

576.25   Kleist] See note 476.17.

580.22–23   sect of the levellers] Popular movement in mid-seventeenth-century England that believed in the people's sovereignty and advocated for expanded male suffrage and other reforms.

587.8   idées reçues.] French: received ideas; clichés.

587.15   V-J Day.] Public holiday in the U.S. to celebrate the victory over Japan declared with the announcement of the Japanese surrender, officially scheduled for September 2, 1945; celebrations took place as well on August 15, the day after the announcement had been made.

591.8   one-eyed . . . king] Cf. the adage "In the country of the blind the one-eyed man is king," often attributed to Erasmus.

591.22   The Dong with the Luminous Nose] The title is from Edward Lear's 1877 poem of the same name. Ashbery's poem is a cento containing lines by, among others, Lord Byron, Gerard Manley Hopkins, T. S. Eliot, Thomas Gray, Alfred, Lord Tennyson, Shakespeare, Matthew Arnold, William Wordsworth, and Robert Bridges.

GIRLS ON THE RUN

599.2   Henry Darger] Girls on the Run is a poem inspired by the work of the American outsider artist Henry Darger (1892–1972), which was discovered shortly before his death and exhibited posthumously to great acclaim. Darger spent much of his adult life working on an enormous illustrated saga entitled "In the Realms of the Unreal," depicting the adventures of an intrepid band of children called the Vivian Girls.

601.6   dehors] French: outside.

625.1–2   "some in rags, some in jags, and some in velvet gown,"] From the nursery rhyme "Hark, Hark, the Dogs Do Bark."

644.16–17   "She gave them some broth, without any bread] From the nursery rhyme "There Was an Old Woman Who Lived in a Shoe."

YOUR NAME HERE

650.15–16   "Poor thing but mine own,"] Cf. Shakespeare, As You Like It, V.iv.57–58: "an ill-favor'd thing, sir, but mine own."

656.28   Sam Rayburn Lake] A reservoir in Texas named for Sam Rayburn (1882–1961), a Democratic congressman from Texas, 1913–61, and Speaker of the House, 1940–47 and 1949–61.

659.13   Mattia Preti] Italian painter (1613–1699).

659.14   Luca Giordano] Italian painter (1634–1705).

660.13   Henny Penny . . . Turkey Lurkey] Characters in the children's story "Chicken Little."

662.3   James Tate] American poet (1943–2015). "The Horseshoe" was published in his collection *Constant Defender* (1983).

663.14   Weird Sisters] The three witches in Shakespeare's *Macbeth*.

664.20   Old Goriot."] Titular character of Honoré de Balzac's novel *Le Père Goriot* (1835).

664.28   sugar falling gently . . . red eggs.] Cf. *Nouvelles Impressions d'Afrique* (1932) by the French writer Raymond Roussel (1877–1933), canto II, lines 178–79: "And snow is falling, a heap of red eggs, / For strawberries being sugared" (trans. Mark Ford).

664.35–665.1   the poet Lenz . . . rosy firmament] The German writer Jakob Michael Reinhold Lenz (1751–1792), who was described by Goethe as "a shooting star, only for a moment passing over the horizon of German literature and suddenly vanishing without leaving any trace in the world."

665.10   Robert Walser] Swiss writer (1878–1956) who wrote in German; "The One of Fairy Tales" was published in 1924.

667.1   *L'heureuse*] French: The happy woman.

667.19   *The History of My Life*] Title of memoir by Henry Darger (see note 599.2).

668.5   *Toy Symphony*] Eighteenth-century musical work featuring toy instruments that has been attributed to Mozart, among others.

668.8   Valéry, *Alphabet*] The French poet, critic, and essayist Paul Valéry (1871–1945) wrote the prose poems that make up the posthumously published *Alphabet* in the 1920s.

668.11–12   Miss Marple . . . Boston Blackie or the Saint] Miss Marple, detective in many Agatha Christie novels and short stories; Boston Blackie, character created by American writer Jack Boyle (1881–1928), who is best known as the thief-turned-detective played by the American actor Chester Morris (1901–1970) in fourteen films in the 1940s; the Saint, nickname of Simon Templar, a detective who features in a series of books and stories by the British writer Leslie Charteris (1907–1993) published beginning in 1928, as well as a series of films (1938–54) and a television series of the 1960s.

669.8–9   Dewey took Manila . . . decimal system] The American naval officer George Dewey (1837–1917) commanded the squadron that defeated the Spanish in Manila Bay on May 1, 1898; the American librarian Melvil Dewey (1851–1931) invented the library classification system known as the Dewey Decimal System in 1876.

672.17 *The File on Thelma Jordan*] *The File on Thelma Jordon* (1949), film noir directed by the German-born director Robert Siodmak (1900–1973), starring Barbara Stanwyck (1907–1990) and Wendell Corey (1914–1968).

675.9–11 raven . . . Edgar Allan Poe] Poe's poem "The Raven" was published in 1845.

679.26 "*La Folia*"] Anonymous musical theme first published in 1672.

680.3 Clement Attlee] English statesman (1883–1967) and Labour Party leader, British prime minister, 1945–51.

680.8–9 man named Silhouette . . . stinginess.] The French government official Étienne de Silhouette (1709–1767) restricted state spending in France as controller general under Louis XV.

680.19 hoosegow] Slang: jail.

681.8 De Senectute] "On Old Age," title of an essay by Cicero written in 44 BCE.

685.22 *Here We Go Looby*] From the nursery rhyme "Here We Go Looby-Loo."

686.5 Miles Standish, or Priscilla—] Myles Standish (1586–1656) was military adviser to the colony founded by the Pilgrims at Plymouth. Henry Wadsworth Longfellow's narrative poem *The Courtship of Miles Standish* (1858) describes his wooing of Priscilla Mullins (later Alden, c. 1602–c. 1685).

687.14 *Life Is a Dream*] Title of play (1635) by the Spanish playwright Pedro Calderón de la Barca (1600–1681).

688.11 *Beverly of Graustark*] Title of novel (1904) by the American writer George Barr McCutcheon (1866–1928), creator of the fictional Eastern European country of Graustark that is the setting for several of his books; it was adapted as a silent film in 1926.

690.11 *The Pearl Fishers*] Title of opera (1863) by French composer Georges Bizet (1838–1875).

693.10 Rimbaud's Les Voyelles] "Voyelles" ("Vowels," 1871), sonnet by the French poet Arthur Rimbaud (1854–1891).

695.1 *A Descent into the Maelstrom*] Title of Edgar Allan Poe's short story (1841).

695.23 *Sonatine Mélancolique*] French: Melancholy Sonatina.

696.5 *Little Dorrit*] Novel (1857) by Charles Dickens.

697.24 film *Careful*, by Guy Maddin] Canadian film director (b. 1956); the quotation that serves as the epigraph for this poem is not from *Careful* (1992) but from Maddin's *Tales from the Gibli Hospital* (1988).

NOTES 807

698.28 'It bloweth where it listeth,'] Cf. John 3:8.

700.18–20 Be kind to your web-footed friends . . . somebody's uncle.] Cf. the children's song "Be Kind to Your Web-Footed Friends," sung to the tune of John Philip Sousa's march "The Stars and Stripes Forever": "Be kind to your web-footed friends, / For a duck may be somebody's mother."

704.1 "old dark house" movies] Ashbery's play *The Philosopher* (1959) spoofs this popular movie genre.

705.14 Casper David Friedrich] German painter (1774–1840).

708.1 *Amnesia Goes to the Ball*] Cf. the title *Amelia Goes to the Ball* (1937), opera by the Italian-born American composer Gian Carlo Menotti (1911–2007).

713.3 this Dreyfus business."] The French-Jewish artillery officer Alfred Dreyfus (1859–1935) was wrongfully arrested on charges of treason in 1894 and was sentenced to life imprisonment. The intense controversy that followed resulted in the case being reopened, and in September 1899 Dreyfus was pardoned by French president Émile Loubet. He was fully exonerated by a military commission on July 12, 1906, and one week later was publicly decorated with the Légion d'Honneur.

713.31 ultima thule] Medieval geographers' term for a place beyond the borders of the known world.

715.19 So I wandered fleecy as a cloud] Cf. William Wordsworth's poem "I Wandered Lonely as a Cloud" (1804, rev. 1815).

721.28 *Vendanges*] Grape harvests for wine.

725.3 Flaubert, *Dictionary of Received Ideas*] Satirical dictionary compiled by the French novelist Gustave Flaubert (1821–1880) in the 1870s, published posthumously in 1911–13.

727.12 Marie de Médicis] Marie de Médicis (1575–1642) was the second wife of Henry IV of France.

729.27 *Doucement, doucement*] French: Gently, gently.

732.21 *ma jolie*] French: my pretty one.

736.5 Tosca . . . Isolde] Heroines of operas: Puccini's *Tosca* and Wagner's *Tristan and Isolde* (1865).

737.25 *plats*] French: dishes.

737.27 Mme de Staël by Overbeck] French writer Anne Louise Germaine Necker, Madame de Staël (1766–1817); German painter Johann Friedrich Overbeck (1789–1869).

738.20 *Jean-Christophe*] Novel in ten volumes (1904–12) by the French writer Romain Rolland (1866–1941).

UNCOLLECTED POEMS

741.1 *Hoboken*] This poem is an early uncollected poem from an undated issue of *Semi-Colon*, c. 1954, published by the Tibor de Nagy Gallery in New York City.

746.5 Le singe d'une nuit d'été] French: The monkey on a summer's night. Cf. the French title of Shakespeare's *A Midsummer Night's Dream*: *Le songe d'une nuit d'été*.

761.14 *Vauban*] The Marquis de Vauban (1633–1707), military engineer and Marshal of France.

Index of Titles and First Lines

Abe's Collision, 426
About a year ago around lunch time, 761
About to Move, 353
Abruptly, unassertively, the year starts, 594
A cautionary mister, 585
Accept these nice things we have no use for, 710
According to most of these people, a good "ladle," 508
A chance balloon drew these settlers nigh, 662
A couple of shivers of attitude, 573
Across the frontier, imperfect sympathies are twinkling, 732
Acts have been cleaned up, 361
Actually it was because you stopped, 272
Actually the intent of, 400
A cup drips air, 556
Added Poignancy, 545
A few things came to observe me, 721
After it had jiggled down it came out OK, 312
After only a week of taking your pills, 566
After ten years, my lamp, 355
Again, what forces the critic to bury his, 506
A great plane flew across the sun, 599
Ah, the farts, 764
A hears by chance a familiar name, 431
Alborada, 345
Alive at Every Passage, 551
All of us getting our licks, 369
Allotted Spree, 426
All that we are trying most defiantly to unravel, 254
A loose and dispiriting, 423
Although I have known you for a long time, 692
Always / because I saw the most beautiful, 321
A man walks at a city, 336
American Bar, 258

Am I to be allowed to go back? 754
Amnesia Goes to the Ball, 708
And Again, March Is Almost Here, 693
And for all the days it doesn't happen, 436
And Forgetting, 227
And he would say, "You ought to write him and thank him for it," 690
And it was uniquely the weather, O *bombes-glacées* university! 297
And of course one does run on tooling, 712
And one wants to know everything about everything, 460
And patient, exacting, 375
And Socializing, 337
And sometimes when you want it to it won't, 339
And the bellybuttons all danced around, 353
And the failing panopticon? 424
And the ignorance on your hands is August, 395
AND THE STARS WERE SHINING, 349
And the Stars Were Shining, 403
and they can't all be prayer too, 755
And they have cooler armchairs, 474
And when do we get to the threadbare house, 763
And when some sidle awkwardly, 257
And when they had mounted it on the flatbed, 453
And who, when all is said and done, 314
And you forgave the bastards, 245
Angels (you, 427
An immodest little white wine, some scattered seraphs, 541
Another Aardvark, 725
Another Example, 261
Another Kind of Afternoon, 555
Anxiety and Hardwood Floors, 428
Any Other Time, 573
Anyway, sleep came that day, 270
Archipelago, The, 384
Art of Speeding, The, 257

As a fish spoils, 589
As inevitable as a barking dog, second-hand music, 656
As it unfolded and took on something of the aspect, 303
As Oft It Chanceth, 311
As one turns to one in a dream, 351
As rain cobbles itself, 586
Assertiveness Training, 378
As structures go, it wasn't such a bad one, 307
A tad triste I too found it, 459
A talent for self-realization, 687
A tall building in the fifteenth arrondissement, 721
At First I Thought I Wouldn't Say Anything About It, 428
At Liberty and Cranberry, 429
Atonal Music, 430
At the Station, 554
Autumn Basement, 702
Autumn in the Long Avenue, 588
Autumn on the Thruway, 249
Autumn Telegram, 231
Avant de quitter ces lieux, 262
Avenue Mozart, 687
Avuncular and teeming, the kind luggage, 494
Awful Effect of Two Comets, 430
A yak is a prehistoric cabbage: of that, at least, we may be sure, 232

Back from his breakfast, thirty-five years ago, 337
Baked Alaska, 265
Baltimore, 542
Because if all of life is just a blip or some kind of exclamation, 279
Beer Drinkers, The, 333
Befuddled, 764
Be kind to your web-footed friends, 700
Beverly of Graustark, 688
Bloodfits, 656
Blot People, The, 489
Bobinski Brothers, The, 650
Bogus Inspections, 568
Boy I can remember when February, 580
Brand Loyalty, 654
Bromeliads, 398

Brute Image, 293
Bug-eyed at the possibilities, 717
Burden of the Park, The, 552
But how can I be in this bar and also a recluse? 737
but my advice is—be comfortable, 560
but then I thought keeping quiet about it might appear even ruder, 428
. . . *by an Earthquake*, 431
By Forced Marches, 248
By Guess and by Gosh, 435

Call for Papers, A, 278
Call It "Untitled," 745
Candid jeremiads drizzle from his lips, 566
Cantilever, 436
CAN YOU HEAR, BIRD, 421
Can You Hear, Bird, 436
Captive Sense, The, 490
Caravaggio and His Followers, 659
Central Air, 290
Cervantes was asleep when he wrote *Don Quixote*, 484
Chapter II, Book 35, 437
Charges about this unhappiness, 398
Cheerio. Nothing on the shore, 715
Chronic Symbiosis, 438
Cinéma Vérité, 700
Coldly, we put away the cabin flatware, 672
Collected Places, 439
Come On, Dear, 593
Come on, Ulrich, the great octagon, 234
Coming Down from New York, 440
Commercial Break, 399
Confronters, The, 491
Continually detouring among the mountains, 734
Conventional Wisdom, 692
Cool enough. Granted, 357
Cop and Sweater, 241
Cousin Sarah's Knitting, 543
Coventry, 402
Cream margarine; add sugar gradually, 748
Crossroads in the Past, 698
Crowd Conditions, 732

Dangerous Moonlight, 440
Dark days, lit by a falling flame, 766

INDEX OF TITLES AND FIRST LINES 811

Day at the Gate, A, 423
Dear ghost, what shelter, 227
Dear Sir or Madam, 566
Debit Night, 442
Decline of the West, The, 383
Deeply Incised, 558
Departed Lustre, The, 301
Descent into the Maelstrom, A, 695
De Senectute, 681
Desolate Beauty Parlor on Beach Avenue, The, 492
Desperate Hours, The, 382
Dewey took Manila, 669
Didn't you get my card? 652
Did you want it plain or frosted? 675
Dinosaur Country, 392
Discordant Data, 567
Dissolving Bride, The, 752
Disturbing news emanates from the wind tunnel, 671
Do Husbands Matter?, 445
Dong with the Luminous Nose, The, 591
Do not go into Hawaii, 455
Don's Bequest, The, 728
Don't cry it's lentil soup, 526
Don't just stand there, Kiki, 451
Do you know where you live? Probably, 678
Dream Sequence (Untitled), 657
Driftwood Altar, A, 286
Dull Mauve, 446

Each is truly a unique piece, 552
Earth-Tone Madonna, The, 564
Edith and Julian / waiting, 380
Elephant Visitors, 299
Enjoys Watching Foreign Films, 733
Erebus, 305
Eternity Sings the Blues, 447
Even so, we have forgotten their graves, 435
Everyone seemed pleased, even the then-invisible statisticians, 324
Excitation, excitation of feeling, 741

Fade In, 734
Faint of Heart, The, 493
Faithful I keep coming over to address the issues, 273
Falls to the Floor, Comes to the Door, 363

Fascicle, 450
"Father, you're destroying the Collectibles!" 654
Feather in your cap? Not from heeding, 320
Fifty years have passed, 498
File on Thelma Jordan, The, 672
Film Noir, 331
Five O'Clock Shadow, 451
Floatingly, 570
Flotsam, I told you, isn't the same as jetsam, 244
FLOW CHART, 1
Footfalls, 374
For a little snow you get your asking price, 570
for me now, 485
Fortune Cookie Crumbles, The, 677
Free Nail Polish, 357
French Opera, 316
French Stamp, A, 583
Friend at Midnight, The, 560
Friendly City, The, 381
Frogs and Gospels, 662
From a dark land of figs, 472
From Estuaries, from Casinos, 239
From Old Notebooks, 586
From Palookaville, 259
From Such Commotion, 548
From the Observatory, 452
Fruit and Tea, 747
Fuckin' Sarcophagi, 453
Full Tilt, 671
Funny, it says "hidden drive", 734

Garden of False Civility, The, 230
Gentle Reader, 594
Get Me Rewrite, 664
Getting Back In, 454
Ghost Riders of the Moon, 354
GIRLS ON THE RUN, 597
Girls on the Run, 599
Gladys Palmer, 455
Go ahead, plant that tree, 750
Gods of Fairness, The, 683
Going Away Any Time Soon, 578
Gracious exterior, but the rooms are small and mean, 359
Greased Lightning, 762
Great Bridge Game of Life, The, 300

INDEX OF TITLES AND FIRST LINES

Green Dress, The, 756
Green Mummies, The, 494
Gummed Reinforcements, 385

Hailstorm in Belgrade, May 24th, 1937, The, 755
Hang-Up Call, 702
Happy thoughts weren't made to last, 458
Harbor Activities, 341
Has to Be Somewhere, 726
Haunted Stanzas, 318
Have a care lest, 272
Haven't you arrived yet? 356
Having escaped the first box, 726
Heartache, 676
Hegel, 456
Held Thing, A, 366
Hell no, the creators were anguished, 695
Hello, Blubberface. You can come in now, 464
Help, when it came, came from an unexpected place, 255
Here We Go Looby, 685
"Her name is Liz, and I need her in my biz," 650
He was a soldier or a Shaker, 437
Hi. I'm Bob, 316
Hierarchy of the Unexpected, 757
History of My Life, The, 667
Hoboken, 741
Hole in Your Sock, A, 336
Homecoming, 595
Honored Guest, 710
HOTEL LAUTRÉAMONT, 225
Hotel Lautréamont, 235
How Dangerous, 704
However it may come back to you, 529
How funny your name would be, 395
How little we know, 378
How the past filled its designated space, 426
How to Continue, 346
Humble Pie, 705
Hundred Albums, A, 361

I, Too, 458
I am always shaking deliquescent bonbons, 756
I am going to be your host tonight, 465
I cannot recommend your curls too highly—, 725
I cannot remain outside any longer, 508
Ice Cream in America, 369
I did not, then, 503
I don't really understand why you object, 716
If all you want is kittens, 684
If it is spring it matters a little, 735
If I were a piano shawl, 504
If I were a tree you'd say, 693
I Found Their Advice, 315
If this is July, why does it look like August? 558
If You Said You Would Come with Me, 649
I had a voice once, 703
I have to sign my name, 394
I knew we should have stopped back there, 436
I like napping in transit, 358
I like the integrity of what you have to say, 378
I'll see you in my dreams she said, 578
I'll tell you what it was like, 286
I lost my notes, or they were useless. Luckily, 702
Implicit Fog, 657
Improvement, The, 365
Impure, The, 731
I must proceed unflustered, 386
In an Inchoate Place, 459
In Another Time, 272
In autumn things swell, books or leaves, 760
Industrial Collage, 660
In My Head, 576
In my original philosophy for the age of gink, 398
In My Way / On My Way, 327
In Old Oklahoma, 459
In other places where it was found, 542
In rainy night all the faces look like telephones, 246
In Scandinavia, where snow falls frequently, 691
In some of the stores they sell a cheese rinse, 473
In sooth, I come here sadly, 729
Instant insufficiency edged eerily over our oasis, 688
In the avuncular waiting rooms, 708

INDEX OF TITLES AND FIRST LINES 813

In the days of French film and infanticide, 476
In the eighteenth century, many avenues of expression were open to monkeys, 746
In the end it was their tales of warring stampedes, 678
In the Meantime, Darling, 397
In this childhood you can, 526
In town it was very urban, 649
In truth there is room for disgust, 716
In Vain, Therefore, 332
Invasive Procedures, 665
Invitation to a Wooing, 759
Irresolutions on a Theme of La Rochefoucauld, 276
I Saw No Need, 456
I saw no need to paint the sky, 456
I see and hear the wind, 588
is requested." That's where it began—, 366
Is that where it happens? 365
Is there another person you would like me to invite? 459
It ached to cross the Crimea, 756
It buttered no parsnips that it was raining, 278
It crossed the road so as to avoid having to greet me, 650
It has been raining on and off for a week now, 318
I think it's nice of me, 505
It is true that I can no longer remember very well, 471
It Must Be Sophisticated, 341
It's about this undulation thing, 241
It's almost two years now, 239
It's an art, knowing who to put with what, 352
It's a question of altitude, or latitude, 293
It seems very unlikely that my wishes will, 481
It's often more crazy like this, 728
It's one thing to get them to admit it, 208
It's only a matter of days now, 396
It's so easy to be attractive when, 486
It's wind, it's sleeting, 688
It was another era, almost another century, 593

It was great to see you the other day, 578
It was the solstice, and it was jumping on you like a friendly dog, 403
It will do. It's not, 265
I walk out over the moors, the hills, the sand valleys, 576
I was lying, lying down, 547

Job on the hills, 708
John came into town at night, 584
Joy, 276
Just for Starters, 398
Just how I feel, 697
Just the washing of the floors, 331
Just Wednesday, 325
Just What's There, 356
Just when I thought there wasn't room enough, 467

Kamarinskaya, 297
Keeping in mind that all things break, 560
Kill the white beaches, the hotel, bugs! 570
King, The, 245
Knowing John, it might have been, 495
know who you are), come back, 427
Korean Soap Opera, 284

Large Studio, The, 228
Last Legs, 712
Last Night I Dreamed I Was in Bucharest, 545
Last Romantic, The, 562
Latvian, The, 495
Laughing Gravy, 547
Laughter of Dead Men, The, 566
Leap in Time, A, 763
Leeward, 393
Lemurs and Pharisees, 712
Let it come back to this, 747
Let's get this going again. It might work, 445
Let's make a bureaucracy, 237
Let us leave the obedience school, 471
Life in Japan is one of the most famous with all these, 369
Life Is a Dream, 687
Light Turnouts, 227
Like a coffee table, the chair slides, 456

Like America, 580
Like a Sentence, 378
Like a summer kangaroo, each of us is a part, 704
Like you've done it before—, 574
Limited Liability, 460
Linnet, A, 650
Little Black Dress, The, 254
Livelong Days, 320
Local Time, 370
Lost Profile, 703
Lot of Catching Up to Do, A, 766
Lounge, The, 364
Love in Boots, 462
Love Scenes, The, 355
Love's Old Sweet Song, 279
Love's Stratagem, 463
Lyricist, The, 766

Mandrill on the Turnpike, The, 352
Man in Lurex, 396
Many Are Dissatisfied, 464
Many Colors, 587
Many couldn't stop being in love with you, 725
Massachusetts rests its feet, 665
Maybe it only looks bedraggled, 697
Maybe untwine my breath, like, 535
Meanwhile, back in / soulless America, 537
Media Runner, 754
Melodies of the past, fibers, tangled tracings, 454
Memories of Imperialism, 669
Men duly understand the river of life, 424
mensonge de Nina Petrovna, Le, 282
Merrily We Live, 653
Military Base, The, 496
Military Pastoral, 464
Moderately, 549
More and more obviously, the trainer won't handle things, 583
More Hocketing, 706
Mourning Forbidding Valediction, A, 314
Musica Reservata, 242
Music lovers everywhere, 447
Mutt and Jeff, 400
My country is but scrubland, 473
My Favorite Dress, 750

My friend, how are you? 345
My Gold Chain, 373
My Name Is Dimitri, 465
My nephew—you remember him—, 712
My Philosophy of Life, 467
Myrtle, 395
My sister and I don't seem to get along too well anymore, 284

New Constructions, 580
New Octagon, A, 423
Nice Morning Blues, 469
Nobody Is Going Anywhere, 716
No Earthly Reason, 469
No Good at Names, 330
No longer available is the hare, 532
No Longer Very Clear, 471
No more absenteeism, 758
No more odes, the good doctor said, 476
No one ever had to face such turmoil, 450
No one ever oversleeps, 317
Not all the buds will open, this year or any year, 290
Notes from the Air, 232
Nothing I'd ever want to own, 490
Not Now but in Forty-Five Minutes, 270
Not Planning a Trip Back, 395
Not to stumble, to get to tell you something simple, 562
Not You Again, 651
Now, in summer, the handiwork of spring, 496
Now another one who said it is gone, 679

Obedience School, 471
Ode to John Keats, 472
O did he see something yesterday? 374
Oeuvres Complètes, 324
Of a Particular Stranger, 473
Of course you will. It happens even after you're dead, 440
Of Dreams and Dreaming, 294
Of handedness and the Brothers Handedness, 583
Of Linnets and Dull Time, 284
Of our example, earth, 261
Often in Sorting Out, 752

INDEX OF TITLES AND FIRST LINES 815

Of the Light, 736
Oh I am oh so, 301
Oh there once was a woman, 346
Old Complex, The, 307
Old House in the Country, The, 701
Once, out on the water in the clear, early nineteenth-century twilight, 289
Once after school, hobbling from place to place, 670
Once upon a time there were two brothers, 667
One day he said to me, 746
One Man's Poem, 584
On First Listening to Schreker's Der Schatzgräber, 391
Onion Skin, 678
Only a breath of this region, 428
On she danced, but had forgotten, 730
On the Empress's Mind, 237
O Oswald, O Spengler, this is very sad to find! 383
Operators Are Standing By, 473
Others Shied Away, 474
Our first assignment was to make a square, 462
Our Leader Is Dreaming, 710
Our worst fears are realized, 351
Out on the terrace the projector had begun, 668
Outside My Window the Japanese . . . , 571
Outside my window the Japanese driving range, 571
Over a cup of flaming tea, the ogre assessed, 423
Over at the Mutts', 734

Pale Siblings, 715
Palindrome, 476
Palindrome of Evening, 542
Paperwork, 666
Paraph, 394
Pardon my appearance. I am old now, 327
Part of the Superstition, 255
Pastilles for the Voyage, 735
Pathetic Fallacy, The, 585
Pathless Wanderings, 390
Peace Plan, The, 497
Pearl Fishers, The, 690
Penitent, The, 497

Penthesilea, 476
People are buying store-dolls, 580
Phantom Agents, The, 238
Plain as Day, 477
Pleasure Boats, 388
plunge into distress, 753
Poem at the New Year, 289
Poem of Unrest, A, 424
Poem on Several Occasions, 716
Point Lookout, 478
Poor Knights of Windsor, 479
Postcard from Pontevedra, A, 697
Pot Luck, 719
Preposterous. That was the word she used, 702
Pretty Questions, 389
Private Syntax, 269
Probably Based on a Dream, 574
Problem of Anxiety, The, 498
Proximity, 578

Quarry, 547
Quartet, 321
Quick Question, 480
Quietly as if it could be, 696

Railroaded, 708
Raindrops fall on the treetops. A rainy day, 655
Rain in the Soup, 655
Reading this folderol, 762
Really? Uncle Pedro is coming, 683
Redeemed Area, 678
Remotely the unnamed keeps up with me, 555
Renewed by everything, I thought, 554
Research has shown that ballads were produced by all of society, 235
Retablo, 312
Reverie and Caprice, 481
Revisionist Horn Concerto, 338
Ridiculous Translator's Hopes, The, 359
Roll up your sleeves, 551
Run water from a tap into one of the pipes, 749

Sacred and Profane Dances, 684
Safe Conduct, 481
Salon de Thé, 482
Say it was any day, 479
Say that my arm is hurting, 249

INDEX OF TITLES AND FIRST LINES

Say that this is a street therefore people walk down it, 576
Scramble the "Believer" buttons, 699
Sea, The, 499
Seasonal, 296
Sedentary Existence, A, 304
See How You Like My Shoes, 483
seeking to convince the supreme Jester, 545
Seen on a beach this morning: a man in a gray coat, 231
Shadows in the Street, 563
Shadows on the Street, 753
She bit the bridge. A photograph can stomach it, 563
She plundered the fun in his hair, 509
She wasn't having one of her strange headaches tonight, 362
Shocker, The, 500
Short-Term Memory, 721
Sicilian Bird, 400
singe d'une nuit d'été, Le, 746
Sir Joshua Lipton drank this tea, 714
Sleepers Awake, 484
Slowly he is eating the stars—, 538
Slumberer, 717
Small City, 723
Small city where I lived for some years in total darkness, 723
Snow, 589
So, with a bath and tin words, 392
So it likes light and likes, 325
So I was bewildered, OK? 766
Some of the finest and most spectacular, 748
Some of these houses are startlingly old, 687
Something's not right. There were vibrations, 489
Something Too Chinese, 485
Some time before you wore that belt, 482
Sometimes a dangerous slice-of-life, 676
Sometimes in Places, 375
Sometimes it's more time than we care to be, 368
Sometimes the drums would actually let us play, 653
Sometimes you overhear them discussing it, 304
So much energy deployed, 426

So much has impaired here, 492
Sonatine Mélancolique, 695
So what if it's brackish my love, 533
Spacious Firmament, The, 576
Spotlight on America, 386
Spring Cries, 351
Stanzas Before Time, 696
Star Belched, A, 730
Stifled Notation, A, 317
Still in spring, my coat, 567
Still in the published city but not yet, 3
Still Life with Stranger, 234
Still no this morning, 759
Story of Next Week, The, 360
Strange Cinema, 729
Strange Occupations, 670
Strange Things Happen at Night, 368
Stung by Something, 560
Suddenly all is quiet again, 264
Suit, A, 697
Surely it was the same blank wall of twenty years ago, 507
Surely the lodger hadn't returned yet, 525
Susan, 244
Swan filets and straw wine, 663
Swaying, the Apt Traveler Exited My House, 486
Sweet Young Thing: "Why are you all down in the mouth?" 299

Tahiti Trot, 748
Take care of values. The rest is shopping, 399
Tangled Star, 556
Taxi in the Glen, 488
Tell me more about that long street, 294
Tenebrae, 570
Terminal, 652
That arrival, a foretaste of which appalls some, 363
That article I'd meant to read—, 724
That it was a relief to him, my lord, 364
That night the wind stirred in the forsythia bushes, 698
That watery light, so undervalued, 736
That You Tell, 334
The binding clause—, 500
The boss made it official, 308
The cannons waved summer goodbye, 334

INDEX OF TITLES AND FIRST LINES 817

The car bounds forward eagerly, and for a moment, 429
The coast is clear. Bring me my scallop shell of quiet, 481
The comparison says enough, really, nay is eloquent on the subject, 463
The crisis has just passed, 547
The dress code is casual, the atmosphere relaxed, 548
The failure to see God is not a problem, 683
"The Favor of a Reply, 366
The fear was that they would not come, 706
The fire betokened it, 387
The fox brooding and the old people smelling, 549
The / ghoulish / resonance, 664
The gray person disputes the other's clothes-horse stature, 292
The hamlet stroked its reflection in a, 430
The harshness isn't intentional, 440
the jetsam sighs, 332
The man, someone's uncle, went down, 382
The man behind you spoke to the tracery, 501
Theme, 504
The midgets stand on giants who stand on midgets, 259
the most beautiful combination appeared, 527
Then, everybody loved what they saw, 745
the new production, 752
Then he sort of lobbed it, 366
Then I reached the field and I thought, 242
Then I walked on a ways, 695
The object of the game is, 478
The obligation I have assumed is an unprepossessing one, 269
The perfume climbs into my tree, 400
the prodigal returns—to what mechanical, 248
The promised "great getaway" turned out to be, 469
The prospect: roofs and more roofs, 341
The rain fell with startling regularity, 375
There are additional reasons having to do with security, 469

There are attics in old houses, 341
There is a chastening to it, 587
There is still something I'd like to explain, 757
There was one who was put out of his house, 402
There will not always be a step, 430
The room I entered was a dream of this room, 649
These are the eyes I have stared out—, 497
These Symptoms I Know So Well, 760
These things can be arranged, he said, 438
The tea is too hot, 591
The things that were in the drawer were dispersed a long time ago, 568
The time is for going out, 397
The two parks interfaced, 389
The walls are whitish, 701
The woman with the confused soul keeps calling, 391
They Don't Just Go Away, Either, 691
They watch the blue snow, 262
Think of it as some god-liberating whimsy, 276
Think of it as something that is happening, 333
This Room, 649
This slave brings me tea, 282
Thought I'd write you this poem. Yes, 651
Three Dusks, 505
Till the Bus Starts, 358
Tin Steamboat, 749
Title Search, 357
Today I would leave it just as it is, 354
Today's Academicians, 506
To Good People Who Should Be Going Somewhere Else, 725
Token Resistance, 351
Tonight we are going to try a different dish, 305
To stay here forever. To lie down, 733
Touching, the Similarities, 507
Tower of Darkness, 508
To whom it may concern: Listen up, 371
Toy Symphony, 668
Tremendous Outpouring, 508
Tropical Sex, 558
Tuesday Evening, 509

INDEX OF TITLES AND FIRST LINES

Twenty miles away, in the colder, 446
Twilight Park, 525
Two for the Road, 675
Two Norwegian Moods, 748
Two Pieces, 380
Two twisted dry turds on the sidewalk, 483
Two were alive. One came round the corner, 542

Umpteen, 526
Under the big Greenaway hat, the Diva, 373
Underwriters, The, 714
Unless you put it away, 381
[untitled], 324
Up, up it rises, 393
Up there our leader is dreaming again, 710

Variations on "La Folia," 679
Various flavors recite us, 705
Vauban, 761
Vendanges, 721
Victrola floribunda, 756
Village of Sleep, The, 574
Villanelle, 303
Vintage Masquerade, 724
Voices of Spring. Vienna Bonbons, 357
Vowels, 688

Waiting Ceremony, The, 500
WAKEFULNESS, 539
Wakefulness, 541
Waking Dream, A, 424
Walkways, The, 501
Waltz Dream, A, 362
Wash it again, 388
Waste time on these riddles? 666
Water Carrier, The, 503
Water Inspector, The, 699
We are constantly running checks, 660
Weather and Turtles, 375
Weather drips quietly through the skeins, 595
We bake a dozen kinds of muffins every day, 258
We began adulating, 657
We carry our anxiety about the land with us, 499
We close in on ourselves, 748

Weekend, 663
Welcome to Entropy, 758
We leave out old regrets, 276
Well, folks, and how, 384
Well, let's see, 752
Well, Yes, Actually, 371
We need more data re our example, earth, 238
were always right, 493
We took to the lake, 480
We've been out here long enough, 330
We were coming down from the city, 442
We were staying at the Golden Something-or-Other, 530
What are these apples doing here? 497
What can we do, / except, 370
What could I tell you? I couldn't tell you any other way, 545
What does the lengthening season mean, 296
What Do You Call It When, 387
Whatever charms is alien, 681
What Is Written, 658
What is written on the paper, 658
What more clouds are there to say, 338
What the Plants Say, 526
What were you telling him about, 564
What with one thing and another they were all, 300
What would I learn? That this vale, 500
When All Her Neighbors Came, 527
When I last saw you, in a hurry to get back and stuff, 227
When Pressed, 730
When they had climbed the Valley of Thieves, 452
When you come on, 439
When you hear the language, 315
Where are you? Where you are is the one thing I love, 230
Whereas I, efficacious ruin, 390
Where is that tricycle, man? 685
Where It Was Decided We Should Be Taken, 528
Where We Went for Lunch, 308
Which of the incredible lies will prove true? 491
Whiteout, 583
White Shirt, The, 264
Who Knows What Constitutes a Life, 683

INDEX OF TITLES AND FIRST LINES 819

Whole Is Admirably Composed, The, 246
"Why, there's the well where the message fell apart, 281
Why, we must dye it then—, 574
Why has the sailor come in, 730
Wild Boys of the Road, 281
William Byrd, 376
Wind Talking, The, 273
with all its accoutrements, 477
Withered Compliments, 272
Within a windowed niche of that high hall, 591
Within the Hour, 591
Without thinking too much about it, 368
With the precision of one who fights, 376
Woman Leaning, 529
Woman the Lion Was Supposed to Defend, The, 339
Works on Paper I, 369
World's End, 368

Yes, but right reason dictates, 360
Yes, Dr. Grenzmer. How May I Be of Assistance to You? What! You Say the Patient Has Escaped?, 530
Yes, I Have Been Reading, 750

Yes, I have been reading your book, 752
Yes, making a point of using it, 558
Yes, she chopped down a big tree, 657
Yesterday, for Instance, 532
yet the wind from Seattle blows over and over, 464
You, My Academy, 535
You always leave me where we left off, 719
You are my most favorite artist, 659
You Dropped Something, 533
You had but to look at a mound or nut, 311
You have a kind and gentle nature. Not overly, 677
You keep asking me that four times, 543
Young People, 538
YOUR NAME HERE, 647
Your Name Here, 737
Your name here invisible as a headache, 528
Your story . . . most enjoyable, 731
You said you don't want to know any more, 284
You throw matches on the floor, 488
Youth's Magic Horn, The, 292
You Would Have Thought, 537

This book is set in 10 point ITC Galliard,
a face designed for digital composition by Matthew Carter
and based on the sixteenth-century face Granjon.
Composition by Dedicated Book Services.
Designed by Bruce Campbell.